676

THE LIFE OF GRAHAM GREENE

Norman Sherry, a Fellow of the Royal Society of
Literature and the Mitchell Distinguished Professor
of Literature at Trinity University in San Antonio,
Texas, was already an accomplished biographer
when Graham Greene, having read Professor
Sherry's work on Joseph Conrad, asked a mutual
friend to introduce them. Greene was impressed by
Professor Sherry's method of 'literary detection', and
their meeting resulted in Greene asking Professor
Sherry to write his authorised biography, an
exhausting but fascinating task which has resulted
in *The Life of Graham Greene*, Volumes 1, 2 and 3.

Professor Sherry's books on Conrad, *Conrad's Eastern
World*, *Conrad's Western World*, and *Conrad and His
World*, are, thirty years after their publication,
still quoted by scholars as the standard texts on
Joseph Conrad. Professor Sherry honed his skills as
a biographer with *Charlotte and Emily Brontë* and
Jane Austen.

Professor Sherry received an Edgar Allan Poe Award
for *The Life of Graham Greene, Volume One: 1904–
1939. The Life of Graham Greene, Volume Two:1939–
1955* was designated as 'One of the best eleven
books of 1995' by the editorial staff of the *New York
Times Book Review*, who confirmed their admiration
by featuring Volume Two in *Books of the Century: A
Hundred Years of Authors, Ideas, and Literature* (1998).

THE LIFE OF GRAHAM GREENE

Volume One: 1904–1939

─────────

NORMAN SHERRY

PIMLICO

Published by Pimlico 2004

2 4 6 8 10 9 7 5 3 1

Copyright © Norman Sherry 1989

First published in Great Britain by Jonathan Cape 1989

First published in the United States of America by Viking Penguin 1989

First published in paperback in Great Britain by Penguin Books 1990

Pimlico edition 2004

Pimlico
Random House, 20 Vauxhall Bridge Road,
London SW1V 2SA

Random House Australia (Pty) Limited
20 Alfred Street, Milsons Point, Sydney,
New South Wales 2061, Australia

Random House New Zealand Limited
18 Poland Road, Glenfield,
Auckland 10, New Zealand

Random House (Pty) Limited
Endulini, 5A Jubilee Road, Parktown 2193, South Africa

The Random House Group Limited Reg. No. 954009
www.randomhouse.co.uk

A CIP catalogue record for this book is available from the British Library

ISBN 1-8441-3753-8

Papers used by Random House UK Limited are natural,
recyclable products made from wood grown in sustainable forests;
the manufacturing processes conform to the environmental
regulations of the country of origin

Printed and bound by CPI Antony Rowe, Eastbourne

for Elisabeth Dennys
with love

Many years will go by. Many great years. I shall then no longer be alive. There will be no return to the times of our fathers and grandfathers. This would, indeed, be both undesirable and unnecessary. But at last there will appear once more things that have long lain dormant: noble, creative and great things. It will be a time of final accounting . . . Think of me then.

— BORIS PASTERNAK

Contents

Illustrations

LINE ILLUSTRATIONS

Preface

This biography had its origins in a list which Graham Greene kept – and still keeps – of the books he reads. Against my second book on Joseph Conrad, *Conrad's Western World*, he had put in July 1971 two ticks, indicating special approval. Three years later the journalist William Igoe told me, over lunch, 'There is a man who is a legend in his own time and who admires your work.' That man was Graham Greene. When he was next in London we were introduced. I did not know then that he was under some pressure from his family and friends to appoint a biographer, but during lunch, while I was still fascinated by his singular smile and eyes so blue that they gave off a curious sense of blindness, he suddenly said, 'You wouldn't be able to write about me as you wrote about Conrad – you wouldn't be able to get into Saigon' (the setting of *The Quiet American*). I told him that after a ten-year stint on Conrad I was looking for another subject and he immediately backed off: 'Oh I wouldn't like anyone looking into my life.' Then he added with what I am sure was the instinctive decision of a novelist, 'If I were to have my biography written, I would choose you,' and later, as we parted in Brook Street, he made up his mind. I was to be his biographer, and we shook hands on it.

I think he thought I would be suitable because I had shown an objective approach to Conrad and because I had vacated the library to seek my subject in the countries in which he had lived and travelled. He was fascinated by my journeys to the Far East and especially by my discoveries in West Africa about Conrad's *Heart of Darkness* – a part of the world he knew well from personal experience. But he still had doubts and only days later wrote to me from the Royal Albion Hotel in Brighton (where he went when he had a writer's 'block') asking me not to interview certain women he had known. It was only very gradually that a mutual trust developed and I think it was expressed when we were crossing St James's Street in London and narrowly escaped being knocked down by a taxi. He said, 'You almost lost your subject there', and I replied, 'That's not half as bad as losing your biographer.' He laughed and I knew we had become friends.

If it is the aim of a biographer not only to trace the life and career of his subject but also, so far as possible, to penetrate the mystery of his character and personality, then there could be few more difficult subjects than Graham Greene. He is noted for his determination to protect his privacy and to keep secret what he wishes to keep secret. My doubts about being able to penetrate the personal and private world of Greene were increased when I discovered a letter written to a friend in 1977 which stated succinctly: 'When I read Christopher Sykes's *Evelyn Waugh* I felt I had done right in agreeing to Sherry undertaking me. He has the great advantage of not knowing me.' I had to cancel out that 'advantage' by embarking on a search for Graham Greene much more extensive than my search for Joseph Conrad. For one thing I was never able to interview Conrad, but I was able to interview Graham Greene. He was always willing to accommodate me, though sometimes the interviews were uncomfortable and sometimes unproductive exercises for both of us. I recall the occasion at his sister's home in Sussex, when Greene's nephew, Nicholas Dennys, told me of how, on coming downstairs from his bedroom, he had met his uncle and caught on Graham Greene's face a look of terror: 'He thought the footsteps on the stairs were yours, Norman, and that an interview was to be undergone.' Yet, though he never enquired beforehand what questions I would raise, and would answer briefly and at once – 'I will never lie to you Norman, but I will not answer all your questions', he said – I knew that he was re-presenting the pattern of his life as he saw it. I had to widen the perspective.

I gave up my position as Head of the Department of English at the University of Lancaster and began seeking exchange fellowships at American universities in order to research the Greene archives in Boston College Library, Georgetown University Library in Washington D.C., and the Humanities Research Center at the University of Texas in Austin. There was a vast cache of letters from Graham to his mother to be found in the vaults of a London bank in Fleet Street. I visited Berkhamsted School, where he was born and where his father was headmaster for seventeen years; there were many Old Boys, contemporary with Greene, not all of whom lived in England, who had to be found, interviewed, and their memories recorded. Discovering the originals of those boys who tormented him at school led me to Malaya, for I had to find the source of those experiences still painful to Greene. Always interviewing, I visited the large clan of Greene cousins. Graham's wife, Vivien, was especially helpful, while the book could not have reached this state of completion without Graham's sister Elisabeth's help and the willing assistance of his late brothers Dr Raymond Greene and Sir Hugh Greene.

Greene once called me his *doppelgänger* and indeed I had to become that, following his tracks in many different parts of the world. (He once sent me a large map on which the places he had visited were underlined like a red rash in every continent, with the words, 'You are my biographer, *you* date my journeys'.) Risking disease and death as he had done, I went to those places and in most cases found people Greene had met and put into his novels. I made journeys to Mexico (where I contracted dysentery in exactly the same mountain village, living in the same boarding house as he had done), Haiti, Argentina, Paraguay and Panama. In Liberia, a week after I had left that most corrupt of countries, during a revolution led by Sergeant Doe (now General and Head of State), the previous corrupt leader was murdered and his supporters shot or had their throats cut. I had only recently interviewed some of these men. In the interior, the stone age villages that Greene had seen in 1935 in his heroic march through that country were unchanged.

The journeys Greene made, I made, for it was a promise I had given him on our first meeting. I had to experience, as far as possible, what my subject experienced. I have not, any more than he has, reached the end of that experience, but it has taken me, as it has taken him, from the small town of Berkhamsted through the changes of history and some exotic and dangerous parts of the world, and meetings with some very extraordinary people, including one with the original of the Judas figure of *The Power and the Glory*, whom I tracked down in Mexico.

What stands out particularly in my meetings with Greene was his charging me, as we walked across Berkhamsted Common, that I had asked his friends for the names of his enemies. I replied that no one could succeed in life without making enemies – it was in the nature of the human condition. He countered that he did not live and work in an academic institution; he mixed only with friends. But that night, back in London and before dinner, in his room in the Ritz (an astonishingly small room) Graham, shaving, looked through his mirror at the recumbent Hugh lying on Greene's bed and said: 'Norman wants the names of some enemies – what's the name of the man I disliked in Sierra Leone during the war?' and both brothers there and then made me out a list.

Greene may not approve of my judgment of him, but that is inevitable: ''Tis with our judgments as with our watches, none/Go just alike, yet each believes his own', and a biographer's task is an impossible one, biography an imperfect genre.

This book is an imperfect report – how can one enter into the life of another person and re-create the intimate sensations of his experience? There are mysteries in every life and I am especially sensible, in Graham Greene's, of information sought but not found, sources untapped. I have tried to make some inroads, though as John Keats wrote, 'A man's life of any worth is a continuous allegory and very few eyes can see the mystery.' There lies the hope – to be those eyes; to lift the stone and let in light.

San Antonio, Texas   N.S.
1988

Our Man in Antibes

When in the winter of 1983 I was to visit Graham Greene in Antibes, he told me over the phone, in his precise and practical way, that there would be no heating in the small hotel near his home, that I would need a hot-water bottle, and that the cost would be only 127 francs a day. He was then seventy-nine and he still had a youthfulness about him, especially when a look of excitement appeared in his eyes, and there was something disarming about his manner.

I phoned Graham from the hotel and he said he would come and pick me up. When I got downstairs he was in the tiny office listening to the manageress. He was wearing a raincoat with the collar turned up, hands in his pockets. It was difficult to believe he was rising eighty.

As we walked from the hotel to his home, the rain fell heavily upon the black umbrella which he held high above my head. He explained that since it had rained for three days it would be fine tomorrow. It was.

The Avenue Pasteur, less impressive than its name, was a modern block of flats: his name on a plain brass plate was one of many. In the small entrance hall, a mirror stretched across one wall, reflecting my face as I stared into it. Greene, a man with little personal vanity, ignored it. He got into the elevator.

The main room of his flat was modest in size, thirty feet by twelve. There was a bamboo sofa and two bamboo chairs. Above the sofa was an abstract (flowers) given to Greene by Fidel Castro. White bookshelves filled two walls, and on another wall was a muffin-coloured print of Lunardi making his ascent in a balloon in 1789. Near the window a table performed the dual function of dining table and writing desk. There was a black-and-white television set, used mostly to watch the 7.45 p.m. news from Paris. There were some personal touches – eight pictures but no photographs – and if our living rooms are places which reflect our personalities, was Greene's an accident or a calculated revelation of character?

I am inclined to think it was neither – just a statement of what its inhabitant needed in order to live and to work. None of the trappings proclaim a successful writer, merely the basic necessities for writing and living – nothing superfluous, a statement of fact. As Greene wrote of Scobie's room in *The Heart of the Matter*: 'to a stranger it would have appeared a bare, uncomfortable room but to Scobie it was home. Other men slowly build up the sense of home by accumulation . . . Scobie built his home by a process of reduction'.

Writing at his dual-purpose table, Graham Greene faced into the light through a window which shows a fine view of the marina, a few yachts in the winter sun (it had stopped raining) and on the far side of the basin the low-slung, immensely powerful sixteenth-century Fort Carré, mountain-solid.

No sooner had we sat down than Greene wanted to start our interview (a desire to put unpleasant chores behind him). He offered me a drink and I asked him to mix me his own special brand of Martini. After this there was nothing to be done but set up my tape-recorder (I never relied solely on memory) and begin my questions. Greene's face closed down.

As an interviewer I find that it is often the subject's face that has a significance almost as great as his words. From our first meeting, I was struck by the fact that Greene's was a truly mysterious face, his looks can change so much. The front view of him is strong and still. What strikes you are his slightly bulging, blue, speculative eyes, the eyebrows raised in a perpetual questioning. It is a handsome, compelling face, with a stern strength which Anthony Palliser caught in his study for the National Portrait Gallery, but let him turn sideways and his face in profile has changed again. One notices a small up-turned blue-veined nose. The bags under his eyes are 'like purses that contained the smuggled memories of a disappointing life', and there are deep lines running from nose to chin. But when he smiles or laughs he becomes an excited boy, lifting himself out of a trough of sadness – something recalled, a surprise pondered upon, and his face is transformed.

On other occasions I was to meet a different Greene. When staring at the ground, he can look positively wooden – a hopeless emptiness at the core, a haunted look – and his mood can be intimidating by reason of your sense of his withdrawal. Sometimes it is as if he were deaf and did not hear. He stonewalls and does not reply to your question or to the implied suggestion behind your words. Yet in retrospect, I think when he does not respond or his responses are brief, the questions disturbing, this is the time he is listening most intently.

During the following three days, Graham sat quite still on the sofa for long periods, except when I pressed him too hard ('You are grilling me, Norman') and then he would lean back hard in his chair, looking hunted.

The first afternoon rolled on: I would ask another question and he would, almost always, answer briskly and without any evident emotion, but when his friend Yvonne came quietly into the flat with her dog, Sandy, and offered us drinks, he came quickly alive: his pleasure was sparkling, the interview could be terminated and he could relax into friendship. Later, Yvonne got me on my own and said, 'You know you mustn't be disturbed. Graham knows he has to be questioned but it is painful for him.'

On the morning of the last day of my visit, Graham was excited, perhaps because it was 10 a.m. and he felt the scrutiny was almost over, but also because he had had two dreams in the night. He began the conversation at once in high glee and I was conscious of that curious Greene accent, a kind of gurgle in the throat. Words like 'bad' are pronounced 'bed', hand 'hend', background 'beckground', attic 'ettic', and such words bitten off, the jaws grinding them out:

I had two dreams last night. Both of them were about ideas for novels and I felt very relieved for having ideas for novels. The first one I've forgotten completely. But the second one was about a rather odd house, rather ruined house and the story moved from room to room, each room contributing to the story, until the reader became aware that the attic was never visited. So in the final chapter the attic was visited and the attic was full of old newspapers with headlines and those headlines were going to be very significant and would give the final gist of the novel.

We spoke that morning about his religion and his 1949 visit to Padre Pro who reportedly had stigmata. In Malcolm Muggeridge's diaries, he recorded how Greene had just returned from Italy that year and was full of his having seen Padre Pro, describing his stigmata 'in his usual lurid way'. According to Muggeridge, Graham had told him that 'miracles were done constantly by Pro' (though Graham denies this) and that 'heavenly and devilish forces in creation were now exceptionally active in preparation for busting up the universe by means of the hydrogen bomb'.[1] Certainly, there is no doubt of the impact made on Greene by his meeting with Pro. Discussing this thirty-four years after the event, I found him still exercising his characteristic sense of recall.

On going to Italy in 1949, Graham first had an audience with the Pope in Rome and then travelled to the Franciscan monastery where Pro was saying Mass. He spoke to me about him in some awe:

The Vatican disapproved of him and so he had to say Mass in this Franciscan monastery on a side altar at five o'clock in the morning so as to discourage pilgrims. So we went and there were . . . about a dozen women waiting outside . . . The doors opened and what surprised me was that they went straight to the confessional and not to the altar where he was going to say Mass. Once you got there you were supposed to stay on without breakfast and Pro stayed on and heard all of their confessions.

And the curious thing was that I'd been told that it was a very long Mass. He spoke it clearly (he didn't gabble it like some priests do) and I thought it wouldn't take more than 55 minutes, and then finally we came out and found that it had taken two hours. I couldn't see where I had lost the sense of time.

I can recall the stigmata, the dried blood sticking out. It would dry and then it would bleed again and then dry again. He also had to have his feet padded because they also bled. So the blood dried and then it starts again and then there will be a period when it gets rather old. I was as near to him as I am now to you and those hands looked terrible, sort of circular pieces of dried blood.

Normally he hid this by wearing mittens but at Mass you aren't allowed to wear anything on your hands. And so he would try continually to pull down his sleeves to hide it but the sleeve would slip back.

I asked him if he had met Pro personally and he answered: 'No. I got a message and was invited to meet him but I said, "No, I don't want to. I don't want to change my life by meeting a saint." I felt that there was a good chance that he was one. He had a great peace about him.'

There was one other moment, in our three days of talks, when Greene became excited. I asked him if he was still hounded by God (as is his atheist character Bendrix at the conclusion of *The End of the Affair*), and he answered: 'I hope so. I hope so. I hope He is still dogging my footsteps.' Bendrix, in some senses, reminds me powerfully of Greene. He told me that that novel had its beginnings in a phrase from Baron von Hugel and he quoted: 'If we will not own it as a means, it will grip us as our End.' God grips the reprobate Bendrix at the end. It is a desperate fight. And it comes about quite casually when he discovers that ordinary corrupt human love has not finally satisfied his mistress, Sarah, and he faces up to the extraordinary possibilities of sainthood. Greene read the relevant passage to me from the French version, translating into English as he went. His reading was filled with unusual emotion:

For if this God exists, I thought, and if even you – with your lusts and your adulteries and the timid lies you used to tell – can change like this, we could all be saints by leaping as you leapt, by shutting the eyes and leaping once and for all: if you are a saint, it's not so difficult to be a saint.

We can see that even Bendrix is under the sway of what he cannot control. He may still mouth his hatred of God at the end of the novel; he may still speak of foiling God's plans – 'I'll rob Him of what He wants in me' – yet he has begun to enter a phase of life which borders on the miraculous.

Listening to Greene, I was deeply moved, partly because Greene himself was moved. I felt that he was approaching Cardinal Newman's notion that God has a special commitment for each of us, though we may not know what the mission is, or the way God may approach us. And I felt that in his private moments Greene, often in perplexity, must wrestle with the problems of mission.

*

The phone rang. It was a call from Switzerland and while he took it I looked round his flat searching for some impression which I could carry away with me, something reflecting the room and the man, and I seized upon a tall cylindrical wastepaper basket beside his table. It was encircled by brass bands and topped by a secure and heavily padded black lid. It, at least, made a statement.

There was one other impressive object, so tiny as to be almost ignored. It was a carving, a 3,000-year-old piece of stone no larger than a small hand. It had a fat, legless body and a sombre inward-looking face. The face was a mask of composure, and there was within a knowledge which was deeply disturbing. The same carving appears in the portrait of Greene in the National Portrait Gallery.

I left Antibes feeling that I had met Graham Greene to a limited degree on his home ground, but I still had a long way to go to an understanding of him – a distance of over eighty years.

PART I

Childhood

I

Beginnings – Comfort and Fear

Childhood knows the human heart.
— EDGAR ALLAN POE

THE *Berkhamsted Gazette and Hemel Hempstead Observer* of 8 October 1904 carried the following announcement: 'On October 2, at St John's, Berkhamsted, the wife of Charles H. Greene [was delivered] of a son.' The second of October was a Sunday; the weather, after a cold and cloudy September, was fair; and according to his mother's entry in a sixpenny booklet entitled 'All About Baby' (produced by Steedman's of Walworth, Surrey, who manufactured soothing powders for children cutting their teeth, and illustrated with line drawings of some plump and rather sinister-looking young children), the boy was born at 10.20 a.m. and weighed 7½ lbs. He was the fourth child of Charles Henry Greene and his wife Marion Raymond Greene. According to his younger sister, Elisabeth Dennys, it had been a difficult birth: 'My mother had had a number of miscarriages and she had been appalled to find herself pregnant again.' She was to bear two more children.

The future novelist was born into three small worlds – the town of Berkhamsted, one hour north of London by train, the family home attached to the school, and Berkhamsted School itself – the last being a world into which he was gradually absorbed. His father, who was thirty-nine, was second master at the school and housemaster of St John's house, and his mother, then thirty-two, apart from looking after her family, was responsible for the catering at St John's where Graham Greene was born and where, at first, he lay, 'Behind the tight pupils/That have never opened on the world of chairs and walls'.[1]

On Sunday 13 November, five weeks later, the boy was baptised in the school Chapel by the headmaster, Dr Thomas Charles Fry, he whom the school's historian was to call 'the magnificent' and whom the baby he baptised was, much later, to describe as 'my father's sinister, sadistic predecessor'. The Chapel, dedicated in 1895, cost between £7,000 and £8,000, paid for by Edward Greene, Dr Fry's father-in-law, uncle to Charles Henry Greene and owner of the Greene brewery at Bury St Edmunds.[2] It had floors of polished marble and mosaic, electric lighting and seating for 320 people. Peter Quennell in *The Marble Foot* described it as 'repulsive red-brick . . . approached by a range of ill-proportioned cloisters', but the Chapel marked the beginning of a generous patronage to the school which was continued by Edward Greene's nephew (also called Edward Greene), the brother of Charles Henry Greene.

The baby was called Henry after his father and Graham after his uncle Sir Graham Greene and Graham Balfour, a descendant of Robert Louis Stevenson, his mother being first cousin to Stevenson. The small group assembled for the baptism must have been rather lost in the Chapel. One of the baby's godfathers was Colonel Henry Wright. Colonel Wright's wife, the baby's great-aunt Maud, had introduced Robert Louis Stevenson to his 'first great love, Mrs Sitwell'.[3] The Wrights lived at 11 Belgrave Road, and on visits to London the Greene family usually had lunch with them. Afterwards, the Colonel would produce 'a vast chamberpot' from the sideboard cupboard (for the relief of his guests, presumably): 'a relic of Victorian manners'.[4] He was not present at the christening, Charles Henry Greene being proxy for him. The other godfather was a Mr Herbert, who was to be housemaster of St John's at Berkhamsted when Henry Graham Greene was a boarder there.[5] Henry Graham's mother noted in her Steedman's booklet that, among others, her daughter Molly and her sons Herbert and Raymond, as well as Mrs Fry, her sister-in-law Alice, and Mr Simpson, a master at the school, were present.

Henry Graham Greene was later to write: 'Everything one was to become must have been there, for better or worse . . . Here in Berkhamsted was the first mould of which the shape was to be endlessly reproduced'.[6] The family influences (and it was a family proud of its traditions) were of course represented by the parents, Charles and Marion Greene, and their children. Marion had been a Greene before her marriage, coming from the Bury St Edmunds side of the family, and was her husband's first cousin once removed. The baby's Aunt Alice was a progressive and must have been on leave from the school she ran in South Africa. She was a friend of General Smuts and Olive Schreiner. Maud Wright, and Dr Fry's wife, Julia, originally a Greene, completed the family group. Graham Greene's mother was naturally to be an important influence in his life; his father, Dr Fry, Mr Herbert and Mr Simpson were representatives of the school that was to have such a traumatic effect on him; the literary heritage was there in the relationship with Robert Louis Stevenson; and the school and town were the physical settings of his formative years.

Behind the Greenes present at the Chapel stood the long line of Greenes living and dead, who by their existence alone would create in the boy his strong sense of what it meant to belong to that family and against whom he was later to rebel. This strong consciousness of belonging to a family with a long lineage is described by Graham's elder brother Raymond, in an unpublished typescript, as being that of a typical English middle-class family: 'within our knowledge no foreign blood has contributed to theirs since the Norman Conquest'.★ The Greenes were varied in character, ambitions with degrees of success, proud of their history, which included banking, brewing and trading with offshoots into education, literature and the arts, plus a certain amount of real eccentricity. Benjamin Greene III, born in 1780, was to found the Greene King brewery at Bury St Edmunds and bought sugar estates in the West Indies: he and his brother John married two sisters, daughters of Elizabeth Carleton Smith, heiress of the banker Zachariah Carleton. Benjamin Buck Greene (son of Benjamin Greene III) was to become a director and later Governor of the Bank of England (1850–75). The widow of Benjamin Buck Greene's son, Frederick (born 1841), one Lucy Greene, who lived in Jersey, would 'summon her cousin Maud Churchill Greene' to come and attend her whenever she was ill. She never paid her and left half a million pounds, not to Maud, but to the Society for the Propagation of the Gospel.

*

Beyond the 'world of chairs and walls' which was the baby's home society was Edwardian, though only by three years, Queen Victoria having died in 1901. On the whole, Victorian standards and conditions still prevailed, particularly at Berkhamsted School as we shall see, though it was the beginning of a period of change. There were already electric trams running in the town and the *Berkhamsted Gazette* concluded that local workmen were drinking less because they were carried with such rapidity in the trams past places of temptation on their way home from work. By the time Henry Graham Greene was six there was a cinema in most towns in England; when he was ten the First World War began; when he was thirteen there was the

★ His uncle Edward did in fact marry a German, born in Brazil.

Russian revolution; when he was twenty-two there was the General Strike in Britain. In the year of his birth 5,000 Frenchmen attended a demonstration to commemorate the second anniversary of the death of Émile Zola and a small notice in *The Times* reported that Charlotte Brontë's husband (she had died fifty years before) was 'still living, in honoured old age, in an Irish village'.

In the same year, Kipling's *Traffic and Discoveries*, H. G. Wells's *The Food of the Gods*, Henry James's *The Golden Bowl*, John Galsworthy's *The Island Pharisees* and Joseph Conrad's *Nostromo* were published, and Belgian atrocities in the Congo, which Conrad had written about some years earlier in *Heart of Darkness*, were still inspiring letters to *The Times*. Conrad was to influence Graham Greene as a writer. D. H. Lawrence was nineteen that year, Virginia Woolf and James Joyce were twenty-two. On the day before Graham Greene was born, Captain Scott, still six years from his fatal expedition to the South Pole, was at Balmoral Castle showing lantern slides and delivering a lecture to King Edward VII on the work of the Antarctic Expedition.

Poverty and unemployment in Great Britain were increasing the number of emigrants to Australia, New Zealand and Canada – and a third-class passage to Canada cost £2 7s., a not inconsiderable sum for the ordinary working man in those days. A case of child neglect reported in *The Times* on the day before Greene's birth reflects the condition of the poor. The unmarried parents were known drunks whose numerous children were forced to live not in the house but on the outside staircase, scantily clad, and fed by neighbours. On the same day an outbreak of smallpox was reported in Dewsbury.

For the better off, servants were still available and their advertisements in *The Times* for positions suggest a high standard of service: a butler stressed that he was thoroughly sober, honest and obliging – and a good carver; a valet, seeking a post as attendant to a bachelor or invalid gentleman, stated that he was a certified masseur and in character an abstainer, a non-smoker and a good traveller. There was no butler or valet in Charles Greene's home, though there were many servants. At the Hall in Berkhamsted, the home of Graham Greene's uncle Edward, there were twenty-three servants and a chauffeur.

*

Writing of his childhood, Greene claimed that we are all 'emigrants from a country we remember too little of'; though it haunts us and we try to reconstruct it, all that is most important escapes us – 'we can't remember how happiness felt or the quality of the misery; we watch our children's eyes for hints: knowledge has altered the taste of every emotion.' And yet, in his fiction and non-fiction, in forgotten poems, journals and letters, Greene has constantly returned to and remembered his childhood – the good occasions and the bad, the feelings of happiness and misery, the taste of every emotion, memories of blood and death and childish terrors – some which were painful for him but were not much more extraordinary than those experienced by many children, except perhaps that his response was more sensitive, his memory more enduring. Certainly he remembered a great deal of that 'country of childhood'.

*

At Berkhamsted School, St John's was a boarders' house, opened by Dr Fry in 1890 – rather different from an ordinary home. Yet, although both his parents were involved in school life, the ethos and pressures of St John's, or for that matter of the school itself, do not seem to have impinged on his early consciousness; but of course he was not quite six years old when the family left St John's. His earliest memory, if he has it right, dates from his second week of life, perhaps an understandable exaggeration given the circumstances in which he wrote about it, but obviously a very early and possible memory. In 1926, when he was desperately in love with Vivienne Dayrell-Browning★, he wrote to her:

> And in a way perhaps I've always loved you, since I was born . . . because, darling, you are beauty, through and through . . . and so when I was a fortnight old, and loved the glint of a watch dangling in someone's hand, I really loved you, only I didn't know it. And I can never stop loving you, therefore.[7]

Otherwise, all that he claims to remember about his physical surroundings were the 'chintzy drawing-room' where his mother read stories to her children, the nursery where he took his early steps and awkward falls and concentrated silently upon the fire half-hidden behind the fire-guard, noticing how the shadows cast by the flames advanced and receded, and the extra piece of garden they had across the road, with its summer-house and bushes which blocked the view of his home – his 'first experience of a foreign land'. To his child's imagination, his home was 'England', the garden 'France' and to cross over from one to the other was an adventure, involving danger and secrecy but also affording the safety of a hiding place and of knowing that home was not far away. Certainly the mould was being formed.

★ Later she called herself Vivien.

7

What he then had no knowledge of was the boarding area of the house where there were 'such grim rooms' – the schoolroom, the dormitories, the changing-rooms, the lavatories without locks on the doors – a much more unpleasant 'foreign' land (planned by Dr Fry) which was to lie in wait for him for thirteen years. His discovery of that shut-off area in what had once been his home was, as he said, 'climacteric', but it is probably true to say that from the age of seven he was increasingly 'menaced by the approach of school and a new kind of life'.

His infancy went according to nature's – and man's – plan. For four months he was fed at his mother's breast and weighed 11 lbs when he was one month old. He was dressed in his first short clothes on 15 January 1905 when he was three months old and four days afterwards this future nomad took his first modest ride in a cart drawn by the family donkey, Miranda, to the post office to collect the mail. He cut his first tooth on 6 July 1905.[8]

A photograph taken when he was four shows that he had fair curls falling round his neck and, following the fashion of the time, wore a pinafore which gave him 'the ambiguity of undetermined sex'.[9] At that period his adenoids and tonsils were removed, the operation being carried out at home and leaving him with the memory of a tin chamber pot full of blood. The sight of blood was to disturb him into manhood and he sometimes fainted at the mere description of an accident. These incidents of nausea were only conquered during the London blitz some thirty years later.

The first words he uttered appear to have been inspired by a tragic event, the death of his sister Molly's pug: 'It had been run over – by a horse carriage? – and killed',[10] and had apparently been thrown into his baby-carriage by the nurse who 'thought it convenient to bring the cadaver home this way'. In his autobiography Greene makes no comment on the shock of such an incident, and indeed, earlier, in his travel book, *Journey Without Maps* (1936), he wrote: 'There was no emotion attached to the sight [of the dead dog]. It was just a fact. At that period in life one has an admirable objectivity.'[11] There may be some truth in this, but a few months afterwards, when he first spoke, to his mother's surprise he said, 'Poor dog', which suggests an imaginative sympathy with the creature which was both pathetic and impotent. One wonders why he needed to deny the emotions which this event must have aroused, a denial strengthened by his controlled unemotive language: 'no emotion', 'just a fact', 'admirable objectivity' – like splinters of ice. We cannot date this incident exactly, but assuming he was somewhere between eight and ten months at the time, he must have been distinctly aware of the sudden oppression of having a dead dog tossed into the restricted space of his baby carriage – and a pug normally weighs little less than a child. However young he was he must have had an instinctive awareness of death from the carcass, the smell, perhaps blood, perhaps the mouth pulled back over the teeth in the snarl of death. Wouldn't there be a growing sense of panic, even nausea on finding himself shut in, irrevocably committed to sharing the limited confines of a pram with a dead dog? It may well be that the impact of this experience was reflected thirty-eight years later in his novel, *The Confidential Agent*, in a passage describing the hero's horror in recalling the death, not of a dog, but of a cat: 'He felt sick and shaken; he remembered the dead tom-cat close to his face: he couldn't move: he just lay there with the fur almost in his mouth.'[12] Knowledge of death came early to Graham Greene.

There was a second confrontation with death when he was six and he was to return to this event on no less than five occasions in his writings. Each time something is added to the incident. The first account is brief: 'Another fact was the man who rushed out of a cottage near the canal bridge and into the next house; he had a knife in his hand; people ran after him shouting; he wanted to kill himself.'[13] This was followed by a rather more developed version in the unpublished manuscript, 'Fanatic Arabia' (the title derived from Charles Doughty's *Travels in Arabia Deserta*) in which Heinz, the hero, recalls seeing a man 'run into one of the little shabby almshouses, blackened with railway soot, with a knife: he wanted to cut his throat but a crowd of people followed him and wouldn't let him.'[14] The third version appears in 'The Innocent' (1937), when the neighbours pursue the man up the stairs but the suicide is left unconfirmed.

Three years later, in the Prologue to *The Lawless Roads*, a new factor has entered (one which could not have been known to a child of six). The man's desire to end his life stems from his loss of a sense of God: 'He was going to cut his throat with a knife if he could get away from his neighbours, "having no hope, and without God in the world."'[15] These last words were in one of Greene's favourite books, *Apologia Pro Vita Sua* by Cardinal Newman.

The final version, and perhaps the one closest to the truth, comes over thirty years later in *A Sort of Life*, a vivid cameo sketch, the almshouses in Berkhamsted leaning against each other near the Grand Junction Canal, the crowd outside one of the houses, a man breaking away and running into another house – though in this version the crowd does not follow him. Instead everyone stands outside in anticipation of the bloody event. Among the crowd was the child Graham Greene (his age reduced to five) with his nurse.

However vivid and compelling this incident was to Greene, doubts about its authenticity bothered him for many years and were only dispersed when he was writing his autobiography and sought confirmation from his brother Raymond, who told him: 'You did in fact see the man cut his throat, standing by a first floor window, or the nurse may have obstructed your view. Anyway he succeeded.' It is strange that I could find no report of this incident in the *Berkhamsted Gazette* for the years 1908–11. Nevertheless, with his brother's confirmation, we can conclude that powerful experiences of blood and death were part of his early life.

*

Until his schooldays began, Graham Greene's life was nursery-orientated. His brother, Hugh Greene, described the unchanging routine of those early years and the close, secure, busy world of the nursery, with its natural hierarchy of brothers and sisters, its pressures, standards and shared pleasures, secrets and arguments.[16] His older sister, Molly, thirteen when Graham was born, was soon to move out into the adult world, but there were Herbert and Raymond above him. As he grew older and was no doubt more in authority, there were Hugh and Elisabeth below him. They saw their parents for an hour in the evening from 5.30 to 6.30. In the afternoon they went for a walk with their nurse – sometimes with a nursemaid as well. During the rest of the day they lived in the nursery and took their meals there. Even had they wished, their parents, certainly their father, would not have found it possible to spend much time with their children, but in Edwardian, as in Victorian, middle and upper class families, with their large houses and numerous servants, this was the norm. For some children, such as Beatrix Potter, this meant a lonely life, but that was not the case with Graham Greene, and until he was thirteen he was not deprived of company and affection.

He remembered the nursery at School House (to which the family moved when he was six) as: 'a large confused room . . . with toy cupboards and bookshelves and a big wooden rocking-horse with wicked eyes and one large comfortable wicker-chair for the nurse beside the steel fireguard.'[17] He remembered a long succession of nursemaids, but the important woman in his childhood was his Nanny, who had been with the family for thirteen years before his birth, brought in originally to look after his eldest sister Molly. What he remembered of her was her head bent over his bath and her white hair in a bun – what he described as that 'white bun of age'.[18]

A very early and forgotten poem, 'Sad Cure', gives a vignette of the Greene home as seen from a child's point of view and emphasises the child's helpless inarticulateness in face of what he sees and feels. Comfort (with its related security) and Fear (with its related terror) are the two poles of the child's world – the comfort and security of nursery and drawing-room, the fear and terror of the dark stairs and dark bedroom:

> If he shut his eyes, he almost heard
> the butter frizzling on the thick hot toast,
> while Nurse was clattering teaspoons, clinking cups . . .
> He'd sometimes sit and spin the minutes out
> before he dared the dark stair to his bed,
> reading or sometimes tempting Nurse to tell
> of witches, pirates, angels, devils even . . .
> Comfort and Fear – these two alone made Life.
> But while the Fear too often stood alone . . .
> The Comfort always had been mixed with fear.
>
> They could not tell . . . what his feelings were
> when a small wind crept round an ancient poster,
> nor yet the smell that always brought a drawing-room to his
>   mind,
> the spirit lamp, the tea-cups and the jam.
> They could not tell; he could not tell himself.
> What is most strange is if they could relate
> each trivial sight which brought him ecstasy,
> and set his small . . . soul,
> a-stuttering out its happiness to the dark.[19]

He had a mind so sensitive and an imagination so vivid that the coming of evening raised up terrible possibilities and 'all the nerves [were] ajump with the fear of bed-time' bringing him near hysteria. Apart from trying to extend nursery comforts by encouraging his nanny to tell him stories, he remembered that he used to take 'a multitude of soft animals' to bed with him – an indication of fear and insecurity. He remembered two bears, a rabbit and a blue plush bird. He 'kept the bird . . . only for the sake of filling the bed, because [he] disliked the feeling of plush' and had a terror of birds.[20]

To drive away the fear and find security he would drop his teddy bear out of bed so that when his nurse came to pick it up he felt assured that all was normal and he could go to sleep. When the house fell quiet and he had fears of fire or of being deserted by his family, he would get up and sit at the top of the stairs so he could hear the voices from the dining room below: 'the low comforting drone of dull adult conversation which told me that the house was not yet ablaze'.[21] These recollections appear in his autobiography as late as 1971, but as early as 1936 he had used them in 'The Basement Room': 'they saw him into bed and lit his night-light and left his door ajar. He could hear their voices on the stairs, friendly like the guests he heard at dinner-parties when they moved down to the hall, saying good night . . . he was safe.'

The journey to bed (and this was in School House) was one of fear in itself. He had to creep by what he calls a branch line on the main staircase that ran steeply up to his mother's private lavatory. At night this narrow stair was a point of terror – anything might lurk there in ambush. It seemed it was always on landings that he was most in danger. When he was nearly seven, and unhappy at the thought that he would soon have to attend school, he was terrified by a witch, who, he believed, lurked on the nursery landing by the linen-cupboard: 'After a long series of nightmares when the witch would leap on my back and dig long mandarin finger-nails into my shoulders.' Looking back to these genuine terrors in *A Sort of Life* he recalls how, in a dream, he attacked the witch and put her permanently to flight: 'I dreamt I turned on her and fought back and after that she never again appeared in sleep.'[22] Greene was sixty-seven when he wrote his autobiography and we might think his nightmares were the figments of his imagination, but they appear in a review written when he was twenty (and hidden away in a 1924 copy of *The Oxford Outlook*): 'Comfort is not a reality. The real things are terrible things. The stairs to bed, the empty cupboard on the landing, and the witch with white puffed hands and the fleshy face, who waits always round the corner.' Philip Lane in 'The Basement Room' also has nightmares which could well have been Graham's own – 'the inevitable terrors of sleep came round him: a man with a tricolour hat beat at the door on His Majesty's service, a bleeding head lay on the kitchen table in a basket, and the Siberian wolves crept closer. He was bound hand and foot and couldn't move; they leapt round him breathing heavily.'

Minor ailments pleased him for they confined him to bed and brought him a sense of peace, endless time, and a night-light burning in his bedroom, a feeling of security.

Fear of drowning, from which he also suffered, probably originated in an early attack of hay-fever brought on by playing in a haystack. His family was mystified by the illness as he lay awake coughing and gasping for breath all night – 'perhaps during that night I evolved my fear of drowning – I was able to imagine the lungs filling with water'. He had dreams when he would feel himself drawn as if by a magnet to the water's edge and later, in adolescence, they became so strong that they affected his waking life: he would find his feet would be actually attracted by the margin of a pond or river. This fear must have been strengthened by what he heard of reports of inquests in the *Berkhamsted Gazette* on people – often children of bargees – who had drowned in the Grand Junction Canal running through the town. It was believed locally that no one who fell into the locks on the canal could be rescued: 'I cannot to this day', wrote Greene, 'peer down . . . the sheer wet walls, without a sense of trepidation.'[23]

In *The Quiet American* (1955), Greene was to draw on this particular fear when Fowler and Pyle have to sink into the flooded paddy-field in Vietnam to escape the enemy:

the footsteps halted: they only seemed the length of a room away. I felt Pyle's hand on my good side pressing me slowly down; we sank together into the mud very slowly so as to make the least disturbance of the rice. On one knee, by straining my head back-wards, I could just keep my mouth out of the water. The pain came back to my leg and I thought, 'If I faint here I drown' – I had always hated and feared the thought of drowning. Why can't one choose one's death?[24]

That his fear of drowning is rooted in a hay-fever attack receives some confirmation from a description of a nightmare endured by Pinkie, the boy killer in his 1938 novel *Brighton Rock*:

A piece of blanket fell across his mouth; he breathed with difficulty. He was upon the pier and he could see the piles breaking – a black cloud came racing up across the Channel and the sea rose: the whole pier lurched and settled lower. He tried to scream: no death was so bad as drowning. The deck of the pier lay at a steep angle like that of a liner on the point of its deadly dive; he scrambled up the polished slope away from the sea and slipped again, down and down.[25]

Greene makes a distinction between terror and fear, and while fear has an odd seduction, 'one escapes, screaming, from terror'. His terror of birds, his loathing of the touch of their feathers, was inherited from his mother, though it did not prevent his being involved in the burial of a bird: 'I remember the funeral of a dead bird which was coffined in a Price's night-light box. My elders, Herbert, Molly and Raymond, buried him in what was called the Shady Walk [at Harston House, home of his uncle, Sir Graham Greene]. I was only a minor mourner, being the youngest, too young and unimportant to be priest or grave-digger or chorister.'[26] The hairy bodies of moths also terrified him and his abhorrence of bats is vividly recalled when he describes how one came into his bedroom at Harston: 'I saw it poke its furry nose first around the curtains and wait to be observed.' The following night it came down the chimney and Graham shrieked with his head under the blankets until his brother Raymond came and caught it in a butterfly net.[27]

Again he draws on a powerful personal feeling when he uses his fear of birds in describing Arthur Rowe's response to the violent, grotesque character Poole in *The Ministry of Fear* (1943), a novel rich in disguised references to his own life. Whenever he thinks of Poole, Rowe is aware of something 'unhappy, something imprisoned at the bottom of the brain trying to climb out. It frightened him in the same way as birds frightened him when they beat up and down in closed rooms. There was only one way to escape the fear of another creature's pain. That was to lash out until the bird was stunned and quiet or dead.'[28]

The novel's hero, Arthur Rowe, mirrors Greene's character and upbringing in his attitude to pain: 'He was brought up to believe that it was wrong to inflict pain . . . He learned before he was seven what pain was like – he wouldn't willingly allow even a rat to suffer it.'[29] This refers to Greene's boyhood experience of an unskilled dentist: 'I have never suffered greater pain than I did then. I remember rolling on the drawing-room floor in agony from an exposed nerve.'[30]

A sensitivity toward animate and inanimate nature was apparent when Greene was only four years old. On the occasion of his brother Herbert's eleventh birthday during Easter 1909, the family spent some time at the seaside resort of Littlehampton on the Sussex coast near Bognor Regis (it was Graham's first visit to the seaside). His mother wrote to her husband of a glorious day passed with a carriage ride into the woods:

> The primroses were glorious. We picked for 1-1/2 hours. Graham had never seen woods with primroses before. He was so happy: 'I can't help treading on them Mumma' he said quite sadly & was much relieved to hear it would not hurt them.[31]

Again, this aspect of Graham is reflected in Arthur Rowe, who felt pain so intensely that whenever he tried to move his feet 'the earth whined back at him: he couldn't move an inch without causing pain.'[32]

As a child, Greene was a loner, secretive, keeping his fears and terrors to himself. Not even his younger brother Hugh, with whom he had the closest relationship, was taken into his confidence always.

For example, on Greene's eightieth birthday, Sir Hugh Greene, in a piece entitled 'Childhood with Graham' published in the magazine *Adam*, recalled that he had a strange, macabre childhood memory which he felt Graham apparently did not share. Over the wall from their garden (this must have been at School House) was a butcher's slaughterhouse and Hugh Greene wrote: 'I remember the screams of dying animals as a background to our play.' But in fact Greene had been aware of these screams and used his recollection of them thirty years later in *The Quiet American*, transferring his experience to his hero Fowler as he lies wounded in Vietnam:

> another shell exploded on it – they were making quite sure before they came in. What a lot of money it costs, I thought as the pain receded, to kill a few human beings – you can kill horses so much cheaper. I can't have been fully conscious, for I began to think I had strayed into a knacker's yard which was the terror of my childhood in the small town where I was born. We used to think we heard the horses whinnying with fear and the explosion of the painless killer.[33]

Greene's short story, 'End of the Party', is crucial to our understanding of him as a boy since its hero, Francis, who is doomed, suffers from many of the fears of his creator – fear of darkness, of bats, the footsteps of strangers, and also the sense of isolation from adults, including his mother: Francis is amazed at the way in which adults misunderstand the nature of their own children and he has a desire not to 'lay bare his last secrets and end reserve between his mother and himself'. That Greene is drawing on his own character here is confirmed by one example of his determined secrecy. He was at his uncle Graham's home, when he suddenly discovered that he could read – the book was *Dixon Brett, Detective*. Not wanting anyone to know of his discovery, he read the book secretly in a remote attic, though his mother must have had some inkling since, on the train journey home, she gave him Ballantyne's *Coral Island* to read. Stubbornly he refused to read it and during the whole of the interminable journey forced himself to stare at the only illustration in the book – a group of children poised on some rocks.

Unlike the fictional Francis, Greene had several reasons for concealing his new-found ability. His parents had been concerned because he was a reluctant reader. He had shown no interest in such teaching books as *Reading Without Tears* and their 'cat sat on the mat' approach. His mother's offer of *Coral Island* would not have been attractive either – after all, as he said, the detective Dixon Brett had a boy assistant with whom he could identify.[34] But there were other causes for his reluctance. At seven years old he 'feared that reading represented the entrance to the Preparatory School', and he was to go through its 'grim portal' a few weeks before his eighth birthday. He also disliked 'the sense of patronage' which he detected when he was 'praised for something others did quite naturally'.

In Marion Greene's 'All About Baby' booklet there is the following brief entry: 'Started lessons Miss Heseron Jan. 1911.' This marks the beginning, and a very gentle one, of the then six-year-old Graham Greene's formal education. These lessons were private, but in September of the following year, just before his eighth birthday, he went through the green baize door beyond his father's study to enter preparatory school. On his first day he had to read a passage from Captain Cook's voyage and found the eighteenth-century prose dull. His mother, writing to aunt Alice in South Africa, added a few comforting comments: 'Graham seems very happy' and 'today is his birthday and Ben, Ave, Tooter [Edward Greene's children], and his school friends have been to tea and it went very very well.'

The Preparatory Department of Berkhamsted School was established by his father in the year Graham became a pupil there. His mother wrote to Alice that 'Charley' had bought Elvyne House where her sister Maud had once lived (it was in Chesham Road) and turned it into a boarding house for boys of eight to ten and a half years old, but the preparatory classrooms were in the Junior School at Berkhamsted. The Department and the House were run by a Mr Frost. Marion wrote: 'It has started very well with 8 boys. They all seem so happy & Mr Frost is in the seventh heaven.'[35] And in his speech on Founder's Day, 1913, Charles Greene described Frost as a man 'who seemed specially fitted by nature to be a helper and a friend to little boys'.[36] S. R. Denny, Graham's contemporary, remembered Frost, 'surrounded by a cheerful gang of gambolling preppers . . . He was very popular and fatherly'. But not to Graham, the unforgetting (and perhaps unforgiving) who was 'a little afraid of him. He used to sweep his black gown around him in a melodramatic gesture, before he indulged his jovial ogreish habit of screwing a fist in one's cheek till it hurt.'[37] One Old Boy could still recall his impression of Greene as having 'the face of what looked to me a very shy and sensitive little boy above a green and gold Preparatory House tie'. Whether he was as happy as his mother suggests is debatable. He only admits to being 'not unhappy at school' at that period, but he had a tendency to become ill as school days approached and caught measles before entering Preparatory School and chicken pox five weeks after starting school. Such childhood illnesses are of course normal and infections are easily picked up at school, but illnesses that were not too severe would give him an extension of a quiet, secluded existence away from disciplined group routines and activities. He recalls that after he was six but before he went to school, he 'began regularly to steal currants and sultanas out of the big biscuit tins in the School House store-room', methodically putting the currants in his left pocket and sultanas in the right and carefully eating every one – even the fluff-covered ones – to escape detection, perhaps indicating his anxiety about the future.

However reluctant he had been to learn to read, however daunted by the prospect of a preparatory school, having once begun, he read with absorption and intelligence. In his eighth year his mother wrote to his aunt Alice:

> [Graham] was sitting reading poetry very gravely to himself & he looked up & said, 'how different the funerals of Sir John Moore & the Duke of Wellington were. At Sir John Moore's not a drum was heard . . . not a funeral note while at the Duke of Wellington's were drums & music.' Rather curious, don't you think it striking a person of 8?

His reading matter was not always so serious and thought-provoking. He was able to quote from memory the closing twenty lines of the romantic poem, 'The Cavalier's Escape' by G. W. Thornbury: 'But pad, pad, pad like a thing that was mad/My chestnut broke away', and also Alfred Noyes's 'The Highwayman' which tells how Bess, the innkeeper's black-eyed daughter, sacrificed her life to warn her highwayman lover that soldiers were lying in wait for him.

The books Graham read as a child ranged from Charlotte M. Yonge's *The Little Duke*, the Andrew Lang Fairy Books, E. Nesbit's novels, and Beatrix Potter, to romance, adventure and history in Kipling, Captain Marryat, Henty, Rider Haggard, Stanley Weyman and Captain Gilson. One of the advantages of being the son of the headmaster was, he recalls, that on holidays the thousands of books in the school library were available, 'only waiting to be explored'.[38]

For him, it is only in childhood that books have a powerful influence: 'What do we ever get nowadays from reading to equal the excitement and the revelation in those first fourteen years?' he asks, and recalls 'the missed heartbeat, the appalled glee'[39] when he found a novel by Rider Haggard, Percy Westerman or Stanley Weyman, and the fear he felt when, in Preparatory School, he first read *Dracula*: 'The memory is salt with the taste of blood, for I had picked my lip while reading and it wouldn't stop bleeding.'[40] And it was terror that struck him most: the Ugly Wugglies in Edith Nesbit's children's book *The Enchanted Castle* who are made of masks and umbrellas and suddenly come alive and applaud 'the children's play from their roofless mouths, clapping empty gloves'; or the strange attraction of suffering and cruelty when the mad Khan in Rider Haggard's *Ayesha* goes hunting with bloodhounds the man who has courted his wife – 'never shall I forget the scene of those two heaps of worrying wolves, and of the maniac Khan, who yelled in his fiendish joy, and cheered on his death-hounds to finish their red work.'[41]

But reading had other importance apart from providing excitement, fear and escape: 'in childhood all books', he writes, 'are books of divination, telling us about the future, and like the fortune-teller who sees a long journey in the cards or death by water they influence the future.'[42] Indeed Greene believes that early reading has more influence on conduct than any religious teaching.[43] It was Rider Haggard's *Montezuma's Daughter*, the story of the disastrous night of Cortez's retreat, which lured him to Mexico twenty years after reading it and led ultimately to his masterpiece, *The Power and the Glory*. And he is certain that he would not have made a false start, beginning his post-university career with the British-American Tobacco Company, if he had never read Captain Gilson's *Lost Column*; that without having read in Rider Haggard's *King Solomon's Mines* about the witch Gagool he would not have been drawn to Liberia in the 1930s:

> In 1935 I found myself sick with fever on a camp bed in a Liberian native's hut with a candle going out in an empty whisky bottle and a rat moving in the shadows. Wasn't it the incurable fascination of Gagool with her bare yellow skull, the wrinkled scalp that moved and contracted like the hood of a cobra, that led me to work all through 1942 in a little stuffy office in Freetown, Sierra Leone?[44]

But the books for children of that period not only provided adventure and excitement and the strangeness of foreign lands, they instilled standards of heroism, idealism, courage and self-sacrifice, presented in a world that was much simpler than the future was to be for Greene. There were stories of honourable men – Captain Scott writing his last letters home; Oates walking into the blizzard; Pierre Curie's experiments with radium which led to the loss of his hands; Damien working among lepers and contracting leprosy. 'In childhood,' Greene wrote, 'we live under the brightness of immortality – heaven is as near and actual as the seaside. Behind the complicated details of the world stand the simplicities: God is good, the grown–up man or woman knows the answer to every question, there is such a thing as truth, and justice is as measured and faultless as a clock.'[45] It was a world that he, like his hero Arthur Rowe, did not wish to lose and wished to return to. Seeing a garden fête in the middle of London during the Second World War, Rowe is drawn irresistibly towards it: 'The fête called him like innocence: it was entangled in childhood, with vicarage gardens and girls in white summer frocks and the smell of herbaceous borders and security'[46] and he longed to mislay the events of twenty years of adulthood, for in his lean experienced skull lay childhood.

Childhood and the innocent eye, however, are temporary and their loss began for Greene at about the age of ten, when the move from Preparatory School to the Junior School at Berkhamsted made him realise that the world was not as he had imagined – not as he had gathered from his reading. He began to be aware of cowardice, shame, deception and disappointment – the real world, in fact. He began to see that heroes in life were not simple, were not brave, did not always tell the truth and were in the long run often defeated. He began to have reservations about the two white heroes in *King Solomon's Mines*:

> but Quatermain and Curtis – weren't they, even when I was only ten years old, a little too good to be true? They were men of such unyielding integrity . . . that the wavering personality of a child could not rest for long against those monumental shoulders . . . Sir Henry Curtis perched upon a rock bleeding from a dozen wounds but fighting on with the remnant of the Greys against the hordes of Twala was too heroic . . . they were not life as one had already begun to know it.[47]

There comes a moment in childhood 'when the door opens and lets the future in'.[48]

Apart from the Walter Mittys of the world, however, the loss of innocence and childhood illusions is part of the normal process of maturing. In Greene's case it would seem to be the abruptness of his awakening to reality that was traumatic, and yet, from an early age, there was a strangeness about him. A family group photograph illustrates this. Elisabeth is still a baby, which places the photograph in the spring or summer of 1915 when Graham was eleven. Herbert, the eldest boy, is in military uniform, Raymond, Molly and Hugh are all staring normally at the photographer, but Graham is sitting apart and looks as if he is 'somewhere else'. He has the lost, unanchored look of a child, but he also seems different and separated by more than physical distance from the others. This view of him was reinforced by some of his contemporaries at school, who thought that he was 'very different and perhaps a bit bonkers.' (We must set beside this Sir Hugh Greene's comment: 'We Greenes are all a little bonkers!') As a child Greene could become very excited and this was reflected in a language of his own devising which he was still using, on occasions, when he was twenty and in love with his future wife:

> Will you be affectionate in spite of the cold weather? Will you be brazen? I shall be. Will you be scandalous? I shall be. Will you be shocking? I shall be. Gooja Gooja Gooja Gooja. I've not gone mad, darling, but when excited frantically, I always babble nonsense to myself in the Lollabobble dialect.[49]

Graham may not have been 'bonkers' but he was different.

*

It is little wonder his parents did not fully understand the nature of their son, given his ability to conceal his fears and emotions, though sometimes his sympathy for others would move him to tears. A story which his mother would read to the children during their hour with her in the drawing room caused him much distress:

> I remember the fear I felt that my mother would read us a story about some children who were sent into a forest by a wicked uncle to be murdered, but the murderer repented and left them to die of exposure and afterwards the birds covered their bodies with leaves. I dreaded the story because I was afraid of weeping.[50]

This was not just a childish reaction – even today he sometimes finds himself slinking shamefacedly from a cinema with tears on his face, and perhaps this imaginative sympathy with the predicaments of others helped to make him a novelist.

But along with sensibility went integrity. At the age of four, he had a conviction that promises made are promises kept. In the same Easter letter quoted above, Marion Greene recorded how her sister Nora (called Nono by the family) had come up against young Graham's stubborn determination to stand by his word:

> Nora put the boys to bed last night & Molly & I went to Church. Graham refused to say his prayers to Nora & when she embarked on a second try, he said 'Auntie Nono I volunteered before I wouldn't say mustard [wouldn't say anything].'[51]

We do not know why he had volunteered not to say 'mustard' but presumably some peccadillo had been committed by the brothers and because he had been sworn to secrecy he was not going to break faith – in prayer he might have been obliged to do so. Moreover, we have here an example of a child contending with the adult world despite his natural powerlessness. It must have taken some strength of character to refuse Aunt Nono's request.

This child mystified not just his parents. His aunt Eva, who married Edward, Charles's brother, in Santos, Brazil in 1901, was twenty-two when Graham was born. When she was almost 100 years old her memories of the Hall in Berkhamsted where she had lived were still fresh:

> I never found it easy to understand young Graham. Once I remember when he was naughty, he refused to own up to the fact until he had persuaded us to say please. He must have been then 5 or 6 years old. He seemed as a boy completely inexperienced and yet he was not. He was very shy and yet he was not shy. He seemed to respond to us. I never knew, when he called at the Hall, whether he was happy or unhappy. He was certainly *different from any other child I have ever known.* He came over to the Hall very often during the time his father was Headmaster at Berkhamsted. I don't know, I think he just left me puzzled. I just never knew whether he was as a child pleased or unhappy, approved or didn't approve. I never knew. I never knew.[52]

Graham himself remembered how, as a child, he was unjustly smacked for refusing to apologise for things he had done. We can imagine the scene: his family demanding he should apologise and he in return demanding that they say please first – as, no doubt, *he* had been taught to say 'please' when making a request.

But it was not until he was almost thirty, in a *Spectator* book review (30 June 1933), that Greene revealed his sense of hopeless opposition to the injustice of adult behaviour towards children:

> Against the background of visits to grandparents, of examinations and lessons and children's parties, the tragic drama of childhood is played, the attempt to understand what is happening, to cut through adult lies, which are not regarded as lies simply because they are spoken to a child, to piece together the scraps of conversation, the hints through open doors, the clues on dressing-tables, to understand. Your whole future is threatened by these lowered voices, these consultations . . . the quarrels in the neighbouring

room, but you are told nothing, you are patted on the head and scolded, kissed and lied to and sent to bed. Herr Lothar has written the *All Quiet* of childhood, showing what is behind the official posted bulletins: 'X has been irritable.' 'X has been good.' 'X has gone to bed in tears.'

The impression that comes from this is that of a child who was imaginative, fearful of many things, complex, often withdrawn, but with an early developed sense of justice and independence. With this went not only the need for security, but the allied need for solitariness, and the need to defend the territory that provided both. At his uncle's home, Harston Hall, he had the remote attic to read in and the hiding places in the rambling gardens, and was so jealous of them that he refused to reveal them to a small boy who was invited to share his summer holiday there.[53] At St John's he had the 'French' garden from which he could watch the 'English' garden unobserved, and the seclusion and comfort of his bedroom when he was ill and could enjoy the peaceful darkness, endless time, privacy and 'books brought by my mother for me to read . . .'[54]

Though solitude and secrecy were essential to him at times, he was never lonely: 'however occupied the parents might be, in a family of six children, a nanny, a nursemaid, a gardener, a fat and cheerful cook, a beloved head-housemaid, a platoon of assistant maids, a whole battalion of aunts and uncles, all of them called Greene', there was no loneliness, and the 'six birthdays, the Christmas play, the Easter and the summer seaside, all arrived like planets in their due season'. 'The clouds of unknowing were still luminous with happiness.'[55]

He also had pets and toys and engaged in the usual activities of a child, though in his case it would seem that they took on a Greeneian irony. He had a small garden plot at School House, 6 ft square, where he succeeded in growing radishes, but he remembered also the excitement of collecting snails in a bucket and of pouring salt on to them – 'they exploded into foam'.[56] He once owned two white mice, but 'one ate the other and then died of loneliness'.[57] He shared with his brothers a succession of canaries, but one broke a blood vessel singing too loud and long. His favourite toys were a clockwork train and some lead soldiers: 'When the soldiers had lost too many limbs to stand up we melted them down in a frying-pan over the nursery fire and dropped them into cold water as people do now in Sweden on New Year's night, seeking omens of the future.'[58] And he remembered how his uncle Frank, his mother's brother, would make Chinese junks by folding paper and sailing them in his bath. He longed to make his own Chinese junks but did not ask his uncle to show him how. Instead, he tried to find out for himself with the aid of Arthur Mee's *Children's Encyclopaedia* but 'never learned the secret'.[59]

2

Personal Map

Memory is like a long broken night
— GRAHAM GREENE

IT was late in the year 1910 that Charles Greene and his family moved from St John's house to School House. For Charles Greene the move was a milestone in his career: he was the new headmaster of Berkhamsted School.

The November 1910 issue of the school magazine, *The Berkhamstedian*, had reported, 'Within a fortnight of the beginning of the new school year came the announcement that the King had been pleased to approve the appointment of Dr Fry the headmaster to the Deanery of Lincoln.' *The Times* of 28 September announced the appointment and gave an account of Dr Fry's career, and the *Morning Post* congratulated Asquith, the Liberal Prime Minister, on appointing a man not only Liberal in politics but one who had given 'long and meritorious services to the Church'. The name of Fry's successor was not published in *The Berkhamstedian* until the next issue of April 1911, so that the new appointment must have been made in late November or early December 1910, but the editor, late as it was, extended 'the heartiest of welcomes to the Head', whose appointment afforded 'matter for the profoundest satisfaction' since there had been no need to have 'recourse to external aid' in making it.

School House was to be the family home until Charles Greene retired in 1927, and it was here that the latest addition to the Greene family, Hugh, was born in November 1910. Their new home was more in the centre of Berkhamsted than St John's and also much more part of the School. Whereas St John's, a comparatively new building, dating from 1890, was situated in Chesham Road off the High Street, School House was in Castle Street, also off the High Street but where the Norman Church was. It was part of the old Hall, the original 'free school', built of brick and freestone in 1544

24

by its founder, John Incent, Dean of St Paul's, and, inevitably, added to by Dr Fry.

It must have been from the time of the move to School House that Graham Greene began to get to know more intimately the town in which he lived for his first seventeen years and where he was nearer to being rooted than in any other place. If Berkhamsted did not finally hold him – for once he could escape, he did – it nourished him, gave him moving, unforgettable moments of happiness and deep scarring misery, allowed him to experience first love and make his first attempts at serious writing. It was to be his personal map for life: 'Everything one was to become must have been there, for better or worse. One's future might have been prophesied from the shape of the houses as from the lines of the hand.'[1] It was a map not simply of physical features but one on which were traced emotional and psychological contours mapping his development from childhood to adolescence and forming a personal historical addition to the history of the town. Berkhamsted was a place to which, in his long fascination with his childhood, he returned again and again in imagination: he described its streets and buildings and historical events in *The Lawless Roads*, 'Fanatic Arabia', 'The Innocent', 'Across the Border', *The Human Factor* and in his autobiography, most often recalling the same details so that any one of the descriptions points to the specific characteristics that had had significance for him. In his short story, 'The Innocent', the narrator goes back to his home town, Bishop's Hendron, obviously Berkhamsted, and discovers why the town has such a hold on him:

> the old grain warehouses across the small canal, the few lights up the hill, the posters of an ancient film . . . It was very dark, and the thin autumn mist, the smell of wet leaves and canal water were deeply familiar . . . We came up over the little humpbacked bridge and passed the alms-houses . . . little grey stone boxes, but I knew them as I knew nothing else. It was like listening to music, all that walk . . . We passed the school, the church, and came round into the old wide High Street and the sense of the first twelve years of life. If I hadn't come, I shouldn't have known that sense would be so strong . . . but now with the smell of wood fires, of the cold striking up from the dark damp paving stones, I thought I knew what it was that held me. It was the smell of innocence.[2]

Greene's recollections of Berkhamsted and School House have detail and warmth and reflect the innocence of a generally happy childhood. For him, the town, with its short streets running north and its long streets running south uphill and two miles of High Street (as wide as many a market square) holding them together, 'was like a crucifix for a man with one arm too long'. Among the High Street shops and abusing 'its broad dignity' was the New Cinema with its green Moorish dome, built after the First World War. He remembered how his father once allowed the senior boys of the school to go to the cinema to see a Tarzan film under the mistaken impression that it was an educational film of anthropological interest. Soon after the start, Charles Greene stalked out, followed by his wife, but the boys were allowed to stay. Charles regarded the cinema ever afterwards with suspicion and disillusionment.

In the same street was an authentic half-timbered Tudor house (opposite the false Tudor front of the Tudor café where 'four one-armed men [once] dined together, arranging their seats so that their arms shouldn't clash') which was used as a photographer's studio. The Greene family knew the photographer well, for Newman, as he was called, was official photographer to the school. In the unfinished novel 'Across the Border' Graham, calling him Millet and the town of Berkhamsted Denton, takes us into that ancient shop: 'There was a smell of chemicals, and in the dim bare light an antique pillar of plaster with a velvet top to rest the elbows on. Something hooded stood in a corner, and a metal clamp to fix the neck in . . . old Millet had had a flair for character in his day. As much as the crusader he was a relic of the time when Denton was a place in which to live.'[3] There was the ruined castle, the crusader's helmet in the church, the almshouses, the Grand Junction Canal, the warehouse nearby, the faint smell of coal dust blown up from the coal yards and the railway with its twice daily stream of commuters. And there was the toy shop on the High Street kept by an old woman called Figg: 'One climbed down a few steps into something like a crowded cabin, where on bunk over bunk lay the long narrow boxes of Britain's toy soldiers . . . an amazing variety which recalled all the imperial wars of the past century: Sepoys and Zulus and Boers and Russians and French.'[4] In contrast you entered the sweet shop in Castle Street by climbing steps. It was opposite the churchyard and the jewellers on the corner of the High Street. The jeweller was an old man with a white beard who sat behind the window, magnifying glass in his eye, mending watches, looking, Graham thought, like the figure of Moses.[5]

It is interesting that Graham's recollections of Berkhamsted are those important to a boy between the ages of six and twelve, but not to one who knew the town from the inside. He knew it as a middle-class boy from the School – not intimately. His knowledge began with walks supervised by his 'crotchety nurse or the nursemaid', but one walk the nurse would never take them on was along the tow path by the canal which had 'the menace of insulting words from strange brutal canal workers [from the coal barges] with blackened faces like miners, with their gypsy wives and ragged children, at the sight of middle-class children carefully dressed and shepherded'.[6] At the rubbish tips by the canal at the end of Castle Street he made friends with two or three working-class town boys and for a time used to meet them in secret (for his mother would have been deeply disturbed to have found him fraternising with such riff-raff), bringing with him a cricket bat and ball, neither of which they possessed. And then there was the old woman who lived in Castle Street and prepared tripe, 'a far lower occupation than a butcher's', though during the First World War the Greene family of necessity frequently ate her tripe with white onion sauce.[7]

He remembered the faces of the population of the town, recognisable faces 'pointed. . . like the knaves on playing cards, with a slyness about the eyes, an unsuccessful cunning'.[8] And he recalled the photographs in Newman's window of 'wedding groups bouqueted and bemused like prize oxen'. Although he says in his autobiography that his encounter with working-class boys was one of the few 'memories which remain. . . suggesting some social conditioning', it is obvious that social conditioning had begun with his birth: he had been conditioned to a middle-class family life and the public school environment. Remoteness was not only a quality of his relationship with his parents. He was remote from Berkhamsted, the working-class boys, the local people and the gypsy children of the coal barges. But he still owed much of his sense of security as a child not only to the nursery and the garden across the road at St John's, but also to the 'green spaces of a map [as] empty as Africa' – the wastes of gorse and bracken of the great Common of Berkhamsted and the small Brickhill Common and the park of Ashlyns[9] where he was to find privacy, solitude and an escape from the pressures of school life.

*

Another important feature on his personal map of Berkhamsted was the Greene family: Harston in Cambridgeshire, St Kitts in the West Indies and Berkhamsted had been 'colonized' by the Greenes who 'seemed to move as a tribe like the Bantus, taking possession'.[10] On special occasions, they could muster twenty-six relatives. Graham belonged to a wide-ranging family which did all the usual, accepted middle-class things: seaside holidays at regular times, gardening, church, tennis.

At the far end of Berkhamsted, at the Hall, 'the great house of the town', lived the rich Greenes. Those at the School were the intellectual Greenes. Charles Greene's brother Edward, who had been a highly successful businessman in Brazil, chairman of both the São Paulo Pure Coffee Company and of the Brazilian Bank among other companies, had returned to live at the Hall with his wife, Eva, and their six children (just as there were six children at School House), of whom 'Tooter' was Graham's particular friend with whom he would sit, god-like, on the roof of the Hall, surveying the country-side, eating sweets and planning their futures as midshipmen or Antarctic explorers (though it was with Tooter's younger sister, Barbara, that Greene was eventually to travel adventurously through Liberia). Also in the town was his mother's spinster sister, Maud (who had been a nurse) the poor relation, but also 'a walking news-letter' of Berkhamsted, who took him as a child to convalesce in Brighton. He would later travel from London to visit her and hear the Berkhamsted gossip.

Charles Greene's family would spend Christmas Eve with the Edward Greenes. There was the novelty of a German influence (Eva Greene was German in origin) in the shape of a Christmas tree and carols sung in German round it and presents for all the children laid out on separate tables. Christmas began for Graham at his home on Christmas Day with 'a heavy stocking lying across the toes and a slight feeling of nausea due to excitement'. Also Christmas was especially a time for family amateur theatricals. Elisabeth remembered the popularity of Saki's 'The Unrest Cure'. Plays continued in the family for many years as a letter written by Graham when he was twenty-two shows: 'I've had to invent an impromptu play for Raymond and Charlotte and Hugh and Elisabeth and me to act on Christmas night, a sort of acrobatic charade. It's horribly gruesome.'

Graham's sister, Elisabeth, recalled a playtime life of charades galore at home, sometimes by word, sometimes by pantomime: 'for some reason I particularly remember Vivien in an advertisement of "Still beautiful by candlelight".' She remembered another game they played in their drawing-room: 'Each person wrote a question on a piece of paper, folded it down the middle and passed it on and the next person wrote a word. The papers were folded up and each person took one. They then had to write a poem answering the question and bringing in a word. I thought this was hell, but I remember how good Graham was at it.'

Graham excelled in all games of this kind. On one occasion when the family was assembled and the rich Greene cousins were also present, they were asked which two books they would take with them to a desert island if they were marooned. Graham astonished his older relatives by immediately mentioning the essayists Lamb and Bacon. 'How could you cap that?' asked 'Tooter' Greene.

If Greene 'reluctantly' set on his personal map the School, that reluctance stemmed from his experiences after he was thirteen, for his home in School House was a happy one. What impressed him about School House as a six-year-old was 'the long path from the street to the front door, on the right the red-brick Tudor school hall and on the left, divided from [it] only by a flower-bed, the old disused churchyard',[11] whose leaning graves could be seen over the low garden wall. Nobody was being buried there any longer and 'the dim inscriptions on the tombstones spoke of falling asleep and peace and hope of resurrection.'[12] Over the years scraps of bone would move under the wall and the gardener would regularly turn them up when he was re-making the herbaceous border. Rhododendrons pressed up towards the window of the drawing-room and at the end of the path was a tennis court and beside it a small flower garden with a pond full of tadpoles and a buddleia which in the summer swarmed with peacock butterflies. Following the fashion then, he did for a time catch and kill butterflies, but never pinned the corpses out in a case. Later he was paid 'a penny a dozen for killing cabbage-white butterflies with a tennis-racket' just as he had been paid by the hundred for the corpses of snails he had exploded with salt.[13]

Beyond the buddleia were the two greenhouses at right angles to each other and through a gateway by the smaller of the two was a croquet lawn, at the far end of which were apple trees and a revolving shelter, then a wooden fence which separated the lawn from the kitchen garden. Beyond the kitchen garden on the left were the stables which housed only the donkey Miranda and on the right the entrance to the School quad, which lay at the back of School House.

After the move to School House, and when he was twelve, Herbert Greene started the *School House Gazette*, which takes us further into their family life. Apart from Charles, and Hugh, who was less than a year old, the whole family seems to have been involved in it, including Aunt Nono, Herbert being editor and Graham office boy. It is literate, competent, amusing at its level. We learn from it that on Graham's seventh birthday on 2 October 1911, he 'got two tents from me [Herbert], a book from auntie Maudie, a book from auntie Eva, a fort from Mumma, soldiers from Nanna & Da, sweets from Ave, a paint book from Tooter, a shooting game from Molly. The cousins came to tea and we played French and English and egg hat and hide the thimble after tea.' There was a serial, a 'Lost' column (Mrs Greene's Omoto pen. Last seen in Drawing-room of School House), a 'Jokes and Puzzles' section, typically youthful and

unchanging: 'Why is your eye like a schoolmaster using corporal punishment? Because it has a pupil under the lash'; 'Why should a thirsty
man always carry a watch? Because it has a spring inside'; and the
celebrated Detectives Herbert and Raymond Greene offered their
services. There was a 'Table Talk' column in which is recorded a
family discussion about the horses they will ride that day, which is
stilted except for Mrs Greene's injunction, 'Sit up Molly', and Herbert's, 'The craze for notoriety is the curse of the present age', and
Graham's interpolation, 'You are silly, Molly – girls are so silly.'
One feels that this is a deliberate send up of the family by the editor
and it attracted letters of protest: 'The story about our talking at
breakfast was all wrong – 'cept the part that said Molly is silly –
'cause she is silly, girls always are, Graham.'

Two items are intriguing. One is an account, with a full-length
photograph of Charles Greene, M.A., F.His.S. – 'Was educated at
Bedford. Afterwards went to Wadham College Oxford. Has been at
Berkhamsted School for 22 years. Last Easter term was appointed
Head-master in place of Dr. Fry who was given the Deanery of
Lincoln.' The second shows that on his seventh birthday Graham took
part in a competition run by the *Gazette* which involved answering a
questionnaire (he won the second prize of twelve tubes of water-
colours). The questionnaire gives some insight into the cast of mind
of the family with its emphasis on aims, qualities, pastimes, hobbies,
holidays, cricket and reading, and Graham's answers reflect the stage
of his development:

> What is your greatest aim in life? *To go up in an aeroplane.*
> What is your greatest idea of happiness? *Going up to London.*
> Who is the greatest living statesman? *Don't know any.*
> Who is your favourite character in fiction? *Dixon Brett.*
> What are the qualities you most admire in men? *Good looks.*
> In women? *Cleanliness.*
> What is your favourite pastime? *Playing Red Indians.*
> What is your pet hobby? *Collecting coins.*
> What is your favourite quotation? *'I with two more to help me will
> hold the foe in play.'*
> Who is the author you like best and which book? *Scott*, The
> Talisman.
> Who is the cricketer you most admire? *Herbert Greene.*
> Which is your favourite holiday resort? *Overstrand.*

Coin collecting and playing Red Indians are fairly predictable
activities, though his honest confession that he did not know any

living statesmen is in character, but he explains in his autobiography how a seven-year-old would have read Scott's novel *The Talisman*. It was a simplified version published in a series for children by Blackie. For a boy at that period it would be the height of ambition indeed to go up in an aeroplane and in his autobiography he recalls his family waiting a whole afternoon in the garden at St John's House hoping, in vain, to see Louis Blériot (who made history with the first flight across the English Channel in a monoplane on 25 July 1909) make the first London to Manchester flight.[14] But Greene's description in *A Sort of Life* of watching from the nursery an Old Boy of the School called Wimbush crash the first plane he (Graham) ever saw, on the School playing-fields, is a recollection of a much later event. James Wilson, a contemporary of Greene at Berkhamsted (whose schoolboy diaries provide us with a day-to-day account of school life) relates that this incident occurred on 27 March 1918, when Greene would have been thirteen and a half. And it was Wimbush's brother who crashed the single-seater Sopwith Triplane on the fields where heats were being run in preparation for Sports Day. The plane was reduced to matchwood and the pilot died, not at once, as Graham believed, but two days later in hospital. Though this was not a nursery incident, it was one that had a powerful effect on Graham's hypersensitive nerves: 'Often since then watching planes cross the sky, I half-expect to see them fall to earth, as though it were my gaze which had caused that first crash.'[15]

Much later, in 1945, the widow of the author Mervyn Peake met Graham Greene at a bus stop in Oakley Street, London. He had returned by air from a visit to America,[16] and she recalled that he described to her the heart-stopping experience of the plane's engines literally ceasing in flight. But Graham's reaction to this was unexpected. He was deeply sorry the plane had not gone down: 'I would have been happy to die, very happy to die.'

Overstrand, which Graham claimed as his favourite holiday resort, is many miles from Berkhamsted on the Norfolk coast near Cromer and was where the family spent their summer holiday. Littlehampton, which he says meant more to him with its goat carriages, sea anemones and picnics in Arundel Park, was where they went at Easter as his mother thought it was too vulgar a resort in the summer, being visited by the wrong people.[17] And that going up to London was his idea of happiness is totally understandable. Once a year at Christmas, the children were taken to see a production of J. M. Barrie's *Peter Pan* at the Duke of York's Theatre. Graham loved it, his favourite scene being when Peter Pan fought alone against the pirates with his sword, and second to that was the moment of enjoyable horror when the green–lit face of Captain Hook appeared at a service hatch and put poison into Peter's glass. Although the dying fairy Tinker Bell touched him, he would never call out with the audience that he believed in fairies in order to save her as he had a deeply felt need to be honest: 'It would have been dishonest, for I had never believed in [fairies], except for the period of the play.'[18]

Two interesting revelations are his admiration of good looks in men and cleanliness in women. At the age of seven, Graham Greene, like many small boys, had a poor opinion of the female sex. Perhaps his desire for cleanliness in women stemmed from his fate of being at the mercy of aunts and other females who wanted to kiss him. An incident of this kind occurred on his seventh birthday and was reported in the *Gazette* by his aunt Nono. In his autobiography he tells how a Miss Wills, then matron at the school, embarrassed him by kissing him when he took her a piece of his birthday cake: 'I returned to the family circle, angry and shattered by the experience.' His aunt Nono recorded the incident in a parody of 'Jenny kissed me when we met' by Leigh Hunt, entitled 'The Awful Day I Shall Never Forget':

> Miss Wills kissed me when we
>   met
> As I took my birthday cake in
> Ladies you who love to get
> Kisses on my lips, this take in
>
> Though I'm nippy, though I'm
>   spry
> Though I dodged she never
>   missed me
> Though I'm growing old and
>   shy,
> Miss Wills kissed me.

Graham Greene had an uncomfortable feeling then that the incident would not be forgotten because it had been 'immortalized by art', and in a sense he was right, for many years later the *Daily Mail* tried to publish a copy of the poem, but was prevented by Greene's threat to sue them for breach of copyright. This incident was a spin-off from a public campaign against the British Broadcasting Corporation in general and Hugh Greene (who was then Director General of the B.B.C.) in particular, a campaign led by the eldest Greene son, Herbert, who by that time had something of a reputation as the black sheep of the family. He was master-minding a lively campaign from his home in Sussex and invited down a journalist, Miss Olga Franklin, no doubt to help with publicity. Herbert felt that his younger and more successful brother Hugh was, as Director General, too icono-clastic. He had dared to remove the universally loved 9 o'clock News and the powerful chimes of Big Ben which introduced it. To many people, Big Ben and the news at nine were sacrosanct and not to be meddled with by the likes of Hugh Greene. Thus a family quarrel, the first but not the last, was carried out in public.

On that visit Miss Franklin was given the opportunity of looking at a copy of the *School House Gazette* and of reading private letters and early schoolboy poems of Graham's as well as his early diary, which she found appealing but which has since disappeared. Miss Franklin particularly recalled another poem about kissing, written by Graham when he was about eleven, bemoaning the necessity at family teas of kissing his aunts. Miss Franklin recalled Graham's regretting the whole necessity of the family ritual:

He described how the whole family sat round the table at Nursery Tea. He spoke of the 'green baize door' which separated them from the school itself. He did not enjoy kissing one particular Aunt, and enjoyed even less being watched whilst doing it. The poem was competent yet the feelings described were those of a much younger child who, like so many children, resented being kissed . . . by grown-ups. But together with what Herbert had told me of the family teas in early days, I got the impression that Graham's emotional growing-pains had been intensified by the somewhat grotesque family scene of the quite Brobdingnagian members of an excessively tall family (especially the women) closeted together at compulsory tea in that Victorian [sic] background.[19]

If Miss Franklin remembered that poem correctly, it is interesting not so much because it expressed Graham Greene's dislike of being kissed by grown-ups, but because of its very early mention of the 'green baize door' – an actual door which was to become also a symbolic one, and was eventually to open the way for him into the place he set reluctantly on his personal map, the School: 'part rosy Tudor, part hideous modern brick the colour of dolls'-house plaster hams – where the misery of life started . . .'[20] In *The Lawless Roads* (1939) he wrote, 'If you pushed open a green baize door in a passage by my father's study, you entered another passage deceptively similar, but none the less you were on alien ground.' That ground was to become like a sombre theme in a Sibelius symphony, repetitive and each time louder. His experience of it came gradually. It included the matron's room where he had gone with the gift of a piece of his birthday cake, but it also included the old Hall, the original school, the school dining-hall where he and his brother Hugh would push the big tables together and play an elaborate war game based on H. G. Wells's *Little Wars*, and the school library where he was free to read. He had the 'freedom of these regions only out of term' and in his memory they were always empty – 'stony, ugly, deserted', 'grim rooms' like those he had not known of at St John's House, but which must have presaged a threat to him even while he played or read in them. They were certainly alien since they were not part of his normal life, except that they were where his father worked. The green baize door was to become the division between heaven and hell, the gate that separated Eden from the wilderness of the world.

3

Charles and Marion Greene – and Dr Fry

That dear octopus from whose tentacles we never quite
escape.

              – DODIE SMITH

T HERE was a lack of intimacy between Graham and his parents,
in spite of the lively, extended family environment, which
would appear to have resulted from differences in personality rather
than from lack of affection. He associated his mother with a remoteness which he did not at all resent, and with a smell of eau-de-cologne.
'If I could have tasted her,' he writes, 'I am sure she would have
tasted of wheaten biscuits . . . The wheaten biscuit remains for me
a symbol of her cool puritan beauty – she seemed to eliminate all
confusion, to recognize the good from the bad and choose the good.'[1]
His mother was not only remote but had a 'wonderful lack of the
possessive instinct'[2] which, Greene comments, was made much easier
for her to achieve by the presence of Nanny. In spite of his disclaimer
that his mother's remoteness did not trouble him, he yet speaks of
her in terms appropriate to some official dignitary: 'She paid
occasional state visits to the nursery.'

Very often in his novels Graham Greene was to draw on his
memories of childhood, trying to recapture the uniqueness of that
experience and sometimes the personality of his mother. He returned
to that period particularly in *The Ministry of Fear*, which was published
in 1943 but written in 1942, the year his father died, when Graham
was working for British Intelligence in Sierra Leone. The reminiscences form part of the background of the character of Arthur
Rowe who recalls the drawing-room at his home and the memory
of his mother's perfume: 'He remembered afternoon tea and a
drawing-room with water-colours and little tables, a piano no one
played and the smell of eau-de-cologne.' This is a compilation of

35

obvious details, but another passage comes closer to the flavour of Greene's relationship with his mother. In the novel, which contrasts the horrors of the Second World War with the security and innocence of the peaceful life that preceded it, Arthur Rowe, having experienced the blitz on London and also having killed his wife (it was a mercy killing), tries to tell his mother what he has done. The sense of unlistening security established around mother and nurse, unable to comprehend Rowe's distress, could well be a reflection of the experience of the seven-year-old Greene, trying unsuccessfully to communicate his fears to his mother (the setting is the garden at the School House, Berkhamsted):

> . . . he was having tea on the lawn at home behind the red brick wall and his mother was lying back in a garden chair eating a cucumber sandwich. A bright blue croquet-ball lay at her feet, and she was smiling and paying him the half-attention a parent pays a child. The summer lay all around them, and evening was coming on. He was saying 'Mother, I murdered her . . .' and his mother said, 'Don't be silly, dear. Have one of these nice sandwiches.'
>
> 'But Mother,' he said, 'I did. I did.' It seemed terribly important to him to convince her; if she were convinced, she could do something about it, she could tell him it didn't matter and it would matter no longer, but he had to convince her first. But she turned away her head and called out in a little vexed voice to someone who wasn't there, 'You *must* remember to dust the piano.'
>
> 'Mother, please listen to me,' but he suddenly realized that he was a child, so how could he make her believe? He was not yet eight years old, he could see the nursery window on the second floor with the bars across, and presently the old nurse would put her face to the glass and signal to him to come in. 'Mother,' he said, 'I've killed my wife, and the police want me.' His mother smiled and shook her head and said, 'My little boy couldn't kill anyone.'[3]

'If one of us,' writes Greene, 'had committed murder [my mother] would, I am sure, have blamed the victim.'[4] Marion Greene, far more than her husband, made Berkhamsted a secure world for all of her six children. But there is a possibility that her confidence in them and her inability to imagine anything but good for them may have blinded her to Greene's unhappiness in his adolescence, or at least made its sources incomprehensible to her.

Trevor Wilson, at one time British Consul in Hanoi and who provided Greene with some insight into the conditions in Vietnam for *The Quiet American*, called on Marion Greene very late in her life. It was her love for Graham that he recalled: 'She must have been in her eighties then, a very beautiful person. Just said big things of Graham. She said quietly, "Look after Graham".'[5] Until her death, Greene wrote regularly to his mother – very rarely to his father. Even before he encountered his father in the role of headmaster at school, Greene found it difficult to love him or to communicate with him:

> To be praised [by him] was agony – I would crawl immediately under the nearest table . . . my only real moments of affection for my father were when he made frog-noises with his palms, or played Fly Away, Jack, Fly Away, Jill, with a piece of sticking-plaster on his finger, or made me blow open the lid of his watch.[6]

He remembered his father sitting in a deck-chair in the larger of the two greenhouses at School House, where he grew orchids and green grapes, smoking a pipe and 'blowing smoke over the grapes to kill greenflies'.[7] 'As a headmaster,' Greene writes, 'he was even more distant than our aloof mother.'[8] He would sometimes take a winter holiday alone in Egypt, France or Italy with a friend, Mr George, a clergyman and also a headmaster. When the children went off for their Easter holiday at the seaside, travelling with their mother and nurse in a reserved third-class compartment with a hamper-lunch, his father wisely would always come down alone a few days later second-class.[9] It could well be that, as headmaster of Berkhamsted, Charles Greene needed to have periods of relaxation away from children, something that his young son could not have understood, but because he could not believe that his father's interest in him was genuine, Greene did not come to love his father until he had children of his own – only then he 'discovered a buried love and sorrow for him'.[10]

Between his mother's aloofness and conviction of her children's goodness and his father's preoccupation with the school and his conviction of the natural inclination of boys to sin, it is not surprising that Graham Greene's own reluctance or inability to communicate his deepest concerns was ultimately to bring about a crisis.

*

Charles Henry Greene never intended to become a schoolmaster, but, as his son records, slipped into it during a lean period. Born on 12 January 1865, he was a grandson of Benjamin Greene, brewer of Bury St Edmunds, and owner of sugar plantations in St Kitts, West Indies, and a son of Benjamin's fifth son, William, who was sent out to manage those plantations when he was only fifteen. On his return to England, William married the daughter of a master mariner and took up farming and then became a solicitor, but he always yearned for St Kitts and returned there in 1881 and died of yellow fever. His eldest son, Graham, was to have a distinguished career as a civil servant, and was knighted, but his second son, Charles Henry, was less successful. Educated at Bedford School and Oxford University, he succeeded in obtaining only a second class degree in History and a third in Classical Honours Moderations. He intended becoming a barrister and went on, in the traditional way, to eat his dinners at the Inns of Court, but then, in 1889, his cousin Julia's husband, Thomas Charles Fry, headmaster of Berkhamsted, being in need of a tempor-ary classics master, persuaded him to take the post, and the temporary post became permanent and he remained at the school for almost forty years. Photographs of him in his youth show a handsome man, but during his long years as headmaster of Berkhamsted he developed a stoop, becoming a veritable Mr Chips.[11]

He married his first cousin once removed, Marion Raymond Greene, in 1896, the same year in which he was promoted to second master at Berkhamsted. Like most of the Greene women, Marion was 'tall and so thin . . . She had a mild and extremely refined look.' When, after twenty years as a master at Berkhamsted, Charles Greene was chosen from thirty candidates to be headmaster of the school there was no nepotism involved, for Dr Fry was not on the selection committee; but Charles Greene was very much Dr Fry's man and Fry believed, his work at Berkhamsted being as yet unfinished, that only Charles could be trusted to continue running the school on his principles and carry out his aims.

This autocrat, called by the schoolboys of the day 'the presence', literally danced for joy once his cousin by marriage was appointed head of the school. Fry was a bantam cock who had dominated the school, was pugnacious, yet had his fears as an extract from his diary shows: 'They are all against me except Charles Greene.'[12] And something of Charles's formal style (rigorously avoided by his son Graham) comes out when he writes of Fry: 'He gave me the inesti-mable privilege of his confidence and talked over with me all his plans.'[13]

Given the importance of Berkhamsted School as an influence on Graham Greene in his formative years, it is essential to re-create as far as possible the atmosphere of the school at that time and the character and principles of the headmaster. Many of Graham's school-boy contemporaries, in retirement after colonial service or commer-cial work overseas, were strong supporters of their school still. Some had found fame, others were known only in their immediate circles. None was reluctant to speak of his schooldays or of Charles Greene.[14]

Raymond Greene told the story of how he, when still a youngster, met the Bishop of St Albans at the theatre. His father asked him what the Bishop thought about the play and Raymond replied that the Bishop thought the play damned good. His father responded: 'Raymond you must not make up these things. Bishops do not use bad language.' Graham's cousin Ben (a gentle giant of 6 ft 8 in.) stressed that his uncle was unworldly: 'He knew nothing about the world. He was like Macmillan in the Profumo case, you know, bewildered by it.'[15] And James Wilson admitted of his headmaster that he 'was too Olympian. He lived up there somewhere.' But authority in the school rested with the headmaster: he was all powerful. As Eric Guest commented, 'a headmaster's remark or lecture was a kind of decree, an arbitrary order, an ukase, and all obeyed Charles.' Sir Cecil Parrott had no doubt that 'Charles Greene was the absolute law in the land, the only god we knew at first hand.' Yet Charles Greene was a very shy man, and how does such a man handle the position of being a minor god?

By nature and inclination he was a very liberal man (Graham was beaten only once by his father), though by the standards of our day he sometimes acted illiberally; and although he was not by nature a disciplinarian, his job was to impose discipline. According to Anthony Nichols, his problem was increased by the fact that he took over from one of the great Victorian headmasters, but he dealt with the situation in the special way of a very shy man – he created a protective persona mainly through his mannerisms, some of which probably originated in genuine nervousness:

> He could be very irascible and when he was you would see him nervously tying his gown literally into knots and he spat a little, or so it seemed to us, into our heads and he would swing his gown furiously and he would bang desks . . . I remember his tugging at his gown; he never stopped tugging and touching it while talking or he would be twiddling with a quiff of hair at the front of his head reaching it with his arm over the back of his head and he always seemed to be clearing his throat . . . He was someone out of Greyfriars magazine.

He was, also according to Nichols, 'soft and paunchy and his moustache . . . gave him a walrussy effect. He was always, it seemed . . . carrying papers and Charles carried his papers and his books with an air of display. And of course, he had these physical eccentricities; his pince-nez were never on his nose for five minutes at a time and he was always fiddling with them.' He was untidy and boys would look to see if he had egg on his tie. Felix Greene provides us with a gentler picture of an unworldly man: 'He always had ash on his coat. He was constantly lighting his pipe. [It] never lasted more than about fifteen seconds and he'd fumble around and light it again. He never managed to keep a pipe alive, because, well, he was like that.' By exaggerating his innate eccentricities Charles Greene created a caricature which was to some degree comic and on occasions ludicrous. Boys often indulged in mimicry at his expense, yet under it all one senses a natural gentility, and a genuine unworldliness.

Perhaps most important was the fact that his pupils found him unapproachable and with his 'slightly vacant look' he gave the impression (and this is true of his son Graham as a boy) of someone detached from life. But he also believed in, took over and enforced, the Victorian philosophies of his predecessor, Dr Fry. According to Claud Cockburn, Charles Greene's favourite word was 'keenness' and he had a strong belief in doing one's duty, an example of which was given to me by R. S. Stanier. According to school routine, after tea the boys had prep., then supper and went to bed at nine, but the prefects were allowed to stay up until ten, Charles or 'Charlie', as the boys called him, expecting this extra hour to be used for further preparation. He was, therefore, genuinely shocked when he wanted to speak to a particular prefect and discovered that he was having a bath. 'You mean to say,' the prefect was asked publicly, 'that you desert your duty to go and have a bath?'

On the whole Berkhamsted was a humane school. There was very little bullying and the masters were concerned about the boys in their charge. It was also one of the least corrupt of schools due to the influence of Dr Fry and Charles Greene's own character. James Wilson told me that 'the masters backed up Charles one hundred per cent in his purity campaign. Many of his staff were dedicated bachelors and chaste as a dedicated Roman Catholic priest. They were all devout Christians and Charles as their leader was absolutely ruthless in maintaining the moral tone of the school.'

His main concern in this urge towards purity was the dampening down of the sexual urge, particularly the homosexual. Graham Greene himself admits that it is possible that his father believed that masturbation led to madness and perhaps blindness. Following the plans of Dr Fry, the school was organised to prevent the possibility of homosexual relationships developing.

To begin with, 'muscular Christianity' (an idea originating with the Victorian novelist Charles Kingsley) was encouraged. According to Claud Cockburn, the goal was 'to keep us all going endlessly, so that we wouldn't get into all this sex stuff.' Eric Guest recalled that 'no boy was ever allowed to be idle'. The cult of games had been established in many public schools and Dr Fry was not against compulsory games: 'Manliness', he felt, 'is one of the virtues which our public school system is designed to teach, and there is no reason why it should not be taught by compulsion to the few who do not take to it willingly.'[16] So they played cricket all summer and football all winter and then in the spring there was the Officers' Training Corps (the O.T.C.). If you went running or trained with the Corps you could get off everything else. Cockburn (given to special pleading, it's true) asserted that all the military activity of the boys during the First World War had nothing to do with winning the war. It was a way of keeping busy.

There was also a system of perpetual watchfulness set up by Fry and continued by Charles Greene. According to Eric Guest, someone had to know what each boy was doing at any given time. No one was allowed to be alone. Graham Greene, writing of this system in *A Sort of Life*, does not blame his father for it, but he does write contemptuously of the 'authorities' who imposed it, and of course, his father was the ultimate authority. Masters who were heads of houses had great personal authority and could exercise their own censorship. Graham's first housemaster was the old silver-haired bachelor, Mr Herbert:

> To add to my inextricable confusion of loyalties he happened to be my godfather, mysteriously linked at my birth to look after my spiritual well-being . . . Mr Herbert was certainly not a cynic. He was an innocent little white rabbit of a bachelor, dominated by the dark Constance, his sister . . . My only memory of him is seated at a desk in the St John's schoolroom on the first evening of my first term there, while each boy in turn submitted to him, for censorship or approval, any books he had brought from home to read. The danger was in the source – home, where dwelt unreliable and uncelibate parents.[17]

Boys in the houses had individual sleeping cubicles separated by six-foot high wooden partitions with a curtain across the front. No boy ever visited another boy's cubicle and even to stand on one's bed and have a chat with the boy in the next cubicle was the height of daring. Masters and prefects patrolled the dormitories at night, inevitably involved in spying. James Wilson could go back to the day when he had to report on a boy: 'I can remember the occasion well. I came to the conclusion that someone was masturbating and I had to tell the housemaster about it. They kept a very, very tight rein on us.'

Even Sunday walks were so organised as to prevent intimacy. Graham wrote: 'On Sundays we would go for walks, by order, in threes, and the names had to be filled up like a dance programme on a list which was hung up on the changing-room door. This surely must have had some moral object, though one which eludes me today . . . Three can surely be as dangerous company as two, or were the authorities cynical enough to believe that in every three there would be one informer?'[18] All ten Berkhamsted Old Boys interviewed recalled that Sunday walks were organised as Graham Greene tells us but that it was in groups of two not three.

Charles Greene dealt with any suspected *amours* by means of expulsions. According to R. S. Stanier: 'Charles left us with the strong impression that we had to avoid misbehaviour in the dormitories; that misbehaviour in the dormitories was more serious than misbehaviour elsewhere. In my time of five years . . . there were about four cases of expulsion for things of this sort. I suppose Charles would say that if by expelling one or two boys on four occasions in five years, he preserved that innocence of mind, it was worth it.' Claud Cockburn, who greatly admired Charles Greene, was probably speaking with only half a tongue in cheek when he said: 'Being a really Victorian Liberal, he believed sincerely that if people were allowed to be together – between any two boys who might conceivably be alone together for more than twenty minutes – sin would occur.'

Charles strongly hated a sloppy posture and would shout right across the school grounds if he saw an example of it. One Old Boy remembered how Greene had ordered a pupil, because he found him lounging about with his hands in his trouser pockets, to have the pockets sewn up for a week. But another Old Boy thought there was an ulterior motive in this: 'It was all tied up with sex, in case we had holes in our pockets.'

Most of the boys had only the vaguest notion of what was going on. James Wilson felt sure that he just escaped 'getting the sack'. He was found by his physics master, reading Alec Waugh's *Loom of Youth* (1917). The physics master punished him instead of reporting him to the Housemaster, Herbert, who would in turn have reported him to Charles Greene and he would have been expelled. (Wilson's whole generation was fascinated by *The Loom of Youth*. It created an absolute sensation in raising the apparition of homosexuality at Sherborne School.)[19]

Anthony Nichols also described how he just escaped expulsion. There had been an outbreak of Spanish 'flu and thirty boys were despatched to the school sanatorium. On one occasion the boys were talking schoolboy sex when the under-matron came in: 'What we were saying was the usual things – "Look at my oranges – look at my balls or at our bananas" – just ordinary schoolboy sex and we were reported by the under-matron to Charles and Charles called a number of us in. I remember being terrified and he asked me very peculiar questions. He wanted to know exactly what had been said by the boys. "What was meant by banana?" he asked.' And thanks to Wilson we know exactly how the expulsions took place:

> What would happen would be that boys would be called out of class, summoned by the sergeant to report to the headmaster's study and they would be away for a period, and then another boy would be called, and this might go on for a day or two. And then, suddenly, so and so, and so and so, would just disappear. You never said goodbye to them, you didn't know what had happened to them. They simply faded away and disappeared. Their names will never appear in the Old Boys' list and they will never be heard of again.

Sometimes, a less dramatic method than expulsion was used by Charles Greene and Graham was well aware of this. In his novel *England Made Me* (1935) Minty, the seedy, unscrupulous journalist, is gently sent packing: 'it was Minty who left, after long hours with the housemaster, not expelled but taken away by his mother. Everything was very quiet, very discreet: his mother subscribed for him to the Old Boys' Society.'

Charles Greene was, said Ben Greene, 'bewildered by sex. He just didn't understand it.' And Ben gave an example of Charles's swift action to head off the sex bug: 'When I was at school, he expelled one awfully nice boy for kissing a girl up on Brickhill Common. A master saw him kissing, and he was expelled the next day.'

Charles's bewilderment over such matters seemed to find its way into the manner in which, on these occasions, he interrogated the boys. Nichols recalled that he would ask questions such as, 'Do you know what masturbation is?' or 'How many times have you masturbated?' and when the initial fear of the boy being questioned had receded, Charles became for the boy something of a figure of fun: 'He would never say, "Please leave me now", he would say, "You boy, you will go, go, get out of my sight."'

He was also known, affectionately, for his 'jawing'. As a lay preacher he gave a sermon at the beginning of every term – very often on the theme of 'purity'. An entry in James Wilson's diary reads: 'Charles preached a very vehement sermon against filthiness.' There was also a special 'jaw' at the end of term, another when a boy was made a prefect and a very special 'jaw' for confirmation. Yet it was a little like the blind leading the blind. Graham's cousin, Ben, recalled his father Edward telling him nervously of the problems a young man had to face in the world, and suggesting his best plan was to follow the rules of the Church, to study his lessons diligently, and to go to 'Uncle Charles for confirmation lessons'. The trouble was that his uncle was so narrow, had no real experience and only followed church rules. Yet Charles's jawing was tremendously effective. He was an excellent public speaker. One can see how firmly established Charles Greene's behaviour was, and how slightly comic also, in the following incident.

Charles was in Egypt in 1904 and in a tourist way was visiting the pyramids: 'The climb to the King's chamber is half way up, very steep and hot. Two Arabs hold each a hand; another carrying a candle. With the help of the three the journey is quickly done; I gave the men very good backsheesh but with one consent they howled for more. I sat down and gave them a lecture on their sins then and there. I don't suppose they understood a word, but I probably glared at them as you tell me I do when I am angry. They threw up their arms to Heaven and with just as much animation as they had howled for more exclaimed "we are all satisfied".'[20]

Charles Greene's language had an evangelical flavour and he was indeed something of an evangelist. He was, thought one Old Boy, a kindred spirit with the prophets of the Old Testament and like an Old Testament prophet himself: 'The talk given by Charles to new boys was a bit Sinai-like. One felt that something terribly important was being said, but one didn't quite know what it all amounted to.' Another Old Boy remembered his splendid sermons in Deans' Hall:

He was always speaking, as it were, about the blood of Jesus Christ and the Lamb of God. I remember one particular graphic phrase which you would find appearing in sermon after sermon. The phrase was: 'What of the ships, O Carthage, O Carthage, what of the ships'. Whenever he was stuck in would come this kind of pronouncement.

He read the second lesson in the school Chapel and had a particular passion for The Book of Revelation and one particular passage in it, the 21st chapter, and many boys remembered his reading this with the names of lovely sounding jewels which he would roll out, not only because of the beauty of the passage but because of the strength of his personal feeling for its beauty. 'The foundation of the Holy City rolled off his tongue, especially when he reached the tenth stone, Chrysoprasus', recalled S. R. Denny:

And the foundations of the wall of the city were garnished with all manner of precious stones. The first foundation was jasper; the second, sapphire, the third, chalcedony; the fourth, an emerald; the fifth, sardony; the sixth, sardius; the seventh, chrysolyte; the eighth, beryl; the ninth, a topaz; the tenth, a chrysoprasus; the eleventh, a jacinth; the twelfth, an amethyst.

Was it part of Charles Greene's persona or an authentic concern that led him to give some of his pupils, on the day they left school, some words of advice, most of which mystified them? Here they had their last view of Charles, the old-style believer in clean living and the good Christian life. His advice to Nichols was innocuous enough, and advice which his own son Graham has followed throughout his career: 'I remember one of the last things he said to me just before I left school – "One thing you've got to think about – application, application, that will take you to the top of things, application." He was always repeating things of this kind.' And Stanier also recalled his last day: 'His sort of leaving talk to me – he had me into his study – and he said, "I'm sure I've no need to warn you against drink and gambling. I'll just say one thing – see that you come to your future wife clean." And that was that.' E. T. Arnold, a relative of Matthew Arnold, remembers to this day paying his respects to Charles on leaving school to join the Army in 1918: 'I was puzzled then, I am still puzzled now sixty years later, by his advice. It was: "Remember to be faithful to your future wife." I did not know then what on earth he was getting at.' It happened to Sir Cecil Parrott just before his confirmation: 'I remember Charles saying suddenly out of the blue to me: "An army of women live on the lust of men."'

A curious man, Charles Greene, but one beloved by his pupils. According to Eric Guest he was a man of great moral courage and an ardent opponent of all witch-doctors in and out of society. Undoubtedly, he had an obsession about homosexuality but even Ben Greene (who did *not* love his uncle) expressed his strong support for Charles when told that one Old Boy had said that he was a bit phoney: 'A phoney always looks for popularity and this was the last thing that Charles ever looked for. He isn't among my pantheon of two or three people that I feel the better for having known, but he was a man I respected and I wouldn't mind having a hundred thousand of him now.'

R. S. Stanier, prefect, head of the house and later temporary master at Berkhamsted, in speaking of Charles and Marion Greene's relationship, said firmly that they 'were absolutely whole-hearted lovers all their lives'.

> I think [wrote Graham Greene] my parents' was a very loving marriage; how far any marriage is happy is another matter and beyond an outsider's knowledge . . . but I think their love with-stood the pressure of six children and great anxieties.

Raymond, Hugh and Elisabeth Greene confirmed this.

We can gauge the depth of Charles's love for Marion from letters he wrote to her in 1905, when Graham was three months old, after nine years of marriage, from the Hotel d'Angleterre in Cairo. The way Charles addresses his wife – 'Dearest love and sweetheart' – suggests that he retained a boyish freshness in his love. He tells Marion: 'Kiss the children and the dear little baby [Graham] specially because he is so small'; 'Kisses to yourself & the children & an extra one to the baby for comforting you.' But his feelings for his wife are obviously strong.

> Only one thing was wanted – to have you to enjoy it with me. I ache to have you darling. I feel after a day of Egypt as if I must start back again. It is not that I don't enjoy myself, I do intensely. But there is always an abiding want – my dear sweet wife. Although I have been but one day here, a few days after you get this I shall be starting back . . . I shall be thinking of you all day long.
>
> Your loving husband
>
> Nine years have we been married; and you are still & ever the dear Marion I began to love at Cirencester & have gone on loving more ever since.
>
> I miss you more even than when I went to Italy. There is a void where you are not.

Marion Greene was, as her family, friends and the schoolboys recall her, astonishingly remote. Sir Cecil Parrott remembered that she was called 'Ma Greene' by the boys and that she was 'very, very tall [she was exactly 6 ft], thin, remote, nervous and the kind of person you always worried about speaking to in case things went wrong but then you discovered that *she* was worried about you'. Eric

46

Guest had a remarkably similar memory of her – 'so tall, so thin you were terrified to look at her, only to discover *she* was terrified of you. She had a habit of putting her hand up to her mouth, in a nervous gesture, when she talked.'

Anthony Nichols, always a hostile critic, remembering his meeting with 'Ma Greene' on his first visit to the school with his father and having tea with the Headmaster, said that she was a meek woman, physically flat-chested, with thin and pursed lips – she was always dabbing her nose: 'She was talking to my father and immediately shut up in the middle of a sentence because Charles began rumbling in the background. I remember the embarrassment. She was so very shy.'

Few boys had much to do with 'Ma Greene' but prefects did meet her and her equally tall daughter Molly ('they were like hop poles') every Sunday afternoon when school tea parties were held at School House for visitors and prefects. The occasions were disconcerting for the boys, as S. R. Denny recalls:

As the church clock chimed the hour of four about a dozen of us were ushered into the drawing-room – a pleasant long apartment overlooking the churchyard – by a spruce parlour maid, to be greeted by name and handed a cup of tea. No plate. This was the first test! Could we manage a slice of cake on that precarious resting place?

We stood in a line rather sheepish and shy. Those nearest to Charles and Mrs Greene were engaged in stilted conversation, largely on a school subject. One more daring than the rest would pass round the three tiered cake stand to any other guest who might be present, praying that it would not fold up and deposit its contents on the floor.

Those not actively displaying their social graces murmured amongst themselves. One learnt another skill at those terrifying seances – how to dispose of a large chunk of cake which has fallen into the carpet by the pressure of one's heel.

In spite of tremendous shyness, Graham's mother was an enlightened and forward-looking woman – Greene women tend to be so – a good Protestant, who allowed people to be individuals. Sir Hugh Greene's first wife, Helga, recalled how Marion used to read aloud to Charles after his retirement and when he was much older: 'It is difficult to describe the Greene woman's voice, something rather like the Queen's voice, very much of a certain class.'

While she gave the impression of being shy, she did her duty – all those boring Sunday tea-parties are an example. Sir Hugh Greene, in comparing his mother and father, thought that, in spite of his father's range of knowledge, his mother was much sharper and more penetrating. And while a walk with Charles was a splendid experience – he knew intimately the flora and fauna of the area – he was yet, Hugh believed, a bit naïve and bewildered by life.[21]

Most of all Marion Greene had a certain demeanour and Alice Greene (Charles's sister) records in her diary in September 1881 not only Marion's beauty as a child but also her manners at the age of seven as seen from the point of view of an adult: 'Aunt Lally was much struck with Marion's manners, size and beauty. She says she is a child whom no one could dream of taking liberties with and whose manners would befit an empress. The expression on her face – one could almost call it scorn – when she entered the drawing room and found visitors there, Aunt says she will never forget.'

To some degree, the 'rich Greenes' were in awe of Marion and this seemed to have been solely due to Marion's strength of personality and quality of intellect, as well as her superior sense of the nature of local society. They often felt in her presence socially inept. The fact that they lived in the Hall, had several gardeners, a chauffeur, count-less servants, had two to serve at table, had their clothes laid out nightly, did not seem to them as weighty as intellect. There was, according to Ben Greene, a lording it over the rich Greenes by the intellectual Greenes. Ben Greene reinforced this view with an account of a comment by his sister Kate, then aged seven: 'She was heard to say, lisping a little, to some visitors in the dining-room – "I am very stupid and my brothers and sisters are very stupid, and my mother and father are very stupid, but we have such clever cousins." '[22]

Marion Greene had a tight hold over her emotions. Something of the control and the habit of correct form is revealed in a letter she wrote on the death of her husband, to her younger, and favourite daughter, Elisabeth. The letter begins 'My own darling Elisabeth' but even on this sad occasion, her mother ended her letter with her full signature, 'Marion R. Greene'. And this favourite daughter admitted that her mother would never throw her arms round you and kiss you: 'I remember when I went abroad on special duty during the war, she didn't make any fuss – yet she was a remarkable mother. She had certain wonderful qualities in a mother: she was dependable and she was always there. She was very stable and practical. She was rational and had good sense, and she was always interested in what her children did and this extended throughout their careers – she wanted to know but would not interfere with one's decision.'[23]

If Marion had a fault it lay in her remoteness, her inability to show tenderness towards her family in spite of her love for them. Her central passion was for her husband.

Describing her as she was dying on 23 September 1959, at the age of eighty-seven, Graham Greene wrote: 'When she was in an untroubled coma before death and I was watching by her bed, her long white plantagenet face reminded me of a crusader on a tomb.'[24]

*

There was another presage of school beyond the green baize door for Graham Greene in the person of the former headmaster, Dr Fry. Why was it that Graham so hated his father's predecessor? Charles Greene's sister, Mary, known as 'Polly' to the family, described Dr Fry and his wife in her unpublished diary before Graham Greene was born. Mary never married, painted hard, and sometimes well, all her life and though Graham writes of her 'gaiety, fantasy and silliness', her account of Fry seems shrewd:

> Dr Fry was bald, had fine features and a long beard that changed later from golden brown to snowy white. He could hardly be called portly but he had a comfortable figure. He was a very small man but he had such a look of importance that in five minutes after being introduced to him a stranger would think of him as tall. Cousin Julia could not be said to be dominated by her husband because her complete subservience to him was so voluntary and glad.

Several Berkhamstedians, admirers of Dr Fry, have told me of their distress at Graham Greene's criticism of him, in particular Colonel Wilson, older than Greene, a benefactor of the school and author of a booklet on its history, who wrote, 'In my view his comments about Dr Fry, his father's predecessor, were unkind, unjustified, libellous and in the worst possible taste since Fry is not allowed to defend himself.' And he adds, significantly, 'Also, as Fry left when Graham was under five years old [Graham was actually six], I cannot conceive where he collected his impression.'[25] How did Graham obtain any impressions of the man which could bring about such dislike?

Greene's condemnations appear in *A Sort of Life*, published in 1971, and two of the anecdotes he relates are intended to show Fry as 'the absurd figure he has always been'. Dealing, as they do, with the man's weaknesses, they reveal a lack of generosity and sympathy. The first describes Fry's behaviour when visiting the Greenes and must date from some time after Fry had left the school and when Greene was older than six years:

This Manichaean figure in black gaiters with a long white St Peter's beard sometimes came to stay. After breakfast on these occasions it was my mother's duty to clear the hall outside the dining-room of maids and children, so that the Dean could go to the lavatory unobserved and emerge again unseen by anyone.[26]

The second anecdote must come from a still later date:

On [Dr Fry's] last voyage . . . [returning from a lecture tour in America] fate overtook him and showed him up as the absurd figure he had always been. He had suffered a stroke before embarking which damaged his powers of speech and his neighbours at table overheard him asking his son Charley, the Vicar of Maidenhead, for certain shocking objects when all he had in mind was a soft-boiled egg.[27]

But in 1936, thirty-five years before Greene published these anecdotes, he had recorded them in an unpublished diary and the suggestions are that these two stories about the Doctor are hearsay, as is the Doctor's reputation as an unjust flogger. The entry is as follows:

I remember Dr Fry chiefly for his gaiters, & his big white spade-shaped beard, for his rather bullying hearty manner & the reputation he left behind at Berkhamsted as an anal flogger . . . Coming back from a lecture tour in America just before his death, he had a fit and went off his head. I must try & discover the absurd story of the boiled egg his son, Charley Fry, Vicar of Maidenhead . . . wrote home. It was meant to be rather horrifying & pathetic but was simply very funny & a little macabre when you had known [him].

Hugh remembers his fear of being seen using a lavatory. My mother had to clear a way for him to the lavatory, sending all the children away from the hall & passage & shutting herself in the dining room. The only warning he could give was to hang unhappily about the hall. If someone tried the door when he was in the lavatory he would remain there for a very long while. A strong virtuous wicked man.

One wonders why Hugh is brought in as witness since, being six years younger than Graham, he is unlikely to have remembered as much about the Doctor as Graham (he was born in the year that Fry retired) and the phrase 'must try to discover' suggests that the story of the egg was family tradition and not something Graham knew about at first hand. Graham Greene may well have considered the Doctor's requirements as a guest an intolerable imposition on his mother and a slight to the family pride.

But Fry's reputation as a flogger came from Kenneth Bell, Greene's tutor at Oxford, a good friend and an old Berkhamstedian who, as a schoolboy, had his cap snatched from him by a bully and was then beaten by Fry who saw him in the street without it. It does seem that while Fry probably was as unpleasant as Greene thought, his opinion is based on family feeling and tradition rather than Greene's personal experience of the man. Perhaps, and more likely, it is a reaction to his father's admiration of Fry and his perpetuation of Fry's traditions in the school.

Unquestionably Graham saw Fry as the man who, by the force of his personality, had determined the nature of a school which Graham later found so unpleasant that it helped to develop in the young boy suicidal tendencies. Moreover, he would no doubt have felt more kindly towards his father had Charles Greene more seriously modified the Fry mould.

There is a further irony. Fry's success was in part due to his powers as a great fund-raiser. Colonel A. G. Wilson credits Fry and his wife Julia with 'defraying the costs' of building the Chapel. But Fry had no money of his own, and his biographer shows just how financially useful to Fry the Greene family were: 'The Greene family was influential, talented and prosperous, Julia herself having access to considerable private means. On their silver wedding anniversary, Fry paid tribute to his wife, who, he joked, had left a home of great luxury to marry a poor man. It was quite true.' And Fry's biographer also admits that Edward Greene (Julia's father) and his nephews Sir Graham, Charles and Edward, 'the more prominent members of Fry's new family circle . . . in one way and another . . . helped him enormously throughout life.'[28]

In 1929, Fry, still upset by the death of his wife the previous year, went off to Antofagasta in Chile to try to raise money for Lincoln Cathedral, and suffered a stroke there that impaired his powers of speech and forced him to return home. He died on 9 February 1930.

4

The First World War
and the School

The lamps are going out all over Europe.
— SIR EDWARD GREY

IN August 1914, during the summer holidays, Graham Greene was staying at his uncle Graham's home, Harston House, though his uncle was probably not there, being a 'very remote' Greene who was never there when his nephews and nieces were, but stayed 'safely away from any family turbulence' in his bachelor flat off Hanover Square in London.[1] On this occasion he was probably at the Admiralty, where he was permanent private secretary to the First Sea Lord. Starting off with Lord George Hamilton in 1887, he had held this post under successive First Sea Lords – Spencer, Goschen, Selborne and finally Prince Louis of Battenberg over whom he had great influence. Sir Graham Greene foresaw the approach of war, and arranged that the whole British fleet should be on manoeuvres and ready for action. Something of his power is reflected in the *Daily Mail*'s description of him as 'the octopus of Whitehall'.[2] He was also known as Sir Graham 'Secretive' Greene. Greene was right in his prediction, as Britain declared war on Germany on 4 August.

Graham Greene, aged nine, remembered during that holiday being sent out with a basket of freshly picked apples from Harston's orchard for some weary soldiers resting on Harston Green. It was a gesture in the tradition of charity from the big houses to the needy in Victorian and Edwardian times (though George V was then on the throne), but it had deeper significance. Those soldiers were being sent to a bloody war but their young benefactor was to begin his own kind of warfare in the following months which eventually was to destroy his idealism and bring him to a state of 'knowing' – an experience which, set against the devastation of Europe during the next four years and its effect on Berkhamsted School, was minor, though not to the boy with the apples.

We can recapture the atmosphere of Berkhamsted School during the first term of the school year in 1914, when Graham Greene moved into the Junior School, through the memories of Old Boys, *The Berkhamstedian*, and Greene's autobiography. Cecil Hodges, ahead of Graham at the School, was to be called to the colours immediately on leaving, and recalled that, at the beginning of the new term, the boys 'did not notice much change in the daily routine. In 1914 we occasionally heard a rumble of strange heavy traffic, saw a detachment of purposeful-looking soldiers, or heard some item of news that we didn't like the sound of – it seemed we were not advancing at once to victory.' At the same time, 'though in the Dining Hall menu [they] sensed a change' they 'did not realise that things domestic were beginning to get difficult'.[3] They did get difficult. Graham Greene recalls the effects of the food shortage: 'I suppose we were always a little hungry in the war years. There were no potatoes and little sugar and we grew deadly tired of substitutes – rice and honey-sugar'. Because of war shortages, the School tuck shop was open only to senior pupils, and Greene, as a junior, would 'stand outside reciting an accepted formula, "Treat I", to any older boy as he came out, and occasionally one would detach a morsel of bun and hand it over'.[4] Graham's cousin Ben recalled being 'frightfully hungry at school' at that time and Charles Greene was later to shut the tuck shop – a terrible blow to the boys – since he felt that the difference between 'the trench population', as Winston Churchill described the soldiers fighting in appalling conditions at the front in France, and the non-trench population, scarcely suffering at all, should be narrowed; the boys at the school would not do better than the troops – it was immoral, it was the using up of national resources for the wrong purpose.

The heroic attitude to the war – loyalty to one's country, which in the case of a public school that was to provide officers for the army involved total acceptance of personal sacrifice, and devotion to training to meet the demands of war – was reflected in *The Berkhamstedian*: military matters were taking precedence over all others. The November 1914 edition states in its editorial: 'Had it not been for the stern fact of war, the chief point of interest would have been the new playing fields, now really our own' (Edward Greene had shown 'splendid generosity' in his subscription to their cost.) But more important, as the editor states: 'We meet this term under the shadow of war and, as is only natural, all other School arrangements give way to the imperative claims of the O.T.C. . . . No examination for Certificate "A" can be held this term, but lectures are given for the senior members of the Corps on Tactics and Musketry.' The boys were sternly reminded that 'More is required of each cadet than a perfunctory attendance at parades . . . all those who are hoping to get commissions . . . must have as sound a knowledge of the use of the rifle in war, and handling of the smaller units in the field, as he has of manual exercises and parade movements.'

To begin with, two parades were held weekly, but later there was a parade only on a Friday, held after morning school on the Gravel Quad behind the Old Hall. Life became more hectic that day as the boys would be polishing buttons, belts and brass both before and after breakfast. Button sticks were lost and borrowed. N.C.O.s helped the less competent to wind their puttees in such a way that they could avoid ugly bulges. Recruits were advised to acquire second-hand belts for, as every old soldier knows, they take polish more easily. After the parade, the boys marched off to the playing fields to drill and execute manoeuvres.

The first war-time school concert, held on 19 December 1914, was a heavily patriotic affair. The School Song, 'Come what may, we'll be men', and Kipling's ballad, 'The Flag of England' were sung, followed by 'England's Battle Hymn' and the concert finished with an orgy of the national anthems of the Allies – France's 'Marseillaise', Belgium's 'Brabançonne' and the Russian national anthem, 'Boze, carja chrani' ('God Save the Tsar') and finally 'Rule Britannia' and 'God Save the King'. In March 1915, *The Berkhamstedian* reported that 'more and more O.B.'s are flocking from all over the world to join the colours and take the place of the fallen.' Few were disheartened, for only three Old Boys of the school had so far died in battle.

*

During that first year of the war and Greene's first year in Junior School, he took steps, with an independence that must have been fostered in his childhood, to remove himself from the disciplined world of school and continue the kind of existence that his instinct indicated was right for him. 'All life long,' he wrote, 'my instinct has been to abandon anything for which I have no talent'.[5] And those things for which he had no talent – organised games, tennis, golf, dancing, sailing, and gymnastics – demanded a physical co-ordination and an acceptance of established conventions of movement and aims. In later life, while training for intelligence work during the Second World War, he failed to master the intricacies of riding a motor-cycle. At school, too young then to be involved in the O.T.C., he first removed himself from gymnastics by pretending to the gym mistress (the gym master had been called up into the army) that he was ill. The 'evasions and deceits' had begun. He would then slip out on to Berkhamsted Common and, hidden among the gorse bushes, enjoy watching people going by. Having given up the idea of vaulting, climbing a rope or scrambling on the parallel bars, he then went into a more extended truancy, better organised since he had now 'sussed out' the school day, and had worked out a way of circumventing the implications of the green baize door.

On reaching the age of eleven, he no longer had breakfast in the nursery with his five-year-old brother Hugh and the baby Elisabeth, but joined his parents and Molly, Herbert and Raymond in the dining-room. After that he ought to have gone through into the School for prayers in Deans' Hall with the prefect in charge crying, 'Go Down', the rush to collect books and the cardboard sheet against which they were carried and a companion with whom to 'Walk Down' to the Hall and be seated there in reasonable class order. At that time, Major James Parsons, second master and later Mayor of Berkhamsted, took charge. He twittered, he tapped the table with increasing ferocity, demanded silence but did not obtain it; the school prefects patrolled the aisles, seconding Parsons's efforts with little result. Then Charles Greene would enter, gown swinging behind him, and climb on to the platform. He would place his mortar board on the table and up went the sound of schoolboy voices singing Psalm 121: 'I will lift up mine eyes unto the hills'.

So, with an obvious innocence of the power and interrelatedness of the establishment, instead of going into Deans' Hall, Graham would, after breakfast, gather up his school-books as though going to prayers, but instead would wait in the garden until he knew the school was assembled, and he was free. It was a dangerous, exciting freedom. Sometimes he would walk up the High Street to the local W. H. Smith's shop to look at the books. He confesses to having once stolen a sixpenny paperback, Stanley Weyman's *The Abbess of Vlaye*. When he returned home, he would stoop beneath the level of the dining-room window in case a maid caught a glimpse of him and would go cautiously to the croquet lawn where the summerhouse was that could be turned round so that it faced away from house and school and there, sitting in a deck-chair, he would read all day, breaking only for lunch.

In his autobiography, Greene said that he 'carried on his truancy until the last day of term', but a much earlier account, in a letter he wrote to Vivien Dayrell-Browning, suggests that it lasted only two weeks. Yet even this, given the rigorous surveillance in the school, was a remarkable feat. When his truancy was discovered, 'there *was* a rumpus, a most painful rumpus'.[6] A master to whom Graham had reported himself sick to account for his absence asked Charles Greene how his boy was progressing. Knowing of no sickness in his family, Charles Greene came back home and discovered his son in the shelter – 'or rather I think he sent my mother . . . I was told to go to bed, and when I was in my nightshirt my father came up and caned me. This is the only beating I can remember.'[7] He did, however, have the impression that his father used to smack him as a child.[8]

*

By June 1915 the whole of the Senior School belonged to the O.T.C. and the number of Old Boys killed in action rose to fourteen. The death of Captain H. H. Berners is described in *The Berkhamstedian*:

> He was the life and soul of our lot. When shells were bursting over our heads, he would buck us up with his humour about Brock's display at the Palace. But when we got to close quarters it was he who was in the thick of it and didn't he fight! I don't know how he got knocked over, but one of our fellows told me he died a game 'un. He was one of the best officers, and there is not a Tommy who would not have gone under for him.[9]

The phrases and the euphemisms concealed the reality of trench warfare and death, and were all set against the social scale of officers and Tommies, leaders and men. This is also very close to the boys' adventure story, the standards of the public school, the glossing over of the horror of war and the finality of death.

Edmund Blunden, who was a young officer in the war, describes in *Undertones of War*,[10] an 'old trench' – one which had been German but had been overrun by the Allies: 'It was strewn with remains and pitiful evidences. The whole region . . . being marshy and undrainable, smelt ill enough, but this trench was peculiar in that way. I cared little to stop in the soft drying mud at the bottom of it; I saw old uniforms, and a great many bones, like broken bird-cages. One uniform identified a German officer; the skeleton seemed less coherent than most, and an unexploded shell lay on the edge of the fragments.' And then there were the rats feeding on the rotten flesh – dead men, dead horses or parts of both. Sometimes the bodies were not buried for months and became part of the trench parapets.[11] It was such fallen that the Old Boys of Berkhamsted School were flocking to replace, and there were many places to be taken – almost one million British died.

On Founder's Day, Monday, 31 July 1916 (Berkhamsted School was then almost 400 years old), Charles Greene spoke proudly of the fact that 900 Old Boys were serving their country, but also stated that 76 had been killed and 125 wounded. A year later the casualties had mounted to 132.

Although Graham was very young at that time and the war impinged on him only minimally, he was living in an environment which was very much affected by it, both overtly and covertly. The overt signs of war were the expressions of traditionally heroic attitudes and the acceptance of sacrifice for one's country, a sacrifice linked with loyalty to the school. As Charles Greene said of the Old Boys who had been killed:

> However hard it might be to think of their death, it was yet a proud thing and a most touching thing to their old masters to read in their letters, or to hear from their parents, of the love which these boys had for their old school . . . that had been a most uplifting thing.

Graham remembered the whole Junior School pressing up against the terrace whenever there was a rumour that an Old Boy had been decorated with a D.S.O., an M.C. or a V.C., since the first two ensured a half-day's holiday and the last (and there were two of those) a whole day, the matter being settled by the appearance of the Headmaster.

The School's Roll of Honour was the visible record of sacrifice and loyalty to school and country – remembered later by most Old Boys. Graham Greene recalled that 'outside the school chapel there was the list of old boys killed, plaque after plaque in double column, to remind us of the recent years.'[12] One Old Boy remembered that it was the master John Trask (he had a grizzled beard) who was to be seen every morning posting yet another black-edged card in the cloisters, and the deaths were recorded in the 'In Memoriam' section of *The Berkhamstedian*. Cecil Hodges recalled that the beginnings of the reality of war, as the older boys were to know it, came as the losses became more personal to them: 'Reports of casualties on Active Service began to come through . . . the Roll of Honour came inexorably into being. The dead were honoured by name and the rendering of a "Marche Funèbre" (usually Chopin, sometimes Handel) at the conclusion of Evensong in Chapel on Sundays. And it was not very long before we began to hear the names of those whom we had so recently known as part of our life – a House Prefect, captain of cricket perhaps, or a scrum-half or a long distance runner – gone, and we should never see him again. It was very hard to believe.'

The dichotomy between the outward show and the appalling reality was felt by the older boys at Berkhamsted. Cecil Hodges had often wondered, since those days, whether they could have been aware of the numbing effect on their spiritual vigour of the conflict between the apparent and obvious and the true but obscured reality:

We did as we were taught – held our heads high on the parade-ground (O.T.C.) and elsewhere in public; but within ourselves we knew that we should be packed off for training as soon as we were 18, and overseas very soon after. It was a prospect that put an end to any remote ambition or aspiration. No one could count on coming back. And that was how I left Berkhamsted within a few months to sample 'the way of glory', on active service in France. Mercifully I survived. In looking back over a long distance, I feel that I am right in recollecting a period at Berkhamsted (2 to 3 years or so) of unrelieved suspense and oppression: suspense in which we hung day in day out, with no future further than tomorrow, awaiting good news; oppression by a heavy pall of inscrutable mystery which grown-ups assured us must never be allowed to diminish the will to win.[13]

Hopelessly physically unco-ordinated as he was, Graham Greene was in trouble when he entered the senior school at the age of ten and a half and joined the O.T.C. He hated military uniforms and could never learn to put on his puttees neatly – he was unable to tie a necktie until he reached University. Any under-officer of the O.T.C. who had money was allowed to buy specially shaped puttees which looked smart, but Graham did not reach the rank of under-officer, nor would his father have given him permission to buy them, as this might have been construed as a special dispensation and Charles Greene would never have tolerated anything that smacked of nepotism: the Greene boys – Raymond, Graham and Hugh – could receive worse treatment than others but never better. Unlike Raymond who became a senior prefect, head of his house, and was looked up to by other boys, Graham genuinely fumbled. He dreaded parades. He would get out of step forming fours and botch fixing his bayonet. A very sensitive boy, the fact that his physical awkwardness could not be hidden and therefore was obvious to others, filled him with intense shame. He felt found out, and writing to his future wife a dozen years later about people who had known him at that time he asked: 'Do you slink by such people with an inferiority complex? I

do. It's the one thing that it's impossible to forgive one's parents.'[14]
His sense of personal humiliation was to last many years.

*

The period of the war was a testing time for his father also – perhaps
his most testing time. Many of his best masters were lost to the war
machine and he managed the school by bringing people out of
retirement and, according to Ben Greene, taking on women teachers,
many of them 'extraordinarily tough and frightening', and a certain
number of drunken curates. He had to recruit staff wherever he could
find them and he held the school together with difficulty, but the
greatest pain came from the deaths of boys he had only so recently
taught. Claud Cockburn, as a pupil, observed and understood him:
'He'd got all the philosophy of the Victorian age, yet he was trying
sincerely to adapt to all these kids who were, after all, in the middle
of World War I. Most of the sixth form was wiped out, year after
year, and he'd sit there teaching the sixth form, then they were called
up and 80 per cent of them would be killed. I know when I was in
the sixth form, I think only about ten per cent or so of the previous
year were still alive, and we thought that was life. So it was, so it
was, but it must have been an appalling experience for a man of his
great liberal mind.' Distant figure as he was to the boys, one who
spoke in a peculiar voice, gestured with his hand in an odd way,
pulled his hair down in front from time to time and walked across
the cloisters to the Hall with a long stride and a flowing gown, the
war was for him a shattering experience and the deaths of those he
had helped to educate wounded him deeply.

Graham Greene's father, as well as being a simple patriot, was also
genuinely liberal in outlook. He was appalled by the attitudes of
imperialism and militarism which the war engendered: 'You mustn't
confuse the relative militarism of the School with anything on his
part,' Claud Cockburn insisted. 'Charles Greene remained a liberal
throughout the War, and I remember very well he came to see my
father and my father was a real roaring mandarin and he loved Charles
and Charles sort of loved him, but Charles was shocked by my
father's extreme imperialistic opinions. One day Charles Greene came
to our house and he said, "The most appalling thing has happened",
and he had been down on the playing fields where the O.T.C. were
training, and he'd seen or listened to the Sergeant Major training
these recruits, and he'd heard him saying, "Well now when the
enemy come out of trenches and surrender and raise their hands,
remember not to take your fingers off your machine guns." And
Charles came back and said, "My God – we must all protest against

the army becoming as barbaric as those fellows."' Indeed there were signs of local barbarism – a dachshund was stoned in the High Street in Berkhamsted.[15] Eva Greene also had an unhappy and anxious time.

The school during wartime increased in size and to a master on active service Charles Greene wrote: 'We have passed the 500 limit. I have seen the 200, 300, 400 and now 500 limit passed. I should have liked to rejoice, but it seems too trivial for joy just now . . . The 200th boy's name was Dear and the 500th boy's name was Good.'

By Founder's Day 1918, 1,145 Old Boys were serving and 184 had been killed. The war had only three and a half months to run but the number of school dead increased to 230.

*

On Sunday 10 November 1918, James Wilson recorded in his diary: 'Today everybody is expectant of peace soon. It's only a matter of hours, as the Kaiser and Staff and Crown Prince have all abdicated. Charles preached . . . I put five pence in the bag.' The following day he wrote: 'Armistice signed at 11 o'clock! At twelve o'clock as soon as Charles announced on the terrace it was signed, the flag was hoisted and we all sang "God Save the King". Then everyone went out, capless' – a punishable offence.

Elisabeth Greene was four at the time. She could remember the noise of the boys in the quad, their milling about and the shouting. The story prized in the family ever since was that this serious little girl suddenly spoke, above the noise, 'Is this what they call peace?'

Charles took an astonishing stand on Armistice Day. So strongly did he feel about the five million dead allied soldiers that he did not give the school a free holiday. He argued that 'We simply must go on. Now is the time for effort: now is the time for the coming of the world.' And thus he found that he had unexpectedly a revolution on his hands. James Wilson wrote in his diary: '. . . greatest rag of all. 8.30 p.m. in prep. a huge mob of Inns of Court O.T.C. and W.A.A.C.S. [Women's Army Auxiliary Corps], burst into the old hall of the school. [The gates] had been opened for them from the inside and [they] scragged [roughed up] Cox, called for Charles to scrag him. The Inns of Court dragged all the chaps out into a huge procession along the High Street. Charles absolutely convulsed with rage.'

Claud Cockburn remembered that night sixty years afterwards with great gusto. Because Charles Greene refused to give the school a holiday on Armistice Day, certain Berkhamsted prefects, led by a student leader called Webb, plotted with the local O.T.C. to break into the school:

It was my first experience in revolution . . . for some reason, by nature of the fact of it being my bath night, I could get into a section of the building beyond the hall where the baths were. And I was to throw the key of the gates, which were heavily locked, down to the Sergeant Major or some blasted man. I did all this. And I can remember now sitting there – it was one of those foggy nights in Berkhamsted, fog rising from the canal and so on, and suddenly we heard the roar of the distant troops coming up the road. Everybody was quite confident because they couldn't get in. And then in they burst, and we were all sitting at prep. in the Great Hall at about 7.00 p.m. So suddenly all these drunken troops and women came surging in and were planning to throw Charles Greene into the canal . . . and Greene and second master Cox appeared at the end of that little passage, and defended the door, and Greene was persuaded to retire to his study. Cox stood at the door, and drunken troops joined in with the students, and we surged out of school, and marched through the streets of Berkhamsted, and I can remember to this day walking down Berkhamsted High Street and I took off my shoes in order to beat on the drum with them. We then occupied the local cinema and we sprang onto the stage and sang songs and yelled and shouted. And at last the troops retired, and we, rather bedraggled, returned after this enormous elation, this tremendous night, and suddenly realised that we had to face reality. And the reality was Charles Greene who was sitting at the big desk in the Great Hall, and said, 'You're expelled, you're expelled', one after another. He expelled 122 of us – 'This abominable thing that has happened is Bolshevism.' And so we all went to bed expelled. I knew the awful fact that my father thought expulsion from school was an awful thing to happen, so I was quite worried in the morning. We were all brought down to the Great Hall and given a tremendous lecture by Charles Greene.

And because it had been a night on which he had been expelled, Claud Cockburn could even remember Charles Greene's characteristic rhetoric on that occasion: 'This is one more exhibition of the spirit of Bolshevism which is creeping across Europe. Over there in Moscow, there sits Lenin, there sits Trotsky, there they are. The spirit of Bolshevism and Atheism is creeping across Europe. It is breaking out all over. Look at Lenin, look at Trotsky, and look at you. It may reach our shores at any minute, and here right in Berkhamsted School we have the deathwatch beetle already in the beams above us, and the prefects, even our own prefects, betray us from within, and you, Webb, and you, Cockburn: you are a part of this conspiracy of the Bolsheviks . . .'

Cockburn commented: 'In 1918, Marxism was like saying "Rabies," you know.' And well it might have been, for only four months previously Czar Nicholas II and his whole family had been murdered by the Bolsheviks, the Winter Palace had been taken over and their authority established only days before the Armistice was signed.

But it turned out well for the expelled boys. Charles Greene had expelled far too many and finally almost all were reinstated. Two, according to Cockburn, remained expelled because, 'they tried to get the soldiers to break into Charles Greene's study and tear up his books – a really rather shitty thing to do.'

Cockburn suggested that there was some justification for their actions. 'These prefects had been living in expectation of being killed on the Western front some time in the next three months, so they didn't take much interest in the preservation of civilisation or the school spirit and they got pretty rough.'

Three years after the end of the war, when he was in London, Graham Greene went to Westminster Abbey for 'the American ceremony', and wrote to his mother:

> The Abbey itself lighted up brilliantly, but outside the door nothing but a great bank of mist, with now and again a vague steel helmeted figure appearing, only to disappear again. The whole time the most glorious music from the organ, with the American band outside, clashing in at intervals. Then the feeling of expectancy, through the whole people, the minds of everyone on tip-toe. It got back the whole atmosphere of the war, of the endless memorial services. I'd never realised before how we had got away from the death feeling.

The effect of the war on Charles Greene, and the loss of so many boys, was such that he remained very conscious of history, returning to that period of war constantly in his teaching. Claud Cockburn remembered that Charles never forgot the war or the 'peace' that followed, giving rather profound ambling descriptions of history: 'We used to sit there in his great history lessons, and he'd start off with Cicero or something – we had 3 hours, 2 hours were Greek and Latin, and the next hour was Ancient History – but after about the first 20 minutes of Greek, he would be back in 1919 – Treaty of Versailles and so on – he was anti the Treaty of Versailles – he thought they had made a wreck of Europe, which indeed they had, and I remember him so well sitting there . . . and the mortar board used to fall further and further over his face and he would lean back in the chair saying, "When I gaze into the abyss of history, when I see Monsieur Clemenceau, when I observe Mr Lloyd George, I feel that I am gazing into an abyss. I see nothing but disaster." [16]

Claud Cockburn recalled how, when he was a prefect and sitting next to Charles Greene at lunch, he would argue the Tory point of view (for the future Communist was then a Tory): 'Charles thought I was entirely dominated by my father's evil imperialistic qualities, and so he'd argue about this and that, and of course he had the right to cut off argument by standing up and saying grace, so when I felt that I'd really got him, he'd suddenly say, "Well, Cockburn, I don't know how civilisation is going to be saved – Benedictus benedicat." But he was a man of really incredible goodwill.' To Cockburn's account can be added Peter Quennell's which he wrote in a letter to Graham Greene in 1922. Quennell was then seventeen and already a publishing poet. As in the Cockburn account there is some light teasing though there is also love for Charles Greene. Graham, then at Oxford, had sent Quennell a telegram. Quennell's reply was in the *vers libre* manner of his brilliant poem 'Masque of The Three Beasts':

Your father was in the middle of what I think was an English
period. It had become rather historical. The dear old gentleman
was lying comfortably on his back – like an inverted turtle.
  – Have you noticed how like a very dear old
    turtle he is becoming? –
  – and we had become gloomy but sonorous –
    over the future of Democracy
And then of course entered Mrs Edmunds . . .
  – in a tottering hurry
And your father stopped in the middle of a more than
Ciceronian period
  – and heavy gloom and foreboding fell
upon everybody –
  – and especially Peter [Quennell] when he heard
it [the telegram] was for him –
  – and I pictured my father run over in
Theobald's Road
    or my Cockerel at his last gasp
And your father made ineffectual efforts to sit up
and said in a severe and entirely cold and disapproving
way that I might read it at 12

   – and – suddenly relenting – if I was good – that I
might read it now – and immediately and at once
                      lest there was an answer
And I read it in icy stillness and while I was still
glaring at it
     – in astonishment of mind
     – almost alarm –
your father
     asked in a yet more disapproving way if there was
an answer
     but there wasn't
And he slid back to the turtle position
     and the Ciceronian period went on – and the
Democracy of Europe and its fate rolled up again like
storm clouds.[17]

And so it would seem that though Charles Greene was remote as a father, as a teacher, with his mild eccentricities and obsessions, he was able to inspire humour and affection and respect in his pupils, and it does seem strange that, sympathetic as he was towards Cockburn and Quennell, he was unaware of his own son's increasing unhappiness.

Two months before the war ended, and uninvolved, therefore, in the rowdy celebrations at the School, Graham Greene went as a boarder to St John's. He was within a month of his fourteenth birthday.

5

The Greening of Greene

A savage country of strange customs and inexplicable
cruelties.
— GRAHAM GREENE

Literature springs from humiliation.
— W. H. AUDEN

G RAHAM Greene's time as a boarder at St John's was traumatic
for him, but also seminal for his future as a writer. He returns
to it again and again in his work, beginning with his first unpublished
novel, 'Anthony Sant' and continuing with references in *England
Made Me* (1935), *Brighton Rock* (1938), *The Lawless Roads* (1939), *The
Confidential Agent* (1939), *The Ministry of Fear* (1943), 'The Lost
Childhood' (1951) and *A Sort of Life* (1971). Moreover, several
compulsive themes in his novels derive from that experience.

What could it have been about St John's that made his stay there
such a torment and brought the young Graham Greene to successive suicide attempts? In interviews he has been unwilling to go
into that period in greater detail, perhaps because the pain is still
there.

On the face of it, there seems little to justify the emotive language
he has used to describe the situation in which he found himself –
he was a 'foreigner' in a 'savage country of strange customs and
inexplicable cruelties', he was 'a suspect', 'a hunted creature', 'Quisling's son'* and there was 'loneliness, the struggle of conflicting
loyalties . . . a great betrayal'.[1] In fact, he was the Headmaster's son,
had moved only a short distance from home at School House to be
a boarder at St John's where his cousins Ben and Tooter were also

---

* Quisling was a Norwegian politician whose name became synonymous with
collaborator and traitor during the Second World War. Quisling was sentenced to
death on 17 September 1945 by a Norwegian court and executed in Oslo on 24
October 1945.

boarders and his brother Raymond was head boy. Raymond, Ben and Tooter went through the school without being scarred, and one might have expected that through them something of the protective family environment would have been extended. Thousands of children then, such as those whose experiences were recorded in *The Times* in the year of his birth and the children of the canal workers in Berkhamsted, were born to much greater physical and mental hardships. His advantages in terms of wealth and class were considerable. A decline in his living conditions and a certain amount of ragging and bullying at St John's seem unimportant.

His state of health before entering St John's was not good. In 1917 he had a second attack of measles, a threatened mastoid, jaundice and, in 1918, pleurisy. His further troubles are reflected in the character of Arthur Rowe in *The Ministry of Fear* who was 'often ill, his teeth were bad and he suffered from an inefficient dentist'. Some of the illnesses might have been psychosomatic, an attempt to escape from a future whose implications might have been frightening to a timid, excessively shy boy. Moreover, according to Graham's cousin, Barbara Greene, later Countess Strachwitz, there was a family tradition of his having 'crises'. She recalled two occasions when Graham was young on which her mother, Eva Greene, had taken her nephew with her on her travels to recover:

> My mother took Graham off twice. I know that was an expedition with my father and various uncles. Then another time she was going to meet my father at Lisbon when he was coming back from Brazil and Graham had just gone through *another* crisis and she just said she was taking Graham with her. I can't remember which crisis it was. Among the older generation there was much talk. I'm sure they were quite worried about him.[2]

We already know of the fears from which he still suffered as a boy of thirteen: fear of the dark – 'no night-light to make a blessed breach'; of birds and bats which came to symbolise the dark – 'then darkness came down like the wings of a bat and settled on the landing'; and even death – 'the whole room seemed suddenly to darken, and he had the impression of a great bird swooping'. The footsteps of strangers caused a rapid beating of the heart, a sick empty sensation in the stomach. It is likely that he was not in a physical or mental condition to deal with the change that took place in his life.

In 'The Burden of Childhood' (1950) Greene writes, 'There are certain writers . . . who never shake off the burden of their childhood' and they are those to whom life turned 'its cruel side'

66

during the defenceless period of early childhood and all their later experience seems to have been related to 'those months or years of unhappiness'. He cites the cases of three writers to support his thesis: Charles Dickens, Rudyard Kipling and H. H. Munro ('Saki'). He might well have added his own name to the list. For him also childhood was a burden and his experiences had parallels with theirs.

Dickens, Kipling and Munro were uprooted from happy childhood homes and placed in hostile environments. Kipling and Munro experienced this at the age of six, since their parents lived in India and Burma respectively where the climate was not considered suitable for white children after that age, and education in England was necessary. Rudyard Kipling and his sister were left as paying guests with a retired naval officer and his wife who became 'Uncle Harry' and 'Auntie Rosa'. Kipling spent five years with Aunt Rosa and wrote of the experience that the 'wretchedness of those five years lay buried in that inaccessible hiding place, the secret heart of a child' – 'I had never heard of Hell, so I was introduced to it in all its terrors.' Munro was left with aunts Augusta and Charlotte after his mother's death when his father returned to Burma. Dickens was twelve when, his father being imprisoned for debt, he was put to work in a blacking factory to relieve the family's financial difficulties. The owner of the factory was a relative, Dickens was not ill-treated or over-worked by the standards of the day and his experience lasted only four months.

Common to all three boys was the sense of having been abandoned by their parents, but Dickens's experience is closest to Greene's. What was most painful to Dickens was the fact that he was put into lodgings and left to fend for himself on six shillings a week while his family lived close by in reasonable comfort, in the debtors' prison it is true, but on his father's salary and with a maid to look after them. 'No words', Dickens wrote, 'can express the secret agony of my soul.' He felt 'utterly neglected and hopeless' and as an intelligent and well-read boy, he felt he was not only suffering physical indignities and abandonment, but was being deprived of education and a future career. When his sister received a prize at the Royal Academy of Music, tears ran down his face and he 'prayed . . . to be lifted out of the humiliation and neglect' in which he was. For years afterwards Dickens avoided the scene of his humiliating experience, and significantly Greene writes about Berkhamsted: 'Memory often exaggerates, but some twelve years ago [1959], because I had started a novel about a school, I revisited the scene and found no change. I abandoned the novel – I couldn't bear mentally living again for several years in these surroundings.'³ He went instead to a leper colony in the Congo.

Greene's memory does not usually exaggerate nor is he extravagant in his descriptions of places, people and events, and he is always remarkably consistent about his feelings. Once he has established a view of an experience he will be locked into that view and so we have to take seriously his comment: 'Years later when I read the sermon on hell in Joyce's *Portrait of the Artist* I recognized the land I had inhabited.'⁴ Earlier, in *The Lawless Roads*, he had in fact quoted, without attribution, a line from the sermon on hell to describe his school experiences (which I italicize below) tracing in them the beginnings of his first, primitive, religious belief:

> And so faith came to one – shapelessly, without dogma, a presence above a croquet lawn, something associated with violence, cruelty, evil across the way. One began to believe in heaven because one believed in hell, but for a long while it was only hell one could picture with a certain intimacy – the pitchpine partitions of dormitories where everybody was never quiet at the same time; lavatories without locks: '*There by reason of the great number of the damned, the prisoners are heaped together in their awful prison . . .*' walks in pairs up the suburban roads; no solitude anywhere, at any time.⁵

Joyce's hell, though, is so terrible that Greene's comparison of St John's with it is difficult to understand. For example, 'the damned are so utterly bound and helpless that . . . they are not even able to remove from the eye a worm that gnaws it . . . All the filth of the world, all the offal and scum . . . shall run there as to a vast reeking sewer.'⁶ What was it about the situation at St John's that caused him to make such a comparison?

*

What comes through at first from his various accounts of that time is the impression that he had suffered a profound culture shock. Of the various strains in the Greene family, he would seem to have inherited the remoteness of character, the need for privacy and for the security of a warm family environment in which to develop his individuality. His instinctive reaction to his gradual involvement in the public and, in a sense, uncivilised world of school, has been demonstrated by his truancies, but he still had the family life to rely upon then. When he was sent to St John's as a boarder, he was totally cut off from the secure life that had succoured him, but with many added and painful ironies. He had lost his home at School House and he was now living in what had been his home for his first six years, St John's, but he was on the other side of the green baize door. He entered the house now by a side door 'like a service entrance', and the passage that was deceptively similar to the one he had known in childhood was now alien ground. There was no hope of returning through the green baize door. He was in those grim rooms he had not known existed where there was a schoolroom 'with ink-stained nibbled desks insufficiently warmed by one cast-iron stove . . . stone stairs, worn by generations of feet, leading to a dormitory divided by pitch-pine partitions that gave inadequate privacy – no moment of the night was free from noise, a cough, a snore, a fart.'[7]

The seedy experiences of Anthony in *England Made Me* are based on those of his brother Herbert, but Anthony's experiences at school come from Graham's experiences at St John's – the same physical surroundings, the same lack of privacy:

> Feet on the stone stairs, running, scrambling, pushing, up to the dormitory . . . Not a moment of quiet even at night, for always someone talks in his sleep the other side of the wooden partition. I lay sweating . . . unable to sleep . . . waiting for the thrown sponge, the rustle of curtains, the hand plucking at my bed-clothes, the giggles, the slap of bare feet on the wooden boards.[8]

The force of these feelings has not diminished with time. Interviewed in 1979 by Marie-Françoise Allain about his experience at boarding school he burst out with the words: 'But it was horrible . . . The promiscuity, the total absence of solitude, there was the horror.'

Certainly, it was a different world from that of the French and English gardens, the chintzy drawing-room, the secure life of family and nursery, the smell of books and fruit and eau-de-Cologne.[9] It was a communal society which afforded no individual privacy, where even solitary walks were forbidden.[10]

He must also have felt that he had been abandoned and betrayed by his parents – young as he was for his age and used to a cultured, reasonably free and perhaps over-protective environment, one still enjoyed by his parents such a short distance away. And there were other emotional conflicts. He was isolated, disliked and distrusted since he was the headmaster's son. Sir Cecil Parrott told me that all the Greenes had this difficulty at school. They were 'Charles's sons' and the result was that nobody trusted them.[11] Graham had the added disadvantage of not 'fitting in'. He lived within himself, was book-orientated, looked younger than his years, and was 'odd'. R. S. Stanier said: 'Graham was a peculiar boy. There is no doubt about it. He had this rather funny voice, a bit of a lisp I think, and a sort of plummy utterance. Certainly people did make fun of him a bit. He didn't play games well. He wasn't in a school team or a house team. His physical participation was minimal. And Graham found games particularly unpleasant. He was naturally teased.'[12] To his friend Claud Cockburn, Graham was indeed different: 'He looked sort of a little separate – from his family certainly. I think this may have contributed to the view among the boys that he was a possible spy and so on, which he wasn't and which most couldn't have believed because he didn't look in the least like any of his family. There is something strange in him, something unordinary, some element in his mind which is a governing influence . . . I don't know what it is and I don't think anybody else does.' Personal characteristics made him different and therefore a target for torment simply because he was different – the pack drives out the 'sport'; society finds its scapegoat.

It is probable that Graham's failure, where physical prowess was concerned, was exacerbated by the fact that his elder brother Raymond was such a success at school, seemingly in all he attempted. J. B. Wilson said:

> Look, I would say this honestly. Raymond and Ben Greene held their own. They were perfectly normal as regards athletics and everything else. Graham was abnormal. There was no question about it. His brother Raymond – we called him Raye or Rayay – we admired and looked up to. He was head of the house, was in the Rugger XV, was a pretty good runner and all the rest of it. Graham was nowhere to be seen.[13]

Raymond took on every duty, performing with relish, not only as a senior prefect, but as honorary secretary of the school's Debating Society, where he stood no nonsense, as a letter in *The Berkhamstedian* shows. There he suggested that unless more interest was shown in the Society, he would 'move the dissolution' of it.[14] He was an ardent debater, but also a successful editor of *The Berkhamstedian*, where he urged students to 'forsake the jelly for the press' since rumours had reached him 'of wits, of poets, of novelists, of journalists, all at hand within the School itself'.[15] Even in a field where you would think his presence and forcefulness would not aid him – poetry – he succeeded in winning the school's Arnold Medal for the poem 'Great Gable'.★

Graham had shown none of his brother's or his father's competence, powers of command and leadership in the small society of the School. It is no wonder that his sense of failure brought about a breakdown.

*

Some of the mental agony brought about by his lack of popularity and consequently his difficulty in finding companions for the Sunday walks, was relieved when his parents gave him permission to spend Sunday afternoons at home. But it was a temporary relief. In the evening he had to rejoin his companions tramping into the school Chapel and up the hill to St John's, and then at night the stone stairs to the dormitory.[16] It must have separated him still further from the other boys, for was he not receiving a special dispensation because he was 'Charles's son'? And if he tried to gain popularity would that not mean betraying his father? At the same time, his sense of failure in coping with the institution and its standards – which were those of his father – must also have been strong, and in a way a further betrayal. He was, after all, the son who could not deal successfully with his father's world.

When we use the term 'Greeneland' to describe the characteristic landscape of his novels we usually have his concern with betrayal in mind. He treats betrayal obsessively, its source, its nature, its prevalence in the world as a malady, its necessity the unstated part of every man. His first published novel derived from his finding, in an account of nineteenth-century smuggling, an example of betrayal. Writing to his future wife about it in 1926 he describes 'a gorgeous long cold-blooded letter by an anonymous informer to the Admiralty' which gave him the subject of *The Man Within* – 'the hero of the novel has *got* to be an informer'. The letter must have taken him back instinctively to the betrayals involved in his time at St John's.

But he did not betray his tormentors. The determination of the youth in his short story, 'End of the Party', 'not to lay bare his last

★ An indication of Raymond's prefectorial manner has survived in a note, written seventy years ago while he was head of house, and preserved by J. B. Wilson:

You may remember that I said that you could use the Pres' Room when invited to do so. I should have been perfectly willing to grant permission if anyone had troubled to ask me. In my absence leave can be obtained from one of the other prefects.

When you do use the room, I should be obliged if you would remove all signs of your presence. This outburst is caused chiefly by the fact that there were crumbs etc. all over the place and a large hunk of jam on the top of my books.
R.G.

secrets and end reserve between his mother and himself' suggests the reason why he did not take the easy way out and confess to someone – his brother or his father or mother – the difficulties he was experiencing and his deep unhappiness.

*

In his recollections of that period, Graham Greene makes a distinction between physical and mental torture and demonstrates what was for him the 'genuine quality of evil'. And yet what he writes of his experiences does not suggest that he was subjected to great evil. Indeed he wrote in *A Sort of Life*: 'Though children can be abominably cruel, no physical tortures were inflicted on me.'[17] This suggests, of course, that for him it was a mental cruelty which was, in his case, worse. In the earlier *The Lawless Roads*, there is a different emphasis and an increase in emotive language:

> In the land of the skyscrapers [this was his name for the new struc-tures Dr Fry had had put up], of stone stairs and cracked bells ringing early, one was aware of fear and hate, a kind of lawlessness – appalling cruelties could be practised without a second thought; one met for the first time characters, adult and adolescent, who bore about them the genuine quality of evil. There was Collifax, who practised torments with dividers;* Mr Cranden with three grim chins, a dusty gown, a kind of demoniac sensuality; from these heights evil declined towards Parlow, whose desk was filled with minute photographs – advertisements of art photos. Hell lay about them in their infancy.[18]

This trinity, Collifax, Mr Cranden and Parlow, represented for Graham a descending order of evil at Berkhamsted and I shall try to determine the names and characters of the originals who stand behind these figures.

We shall not easily discover the true name of the least evil ('from these heights evil declined towards Parlow'), but that such a boy existed I have no doubt since, in the surviving typescript of Graham's first novel, 'Anthony Sant' (later called 'Prologue to Pilgrimage' un-known and unpublished and written when Greene was a student at Oxford), Parlow, his name changed to Porter, has the same repository of photographs. 'Some disguised their lack of enthusiasm and like Porter, whose chief interest was in his picture gallery of naked ladies, feigned an interest in games.'[19] A further clue lies in *England Made Me*. There the reporter, Minty, dislikes the military attaché Gullie

---

* two-spiked instruments for measuring.

and 'nothing could have more stirred his malice than the sight of Gullie poring over the photographs of naked breasts and thighs'.[20]

Gullie derives from a person Graham knew at school, but what was the real name? Graham calls him successively Parlow, Porter and Gullie. There is a clue to his identity since the other fact about Gullie, apart from his fascination with the female form, is that he was an amateur painter of ships: 'little pictures . . . hung two deep round the white walls: small ships of every kind, barques, brigantines, frigates, schooners . . .'[21] Now there was a prefect in St John's when Graham was there called Henslowe and this rhymes with the name Graham first gave to his young voyeur, Parlow. Could Henslowe be the true name of Parlow? Henslowe was an excellent amateur sketcher, not of ships but of aeroplanes: 'He had always a crowd of youngsters round his desk asking him to draw a Spad or an SE2 or some other esoteric aircraft,' an Old Boy recalled.

Would Greene make such a simple change from Henslowe to Parlow? Possibly. We know, for example, that the hero of *The Heart of the Matter*, Major Scobie, is based on a police official called Brodie with whom Graham worked in Sierra Leone during the Second World War.

*

Graham wrote many years later in *A Sort of Life* about Mr Cranden, his three grim chins increased to four, and called him by his real name, Dr Simpson. It is a milder portrait, probably because Graham felt he could no longer speak of a 'demoniac sensuality' once he was giving the man's true name:

> A popular master in charge of one of the junior houses was called Simpson. He was never properly shaved, the five o'clock shadow was there at morning prayers, and he had four chins, although he was not otherwise a fat man. He rubbed his hands together in a gloating manner when in form he caught one who belonged to his house in a punishable offence. He would refer jocularly to beatings and he very obviously enjoyed them. In a strange way this made him popular. It seemed to me even then that his boys were collaborators in a pleasure.[22]

Many Old Boys have spoken about Dr Simpson. One was highly critical of Graham's description of him. He described T. Dale Simpson ('Simmy'), who was in charge of Overton House, as being like a farmer in spirit who did wonders in the garden growing vegetables during the war, and whose wife was red-faced and sold the boys bantam eggs for tea. Simpson played the double bass in the school orchestra and was memorable for his readings (with an impeccable Cumbrian accent) of 'Owd Bob' by Alfred Oliphant. But he was a flogger: 'Simmy was a disciplinarian and laid about him with a cane left-handed.' He remembered Simmy coming into the class of a woman teacher, who was in tears trying to control the boys, and sending her home and in the next hour beating the whole house. The young ones were caned in the dormitories in their pyjamas, the older boys in the study.

Another Old Boy recalled that Simpson's punishments in his study were with a heavy cane known as 'The Board' which he 'chalked' carefully before the first stroke to provide an aiming mark for those to follow. At night he patrolled the dormitories (but not at fixed hours) silently in rubber-soled shoes and carrying a light, flexible rattan cane up his sleeve which was known as 'The Twitcher'. This was ready for instant use on any pyjama–clad bottom when someone had erred. Simpson greatly enjoyed the nightly chase and the frequent 'kills' which resulted.

There is an interesting postscript to this account of Simpson, who was close enough to the Greene family to be present on 13 November 1904 when Graham was baptised. Early in August 1974, Graham Greene and his brother Hugh were invited by the Berkhamsted Citizens' Association to answer questions about their early lives at Berkhamsted School. During the proceedings, a daughter of Dr Simpson stood up in the body of the hall and said she had travelled a long way from Eastbourne to question Graham's description of her father, Dr Simpson, whom Graham deemed a flogger. Groans came from the Greenes. Both brothers then gave examples of Dr Simpson beating boys for such misdemeanours as being without a cap. It caused laughter when she admitted that she herself had had a birching when caught listening at her father's door. Sir Charles Parrott told me that the girl watched her father flog boys and was in turn flogged.[23]

*

Who was Collifax, practising 'torments with dividers', who bore about him the genuine quality of evil? Collifax's real name was Carter, and it was he who, with the help of a boy called Wheeler, turned Graham's life into a hopeless misery. Because Wheeler was still alive when *A Sort of Life* was published, Greene called him Watson. In 1981 the acting secretary of the Selangor Turf Club, Kuala Lumpur, Kaka Singh, wrote to me: 'It is with deep regrets that we inform you that Mr A. H. Wheeler has left us to be with the Lord many years ago.'

Greene mentioned Collifax's real name as early as 1951 in *The Lost Childhood*. Speaking there of the books of his childhood he discusses

Marjorie Bowen's *The Viper of Milan*, and tells us that the story of
the war between Visconti (Duke of Milan) and della Scala (Duke of
Verona) crept in and coloured and explained 'the terrible living world
of stone stairs and the never quiet dormitory':

> It was no good in that real world to dream that one would ever be
> a Sir Henry Curtis, but della Scala who at last turned from an
> honesty that never paid and betrayed his friends and died dis-
> honoured and a failure even at treachery – it was easier for a child
> to escape behind his mask. As for Visconti, with his beauty, his
> patience, and his genius for evil, I had watched him pass by many
> a time in his black Sunday suit smelling of mothballs.* His name
> was Carter.[24]

Who was this Carter, who was able to torment Graham and change
him from being a trusting child into an untrusting man? Who helped,
along with the living conditions at St John's and his sense of having
been deserted by his family, to bring him to the point of escaping
behind the mask of della Scala? How could Graham have come to
see this boy who was only a few months older than himself† as
Visconti, as one who gave him his first insights into the way of the
world: '. . . perfect evil walking the world where perfect good can
never walk again, and only the pendulum ensures that after all in the
end justice is done'?[25]

Graham, in every respect, was a sitting target for a person like
Carter who 'perfected during [his] fourteenth and fifteenth years a
system of mental torture based on [Graham's] difficult situation'.
Carter had an adult imagination. He could conceive the conflict of
Graham's loyalties, loyalties to his age-group, loyalty to his father
and brother. 'The sneering nicknames were inserted like splinters
under the nails.'[26] The pressure on Graham was to side with the
'forces of resistance' – the schoolboys – against his own family, a
betrayal which could bring him acceptance and popularity, and he
did understand and sympathise with his school-fellows for rebelling:
'Inexorably the others' point of view rose on the path like a murdered
innocent.' Later in life he wrote that 'it has always been in the interests

---

* According to Claud Cockburn every boy had to wear on Sundays a black
coat and striped trousers, though the black coats were relaxed during the war and
boys wore blue coats. After the war, black coats were reintroduced. Cockburn
recalls Graham's father catching him in blue instead of black: 'He gave me a lecture
and finally said, climaxing a rhetorical enunciation, "Cockburn, would you go
through life in a coat not black?"'

† Lionel Arthur Carter was born 12 May 1904; he died 17 May 1971.

of the State to poison psychological wells . . . to restrict human sympathy' and therefore it is the storyteller's task 'to elicit sympathy and a measure of understanding for those who lie outside the boundaries of State approval.'[27] In *A Sort of Life*, he claimed that his cousin had succumbed to temptation: 'My cousin Ben, a junior prefect, one of the rich Greenes, had no such scruples and worked covertly against my brother, gaining much popularity in consequence.'*

It is probable that Graham also was tempted, that he toyed with the idea of betrayal in order to gain release from his situation. 'It is impossible', says the obsessed Rowe in *The Ministry of Fear*, 'to go through life without trust: that is to be imprisoned in the worst cell of all, oneself.'[28] Betrayal could have earned Graham the trust of 'the forces of resistance', and in *A Sort of Life* he admits that Carter continuously tempted him with offers of friendship which were 'snatched away like a sweet, but leaving the impression that somewhere, some time the torture would end'.[29] And he had a reluctant admiration for Carter:

> I admired his ruthlessness, and in an odd way he admired what he wounded in me. Between the torturer and the tortured arises a kind of relationship. So long as the torture continues the torturer has failed, and he recognizes an equality in his victim. I never seriously in later years desired revenge on Carter.[30]

To a certain degree he succumbed to the torture by inventing stories of having been cruelly flogged in order to clamp down the suspicions against him and redeem his poor status in the eyes of the other boys – presumably without success.

Carter's first attack on Graham was physical – 'there was Collifax who practised torments with dividers'. This first published account appeared in *The Lawless Roads* in 1939, but Greene had already dealt with it in an unpublished novel, 'Prologue to Pilgrimage', as early as 1923. Its special value lies in the fact that he was then still a fledgling in disguising the autobiographical sources of his fiction, and I believe we have in the surviving typescript a close record of his life at St John's. The three central characters in the novel – Hardy, Webber and Sant – are based on Wheeler, Carter and Greene. Webber (Carter) first attacks Hardy (Wheeler) and then it is Anthony Sant's turn, and he, in feelings and personality, is a twin of Graham Greene, with the exception of one important and significant feature which we shall

---

* My judgment was similar to Claud Cockburn's: 'He was a great shambling man of total goodwill. He wished everybody well and thought that other people wished everybody well, too.'

come to later. 'Prologue to Pilgrimage' is convincing in its reconstruction of the schoolroom situation:

> Slowly Anthony felt an arm creeping behind his back . . . There was a jerk and a muttered exclamation from Hardy. The hand withdrew itself and Anthony saw that Webber had been using a pair of dividers . . . A quarter of an hour later once again came the disturbed flurry behind his back . . . Furiously he seized his own box of geometry instruments, and prepared to retaliate. Then caution predominated again in his brain . . . But he was too late to disguise the first aggressive movement. Webber had noticed it and Anthony felt a small warning prick in his calf . . . Webber was subtle. He half realized Anthony's character, his fear of precipitating an unnecessary struggle, his passionate desire to be left in peace . . . three or four times during every future evening, Anthony's dreams would be broken by that warning prick . . . Webber did realize the existence of two methods of torture, the physical and the mental . . . to Anthony the last was the most terrible.[31]

A variant of this appears in *England Made Me* where Minty, one of Greene's grotesque figures, nevertheless shares an experience of Graham's at school: 'It was only that Minty had more self-control. The twisting of his arm had taught him it, the steel nibs dug into his calf.'[32] Three years later Greene returned to the theme in *Brighton Rock* where it has lain unnoticed. Pinkie, the boy gangster, is cornered and attacked by another gang:

> [He] . . . saw the faces ringing him all round. They grinned back at him: every man had his razor out . . . the long cut-throat razors which the sun caught slanting low down over the downs from Shoreham. He put his hand to his pocket to get his blade, and the man immediately facing him leant across and slashed his knuckles. Pain happened to him, and he was filled with horror and astonishment as if one of the bullied brats at school had stabbed first with the dividers.[33]

Greene is dealing closely here with Carter's opening shots in a game of mental and physical torment and with his own tremendous sense of being humiliated. A friendly master in the novel, Mr Penley (based on Mr Dale at Berkhamsted School) says to Anthony: 'They don't fight fair . . . they send out their little insidious worms, brain worms, which creep into your mind so softly that you don't notice them but all the time they are gnawing away at the foundations.'[34]

Whenever Sant 'entered the schoolroom, an undertone of mockery seemed to creep into that endless chorus of voices, which was to din, din its way into Anthony's ears for twelve long weeks of term.'[35] And always, Anthony stresses Webber's subtle knowledge of his character. He unceasingly nags Anthony as in life Carter nagged Graham. And surely Anthony's frantic hope, as a new term approaches, that life would be different, that he would find a real friend, and that the torture would cease derives from Graham's own hopes. But there was no change. Deliberately and calculatingly, Webber turns the screw, working on Sant's intense fear of ridicule. From the following passage in 'Prologue to Pilgrimage', we have a good notion of Graham's initial problem of personality:

> And then would come suddenly one of those flashes, not so much of self-revelation, as of self-distortion, when he pictured himself the ridiculous figure which he thought all must picture him . . . If someone insulted him he had not the courage to fight. He was not physically afraid, but was overcome by the mental panic of seeming ridiculous.[36]

Like Sant, Graham's own fear of ridicule and humiliation was more intense than his fear of death.

Possibly he had little ability then to defend himself physically. The evidence is slender but when the agent D, in the novel *The Confidential Agent*, is attacked there is a strong sense that a boy not a man is being attacked by a bully, and it is likely that this records one painful experience Graham had as a boarder at St John's.

> He felt a little sick with apprehension. He hated personal violence: to kill a man with a bullet, or to be killed, was a mechanical process. But the fist was different: the fist humiliated; to be beaten up put you into an ignoble relationship with the assailant . . . he would have been prepared to answer any charge to escape the physical contact. He shut his eyes and leant back against the mirror: he was defenceless. He didn't know the first thing about using his fists.[37]

Like Sant, Graham had no means of establishing himself with his classmates. Everything about him was cause for ostracism and provided ammunition for Carter – his odd appearance and speech, his manner, his inability at games and the physical feats most admired in the school. He records how at O.T.C. parades Carter and Wheeler were always ready to exploit his inadequacies as he fumbled under their 'ironic eyes'. All he could do was to become clever at evasion.

To avoid fielding practice he invented extra coaching in mathematics and even named the master supposed to be teaching him.[38]

An extract from Anthony Sant's diary in 'Prologue to Pilgrimage' gives us the events of two weeks in his life. In all probability it is modelled closely on Greene's own schoolboy diary (now lost) for the last two weeks in July, probably of 1920. It shows signs that he was nearing a breakdown. From 14 to 18 July, the diary records either 'school in morning. Cricket in afternoon' or 'school in morning and afternoon'. The entries then become more detailed:

July 19.	Sat.	School in morning. Felt miserable. Webber at me again. Got off cricket by saying Mr Penley had invited me to tea. I don't know what Crooks will say if he finds out.
20.	Sunday.	Chapel in morning and evening. Hardy wanted me to go for a walk. Said I was already walking and felt like a beast. Went to my usual hiding place. After prep., Webber sang 'darkie' songs at me.
21.	Monday.	School in morning. Cricket in afternoon. Awful house game. Missed two catches . . .
24.	Thurs.	School in morning and afternoon. Said I was kept in and cut practice . . .
26.	Sat.	School in morning. Cricket in afternoon. Webber & Co. gave me a rotten time in changing room afterwards. I wish they'd try and hurt me physically, then I'd fight. Why am I so damnably afraid of being ridiculous?[39]

The significance of Webber's 'darkie' songs is that in transmuting his experiences into fiction, no doubt in order to explain a schoolboy situation which might otherwise seem ordinary, Graham made Anthony Sant black, and therefore at that time a natural target for persecution and one who stood out as different from the pack. It is also possible that scandalous rhymes about the headmaster, of a kind not unusual in most schools, were repeated in his presence. One can imagine the sneering nicknames which might have been applied to Graham, for Carter was, like some dark magician. He was always able to shut down Graham's contact with others, halt a friendship, imprison him in permanent isolation, and like a young Satan entice Graham to betray brother and father.

*

The name 'Carter' appears in a number of Greene's novels, but the characters with this name are not like the actual Carter. One suspects that Carter really appears in the character Hilfe in *The Ministry of Fear*, where the hunted hero, Arthur Rowe, trusts him and is fascinated by him and his very blue eyes – and Hilfe plays with him as a cat does with a mouse. Hilfe controls the situation between them with an adroit cunning; he is unshocked and unshockable. Everything in life is a game. He gives off a blithe innocence, is charming and yet utterly ruthless, and utterly without any belief. He is something new in Rowe's experience. Both Carter and Hilfe are without any psychological scars. They both enjoy baiting for the sake of baiting, for its cleverness. Like Hilfe, Carter was 'good-looking, very young and even inoffensive to look at'. A contemporary recalled him as 'good-looking, clean-cut, blue eyes'. Here is Hilfe, after his part in creating a Ministry of Fear has been discovered by Rowe:

> He was deeply and completely at peace, and so defenceless that he seemed to be innocent . . . The face seemed to Rowe very beautiful, more beautiful than his sister's, which could be marred by grief or pity. Watching the sleeping man he could realize a little of the force and the grace and the attraction of nihilism – of not caring for anything, of having no rules and feeling no love. Life became simple . . . The pale blue eyes held full knowledge of the situation; there was nothing to explain. He smiled and Rowe caught himself in the act of smiling back. It was the kind of trick a boy plays suddenly, capitulating, admitting everything, so that the whole offence seems small and the fuss absurd.[40]

But perhaps most significant as far as the Carter/Greene relationship is concerned was Hilfe's ability to destroy Rowe's illusions about life: 'You've got so many illusions of grandeur, heroism, self-sacrifice, patriotism,' Hilfe says to Rowe, listing the ideals Graham's father had instilled in class and from the pulpit and those Graham had absorbed from his childhood reading, and it would seem that Carter, while introducing him to the possible physical and mental cruelties of life, attacked and destroyed his illusions of man's heroic nature and so wrenched Graham's nature out of true.

Two stories that Graham contributed to *The Berkhamstedian*, both unsigned, reflect his personal crisis at that time. The first, entitled

'The Tick of the Clock', suggests a deep-seated loneliness, being about an old lady, close to death and totally friendless, whose only sense of companionship comes from the ticking of her clock – an unusual conception for a sixteen-year-old boy. Equally curious was 'The Poetry of Modern Life', published in March 1921 at the height of Carter's persecution. The story, in spite of its unemotive title, deals with the effect of Carter's attack on Graham's view of human nature, for there was no longer to be any 'poetry' in modern life:

> It was just a voice in the street that I heard as I passed along 'Poetry and Romance are dead' . . . when I heard that voice, the busy movement of the streets pressed in upon me, seeming to shut out all colour, and changing everything into a dull monotony . . . it penetrated into my slumbers so that I seemed to be surrounded with legions of devils, all crying out, 'Poetry and Romance are dead.'

The narrator is so disturbed that he seeks reassurance from a knight – a traditional, picture book, chivalrous knight – who admits, 'I and my kind are dead', and, as if reflecting Graham's losing battle with Carter, he can only offer the consolation that there is heroism even in the 'poetry of defeat'. The story ends with an example of this: 'Three men lay there. Death through hunger and cold had almost come; yet one was still striving to write some last letters to those at home.'

I suspect Graham has in mind here the death of Captain Scott of the Antarctic, and his comrades Wilson and Bowers. Scott's death in 1912, amidst the snow and ice, made him among British schoolboys an archetypal hero.

Perhaps the dying man's attempt to write letters home reflects Graham's desire to write to his parents about his misery, though he could not. In the face of Carter's undermining of Greene's cherished boyhood beliefs, it is not surprising that he turned to a less romantic vision. The knight in the story offers some hope, arguing that 'as long as the great world struggle between Good and Evil lasts, so long will there be poetry in life.'[41] It is possible that Carter, with his inexplicable cruelties, his nihilism, his ability to feign innocence, put Greene on to his fundamental theme, the nature of Good and Evil and the conflict between them. Thus Graham is seeking an answer to his personal problems in his earliest published pieces. They represent his cry in the night for help. Carter's powerful mockery at this time was sapping Graham's belief in his boyhood dreams and chivalric standards.

*

In *A Sort of Life*, Graham speaks of a 'great betrayal' and tells us that Wheeler deserted him for Carter. J. B. Wilson, who was a boarder at St John's at the same time as Graham and knew Carter and Wheeler, had this to say: 'Granted that Carter looked very young and inoffensive, he could have turned against Graham – there was something sly about him. Wheeler in contrast was one of those no-character people. I mean he was just there. He was an efficient member of the House. He was always cheerful and grinning.'

A no-character he may have been but there is no question that he betrayed Graham. Again Graham gives us nothing of substance beyond the statement that he was betrayed, but the weight of that betrayal, its effect on Graham appears in an interview that Greene gave to Ronald Matthews in 1957 and is to be found in Matthews's book *Mon Ami Graham Greene*:

> One didn't know where one was, and that might be a good definition of nightmare. The world of nightmare is a world without defences because each defence may be nullified. What would be the point in preparing to prevent an attack when your best friend might suddenly without any reason turn into your worst enemy?[42]

There is much feeling here but little factual detail. Yet we can speculate about the betrayal. This was a time in Graham's life when changes in body and mind were taking place. He had reached puberty and was turning towards poetry inspired by love. He found extraordinary beauty and passion in the work of Sir Lewis Norris, in his *Epic of Hades*, for example, where Helen comments on the nature of her love for Paris and her need for freedom:

> Fair with a woman's fairness, yet in arms
> A hero, but he never had my heart.
> It was not he seduced me, but the thirst
> For freedom . . . my child,
> Born to an unloved father, loved me not,
> The fresh sea called, the galleys plunged, and I
> Fled willing from my prison and the pain
> Of undesired caresses . . .[43]

It was from Lewis Norris's poetry that he learnt of the carnal loves of Helen and Cleopatra. To read such poetry, he would steal out of school, miss classes, avoid fielding practice and escape to a solitary lane where he had a secret hideout. It provided him with the age-old security of the womb: 'On one side was a ploughed field: on the other a ditch with a thick hawthorn hedge which was hollow in the centre and in which I could sit concealed and read my book.'[44] This hideout is also described in 'Prologue to Pilgrimage' where Anthony Sant indulges in the 'crime' of reading poetry. Could Graham have trustingly told Wheeler of these things, perhaps confessing such secrets in the first flush of friendship? And if Wheeler carried them to Carter who then made cynical use of them surely this would fill Greene with a sense of ridicule and mortification.

Some support for this view can be found in Greene's first published novel, *The Man Within*. There Carlyon, a leader of the smugglers, makes a curiously unexpected outcry to Elisabeth about Andrews, his one-time friend, now his enemy: 'Was he laughing at me the whole time . . . while we were friends? . . . I told him all the things I liked. I read him things, shared what I loved with him.'[45] The Judas figure, a powerful character in some of Greene's finest novels, could well have derived from Wheeler. The prevalent view then among schoolboys of those who read poetry for pleasure was that they were 'lily-livered girls'.[46] Hardy pleads with Sant to stop reading poetry or he would never hear the last of it.

Greene never forgot Wheeler and he desired, long after he left school, to have his revenge, not only because by his defection his isolation had become almost complete, but because he came to suspect that Wheeler's friendly overtures were made in order to betray him later to Carter. Even the way in which Greene writes about him suggests an anger harboured over long years:

I found the desire for revenge alive like a creature under a stone. The only change was that I looked under the stone less and less often . . . But still every few years a scent, a stretch of wall, a book on a shelf, a name in a newspaper, would remind me to lift the stone and watch the creature move its head towards the light.[47]

What brings Anthony Sant to crisis is the theft of his diary by Webber and the enormous fun Webber gets out of holding the diary aloft as a trophy:

A hand swooped suddenly down and whisked the diary away, and when Anthony looked up, Webber was again at the stove, with the book open in his hand.

'Oh, do just look at this,' he crowed. 'It's Sant's diary. I'll read you some. It's priceless.' . . . 'Beastly unhappy to-night. Webber and everyone teasing as usual. Diddums then.'[48]

Graham has not suggested that his diary was seized in a similar manner (though it could have been) or that as a consequence his life was brought to a crisis, as Sant's was.

In *England Made Me*, there is an account of a gang of schoolboys breaking up Minty's pictures of the Madonna and Child, 'jeering, belching, breaking wind',[49] and perhaps what happened to Graham emotionally was something of this sort. In *The Lawless Roads*, recalling that he 'couldn't sit in the plaza for more than a few minutes without a gibe', he makes a comment which surely looks back to his schooldays: 'It preyed on my nerves: it was like being the one unpopular boy at school.' Graham must have been at breaking point once Wheeler joined forces with Carter.

Throughout Greene's work there are references to a cracked bell, even in such a commercial work as *The Third Man*, which becomes symbolic of a desperately unhappy boyhood. It appears in *The Lawless Roads*: 'In the land of . . . stone stairs and cracked bells ringing early, one was aware of fear and hate', but if we look at Graham's first reference to the cracked bell in 'Prologue to Pilgrimage', and accept that his experience was Anthony Sant's, we can understand that he was on the verge of a breakdown. His hopeless brooding led him to a belief that every boy in St John's (there were forty of them) was in league against him – all potential enemies because his father was headmaster:

Over all these dreams hovered one persistent question, 'Why am I here?' And as yet there was no answer that he could give. But always day by day at a certain hour, with an incredible and almost superhuman punctuality, came the sound of the cracked bell. It would begin with comparative faintness as the ringer strode along the upper dormitory, and then, as he turned to descend the stairs, there would come with monotonous regularity the half choked clang, before the hand fastened on the hammer. Day by day Anthony in his state of semi-wakeness would listen and picture the act with a kind of mechanic precision . . . Anthony longed at times with almost stunning force that the hand would slip, that the bell for once would emit its full cry, as the boy came down the stairs. Anything would be welcome to break the monotonous terror of the routine. Anthony would cower beneath his bedclothes in real physical fear of that inevitable sound, and when it came, it would stab his flesh, like the pain from an exposed nerve.[50]

Graham's sole desire was to remain on the 'right' side of the border, which he expresses movingly in *The Lawless Roads* – Saturday night, the school orchestra playing Mendelssohn, and Graham alone in the dark on the croquet lawn:

> There lay the horror and the fascination. One escaped surreptitiously for an hour at a time: unknown to frontier guards, one stood on the wrong side of the border looking back – one should have been listening to Mendelssohn, but instead one heard the rabbit restlessly cropping near the croquet hoops. It was an hour of release – and also an hour of prayer. One became aware of God with an intensity – time hung suspended – music lay on the air; anything might happen before it became necessary to join the crowd across the border. There was no inevitability anywhere . . . faith was almost great enough to move mountains . . . the great buildings rocked in the darkness.[51]

We can date this 'hour of release' accurately since the only time during his period at Berkhamsted that Mendelssohn was played at a school concert was on 14 December 1920.

But faith was not able to rescue him from his unbearable situation – there was no blinding flash of revelation pointing to change. Like Rowe in *The Ministry of Fear*, imprisoned in the worst cell of all, himself, and realising there would be no release, he decided that, whatever the risk, he must break out. He could not turn to his father with his problems. That would have been treachery against the boys at St John's and would have justified their treatment of him. Also he feared the 'cold confidence of a grown-up's retort'. Kipling, in a very similar predicament, explains, 'Children tell little more than animals, for what comes to them they accept as eternally established.'

His first idea was to inflict an injury on himself which would force his parents to take him home. On the stone stairs to the dormitory, he tried (and fortunately failed) to saw open his knee. The penknife used was too blunt or perhaps, as he suggests in *A Sort of Life*, his nerve failed him.[52] In 'Prologue to Pilgrimage', Sant also draws his pocket knife across the skin of his knee, but the cut is negligible and he hasn't the courage to shut his eyes and stab. What Graham calls 'other forms of escape' should be called what they are: attempts at suicide. He sought a way of dying quietly in a peaceful trance. Perhaps the words of Peter Pan were in his mind: 'To die will be an awfully big adventure':

> I tried out other forms of escape after I failed to cut my leg. Once at home on the eve of term I went into the dark room by the linen-

cupboard, and in that red Mephelophelean glare drank a quantity of hypo under the false impression that it was poisonous. On another occasion I drained my blue glass bottle of hay-fever drops, which, as they contained a small quantity of cocaine, were probably good for my despair. A bunch of deadly nightshade, picked and eaten on the Common, had only a slightly narcotic effect, and once, towards the end of one holiday, I swallowed twenty aspirins before swimming in the empty school baths. (I can still remember the curious sensation of swimming through cotton wool.)[53]

The twenty aspirins he recalled in 1971 were an increase on the fourteen he wrote about in a letter only five years after the event, when he records going for a swim, his legs like lead, then managing to get back home and sleeping uneasily for hours.[54] We can add another attempted suicide to his list. Arthur Calder-Marshall recalled (in 1977) that he met Greene in 1940 and Graham said that that morning he had been reading his schoolboy diary in which he had written: 'Ate a whole tin [of hair pomade]. But it didn't work.' All his attempts had failed.

On the last day of his summer holiday he could not face returning to St John's. 'I endured', he wrote, 'some eight terms – a hundred and four weeks of monotony, humiliation and mental pain.'[55] He decided on a different way out, perhaps the only means of bringing his unhappiness home to his parents. He ran away. He wrote a note and placed it on the black oak sideboard in the School House dining room under the whisky tantalus. It said, he tells us, that he had taken to the Common instead of returning to St John's and that he would remain there in hiding until his parents agreed that he would never again have to go back to his prison.

Once he reached the safety of the Common, 'among the gorse and bracken of [his] chosen battlefield', he felt a wonderful sense of release from all the tension and indecision. He had nothing to do but roam his 'battlefield from bush to bush'; he wanted to be an invisible watcher, a spy on all that went on, and he moved restlessly among the bushes on the edge of the Common, waiting for the search party. He must have known that he had made the move which would guarantee his freedom. Coming down to look at his exposed flank, a steep clay path between oaks and beeches, he moved rashly out beyond the cover of the bushes and turning a corner, came face to face with his elder sister, Molly.

Thus his escape came to an inglorious end for it would hardly have suited the dignity of his protest to run off and he went quietly back home with her.

Graham was unable to remember much more – 'a thick haze conceals all that happened next' and he admits that perhaps he was nearer to a nervous breakdown than he had previously cared to believe. He remembers no reproaches from his parents, only being put into a warmed bed in the spare room next to his parents' room.

In contrast to the life he was escaping from, his actual escape as he recounted it fifty years later, lacks pressure and has an element of child's play about it as if he wished to discount its seriousness. In retrospect, he changes the emphasis, wishing that he could have watched, observed and known how his family took his sudden disappearance – 'what conferences were held, what tactics were suggested, what decisions were made' – and adds, 'it is too late for me to find out. All the protagonists are dead except myself – my father, my mother, my elder sister, even the head housemaid who would have known all.'

But a letter has survived, unknown to Graham, written in 1948 by his mother to his wife and kept secretly by her for forty years. In it, Graham's mother recalls the day he disappeared and his peace-destroying note. Even though she was writing long after the event, her deep concern over her disturbed and sensitive son is apparent:

He went as a boarder to St John's in September 1918. Raymond was still Head of the house but had no idea Graham was being persecuted by a particular boy. In what way I do not know nor did Guest who was a friend of Graham's. I cannot date when the crisis occurred but between 1919 & 1920. I think Graham was not well the morning he should have gone back to St John's – slight temperature and eyes peculiar. Doctor could not understand the eyes. I kept him in bed and went to do house-keeping & returned to find he was not there & a note to say he would not go back to St John's – had tried to poison himself with eye-drops (accounts for eyes) in vain & had gone & we should not see him again.

You cannot imagine how we felt. We did not want to go to the police at once. Uncle Eppy sent his bailiff whom he could trust to hunt along the canal. Dr McB. took me all over golf-links in his car – we searched woods calling all the time. Then after lunch Molly said she had a feeling she should find him & taking Miss Arnell & some food they set out. And they found him sitting in the little wood where M. thought he might be. They brought him home & I put him to bed & told him he should never go back.

This letter confirms Greene's many attempts at suicide and his methods, but whereas he plays down the escape incident as a game of hide-and-seek (thus denying the feeling of terror which drives a youngster to run away), merely holding out on the Common until his parents gave way, his mother's letter shows that it was much more serious and distressing and the note he left was much more disturbing than he suggests. A passage in 'The Basement Room' where a boy runs away from home reflects something of the real terror he must have been feeling: 'The only thing he could do was to get away, by the back stair . . . and never come back again. You didn't think of the cold, or the need of food and sleep; for an hour it would seem quite possible to escape from people forever . . . no one would ever find him again.' Also in 'The Basement Room', the same boy is outwitted by Mrs Baines so that he gives away the fact that her husband is having an affair – with disastrous consequences. Graham had gained his release, but there was an after-math since, as his mother's letter suggests, he revealed the name of his tormentor, probably winkled out of him by parental questioning. He has written, 'So long as the torture continues the torturer has failed,' and the torture stopped, so presumably Carter had succeeded.

Charles Greene visited his son after he returned, 'sitting on the bed and interrogating [him] seriously and tenderly', which led to a misunderstanding between them since his complaints about the gen-eral filth of life at St John's – meaning the unlocked lavatories, the farting, etc., gave his father the impression that he had been the victim of a masturbation ring. Graham adds, in a sentence ominous in its suggestion, that then 'other investigations were set on foot among the innocent inhabitants of St John's'. The differences between father and son, as shown by this, were great. The worst thing that could happen, so far as Charles Greene was concerned, was homosexuality, something the school's system had been organised to prevent. In fact, his son had been subjected to sadistic mental torture, 'the whole dark side of childhood', which was totally outside his father's comprehension.

Greene's attitude to such myopia, though he does not mention his father, comes out in his essay, 'The Old School'. His criticism is of the system but his father was in charge of that system: 'Too often the system interferes with its cult of suspicion and its abnormal fear of sexuality . . . One is alternatively amazed at the unworldly innocence of the pedagogic mind and at its tortuous obscenity.'[56]

Later in his essay he comes back to the same point and is clearly criticising his father, suggesting that a boy, 'his time free, and his speculation endless', will pick up in the field or in the streets know-ledge of sex:

He will have learnt sex more truthfully in a farm yard than in a house-master's study; and if he is a town child the jokes written on lavatory walls are likely to do less harm than the sentimentality, the embarrassment, the intellectual flummery of a set talk before confirmation on 'the facts of life'. They will have taught him at any rate that sexual enjoyment is neither solemn nor dull.[57]

It was Fry who introduced the large dormitories 'broken up by six foot partitions into cubicles'.[58] He also introduced the various other rules intended to abolish privacy. The young Graham Greene must have made the connection, perhaps even the identification, between his father and his father's 'sinister, sadistic predecessor'.

*

L. A. Carter left Berkhamsted School with no great distinction in the Easter term of 1921, without having entered the sixth form or completing his education at the school. His future career was not brilliant, and he retired early in life with a pension from the Cable and Wireless Company, suffering from stomach trouble. The question is, was he expelled from school as a result of Charles Greene's enquiries? It would seem not since he returned to play cricket for the Old Boys against the Masters' team and the most likely explanation for his early departure from the school is that, given the situation, his parents decided to withdraw him. Thus both families were able to avoid a scandal.

In 1985 L. A. Carter's widow, then an old lady living in a home at Worthing, told me that Jacky Hill (a popular master at Berkhamsted) was Carter's uncle on his mother's side. This is another reason why no publicity would have been given to Carter's leaving school early. But given the circumstances, Graham must have felt that he had betrayed his tormentor and his humiliation would have been complete. No one I have interviewed has criticised Carter, but one man who knew him when he was working for Cable and Wireless in Aden remembered him as a satirical man who could always make you feel foolish with a smirk and a turn of the lip.

It is remarkable that a relationship between a few boys at a public school should have had such repercussions, bringing Graham Greene to an understanding of the bond between the torturer and the tortured, of sympathy for the outsider and the recognition that victims change. Writing of his difficulties with Carter and Wheeler in *A Sort of Life*, Greene refers to a novel by Quiller-Couch, a story of a man's revenge in which, during a long, drawn-out pursuit the characters change places: 'the pursued took on nobility, the pursuer the former vulgarity of his enemy'.[59] Could it be that the burden of his youth, after the Carter experience was over, was that of guilt and betrayal, never successfully exorcised?

Oddly enough, most contemporaries of Graham at school could not clearly recall him. Those who did thought he was something of a softy. Raymond Greene they all remembered and, in spite of his condescension of manner, they greatly admired him. They had heard of Graham Greene, the famous writer, an Old Boy and son of the headmaster, but at school he had not been noticed. When asked to read *A Sort of Life* and give their reactions to the account of Berkhamsted, the Old Boys' response was that Graham had not had enough true grit: 'schoolboys fart and what's the fuss about?' Moreover they felt that he should have praised their school – after all, damn it, his father *was* headmaster. They considered he had let the side down: he had spit into his own soup – a distasteful culinary habit. But then he was young for his age and very shy. The schoolmaster Sunderland-Taylor said, 'He was the shyest little boy who ever passed through my hands.'[60] In photographs of Graham at St John's what we see is a very shy boy peeping out from a crowd of boys, unnoticed and seeming half afraid to be noticed.

Graham was only too aware that there was a total contrast in standing between himself and Raymond on the one hand and himself and his father on the other. This is expressed in *The Man Within* when Andrew cries, 'haven't I a mind? Wasn't my brain of any use to them that they should treat me like a child, never ask my opinion, have me there on sufferance only, because my father willed it?'[61] And also, 'I could see how they wondered that such a mountain [Charles Greene?] could bring forth such a mouse [Graham?].'[62]

His breakdown was, therefore, the result of many pressures which brought him near to manic depression, of which he was showing the classic symptoms – loss of interest in or ability to experience pleasure; increasing feelings of worthlessness, and thoughts of suicide. There was also, I suspect, the delusion of being persecuted because of his apparent inadequacy. He was, of course, being persecuted, but he began to see persecution everywhere, as Anthony Sant's comments reflect: whenever he 'entered the schoolroom, an undertone of mockery seemed to creep into that endless chorus of voices . . . for twelve long weeks of term'.

He was also turned inward, unable to tell his family what was happening or how he felt – not even his favourite aunt Nono could be confided in, even though she was living in London when he was having psychoanalytic treatment. In 1971, soon after the publication of *A Sort of Life*, Aunt Nono, in a nursing home, lay slowly dying of old age. Graham's sister, Elisabeth, visited her daily and it was her aunt's wish that she read her Graham's autobiography. Elisabeth takes up the story:

> I went on reading *A Sort of Life* and one day I'd read to her for a long time, and with only one chapter left, I said to Aunt Nono, 'Look, aren't you tired? Should I come in tomorrow, and read you the last chapter', and she said, 'No, I want you to read it to me now', and she died during that night. I remember her saying that Graham was such an enchanting little boy, it made her very sad to think he'd been so unhappy at school.[63]

This would suggest that Marion and Charles Greene had not told even close relatives about the matter, perhaps because of Charles Greene's interpretation of it.

Always after this we will witness Graham's tremendous sympathy for the hunted man (for he had felt hunted); the hunted man would become the staple of his fiction and he would have a profound interest in, and compulsive love for, the down-trodden everywhere. After Carter he would no longer look at the world in a child's way and he would discover his appointed task on earth: to be a writer. He puts it this way in *A Sort of Life*: meeting Wheeler in 1950 in Malaysia he wonders on his way back to the hotel if he would ever have written a book had it not been for 'Watson' and Carter, if those years of humiliation had not given him an excessive desire to prove that he was good at something, however long the effort might prove.[64]

In *The Lost Childhood* he puts it differently, attributing his desire to write to Miss Bowen's *The Viper of Milan*, but then the value of the Viper, as he mentions there, was that he made the evil of Carter understandable.

Thirty years after the events which drove him to breakdown, Graham Greene, writing on Charles Dickens, said, 'the creative writer perceives his world once and for all in childhood and adolescence, and his whole career is an effort to illustrate his private world in terms of the great public world we all share.'[65] He had found his subject:

> In the lost boyhood of Judas
> Christ was betrayed.

6

Psychoanalysed

Without nervous disorder there can be no great artist.
— PROUST

IN *A Sort of Life* Graham describes the panic in his family after
he ran away: 'Raymond . . . was hastily summoned home for
consultation; my father found the situation beyond him . . . My
brother . . . suggested psycho-analysis as a possible solution, and my
father – an astonishing thing in 1920 – agreed.'[1] Moreover Raymond
suggested the psychiatrist – Kenneth Richmond. I doubt, however,
that Graham was treated by Richmond in 1920 or that he went to
Richmond at the time he was most suicidal.

To begin with, he writes of his experiences at St John's as lasting
'for some eight terms – a hundred and four weeks',[2] and we know
from his mother's notebook that he went to St John's as a boarder
in September 1918 so that the eight terms would take us to the end
of the Easter term 1921, not 1920. His crisis must have taken place
just before the summer term 1921. This date is more likely from
Raymond's point of view since he did not start his medical studies at
Oxford until the autumn term of 1920, and by the end of the Easter
term 1921 he would have completed two terms and could have been
in a position to advise. The determining factor is a report in *The
Berkhamstedian* which records that on the evening of 4 June 1921, the
St John's Dramatic Society presented Lord Dunsany's play *The Lost
Silk Hat*, with H. G. Greene playing the part of the poet. It would
seem therefore that, his tormentor having departed, Greene returned
to St John's, though not as a boarder, for the summer term 1921 –
or part of it – and acted in a play, and his psychoanalysis began at
the end of that term – his earliest surviving letter to his mother from
Kenneth Richmond's house is dated by her 1 July 1921. We can
conclude that, given the changed situation at St John's and some
improvement in Greene's mental state, his parents decided to post-
pone the psychiatric treatment.

Raymond Greene recommended Kenneth Richmond to help his brother not only because he had gained a reputation at Oxford for his successful treatment of disturbed schoolboys, but also because he had a strong literary bent – a suitable mentor for a future writer. Yet Richmond might have been considered a strange choice, and it is unlikely that Greene's parents had any idea what the treatment would involve. It is uncertain whether Graham, at that point, really needed psychiatric treatment; but it is clear that Raymond Greene had hit on a winner with Richmond and his wife Zoe, because they were worlds apart from the Charles Greenes and Berkhamsted School.

Richmond had had several unpropitious starts in life. He and his mother had tried running a private school, but his mother suddenly decided against it and left her son with a building of boarding house proportions. His next venture followed logically from this. He and his wife Zoe established a boarding house there, which was only moderately successful. Then their lives turned in another direction – Richmond became a psychiatrist. It came about by chance. He had been reviewing for the *Observer*, *The Times*, the *Weekly Westminster* and the magazine *Land and Water*, and in 1917 he reviewed a book by Maurice Nicoll entitled *Dream Psychology*. Nicoll, who acknowledged his great debt to Jung, was becoming well known as a pioneer in psychological medicine and was so impressed by Richmond's review that he visited him in Cornwall and made the singular suggestion that Richmond would make a natural psychiatrist – natural indeed since he was without training or qualifications. It was Nicoll who sent him his first client, a dear friend of his, an American actress. She went to the Richmonds as their first paying guest. A friendship developed between her and Zoe, and through her the Richmonds were brought into close contact with Carl Jung, when, some years later, the actress was hostess to Jung during his visit to London.

Richmond and his wife had already become spiritualists, being greatly influenced by W. H. Myers's *Human Personality and its Survival of Bodily Death*. They accepted that some people were mediums who were sensitive to vibrations from the spirit world and could receive messages, and that a 'control' was needed – a spirit guide, a soul who had gone ahead, and who would convey messages. Zoe told me (she was then ninety-six but still forceful and with a lively mind) how her husband became a medium. She had an only brother called Miles and had 'a strong positive fixation to him', but he died during the First World War:

He was a darling. And he came to me immediately he died to say he wasn't dead, and we walked up and down the beach I remember and then he said he would be able to teach us things and he did through Kenneth and that's how Kenneth became a medium. And that has gone on, you see. I don't mean to say my brother told him . . . Somebody told him what to say to his patients because they mostly got well.[3]

In the same interview she was very insistent about the source of her husband's help in treating patients:

> Z.R.: 'Anyhow, he was told exactly each time how to treat each patient.'
>
> N.S.: 'By whom?'
>
> Z.R.: 'By communicators. You see, we had begun our experiments in spiritualism.'

The closest Graham comes in *A Sort of Life* to suggesting that the Richmonds were spiritualists is in the following passage: 'On Sundays . . . Richmond and his beautiful wife Zoe went to a church in Bayswater of some esoteric denomination, where the minister asked the congregation to decide by vote whether they would prefer that evening a sermon or a lecture on a psychological subject.'[4] Zoe explained that this was the spiritual church, The Seekers: 'They used to be in Queen's Gate. They had a marvellous medium – the man we went to see. He had a doctor communicator and he used to heal people through the doctor. They used to teach healing.'[5]

Richmond was quiet, reserved, intuitive, very intense and given to agonising over another's pain. A man of wide intellectual interests, he was a close friend of many of the leading writers of the day. He was thirty-six when Graham went to him (Graham thought he was in his early forties), and he had, four years earlier, been afflicted by a sense of failure and lack of purpose: he had had to fight his own battle against depression and find his own way out of darkness. He suffered much of his life as an alcoholic, though this rarely showed and his patients were not aware of it. Perhaps most significant, in dealing with Graham as a patient, was the fact that he was the rejected son of Canon Wilfred Richmond of Winchester. Canon Richmond, when he was no longer young, had married a seventeen-year-old girl who did not want to marry him, never loved him or their only child Kenneth. At the age of fifteen, Richmond escaped from his tormentors at public school by getting drunk and consequently being removed. He must have been deeply sympathetic to Graham's situation.

Graham believed that his analyst 'belonged to no dogmatic school

94

of psycho-analysis . . . was nearer to Freud than Jung, but Adler probably contributed.'[6] Thinking back to those days, Graham asked himself, 'was there a couch, the stock-subject of so many jokes? I can't remember.' But there would not have been a couch since Richmond was a practising Jungian. Zoe Richmond was quite adamant that her husband was not Freudian. 'Oh certainly not Freudian,' said she firmly, 'he was a Jungian.'[7] Jung's method was to have a face-to-face interview between patient and psychiatrist, sitting opposite each other – two human beings attempting to solve a problem between them, as friends, a problem shared and therefore halved. Freud's method of consultation, in contrast, was to have the patient stretched out on a couch with the psychiatrist slightly behind him listening to what the patient had to say, and rarely taking part. A basic difference between Jung and Freud lay in Freud's insistence on the sexual basis of neurosis. This Jung opposed. He felt that only if we can discover our own myth as expressed in dreams, can we become more complete personalities.

It was as a Jungian that Richmond placed importance on dreams. He believed, like Jung, that the motivation always derives from the unconscious and that dreams are part of the unconscious making itself manifest in sleep and therefore having meaning, reflecting a hurt, rejection or mental disturbance. But the dream has to be decoded. There are recognisable elements, but the key to understanding is there only if the signs can be read correctly. As a good spiritualist he listened to his own inner voice and acted according to its promptings.

Jung thought that only a psychiatrist who had his own problems could heal: 'In the end, only the wounded physician heals.' Whether or not Richmond healed Greene, whether or not Greene was in need of healing, Richmond was well-qualified, in his own way, to heal him.

*

Graham went to the Richmonds at 15 Devonshire Terrace, London, late in June 1921 and his description of Richmond's physical appearance is sharp and accurate:

> [He] had more the appearance of an eccentric musician than anyone you might suppose concerned with curing the human spirit. A tall stooping figure in his early forties, he had a distinguished musician's brow with longish hair falling behind without a parting and a face disfigured by large spots which must have been of nervous origin.[8]

Ave Greene, Graham's cousin, also went for treatment, near the end of Graham's stay, and Richmond's facial disfigurement troubled her:

'He had spots all over his face and sores. He said, "I can make those spots go by self-hypnosis."'[9] According to Zoe, her husband suffered from psoriasis: 'Do you know what that is like? Well, when you get out of bed it looks as if you had upset a packet of Lux [white soap flakes]. All the skin comes off in bits just like Lux. And when he was bad and he got out of bed it sort of spread over on to the floor.'[10]

Ave Greene never really knew why she had been sent to Richmond but she hazarded a guess:

> Graham was unhappy and suicidal. My family never told me why I had to go there. I knew Graham had to go because he was unbalanced and I felt then that I'm being sent because I'm unbalanced. And so the two of us were unbalanced people . . . My father and Uncle Charlie were very close, and he felt if his brother sent his dippy son to Richmond, perhaps he'd better send his dippy daughter.[11]

Richmond's treatment was simple and regular. Every morning, at eleven o'clock, Graham would present himself at Richmond's study and relate to him the dream he had had the previous night. Graham describes his experience:

> There he would always be, sitting behind the desk with his marred musician's face, stop-watch ready, waiting for my coming . . . I would begin to read out my dream, and he would check my associations with his watch. Afterwards he would talk in general terms about the theory of analysis, about the mortmain of the past which holds us in thrall. Sometimes, as the analysis progressed, he would show little hints of excitement – as though he scented something for which he had been waiting for a long while.[12]

These daily sessions of dream analysis were a worry to both Graham and Ave, because if they could not recall a dream they were asked to invent one. Ave Greene recalled: 'To begin with I could never remember my dreams, so Graham and I used to get together and I'd say, "Look, can you remember your dreams?" and he'd say, "No." And so he and I used to concoct dreams, but very likely he could remember his dreams more vividly than I could. And so, he and I used to sit together and concoct our dreams, and then I'd go and be interviewed by Richmond and tell him all my dreams. I loathed every moment of it.'[13] Whenever Graham had to invent a dream it always began with a pig. (Perhaps one reason was that at the end of the summer term in which he started going to Richmond for treatment, he attended the Berkhamsted School fête where one side-show was bowling for a pig.)

A review by Graham in the *Spectator* in 1941 of a diary kept by a Dutch boy refugee suggests something of Richmond's method as an analyst: 'We watch all the repressions of experience which will help to form the adult character painfully initiated. Here are the vivid scraps of childhood-horror which the psychoanalyst, stop-watch in hand, may later have to lead his patient back to by way of dreams or faulty memories.'[14]

In spite of the 'hints of excitement' on Richmond's part, the patient was not provided, according to Greene, with any response to, or analysis of, his dreams or associations: 'so far as my own dreams and associations went, he *told* me nothing; he patiently waited for me to discover the long road back for myself. I too began to feel the excitement of the search.'[15] It was Richmond's way to work slowly with a patient. He did not foster introspection in the direction where a patient's difficulties lay until he thought the inflammation of the hurt or crisis had subsided. He was always reluctant to proceed too fast and too far. It was, in his view, of paramount importance that the patient recognised the problem for himself and how it could be solved. His way was, according to his wife, never to force anything, to allow the person to learn about himself, make his own discoveries:

That's what he transferred to Graham you see, this life-giving thing. You had to decide all by yourself. That was the whole treatment. To listen to the God in you, and you are told what to do. Kenneth would have told Graham to listen to his own voice – listen to the God in him. That's the whole point of Jung's analysis – to unite your conscious mind with an unconscious God in you.[16]

While we know that Richmond was 'extraordinarily good' at interpreting dreams, we have no record of his interpretations and although Graham kept a dream diary at the time it has not survived; yet he recalled some of his dreams in *A Sort of Life*. In one of them there were colours of great beauty and towers and pinnacles and then a bodiless voice intoning, 'Princess and Lord of Time, there are no bounds to thee.'[17] The Princess of Time haunted Graham's sleep. In her service was 'a troop of black-skinned girls who carried poison flowers which it was death to touch'. Writing of this dream in *Journey Without Maps* Graham admits he could still recall the dull pain in his palms and his insteps when he deliberately touched the flowers.[18] He was always trying to escape her, for she was a symbol both of kindness and destructiveness. Once he was incited in a dream to kill her. He was given a book of ritual, bound in limp leather, and a dagger, but she survived into many later dreams. Indeed, any dream which opened with terror, with flight, with falling, with unseen presences and opening doors usually ended with her presence both 'cruel and reassuring'.[19]

Another was a nightmare in which Graham, pursued by sinister Chinese agents, took shelter in a hut with an armed detective. At the point when he began to feel secure, he looked down at the hand of the detective and saw that he had the long nails of a Chinaman.[20] This kind of nightmare recalls Greene's statement to Ronald Matthews: 'The world of nightmare is a world without defences because each defence may be nullified.'

Other dreams at a later date followed: a man with his throat cut dragging himself across the carpet to the bed; the old woman with ringworm; the man with gold teeth and rubber surgical gloves.[21]

We do not know what Richmond would have had to say after being told of such recollections. However, it is possible to discover something of his beliefs through a study of his writings, in particular, from a biography purporting to be about a man called W. E. Ford written by Richmond and his friend J. D. Beresford.[22] According to his wife Zoe, this biography is in fact about Kenneth Richmond's life and views. The portrait of him is of great interest for he held views on education and on the nature of psychological crisis in advance of his time.

To begin with, he was in every way different from Graham's father. He was not on the side of respectability and social correctness. These were not spiritual forces. While the Greene household was highly literate there were limitations on what could be discussed. In the Richmond household there were no such limitations and for sound psychological reasons. Inhibition only succeeds, Richmond felt, in driving things underground. How refreshing it must have been for Graham to discover an adult who held the view that faults of character become magnified and ingrained by perpetual 'don'ts'. Also, Richmond was utterly opposed to boarding schools, seeing them as artificial orphanages. Finally, he did not equate sex with sin.

*

Graham's account of his treatment is so light-hearted as to deny the importance of his breakdown, and he expressed doubts as to his need for analysis. He conveys no feeling that he was ill, close to despair or even suicidal. He could be playing down the severity of his breakdown but he did appear at the time to be quite normal. When Ave Greene went to Richmond for treatment, she did not think Graham was ill – to her he seemed absolutely normal. But we have to remember that Ave Greene went to Devonshire Terrace in December 1921 when Graham's treatment was nearing its end. If he had recovered by then, he would have seemed 'absolutely normal'.

Zoe Richmond stressed that Graham 'was almost the easiest of all to live with . . . most polite and very pleased with what he'd got – he was no trouble at all.' Though she added, 'You have to keep in mind that I've always found that people are not disturbed when we meet. And if you treat them as if they weren't disturbed, they're not disturbed. Kenneth and I didn't make any difference between Graham and anybody else. I mean he was just a guest of Kenneth's.'

There are no surviving letters to allow assessment of the physical and mental condition of Graham at this time – though there is some significance in the fact that although Marion Greene always kept her son's letters, there survive for this period one dated 1 July 1921 and no more until October – three dated Autumn 1921 and two cards dated 25 November and 12 December respectively, the last announcing Ave's arrival. But I think we can hazard a guess that Graham, with his public school training in good manners and his need to suppress emotion, was at least initially concealing his despair and his deeply-felt uncertainty about himself.

Richmond, 'the wounded physician', must have brought Graham to a form of confession through dreams, thus releasing him from his inhibitions and habits of suppression. Also, he taught Graham to sift his own motives fearlessly, encouraging him to make use of intuition and intellect. In this way he reduced his sense of guilt.

When Graham returned to school he no longer looked upon the rules as anything other than temporary ordinances. As a shy responsible person he would not openly revolt against his father, but his characteristic response towards authority, which his father represented, changed and this turned him ultimately into a rebel in religion and in politics. Richmond liberated Graham and helped to start him on his long road as a writer. Thus he must have felt for Richmond, as he writes in *The Confidential Agent*, 'a tremendous gratitude that there was somebody in the warring crooked uncertain world he could trust beside himself'.[23]

*

It was not simply through those morning sessions in analysis that Richmond helped Graham. He and his wife, at a crucial moment in the boy's development, introduced him to a more relaxed, uninhibited and intellectual way of life. As Graham himself wrote: 'My life with [Richmond] did me a world of good, but how much was due to the analysis and how much to the breakfasts in bed, the quiet of Kensington Gardens, the sudden independence of my life I would not like to say, nor whether the analysis went deep enough.[24]

Breakfast on a tray was brought in by a maid wearing a white starched cap, and after analysis he was free. He spent the mornings studying under the trees of Kensington Gardens. London was not a train journey away, but merely just down the street and he would go in search of youthful adventure. He could indulge his passion for the cinema and theatre and when his cousin Ave came they went to see Eugene O'Neill's *Anna Christie,* and also visited the London Assizes together: 'It was Graham's idea to go to the Old Bailey, because we didn't have enough money to go to the theatre often. Graham would ask the Bobby on duty in the forecourt which were the most exciting cases on and we'd go and spend the whole afternoon there.'

Before Ave Greene's arrival Graham had been exploring London's museums. On 1 July he visited the Imperial Institute, the Natural History Museum and finally the Science Museum. Next he visited the London Museum and outside St James's Palace, on the stroke of twelve, he watched the changing of the guard. With his favourite aunt Nono he visited the Tate Gallery to see the war paintings of C. R. W. Nevinson. In October, he and his aunt bought tickets for Gilbert and Sullivan's *The Gondoliers* ('our seats were excellent . . . a large proportion of evening dresses . . . Lytton and Sheffield were wonderful'), and they went to see the play *Christopher Sly:* 'The show was the best I've ever seen. Matheson Lang acted beautifully. Florence Saunders was an extremely pretty girl . . . Arthur Whitby . . . awfully good as a strolling player . . . The end was wonderful. The dead body of Christopher Sly lying in the dark cellar, and slowly the light of a lantern approaching and the voices of the guards, coming nearer, singing a drinking catch, coming to let free Sly, to let him return to his tavern and bottle.' What Graham did not mention to his mother was that Florence Saunders wore a long white silk nightdress, and moved him sexually.[25] Graham, having reached puberty, was alert for possible adventures with the nursemaids out with their charges in Kensington Gardens, but his only adventure was one he could well have done without. Here is the first of his seedy characters stepping for a moment into his life and perhaps contributing to his interest in, and creation of, such characters in his later novels:

An elderly man, with an old Etonian tie and a gaze unhappy and shifty, drew a chair up to mine and started to talk of schools. Was there corporal punishment at my school, and did I suppose there were any schools left where girls were whipped? He had an estate, he told me, in Scotland, where everyone went around in kilts, so convenient in some ways, and perhaps I would like to come for a holiday there . . . Suddenly he sloped away, like a wind-blown umbrella, and I never saw him again.[26]

One of the Richmonds' many callers was a ballet student. Graham was ready to fall in love with her but was too shy to make an approach. He wrote three imagist lines under the influence of Ezra Pound's early romantic poems – he had found a copy of Pound's *Personae* in a little bookshop on the embankment near Albert Bridge. While he could write enthusiastically to his mother about the girl, whose name was Isula, saying she was 'a future Pavlova', he could not find the courage to present her with the poem.

Something of his attitude towards women (he was sixteen when he went to Richmond and two months into his seventeenth year when he left) is reflected in a piece he wrote at the Richmonds' called 'The Creation of Beauty'. He told his mother jubilantly: 'I hope soon to blossom into the Saturday Westminster. "The Creation of Beauty: A study in sublimation", by H. Graham Greene. Ahem! Ahem!' And it did appear, though without a by-line. It is a story in which, after the seventh day, the chief architect of the universe comes into the presence of God unhappy because, while on God's orders he has created man, God has given man no happiness other than a woman to love. Set against that he has given man darkness which is full of fear. He has given him sleep but in sleep there are evil dreams. Everything it seems has the power to hurt man – with the sun he will moan with the heat or cry aloud in the cold. Birds will ravage the fields, beasts will wage perpetual war. So speaks the chief architect; but God answers him:

> Can you not see, that because you have given him the beauty of woman, you have given him the beauty of the universe? He will worship the moon, because it is as pure as his love. He will worship the sun because it is aflame with the glory of her spirit. He will love the cold, because it is like his wayward mistress; he will love the heat, because it is as warm as her breast. He will write songs to the dark, because it is as deep, unfathomable and mysterious as love, and drowns him in the blackness of her hair. He will let himself down into sleep with a fear, because, though it bring evil dreams, yet will it also bring dreams of her for whom he lives. He will glory in the birds, for he will decorate her in their feathers, and, when she speaks to him, he will sing with them in the tree-tops; he will slay the beasts to clothe her in their skins, and love them for their lithe forms, which rival hers in grace, and the darting movement of

the fish will remind him of the flutter of her hands. But the seas he will worship forever, for the waters are motherhood.

If nothing came of his love for the young ballet dancer, there was another whom, at least in dreams, he could love, an older but beautiful woman – Kenneth Richmond's wife. Here was a dilemma for a shy boy: having dreamt of Zoe Richmond he was duty bound to reveal his dream to his analyst. For the first time he feared his eleven o'clock visit, yet his passion for analysis prevented him from lying. Graham's record of that session with Richmond is revealing of his new-found daring and of his analyst's character:

'And now,' Richmond said, after a little talk on general theory, 'we'll get down to last night's dream.'
I cleared my dry throat. 'I can only remember one.'
'Let's have it.'
'I was in bed,' I said.
'Where?'
'Here.'
He made a note on his pad. I took a breath and plunged. 'There was a knock on the door and Zoe came in. She was naked. She leant over me. One of her breasts nearly touched my mouth. I woke up.'
'What's your association to breasts?' Richmond asked, setting his stop-watch.
'Tube train,' I said after a long pause.
'Five seconds,' Richmond said.[27]

Zoe Richmond laughed over this passage in Graham's autobiography, and well she might, for she would know (who better than the wife of an analyst?) that here we have a clear example of the great mother dream. Graham's mother was, as we have seen, remote to her children and closest to her husband. To Graham love, expressed through touch or kiss, did not come from her but from his Nanny.

Then, in Kenneth Richmond's home, he had this dream of a relatively older woman (Zoe was thirty-one) coming to his bedside to give him the supreme evidence of motherly love by offering her breast, unlike his mother, who came to the nursery to supervise while retaining immense reserve. Surely the dream's message was his need for love, a mother's love which was never sufficiently expressed. 'What we offered,' Zoe told me, 'when Graham came to us was something very different. We all do love each other in this family. I was to Graham a mother substitute. I suppose he felt the difference and it reflected in his dream of me as a mother when in his dream I offered my breast to him. But Kenneth would also offer him a plan to see the other side; to see the un-seen world; that you can be developed from there and not from here; that God in you does tell you what to do.'[28]

In spite of Graham's describing Richmond as 'our bizarre and spotty analyst', he must have been for Graham something of a substitute father. His father, unquestionably a good and liberal man, had yet misunderstood what had happened to him at school, and his authority had been unable to protect Graham from the bullying.

Zoe Richmond had her own notion of what was wrong with Graham and why he was in need of treatment, and she did not mince her words:

People are often suicidal and unbalanced if they have impossible parents. People must be loved and the awful thing is when a son is not loved then trouble begins. In Graham's case he was always a very sensitive person. Some people are more sensitive than others. Graham was very intellectual and very sensitive. His father had a frightful instinct against homosexuality. Graham wasn't homosexual but he was feminine and sometimes you can't tell the difference. To be sensitive is feminine and the unsensitive and warlike is extremely male. A lot of the patients who came to Ken were homosexuals. In Graham's case, he wanted to commit suicide in the end because he couldn't love himself or anybody else. And he was never openly loved and you see he was frightened of his own sensitivity. Lack of love creates the kind of disability Graham had. Graham's father was all negative and that's what he was bred into. The fact that his father thought Graham was involved in a homosexual ring when in fact he was being bullied – why his father was barmy. He had an obsession. I always knew it was the father's fault.

And Kenneth was good for Graham because they had in them, in some ways, a suitable similarity.[29]

The Richmonds did much to encourage Graham's interest in writing by introducing him to writers and editors, as his letters to his mother show. Already, before he went to Richmond, and when sixteen years of age, he had had some success as a writer. His 'Tick of the Clock', published in the school magazine, he had cut out and sent to the London newspaper, the *Star*. In a letter written to his future wife, 16 August 1925, he recalls his first literary success: 'I was delirious with joy . . . when I was sixteen, when I got my first money from a paper the Star(!!) for a terrible sentimental sketch.' The story appeared on 18 January 1921. He received a cheque for three guineas:

I took the editor's kindly letter and the complimentary copy up to the Common, and for hours I sat on the abandoned rifle-butts reading the piece aloud to myself and to the dark green ocean of gorse and bracken. Now, I told myself, I was really a professional writer, and never again did the idea hold such excitement, pride and confidence; always later . . . the excitement was overshadowed by the knowledge of failure, by awareness of the flawed intention. But that sunny afternoon I could detect no flaw in The Tick of the Clock. The sense of glory touched me for the first and last time.[30]

His excitement continued when he showed the story to Kenneth Richmond. To his mother he wrote: 'Mr Richmond was quite bucked with my Tick-Tock. He showed it to Mrs R. and asked her whether she could recognise who wrote it and she said J. D. Beresford. Hah.Hah.Hah.' He was to meet at the Richmonds' J. D. Beresford, a novelist crippled by poliomyelitis and author of the remarkable novel *The Hampdenshire Wonder*. 'I hope to see Walter de la Mare

---

THE STAR, TUESDAY, JANUARY 18, 1921.

The Star

Telephones : 313 Central (7 lines),
6420 City (6 lines).
Telegrams : " Star, London."

WHAT WE THINK.

The Old Sham.

The Hour has come and with it the Man ! Several men, in fact. Not to put too fine a point upon it, the London Municipal Society and that fine old Roman, Lord George Hamilton. The note is struck, the standard hoisted, the flag is nailed to the mast in to-day's "Times," where we read that there is to be "no more apathy" in local government elections. A vigorous campaign against municipal waste is to be initiated this week by our old friend the London Municipal Society, the ground landlords' pet organisation. The opportunity to grind its axe on the subject of high rates is not to be missed, and the Society is going to call a "conference" and to guarantee all its candidates to support the crusade against the "twin dangers of waste and Bolshevism."

How familiar all these stage "properties" sound. There is the "reduction of debt," "municipal trading," and, of course, the limitation of rates to the lowest possible figure "compatible with efficient administration." The main causes of the increase in rates is the increase in the cost of materials and of labour. Will the London Municipal Society force the contractors to

SEA SNOW.

The Hebrides Under Their White Winter Quilts.

By "SEAMARK."

THOSE who have never slipped down coast on a bright sunny morning after a heavy snowfall only know half the story of British coastal scenery. To see it at its best one should be coming down the western run of the Sutherland coast towards Cape Wrath, or, preferably, threading the glorious maze of the Hebrides. Nominally, of course, they are islands, but in reality they are magnificent mountain tops rearing perpendicularly from the water's edge: and in the tiny channels between these vast walls there is often only room for a very small boat to make steerage way.

Dawn on the Hebrides.

A heavy snowfall softens much of the shaggy ferocity of the Hebridean crags, but even so, in their spotless white quilts they are grimly perfect. They give of their best in the early dawn when a rose pink sunrise reaches across from the horizon and tints their glaring white with the faint colours from the palette of the morn. Eunessan swims in a pool of amber half-light, at the base of its own high battlements. Iona looms solitary and desolate across the way, shadowed in grey where the sea frets its edge but burning redly at its crest as a scarlet shaft from the east bursts upon it. Staffa is on fire in the distance like a row of snow torches rising from a cold blue lake : and

THE TICK OF THE CLOCK.

A Legend.

By H. GRAHAM GREENE.

" The tree was life, and the fruit death, and the hid seed was love."—
Sir Lewis Morris.

"TICK-TOCK, tick-tock," said the old clock in the attic, and the little old servant dusted it and polished it and wound it up just as if it stood in the drawing-room down below and told the time to all the house. Really it stood in the corner of her own cobwebby bedroom, and the time it told was—well, it was anything from ten to ninety minutes out. But every day before she cleaned the silver this peculiar old woman attended to the clock, just as if she was performing a sacred ceremony.

* * *

Indeed, she meant it as a sign of her worship, for every night it seemed to be on the point of telling her something, what she did not know, and she wished by her service to persuade it to speak. But the clock only said, "Tick-tock, tick-tock."

She was so old that the children said she was a witch. They fled when they met her alone, never realising the pain they were giving to her, for she had always longed for a child to love. So the affection which she could not lavish upon them she gave to the clock, which was older, far older, than she.

* * *

soon', he wrote to his mother. 'Mrs Richmond has promised to ask him to tea, before I [return home].' De la Mare was his favourite poet and also a remarkable short story writer with a sensibility attuned to the macabre, who was able to bring innocent and supernatural visitings delicately together. The poet came with Naomi Royde-Smith who was editor of the *Weekly Westminster* and whom Graham had already met in July: 'A few evenings ago the Lady Literary Editor of the *Saturday Westminster* came to dinner.' He showed Richmond his piece 'The Creation of Beauty' and again Richmond tried to help him: 'Mr Richmond is going to thrust it before [The Lady Editor's] eyes and thinks she'll accept it.' After he returned to school he was to bombard her with fantasies written in poetic prose.

Undoubtedly the Richmonds helped Graham by understanding his emotional conflicts, his creativity and his ambitions and by introducing him to an adult world more exciting and stimulating than that of School and the society of aunts and uncles – an important part of the cure.

There was one slight lapse in health. It was not thought by Graham to be of importance, yet it was to have repercussions five years later and then caused him great anguish of mind and lessened his trust in and affection for Richmond. It seemed a simple enough, even natural incident. One night, a guest at dinner was describing an accident and Graham's imagination ran away with him. As he listened, his mind went back to a story he had heard when he was six years old, of two ladies on the Royston road in a carriage. The horse had run away, and one of the ladies had fallen out of the carriage and her long hat-pin pierced her brain. Suddenly, in the Richmonds' dining room, Graham had a black-out and fell to the floor.

Graham explains that his imagination had a way of showing him details of an accident not fully described and when that happened he would faint, 'like a medical student at an operation'.[31]

Richmond, disturbed by this event, took him to a Harley Street specialist friend of his, George Riddock. He then wrote to Graham's mother and gave her the specialist's opinion that her son was probably suffering from incipient epilepsy. It was a time-bomb which was to tick quietly away. Graham's lack of knowledge of the diagnosis is revealed in a card he sent his mother in November: 'Have been to Doctor Riddock, and am taking malt and another medicine which I may have to continue for 2 years.'

Zoe Richmond suggested a different interpretation of Graham's acute sensitivity to such events when she stressed that while the world might have gained a great novelist in him, it had lost a natural medium. Graham Greene was born, Zoe asserted, with mediumistic powers, for it was at Devonshire Terrace that he had a precognitive dream which impressed his analyst. To his mother Graham wrote:

A night or two ago I had a shipwreck dream, the ship I was on going down in the Irish Sea. I didn't think anything about it. We don't have papers here as the usual thing, and it was not till yesterday, looking at an old paper, I saw about the sinking of the Rowan in the Irish sea. This made me quite excited and when I got back I looked at my dream diary and found that my dream had been Saturday night. The accident had happened just after Saturday midnight.[32]

This was not the first time Graham had had such dreams of disasters of which he could not have known. When he was seven and on the night of the *Titanic* disaster, he dreamt of a shipwreck: 'One image of the dream has remained with me for more than sixty years: a man in oilskins bent double beside a companion-way under the blow of a great wave.'[33] When he was twenty-one and living in Nottingham, he wrote to Vivien Dayrell-Browning recalling a third disaster:

On Wednesday night, I did not dream of a wreck, but I was on a ship and I was going to be faced with a punishment for something, to jump overboard, and what I feared was not so much the drowning as the wind of the fall from the liner's upper deck. In today's [Nottingham] Journal I find that on Wednesday night there was a terrible crash off the Yorkshire coast in a storm and the Captain ordered his men to jump into the sea, as the only hope, and all but two were drowned. It's awfully strange. Of course on an occasion like that there must be terrific mental waves of terror, and my mind seems to be particularly attuned to the terror of drowning wave.[34]

Greene wondered in *A Sort of Life* 'whether the analysis went deep enough', and Zoe Richmond said, in January 1985, that his treatment was not properly finished:

I wrote to Graham once and said I wish to goodness we had known more about things when he was being analysed because we didn't know very much – we had just begun. I don't think he was ever finished properly. He got all right again and went home. It's very difficult for an analyst and the people at home don't understand any of it. They don't see why, if it seems all right and the patient carries on all right they should pay any more either, quite reasonably. But that's how it is.

Perhaps the treatment was not entirely successful. For one thing, he discovered afterwards that he could no longer take an aesthetic interest in any visual thing – staring at a sight that others assured him was beautiful, he would feel nothing.

Even so, it was true that this short period of six months at Devonshire Terrace had a remarkable influence on Graham's life. Sixty-three years later he wrote to Zoe, soon after his eightieth birthday: 'Please believe that you represented one of the happiest periods of my life with your kindness – your beauty.'*35

*

It is possible also that Kenneth Richmond's philosophy and beliefs, 'wounded physician' as he was, stretched far into Graham's future as an influence. The experience of that change of environment, from the sense of imprisonment at St John's to the enlightened freedom of Devonshire Terrace, may well have established his life's pattern of escaping from the impossible or the boring into unknown and dangerous environments which would stimulate, offer fresh experiences and also provide copy for his novels.

Possibly, too, Richmond, with his emphasis on 'the God within you', set him on the path to his eventual conversion to Catholicism.

It is almost certain that, in releasing him from the thrall of his father and the school, Richmond gave him the freedom to express his opposition to public schools and the courage to question the notion of 'loyalty' – to the school first, but to other accepted 'loyalties' later, thereby opening the way for Graham to embrace 'disloyalty' as a principle.

Although Graham was to become reconciled with his father, he never relented in his opposition to public schools and some, at least, of their products, though extraordinarily he sent his own son Francis to one. Proof of this can be seen in a 1938 review in the *Spectator* in which he questions the motives of men who return to their old school and seek out their old masters:

> There is a kind of hollow bombast in their manner . . . a patronage which doesn't quite come off. They are the great world, of course, but the great world has turned out to be only a place on the Stock Exchange, lodgings in Aldershot or a general store in Sierra Leone – if they had been more successful, you feel, they would not have

---

* Zoe Richmond died on 26 November 1986 at the age of ninety-eight. She retained her alert mind, and remained a spiritualist, until the end.

been here at all. A more imperative loyalty, a deep affection would have detached them from their school. Pity them a little, with their nostalgia for childhood and their unconvincing swagger.

Four years earlier, Graham's dislike of school games, the area of school activity in which he was a disastrous failure, had hardened into a principle:

> Games and school I should like to see kept rigidly apart, for games are used more than anything else to teach him narrow loyalties (that they do not teach him sportsmanship is obvious in any football match between rival public schools). It is at least better that he should learn loyalty to a town which includes all classes and both sexes than to an institution consisting only of his own sex and his own class. Why, in any case, he should feel more loyal to a school which is paid to teach him than to a butcher who is paid to feed him I cannot understand.[36]

Graham is still distressed by the unquiet of an old hurt.

Thirty years later, in a speech of considerable distinction on receiving the Shakespeare Prize from the University of Hamburg in 1969, the principle is carefully enunciated: 'Loyalty confines you to accepted opinions; loyalty forbids you to comprehend sympathetically your dissident fellows; but disloyalty encourages you to roam through any human mind.' His unrelenting disloyalty towards and distrust of his own school has remained. On 11 September 1977, the *Sunday Times* tells us:

> Berkhamsted School's current Appeal, which involves the sale of inscribed chairs, has met its match in old boy Graham Greene, whose memories of his school days are none too nostalgic. Asked if he would like to sponsor a pair at £12.50 each, to furnish Deans' Hall, Greene said he would be delighted – if the chairs were dedicated to Diana Dors. I understand the school will not be pursuing the matter.

Nine days after this appeared Graham Greene sent the cutting to his brother Hugh:

> See enclosed cutting! Who was the Sunday Times informer – you, Sherry, or the schoolmaster? Anyway I said Brigitte Bardot and not Diana Dors.

7

Realism and Fantasie –
a Reconciliation

Human kind
Cannot bear very much reality
– T. S. ELIOT

'I wish,' Marion Greene wrote to Graham's wife, 'I had not torn up Kenneth Richmond's letter about [Graham]. I cannot now remember how we took Graham to him but he was a different person after that treatment . . . Kenneth R. felt being able to express himself in writing would help so much.'[1]

Not everyone approved of the change in the young Graham. Eric Guest commented, 'Before psychoanalysis he was shy, he was diffident, he was insecure socially of himself. Afterwards he was much surer, and much less delicately minded.' Ben Greene also had an opinion about the 'changed' Graham: 'Graham was not a man gifted with intimacy but the one I remember and liked best was Graham before the psychiatrist. He was as a boy a very withdrawn separate kind of person getting really in touch with comparatively few people, but if he did, the sort of depths of his mind soon became apparent and he was then most fascinating.' Ben Greene argued that 'if you are a perfectly ordinary diffident boy' you could be 'corrupted by, twisted by, a psychiatrist, so that dangerous fantasies are put into your head.'[2] Afterwards, according to Ben Greene, Graham remained almost equally detached but he was much more meaty and turned his attention more to living than to the sort of mental climate which he had favoured before.

Graham, much later, was able to assess the change in himself from the point of view of others: 'I had left for London a timid boy, anti-social, *farouche*: when I came back I must have seemed vain and knowing. Who among my fellows in 1921 knew anything about

109

Freud or Jung?' He now listened avidly to his parents' accounts of their dreams and analysed them, as Claud Cockburn recalled:

> As was the custom of many old-fashioned people at the period, the Greenes used at breakfast innocently to describe to one another anything interesting, bizarre or colourful they had had in the way of dreams during the previous night. Mr and Mrs Greene were unaware that their third son, Graham, had at about this time discovered Freud. He would leave the bacon cooling on his plate as he listened with the fascination of a secret detective. When necessary he would lure them on to provide more and more details which to them were amusing or meaningless but to him of thrilling and usually scandalous significance.
>
> 'It's amazing,' he said to me once, 'what those dreams disclose. It's startling – simply startling', and at the thought of it gave a low whistle.

Looking back, Graham was able to wonder whether the excitement of the search for hidden motives did not gain too great a hold over him, fostering in him a desire to turn up every stone to discover what lay beneath, to question motives, to doubt.[3]

He had friends in the London literary world now and could show them off at Berkhamsted: 'That summer [he] invited Walter de la Mare to a strawberry-tea in the garden with [his] parents . . . [he] posed proudly as the poet's friend.'[4]

His life at school had been transformed: he was no longer a boarder at St John's, but a day boy, living with his parents and going to school each day. He had real friends, among them Eric Guest, Claud Cockburn and Peter Quennell. And he no longer feared school games and gymnastics. Richmond had written to Graham's mother (no doubt after his fainting fit) suggesting that he must not be involved in heavy physical exercise. He also escaped the O.T.C., and in the company of Peter Quennell, he took instead riding lessons from Sergeant Lubbock, gym master at the school and an ex-cavalryman: 'Sometimes [Graham wrote] returning at a walk down the long road from the Common . . . we would pass on a hot summer's day the sweating trudging ranks of the O.T.C. singing a gloomy military song, "We're here because we're here because we're here".'[5]

This did not go unnoticed. Years later, in a doctor's surgery in Berkhamsted in November 1976, a contemporary of Graham's at school told another Old Boy of how there was tremendous keenness for the O.T.C. and that every boy in the Senior School was in it, with the exception of four: 'Two of them were congenitally lame and the other two', he said with some asperity, 'were Graham Greene and Peter Quennell.'[6] Quennell and Greene had other interests. Graham, for example, recalls the two of them, both in their bold teens, sitting on a gravestone in the old disused churchyard reading aloud to each other from *The Yellow Book* 'with a sense of daring and decadence'[7] and no doubt fascinated by Aubrey Beardsley's brilliantly risqué drawings. Peter Quennell remembered Graham reading:

> *Madame Bovary*, not the kind of novel that either his father or mine would have encouraged us to open. His talk had an exuberantly sceptical and blithely pessimistic turn; and his contemplation of the horrors of human life appeared to cause him unaffected pleasure. His pessimism did nothing to sour his temperament; while Evelyn Waugh would change beyond all knowledge, the young and the old Greene have remained relatively consubstantial. At each fresh insight he obtained into human absurdity or wickedness, his pallid, faintly woebegone face would assume an air of solemn glee.[8]

R. S. Stanier recalled Graham's return to Berkhamsted and it does seem that a cheeky, self-assured, rebellious adolescent had taken the place of the shyest of shy boys. Even Stanier used to think that Graham was getting away with it, on his return, because he was the headmaster's son, but with hindsight, he realised that the masters were handling him with kid gloves as a boy who had had a nervous breakdown, quite regardless of whether he was the head-master's son or not:

> You couldn't just whisk him off and beat him or something of that kind if he was cheeky, but he could be rather annoying. I remember in those General Science things we were doing the origin of species and heredity and that kind of thing and we used to have a test from time to time to see how much we knew. I remember Graham Greene producing a facetious answer in verse, beginning something like 'Old Mendel was a funny man who used to play with peas', which of course he did very well, and that did get a raspberry from the very sensible science master A. G. Coombs.[9]

In creativity and competitiveness, Graham was also developing. Strangely, for a fundamentally shy person, even before his psychoan-alysis he had wanted to act: 'When I was sixteen,' he wrote to Vivien Dayrell-Browning, 'my greatest ambition was to be an actor.'[10] And in the same letter, he admits that while he always found it embarrassing to read aloud an essay or poem before others in class, he did not mind in the least acting in a much larger group in the Deans' Hall. He acted not only in *The Lost Silk Hat* but also in the interlude of 'Pyramus and Thisbe' from *A Midsummer Night's Dream*.

Thanks to Charles Greene there had been a revival of drama at the school. The editor of *The Berkhamstedian* wrote: 'One phase of school life has certainly revived during the past few terms – to wit, the Dramatic Art.' Perhaps it was this that stimulated Graham into writing plays:

> I began to write a fantastic play of which I cannot even remember the title. It celebrated what I liked to believe was the sense of poetry inherent in the ceremony of afternoon tea. In 1920 tea was still one of the important meals of the day, and the most aesthetic. The silver pot, the tall tiered cake-stand, like a Chinese temple, two kinds of bread and butter, white and brown, cucumber and tomato sandwiches cut razor-thin, scones, rock-buns, and then all the cakes – plum, madeira, caraway seed – the meal had about it the lavishness of a Victorian dinner. My play, I don't know why, except that Dunsany's had taken much the same road, moved from London to Samarkand.[11]

Such a subject is un-Greeneian and yet not unexpected, given Olga Franklin's remarks in 1980 on his aunt's poem written on his seventh birthday about his being kissed, and his later poem on the same subject when he was eleven expressing disapproval of this Victorian family ritual. Perhaps his lost play was equally critical though his comments above suggest otherwise. Nevertheless, it does point to one curious aspect of Graham's character: the way in which a subject first thought of in early youth is not wasted but is returned to as a topic to be written up at a much later date. There are numerous instances of this astonishing continuity of ideas throughout his long life.

Whatever the quality of that first play, it was accepted – in a way. Graham gives a droll account of it:

> I sent the play to one of the many dramatic societies which existed in 1920 . . . and I was excited to receive a letter signed with a woman's name accepting it for production. So up I went to London one morning to meet my first management. The address was somewhere in St John's Wood, a district which in those days still retained the glamour of illicit love-nests. There was a long delay, after I sounded the bell, and when at last the door was opened, it was by an over-blown rosy woman holding a dressing-gown together, who was watched from the end of the passage by a naked

man in a double bed. She looked with astonishment at my blue
cap with a school crest while I explained that I had come about my
play. Then she gave me a cup of rather weak Mazawattee tea . . .
and she became carefully vague, as she scrutinized me, about
casting and the date of production. I don't remember that I ever
heard from her again, and the society, I am sure, soon ceased to
exist.[12]

We know that he had written many imitations of *The Viper of
Milan*, 'stories of sixteenth-century Italy or twelfth-century England
marked with enormous brutality and a despairing romanticism',[13]
but he also decided to enter the school essay competition. He wrote
to his mother from Richmond's house on 6 October 1921 asking for
details: 'If Da does happen to get particulars, would you write. If
not, I'll just wait till I return. By particulars I mean whether there is
a word limit, whether you can send any type of prose, plays or
anything. I haven't got that number of the *Berk*.' The story he
submitted was entitled 'Castles in the Air'. The setting is a fair, the
central figure a grotesquely ugly piper who, on the concert manager's
accidentally saying, 'in the devil's name', takes this as a password
and plays such notes that the noise and fun of the fair cease forthwith
and everyone listens utterly entranced, for the tune brings to each
the 'pangs of mortal sadness'. Afterwards the piper disappears like
an apparition and the suggestion is that people, without knowing it,
have been witness to a visitation of the devil to earth. It is a beautifully
told tale for a seventeen-year-old and it gained Graham, as an 'Essay
in the Imaginative or Descriptive Writing', first prize.

Graham was coming into his own. Even while under treatment,
he continued his school work. He wrote to his mother asking her to
ask Eric Guest to get his Warner and Martin [History] from his locker
in the library and have it sent to him. In another letter he asked his
father to send him a Latin Loeb Classic to read and in yet another he
enclosed 'two more history essays for Da' – evidence that he had his
future as a student at Oxford in mind.

He gained his School Certificate, reached the sixth form, and
dropped mathematics, Latin and Greek in favour of the modern side
with French, History and English as his main subjects. There were
only a few boys in the sixth and they enjoyed frequent free periods
and were allowed to work alone in the library.

In his last year at school there appeared another story of his in *The
Berkhamstedian*, the first piece to carry his initials H.G.G. It was
entitled 'The Tyranny of Realism'. A child lies bound in a cold marble
hall. There is the smell of a prison, of discipline, repression and

corruption. In the distance is the throne of the tyrant King Realism. At the feet of the imprisoned boy lies a maiden with mournful lips – her name is Fantasie. The boy asks the King why Fantasie has been taken from him – she whom he loves more than life. He also asks why he had sent Spiritualism to drive away his dreams – the ghosts who used to kiss his lips and hair. 'Once I loved in a great unknown country of dark caves and hidden ways . . . where every morning . . . found new beauties and new terrors. And even the fears were sweet. Now you hold me bound, cramped, within a small room and never is anything new.' But the King indicates that he is not bound, and thus the walls of his prison melt and beside the King on the throne now sits Fantasie, their lips pressed together in a long passion of joy.[14]

In this allegory, Graham is obviously trying to come to terms with his new world after psychoanalysis – his earlier character and his developing one. It also shows that Graham began early as a writer to use his personal difficulties as fictional material on which to build. The term 'spiritualism' is interesting when we remember the Richmonds were both spiritualists. At a literal level, the allegory is probably a pointer to Graham's hope that because he felt he must in the future write in a more realistic vein it did not mean (as clearly he had feared) that his fantastic imaginings could not also flourish.

*

No match for his brother Raymond at school – he never became a prefect – Graham was nevertheless establishing himself in his own way. He even took part, not with great success, in two debates.

The first was on the motion: 'That in the opinion of this House the Government's Policy of reprisals in Ireland is unjustifiable.' As today, there were appalling atrocities being committed by the military wing of the Sinn Fein – the burning of houses, the killing of people – but the difference lay in Lloyd George's response. That wily Welshman enlisted retired army officers and men, called locally Black and Tans, and they decided to beat the Sinn Fein at their own game. They were a ruthless auxiliary police used against the Republicans from July 1920 to July 1921 so that when the debate took place on 12 February 1921 reprisals were still going on. R. S. Stanier recalled, fifty-six years afterwards, that Graham spoke with great passion: 'He made an eloquent speech referring to the Indian Mutiny and how useless the atrocities had been then. He mentioned the Indian mutineers being blown from a gun and whatever one thinks of that as a method of dealing with a massacre, it certainly didn't go on and on as things have in Ireland.'[15]

The only report in *The Berkhamstedian* of Graham's being involved in a second debate is short indeed. On 18 February 1922 the motion was: 'That in the opinion of this house science destroys beauty.' The motion was lost by 17 votes to 20. All Graham's friends spoke – J. B. Wilson, Claud Cockburn, Eric Guest – and it was recorded that they distinguished themselves. Of Graham the report simply stated: 'H. G. Greene spoke at some length and somewhat off the point.'[16]

Graham had one final piece in *The Berkhamstedian* before leaving school. It is a satirical poem, brilliantly executed and entitled, 'An Epic Fragment from The Dish Pioneers'. It deals with Sarah Beeton, the famous Victorian cookery expert. Before her entry into heaven Sarah Beeton sings:

> Roll the little oysters in the bacon,
> Never heed their childish woe;
> Fry them in their little shrouds, three minutes;
> Gently to their mothers break the blow.

> Lay the little corpses out quite gently,
> On their coffins of fried bread,
> Garnished with the lemon and the parsley.
> Weep no tears, for they are happy dead.

> Then Peter oped the loudly clanging gate,
> And all the mighty host rushed in to peace,
> But Sarah Beeton slowly went, for she
> Was just inclined to adiposity.[17]

Graham was trying now to connect with, and stretch out to, others, but still sometimes he would suffer a relapse, an abrupt breaking away, a shutting himself off and living within his own loneliness. The shy Greene still remained, protected now by a carapace of self-possession, self-knowledge, confidence and the appearance, at least, of fearlessness – everything played in a low-key and self-deprecating fashion. He was to become rather intimidating himself, but he would never again be intimidated. Instead he would face every situation – and even seek out, deliberately, the most dangerous ones, not only to overcome boredom or find copy, but to prove himself to his own satisfaction, and his blue eyes would outstare the world. Never again would he confess easily to a Wheeler (though women and priests there have been many). He would 'Set a watch, O Lord, before my mouth and a door round about my lips . . .',[18] such discipline was now his.

One other attribute his school crisis left him with was a sympathy with the suffering and difficulties of others and the urge to help them.

Perhaps J. B. Wilson, Greene's contemporary at school, describes with most insight the sea-change that Greene had undergone:

I have thought over the years that it does almost look as if the boy who is withdrawn at school, who is an observer, who isn't a go-getter, who doesn't take part in things, isn't a doer – maybe he's reserving his energy and building up his potentiality and then afterwards he suddenly blossoms, and makes a tremendous impact in whatever branch it may be: law, diplomacy, finance, literature, what-have-you. And I can see that so many of the boys who were leaders at school, and popular at school, haven't necessarily done anything after they left school.

Graham at school was not in the picture at all. And then he developed his potentiality, which must have been there at the start, after he left school. To keep it in the family, his brother Raymond was brilliant at school. Now he did become an outstanding surgeon – he did do certain outstanding things. But it is no equation: Raymond's final achievement is not equal or comparable to his potentiality as that was demonstrated at school. Graham's potentiality as demonstrated at school was almost nil and has become almost infinite.[19]

PART 2
Oxford

8

Freshman at Balliol

God be with you, Balliol men.
— HILAIRE BELLOC

A tranquil consciousness of effortless superiority.
— HERBERT ASQUITH (on Balliol men)

'I went up to Oxford for the autumn term of 1922 to Balliol,'
Graham Greene records in *A Sort of Life*,[1] and, several pages
later, 'Finals came . . . I managed to get a moderate second in Modern
History'.[2] Between these two cryptic statements he recalls some
events which were important to him, but he gives us little idea of
the real significance of those three years.

University students (as always) celebrated their new-found freedom by kicking over the traces of conventional behaviour in their
own way. Particularly at that time they formed clubs. One of the
most notorious at Oxford was the Hypocrites' Club of which Evelyn
Waugh, John Sutro, Claud Cockburn, Harold Acton and Peter
Quennell were members. Quennell recalled it as 'a kind of early
twentieth century Hell-fire club'[3] and Cockburn described its prem-
ises as a 'noisy, alcohol-soaked warren by the river'. Sutro was its
'accomplished mimic'[4] and Harold Acton was already an established
student poet, renowned for his method of reciting his verses in rooms
overlooking Christ Church Meadows and, having provided his guests
with 'an opulent luncheon, accompanied by large quantities of the
steaming mulled claret', he would declaim 'from his balcony . . . his
latest poems, through a large megaphone to crocodiles of Oxford
school-children trotting back and forth among the trees.'[5]

Tom Driberg wrote that the Club had been the scene of some lively
and drunken revels, mainly homosexual in character: 'I remember
dancing with John F., while Evelyn [Waugh] and another rolled on
a sofa with . . . their tongues licking each other's tonsils.'[6]

Certainly, it would seem, homosexuality flourished. Maurice

Bowra, a future Vice-Chancellor of Oxford University but then a young don at Balliol, talked, according to Anthony Powell, 'as if homosexuality was the natural condition of an intelligent man.'[7] And there was 'Sligger' Urquhart, Dean of Balliol, who was to become one of Waugh's hated men. Should Waugh pass through Balliol at night he would assure the college in a thunderous voice, 'The Dean of Balliol sleeps with men,' sung to the tune of 'Here we go gathering nuts in May'.[8] But I think we can agree with Dacre Balsdon when he writes of Oxford homosexuality: 'It may be doubted whether much went on . . . which could have interested the police. There was a pretty elegance and affectation about it.'[9]

*

Into this environment, in 1922, came Graham Greene just turned eighteen, 'a muddled adolescent who wanted to write but hadn't found his subject, who wanted to express his lust but was too scared to try, and who wanted to love but hadn't found a real object.'[10] He was young both in appearance and outlook. Acton remembered him as a 'thin, tall, blue-eyed, gangling boy, after any adventure',[11] and Claud Cockburn said that he had told Graham he was the greatest case of arrested development he had ever met. Possibly it was not only immaturity in his case: it may also have been an early sign of a great artist's almost magical ability to stay in touch with his own most vivid youthful instincts. Certainly Greene's initial and personal celebration of freedom from school and family life (though the latter ties remained strong) was more juvenile and unsophisticated than that of many of his contemporaries.

The youthfulness was demonstrated during his first month at Balliol. He wrote to his mother of a party in 'a certain Fergusson's rooms': 'We played Chicken Food, and then "Dicky, Dicky show a light," round the quad, until the Dean informed us that we were turning Balliol into a nursery.'[12] Eighteen days later, to commemorate Armistice Day, students played football with tin trays down the High, and with a bucket up Saint Giles. In the process, Greene cut his ankle getting it wedged in the bucket and tripping up on it. On another occasion he went to the Hysteron Proteron Club which, as he told his mother, once a term had a backwards day, with breakfast at eight o'clock at night: 'The meals . . . started with toast and marmalade, then bacon and eggs, and lastly porridge. We then returned backwards to Balliol . . . This morning started with bridge in dinner jackets . . . before working backwards through dinner.'

Although he looked slightly frail (his father chose to send him to Balliol because it was then anti-athletic),[13] he had a deceptive energy shown by the sheer volume of his activities. On 24 October 1922 he wrote to his mother: 'On Sunday I went for a sixteen mile walk with Turton. I am going to the theatre, "The Wandering Jew" with a certain Howard . . . Went and heard Lord Robert Cecil at The Union. This evening I'm going to a meeting of the Mermaid, a University Literary Society.' During his first term he started to play golf with Claud Cockburn, who recalled the experience ending abruptly:

> The only time I played golf was with Graham. We teed up and Graham took a tremendous swipe and struck his caddy by accident because he swung round too far, and the caddy reeled and recovered himself. Then it was my turn and I unfortunately swung round much too far and hit the ball straight into the bus to Headington or whatever bus was passing, and it shot through the driver's seat, narrowly missing the driver, the bus nearly crashed, and so I said to Graham, 'Let's get the hell out of here.' And that was our last golfing experience.[14]

Not surprisingly, Graham was not a member of the Hypocrites' Club. 'When I met Greene at Balliol, I can't say we clicked,' said Acton. 'I fancied him a crude puritan – he did rather look like one, yes. He did look puritanical and rather disapproving.'[15] But he did belong to a club, one of his own making. Writing to Evelyn Waugh on 10 September 1964, he explained why they had not met at Oxford: 'I was not suffering from any adult superiority at Oxford to explain our paths not crossing, but I belonged to a rather rigorously Balliol group of perhaps boisterous heterosexuals, while your path temporarily took you into the other camp.'

This 'rigorously Balliol group' was small. Chiefly, it consisted of Greene and his friends – the late George Whitmore, the late (Sir) Robert Scott,[16] the late Robin Turton (Lord Tranmire) and the late Joseph Gordon Macleod, well known as a radio announcer during the Second World War.* It was called the Mantichorean Society and had its own tie – blue and silver with black stripes.

Many of the exploits of this Society were prompted by Graham. They were 'rather below [those of] the normal adolescent age.'[17] Certainly they took a schoolboy form of games, tests and competitions.[18] On one occasion the Mantichoreans had a competition to see who could collect with the aid of a screwdriver at night the most metal plates with the words 'No hawkers, no tradesmen'

---

* Macleod received an honourable mention in Graham's thriller *The Ministry of Fear*. 'And just at that moment the news began – "and this is Joseph Macleod reading it." The stranger crouched back in his chair and listened.' (p. 23.)

or 'Beware of the dog' printed on them from those little villas in Oxford.[19] Greene later recalled how some of them had decided to enliven the little town of Wallingford.[20] Robert Scott, disguised as a middle-aged clergyman hunting for a runaway wife, called at the rectory and 'took tea with the sympathetic wife of the rector. She urged him to be generous and forgive, and after tea they prayed together.' Meanwhile, Greene was sitting at an easel in Wallingford drawing 'souls' at 6d. a time and writing 'verse on any subject to order'. 'I'd got quite a crowd before the end,' he told his mother.[21]

Then there was the 'Moorish' exploit when they dressed as Moors and went to a Moorish café for a Moorish meal, pastry done in layers, a mixture of dates, nuts and honey. There was one common dish, from which each of them tore portions. Afterwards, they marched out and, followed by about sixty people, created a sensation by carrying a censer in front of them, and, turning to Mecca, praying on their knees. Later they prayed again outside the Clarendon and had dinner on poufs in a room through which all the customers had to pass to get to the restaurant and lounge. They concluded the event by throwing morsels of food at Robert Scott (who again appeared as a clergyman) which frightened away several elderly lady customers.[22]

Some of their exploits were of a more testing and adventurous kind: 'Yesterday morning [Greene wrote to his mother] I spent on a competition to see how far one can get in six hours, without paying and not walking more than a quarter of a mile on foot between each change of vehicle, with no lifts allowed from a friend. One mark is given for each mile, and one for each vehicle . . . I did twenty five miles, with six changes. I used a coal lorry, a side car and lorry with rocks and bricks, and a private motor car.'

In the same spirit, he made his first trip in an aeroplane and saw Oxford from the air: 'It was a perfectly glorious sensation. I've never felt anything so lovely before.'[23] We have to take into account that flying was then considered a dangerous pastime and that John Galsworthy had written to *The Times* two years earlier suggesting that aircraft should be banned 'for any purpose whatsoever because of the danger involved'. In 1925 Graham tried to persuade his future wife to take a flight, but, since she refused, he took it himself and threw oranges at Oxford's dreaming spires.

There were also some skirmishes into public morals and politics. When Aleister Crowley (Beast 666), a self-styled saint and drug-addict dedicated to a life of debauchery with overtones of witchcraft and black magic, visited Oxford, the Mantichorean Society was worried that he might seduce the whole of the University and tried to lure him and his companion, Betty Loveday, away from Oxford 'to prevent this most awful world-wide tragedy'.* They did not succeed in removing Crowley even though they went so far as to seek the help of Scotland Yard, where they were told there were no grounds on which they could turn him from Oxford.[24]

Politically, Greene's attitude at this time reflects a youthful urge to 'send up' the whole business. He wrote to his mother: 'I have now turned violent Conservative and wander round canvassing the unfortunate poor. I am getting quite good at admiring babies.' This did not prevent him going to the Labour Club to listen to Ellen Wilkinson, the new member for Middlesbrough, who made a charmingly left-wing speech: 'She *would* make school-girl eyes in the middle of the most violent and revolutionary statements.' Political candidature was treated as something absurd. In 1922, he wrote to his mother about a bogus candidate called Jorrocks and was enough impressed by the sheer drollery of the situation to send her two skits on political publicity sheets, which she kept. It seems Jorrocks appeared in town and made speeches wearing a mask: his platform was that he belonged to no party and supported no politics. The sheets proclaimed that he was 'the only triangular candidate', 'the only candidate keeping silent' and asserted the need to give up nothing – 'Let Jorrocks hold what Jorrocks held.' Graham admitted to his mother that the local people thought Jorrocks a real candidate and several scrimmages took place as a consequence. It was all good undergraduate fun of a juvenile kind, but Greene was concerned with the success of these adventures: 'I'd got quite a crowd before the end', 'we were followed by quite 60 people' and 'the local people thought Jorrocks a real character'.

*

Other exploits suggest a deeper and more serious commitment to emerging aspects of Greene's character. The 'barrel-organing' episode was an example. In 1923 Greene wrote with seeming innocence to his mother: 'I hear that The Daily Mail last vac. had a paragraph on two undergraduates who were touring with a barrel-organ.' The two in question were Graham Greene and Claud Cockburn, and fifty-five years later Cockburn recalled:

Graham suggested that we might go on a barrel-organ trip through territory which we both knew very well, like the Berkhamsted

---

* Betty Loveday's husband, Raoul, had been a secretary of the Hypocrites' Club. He 'left the university suddenly to study black magic and died in mysterious circumstances at Cefalu in Aleister Crowley's community.' Evelyn Waugh, *A Little Learning*, 1964, p. 180.

territory, so with enormous difficulty, we hired a barrel-organ and disguised ourselves as sort of tinkers, and in those days barrel-organs were rather more common – so it wasn't quite so spectacular to have a barrel-organ, but anyway there we were, in sort of semi-rags, and faces painted up and looking we hoped, like tramps and apparently we did, because we went to Berkhamsted and we went all round the school, the school gates and the gates of the various Houses, and so on, and nobody recognised us, and if anybody said anything, they said, 'Who are these two tramps?', and this caused a good deal of glee . . . as far as I remember we made a little money, and anyway it paid for the trip, and caused a most frightful scandal among everybody who discovered who these two tramps were that they'd been giving money to.[25]

It was part of the ground-rules that they would take no money with them and try to live on their scanty earnings: 'four separate elderly ladies gave us four separate sixpences on condition that we moved on to a neighbour's house.' Thus after three bitter December days, Cockburn and Greene finished up with a few pence profit. More important, they made the discovery that only the obviously poor gave money to tramps.[26] They were not allowed in any inn in Langley near St Albans because of their dirty faces and rags; they tried to sleep in a field 'iron-bound' with ice and then found shelter in a half-built house, the wind coming in chilling gusts through the gaps for windows.[27]

Greene was to return to this episode, which retained significance for him, many years later in the *New Statesman*, 31 May 1968, when he brought out the element of disguise involved. Apparently at one point in their journey they both wore 'Christmas masks', Claud Cockburn's being a Billy Bunter mask with a perpetual toffee-fed grin, and the effect of these masks was that each of them became enraged by the other's false face so that they began to defend the respective attitudes on life of their adopted personae and 'would most certainly have come to blows . . . if [they] had not . . . taken off [their] false faces and changed [their] clothes'. They 'parted, not quite such good friends for a while as [they] had been.'

The excitement and secrecy involved impressed Graham and he was to continue to seek such experiences. It was his way of carrying on 'the life-long war against boredom' and of trying to get behind the façade of conventional life.

Lord Tranmire felt Graham was both younger and older than his contemporaries at University: 'He would wrinkle up his eyes, which you get in a child, and you don't really get so much of in an adolescent. He had a very well-developed sense of fun, like you get in a child, but in some ways he was older than all of us.'[28] The youthfulness, energy and adventurousness were to be permanent characteristics. 'He remains', Acton said, 'an adventurous boy, ready to go to any country immediately something starts – a revolution or something. [He is] not a Dorian Gray type of youth, and is a bit raddled now in appearance but the mind and the eye are still those of a boy on the chase, on the look-out.'[29] Tranmire recalled meeting him after thirty-five years, in 1961: 'I asked him to lunch in the House of Commons. He walked in and looked exactly as he had at Oxford. I thought how terribly little he'd changed. And he talked exactly the same: the same rather lively banter that he always had. Very frank and not dissembling. He's a very involved character but he wouldn't dissemble.'[30]

This lively banter and youthfulness shows itself in a poem he probably wrote when he was eighteen, called 'Irritation', published on 24 May 1923, indicating perhaps not only the comic influence of Edward Lear but the concern of his parents as to what Graham was going to do with his life. The poem carries no by-line but his initials H.G.G. are written in ink in a hand recognisably his mother's:

Irritation

Father muttered 'The Home Civil',
　　Mother she said 'No.'
Then she talked a lot of drivel
　　Of a House in Paternoster Row.

Sister squeaked, 'Why not a Vicar,
　　Or a manufacturer of cork?'
But I did not wait to kick her,
　　So I went and left them to their talk.

Then I spilt a lot of treacle on the stairs,
　　And I emptied the slops,
　　In a number of shops,
And I broke the Bank Manager's chairs.

I wasn't angry, Oh, no! Only a trifle put out.
　　I got hold of a halbert,
　　And seized on Prince Albert,
And fed him on golf balls and stout.

You see I was young and saw nothing wrong
　　In setting fire to the High,

With a pink-spotted tie,
And half of a vulgar song.

I shall not boast. There was nothing in that –
    I got hold of a Dean,
    And painted him green,
And gave him a three-cornered hat.

I wasn't angry. Oh, no! Only a trifle hurt.
    I called on the Master
    And mixed all his castor
Sugar, with best London dirt.

I returned to my family much relieved –
    You may take it as true,
    If I tell you, too,
I *had* been a little peeved.

Father said, 'What's it to be?'
    Mother, she said 'What?'
'I'd like to be Sir Herbert Tree,
    And endow an infant's cot.'

But since it's rather hard to change
    My virtuous heart to sinister,
I'll take a post with larger range
And be a Baptist Minister.

We are used to the Roman Catholic Greene, but at University he was a convinced atheist, his psychoanalytical experience having reinforced his disillusionment with the Protestant church. His first published story in the *Oxford Outlook* (February 1923), entitled 'The Trial of Pan', was about a pagan who outwits God and takes over heaven – much to the relief of its inhabitants.[31]

In the following year a curious story by him (signed 'G.G.') appeared in *The Cherwell*[32] entitled 'The Improbable Tale of the Archbishop of Canterbridge'. Satan has come to Britain and 'this lunatic' has led her 'to dabble her feet in blood'. 'The madman with his talk of the joys of war has bewitched mankind' and it is expected that the world 'will be fighting like a pack of mad dogs'. The Archbishop takes it upon himself to shoot Satan and then fears God's justice, but the dying Satan quietens his fears:

'You need not be [afraid] – you will find no God.'
'Will you blaspheme even as you are dying? Who are you to say there is no God?'

'I am God,' said the man, and choked up fresh blood.
'But if you are God . . . how can you die?'
'I made myself man . . . a miracle . . . Very rash . . . I've done
   better in my day . . . such miracles I've done . . . Woods, and
   wars, and sheep paths, and – you, my dear Canterbridge!'
And in a bubble of bloodstained laughter God died.

In a poem entitled, 'Après Vous' (*The Cherwell*, 22 November
1924), Greene writes of going to heaven – though not before his
loved one, 'for I am shy and hate strange company', and he says to
her, 'when I skate on thin ice talking of Satan,/Warn me with that
little twisted frown of yours.' She must tell St Michael:

Do not mind his rudeness, he is shy.
And do not be offended if he does not listen to your talk.
He thinks too much on me.
And do not, do not let him talk to God
Of the superiority of Hell's constitution!

According to Tranmire, 'It was not like Graham to argue for argument's sake. Careful thinking led him to it and he would propound his
own strong atheism. I think in my life I've never heard atheism put
forward better than by Graham, although one was fighting it at that
time. But he was, apparently, a convinced atheist – not arguing it but
merely explaining it. That's why it wasn't undergraduate argument.'[33]

*

In *Ways of Escape* (1980), writing of *Stamboul Train* and *A Gun for
Sale*, Greene says: 'I can detect in both books the influence of my
early passion for play-writing which has never quite died,'[34] and
certainly his interest in the theatre, which started at school, increased
at University where he went through the whole gamut of theatrical
experience as actor, playwright and entrepreneur. He wrote to his
mother during his first month at University: 'A new dramatic society
has just been formed at Balliol for the production of plays by
undergraduates . . . I just missed getting mine taken.'[35]

Six months later there was a Balliol drama competition. Graham
submitted a second play (we do not have the titles of either) and one
of the judges, possibly Harley Granville-Barker, found it 'marred by
sentimentality', though stressing not 'banal sentimentality'. He found
that it was competent within its own limits, and had a certain charm.
He added: 'If, as I venture to suppose, you are as yet fortunately

young, it is exactly as it should be for your future development. I feel fairly sure that . . . we shall hear of you again.'[36]

At Oxford he tried to form his own drama company. He wrote to his mother: 'the first week of next vacation we are going for a tramp, acting plays in small villages.' Typical of his energy is the extraordinary speed with which he put this idea into operation. His letter continues: 'Raymond may be coming. Otherwise it consists of self, Fergusson (Balliol), Guest, Cockburn, York-Lodge (Keble). I got going fairly quickly, as I formed the idea at 11.15 Tuesday morning, and had got the company together by tea time; and had decided on one play. We are doing three one acters, of which one is the *Monkey's Paw*.★ Guest is taking any properties we need in his side car.' Financially alert, he asks: 'P.S. To get off the Entertainment Tax, must all takings go to charity? Or only profits?'[37] Though that particular venture fell through, another was started, a purely Balliol affair with more ambitious plays. They decided on *Macbeth*, with cuts: 'I'm taking [the part of] Banquo, and an English doctor', wrote Graham, 'and Wilde's *The Importance of Being Earnest* which I am stage managing, and acting a young bounder.'[38]

Joseph Macleod recalls that Greene acted in a play of his at Oxford in 1924: 'My play, *The Fog Spider*, was a psychological-symbolical-something-or-other protest against suburban family life. I played the Father, Peter Quennell my Wife . . . and Graham my Son. The action really took place inside the Son's neurotic brain, and Graham did try to establish some atmosphere of terror with eyes staring, hands clutching and extending, and back bent. But we all lacked experience. What was meant as dead tragic was found by the audience killingly comic. It was a disaster.'

Greene's literary tastes at the time appeared decided. According to Sir Harold Acton: 'He espoused the cause of people that I didn't particularly care for, like the Georgian poets. He was then for de la Mare, those delicate rural poets. I belonged to what I thought to be avant garde, the Sitwells, Aldous Huxley and so forth. He was intensely Berkhamsted English and I was intensely non-English from Italy and loved Latin culture.'[39]

But Acton was only partly right: Greene's literary tastes were more complex than this. Just before he went up to Oxford, in a poem

---

★ Written by W. W. Jacobs, the popular short story writer and humorist. Jacobs grew up in the dockland at Wapping but in later years lived at Berkhamsted, visited the School and was known to the Greene family. A contemporary of Graham's, S. R. Denny, recalls Jacobs living above the prep. school: 'He was a pink-eyed, unobtrusive little man who could be seen every noon making his way to the town for his morning draught.'

published in the *Weekly Westminster* (30 September 1922) and signed H. Graham Greene, he wrote of being tired of old authors – Browne, Herrick, Wotton:

> . . . No Browne brings me such pleasure,
> As my loved Barrie; Conrad, Bernard Shaw.
> My Rupert Brooke, my Yeats, my de la Mare,
> Hold memories and scents in richer store.

A letter to Vivien Dayrell-Browning, his future wife, reveals an unexpected passion for a minor poet, T. E. Brown:

> I had his large green Macmillan Collected Poems. People used to come into my room and look at the shelves, and say 'Brown? What on earth have you got that for?' And I would grow wild and frantic and leap on chairs and declaim excitedly, 'He's somebody I'd like to anthologise' . . . I always think a lot of the excitement comes from his prosaicalness. When one's read the first three lines of a Shelley, one knows whether it's going to be good or not. But one reads a Brown poem, as rather interesting, well-knit, masculine prose, and then suddenly at the end, he'll catch his breath in a kind of gasp and one's miles above the ground . . . I warn you, darling, you've hit on one of my enthusiasms.[40]

Balliol was a fine college: the life of an undergraduate entirely desirable. It was possible, so long as it was arranged in advance, to order excellent lunches, as Graham explained to Vivien in 1927: 'Your description of the iced pudding suddenly gave me a wave of greedy longing to be back to the summer of 1924 when I was still in Balliol & could give lunch parties in college. One could arrange a really topping lunch. One got a card from Sligger authorizing it & then went down into the kitchens & interviewed the chef & collaborated in a fascinating menu. I wish I'd known you then.'

Graham also showed himself to be a typical student of the 1920s in drinking to excess, though without losing control. The justification was, as Kenneth Bell, his tutor, remarked one evening to the freshmen: 'Gentlemen, you have come to this ancient University to study a very large number of different subjects. It is our duty to see that you get the best opportunities for studying [them]. But there is one . . . which you will have in common, and that is what we propose to teach you in this college. And that is to take your drink like gentlemen.'[41]

Graham recalled to Evelyn Waugh that for a considerable period of his time at Oxford he lived in a general haze of drink. 'I've never drunk so much in my life since!'[42] In *A Sort of Life* he gives an example from his final year: 'For nearly one term I went to bed drunk every night and began drinking again immediately I woke.' He had given up going to lectures after his first term, judging them less useful than reading. He was within a few terms of his final exams, and had only to be sober once a week when he read an essay to his tutor, but even that demanded more discipline than he could muster. He was drunk at the end of term ceremony called 'The Handshake', when each student had to sit opposite the Master and Dean while his tutor commented on the work he had done during term:

> I was helped as far as the door by two of my friends, Robert Scott and George Whitmore, who held me on a steady course through the quad. Then I slumped into a chair beside Kenneth Bell and faced the Master and the Dean. I don't think it occurred to either of these two that an undergraduate would appear before them drunk at that early hour and on such a serious occasion and they probably put down any strangeness in my manner to nerves. My tutor recognized my state, but he was sympathetic. . . Bell's pupils were aggressively heterosexual and were inclined, like himself, to drink large quantities of beer. So he stage-managed skilfully what might have been a disastrous Handshake, and I was released safely into the care of my friends who had a taxi waiting and they lodged me as though I were something breakable in the train for Bletchley.★[43]

A television team, interviewing Claud Cockburn, referred to the fact that Greene had said that he was in his first term at Oxford 'dead drunk every day' and Cockburn answered, 'Well, I didn't notice.' The interviewer asked, 'You mean he wasn't?' and Cockburn's reply was, 'No, Greene is a very truthful man and if he said he was dead drunk every day, he was and the fact that I didn't notice it must have meant that I was equally drunk.'[44]

Greene did also have some special and moving experiences as a student. For example, he told his wife:

> That July I went for a marvellous walk. I only wish it had been with you, but I didn't know you then. I'd had dinner at the Hall

---

★ 'Do let me most seriously advise you to take to drink. There is nothing like the aesthetic pleasure of being drunk and if you do it in the right way you can avoid being ill next day. That is the greatest thing Oxford has to teach.' Evelyn Waugh to Tom Driberg, *Letters of Evelyn Waugh*, p. 10.

and it was a hot evening. And Tooter said, 'Come for a walk', and I said, 'Let's go to the Bridgewater Arms. We'll get there just before tea!' And then Ave joined us, and we went and we had a drink at the B.A. and it was dark. And I, not expecting to be taken at my word, said, 'Why go home on such a lovely night? Let's go to the Beacon.' And they agreed. And just before midnight we got there. It's the highest point of the Chilterns and a great windy whaleback, very grim at night, and the road to it passes through woods, until it comes out with a sudden white sweep on the edge of the downs. And we told ghost stories as we walked and thoroughly frightened each other. And sitting rather chillily close on the top of the Beacon, we forgot that we were a sophisticated girl of twenty one and still more sophisticated youths of nearly twenty, and at midnight I scrawled a rhyme on a scrap of paper, and we made our marks and we buried it in a little cairn of stones, and we got home very tired at 2.30 a.m.[45]

The schoolboy who was so solitary and disturbed, at Oxford threw himself whole-heartedly into a busy social life. The loneliness of personality, essential to a writer, was taking a rest. It is not surprising that the main object, getting a degree in history, was rather pushed to one side. He was cocking a snook at convention, challenging accepted principles, and experiencing life outside the bounds of society's protection, which involved hardship and danger (on a minor scale as yet), secrecy and disguise.

9

The Art of Spying

Adventure is the vitalising element in histories, both
individual and social.

— WILLIAM BOLITHO

'ESPIONAGE is an odd profession,' Greene wrote,[1] and as a profession it has fascinated him. He has dealt with it in his novels
from the comic point of view in *Our Man In Havana* and from the
serious point of view in *The Human Factor* and he has shown a
sympathy with Kim Philby. As a profession whose purpose was to
obtain secret political or military information about one country on
behalf of another, he did not condemn it. It was either a farce from
both points of view or an indication of commitment either to a
particular loyalty or to money of such strength that it wiped out all
other concerns. He also conceded that there was another form of
espionage – 'for some it is a vocation, with an unscrupulous purity,
untouched by mercenary or even patriotic considerations – spying
for spying's sake.'[2] This last defines his own fascination with a form
of espionage which evinced itself as early as his return from the
Richmonds in his analysis of his parents' dreams.

His parents' life was limited to that of their own class which
allowed a specific range of friends and of accepted social activities.
Servants and tradesmen were, of course, beyond the pale. Graham
admits that his mother was socially prejudiced. During the First
World War, although the Greene family had been happy to patronise
the tripe-seller in Berkhamsted since they needed food, Marion
Greene was deeply offended when the tripe-seller's daughter, living
in Castle Street, married an officer in the Inns of Court O.T.C.,[3]
and Ave Greene remembered that when as a girl she had enjoyed the
excitement of riding into Berkhamsted on a cart, she had been sharply
punished after Marion Greene had verbally chastised Ave's mother
for allowing her daughter to indulge in such unladylike behaviour.[4]
What Graham felt the need to do was to enter into 'espionage' not

for spying's sake but in order to obtain a knowledge of the lives of others so necessary to a novelist and especially this novelist born into the irksome restrictions of his class. He was forced to take the plunge and 'dive below the polite level to something nearer common life'.

It was at University that he took his first tentative steps in this direction when he and Claud Cockburn travelled from Oxford to Tring with their barrel organ, so well disguised that they were unrecognisable even in Berkhamsted among parents, relatives and friends. This episode was of great significance – it was the first venture to include all the basic elements of Greene's later 'spying' travels – a blueprint for the future novelist in search of material.

Anonymity, disguise, secrecy, the experiencing of other lives and conditions, however unpleasant that experience, were all involved. Implicit was a concern for the oppressed and rejected. 'Graham is a real crusader for the underdog – absolutely true,' Claud Cockburn said. 'If a man's having a raw deal, Graham would honestly rush out into the street and get killed.'[5] With customary honesty, Greene wrote: 'I was easily aroused to indignation by cruelties not my own.'[6] He discovered early, certainly by the time he was eighteen, that when under the necessary element of danger, when fear arose in him, whether it came from the possibility of losing a loved one or from going into dangerous unmapped places with the determination of a Victorian explorer, he could do incredible things.[7]

Finally, on the practical side, there was the need in the process of seeking copy to be funded. At first it was not easy, and he simply travelled in hope. The barrel-organ incident provided him with material which took him a long time to convert into cash. Six years later (while working for *The Times* as a sub-editor) an article on that escapade appeared and no doubt Graham received a modest sum for it. Later, when he was more successful, he would persuade leading newspapers to send him out to some political trouble spot and in return would offer vivid articles about his experiences. Specific parts of the material for articles, those which registered his most crucial concerns, would find their way into his novels. A good example of his method of work is *The Quiet American* (1955), of which Frances FitzGerald could argue in *Harper's*, even thirty years after its appearance, that 'there has been no novel of any political scope about Vietnam since Graham Greene wrote *The Quiet American*'.[8] The novel is based on four separate visits to Vietnam, and material in articles appearing in leading periodicals in France, Britain and America do double duty by being subtly introduced into the novel itself.

All these considerations come out in his first important trip abroad. He tells us in *A Sort of Life* that this was to Paris and gives, in separate publications, two conflicting dates, Christmas 1922 and Christmas 1923.[9] In fact, his first visit abroad (apart from a convalescing trip to Lisbon with his aunt Eva), was to Ireland at the end of his first year at Oxford in June 1923. To his mother he wrote: 'On Friday I'm going to Ireland for a week. I'll be perfectly safe.' He always played down danger when writing to his mother, but there *were* dangers in Ireland, then as now, and his instinct for trouble spots revealed itself for the first time, as did his reporter's eye for significant and telling detail.

In 1922 the Irish desire for independence forced the British to give them self-governing dominion status. Michael Collins, who became the state's first Prime Minister, was denounced by de Valera and other Republicans, and was assassinated in August 1922. Retaliation followed. On 20 December, the *Daily Mail* reported: 'seven men executed in Dublin', which brought the total of executions for being in possession of arms 'without proper authority' to nineteen. Ireland was thus lively enough to attract young Greene as soon as he was free at the beginning of his first long vacation.

Establishing the pattern which was to hold good for his future journeys as a writer seeking material, he first made contacts in the area to be explored. To his mother he wrote: 'I've got an introduction to a Free State senator, also I've got at one of the big Sinn Fein Johnnies through the Irish Nationalist here. Moira O'Neill is putting me up.'[10] Second, he sought an outlet for articles, with remuneration to help defray his costs: 'I hope to have more energy with this than with the barrel-organing, as the Daily Express hold out hopes of taking a series of articles on the State of Ireland under the Free State.'[11] As it turned out the *Daily Express* did not publish his articles, but his old stand-by, the *Weekly Westminster Gazette* did ('Impressions of Dublin' 25 August 1923) and paid for his journey ('a free holiday from the W.W.'),[12] a journey which demonstrated again his stamina and determination. He was to write to his fiancée two years later about the long walks he had done. 'I told you of my Irish 32 miles with a pack', and with typical modesty added 'under the influence of funk',[13] and of 'drunken republican innkeepers'. There was certainly something to be scared about since any young man with his British accent would have been immediately recognisable to the Republicans. Nevertheless, he walked from Dublin to Waterford making enquiries, finding out how strong Republican feeling was, at a time dangerous to all meddling Englishmen.

His article is not good, but it shows promise of the future novelist in its observation and style. He notes a mother suddenly leaving her baby in the railway carriage just before the train's departure; an old gentleman in a top hat 'slowly stirring like a piece of disused machinery'; deplorable food – 'liver the colour of good gorganzola cheese'; beggars 'as numerous as in a Continental port'; the midnight painting of slogans, 'The greater number of them . . . written up at nightfall by young girls, still at the "flapper" age, the only active Republicans in the city' (how the word 'flapper' recalls the style and feeling of the 1920s!). The fundamental impression is of unchanging Irish republicanism. 'If they are put in jail, they hunger strike and become martyrs. Thirteen women are qualifying for this heavenly crown.'

*

Greene's second excursion into 'espionage' was a trip to the Ruhr a year later. He had read a book by Geoffrey Moss called *Defeat* which dealt with a complicated political situation, an aftermath of the First World War. Moss described an attempt by the French to set up a separate republic (known as the Revolver Republic) in one of the occupied zones of Germany, the Ruhr, because of Germany's failure in 1922 to continue to pay 'indemnities' to France and Belgium.* To make up a Separatist army, the French brought into the area 'German criminals . . . from Marseilles and other ports – pimps, brothel-keepers, thieves from French prisons – to support the collaborators.'[14] They created flying pickets who moved from place to place, shouting for an independent Rhineland which would break away from the rest of Germany. Moss describes the murder of a policeman by a crowd – an event first reported in *The Times* of 30 September 1923:

> I had just re-entered the hotel, thinking everything was over, when perhaps the most horrible incident of Düsseldorf's 'Red Sunday' occurred. Twenty French Cavalrymen led by a dozen men of the 'Reinwehr' galloped up to a Green policeman and disarmed him. When this was done, the Separatists turned on the disarmed man with leaden pipes and beat him to death. The doomed policeman covered his face with his hands and sank to the ground. A score

---

* After the First World War, indemnities, known as reparations, were imposed on Germany. In April 1921, these were fixed at £6,600,000,000. Germany paid a first instalment but, with inflation, suspended payment in 1922. This led French and Belgian troops to move into the Ruhr basin (the manufacturing region on the right bank of the Rhine) in January 1923, to the passive resistance of the Ruhr workers. The occupying forces encouraged Separatists to proclaim an independent Rhineland Republic on 21 October 1923. Its first (and last) President, Dr Heinz, was assassinated in January 1924. The French gained little benefit from their occupation but did not wish to lose face. They withdrew, after 2½ years, on the eve of the Locarno conference in October 1925.

135

or more blows were rained on him during the half-minute it took to kill him. The French remained impassive and when it was over the Separatists shook hands with them.

This was just the situation to arouse the wrath of Cockburn and Greene: 'We decided to go and do something about it. When you say to Graham, "Let's go somewhere",' Cockburn explained, 'and you mean next month, he means tomorrow afternoon.'[15] They had no money to finance the trip, so Claud wrote articles to collect a little in advance and Graham took a daring step in order to go abroad without expense: 'Just on a blind & impudent off-chance I wrote to the German Embassy,' he told his mother, 'described pro-French feeling in Oxford, & offered to write a series of articles in the University papers, if they would put me up in the Ruhr. I got a letter back from Count Bernstorff . . . saying that he would be down in Oxford and would come and see me.'[16] Graham describes the Count's subsequent visit:

> Coming back one early evening to my rooms in Balliol I found my armchair occupied, my only bottle of brandy almost finished and a fat blond stranger who rose and introduced himself, 'Count von Bernstorff.' He was the first secretary of the German Embassy . . . a man who loved luxury and boys and who frequented a shady club called the Abyssinia in Archer Street, Soho. No one could have foretold that hidden in those folds of flesh was a hero who was to run a Jewish escape-route from Germany to Switzerland during the last war and be executed in Moabit prison.[17]

His days after that seemed to be filled with Germans, and Greene jubilantly wrote to his mother: 'I am going to be supplied with a chain of introductions.'[18]

Although it was inspired by a genuine concern about what was happening in the Ruhr, this trip was in effect another Balliol escapade, undergraduates taking on – and doing it very successfully – the Establishment, and deriving much fun from it. The two worlds – that of the undergraduate 'getting an opportunity of going abroad without expense' and the more serious world of actual human suffering and bravery – come together, a foreshadowing of the tragic underwritten by the comic which was to be a characteristic of some of Greene's novels.

The handing over of the money for the journey illustrated the German secret service's extravagant secrecy and the undergraduate appreciation of its futility. Greene recalls that he received the money at Carlton Gardens, Count Bernstorff handing him a packet and advising him to burn the envelope – which, of course, he kept for some years as a souvenir. Inside were twenty five pound notes, more than sufficient 'for a fortnight's holiday down the Rhine and the Moselle'.[19] But Cockburn's detailed recollection of this event is more farcical and telling:

> It was arranged that we were to be financed for the trip but it was all to be secret. So they turned on one of these ridiculous sort of secret service types, who made everything far more absurd than it needed to be. Instead of just handing over the money, Graham and I were to be at a musical comedy and this man would meet us. So there we were sitting, Graham and I and this agent, who had arrived wearing a sort of Hitlerian mackintosh, and this peculiar trio and two women sitting in the front row of the dress circle. Suddenly this man produced this satchel – which of course he dropped like all secret service men – and started to distribute the marked notes. More attention could not have been drawn to our activities – those strange notes being passed back and forth. However, finally we managed to collect sufficient notes to take off and we got to Essen.[20]

The absurdity of German intelligence was matched only by similar absurdities in British intelligence as Graham would discover during the Second World War. No wonder his novel *Our Man In Havana* (1958) is such a delicious farce bordering on tragedy.

The pair arrived in Essen with a third man, Greene's cousin. Tooter was taken along because, according to Greene, neither Claud nor he could speak German[21] (though Claud Cockburn insists that he 'spoke German damn nearly as well as Tooter').

They visited Cologne, Essen, Bonn, Trier and Mainz. At Cologne they met a Dr Hennings, owner of a great dye factory, who took Claud and Graham to Leverkusen and gave them a huge dinner. To his mother he was expansive about Hennings: 'He's a very charming man, very English in appearance, not at all ostentatious',[22] but in his autobiography written almost half a century later, while Graham recalls the meal accurately, 'a gargantuan feast in Leverkusen', his attitude towards his host was less friendly. Hennings, it seems, 'talked glibly of Germany's starvation'.[23]

Essen was more dangerous. Greene remembered the menace there where most of the factory workers were on strike – the badly lit streets, the brooding groups.[24] To his mother he commented: 'Everybody glowered at us, and there was a very delightful sensation of being hated by everybody . . . all foreigners were taken for French officials. In the evening we went to a Cabaret show, where . . . a dancer did a symbolic dance of Germany in chains, ending in an exultant breaking of her fetters.'[25] In his autobiography he adds a touch he must have felt he had to withhold from his mother – the dancer was a 'rather fat naked lady'.[26] What exactly the naked lady was doing in symbolic dance apart from breaking chains we do not know, but its crudity remained in Graham's mind, for in a letter written three years later to his future wife he speaks of how much coarser were German cabarets than French.

The trio flirted with fear and, while on their journey, began to plan a thriller together in the manner of John Buchan; they sought danger most earnestly, as Cockburn remembered, but they came to no harm:

> So we got there and Graham, again with his tremendous sense that he must do something. It was a very dangerous place, the French trigger-happy, and the thugs from the separatists and so on. My plan was to stay in the hotel, examine the situation and in broad daylight go out and see what was going on. Not so Graham – 'It's at night things happen' – and so, against my will, we set out. We walked through the streets of Essen and under some awful railway bridge. It looked like some recipe for murder, shots going off at intervals. I suggested that it was more prudent to survive and get back home with our story, but it was no use. I think Graham had a pistol, so we trekked on under endless railway bridges and underpasses and God knows what and I was scared shitless. Graham striding boldly along, oblivious to danger.[27]

In Bonn they took rooms in a little Gasthaus in the market place, built about 1649, for 2s.6d. a night – 'one could get replete on 1/6d'[28] – and they followed Senegalese soldiers about in the hope (unfulfilled) of seeing a rape.[29] At Trier, where there was a much greater sense of occupation – the streets full of Spahis – the editor of the local paper 'for an hour and a half . . . poured atrocities into [their] ears' and at Mainz 'the streets [were] full of drunken French soldiers'. It was in Heidelberg, out of the occupied zone, that they met Dr Eberlein who admitted to them that he was a kidnapper involved in murder commissions: 'He recruited young men to drive fast cars across the frontier into the French zone where they seized mayors and officials who were collaborating with the French authorities and bundled them back into Germany to be "tried" for high treason.'[30]

*

For some months after his German trip, Greene was certainly preparing himself to become a secret agent, his intention being to return to the French zone of Germany, get in touch with the Separatist leaders and try to obtain information about their plan for the future. 'It was', he comments in *A Sort of Life*, 'a heady thought for a boy of nineteen.' Count von Bernstorff and the Berlin Foreign Office obviously had him marked out as a possible recruit and kept in touch with him, as Greene's letters to his mother at that time show:

> After lunch, Bernstorff suddenly put his head round the door, and he & his cousin & sister came to tea. They had all motored down for the day. Also, one of the Secretaries from the Austrian Embassy came. (27 April 1924)

> Count Bernstorff turned up last Sunday, & was hopeful of a new trouble in the Rhineland soon. (15 October 1924)

> A man from the Berlin Foreign Office . . . A real pre-war Prussian . . . I felt all through lunch . . . that he was trying to discover [my] weak points. However, his weak point was adiposity, and I quite broke his spirit and dominated him thoroughly by dragging him round Oxford at the speed of an express. (17 October 1924)

He also mentioned to his mother the possibility of his returning to Germany: 'I'm wondering vaguely whether I will not go for a few weeks in the long vac. to my nice little cheap pub in Bonn.' And he was certainly, at this time, taking lessons in German from a woman in North Oxford, 'finding old fraulein Wurchshack an excellent teacher. She races through the grammar, & concentrates most on the conversation.'[31] The fact that Graham was becoming as thick as thieves with the German Embassy was beginning to disturb his father.

But his parents had little to worry about for Greene was not destined to become a professional secret agent then. The problems of the Ruhr were solved: 'The Dawes Plan* was formulated . . . agreements were reached . . . and one insignificant recruit to the ranks of espionage was told to fall out – his services no longer required.'[32]

It had been an adventure, however, and for Greene surely a sortie into a future Greeneland, and it left the three students with memories. Greene was to recall in the *Oxford Chronicle* (June 1924) seeing 'a

---

* A report on German economic conditions providing a scale of payments for reparations coupled with large foreign loans to Germany, thus enabling Germany to meet its treaty obligations for the next few years.

small Spahi with ragged beard and khaki cloak lounging beneath the Porta Nigra, the great Roman gateway that had stood there for sixteen hundred years'. He retained one strong impression – a walk in Heidelberg to a restaurant on the top of one of the hills: 'It was very lovely and quite creepy coming down again through the pinewoods in a rather tenuous moonlight.'[33] Writing to his future wife, two years afterwards, he recalled that Heidelberg evening: 'When I think of the loveliest times in my life, there always comes first a long, long visit of times with you – and then a few odd scattered days, like the pinewoods at night above Heidelberg.'

Tooter's recollections were more fundamental, more comic: 'Don't forget we were very young men at University . . . [and] there was a great craze for limericks at that time . . . I remember that Claud Cockburn coined one for us which went something like this':

> While in a boat with Eva
> She went into a sexual fever
> She opened her thighs
> And to my surprise
> A man on a bank called, 'Beaver!'[34]

10

Apprenticeship

It's the white stag, Fame, we're hunting . . .
— EZRA POUND

THE importance of Oxford for Greene was not the academic seal
of approval it could give, it was the freedom of an apprenticeship
into whatever area of skill he chose. In his case not only 'espionage',
but also making literary contacts, editing, publishing, and selling
what he had edited and published, and making an excursion into the
newest medium, radio, which he succeeded immediately in mani-
pulating for his own purposes.

One of his most important literary contacts was Edith Sitwell. He
had come to admire her and had made her a friend. He wrote in
March 1923 of being 'converted to Sitwellianism' and in June he
wrote to his mother that he had read Edith Sitwell's last volume of
poetry and was 'absolutely out middle stump'.[1] This must have been
Bucolic Comedies (1923): 'When/Sir/Beelzebub called for his syllabub
in the hotel in Hell/Where Proserpine first fell/Blue as the
gendarmerie were the waves of the sea/(Rocking and shocking the
barmaid).' As usual it was no sooner the word than the blow: 'I never
realised she could write like that,' he told his mother, 'I thought I'd
strike while the iron was hot, so I posted off an essay on her to the
WWG.' Although the *Weekly Westminster Gazette* decided not to
publish the essay – they had had enough Sitwell for the time being –
they promised to send him Edith Sitwell's next book of verse to
review, 'and you can embody this article in that review'. Best of all,
the editor sent Greene's essay to Miss Sitwell. She then wrote to
Graham: 'I am not used to people understanding anything whatever
about my poetry, excepting perhaps an occasional image, and that
only partially, as they do not understand the spiritual impulse behind
the image. You have understood it all. Your comprehension appears
to be absolutely complete' (19 June 1923). And she thanked him for

defending her poetry at a time when she felt herself to have been vulgarly abused in the *Weekly Westminster*.

Greene was delighted and told his mother that Edith Sitwell's autograph might some day be valuable, and that he might now have a chance of getting into her poetry magazine *Wheels*. But as there were no issues after 1921, she could not publish anything of Greene's.

Greene wrote in the *Oxford Outlook*, 'In Miss Edith Sitwell we find the style of the Decadents ['Wilde and his insane school'], broadened in outlook, shorn of its madness, and intensified in emotion and beauty, there is no more room for progress here.'[2]

At the end of his freshman year, Greene was elected President of the Modern Poetry and Drama Society, and as a result met many of the literary celebrities of the day. He told his mother that he hoped to invite 'Drinkwater & de la Mare down'. He also made friends with the writer, Clemence Dane, and a useful contact she turned out to be. With a direct honesty, though a little patronisingly, Greene wrote: 'My poetry society had Clemence Dane to tea . . . a very handsome woman and much younger than I had expected . . . I can't conceive how she ever wrote a play like *William Shakespeare*. A woman who can talk of different people as "such a dear".'

A number of female writers took an interest in young Greene – Naomi Royde-Smith, in the 1920s, as we have seen, who published him in the *Weekly Westminster Gazette*; in the 1930s, Mrs Belloc Lowndes, sister of Hilaire Belloc and author of the thriller *The Lodger*; and the famous hostess of the famous, Lady Ottoline Morrell.

*

The Dean of Balliol ('Sligger') was Graham Greene's tutor for a time. Once, having listened to a debunking essay by Greene on the younger Pitt, he was silent for a while, 'then he sniffed, then he kicked a coal, and then he said, "You ought to get on as a journalist, Graham," with bitter scorn.'[3] The Dean was right – Greene did get on as a journalist at Oxford. Shy he may have been, but at Oxford he showed a flair for publicity.

The most obvious outlet for his talents was the *Oxford Outlook*, a magazine established by Beverley Nichols in 1919. He recalls: 'As soon as I went to Oxford I decided, in company with a little band of equally impertinent young men, that what Oxford needed was a new literary magazine which should reflect the new spirit of the university after the War . . . It was to be called the Oxford Outlook and people were to pay half a crown for it.'[4] Greene, in his time, became acting editor and his first contributors were Edmund Blunden and Louis Golding. Louis MacNeice, W. H. Auden, C. Day Lewis, Rex Warner and Emlyn Williams all published early work in the *Oxford Outlook*, some receiving their first acceptances from Greene when the editor, C. H. O. Scaife, was out of the country. He brought to this position initiative, energy – and some misgivings, for, not satisfied with simply editing the magazine, he took it over, changed its image and tried, incredibly, to make it pay – 'I don't know what the other editor will say when he returns from America at our changes,' he wrote to his mother. He not only worked with tremendous enthusiasm and a dedicated attention to detail, but showed a singular ability in promoting the *Oxford Outlook*.

On 15 October 1923 he wrote to his mother: 'I am editing [the *Outlook*] this term and wish to make it partly political, as this will give it a larger circulation. Unfortunately, the owner is averse, but if I get a Trevelyan article, I think he would agree.' G. M. Trevelyan, well known then for his work on Garibaldi,[5] was, fortuitously, a friend of Greene's father and so Graham set the wheels in motion: 'Do you think Da could get George Trevelyan to write some short thing on Italy, on the Corfu business* or something of that sort?'

Thanks to Greene's efforts, the November issue was a remarkable one. Many of the contributors were his contemporaries and friends: 'The Outlook is getting on fairly well, though it's hard to get anybody to write prose. We've got a poem in rhyme by Quennell, the best thing he's done.[6] . . . I've done a piece of verse to J. G. Walker [and] I've brought in Claud Cockburn to do the political side, so that it will be quite an O[ld] B[oy] magazine.' Greene's piece of verse, 'The Coming', inscribed to 'J. G. Walker', disturbed one student friend. Joseph Gordon Macleod in 1977 recalled: 'It was about a man with a stern face looking at a sunset, and I was somewhat jealous because I remembered a sunset with Graham, and the poem was inscribed to J.G.W. I told Graham of my jealousy, wishing the initials had been mine – J.G.M. He didn't answer.' J. G. Walker was the name of the baby recently born to his elder sister Molly. The poem was accepted also for the magazine *The Golden Hind* (April 1924) by the playwright Clifford Bax (who recommended to Greene his first literary agent, A. D. Peters) and it also appeared in Greene's first book of verse, *Babbling April*. The poem can be seen, in some ways, as prophetic:

> And while we other poets sit at winter dusk
> And softly whisper each our little dreams,
> You'll rise and with the ardour of your youth

---

* In 1864 Corfu was ceded to Greece, but in 1923 after the murder of an Italian boundary delegation, Italian forces bombarded the chief port Kerkira.

Stride from the warm glow of the flickering fire
To carve your dreams in facts across the world.

In his November issue, Greene went in for some big names. Apart from pressing his father on the Trevelyan article – 'If Da can get some sort of promise from T. I should be glad to hear by Friday, as we have a meeting then' – he received a story from the novelist Louis Golding on the promise that he review Golding's latest book,[7] and a poem from Edith Sitwell: 'I've just received a rather beautiful poem from dear Edith. It's part of a very long poem called 'The Sleeping Princess' . . . so we shall have two celebrities.' The Sitwell extract is entitled 'La Rousse': 'When reynard-haired Malinn/Walked by the white wave/The Sun, a chinese mandarin,/Came dripping from the wave.'

Thomas Hardy's play, *The Famous Tragedy of the Queen of Cornwall* – he was then in his eighty-fourth year – was reviewed: 'written by a great man . . . it will always have an unfortunate immortality', and indeed, it is no more than a dramatic curiosity.

Apart from finding suitable contributors, Greene was concerned with increasing the sales of the *Outlook*, and he was not naïve when it came to summing up a person and arranging financial matters. Of Linaker, the owner of the magazine, he wrote: 'A delightful man, so candidly unscrupulous', and although Greene had 'no financial responsibilities in the paper', he took the finances in hand:

It is not in best condition [he wrote to his mother] . . . so far I've succeeded in raking up four more pages of advertisement, which will help considerably. So far the losses have averaged seven pounds an issue, the four extra pages bring them to £2.10.0 and we have a covering guarantee of £5.5.0 an issue this term from Frank Gray. Result all serene.

I think I shall risk some of the remainder of the subsidy on posters, which we've never had in the past, and with their help I hope we may cover expenses on the first number, while Quennell is still a big draw.

When it came to selling the November issue, Greene first approached the members of his own family: 'Would you [his mother] and Aunt Eva send your subscriptions c/o Oxford Chronicle stating that you wish to become subscribers for a year', and in the same letter he says that he has 'written to Aunt Nono and asked her to ask Uncle Frank'. Being a relative of Graham had its disadvantages!

Dissatisfied with the attitude of the *Outlook*'s owner, he took steps to replace him: 'Blackwell . . . is thinking of buying [the *Outlook*], and pushing it . . . If we can get one or two juicy promises to impress him . . . I think he'd stump up.' And Greene succeeded in persuading Blackwell to take over the production and risks of the *Oxford Outlook* in the following term, and have it produced 'in a really first class format'.

He expected 'ructions' on the editor's return from America and humorously considered that the editor would resign 'in hopeless wrath at our shocking materialism'[8] but, though the editors Scaife and Greene were sometimes at loggerheads, they did not fall out. After Scaife's return Greene could write, 'we haven't flown at each others' throats.' In fact, Greene had his own way for he adds: 'We are bringing in two more people, one as Advertisement Editor, and the other as Subscription Manager, on a 10% commission basis.' Of the publisher, Linaker, Greene confessed to his mother that he 'made a great show of humouring our childish desire for advertisement'. But it was more than play and Greene, deadly serious, succeeded in introducing on to the Oxford streets sandwich men to advertise the issue.

Scaife went down in the summer of 1924, and Greene became editor: 'I hear today that Scaife goes down after this term, and then at last I shall be able to do what I like with the Outlook.'[9] But there was trouble finally between them over the last issue of Scaife's editorship. As he explained to his mother: 'There's going to be a great bust up. Scaife tried to put in some parodies of what I imagined was the Sitwells without my knowing. He sent a note to the printer telling him not to send me those proofs, but the printer sent them me with Scaife's note enclosed. I kicked up an almighty fuss, as I didn't want my position with Edith Sitwell damaged, and forced his hand by threatening to resign.'

Fifty-six years later Scaife lamented that Greene 'did one thing at the end of our association of which I deeply disapproved. It was the last number of my editorship, June 1924.' According to Scaife, the parodies were not of the Sitwells but chiefly of Harold Acton (a brilliant student but one easy to guy and no friend at that time of either Scaife or Greene) and instead of putting his initials to the introduction, Scaife had put four asterisks which Greene corrected in an erratum – 'For **** read C.H.O.S. [Scaife's initials].' 'This', confided Scaife, 'left me with a low opinion of the chap.'

*

It was a storm in a teacup, but it does reveal Greene's determination when it came to having his own way and not having his relationship with others harmed. Though he had been a rather difficult assistant editor, he was now looking out for 'a nice, subdued, tame, harmless sub-editor'. In his last year at Oxford, he re-made the magazine according to his lights, changed the publisher, and pressed on furiously with his own ideas. He had Basil Blackwell to tea and tried to persuade him to allow wood-cuts to be introduced into the magazine and, for the first time, to pay contributors (excluding himself) '5/- a poem, and half a guinea a story or article, beginning only with the fourth contribution, so as to encourage regular people'. The business acumen revealed here is entirely Graham Greene's.

Blackwell agreed to illustrations, and Greene in his editorial wrote: 'For the first time in its history, the *Outlook* has illustrated itself.' During Greene's editorship a thousand extra copies were printed: 'We shall be the only paper in Oxford that can guarantee being in the hands of every fresher,' he wrote excitedly to his mother on 15 October 1924: 'We are going in for quite Napoleonic methods in order to make a splash with the Outlook this term.'

He had yet another idea for promoting the magazine: to offer its readers 'a free insurance against failure in examinations'. Two coupons – one from the first and one from the second issue of the term – had to be sent in before examinations (thus ensuring that two issues were bought) and in the event of failure in examinations the student would 'receive a free champagne dinner for two at one of the Oxford restaurants'. Graham Greene's editorial explained the scheme:

The main purpose of these editorial remarks is to expound the *Outlook* scheme for Intellect Insurance; and I address them to all freshmen, except a very fortunate few. One of the disadvantages of University life is that you are compelled to take examinations in a term or two, before your mind can be expected to settle down to its best; fell instruments of torture, speciously disguised under the name of 'Preliminaries' or mendaciously as 'Moderations'. With such an ordeal to face, who, even the most erudite, can feel confident? Who can be sure of success? Who can disdain the chance of a consolation prize if he finds himself left at the post? It is this consolation which the *Outlook* scheme hopes to give.

The *Outlook* proposes to give a free dinner to all insured subscribers who fail to pass in History Prelim., Law Prelim., Divinity, or Pass Mods. A copy of the first number of this term is being sent to all freshmen: and with it an order form for the rest of the academic year. On this, those wise enough to insure with us will write their names, colleges, and the examination in which they anticipate disaster; and return the whole, with their annual subscription. The several dinners will be held at the beginning of the terms subsequent to the examination in question, on a date to be made known later; all claims to be sent in ten days before the day appointed.

He was able to tell his mother that the *Oxford Outlook* had leapt into popularity.

As editor of the *Outlook* Greene showed his ability not only to develop his own talents but to recognise those of others. Joseph Macleod recalled that he had a flair for this: 'I remember he was going to ask a Christ Church man called Williams, who was interested in theatre, if he had a play – to publish an extract in the *Outlook*. This must have been to Emlyn Williams valuable encouragement at the outset of his theatrical journey.' I suspect this was Emlyn Williams's short play, *Vigil*, which was performed by O.U.D.S. in November 1925. Graham also published four poems by the Greek poet Cavafy (translated by Cavafy's friend George Valassopoulis) when the poet was then almost unknown to the British public. One of the poems was called 'Come Back': 'Come back often, at night, and take me/ When the lips and skin remember . . .'[10]

In 1961, in a letter to Joseph Macleod, Graham nostalgically recalled those days:

I've just come back to England for a couple of nights from France and found your night letter telegram. How it brought back the days when you would leave in my room a new poem for the Oxford Outlook . . . I have put the night letter poem into my copy of the Ecliptic [a long 1930 poem, by Macleod] which has survived all these years and the blitz.

And he quoted from Macleod's poem: 'the dust is laid and the wet sand is clean.'

*

Apart from the *Oxford Outlook*, there was the newly established British Broadcasting Company which put out its first programme from Savoy Hill, London, on 14 November 1922 with its call-sign, '2LO calling'. The medium was new and amateurish in those less free-spoken days of radio; for example, a 1925 directive sent out to comedians banned jokes about drink, parsons, Scotsmen and Welshmen! Anyone straying from the path of righteousness was sacked.

Characteristically, the undergraduate Greene took on the new popular medium and the *Radio Times* of 22 January 1925 announced:

The Oxford Poets' Symposium

Harold Acton
Graham Greene
Brian Howard*
J. G. Macleod
Patrick Monkhouse
A. L. Rowse

will each read one of their own poems
S[imultaneous] B[roadcast]

Afterwards Graham wrote to his brother Hugh about his first experience in front of a microphone: 'I felt very nervous . . . We sat in a kind of sumptuous drawing room, with beautiful armchairs and sofas, and each in turn had to get up and recite in front of a beautiful blue draped box on a table. I felt like Harold swearing on the saint's bones.' And no doubt his nervousness led to his smoking. That he did smoke cigarettes then is shown in the postscript to his letter: 'Here's a cig. card for Elisabeth.'[11] There was little chance, given the high dignified moral tone of the B.B.C. then, that six rumbustious students would not cause, even unwittingly, something of a rumpus. Acton gave no offence with his reading of a poem called 'After', and Macleod recalled Acton's admirable, caressing diction: 'The g-rass is ve-rey g-reen today.' But, as Greene wrote to his brother, 'the BBC got very nervous when Brian Howard started on his naked lady. They say they have to be very careful.' Joseph Macleod believed though that the trouble came less from Brian Howard than from Patrick Monkhouse (later literary editor of the *Manchester Guardian*) who had substituted another poem for the one accepted which contained the word 'Damn'. Greene wrote an account of the affair for the *Oxford Chronicle*, tongue in cheek, soon after the broadcast: 'Mr Monkhouse voiced the feelings of the whole room towards that confounded box when he swore at it very loudly. "Had I the heart to call you a damned fool?" he cried and proved very conclusively

* Brian Howard was used by Evelyn Waugh in part as the model for Anthony Blanche in *Brideshead Revisited*, more fully as the source for Ambrose Silk in *Put Out More Flags*. Michael Davidson recalls him in the 1940s in London: 'Another drunken poet who came to the Swiss was poor Brian Howard, a haunted soul hungry for tragedy, racked by the tormenting ecstasies of seeking "the divine friend much desired". He too was tiresome when drunk; but a vivid, susceptive person beneath the obfuscations of escape. And Brian, like so many of that delirious generation, later took his own life' (*The World, the Flesh and Myself*, 1962, p. 208).

that he had the heart. The box seemed quite insensible to his oaths; not so the British Broadcasting Co., who were filled with visions of enraged persons breaking their earpieces. They pictured themselves damned . . . bankrupt, starving. The storm in their hearts was still raging when Mr Rowse proceeded to calm them . . . in that deep mellow voice which has so often stilled the Conservative frenzy of the Oxford University Labour Club.'[12]

Only Rowse received a fan letter, from 'an old invalid lady who had found his verses "consoling".'[13] But one listener wrote to the press and (according to Macleod) gave them 'one accurate and deadly epithet each, and ended, "There was then an interval of five minutes' silence. It was not enough."'

Greene's energy is again apparent for not only had he organised this event (and enjoyed the consternation it caused), but wrote it up in an article, and was able to make his B.B.C. contribution do treble duty. His poem appeared in the *Weekly Westminster* two days after the broadcast – 'I'm rather glad, as their rate of pay has gone up,' he wrote to Hugh – and it was also part of his Newdigate entry.★

But there was yet a fourth dimension to his contribution. It was, as Rowse recorded in his diary, an extract from 'a 250-line poem on Byron . . . He . . . dealt with Byron from the point of view of women and love, and to that extent it is a much truer picture than that I give.'[14] The poem was called 'The Godly Distance':

> I could have been so happy had I kept
> A certain godly distance from the world . . .
> Not dust, but only memory of dust,
> No love, but reminiscences of love . . .
> But out I peeped and met a witch's eyes.
> 'I do not want,' I cried, and felt her hair,
> 'I have enough,' and oh, I longed for lips.
> 'Poetry is mine and mastery, I need no more.'
> A finger gleamed and so I swayed to you.
>
> I drove along the road, I walked the lane,
> I felt the ecstasy, I knew the pain.

Rowse, who also described Greene's extraordinarily youthful appearance at this time – 'curly flax-gold hair and the odd strangulated voice . . . those staring, china-blue eyes, wide open to the world' –

★ A prize of 20 guineas known as 'The Newdigate' for English verse entries and confined to Oxford undergraduates. It was first awarded in 1806 and won by, among others, John Ruskin, Matthew Arnold, Oscar Wilde, John Buchan and Julian Huxley.

was right to be struck by Greene's poem, for he had chosen it for a particular and secret reason. 'My sentimental blank verse lines had nothing to do with Byron – they were directed at Berkhamsted.'[15] In fact, this poem was a private message to his first love. Listening to the broadcast at Berkhamsted, as his sister Elisabeth (then eleven) recalled, were a group of people: 'My parents didn't have a radio in 1925 and we all (Da, and Mumma, Hugh and myself and I suppose the governess) went to the matron's room to listen to the broadcast on her wireless – she was the only one in the school who had one!' It was Elisabeth's governess* who was the object of Greene's first passionate love and who sat listening, as she had been warned to do: 'Poor young woman,' Greene explained much later, 'it never occurred to me what embarrassment she must have suffered, seated before the radio set with my father and mother.'[16] In *A Sort of Life*, he does not mention her by name, but she was called Gwen Howell. She was governess at Berkhamsted for about eight months, a tumultuous period for both Miss Howell and young Graham Greene.

---

* According to Elisabeth Greene, Gwen Howell was not actually a governess: 'Up till the time she came there had been nannies (always called nurses then) and she was pure heaven. I adored her and life became much less boring. [She would] oversee nursery meals, take one out, oversee bed time and getting up, that sort of thing.' (Letter of 24 April 1982.)

I I

Love and Death –
a Flirtation

To die will be an awfully big adventure.
— J. M. BARRIE

ON 19 May 1924, Greene wrote to his mother, 'I'm glad Miss Howell is satisfactory', and mentioned that he was looking forward to going down to Sheringham for the vacation, but in his autobiography he recalls how reluctant he was to join his family on the Norfolk coast. If he had had enough money he would probably have gone to France but he had got himself in debt at Oxford and at least at Sheringham he could live at his parents' expense. His debts were what you would expect: 'so many barrels of beer, so many books, shelf upon shelf of them, which had nothing to do with work. At Blackwell's bookshop credit seemed to a newcomer endless (though they liked a little bit sometimes on account), but drinks were ordered through the college buttery and appeared on battels, as college bills were called (there was no credit given there) and . . . there had often been taxis at midnight.'[1]

So events came together and Greene met the 'satisfactory' Miss Howell during the family holiday at Sheringham, and fell in love with her. Fifty years later he recalled the very circumstances – the stretch of beach, his mother reading and the angle from which he examined Gwen Howell's body: 'She was lying on the beach and her skirt had worked up high and showed a long length of naked thigh.' After that, he lived only for moments with her.[2] His love was intense, but was to be short-lived – 'the reality of a passion should not be questioned because of its brevity. A storm in the shallow Mediterranean may be over in a few hours, but while it lasts it is savage enough to drown men, and this storm was savage.'[3]

During vacations he would visit Gwen Howell in the nursery at Berkhamsted, 'where she sat alone and the slow fire consumed the coals behind an iron guard'.⁴ It would seem, at first, not to have been such a sudden attraction on Gwen's part. Elisabeth recalls, when she was twelve, Graham coming up to the nursery in search of Gwen Howell: 'She and I used to hear Graham coming up and we used to hide together in the big school laundry basket that stood between the nursery passage and the entrance to the boys' dormitory. We giggling and listening to Graham putting on gramophone records in the nursery – *Pasadena* and *Last Night on the Back Porch* and something I thought very funny which went like "If you were the bug in the cabbage of life".'⁵

Graham's experience of first love is surely reflected in *The Ministry of Fear* (1943): 'All the way upstairs to his room, he could smell her. He could have gone into any chemist's shop and picked out her powder, and he could have told in the dark the texture of her skin. The experience was as new to him as adolescent love: he had the blind passionate innocence of a boy: like a boy he was driven relentlessly towards inevitable suffering, loss and despair, and called it happiness.'⁶

To please Gwen, he took his first dancing lessons and went to 'hops' at the King's Arms in Tring. To keep up appearances he had to dance occasionally with the wife of some master at the school and 'surrender her to other arms. Sometimes in the dark schoolroom out of term, on the excuse of teaching [his] brother and sister to waltz and foxtrot, [they] had dances of [their] own when half-kisses could be exchanged without the children seeing.' He did not remember the first kiss or 'the hesitations and timidities which surely must have preceded the kiss'⁷ but when in *The Ministry of Fear* he wrote: 'When he thought of her it was with an absurd breathlessness. It was as if he were waiting again years ago outside . . . and the girl he loved was coming down the street and the night was full of pain and beauty and despair because one knew one was too young for anything to come of this . . .',⁸ he must have had Gwen in mind.

In a diary entry of 2 August 1932, seven years later while living with his wife in the Cotswolds, Graham recorded: 'At night I dreamed, strangely, of Gwen Howell, whom I loved with such unreasoning passion in 1924–25.' In providing Arthur Rowe in *The Ministry of Fear* with a past, Graham went back to his love for Gwen Howell:

He was in the main street of a small country town where he had sometimes, when a boy, stayed with an elder sister of his mother's. He was standing outside the inn yard of the King's Arms, and up the yard he could see the lit windows of the barn in which dances were held on Saturday nights. He had a pair of pumps under his arm and he was waiting for a girl much older than himself who would presently come out of her cloakroom and take his arm and go up the yard with him. All the next few hours were with him in the street: the small crowded hall full of the familiar peaceful faces – the chemist and his wife, the daughters of the headmaster, the bank manager and the dentist with his blue chin and his look of experience, the paper streamers of blue and green and scarlet, the small local orchestra, the sense of a life good and quiet and enduring, with only the gentle tug of impatience and young passion to disturb it for the while and make it doubly dear for ever after.[9]

A poem he wrote at this time records how he would sit in the room below Gwen's, his family around him, and while pretending to read, listened to the sound of her moving about on the floor above:

> If you were dead, I should not listen
>   To every sound of your foot upstairs.
> I should not hide where the wet leaves glisten,
>   Hunting my mind's thoughts, coursing its hares,
> Dreaming *that other* [my italics], who will see
>   The whole of your body's secrecy.

And what of Gwen Howell and 'that other'? She was ten years older than Greene and died in 1974, but her husband, Conway Spencer, has explained something about their situation at that time.[10] He met her in Malta in 1918 when she was in the WRNS*, and they became engaged. In 1920 she returned home and her fiancé, who worked for Cable and Wireless, was posted to Aden, then Mauritius and then Rodriguez Island in the Indian Ocean. There were family objections to the engagement and it was broken off. Contact was difficult – there were only four mails a year to Rodriguez. Although the engagement was renewed, they had been separated for about five years when Gwen went to Berkhamsted as governess, but her fiancé was due to return to England in February 1925. Greene's many verses to Gwen, his bombardment of love letters (during term they wrote to each other every week) and especially his broadcast in January 1925, were part of a struggle to win her away from her fiancé, 'who had become a stranger to her'.[11] Gwen had her own struggles – once she spoke of marriage, but what could a student at Oxford do about that? He could only urge her to break off the engagement – to be free.

* Women's Royal Naval Service.

Her husband recalled that on his return 'there was uncertainty in picking things up again . . . it was all a very quick business and the marriage was scheduled to take place at St George's Church, Bloomsbury on 25 February 1925.' Many years later, Elisabeth Greene visited Gwen Howell, who told her that the day before her wedding her mother made her burn all Graham's letters.[12] Graham's mother went to the wedding; Graham did not. His bitterness was expressed in poetry:

> It is not that he gains your craftiest smile,
> The second best was good enough for me.
> Nor that his craving mind will hold awhile
> The transient secret of your intimacy.[13]

Greene had lost the battle but on recovering was to fall more deeply in love again some months later. The following year he won his first prize, apart from his school award, for a poem published in the *Saturday Review* (25 September 1926). The sonnet appeared under the name of H. Graham, and suggests that he was emotionally free of Gwen:

> First Love is but the learning of a lesson,
> A fumbling, faltering, missing of the lips,
> Blind with the wonder of a new oppression
> That drives to exile old cool fellowships . . .

> How could we know, who were so young, dull-witted,
> Dazed by a happiness too full of pain,
> That these our gestures fitted and refitted
> Would lose their passionate errors and attain
> Perfect control of voice, lips, hands and eyes . . .

Nevertheless, such was his love for Gwen Howell that when his play *The Living Room* was a success and he received a letter from her ('I was a man of over fifty and she, by now, well into her cruel sixties'),* he recognised her handwriting on the envelope and his 'heart beat faster'.[14]

*

It was at this time that he began playing Russian roulette. According to his own evidence, he played this game on six different occasions within a period of six months, but if suicide was his intention he was unsuccessful.

* Greene was actually forty-eight.

He had read about Russian roulette in a book by the Russian writer, Ossendowski, which described how White Russian officers tried to escape boredom: 'One man would slip a charge into a revolver and turn the chambers at random, and his companion would put the revolver to his head and pull the trigger. The chance was . . . five to one in favour of life.' It may well have been Ossendowski's book that led Greene to play Russian roulette (though the only episode even approximating to Greene's occurs in his *Man and Mystery in Asia*), but the possibility of playing it came from the accident of his finding a revolver in his elder brother's cupboard. Talking about it in 1981, Graham seemed at pains to find fault with, not his own behaviour, but his cousin's:

> I discovered the revolver. And it had live ammunition – a cardboard box of bullets. And the most astonishing thing, Raymond was given it by a cousin St George Lake who was killed in France. And before he went back to France the last time, he gave this revolver to Raymond, and Raymond could only have been – supposing he was killed in 1917, say, I would have been 13 and Raymond would have been 16. At the most he could only have been 17. It was the most extraordinary thing to do. St George gave me a helmet with a possible bloodstain on the inside, which I kept for many years.[15]

Raymond was away climbing in the Lake District when Graham took his first gamble:

> I slipped the revolver into my pocket, and the next I can remember is crossing Berkhamsted Common towards the Ashridge beeches . . . Beyond the Common lay a wide grass ride known . . . as Cold Harbour . . . and beyond again stretched Ashridge Park, the smooth olive skin of beech trees and the last year's quagmire of leaves, dark like old pennies . . . I slipped a bullet into a chamber and, holding the revolver behind my back, spun the chambers round . . . I put the muzzle of the revolver into my right ear and pulled the trigger. There was a minute click, and looking down at the chamber I could see that the charge had moved into the firing position. I was out by one.[16]

Graham emphasises the casual way in which he began playing this dangerous game, but the urge to play it must have had its roots deep in his psyche, and the timing of it is particularly significant. In his essay, 'The Revolver in the Corner-Cupboard' (1946), he says it began in the autumn of 1922, but twenty-five years later he gives a different date, autumn 1923.[17] In his autobiography he describes how he gave up the game quite suddenly during a Christmas vacation and told his parents that a friend had invited him to Paris.[18] Working backwards from this piece of information, we can give a more accurate dating. He went to Paris in the first week of January 1925, as a letter of 12 January testifies,[19] so that his first experiment probably took place in July 1924 – when he was in love with Gwen Howell.

He was then living a full life – he was in love and fighting for his love; he was deeply involved in activities as an Oxford undergraduate; he was planning a programme for the B.B.C.; and he was editor of the *Oxford Outlook*; yet, after the summer vacation of 1924, he took the revolver back with him to Oxford in order to continue playing the game:

> There I would walk out from Headington towards Elsfield down what is now a wide arterial road, smooth and shiny like the walls of a public lavatory. Then it was a sodden unfrequented country lane. The revolver would be whipped behind my back, the chamber twisted, the muzzle quickly and surreptitiously inserted in my ear beneath the black winter trees, the trigger pulled.[20]

Greene is describing his own actions with the objectivity of a narrator in a work of fiction. It is as if someone else is doing this to him or that the revolver had a will of its own exacting that penalty from this particular ear.

It was a long-drawn-out gamble with death and, furthermore, to others it looks like an obvious desire to commit suicide. This is what Greene denies. For him it was always a gamble with a five to one chance of failure. But what could have been his motive?

Claud Cockburn has suggested that: 'He wasn't trying to get out of life, he was trying to get more kick out of life. After all, if you take LSD, the chances are that it is going to kill you, but equally there is a possibility you'll suddenly have some fantastic new experience, and I think it was like that for Graham. I think it was premature LSD.'[21] Greene's experiment was not, however, the same as taking LSD – it could have resulted in instant death – but he was trying to get more out of life, and what he got were moments of extreme excitement. He brings out the nature of his 'experiment' in his poem, 'The Gamble':

> I slip a charge into one chamber,
> Out of six,
> Then move the chambers round.

One cast of the dice for death,
And five for life.
Then, eyes blind and fingers trembling,
Place the revolver to my head.

And pull the trigger.
Will it be mist and death
At the bend of this sunset road,
Or life reinforced
By the propinquity of death?
Either is gain.
It is a gamble which I cannot lose.[22]

He could not lose because, incredible though it may seem, whatever the outcome he won the battle against boredom, 'boredom . . . which had reached an intolerable depth . . . boredom . . . as deep as love and more enduring'.[23] (It was not only boredom – he has a neurotic terror of passivity.) He either died or experienced 'an extraordinary sense of jubilation, as if carnival lights had been switched on in a dark drab street. My heart knocked in its cage, and life contained an infinite number of possibilities. It was like a young man's first successful experience of sex – as if among the Ashridge beeches I had passed the test of manhood.'[24] Graham didn't feel he had passed such a test when faced with Carter at school. There his attempted suicides were attempted escapes from the misery Carter caused. Alone on Ashridge Park or in a country lane near Elsfield, he was testing his own courage.

Edward Sackville-West wrote that Greene's 'curious confession [of having played Russian roulette] is disturbing, as any sign of desperation always is, but when Mr Greene concludes, after finally returning the revolver to the cupboard, that he simply went off to Paris, because "the war against boredom had got to go on," we do not feel that we have been told the whole truth about the episode.'[25]

What strikes one as strange is the reason Greene gives for attempting suicide: boredom, it seems. As V. S. Pritchett put it: 'It's a young man's disease to be bored to death, and it carries its own agony, as terrible as anything in childhood . . . you feel strongly the meaninglessness of life, something like total and real boredom, something that can come upon a prodigy.'[26]

Greene seems to have endorsed V. S. Pritchett's opinion: 'A death wish, I suppose; a sense of dissatisfaction with myself. I remember myself as an adolescent, not knowing who or what I was. I would look in the mirror and think, "What in heaven's name am I?"'[27] To

Christopher Burstall,[28] Greene gave a moving account of the terrors of boredom: 'At puberty boredom was very acute. It had almost a physical feel about it, the boredom, like a balloon inside my head which swelled and swelled and swelled, until I felt it might break finally!' To put a stop to such a physical feeling might well have been one reason for taking up Russian roulette. And there is in Greene a strong streak of perversity. Speaking of this time he wrote to Vivien Dayrell-Browning:

> I assure you that I have a very strong will. There was a time at the end of the last Christmas term, & at the end of my brief period of lucidity, when Kenneth Bell secretly approached some of my friends – I only heard it a lot later – & told them to quiet me down the next term. *But*, & here's the testimony to my will, they said that they had no influence with me . . . I'm very proud of my will.

We have here the perversity of a character attracted to death as the ultimate way of escape. In his 1926 poem, 'Sad Cure', published in *The Cherwell*, Graham admits, under the guise of John Perry-Perkins, how, 'from the earliest times he could remember/The great witch doctor had been Death.'

Two poems in the same issue of the *Oxford Chronicle* (January 1925) – 'If You Were Dead' and 'Death and Cosmetics' – reveal his morbid interest in death. In the latter he writes, 'Death being but a little while away,/I salve my lips and powder up my face', a Jacobean influence perhaps, but the poem appears under the pseudonym of 'Hilary Trench' which is a name used by Greene when he is at his most morbid. Moreover, these poems were published during the period of 'lucidity' when he was experimenting with Russian roulette.

I questioned Greene about the curious fact that at the time of first love he took to Russian roulette:

N.S.: I can imagine one doing this for all sorts of reasons but when you're in love doesn't seem to be the time to do it. You were in love with Gwen Howell then.

G.G.: Yes, but I think it may have been just after she'd gone away that I began it. I don't know. And the boredom – with one's interests gone as it were – the interest of being in love gone – the boredom had full scope.

It was not only boredom but depression, what he calls in another letter 'this horrid climbing down'. What was intense were the heights of happiness followed afterwards by depression, the nature of which is best expressed in *Brighton Rock*: 'A dim desire for annihilation stretched in him: the vast superiority of vacancy.' Yet we have to add that there is in Greene a strong desire to dare what few others are willing to dare. His practising Russian roulette was in part a very private test of screwing his courage to the sticking place, taking himself up to the wire, what he calls in a 1925 letter 'a final blast in the adventure line'.

Some of his friends at Oxford knew of his attempts at suicide and some did not. Claud Cockburn, who did not know, commented that: 'Either at school, or at Oxford, where people are much more unbuttoned, it would never have occurred to me that Graham was in that state of depression, or that he was anywhere near suicidal. The ordinary gloom, and saying, "Oh my God, what's it all about?" all that, you know, but I was staggered when I read his own accounts of his various attempts at suicide.'[29]

And Sir Harold Acton confided: 'I don't believe that most people who talk about suicide and write about suicide ever intend to commit it. It's a sort of pose, an act.'[30] Certainly one of Greene's poems in *Babbling April* suggests that he might not have been in danger: 'we make our timorous advances to death, by pulling the trigger of a revolver, which we already know to be empty. Even as I do now.' But Greene explains this in his autobiography: 'I wrote a . . . piece of free verse . . . describing how, in order to give myself a fictitious sense of danger, I would "press the trigger of a revolver I already know to be empty." This verse I would leave permanently on my desk, so that if I lost the gamble, it would provide incontrovertible evidence of an accident, and my parents, I thought, would be less troubled by a fatal play-acting than by a suicide.'[31] If we find some difficulty in accepting this perhaps we can more easily accept Greene's statement with its implied reference to Russian roulette, when writing to his future wife about having lied to her over a small matter: 'And sorry's no good as a word. I'd rather have killed myself, been successful, last January than have done it.'

Friends who knew about his attempts at suicide at Oxford did not doubt his intention. Lord Tranmire told me in a hushed voice, fifty-two years after the event, and looking very serious: 'Graham's room was off staircase 24. We were very worried over his attempts at Russian roulette. And in the end we made him promise he would never do it with more than two shots out of the five chambers. Robert Scott talked it over with me and he was the one, rather than I, who had to say to Graham, "Now really this has got to stop."'[32]

And it did stop, but the fascination with the great witch-doctor, Death, and the fight against boredom were to be permanent concerns and, in part, the twin forces behind Greene's writing and travels. The psychoanalysis he had undergone in adolescence had helped but it was not of permanent value – it only suggested another cul-de-sac. Rilke, as Greene pointed out, wrote: 'Psychoanalysis is too fundamental a help for me, it helps you once and for all, it clears you up, and to find myself finally cleared up one day might be even more hopeless than this chaos.'[33] There was no 'perfect cure'.

12

A Seminal Year

. . . no year will seem again quite so ominous . . .
— GRAHAM GREENE

GREENE writes of the 'odd schizophrenic life' he lived during the autumn* term of 1924, but then few young men would have had, like jugglers, so many balls in the air; few would have had the mental, physical and intellectual energy to have kept so many activities going at the same time.

On the one hand, he was the usual student – attending tutorials, drinking coffee at the Cadena, writing an essay on Thomas More, studying the revolution of 1688, taking part in debates at the Union. At the same time, following his trip to the Ruhr, he was learning German in the hope of going into espionage, declaring his love for Gwen Howell, editing the *Oxford Outlook* and operating on the edge of life and death, risking all by playing Russian roulette.

In 1925 he and Claud Cockburn joined the Communist Party of Great Britain, being paid up members for four weeks. In the whole of Oxford there were probably no more than half a dozen members. Joseph Macleod recalled the effect of his friend joining the Communist Party: 'I couldn't believe this. It was a surprise beyond all words. And I said "What for?" and he replied, "Well, I think it's the only future." It shook me to the core. Graham was more stirred and activated by individual victimisation than by class or wage exploitations.'[1] In fact it was a ruse to allow Greene to visit Paris and the Communist headquarters there – another student escapade, but one which, many years later, led to his arrest when he tried to enter American territory. He was by no means a Marxist but he needed an adventure to keep up the excitement level and escape from

---

* 'Why don't we call Autumn the fall like Americans? It's a lovely expression.'
(Letter to Vivien Dayrell-Browning, 28 February 1927.)

the conventional and this is reflected in a letter written a year after his visit to Paris:

> I longed to take fifty pounds out of the bank – overdrawn of course
> – & disappear completely like a conjuror. I always feel that when
> I see these advertisements for 30 pounds single class passages to
> Australia . . . Mexico would be much nicer. Alas! I've never done
> it. The nearest to that sensation was suddenly overdrawing 15
> pounds & departing to Paris. But even then I decided on it three
> days beforehand which is too long, & let my people know two
> days beforehand, which was an arrant weakness in the face of
> convention.[2]

Of course, after failing to capture Gwen Howell, after his flirtation with death through Russian roulette, suddenly going off to Paris would seem to provide another and less final means of escape. But what is missing from this letter is the suggestion that he had ever flirted with death. Doing that had, however, left him still immature, his character seemingly unchanged by his attempts at self-destruction.

He started in January for Paris and the Communist headquarters; and something of his sense of, and hope for, further excitement comes out in a letter describing his rail journey to the coast: 'Going to Southampton the train had to walk through floods halfway up the wheels, feeling its way along invisible rails. An exciting prelude to Paris Communism.'[3]

Greene arrived at the Gare St-Lazare at 9 p.m. and went to the Hotel des Étrangers in the Rue Tronchet to a small back room smelling of urine. But it was not to be all Communism. That first night he visited the Casino de Paris to see Mistinguette, one of the most popular French music hall artistes of the first two and a half decades of the century: 'the thin insured distinguished legs, the sharp "catchy" features like the paper faces of the Ugly-Wugglies in *The Enchanted Castle*'.[4]

The next day he went to the Communist headquarters, where officials, though puzzled by his youth and bad French, on the strength of his being a card-carrying member, invited him to a workers' meeting that night near Menilmontant. But the meeting bored him. It took place at the end of a cul-de-sac in the slums: 'They kept on reading out telegrams from the platform and everyone sang the *Internationale*; then they'd speak a little and then another telegram arrived. They were poor and pinched and noisy; one wondered why it was that they had so much good news coming to them which didn't make any difference at all. All the good news and the singing were at the end of an alley in a wide cold hall; they couldn't get out; in the little square the soldiers stood in tin helmets beside their stacked rifles.'[5]

Graham slipped away and probably that same night went to the Concert Mayol to excite himself 'with naked breasts and thighs'. On his way back to the Rue Tronchet he passed the Madeleine, where prostitutes gathered, but, as he says, he was 'too timid to make [his] first experiment in copulation . . . or else [the girls] were not young or pretty enough' when compared 'with the girls of the Concert Mayol'.[6] This note appears in *A Sort of Life* and immediately afterwards he confesses with characteristic honesty: 'It was certainly no sense of morality which restrained me. Morality comes with the sad wisdom of age, when the sense of curiosity has withered.'

That night, from the window of his hotel, he saw a man and woman copulating: 'they stood against each other under a street lamp, like two people who are supporting and comforting each other in the pain of some sickness'. Greene's clinical horror yet fascination lingered in his mind and surfaced six years later in his second novel, *Rumour at Night Fall*:

> The courting couple came directly below his window into the light of the inn door. He could see the man's lubricious face, the girl's stare of stupid ignorance. A word came up to him . . . 'Mañana' – tomorrow. That was what mañana meant to them – a closer meeting . . . against the wall in a dark street.[7]

Thirteen years after his original shocked observation, he returned again to the event and gave it as the visual experience of Pinkie in *Brighton Rock*:

> The new raw street . . . was empty except for a couple pressed against each other out of the lamplight by a wooden fence. The sight pricked him with nausea and cruelty.[8]

Greene made the most of his short visit to Paris. He bought for 200 francs at Sylvia Beach's bookshop James Joyce's *Ulysses*, then still banned as a work of vice in every English-speaking country: it was a 'huge blue copy . . . the size of a telephone directory'.[9] Also, he had French conversation lessons with a French matron who had clearly decided that the twenty-year-old Greene was a suitable match for her daughter – whom he had not seen. He wrote to his mother of the match-making carried out 'in a most brazen and terrifying manner'. His enjoyment of the situation comes out in the letter:

> She has described her daughter most intimately with regard to character and looks. She has even insisted on my meeting her this afternoon, and corresponding with her from England when I return. She has had the barefaced impertinence, though I assure you I gave her no encouragement, to inquire into my prospects. As though I had asked her blasted daughter in marriage! At any rate she confessed that her daughter was *plus tranquille et plus timide* than herself. And at the end, as she left the room, leaving me limp and helpless, a poor fly hopelessly entangled in the web, powerless even to struggle, she let out her only words of English, 'Pardon me, but you see – I am a mozzer.'[10]

But the fly escaped. 'It's lucky I'll be leaving on Wednesday. She can't possibly make me propose in three days. And yet – the Lord knows what she can't do.'

The rather juvenile aspect of Greene's character at this time, a certain lack of sympathy for the feelings of others and a certain intellectual snobbery, comes out in his attitude towards a provincial literary dinner, when he shows his contempt for cultural pretenders: 'went to dinner with the editor of the *O. Chronicle* yesterday. A most frightful mock. Kind of suburban salon effect, with the kind of literary conversation one gets in Babbitt. Mrs Editor was soulful and talked of the Creative Spirit (with capital letters) – she writes little essays in *Home Chat* . . . and *simply adores* French poetry.' Greene's reponse was to convince them that he was a Philistine by running down literary work for all he was worth, and talking about Einstein and the effect of Gravity on Light, and Planck and the Quantum theory: 'I even convinced an elderly daughter of Professor Soddy (the radium man) that I was studying science!'

*

Another aspect of his schizophrenic life at this time was his urge to become a successful writer, though he complained to his mother of not having time to do anything during that final autumn term at Oxford, he had begun a novel and was concerned about publishing his first book of verse.

Greene had sent Basil Blackwell a volume of prose and verse some time in May 1923. In November Greene, overwhelmed with excitement, told his mother that Blackwell 'was very anxious to publish a volume of mine, but he would have to make one condition, that I contract to sell my next two books of whatever kind to him. I don't think I'll raise any difficulty about that!'★ Blackwell rejected Graham's prose but accepted a small book of verse, the title of which comes from a poem by Edna St Vincent Millay: 'Babbling April I'm thinking of calling it,' he wrote to his mother: 'It is not enough that yearly, down this hill, April/Comes like an idiot, babbling and strewing flowers.'[11]

Blackwell must also have been impressed by Greene's prose for he asked him whether he had ever thought of writing a novel. Did Graham Greene's transparent blue eyes shine? Did the 'gaffer', as Blackwell was called even in his early days, know the significance of his thrown-off remark? We do not know, but Greene knew how to react. To his mother he wrote: 'I said I'd got about a quarter of one written, and he told me to send it along for him to look at. It would be great if he took it on the strength of the quarter. It would give me the necessary urge to finish.'[12] Three months later Blackwell had Scaife and Greene, as editors of the *Oxford Outlook*, to dinner: 'He didn't say anything about my original book [of poems]', Greene reported back to his mother, 'but he said he liked my novel very much and told me to hurry up and finish it.' Blackwell had, all unwittingly, let the genie out of the bottle, and this moment for Greene confirms Novalis's statement: 'my conviction gains infinitely the moment another soul will believe in it.'

With a typical need for privacy, Greene kept his novel a secret from all his undergraduate friends except one. Joseph Macleod recalled: 'During our last months at Oxford, I asked him what he was going to do for a living. He said he would probably take a job under his uncle but that what he hoped to do was to write novels. This astonished me, for none of us so far as I knew had any inkling of any such interest. When I said "What kind of novels?" the reply was "Novels that pay of course. If they don't pay, I won't write them." I took this literally, and for a time thought the less of him. I hadn't realised it was a mere defensive cover for his inner being.'[13]

Greene did as Blackwell bid and worked hard on the novel, entitled at this stage 'Anthony Sant', and the writing of it involved a difficulty he was to have with future novels – it was always the middle portion of a book which caused him the most trouble: 'I've got a bad stretch in front,' he wrote to his mother. 'The first 20,000 words were easy enough, and the last 20,000 will be. It's the bit in between I don't like.'[14] He completed his novel before November 1924. Alas, Blackwell's

★ Basil Blackwell made this a condition of acceptance having first found so many student authors and then lost them when the students went down.

initially warm response was not sustained and the novel was rejected. But Greene did not allow a single rejection to end the matter.

Through the playwright Clifford Bax, the literary agent A. D. Peters was persuaded to take Greene on and soon came to believe in the young man, though Peters was unable to bring his author to success. He sent the novel first to John Lane and when it was rejected,[15] to Heinemann. Greene himself tried to influence events. At Oxford he had known a student who was now at Heinemann's: 'I heard from Katherine Monro,' he wrote to his mother, 'and she has given [the novel] a good report, but says not to build on it as it has to pass four people of various temperaments, of whom she is the junior. However, she's doing her best to boost it!'[16]

Heinemann rejected the novel. Still Greene did not give up. He sent his agent a second volume of verse entitled *Sad Cure* and though Peters did not normally handle verse he made an exception and sent it to John Lane, where J. B. Priestley, a client of Peters, was Lane's principal poetry reader.[17] Three months later Greene was still pressing ahead with 'Anthony Sant' and had started to revise it. Moreover, he and Peters had a plan of campaign: 'In the Vac. I'm going to be introduced to Gerald Cumberland, who is the principal reader for Grant Richards . . . I'm having my novel back and rewriting the end, as my agent thinks my chief difficulty is in the unhappy ending. Then directly after I've met Cumberland, he's going to send it off to Grant Richards.'[18] By August, he was less sanguine, it had after all been rejected by too many publishers and, coolly and accurately, he assessed the novel: 'I've come to the conclusion that the first two thirds is good(!) but the last bit very bad.'[19]

*

There were two shadows looming in those last two terms in Oxford: finals and the need to find a job. The latter involved him in an amazingly wide range of possibilities which suggests that at a conscious level he did not understand the basic drives of his nature, except the need to earn a living. He must have astonished his mother when he told her on 8 February 1925: 'I've just been offered a job at £350 a year (& commissions) in the Oxford & Cambridge Branch of the Lancashire General Insurance Agency, directly I go down . . . Captain Harris, the Oxford Manager, says that that ought easily to mean £800 a year but I have *ma doots!' The Times* was a possibility, but in spite of his journalistic interests at Oxford he appears to have rejected this, partly because of his admired history tutor, Kenneth Bell: 'Kenneth's going to run through my foreign period with me . . . He's very struck with the Levant Consular scheme [presumably another possibility]. He thinks I'd enjoy it far more than *The Times* & I agree.'[20] In March he struck out in another direction: 'A man came down from the Foreign Office the other day & I had an interview. Apparently there are lots of vacancies in the Far East.' And in April he was trying to use the influence of his uncle Edward (head of the Brazilian Warrant Agency) for a job with Asiatic Petroleum:

I wrote to Uncle Eppy about the Petroleum Co., & got a telegram yesterday morning, asking me to meet him at Little Wittenham . . . Tooter, Ave, & Aunt E[va] were there with one or two other vague people & we had lunch at the cottage. I hadn't been in it before, its awfully nice. Uncle E. was rather surprised at my wanting to go into business. As a matter of fact, I've had a desire that way for some years, but imagined the salary was bad. When I heard of this man in the Petroleum Co. starting at £450, I was very attracted. Uncle E. thinks its probably run by Shell & he knows one of the big pots in that & is going to speak to him about me. I only hope he keeps my 'orrible literary past a secret!!'[21]

The other shadow was the final examinations and trying to catch up with neglected academic work. On 26 March he writes of having to 'do a concentrated cram for the next month or two before Finals', though in the same letter he says, 'On Saturday night I danced. Also yesterday . . . I'm just off to see the latest Jackie Coogan [film].' In spite of 'all this frivolity' he was 'keeping up an average of five hours [study] a day' and had 'broken the back of [his] special subject'. He had a rehearsal for finals on 13 March and managed a B on Constitutional History and thought he 'might pull off an alpha' in English History. Foreign and Political Science were his weakest subjects and he was 'hoping for a moderate 2nd now, which I certainly wasn't at the beginning of term'.

Graham's final term was extremely busy, even for him. He was active on the academic side but other interests, more fundamental to his nature, continued to absorb him when he should have been concentrating on his studies. It is true that he had given up the editorship of the *Oxford Outlook* though not his interest in it. To his mother he wrote, 'I've paid my pathetic farewell to the Outlook!' but his next letter home expressed pleasure in its success: 'Extraordinary! The Outlook's sold out again, in spite of increased numbers.'[22] He was looking forward with tremendous anticipation to the publication of his first volume of verse. He could not have known that it would be forty years before he would publish a second in the public domain.* He wrote to his mother in March: 'When my book does come out will you try & get a copy from the library, & ask Aunt Maudy to try & get one out of Boots [library] . . . I must get Aunt N[ono] to do the same' – thus forcing both libraries to buy copies. Also he looked forward to getting 'a little advance advertisement' in *The Berkhamstedian*. Being Greene, he took a careful look at his contract: 'I get 10% on every copy sold & the edition is to be 500 at 4/6d, so I get about 5½d on every copy sold.' He thought that the price of the book at 4s.6d. a copy was scandalous, it being 'very small indeed'.

Babbling April was published on the first of May, and writing to his mother that day he added: 'I've heard from the [Levant] Consular. The Selection Committee is on May 12. I may as well stand in order to have as many irons in the fire as possible.' But on the day before his interview a first review appeared in the *Oxford Chronicle*. Naturally, it stressed that some of Greene's work was first published there, 'the first fruit of a talent which, ripening, should yield a rich harvest.' The influence of Baudelaire and Verlaine was pointed to, but the conclusion was that Greene was not derivative: 'He is singularly original.' It interested Greene that: 'Most people go definitely for "All these things belong to youth"', which was a sonnet listing the disadvantages of youth – 'short-lived loves that yet are over strong . . . Fighting beneath no banner, with no song' – and the disadvantages of age – 'The wheel is broken: there's no course to lay.' The poet, Robert Graves, then rising important, as Greene told his mother, plumped for 'I shall be happy again, when you are gone/ Happy as the insentient stone' – both of these poems in fact recalling his love for Gwen Howell.

Then there came a slashing attack in *The Cherwell* from Harold Acton, at Christ Church, and Graham was immediately involved in controversy.

*

The battle that followed was between two brilliant young men. Harold Acton's stance was that of an aesthete – subtle, knowledgeable, whimsical; his review is well sustained and enjoyable. 'Mr Greene', he says, is 'modest in spite of the multitude of his egos, young in spite of his homesickness for old memories.' He belongs to 'the Centre party, the genius of which is practical rather than adventurous . . . Mr Greene . . . prefers his glass of clear sterilised water . . . is always able to walk into the garden, play tennis . . .

* Greene published privately two small volumes of poetry in 1950 and 1958.

and bridge, enjoy his tea (especially the scones, muffins, crumpets and tea-cake) . . . A girl's red lips are also in the neighbourhood. Thus happy, healthy, lucky, sane, and extremely sentimental, Mr Greene ought to impart much pleasure to reviewers . . . *Babbling April* is a diary of average adolescent moods.'

There is much truth in this, but then Acton comes to the poem about Russian roulette. He sees here a 'repulsive modesty'. 'This false modesty is particularly exasperating, and is often apt to crystallise into cowardice.' What troubled Acton was not that Greene had placed a revolver to his head, but that he did so with 'eyes blind and fingers trembling'. Acton felt a desire 'to throw down the book with disgust, to cry aloud: "For God's sake, be a man!"'

Greene's response appeared in *The Cherwell* on 16 May and he argued that an 'attack by Mr Acton is a recommendation to most readers'. Far from being dismayed at being classed with the Centre party, he accepted the classification since 'reviewers have succeeded in making the poetry of the Centre party sell, and I must confess that I find a strong pleasure in the making of money' – a 'strong pleasure' which has continued throughout life. He concludes by noting how comic it will be to most readers to see 'Mr Acton as a professor of Manliness'.

Acton's reply came two days later. It is more personal and speaks of Mr Greene's 'journalistic nib'. He suggests he should not have written at length about Greene's book but 'dismissed it in a . . . few appropriate words with the vast contempt I feel for Mr Greene . . . with personal knowledge of Mr Graham Greene's grim stolidity . . . I have no doubt he employed his whole week pondering a retort through the crumbling of some bread (Hovis?) during high tea at his lodgings in the Thorncliffe Road.'

It is doubtful that Greene was immediately disturbed by Acton's review; rather he considered the whole business to be good publicity for his book, as his letter to his mother reveals: 'I enclose a page from last week's Cherwell. It was a good advertisement, as there were posters through Oxford with "The Poet's Fight" on them.'[23] The quarrel appeared in the *Westminster Gazette* and 'some Olympian paras' appeared in the *Oxford Chronicle*. 'All grist', writes Greene to his mother, 'to the mill of advertisement.' And yet in some ways, the emotion involved in the episode must have gone deeper. Greene could feel contempt for Acton's supporters ('I only knew Fernauld at second hand and disliked him at second hand extremely. Besides he was a junior subaltern in the enemy camp! Oh these intrigues!') but Acton was a different kettle of fish. Six months after leaving university when Greene wondered, 'what could be more *unimportant* than Oxford and all their little papers,'[24] he could yet flare up over another review by Acton: 'simply inexcusable. It's not a review at all, but a piece of bad-mannered Bystander prose. I wish someone would teach him manners in the method of Lord Queensbury and Wilde . . . It is a piece of gross impertinence.'[25]

Certainly Harold Acton had a sense of his own superiority – a conceit that had something grand about it. Here are two short extracts from letters written by him to Greene when he was editing the *Oxford Outlook*:

19 July 1924
I enclose 'As Dimitri Karamazoff sang on the way to Chaos' for the Outlook. Please do not print it at all if you will not give it the first and most important position in the paper, as I have little desire just at present to see poems of mine in print unless they are noticeable . . . this I consider an important poem.

Monday
I hope that you will receive this enclosed poem in sufficient time to allot it the prominent position it deserves.

Yet Greene recognised Harold Acton's deserved distinction when he described him as the only man in Oxford who could 'mount the guillotine like an aristocrat' and after University when Greene was culturally stranded in Nottingham, he looked back nostalgically to his battles with Acton. Writing to his fiancée he admitted:

. . . the person I miss most now . . . is Harold. It was such intense fun, our mutual 'hate'. And I do respect him. Although I wouldn't admit it to anyone else, his attack in the Cherwell was the best & most awful criticism I've ever had, & my alterations I try to make in my stuff are founded on it. It would have been quite unanswerable, if he hadn't spoilt it by personalities. I've got no one yet I can fight here, & feel empty as a consequence.[26]

Twenty-five years later he was to write to Evelyn Waugh: 'In Italy we saw Harold. How nice & dear he is, & how I didn't realise it at Oxford.'[27]

Alas, Greene's attempts at publicity were not successful. In 1980, Sir Basil Blackwell admitted to me that though he 'published 500 copies of *Babbling April*, [only] 62 were sold in the first year'. And Greene sympathised with his publisher: 'Poor BB lost too much on B.A. to adventure further without financial aid.'[28] Six months later when Blackwell had remained obstinately silent about a second collection of

poems entitled *Sad Cure*, Greene confided to his mother that if
Blackwell kept the manuscript much longer, he would want to scrap it,
'even if he does take it, as I should have scrapped B[abbling] A[pril].'[29]

But the limited sales of his book could not have depressed him too
much. He was writing another novel, he was trying to find a job, he
was studying for finals, and he was in love again.

*

On 18 May, with a student called Harding, Greene went to London
for the Consular interview, which he found not at all frightening:
'They tried to catch me out by shooting out a question, but I caught
them out & they had to apologise!'[30] After this he heard from the
Asiatic Petroleum Company (Uncle Eppy had done his best for his
nephew) and he was enthusiastic about joining them: 'I should be
most tremendously pleased, if I got in. I keep hearing about it from
people, & apparently it's a plum amongst businesses . . . if I have the
luck to get taken, [it] might mean Calcutta, though I should hope
for China or Egypt.' It would seem that the prospect of travel was
what attracted him and that he was trying to avoid his most obvious
route: 'I think even India would be preferable to journalism.'[31] In the
same letter he reported that he had heard from the Consular, that he
had passed the Selection Committee: 'I see the A.P.C. on Thursday
morning . . . I'm seeing the Editor of The Times also on Thurs.'
Meanwhile, he spent his time either working or walking in the
Oxford sun trying to get a suntan.

Disappointments followed. 'I'm afraid nothing will come of [the
A.P.C.] though. Mr Whitehead had mentioned "talent in writing"
in his testimonial, & the man pitched on that. I did my best to
convince him that I'd given all that up months ago. He kept on
harping on the fact that no one could have outside interests in the
A.P.C., with which I most heartily agreed. I shall hear the result in
a day or two, but I misdoubt me . . .'[32] The Asiatic Petroleum
Company offered, if pressed, to take him on for a couple of months'
probation in London – 'in which time I might be able to prove to
them that I had no outside interests', but there was another problem.
His elder brother, Herbert, had applied to the same company and
they were reluctant to have two brothers working for them: 'How
extraordinarily silly. Surely they could segregate us a thousand miles
apart. I hope Herbert gets in all right anyway. It's more important
for him than me.'[33] (More important because Herbert never went on
to University and therefore looked a less attractive bet – which in
later life he proved with singular success to be true.) And so hopes
of China, Egypt and India disappeared.

At *The Times*, he saw Geoffrey Dawson, the Editor, 'an awfully nice man', but Dawson was taking on no one without experience: 'He could promise me a job, if I took a year on a provincial paper first. That's all very well, but that probably means a year without a living wage. The Yorkshire Post he thought the best paper for the purpose. Have any of our family any pull there?'[34]

His hopes of an exciting life in foreign parts were fading. His talent as a writer was the stumbling block to a business career and while it promised a career in journalism, that career would have to start at the bottom of the ladder: 'The worst part of The Times is that it means settling down definitely to spend all my time in England, as Dawson says there is a glut of foreign correspondents & what they have really great need of is leader writers on home politics, which don't seem to me to be particularly fascinating.'[35] Rather desperately, he wrote to his mother on 3 June: 'Another plan which has been suggested to me, if I can't get into a foreign business, is an American Lectureship. There seem to be lots of them going at their small Universities, & thought I might slip through a back door into American journalism.'

But he had reconciled himself to a beginning in provincial journalism. He wrote to a friend on the *Glasgow Herald* on 25 May and probably also to the *Manchester Guardian*: 'The Manchester Guardian is a very bad paper as far as the news side is concerned. It lives on its leader writers.' He also wrote to 'some people, who I think may have influence with the Yorkshire Post.'[36] And keeping in mind his relationship on his mother's side with the family of Robert Louis Stevenson, he decided to approach his Aunt Nono to write to Graham Balfour: 'He might have influence with the Scotsman.' None of these efforts came to fruition, and by 11 June 1925 his final examinations were upon him. He gave his mother a very rational assessment of his chances:

Exams are over for the week. On Thurs. I had English Political History to 1485. I thought that that would be one of my strong papers, but I did mediocrely. In the afternoon Later Constitutional (poor, but I had expected it). Friday morning: Charters & Early Constitutional (poor but less poor than I had expected). In the afternoon Economic History, which was a very pleasant surprise. I think I did a good paper. This morning [Saturday 13 June] Political Science – another pleasant reprieve . . . This afternoon a nice, slack & quite unimportant French Translation paper. So far I think I am a sound, but not good 2nd. Next week however is the tough time; when I may drop into the 3rds.

Although Greene was to write that 'no year will seem again quite so ominous as the one when formal education ends and the moment arrives to find employment and bear personal responsibility for the whole future',[37] 1925 was a seminal year for him in many ways. His first novel had been turned down but his first book of verse accepted. And, had he not involved himself in so many activities at Oxford, he might have become a don (he has a don's passion for accuracy), but apart from his concern at this time about his future, another consuming interest was developing – he was again, and much more obsessively, in love, as a cryptic telegram of 15 March 1925 shows:

> More than earth
> more than fire
> more than light
> Darling.

PART 3

Collector of Souls

13

'Some Ardent Catholic'

Collecting Souls . . . Last addition to collection, undergraduate Versifier.

— GRAHAM GREENE

'A s we grow old,' Greene wrote in his autobiography,[1] 'we are apt to forget the state of extreme sexual excitement in which we spent the years between sixteen and twenty', and he characterised the mess of those years as a mixture of lust, boredom and sentimentality. Also, he spoke tantalisingly of events or affairs *almost* begun: 'a frightened longing for the prostitute in Jermyn Street, where there were real brothels in those days, an unreal romantic love for a girl with a tress of gold and a cousin who played tennis when it was almost too dark to see the ball.'[2]

The cousin was Ave Greene, beautiful then and still beautiful in old age. Herbert, Raymond and Graham all entered into a rivalry for her. The emotion generated by those games of tennis is reflected in 'Prologue to a Pilgrimage',[3] Greene recalling the 'twilight world of calf-love' when the 'wind blew her skirt tightly round her knee.'[4] 'Dusk . . . dropped down till Anthony could see little more than a vague and mothlike flitter of white, across the shadowy net.'[5] When he came to write *The Ministry of Fear* twenty years later this vision of Ave remained unchanged: 'He was waiting for someone at a gate in a lane: over a high hedge came the sound of laughter and the dull thud of tennis-balls, and between the leaves he could see moth-like movements of white dresses.'[6] Thinking of her, Anthony Sant, a black boy, recalls in a phrase which has masturbatory connotations that he was a 'nigger': 'Yet in bed he beat his sheets in an excitement of uncertainty . . . she was attracted by him.'

In a letter written to Greene in their mutual old age, Ave recalled the innocence of those tennis games, hardly realising (though in retrospect wishing she had) the intense emotion she generated in the three Greene brothers.

As for prostitutes in Jermyn Street, Ave's brother 'Tooter' told me that he used to go with Greene to London: 'We were both young men obsessed with sex, and we went on the razzle dazzle.' In Jermyn Street in 1977 with his brother Sir Hugh, Graham recalled that he was once in a brothel there. He patted the original building as he passed and was much taken by the notion that his older brother Raymond, already well-established as a medical man, was at a medical conference next door – on the other side of the wall in the same building.

The 'girl with a tress of gold' was Clodagh O'Grady, daughter of Haddress O'Grady, a master at Berkhamsted. Many schoolboys were in love with Miss O'Grady, including Greene's special friend, Eric Guest. Clodagh O'Grady herself has denied both her golden tresses and beauty – 'my hair was in pigtails and I had broken my nose at the age of seven'. But Greene remembers getting his aunt Maud to pass a letter from him to the girl with golden hair.[7] Alas, no early love letters survive, since, as Clodagh O'Grady told me, she destroyed them, 'very properly, as I then thought', when Greene married.

While at Oxford Greene tried to persuade himself that he was in love with a young waitress at the 'George' in the Cornmarket,[8] and H. D. Ziman, a contemporary of Greene at University and later literary editor of the *Daily Telegraph*, remembered that an attractive waitress he knew at Oxford 'mentioned that she had been out with Graham, among others, and described him as "soft". Her name was Rose.'

Just as Greene's feelings for Ave Greene appeared in his first novel, so his feelings for Miss O'Grady, and possibly the waitress, provided the inspiration for his 1937 story, 'The Innocent',[9] which brings together the child's innocent acceptance of sexuality with the adult's worldly experience of it.

The hero (so like Greene as to be indistinguishable) takes Lola, a girl he picked up in a bar, to his home town for a night of love-making. The hero is seeking the sense of his first years – the 'smell of innocence' – and he finds it when he sees children coming from the same dancing teacher's home he had visited as a child. He remembers when no more than six how he loved his partner on those occasions with an intensity he had never felt since – 'children's love . . . has a terrible inevitability of separation because there *can* be no satisfaction'. He remembers also games of blindman's buff at birthday parties 'when I vainly hoped to catch her',[10] and he recalls in *A Sort of Life*: 'the black shiny shoes with snappy elastic and the walk down King's Road [after dancing lessons] . . . holding someone's hand for fear of slipping.'[11]

In the story, he recovers a message he left his first love in a hole in the woodwork of a gate twenty-five years before – the scrap of paper has his initials below 'the childish inaccurate sketch of a man and woman. It was a shock to see . . . a picture of crude obscenity.'[12] Later that night, he 'began to realise the deep innocence of that drawing. I had believed I was drawing something with a meaning unique and beautiful; it was only now after thirty years of life that the picture seemed obscene.'[13]

Between the innocence of the child's transitory love and the young man's casual sexual encounters, there was the experience of true romantic love which Gwen Howell had inspired. It came again to Greene when he met Vivien Dayrell-Browning in 1925.

*

Their meeting came at a time when the safe life of Oxford was coming to an end and he had to face a future outside the secure bounds of home and university. And he was in a mood for change, 'feeling frightfully bored . . . absolutely fed up with the amusements Oxford provides. It was just like a Paris back street.'[14]

In this frame of mind he wrote an article for the *Oxford Outlook* which linked sex, religion and the cinema. His thesis was that most people were 'considerably oversexed': 'We either go to Church and worship the Virgin Mary or to a public house and snigger over stories and limericks; and this exaggeration of the sex instinct has had a bad effect on art, on the cinematograph as well as on the stage.'[15] This sweeping statement brought him a short, sharp rebuke – linguistic and religious – from Vivien Dayrell-Browning. She wrote to him that one did not 'worship' the Virgin Mary – one 'venerated' her, the correct term being 'hyperdulia'. He replied, the letter undated, to 'Miss Dayrell' on Balliol Junior Common Room notepaper:

> I most sincerely apologise. I'm afraid any excuses will seem very lame. But I wrote the article in a frightful hurry, and without preconceiving it, as the paper was already in press. At the same time I was feeling intensely fed up with things, and wanted to be as offensive all round as I could . . . I really am very sorry. Will you forgive me, and come and have tea with me as a sign of forgiveness?

On 6 March 1925, he wrote to his mother:

> I got a furious letter from some ardent Catholic in Blackwell's publishing firm about a chance remark I made in my article on the

cinema. So I wrote a *sweet* letter back apologising & asking her to tea. She's turned out very charming & not nearly so religious as her furious letter made me believe. So once again out of the lion has come forth sweetness!

This was not the first time Vivien had corrected his work, nor, as he was to realise, was it their first meeting. She had earlier found 'a curious lapse . . . in a poem of his – he spoke of birds' eggs pressed between blotting paper, next to a reference to something that could have been pressed between blotting paper.'[16] This must have been in the poem 'Sensations' in *Babbling April*, and the emended lines were: 'How timorously, like an old fashioned collector of/wild flowers do we gather our sensations and press/them in the damp blotting paper of our mind.' They first met on one of Greene's visits to Blackwell's. He was to give the date as 17 March 1925, but it must have been earlier. Vivien was taking dictation from Basil Blackwell. Her account of this meeting – fifty-five years afterwards, when they had been separated for many years – was rather cool and detached: 'I did not take especial notice . . . He wore, I think, the usual grey flannels and probably a blazer (Balliol) but I'm not sure . . . He had fair hair with a sort of quiff or rather wave on the top, was pale with pale blue eyes. I don't remember anything of [his] conversation with Basil.'[17] But Greene remembered that when he left Blackwell's office that morning 'and started over to Berkhamsted with [Eric] Guest', he mentioned 'with a sense of exhilaration that [he'd] just seen an awfully pretty girl at B.'s!'

Their second meeting, in his room at Balliol, was decisive. He fell in love with her and that, for the young Greene, meant complete devotion. It must have been a stunning surprise that the girl he had spoken to Guest about should be the same girl to come to his room for tea. In a letter of 26 June 1925, he recalled with some ingenuousness his feelings at the beginning of their relationship:

When I got your letter about my article in the Outlook, I was feeling frightfully bored . . . and I read your letter, and this seemed something fresh. And I made a vow with myself that if you were pretty, I'd suggest myself into love with you whatever else you might be. Just as a change from Oxford. That's why I was so anxious for you to have tea with me, and there was only one small scrap of real apology in that first letter. I suppose it was the right punishment to fall really frantically in love with you, without any suggesting at all. And I deserve what I've got. If I'd known what was going to happen, I should never have answered that letter at all, never apologised. I daresay I shouldn't if I'd been feeling merry at the time I got it.

Vivien remembered having tea with him at Balliol. Later he took her to see Greta Garbo at the Super Cinema and then there was tea at the 'Candied Friend' which was a 'beautiful tea shop on the first floor in High Street with home-made elaborate cakes'. Greene's letters suggest a mind agile in recalling these meetings and remembering anniversaries. 'Darling,' he wrote, 'will you think of me at – say 10.30 on Wednesday morning – I think that's about the anniversary [of their meeting.] My dear, you were not looking plain that morning; you were at your second best I admit but your second best is a good reach above other people's best . . . That morning you were merely awfully pretty, & not as you are usually awfully beautiful.' He went over their early meetings with fervent emotion. On 13 July he wrote:

It was in that strange time, when I only knew you a little, even though I loved you a lot. And your name was Miss Dayrell then, and I only thought of you as Vivienne to myself. And you'd just been to Paris, and I wanted you to come to a long forgotten play called The Ship, by . . . Ervine . . . and you nearly didn't come, because you'd been to a dance the night before, and you wrote a very firm note about it (I have it still, the ink faded, the paper yellowed – it was in the days of the three-halfpenny post), and it was to Dear Mr Graham Greene, and luckily I didn't get it till after I'd telephoned . . . and 'You were a Queen in Jerusalem, and I was a heathen slave.' . . . And you'd been looking more lovely than I'd ever seen you before *then*. And what was as good, I began to feel that evening that we really knew each other. I wonder if you began to feel that too. The result was that . . . I couldn't go to bed, and walked two miles beyond my digs . . . wondering how long I ought to wait before asking you to come out again.

Nine months later, in Nottingham, he checked the date of the St John Ervine play: 'I looked up the date of The Ship. It was April 17 [1925], so that Sunday will be the tenth anniversary of my meeting you and the ninth of the certainty that I was in love with you! A whole month before I was certain . . . but I plead . . . in defence of my own slowness that until The Ship I'd only seen you twice for a few moments of business in the office, once at tea and once at The Three Women.'[18]

Greene pursued Vivien with unremitting energy. He bombarded

her with letters (sometimes he wrote three times a day) and telegrams. In those early days of their relationship, he was to remember vividly the briefest of meetings, such as going into Blackwell's and having 'G[ladys] L[oveless] say, "Come in James," and her laughter and apology brought you out of your [cubby]hole for about three seconds. I had to feed on that for days!'[19] Although his first few letters to her have an undergraduate flavour – flippant, bumptious and sometimes outrageous – his infatuation is apparent in every one. 'If you are a fanatic, I admire your restraint. I'm a fanatic on one subject (you), and all my letters have been full of it. I can't keep off it.'[20]

There was often an imaginative lightness to their correspondence. Vivien wrote to him on 2 June 1925: 'Do you know you've had a letter every day this week? I shall appoint myself chairman of a committee empowered to look into the matter & draw up a report', which brought Greene's reply, speaking on behalf of mythical shareholders, that they were fully satisfied with the Chairman, and he added privately: 'I can't say this in the Board Room, but the Chairman is the most wonderful person in the world.'

*

The object of his love was nineteen years old. According to Sir Basil Blackwell Vivien had begun working for him in 1920, when she was only fifteen. She was remarkably precocious, having published verse in *Poetry Review* when she was only thirteen and a volume of verse with Blackwell's, *The Little Wings*, when she was sixteen. G. K. Chesterton wrote an introduction to this book in which he said: 'I should not write an introduction to any work which I did not think promising and beautiful; and I think this work very beautiful and still more promising. The child who has still some touch with the fairies is not only more admirable, but really more terrible than the *enfant terrible*': a rather avuncular pat on the head for the young writer. Here is an example of her work written when she was fourteen:

> Cold lucent depths where fishes swim,
> Crimson floating flowers of the sea,
> Ribbons of silver, long and slim,
> Coral caverns rosy and dim . . .
> These are the things I see.

The book was dedicated 'To Mummydar who has shown me beauty everywhere' and her mother added the following note: 'All the work of my young daughter contained in this first collection of her verse is original and has been written without aid of any kind. I wish to acknowledge the immediate recognition and subsequent kindness shown in respect to my little girl's work by the *Poetry Review* since 1918. Vivienne's present age is 15½ years.'

Whatever the disclaimers, there is the suggestion of maternal influence and patronage and Vivien recalled the shame and mortification the publication of the book brought her. Her mother had collected the poems without telling her and had written the dedication herself: 'I felt', she said, 'as if I should go up in flames.'

When she was seventeen, Vivien became a convert to Roman Catholicism and Catholicism was the subject of her poem entitled *Lux Mundi*, published in *Blackfriars* magazine – one of her more mature poems to survive. The following lines are from the third stanza:

> Like acolytes the candles stood
> Ranged with their flames of restless gold,
> Above them hung the glimmering Rood,
> Below, the Body and the Blood,
> O Mystery no words have told!
> Nor have men's hearts yet understood –
> (O strange and still Beatitude!)
> The Holy Thing their hearts may hold.

She has remained a devoted Catholic.

While Greene's obsession with her can be traced through his avalanche of letters, her attitude to him has to be discovered through those same letters, for few of hers have survived. Certainly they had interests in common and she was a young woman of independent mind, though confined by the stricter conventions of the time, and obviously not a rebel. She told me: 'My mother chose my clothes and I was never consulted and at that time I wore a hideous black hat, suitable for a woman of forty and felt ill at ease in it', though photographs of the time show that she was attractive (what was once called 'well-endowed'), with black hair. Greene wrote to her: 'You carry magic with you always . . . it is in your eyes, & your voice, & your long dark hair, & your whiteness.' In the same letter he described the images of her that he was taking away from a weekend spent together, 'one of them will be you washing in the bathroom . . . your face so perfectly angelic when it looks pink & scrubbed & glimmery with water.'[21] The impression she made on him was best expressed in terms of a 'Wanted' notice which he sent to her:

Wanted – by Me. Miss Dayrell

Alias Vivienne, Dear one, Darling, darling heart, marvellous wonderful, adorable one, Angel, Loveliest in the world, Sweetest
Heart, Dear only love for ever, sweet one, old thing, dear desire.

Description: Hair – dark & lovely & long; eyes, grey-green &
more beautiful than any other eyes; figure, perfect; complexion,
wonderful; skin in texture as a rose petal; feet: very small & very
adorable; disposition: sleepy. Known to her companion in crime
as My Love. May be infallibly recognised by her stars [Vivien's
code word for kisses].

Behind this adulation, one has the impression of a girl excited and
flattered by Greene's courtship of her, but not emotionally involved
with him – enjoying her power, but keeping him within bounds. It
was to be a long wooing. 'His letters were most beautiful and
touching and these showed me his emotions and feelings more than
he could do personally and made me understand him and care for
him gradually.'[22]

One undated letter preserves, as in aspic, a day's experience of love
and college life for Greene:

It was a really marvellous spring day, sky eggshell blue. And I had a
riotous lunch at Thorncliffe Rd [Greene's digs] with Braine-Hartnell
(do you know him? He writes quite good poetry), George [Whit-
more], [Robert] Scott & Bill [?] . . . About 2.30 we staggered down
to the river, got into a punt & steered a strange & erratic course to
Tims – I can't imagine how we kept our balance – as it was we
smashed into every other boat we met. And we got back to Balliol
just in time for dinner, & the trees in the quad were beginning really
to smell like early summer, & in my pigeon hole were TWO notes
from you, which was enough to add a climax to the day, & the
Outlook, & I tried in vain, standing rather precariously on the hall
steps to understand the introductory paragraph, & B. H. tried to
explain it but his brain was equally befogged, & he only made it more
muddled. And dinner made us more 'happy' still, so much that I
can't remember what happened later. I've just looked up the two
notes I found. Even you commented on the day – 'What a heavenly
day it was yesterday! And to-day! I've had to send home poste haste
for summer frocks – I *do* hope it will be like this for Eights Week . . .'

Some of Greene's friends and relatives – not themselves under the
spell of love – have given a rather different impression of Vivien

and Greene's love for her. While Eric Guest confirmed that 'She had the most wonderfully creamy complexion, and was handsome', Greene's cousin, Ben Greene, described her this way:

> She was very velvety, with a feline manner, but I shouldn't have thought claws: she had a rather too consciously sweet manner for me and I like dry drinks, but she was beautiful, and I think desirable . . . but there was more than that in her, much more, and of course I felt discomfort with her, only because she was a deeply religious Catholic and I don't know anything about it and don't want to.

Ben's sister Ave, recalling the days of Greene's heady love for Vivien, said, 'Graham was probably very under-developed. He was completely infatuated and it was like a schoolboy thing – he had a crush on her.' And 'Tooter' Greene concluded, 'Graham, as I remember him, then as now, was always looking for what was not there.'

There is a bittersweet taste to some of his letters, as though he regretted being in her power:

> It must be rather fun collecting souls, Vivienne. Like postage stamps. Last addition to collection Undergraduate Versifier, a common kind. Fair specimen, but badly sentimentalised. Colouring rather faded. Will exchange for Empire Exhibition Special Stamp, or ninepence in cash . . . you will never be more than mildly interested in that blasted non-existent soul of mine. This letter will help you analyse the specimen won't it . . . I've never really been in love before, only suggested myself into a state of mild excitement in which I could draw fifteen bob out of the Westminster Gazette for a piece of verse. I can't do that now . . . I can't think nearly clear enough to fit anything into a metre. You wouldn't expect me to write verse, when I was blind drunk would you? . . . You can't sympathise I suppose, any more than I can with the excitement and scurry of ants.

Vivien's reply has not survived, but on 28 May, Greene returned to the subject of his 'blasted non-existent soul' which she must have taken up:

> *Soul.* Forgive my heavy sarcasm. When I'm just going to die, I daresay I shall find the Earth saltless, & I daresay that I shall turn a trifle religious, as a kind of insurance, in case there *is* something in it. I know I shall, as I did do once when I thought I was in danger of a sudden finish. You see I haven't the courage of my

non-faith. I'm sorry I was dogmatic about my lack of soul. I'll give you even chances that I may have one, in which case it's a small dirty beast not worthy of your trouble. And that's only 30% sarcastic.

Greene ought to have been working for his final examinations yet he was distracted by love and regretting the time he had wasted:

I went out to Abingdon this afternoon, and am now making a pious resolution to do two hours work after tea. I wish I could do all the stuff I should have done in the last two years, so I could get a first and stay on in Oxford. I keep on being haunted by the fact that in a month's time I shan't be here and you will be here . . . I wish you weren't so frantically good at weaving spells, Vivienne.

Returning from an unsuccessful interview – possibly with Asiatic Petroleum – he wrote: 'When will you cheer me up again? As a Catholic you ought to like doing good deeds. And I do need cheering up, something terrible. I've just come back from town & I feel I shall never, never, never be a successful businessman. And it's a horrid feeling.'[23]

On 5 June, only six days before his final examinations began and before leaving to visit his parents ('I've got something a bit unpleasant to go through then, which I can't tell you about'), it is the need to see her which obsesses him:

I want to see you again just once before I go home. It's selfish of me when you . . . promised all those days running after Finals. But quite literally I can't bear not seeing you, if it's only for half an hour . . . I'm just appealing for mercy. You must have lunch or tea or dinner or something free today or tomorrow . . . Do Please. It's no use my trying to tell you how desperately I want you to. The lucky fellow Macleod looked in here [Balliol] for a drink a moment ago – he's in love with someone who's in love with him. It's no use my trying to go to bed. You gave me such a glorious time tonight that I'm down in the depths again now . . .

Do come out today if possible even if you'll be bored. I want you to come so frightfully badly, & I'm ashamed of myself. I didn't think I'd ever need any one so badly.

Greene then attached a piece of verse he had written explaining why he had been unable to write poetry since he had met Vivien. It is a curious piece: 'Consciousness comes creeping down the stair/In the dark well of Mind . . . formed but of a morning and an afternoon'; and he questions: 'How dare I bring this thing into the light,/Place it in a Pawnshop, where the world may see?/Constable, Sergeant, O God there, in the night,/Bring your own manacles & handcuff me.' Following this passage came a final plea: 'Won't you be merciful and make it lunch between office and office this morning? I shall be in Balliol all this morning, if you can send James with an answer. I'm awfully ashamed to have crashed like this, from my self-centredness, but I can't help that.'

Her reply that she would see him brought an immediate response: 'You glorious, marvellous, most beautiful, most adorable person in the world. You are simply the symbol of the Absolute.'

It appears he pressed for that meeting in order to propose marriage, perhaps inspired by Macleod's success,[24] but he was not accepted and his letters on 6 and 8 June give some insight into what must have been a fraught encounter.

Greene's self-deprecation suggests a deep personal uncertainty. 'I must have seemed pretty futile in my burblings, but I haven't had much practice you see. I've never loved anyone before enough to want to marry them.' But part of this disparagement is a reaction to Vivien's response to his proposal: 'You've made me feel an awful brute, Vivienne. I don't in the least want to be the first person to depress you. And for God's sake, don't be. There's nothing you've got to "repay" me. It's all on the other leg. And what does anything matter, if we are never going to see each other again, after the next fortnight?' And he goes on, with some percipience:

> You know it's all rot about things being quickly over when one's young. It's the middle-aged who don't feel as deeply. They couldn't go on feeling things hard for twenty years and live. And besides it's not a question of how many months one feels things at their strongest, it's a question of what one gets away to in those months, and whether one can get back afterwards. I don't want anyone to be 'gentle' to me, I feel I want someone to hit me, so that I could hit back, or else get into a rugger scrum or something. When I get really excited or frightened, then I can think about nothing but my own skin.[25]

Perhaps the most poignant indication of the emotion of that meeting was his comment: 'I'm awfully glad you *didn't* cry the other night; I was just keeping hold of my own feelings, and I couldn't if you had. And that would have been ridiculous.'

We can trace some of Vivien's reasons for refusing to marry him in these two letters. 'Of course,' he wrote, 'it's not the danger that's the objection, because if I could make you love me, it would seem . . . paltry. When I really think about myself, I realise the impossibility of that. I know I'm soiled goods, even though I've been trying to put on paint since I met you. And I'm grateful for what you've done for me, even though I know the paint won't last, when I can't see you again. Probably I shouldn't be in Oxford now, if I hadn't met you. The thin ice was showing visible and audible signs of cracking.'[26] The suggestions of 'danger' that come through here are Greene's imperfection – instability, rather – in Vivien's eyes. Instability there certainly was in his emotional state and in his prospects for the future – the uncertainty of that future could be a danger for her. His protestations suggest that he had tried to 'paint over the cracks' and remain stable. But there is also a suggestion that she was afraid of marriage:

> If you are fond of me, I don't see why you won't do what I want. I know you are fond of everybody (except Cockburn! . . .). But even though you are fond of everyone, are you never going to marry anyone? Couldn't you say there'd be a chance of your consenting, if you still like me at the end, say, of a year? Marriage doesn't mean seeing just one person all day long. You'd see far less of me than you do of someone like Mott [editor at Blackwell's] or Blackwell.[27]

But Vivien's basic objection to marrying him would seem to be a matter of her religious beliefs and his unsatisfactory attitude towards those beliefs.

> I do recognise that you have your own work to do, I mean your religion's more important than mine . . . I do admire . . . you for it, even though I have pretended to laugh sometimes. You might not approve of my principal reason for becoming a Catholic, before I know anything about it. There'd be no reason to be frightened, which was what you said the other night. Isn't it just possible (and I'm not laughing, or being wily, but asking a question on something which you know more about than I do), isn't it possible that the breaking of your crucifix meant that perhaps you weren't right?[28]

No doubt Vivien had many good reasons for not accepting his proposal of marriage, but Greene had hit upon the nub of the matter – religion. The young atheist had fallen in love with the young convert, and already was beginning to interpret the symbols of the Catholic faith.

Although Vivien had decided to end their relationship 'after the next fortnight', Greene, being, as he described himself, 'a cowardly opportunist', did not give up. His reason told him that it was much better not to see Vivien again but he could not bear that. He wanted to put off 'the worst miserableness' as long as he could.

Returning to Oxford after three days of swotting at Berkhamsted, his arrangement with Vivien was that they should continue to meet until, as a note from Vivien said, the final goodbye 'on Friday 20th by the river at Wolvercote', and a small present from her was waiting for him: 'But what a lovely seal, Vivienne. It appeared so opportunely and in place, as I was reading all about the 1810s. The plain but beautiful Jemima on the letter back, the Prince Regent bowling down the Brighton road, and Jane Austen young women chatting to Jane Austen young men in Jane Austen parsonages.'

He refers to their brief separation: 'Can you realise how awful this long absence has been? With the continual heat dancing on tropical leaves, like a solid mass of May flies, and the stench of decay coming up from the Orinoco.' But he was mainly 'on edge to hear about the 13th . . . Will you make it five minutes to seven at Carfax? Because the bus goes very punctually at 7. And pray, pray that it may be fine. And remember to give God the exact date this time, because I'm not sure that he hasn't antedated it again.' The next day, a Sunday, they met again:

Do you mind very much my being disreputable this evening? I have to tea with people down in the town, and shan't have time to . . . change . . . Anyway the Elizabethan Singers is quite a bourgeois show . . . Eight o'clock outside the Y.W.C.A. I spent five minutes . . . in sensible, sober consideration, wondering quite inhumanly and without prejudice, in pure aesthetic argument, which was the most beautiful – you or the sunset behind us on the road from Wytham. Of course I decided on you. The strange thing is that I can't be very depressed, when I'm with you, even though you insist on not marrying me. It's strange that just seeing you is so satisfactory.

Perhaps he had an inkling that she would not hold to the date of their final separation, and he must have been encouraged in this when she sent him flowers during the final week of his examinations: 'You darling! And roses are my favourite flower they really are. With them as a gage I shall do frightfully well in the battle tomorrow . . . I shall be gloriously happy tonight . . . 7.45 at the corner of Balliol then.' (6.45 p.m., 16 June 1925.)

The next day, after examinations and after the history dons had given dinner to students going down, Greene admitted in a letter written half an hour before midnight that during the whole time he was thinking about Vivien. The next day there were more examinations, yet his mind was firmly on how to arrange another meeting with her: 'we could catch the 6.2 to Didcot and get up on the Berkshire Downs. And in case there wasn't any hotel or anything, I could bring strawberries and bananas and apples and oranges and lump sugar and soft sugar, and we could picnic on the Downs. I think they are just a stroll from the station. And I won't chatter, if you don't want me to. Can't you manage it? Say yes.'

He finished his examinations at 5 p.m. on Thursday 18 June and sent Vivien the following telegram at 5.07 p.m.: 'New plan. Meet me 6.30. Do please. Graham.' In two days' time, they were, by her decree, to part for ever. Because examinations and his student days had ended, when they said goodbye at Wolvercote she allowed him to kiss her – after three months of intense wooing – but Vivien's intention was to make the parting final. The full strength of his hopeless love comes out in the first letter he wrote on returning to Berkhamsted:

You were quite right about saying goodbye outside Oxford. I couldn't have stood the bus journey back. And it is of value to have been the first person you've kissed. But it doesn't make me feel a bit pleased with myself. It only makes me wonder how somebody like you can exist, who's willing to do something you don't want to do, just because a friend of yours is so mundane that he can't do without it. And even if I can't say as much, I can say that I've never kissed anyone I've wanted to really badly before, or held off for so long, for fear of offence. You are so precious that I am afraid of doing or saying anything which might prevent me seeing you . . . It's all so silly that I should love someone, whom I should want to marry, whatever conditions she might choose to make, but just the someone who wouldn't marry me on any conditions. It's bad luck at the least.

He describes in this letter a dream he had about her on the train: 'I was on top of a bus with you at Carfax, and I could actually feel you there . . . your voice in my ear. It made me feel extraordinarily queer when I woke up, because there were no sense values left to show which was the dream, the train or the bus. Both had touched all my senses. But the train won in the end . . . my head's just buzzing with you the whole time "Vivienne, Vivienne, Vivienne," like the endless train wheels that go round and round when one's under gas.'

Once at Berkhamsted, Graham asked Vivien to see him again: 'Make it as soon as you can. And it will be the You-Graham, because now the Oxford one's gone, it's the only one that's left.' At the same time, his style is calmer – perhaps the Oxford Graham *had* gone – and his mind is already turning to different things: 'I wish I could work at something or other . . . but I can't. All the beginnings of novels and things . . . were started before I met you, and they don't seem to be me at all. And I haven't got any new ideas . . . I wish you could supply me with some plots . . . It would be fun to have Vivienne Dayrell and Graham Greene on the title page. I should feel I'd got hold of a bit of you then.'

Although he could still write: 'Goodbye, dear love for ever, I'm yours every scrap of me for ever . . . Do tell me that you'll let me see you again soon', he could also write: 'I've succeeded at last in getting to work on a novel. I'd only done about two pages of it last January, and so I've just altered the plot completely to fit in with my new state of mind. I really think it's good so far, much better than that awful thing which is reposing in your office now. When I'm working at that, I can nearly forget you altogether. But as I cannot do more than 1500 words a day, it only fills out three or four hours. But that's better than nothing.'[29]

One has the impression he is settling down and coming to terms with his passion, and perhaps even with his loss of Vivien. Not only is his style more collected, his imagery is powerful but more cerebrally controlled – neater:

I know that I'm 80% mundane, and therefore I shall probably marry someone some time. And I shall probably also be in love with her. But I shall not love anyone more than you, because one can feel perfectly well when one has reached the ultimate point of an emotion. It's like putting one's hand on a wall, but a wall that is so thick that there's nothing on the other side . . . I've been quite a lot in love [before], but I've never got as far as touching that wall, which is the end. I don't suppose one does it often in a lifetime, and so I dare say I shan't again.[30]

There is also a sense of depression in his assessment of his talents and his prospects, which could be the result of exhaustion, mental and emotional, after those last months at Oxford:

> I don't think I shall ever do anything much. If I do it'll be all your doing, because you made me want to do something big, as a kind of way of keeping in touch with you. Otherwise I shall just sink into a crowd of nonentities abroad, and you'll forget all about me . . . If I go on publishing things, or do anything else more worthwhile, it will be simply a signal to remind you not to forget me entirely, a ring on your mental telephone.[31]

Judging from his letters to his mother, Greene does not appear to have told her at this time of his love for Vivien, but there is one reference which suggests that by 18 May, the pressure of Vivien's Catholicism was having some effect on him. He wrote: 'Yesterday I was very energetic. Not only did I sit through a long R.C. service, which was rather fun!! but also went for a long walk' and he added rather cryptically: 'I went out with someone to Eynsham for lunch.' It could be this visit to a Roman Catholic church that he described to Vivien in a letter of 30 May 1925:

> I went and lit the candles, although I felt fearfully nervous, as I thought I ought to be doing genuflexions and things. And there was a very bourgeois looking woman praying, and she watched me out of the corner of the eyes. And I felt like a disguised heretic being examined in the rites of the Church by a hooded Inquisition. I explained (mentally) that the candles were yours, in case I got Grace or something queer on false pretences, and then I wished for the usual thing that I wish for every time I eat my first fruit, or go under the alternative ladder, or swallow a plum stone.

There is no suggestion here that he was on the road to conversion – but the figure in the background of the incident is Vivien. In the same letter he had written: 'I'll do anything you want (almost. I won't go into a monastery, even if you ask me to).'

Perhaps Claud Cockburn, who remained a friend of Greene all his life, was the one person who understood Greene's dilemma at this time:

> I knew him before Vivien. Quite early on, Graham said to me that he had fallen madly in love with this girl, but she wouldn't go to bed with him unless he married her. So I said, 'Well, there are lots

of other girls in the world, but still if that's the way you feel, well go ahead and marry her. What difference does it make?' And then he came back and said (this went on over quite a number of weeks), 'The trouble is that she won't marry me unless I become a Catholic.' I said, 'Why not? If you're really so obsessed with this girl, you've got to get it out of your system.' He was rather shocked, because he said, 'You of all people, a noted atheist.' I said, 'Yes, because you're the one that's superstitious, because I don't think it matters. If you worry about becoming a Catholic, it means you take it seriously, and you think there is something there.' I said, 'Go right ahead – take instruction or whatever balderdash they want you to go through, if you need this for your fuck, go ahead and do it, and as we both know, the whole thing is a bloody nonsense. It's like Central Africa – some witchdoctor says you must do this before you can lay the girl.' And then to my amazement, the whole thing suddenly took off and became serious and he became a Catholic convert. So then I felt perhaps I'd done the wrong thing.[32]

14

The World Well Lost

Women are like dreams – they are never the way you
would like to have them.

               – LUIGI PIRANDELLO

'I'M seeing B.A.T. [the British American Tobacco Company] at
3 o'clock tomorrow . . . afternoon,' he wrote to Vivien. 'Please
send your black cat which I return herewith (X) to sit on the manager's
shoulder. Do please *will* hard that the man likes me and takes me on.
You see I really do believe that you are a talisman.'[1] He was desperately hoping he would get the job.

Apart from hoping Vivien had talismanic powers, he took the
precaution of having with him a special photograph of himself: 'I
posed at Gillman's, stuck my jaw out, & looked as though I'd just
ordered a lot of coolies to be thrashed. Quite the White Man's Burden
touch.'[2] Having deliberately created the right photographic image,
he felt he would have 'to live up to [it] at the interview'.

The B.A.T. is still in Millbank overlooking the Thames. Graham
was daunted 'by the great concrete slab . . . with the uniformed
porter like an officer of some foreign country demanding credentials',
and in the lift were 'several middle-aged men . . . carrying files
carefully like babies.'[3] Aided by a reference from his Balliol tutor
Kenneth Bell ('though not properly developed, there are in him
qualities of leadership'),[4] and Vivien's support, he was able to send
her a telegram after his interview: 'You Angelic Talisman believe
have pulled it off.' And Vivien would have been deeply interested
since her father worked for the Company in Rhodesia and was to die
there in harness.

Archibald Rose, a director of the firm, whom Greene described to
Vivien as being like 'a nice Miss Nesbitt rich uncle from India, who
remembers when he was young', took to Greene. Rose touched on
all the points which would interest an adventure-seeking young man
and made working in China sound fascinating: 'Right up in the

interior and no indoor office work hardly, but riding about the place inspecting things, never doing the same thing for more than a week.' And whereas the director of Asiatic Petroleum objected to Graham's interest in writing, Archibald Rose stressed that 'people with outside interests . . . found the loneliness least trying'.

There were numerous applicants but once Greene was invited by Sir Bruce Porter for a stiff medical examination ('they won't afford first class sailing tickets to men who are going to get cholera at the first opportunity') he knew the B.A.T. wanted him. But the fact that he was now set to go to China was not a clear victory for Greene, for his going could only help to bring his relationship with Vivien to an end. Vivien herself continued their meetings only reluctantly.

Greene next tried to persuade Vivien to spend the night at Aylesbury so that they could meet, but the impropriety of such a meeting, which Graham recognised, made it impossible: 'I know those ghastly people. They carry a great *Why* on their foreheads, like the Jews Ephods . . . I'm sure their (whoever they are) objection was to your staying the night alone there. I must say I had a few faint qualms about it, one is so soaked from the age of one upwards in the "poor defenceless female attitude".'

Their final meeting was planned for London, the time arranged to the minute: 'It seems too good to be true that I'm going to see you at the entrance of Piccadilly Circus Tube at 4.15 on Saturday.' He was very anxious and doubted, in spite of their firm arrangement, that they would meet: 'You know, I half believed I *was* never going to see you again, and that's why I was so unhappy. Saturday will break the evil spell.' Facing three years in China, he was not going to allow his exile to end their relationship: 'When we do . . . say goodbye, I shall be really certain I am going to see you again, after only 3 years. Unless you go off into a convent [a real possibility in Vivien's case] and then I shouldn't trouble to return home at all.'

Letters following his acceptance of a post with the B.A.T. reveal Greene's erratic changes of mind. If he could not have Vivien, well why not China, and something of the end–it–all mood that previously led to his playing Russian roulette surfaced again. Moreover, neither of them contemplated a long life: 'I simply can't stand the thought of England for any time,' he wrote to Vivien. 'I want to get well away from the place, because I can't help longing for you, when you are anywhere near. And that's fairly miserable at times. China would be a splendid sort of suicide–without–scandal–touch. And I agree with you that one doesn't want to go on much longer.'⁵

Yet nine days later when Greene was preparing to visit Oxford for his viva voce he was in raptures about seeing Vivien again: 'I give wild inward hoots of joy, whenever I think of it. Once it came out loud by accident, and puzzled parents asked what was the matter. So I had to say it was a twinge of rheumatics. And I can't keep still at all. I go for long walks and think about it. All the grasshoppers were out yesterday on the Common, all the gorse aflame with them, crackling like a bush fire.'

The night he met Vivien in Oxford, the sky was rent by lightning and her nonchalance in the face of it moved Greene deeply: 'it was just as brave as for someone else to pass through a barrage of shrapnel'. And how little he was asking from life: 'I think my idea of Heaven is sitting still in a half dark, feeling your hand there' – and how much: 'and sometimes talking about anything which comes into the head. And with nothing to worry about for ever.' Greene wrote the above at 11.25 p.m. in Oxford on 21 July and as soon as he was awake next morning, he put pen to paper and his letter takes us close to one aspect of his desire for suicide:

> How wonderful it would have been to have been struck by the lightning, and gone out on a real point of joy. To have reached the absolute pinnacle of happiness, and then have fallen over the edge without knowing any of this horrid climbing down. Why can't one be satisfied with a patch of happiness without feeling depressed afterwards . . . You dear, you dear, I won't write any more. I shall start getting hopeless and morbid, if I do.[6]

Before leaving, Greene dropped his letter off at Blackwell's as the new day was dawning, so Vivien would find it on arriving at work. His emotions swung about most violently and he could write jubilantly, 'China's much the best place for me and I'd bring you home all sorts of Chinese silks, and the very best of China tea.' And he concocted a beautiful, though juvenile fairy tale with Vivien as the sleeping princess: 'I'd like to live in "Afternoon" because of the mysterious stairs, which climb up under the sign. The sort one defends with a rapier from a whole pack of dirty pirates, who can only come up two-a-breast. But then I simply can't surrender the turret window of Afternoon, and the great blue front door . . . And sometimes in the evening you'd let me walk in your garden, though you would always escape indoors. But one evening you would have fallen asleep over an Andrew Marvell, & I should find you still there, under the ash, with the rose bush behind your right shoulder, & a long black finger of shadow between us from the tall tree.'

Even a visit to the dentist is put to service: 'Did I slip secretively into your mind about twenty or a quarter to eleven? You see I had to have some teeth out and had gas. I got your face beautifully focussed with you sitting in your little cubby hole at Blackwell's and kept that picture of you clear, and it was still in my mind, when I woke up. So I wondered whether I'd been able to project my astral self . . . across to you.'[7]

Returning to Berkhamsted, he learned that he was to start work at the B.A.T. on 4 August.

Their last meeting in London had come and gone. Their last meeting in Oxford was over but still Greene couldn't bring himself to believe that this was the end. He asked Vivien to see him once more: 'Don't say you won't see me and talk about my own good', and he ended his letter with words which would touch most hearts: 'I should love you now, if you developed a squint and a hunchback and red hair or anything.' He then telephoned her (something rarely done in the 1920s), hopes high, but she sent a firmly worded telegram: 'Not this time Graham. Sorry.' His reply expresses his anguish: 'I was feeling a bit hysterical and off my head, and then I was wildly jubilant, after telephoning, and then when I got your wire I must have been pretty unbearable. I wreaked all my annoyance on my poor family and was quite impossible . . . It was partly the weather. I can't stick this oppressive heat. It seems to eat away at the brain. I can't imagine why more murders aren't committed in it.'[8]

What made him realise more fully that he was leaving was selling his books ('getting on for five hundred') except for about half a dozen. He was letting go volumes he loved – 'de la Mare's and Masefield's and Conrad's all disappearing'. He felt rather like the people in the last act of *The Cherry Orchard*, 'their homes sold, the furniture covered up in dust sheets'. He was stunned by the thought that he was losing Vivien for three years as soon as his initial training was over. Cryptically he adds, 'or if I got my original intention before I met you, for ever', which I take to mean if he had been successful at Russian roulette, he would not have been alive.

Greene was frightened that Vivien, once he was away in China, would rarely write: 'If you write to me, it'll be only a very long conversation in a very darkened cinema, and the lights will go up again, and there we shall both be still . . .' Moreover, he was disturbed by the impression that Vivien was saying goodbye for ever: 'If I come back, you've promised to let me see you, even if it's only for long enough to tell me that you don't want to see me again . . . and even if you've got married . . . in the interval.'[9]

Greene's letters, painful in their indecision, alternate between wanting and not wanting to leave for China according to the type of letter – kind or indifferent, warm or cold – he received from Vivien.

Although he considered it a real possibility that Vivien would marry another while he was away, he refused to countenance the same possibility for himself: 'Don't make any silly remark about my coming back married. A letter once a month from you, six thousand miles away, is enough to fill my mind until the next one comes. There's no room for anything else. You see, you are the whole world. No one else counts.'

Greene originally wanted to go to China because he was sick to death of all the silly small things which were continually getting on his nerves in England: 'I wanted a job where I could get just physically fagged out every evening and not think at all.' But then he met Vivien and he could not countenance losing her for three days let alone three years. Without her he found England 'a pretty restless sort of disjointed, second rate show.'[10]

He went up to London to look for cheap rooms before beginning work and found them in Smith Street off the King's Road. He was left with one further week of his vacation. In Berkhamsted the weather was atrocious: 'It's pouring with rain and there's nothing to do, but sit and think about you . . . I keep on saying to myself "Why the devil did I ever answer that first letter?" '[11] At the same time he was visualising receiving Vivien's letters when he was in China: 'I always . . . read your letters when I'm by myself. I suppose at Christmas I shall have to go and hide from my interpreter in a paddy field or a pagoda or something . . .'[12]

Greene's family began preparing for a month's holiday in Filey, Yorkshire, and he wrote to Vivien: 'Peace is just beginning to descend again after the awful turmoil of shunted boxes, and misplaced umbrellas, and where's the green trunk? I'm feeling most unfamiliarly glad, because now I'm all alone with you, and I can smell the jasmine at my elbow . . .' He felt guilty that he was disappointing his family by his readiness to enter business: 'My father still murmurs that of course I could always chuck up the B.A.T. after a year and come back to take the Consular, and my mother has been very seedy, and looks depressed, and I feel like a rat leaving a sinking ship.'

Greene's interest in being a businessman turned out to be a deliberate pose on his part, which they recognised, and something of his wilfulness is revealed by his involvement in business in the first place, even though everything he had done in the last few years pointed to his becoming a writer. To begin with, his family never believed he would get the job, but the more they insisted on looking on him as a promising young littérateur, the more he felt the need to pose as a businessman. When he got the job, his parents became worried, anxious and disappointed. But it was not only his family who questioned the advisability of becoming a businessman abroad. Vivien herself wondered if he would not miss the subject he had graduated in – history. Graham answered her question lightheartedly, turning his response wittily in Vivien's direction:

> I think History's rather fun, but my masters and tutors say I'm not *very* good at it. They say I'm too vague, but that's not true at all. I know all the facts and dates and things of the last hundred years. I'm thinking of writing a history and have been making up a time chart of events. I really know rather a lot, though I'm best on the 20th Century, I think. Here goes.

> 1815 Wellington won the battle of Waterloo.
> Then lots of [indecipherable] and corn bills, and Catholic Emancipation, and the Peterloo massacre and Reform Bills, and the Industrial Revolution, but I'm not quite sure of the dates.
> 1857 The Indian Mutiny and then sometime in the eighteen sixties The Crimean War and the Poet Laureate publishes Maud, and the Alhambra becomes a Music Hall, but I'm not absolutely certain of the dates.
> And then lots of people publish lots of things, and sometime at the end of the century comes Kipling and the Boer War. Now I begin to know even more.
> 1901 Death of Victoria.
> 1902 End of the Boer War.
> *1905 Aug. 1. Vivienne Born.*
> 1914 Great War.
> 1918 Armistice.
> 1925 March 17. I met you.
> March 21. I had tea with you.
> April 4. I saw Three Women with you.
> April 17. I went to The Ship with you.

and that's where my knowledge of contemporary history becomes really detailed.[13]

Letters to his mother at this time are calm and show no sign of the love-stricken young man, for he rarely shared his private emotions with his family. He wrote at least one sober letter to Vivien: 'I saw in yesterday's Express that of the three thousand men usually employed in China by the B.A.T. all but fifty are on strike . . . seem to be cutting down my time in London . . . Rose is fitting me into [the] Liverpool [tobacco factory] on the 17th of this month.'

Two days before he began working at the B.A.T., Greene sent Vivien a poem, the first lines of which ran 'Lord Love when will you weary of this war/Fighting with banners and a few high words?'[14]

The B.A.T., however, was no sanctuary for the love-sick. It was rather an initiation into a life of soul-destroying dullness: 'I feel I've earned my salary to-day by the utter boredom of things. The new people have got literally nothing to do but sit on stools & pretend to look through months' old balance books, which convey nothing. Apparently we never shall have anything to do not even at the factory but just stand and watch machines from 7 a.m. to 7 p.m.'

He had to break off writing to Vivien to listen to a talk about China by Lord Gaysford, but Gaysford's talk did not inspire him. He discovered his contract would be for four not three years: 'Three years without you sounded bad enough, four is hellish.' Also, he realised that his salary would initially be only £50 a year. Moreover, 'Lord G. went the wrong way about making the show attractive, emphasising the smallness of personal danger, when the only attraction left seems a fading hope of petering out before the four years are up.'

Greene was troubled as well by the lack of social standing and breeding among his companions: 'There is one conceited & unintelligent individual, who, from his exaggerated Oxford trousers is, I imagine from Durham University. At my own desk there is a hearty fellow, ploughed in Cambridge finals, & quite a good sort, *but* there is one terrible young man, who has been in a bank the last five years, & sticks to me like a limpet. He knows everything about book keeping, motor bicycles & wireless, talks about "johnnies" & says your "label" when he means your name. He'll take the devil of a lot of shaking off.'

And he was filled 'with something very nearly like horror' that there would be no one to talk to about things which were important to him, 'like books and there'd be nothing to keep the mind sharpened'. He feared he would fall 'into a sort of ghastly bluntness', which he would only realise when he had returned from China. Seeing Vivien again on Saturday, he thanked God, for he knew that there was no one else with whom he could talk things over[15] – certainly not his parents who he suspected would take up an attitude of 'I told you so'.

Greene wrote to Vivien again that Saturday night (in pencil and rather illegibly) almost at the end of his tether:

I don't want adventure much. I only want to see you. Oh why in Hell weren't we made relations & I could see more of you? It seems a pretty dirty trick of fate to have shoved us together only to separate us again. I know I shouldn't be able to go on seeing a lot of you, even if I took a job in England but why in God's name should we ever have met? It wasn't natural. And now that we have met, I can't even have recourse to my old methods of curing depression. Lord knows in comparison before this I didn't need much, & then I could get blind drunk for twenty-four hours on end, or else practise the revolver trick, which was warranted to cure for quite a time. Now I can't do either. I've tried to do both last term, & found I couldn't. You've changed all my mind. And now I'm a coward without armour & come whining.

Greene's letters make painful reading as we watch him striving to come to terms with a reluctant sweetheart.

Reviewing Ford's novel *The Good Soldier*, which deals with a broken marriage, he wrote: 'one cannot help wondering what agonies of frustration and error lay behind [it]'.[16] Something of his 'agonies of frustration' is apparent in the extraordinary solution he ultimately offered Vivien of a celibate marriage:

What I long for is a quite original marriage with you, companionship & companionship only, all the Winters evenings past, & to have someone worth fighting for. And you would go on holidays when you liked, & see your mother when you liked, & I should share your companionship. I shouldn't grumble if it was a less share than your mother had. You could work too if you wanted to. There'd be no domestic tying down, & you'd always keep your ideal of celibacy, & you could help me to keep the same ideal.

As he developed his argument for a celibate marriage, he made extraordinary comparisons: 'Darling, it sounds fantastic, but the fantastic is often wildly practical, as when Columbus put out from Spain.' Moreover, the whole thing would be 'an adventure finer than the ordinary marriage' because of a shared ideal and there would be no reason why it should ever end, because no sex was involved (though Graham put it more obliquely, arguing that it would never end because it was very different from the other form of marriage). And, taking up a phrase of Vivien's – the need to 'round off' their relationship, by which she meant a clean break from each other – Greene provided her with a different meaning to the phrase: 'Suppose God *did* make us come together, & the rounding off was as I've imagined, & that He brought us together, in order to strike out together across this new country.' He went on to make still greater claims: 'it would be new country, & perhaps even the kind of promised land to which people have really been aiming, though they didn't know it, & they'll follow us in.'

One gets the impression that Greene is himself amazed to be writing such a letter: 'I could not have believed six months ago [when he was still an atheist], that I should write a kind of religious letter. But I can't help it. I've been wanting to say this for a long time now. O my dear, if you only made it true – this monastic marriage – then it would be goodbye to business in China, & there'd be something more than money in the future.'[17]

Out of his despair, Greene struck the right note and unknowingly found the right formula to touch Vivien's heart. She was intrigued by the idea of a monastic marriage: 'You asked me why I hadn't told you before. I don't know, but last night it all came out . . . I'm not asking you to surrender any of your other greater loves, religion, family, anything. I shall always be satisfied to come third or fourth.'[18]

Greene then presented Vivien with a Dickensian idyll of married bliss: 'And there'll be winter evenings, when we can make hot buttered toast for each other (do you like roast chestnuts? I do), & there'll be summer days with the sea sparkling blue . . . & days on the down, & night expresses, & evenings sometimes, when we are both sleepy and tired & we'll just read, or I'll write & you'll put in a few touches to a design.'

We can see Greene not only readying himself for withdrawal from the business world: 'Darling, I don't want to rush you. You needn't even tell me on Saturday, if you don't want to. If it's Yes sometime (& I pray God it will be), I shall send in my notice straight away to the B.A.T.,' but also contemplating a future as a high-class journalist: 'Then I'll strike out for a better job, &, with you to keep me up to the mark, even the Times might not be fatal. After all (he said with ineffable conceit!) Chesterton & Belloc have been journalists. My miracle, we could do marvels together.'[19]

He was discovering, it seems for the first time, just how strongly he wanted to be a writer: 'When I had plenty of time to write, I liked to despise it, now I know that, though I love you far more than writing, *I love writing more than any other thing.*' He expresses, in a fanciful image, the sense of being born, of being given life itself, by this transforming love:

I feel like a character in a Hans Andersen story. For in a way I have been made out of your breath, this me. The princess very carelessly puffed a big breath on a Winter's day (it *was* snowing)

& the breath froze in the air & made an image, & the princess warmed it with her hands, so that it became alive. So that if you didn't exist, I don't feel as if I could exist either. I should vanish in a breath of mist.[20]

Greene's next letter seems to indicate that Vivien had responded warmly to his suggestion of a celibate marriage since we find him trying to anticipate possible criticism from their respective families, should they commit themselves to a monastic union. Greene drew support for their special kind of love from a popular song of the time: 'Other people won't understand our point of view, at any rate at first. We do. Like the really good line in IT AIN'T GONNA RAIN NO MORE "How in Hell can the old folks tell –"'

He wrote to Vivien three times a day, before he left for the office in the morning, again while at work ('we five China people are considered too delicate plants to do any work whatsoever') and finally in the evening from Smith Street. It must have been his sheer persistence that persuaded Vivien to grant him yet another last meeting. With romantic seriousness he concocted a ruse whereby he would know, without words being spoken, that all was not lost. They were to meet at Oxford station: 'Suppose, if there's hope for me still, you slip a petal of some flower into my hand, when we meet on the platform?'

Greene's desire to increase, if only by minutes, the time he has with Vivien, has something manic about it: 'I hope the train's not late. Don't forget 3.4, & do get a platform ticket & come up on to the platform. It might make a difference of two or three minutes. And I can't afford to lose anything, when I'm not going to see you afterwards for such ages.'

Though the future 'China hands' had very little to do, there is evidence that Graham was studying Chinese. Often, Chinese characters are scribbled in the margin of his letters. So clearly preparations for departure were proceeding. Also he was studying book-keeping: 'I've copied out a typewritten script called Notes on Book-keeping . . . It sounds absolute gibberish. The entries on *Dr.* side of Cash Book are posted to the *Cr.* side of proper A/cs in the Ledger – "By Cash" (C.B. folio no. quoted.) The entries on *Cr.* side of Cash Book are posted on Dr. side of ledger – "To Cash." Does that mean anything at all, I ask you?'

While at the B.A.T. office he began working on his second novel entitled 'The Episode', which, like his first, 'Anthony Sant', remained unpublished and now rests in the vaults of Hoares Bank in Fleet Street: 'I shall try & go on with the novel now, though it's rather hard with a bank clerk chattering at my right hand elbow, & a general fretful buzz of talk, & about twenty typewriters clacking.'

That night he had to go to Archibald Rose's house for dinner along with the other 'China' recruits, but what he wanted to do was stay at home and hold the latest letter from Vivien tight in his hand as if it were her hand and whisper over and over again, 'My love, we'll be brave, be brave, be brave . . . what have you done to my heart, Vivienne?' And even a heavy rainfall was given a fanciful use: 'It's raining hard outside, but it's not raining here. Shall we stop the rain for ever & ever, like Joshua the moon?'

The next day brought him three letters – from his father, his tutor's wife, Mrs Bell, and from Vivien – and his thoughts of the dinner the night before made him as confused over the decision he had to make as he had ever been: 'There was dinner with Rose last night, when he was so charming that I felt a rather mean skunk, considering chucking the business. And then there was a letter from my father saying, "We hate your going, but of course it will be exciting for you." And a . . . letter from my tutor's wife, regretting past talks & extolling the adventure side of the whole thing.' Vivien's letter told him that he was 'worrying' her and he again felt that China was the best place for him. His mind was 'pretty well moiled up' for he just had to place in the balance the fact that he wouldn't see Vivien for four years and the whole business was too ghastly to contemplate and, in some self-pity, he could even envy the treatment Vivien's cat would receive when he was in China: 'And when I think of William having his paws buttered by you by the fire, & that crumbly kiss. O my darling, don't give me a definite No, just because you don't want me to chuck the B.A.T. . . . You see it's such ages till Saturday, & every hour I feel the web of this place growing round me.'

It is the nature of our response to time that the clock moves most slowly when we are involved in tedious activities, but for Greene a dull occupation has a horrifying intensity, like an unending prison sentence. Time for him also mercilessly extends itself when he is separated from that which he loves or needs. But now the approach of his departure was looming in front of him: 'In an hour I'm going up to Rose to get my letter for Liverpool, & suppose he tells me then that he's succeeded in arranging our passages? . . . The first desperation about going is the absolute loss of you . . .'

We can perhaps get some indication of Vivien's rather more pessimistic argument in his reply to her now lost letter:

we are shut in by two gates even now as far as the world's concerned. Any decision we make, even small ones, have some irrevocable effect, so that we pass into a new landscape. You say it's irrevocable. But anything you've ever done is irrevocable. You can't get back to the country you were in, before you went to Blackwell's, even. It's gone, though bits remain, as bits will always, through whatever gate you go.[21]

And all the time his sensitive, snobbish nostrils were quivering in the company of people he looked down upon, for Greene takes offence when his nerves are rubbed up the wrong way: 'Oh chatter, chatter, chatter. I can't, I won't believe that all my life is going to be spent with these people. O God, the bank clerk's reminiscing about his "pals" & his "girls", & I want to kick him or snub him, but I can't. I've got to remain friendly & say Yes? & No? & Really?'[22]

On 12 August, Archibald Rose brought forward the departure of the five future China hands. They were now scheduled to leave on 26 September. Greene then knew for certain that he would not even have a last weekend with Vivien: 'They'll only give a few days between the [Liverpool] factory and sailing.' And in a last letter to Vivien that day, he gives some indication of his turmoil as the time came to sail. He made two lists, one stressing the advantages, the other the disadvantages, of continuing with the B.A.T.:

FOR.	AGAINST.
The adventure	Will the sense of adventure last four, leave alone twenty years? Shall I like the work? I don't like my companions so far.
The B.A.T. with all its faults is a good company. If I do well, I shall do very well as far as money's concerned.	
	Whether successful or not, it practically means giving up writing.
	Opposition of my people, though passive.
The experience.	The experience is not much good by itself. After four years, it will be rather late to start again with something else. It practically means China for life.

And then the last bit For, Sense of Pride.
You see it's rather difficult. The balance in my mind, now I've

205

written it down, tips a little to 'against', if it wasn't for that damnable Pride part, Conceit is perhaps the better word. And it seems so inconceivable that after you becoming so much to me (& perhaps I may have become a trifling bit to you), we should lose it all for ever, even friendship.

Forgive the stickiness of the paper, but I'm sucking caramels to try & get a bit calmer.

So concerned was Greene to write the above that he had not realised that he had written it on a used sheet of paper – a list of people to contact and things to do, the notes appearing upside down.

Macleod
Molly
Ink
Wash
Socks
Bath
Edward [Tooter]

That night he bought flowers and then wrote his third and last letter of the day at 9 p.m., three hours after his previous one: 'I got the violets from an old man outside the Empire, as I was wandering back after getting my dinner. Oh how I wish I could have you with me at dinner all these nights. He was calling "Violets. Lucky Violets" & the lucky caught my ear.'

After lunch the next day, while his future colleagues talked of Gilbert & Sullivan – 'someone recited all the words of nearly all the songs in the Mikado' – Greene went out '& played shove halfpenny in Victoria Gardens with the bank clerk & lost four pence' but soon his irritation towards the bank clerk grew again – and no one could deny that Greene has a wealth of irritable nerves in his body:

He was on a 'spree' last night &, damn him, at Hampstead. It's ridiculous but it makes me furious to hear the little swine mention Hampstead. I can never see the name anywhere, without thinking of you. You & the St Joan photograph. [Greene loved Bernard Shaw's play 'St Joan' and saw Vivien as comparable with St Joan.] I've never been on Hampstead Heath, but I've got my own picture of it with you on it.

Greene knew that he had few excuses for withdrawing from his job and the reasons he could offer Archibald Rose would not be understood by him: 'I can't mention you; I can't say I dislike my companions, as he'd put me down as a snob & he wouldn't understand about my desire to write. Rose'll think that I've just been playing about with the company, taking their money.'

At home that night Greene wrote a letter which gives us a picture of himself in lonely digs in Smith Street, crazily in love and faced with an impossible decision: 'I haven't the heart to play my gramophone now, because it would break the stillness, & while I sit very quiet & don't look too much round me, I can believe that you are just behind my shoulder.' But he did seem to be on the point of making a decision: 'I'll write [my notice] out, & seal it up. I don't suppose I shall post it. There's this damned pride in the way.'

The next day, a Saturday, was his last morning of work in London. He was to report to the B.A.T.'s Liverpool tobacco factory on Monday. He spent his time writing a letter to Vivien, beginning at 8.45 a.m. and continuing it on the train to Oxford – and Vivien. It began with a decision taken: 'I've sent up a note to Rose & am now waiting for the "wrath" to come . . . I can't say I'm looking forward to the interview. One feels ridiculously like a schoolboy being sent up to the Headmaster . . .' – a curious analogy this – do the sons of Headmasters also fear Headmasters? The whole letter is punctuated, not with the time of day but by the number of hours (and ultimately minutes) he has to endure before he meets Vivien at Oxford: '. . . only six & a quarter hours before I see you . . . I wonder if I shall catch sight of you on the platform before I get out in the distance.'

He creates a highly dramatic picture of his present plight giving a blow by blow account of his thoughts: 'The hour of execution must be approaching very rapidly. Suppose Rose doesn't get my note. It will be far worse to have to take the initiative & go up to his room . . . Poor B.A.T. what a lot of trouble I'm causing them.'

As the clock reaches 11.30, Greene notes that he will be with Vivien in four hours. We also learn that Rose has had him up to his room and that Greene has shown himself to be 'a marvellous shillyshallyer': 'I've delayed the final decision. I know I shall feel whatever I decide is wrong.' Rose had used shrewd arguments to persuade him to stay with the firm, pointing out that no other business would take on a man who could only stand the B.A.T. for a fortnight and he pointed out that there had been over two hundred applicants, fifty from Oxford, and five only taken on the strength. Fearing the wrong decision, Greene wrote his fears in the letter which, since it continued until the train was approaching Oxford, must have been handed to Vivien on his arrival: 'They can't have judged just hastily. They must have thought I was suitable, & they've been choosing people for years. Suppose they are right?'

Then he wonders why he is writing to Vivien when it is less than three hours before he sees her and the passage is punctuated by a further fear: 'an awful thought has just struck me. Suppose your mother hasn't been able to bear not seeing you, & has come down to Oxford & snatched you up . . . only allowed me a stolen hour or so. Suppose that's what you tell me on the platform . . . it can't & mustn't be true. And yet sometimes my premonitions have been right.'

Greene left the B.A.T. office at 12.45 and caught the train to Oxford at 1.40 and carried on writing, this time in pencil. The swaying of the train made his writing almost indecipherable:

I'm at Reading & I'm going to see you in exactly half an hour . . . the whistle's gone & we're off. All's well. Fate has given us a lovely day. The flowers at the seed place at Reading were looking lovely & I could almost smell them from the train . . . I knew Fate would do something silly. The train's stopped. Now it's slowly going forward, bumping restlessly.

Then follows a description of the five passengers in the railcoach (and a compliment to Vivien is deftly turned): 'Five of them. On the whole the three men look less hideous than the women . . . But that may be because I haven't a standard for them to live up to while the poor females – well, it's hopeless for them.'

Even the train is given emotions of anger because he is reaching his love too soon:

O dear, the train's getting horribly angry. It doesn't want me to write to you. It bumps indignantly & says that it's selfish of me, when I'm going to see you in – nineteen minutes . . . soon it will be seconds . . . it's going fearfully fast. It wants to see you about as much as I do.

And the river desires to see Vivien too and is in competition with the sun: 'the river is laughing with wild excitement: "Keep out sun. Don't you realise you are an oven"' and it is the river who speaks: 'only fourteen minutes to go . . . only fourteen minutes to go.'

Greene's last words run at a furious pace:

9 minutes only darling. You'll have started to the station . . . Here's Cholsey, but we aren't stopping. Final Stop Oxford shouted

the porter at Reading & my heart shouted Final Stop Vivienne
. . . only six minutes to go. We are going to be punctual. Four
minutes to go.

And there the letter ends, the first of Greene's many 'train' letters.

Without doubt, Greene was fascinated by trains – he wrote his best
letters to Vivien in trains, both when he was approaching and leaving
her. His first best-seller is based on a train journey and his first
children's book was entitled *The Little Train* (1946).[23] Perhaps the
lure of trains lies in the fact that, in those days, they had an exotic
quality of escape about them: one was conscious of meeting destiny,
approaching fate in the shape of the person waiting at the other end.

Greene could not possibly have left his decision over the B.A.T.
much longer, as a letter to his father indicates: 'I & the bank clerk
depart for Liverpool on Sunday. I'm going down to Oxford for
Saturday night & through from there . . . My address in Liverpool
from Sunday on will be c/o Mrs Grant, 44 Manor Avenue. Great
Crosby. Liverpool.' It was not to be.

In an interview for the *Paris Review* Greene put the blame for his
leaving the B.A.T. on the poor bank clerk who, as we have seen,
disturbed and irritated him, though Greene never offered the man a
critical word to his face, indeed he never gave any indication, at
the time, of his dislike: 'What finally got me,' said Greene to his
interviewers, 'was when he said "We'll be able to play this [double
noughts and crosses]* on the way out, won't we?" I resigned
immediately.'[24] No doubt this was an element which weighed in the
balance, but this chapter bears witness to the fact that his decision
depended almost solely on his infatuation for Vivien and on her
reception of him in Oxford. Clearly Vivien was kind, for while she
did not at the station slip a petal into his hand as a symbol of hope,
she did provide him, when later they went walking together in a
wood, with a white bud (symbol of purity?). Afterwards he wrote
of 'heaven on a tree stump at the end of only a week's purgatory'.
The following day he left, not for Liverpool and tobacco planting in
China, but back to his London digs. The terrors of indecision were
over. He sent Archibald Rose a telegram telling him he would not
be returning to his office. To Vivien he wrote: 'If you only knew
how happy you've made me. After all, forlorn hopes have won
through sometimes, & what excitement . . . eternities of love.'[25]

It was in an exultant religious mood that he spoke of God's part
in directing him to know Vivien's significance to him: 'You've made

---

* The American version is Tic Tac Toe.

me *know* that Saturday won't be the last time. It can't. I don't believe God would allow it, even if I tried to make it so. He led me into the B.A.T. just so that I might learn how inexpressibly dear to me you are.'

Yet Vivien, at this stage, had offered him no more than a slim hope for the future. This seems to have been enough. Back at Smith Street he was deliriously happy, a state which lasted two whole days. Vivien sent him a note, accompanying a photograph, and he was in seventh heaven: she had asked that the note be destroyed and he had done as he was bidden: 'I wish you hadn't forced me to tear it up . . . My lashes are all clogged up . . . Though I've had to throw the writing and the paper and the envelope away into the black stream, the words haven't gone': and he recalled the only two previous occasions when he had felt such ecstasy – when he published a story in the *Star* at sixteen and when he won his exhibition at Balliol: 'It's a marvellous feeling – of *wanting* to go on living . . . My miracle worker . . . You've given trees shade, and the flowers scent, and the sun a gold it's never had before.[26]

15

Late Summer at Ambervale

I love you more than I love this wretched self.
— GRAHAM GREENE

THE world looked good the following day: 'I leaped out of bed and had my breakfast, and finished off a book [of poems] called Sad Cure, and took it round the corner to be typed . . . It's really the death of Hilary Trench,' he added cryptically.

Greene continued to write to Vivien. He began his second letter of the day: 'My lovely one, I can't help it. I must write to you again.' The cinema and dreams of Vivien helped to fill his London days: 'I went and had a kind of high tea at a cabman's place this afternoon and then went to the cinema to see Jekyll and Hyde. I saw it four years ago and thought it marvellous, but it seems very poor now. When it was over . . . I went for a long walk, thinking of you, up Sloane St and along Knightsbridge, past Hyde Park Corner, until Piccadilly climbed up in front to a blue Whistler mist of sky.'[1]

But soon, a letter from Vivien brought him low. She regretted that he was not going abroad and there are indications that she loved the letters more than the letter-writer. With such harsh knowledge Greene replied hastily: 'All right. I'll do my best to get a job abroad before the end of September. If I can't get anything else, I can write to my father that I've changed my mind again & am going in for the Chinese consular. Then I can go to France till Christmas, & to Germany till Easter & with luck get off finally by the autumn. And as leave doesn't come for five years, I shall have plenty of time to get over you.' But in the same letter, he promised to write to her often because she liked his letters, but promised also, with some bitterness, that she would not be troubled again by his wanting to see her. He was deeply hurt. His last meeting with her on the previous Saturday had been 'a perfect memory' – this had been the day in Oxford when she had slipped into his hand the white bud of promise. His sense of betrayal welled up: 'the white bud was a white lie, & didn't even mean the one chance in five hundred, but was slipped in my hand because you didn't think that business [B.A.T.] would be good for me.'

Yet Graham was willing to accept any conditions if contact could be maintained:

> . . . if you like then you can have my letters. I'll do anything that pleases you, & you needn't see me on the 26th [September], if you don't want to. And this can be Goodbye as far as seeing each other's concerned, if you would prefer it so. Though I'll go on writing, just as long as you like.
>
> I'll even give you your chance of a melodramatic cut away if I can get a job abroad. I won't write again till this Trench mood is over.

What troubled Greene, as well it might, was a phrase from one of her letters, 'I just love you like I love everyone else.' Vivien was young, though more mature than Graham. She was attractive to others and was, at this time, as a letter written fifty-five years later indicates, drawn to another whom she designated 'X': 'On one special occasion, I forget which, a terrific gift of flowers – masses and masses of them and afterwards I was so ashamed of myself that when I first saw them I was disappointed that they were not from X. He [Graham] had not much money, I think, and it was extravagantly generous.'[2]

It is necessary to know something of Vivien's background to explain why she was so taken by Greene's notion that the best marriage is a monastic one. Vivien did hold surprising views, particularly her opinion that 'the world soils what it touches', which probably had its origin in witnessing, as a child, the break-up of her parents' marriage. A letter has survived from mother to daughter, dated 4 October 1925:

> There were *no* compensations in my marriage, but you and Pat [Vivien's brother] . . . I gave you two good care because I cared for *nothing* else & was shut up & deliberately balked of every other outlet for interest by the narrow views plus narrow pocket of a narrow little man . . . that *awful* caged feeling I had with S.B[rowning – Vivien's father] like being in a small dark room furnished in bamboo. I've locked up the drawer in my mind where every memory of it is only too damn clear & try to start at Oct. 30, 1915 when I burst the door & left him [Vivien was then 10 years old].

I don't in the least blame a man of that type for taking anything he could get when his wife refused to have anything to do with him. Yet I couldn't stand it & for a proud person to feel continually humiliated is simply Hell with the lid off.

Having finished the long poem 'Sad Cure', Graham returned to his second novel. Without a job, it must have seemed to him, and to others, that his future promised little. He had a girlfriend only marginally interested in him and he was writing 'The Episode', a novel he did not believe in. He was to wonder how he could have abandoned the chance of being a businessman when it offered him his only escape from the hated obsession of trying to make imaginary characters live.

And there was the problem of money. He needed a job: 'It was Sackville Street or nothing.' To the young men of Graham's generation, down from University without work, recourse to Sackville Street and Gabbitas & Thring was a necessity.

Greene recalled in *A Sort of Life* an interview at the offices of Gabbitas & Thring, educational specialists offering graduates the possibility of teaching posts. There was about Sackville Street a 'Dickensian mustiness', and on either side were old-established tailors' shops while prostitutes kept flats on the second floor. The office itself reminded him of an old family solicitor's ('with strange secrets concealed in the metal file-boxes'). It was not the haunt, he realised, of men with first class degrees. Gabbitas & Thring 'were the last hope of those needing a little temporary aid. You pawned yourself instead of your watch.'

Greene, mindful of the accidental manner in which his father, intending to be a barrister, had slipped into teaching, had a horror of following the same route, of feeling the trap close: 'I wanted nothing permanent, I explained in near panic, to the partner. Was there not, perhaps, some private tutoring job which was available just for the summer? He opened his file with an air of disappointment . . . As for private tutoring I was too late in applying, such men were needed immediately after the schools broke up (he whisked over page after page), there was really nothing he could offer for someone of my qualifications . . . I would hardly be interested in this (he had detached a page with the tips of his fingers), a widowed lady living at Ashover, a village in Derbyshire, who required someone to look after her son of eight during the holidays. I would not be asked to live in the house: I would have a room in a private hotel with all my meals, but there was no salary attached.'[3] When Greene accepted the post, the interviewer, Mr Bickford-Smith, looked at him with disappointment and suspicion as if there were something disgracefully wrong in Greene's background. However, it was just the post Greene wished to land – a temporary job, filling the vacuum which stretched ahead until Vivien, then holidaying in Italy with her mother, returned – though he had pawned himself more cheaply than a watch.

The card Greene completed has survived at the office of Gabbitas & Thring. It gives his full name (Henry Graham Greene), his age (20 years), his height (6'1"), his religion (C. of E.) and in the far right corner of the card the comment 'not much games'. Apart from offering History and English, he also offered French, Mathematics, Latin 'and some Classics'. Greene went to Ashover on 25 August and left on 15 September 1925. It was a curious interlude during which he again came close to a breakdown, though very little evidence of this appears in his autobiography.[4]

While he waited for the 25th, Greene went on writing his novel in his digs in Chelsea, and continued also his letters to Vivien. To Venice he wrote, 'I have sent a London Pigeon to St Marks [Square], to tell you when you get there, how happy I am & how I love you, & how I am trying to work at what you want. I wonder if you'll realise which it is of all the ones that flutter round your feet.'[5]

He had tea with Kenneth Richmond, as he had done earlier, in May, at which time he thought Richmond himself in need of treatment (a shrewd guess): 'He is becoming more & more a case of "physician cure thyself". He is much more nervy than he used to be.'[6] But in August he had other concerns. To Vivien he wrote: 'I went out to tea today with my psycho-analyst to meet some terrible female novelist, of whom I'd never heard, but I felt I better go, as her husband is a critic on The Times. As a matter of fact she was quite pleasant, and didn't talk shop, as writers, like medical students, always seem to do . . . they are going to try to get me some reviewing for the Lit. Supp.'*[7] This was a straightforward letter showing only that Greene was willing to use influence as it came to hand. Richmond himself was probably watching over young Greene, no

---

* This was a happy letter: 'I've found . . . a lovely book in my digs published in 1893. Enquire within upon Everything . . . I Proposed to you quite wrong [sic] both in June and August . . . Listen: "When a gentleman presents a fan, flower or trinket to a lady, with the left hand, this . . . is an overture of regard; should she *receive* it with the *left* hand, it is considered as an acceptance of his esteem, but if with the *right* hand it is a refusal of his offer. Thus, by a few simple tokens explained by rule, the passion of love is expressed: and through this medium the most timid and diffident man may, without difficulty, communicate his sentiments of regard to a lady, and, in case his offer should be refused, avoid experiencing the mortifications of an explicit refusal."'

doubt looking for evidence of tension or depression. And depression he certainly did suffer with Vivien away and her strong hints that she was not in love with him.

*

Greene left for his stint of three weeks' tutoring perhaps reluctantly. First, he lost the rail ticket which was to take him to Chesterfield and Stretton. Then, while on the train, he discovered he had lost a second: 'Darling, what's happening to me. I've lost a second ticket to Stretton. It's simply unexplainable . . . I'm more nervous than I was of the B.A.T.' On arriving at Chesterfield: 'O dear, I've got to wait feeling nervouser & nervouser for the Stretton train [and] then I have a drive by taxi to Ashover.'[8]

As usual Greene's powers of observation (not necessarily sympathetic) were to the fore. He arrived at the Ambervale Hotel, Ashover, and sent his mother and Vivien his impressions:

> This is a comic little hotel. Mostly elderly people with Manchester accents, except for a pale weedy, slang-ridden school boy, & a bobbed flapper, who is preening herself for a hotel flirtation. [The bobbed flapper was about sixteen or seventeen.] (Letter to his mother, 25 August.)

> I have to sit at a table with the BF [bobbed flapper] with her mother. Her mother is fat, shy & with an accent, which her daughter escapes by the skin of her teeth. Every remark I made to the mother at dinner made her half jump out of her seat . . . I wish you were here and not the idiotic flapper. (Letter to Vivien, 25 August.)

> There's a rather piercingly loud air of bonhomie in the place, laughter & pokes in the ribs & raucous jokes about the weather & food . . . After seeing Mrs Knyvet [the boy's mother] I got caught & had to play ghastly games with everyone till 11. Darling, they are awful people, though terribly friendly. (7.50 p.m. undated letter to Vivien.)

The boy turned out to be tractable and Greene's biggest task was keeping his charge entertained: 'I gave him a quarter of an hour's Algebra so as to keep up appearances & after tea we had a furious game of hide & seek, till 6.30 when I returned here [Ambervale Hotel],' he wrote to his mother. He tried also to teach the boy some Latin: 'Darling you should have seen me growing lyrical over qui, quae, quod and relative clauses. After tea the child grew tired of hide & seek & so I had to pretend that we were Bruce climbing Mount

Everest★ which meant climbing up nearly every tree in a large park, & then trying to haul the creature up after me . . . I have successfully settled the child down with a copy of Treasure Island.' The following day it was 'up on the Trossachs and exploring the Unknown Beaches of the Amazon!' With a sense of relief he confides to Vivien, 'my animal is going back to school on Sept. 16.'

His next venture with the boy (who was ten, not eight as Greene has it in *A Sort of Life*), was to build a toy theatre, but the boy's grandfather didn't think it suitable for a Sunday: 'He's an ancient (88), humourless man of tremendous wealth. He manufactures all England's tape measures & his name . . . is Chesterman.' Greene's next exploit was to light a fire on the moor, and though it was a strain inventing amusements, the boy in Greene enjoyed it. He wrote to Vivien: 'be proud of me. I may not be able to write novels, but I lit a fire at the first attempt in the open air with a strong wind blowing, in order to boil a kettle.'

Nearly twenty-one years old, Greene still retained a boyish streak: the novelist whose fictional characters are often seen as reflecting his world-weariness and cynicism had yet to be born: 'I suddenly found myself engaged in a delicious, undignified and joyful cushion fight with my pupil.' Three days before Greene's services ended, the boy developed knee trouble and was unable to go for walks or climb trees or run races:

> All this morning we sat in the garden & did ridiculous paper games, until we were both too bored for words. Then, as a lesser evil, I imitated the Ashover Light Railway, a tiny, shaky & very perilous railway here, bundled him [this boy of ten and this boy of twenty!] into an old pram, & rushed him about the garden, nearly killing him twice, the second time just as his mother came round the corner . . . the mother, aunt, great aunt & grandfather . . . I'm getting really fond of them.[9]

Outside his work as a tutor, Greene carried on a slight flirtation with the B.F. (Bobbed Flapper) which led to his inheriting a dog: 'She went with me to the pub where the landlord showed us into a private room, where we sat gingerly on the edge of a table and kissed dryly, then took refuge in a half of bitter and a gin and lime. She offered me a mongrel wirehaired terrier as a souvenir, which was to be sent by rail from Leicester to Berkhamsted and was to prove the bane of my life.'[10]

★ Charles Granville Bruce (1866–1931) led the Everest expeditions of 1920 and 1924.

Also while at Ambervale, to escape the 'oppression of boredom' he walked over the hills to Chesterfield and found a dentist:

> I described to him the symptoms, which I knew well, of an abscess.
>
> He tapped a perfectly good tooth with his little mirror and I reacted in the correct way. 'Better have it out,' he advised.
>
> 'Yes,' I said, 'but with ether.'
>
> A few minutes' unconsciousness was like a holiday from the world. I had lost a good tooth, but the boredom was for the time dispersed.[11]

This is a macabre indicator of character, but what was the background to this incident? The letters to Vivien show that he was in poor health at this time – he speaks of Derbyshire not agreeing with him; of dosing himself with aspirin; of promising not to indulge in Veronal. He had a serious boil in his mouth which turned out to be a cyst about the size of a hazel nut which the local doctor realised needed more than lancing and would have to be cut out. Physically low, he was suffering from monotony – 'the cord of monotony is stretched most tight,' a quotation from G. K. Chesterton which was on Greene's lips at this time. 'I feel', he wrote to Vivien, 'like a mummy suddenly crumbling up inside, because the damp has got to it.' It was with such feelings predominating that on 8 September he walked before breakfast the eight miles to Chesterfield to have his undecayed tooth out.

*

At this time, even though he was disappointed in the work he was producing, he was still dragging himself to the writing table in the billiard room of the Ambervale Hotel – where his invariable presence became a stock joke. To cope with his sense of failure as a writer, he resolved 'to do a minimum of 500 words a day' – the habit first begun in his digs in Smith Street just before he went to Ashover. He promised himself to write 500 words daily for three days only.* Perhaps it was his method of keeping at bay depressions which descended arrow-swift upon him. He had no belief in himself as a writer, and was conscious only of lack of talent: yet he still hoped for popularity: 'I felt intensely depressed when I went up to bed last night, and struggled through the allotted span of the novel . . . I'd

---

* In this way a life-long routine was established, which was to lead to over fifty books.

been reading through things I'd written & I felt that I'd never be able to do anything which was even low second class. And I even envied Alfred Noyes for his safe position in the third rate:'* 'I've finished about 13,000 words of the novel . . . oh it's so bad . . . there's not a properly sane individual left in it now.'[12] Perhaps the lack of sanity in his created characters reflected his own bizarre feelings. And while he felt strongly his own personal unworthiness set against that of Vivien – 'You are so wonderful, & I'm so paltry. I crawl about on the ground' – he persisted in writing:

> I'm so tired of writing second rate verse. Why can't I write you a really fine poem, which would be worthy of you? I shouldn't mind then, if I never wrote another word in my life. But it doesn't come & I go on jangling words, & at times I feel the whole thing's hopeless, & I shall never ever have the advantage of popularity which Noyes has got. And even William Watson has written one first class poem . . . If only I could do something, something for you.[13]

Greene did in fact write a poem for Vivien. At the beginning of the year, he had written a last poem to Gwen Howell expressing his distracted love. That poem's first line began with the odd assertion: 'If you were dead, it would not matter'. The poem for Vivien parallels this, is more detailed, and is a further indication of his troubled condition:

> If you lay dying in a very quiet room,
> No sound to break the long & lapping stillness,
> And no one there but I, to watch the encroaching gloom
> Cast its first shadows over your adventurousness,
> I should not weep or mutter prayers or bow my head;
> I should not even hold your hand & rest in quiet,
> To catch the fading syllables of breath, instead,
> Standing at window, watching the colours riot
> Over a case of apples in the yard, I'd say,
> 'The sun is warm. The lane is scarlet with the hips,'
> And turning round to catch once more your eyes at play
> Find hovering death aquiver on your lips.
> And because death closing your breath, had closed my brain,
> Adventure done & all long voyaging, left only calm,

---

* Alfred Noyes (1880–1958) published his first book of verse while still a student. He became a convert to the Roman Catholic Church in 1925. His work has not survived early admiration and is too facile for modern tastes.

Like a poor music box, no hand to alter, tells the same old
    tune again,
I'd stand & say to all that came, 'The sun is warm.'

If he contemplated Vivien's death, he considered also his own suicide
by drowning at the very height of his love:

Loving you is like being drowned in a moment of ecstasy, during
a clean, swift stroke, when the whole arc of blue is caught up by
the eye, & death comes & leaves eternally pictured on the mind the
clean blue sweep of the sky, & indelibly carved on thought, frozen
in death, your head & eyes & hair, & all things nearly worthy to
be your rivals, shade & scent & sun. And the mind dwells on these
eternally, knowing there is to be no awaking.

In his later novels his style is pithy and controlled; in these letters
his language is more extravagant: 'My angel, I haven't got to the top
of the hill yet, & I may never get to the top, though I'm going to
fight hard . . . And there'll be no question of getting to the top and
seeing the view, & then turning back the way I came. There'd be the
blinding ecstatic moment on the summit, with the wind in my ears,
& the sun on the sea, & then I'd start down the other side. And on
the downward slope the poppies would blink red fox eyes through
the corn, & a lark would sweep singing from a yellow gorse bush.'[14]
The images become confused but his seriousness is never in doubt:
'& then there'd be the endless country on the other side to explore,
with a fresh adventure & a fresh period every day, until the end of
all, swimming out through the warm, dusking sea to the red ball of
the sun setting.' He could even be comic:

I love you more than John Donne, more than the Pennines, more
than pinewoods; more than 'No No Nanette'* & Joseph Conrad
& wet laurels; more than St Joan & Claud Cockburn; more than
shrimps, raspberries & cream, & song in the dark; more than dusk
in Piccadilly from the top of a bus,† than the sun on the Needles
below Southampton, or Leslie Henson.‡ I love you more than I
love this wretched self even.

* 'No, No, Nanette' (1925), a musical comedy by Otto Harback and Frank
Mandel. It was presented at the Globe Theatre on 16 September. It started out as a
disaster and ended up as one of the most successful musicals of the 1920s, running
for 321 performances.
    † A description of 'Piccadilly from the top of a bus' appears in the unpublished
novel 'The Episode' which he was writing when living at Ashover.
    ‡ Leslie Henson was a popular comedian during the 1920s and 1930s.

But, more important, he was moving slowly towards Catholicism:

> Darling, I could worship *with* you, if you had your arms round me
> . . . You see, when I see that Catholicism can produce something so
> fine all through, I know there must be something in it.

Vivien returned from Italy on 7 September. Greene tried to arrange
a meeting for the 15th but she resisted. His anxiety shows in his
enquiring about a certain Dick Ellis. Also, there are references to
older men interested in Vivien. He draws a pathetic picture – the
unathletic young graduate set against someone who excels in games:
'Is he a young hearty athlete who will discuss Rugger prospects, or
one of the ancient hearty, I haven't played Rugger for three & a half
years, though I did used to like it . . .' Honest as ever, he added: 'I
was never much good.'

Greene must have felt that no matter what he said or did, Vivien
would not accept him. He had, after all, agreed to her notions of
married life, in which the principal component was companionship:
'I entirely agree with what you say about marriage, neither person
should be tied to the other. Marriage doesn't mean it necessarily.
Why should we follow tradition? My darling we'd be originals.'
Vivien's reluctance to see him was all too apparent: 'You are anxious,
aren't you that I shouldn't pick up any stray scraps of hope from
your letters. You didn't want to see me on the 15th, & I want it so
much myself, because I don't know at all whether I may not be
packed off to Glasgow or somewhere *any* day. You put love in
inverted commas, as if I was a poor fool ready to misunderstand
every word you uttered. I thought that I had made it clear before,
while I was still B.A.T.ing that I was satisfied, more than satisfied
with your kind of love; can't you believe that I understand & love
you a great deal in your own way too, an awful great deal? But of
course if you'd really rather not, it shall be the 26th . . . I've been
looking forward to the 15th all the time you've been in Italy, marking
off a calendar of days.'[15] The above was written at 9.30 a.m. By
1.30 p.m., he had written a second letter and a third by 7.30:

> I'm in one of those moods when one feels simply futile & a waste
> & no good to anyone, merely an expensive luxury for my parents.
> If I'd gone to China I should have been unhappy & hated the job
> but I should have been doing something. Though the only thing
> worth doing at the moment seems to be to go & get killed somehow
> in an exciting manner. Then at least there is one clean, certain
> sensation. Don't take any notice of all this morbidity . . . I'm

getting to know these moods. I've had them nearly as long as I can remember, & have found different cures. At sixteen I made myself ill for three weeks by drinking quantities of stuff out of red labelled bottles – very childish & laughable. And then later I got out of it by my Irish tour for the W[eekly] W[estminster] – & then there was the trip in the Ruhr, in the hope of getting into trouble with the French, Cockburn (that's why I like him) being of much the same temperament as myself. And then there were the Paris Communists in January [what follows is crossed out but is easily read] & last, about what I told you in the Cinema. They were all just, cowardly, if you like, cures for this beastly mood . . . this is a beastly sort of letter to write . . . but I can't help it.

This letter, and the two which follow, offer us an insight into Greene's psychology which future letters do not reveal, for he becomes more guarded in later years. From them we can see that examples of courage in later life probably stem from a desire to take risks, to invite disaster, to bring about death by misadventure. His is a brilliant mind, yet he has a compulsion when suffering from depression to put his mind totally to sleep, to let events determine fate: 'One can't help envying the people of my age in 1914. Everything at any rate was absolutely settled for them. Nothing they could do could alter their fate. They were either going to die or live, & they could just drift with the crowd. I should like the Germans better than ever, if only they'd start a show [war] now again.' Greene likes war on the curious ground that he can have his life determined for him. But also, the strenuous nature of war, the sense of living dangerously, of feeling preternaturally alive, appeals to something deep in him.

In a fourth letter to Vivien that same day the character of Greene's depression becomes apparent:

God . . . I haven't felt as bad as this since January [the time when he suffered from his hopeless passion for Gwen Howell and tried Russian roulette]. I suppose if I analyse it, it's liver or something, but my mind's like a bubble & it's getting bigger & bigger, & if it bursts I feel I shall simply shriek & shriek & not be able to stop. I'm feeling so blastedly hopeless . . . as if that one in fifty chance has gone. It's been your last two letters. I felt that . . . you were feeling less fond of me than ever before & the bubble gets bigger, & I want, oh God, how I want to be dead, or asleep or blind drunk or anything so that I can't think. Not merely not think of you drifting away into a one in a million chance but not think of anything at all . . . if my intuition's right, & there's not even a one in fifty chance, say so for God's sake straight away. But don't think it's you that are making me worried like this. I got like this, long before I knew you. What you've done is to make it come seldom instead of often. If I hadn't met you, I shouldn't have known how long it would go on for . . . It's easy enough for depression to find a cause. If it weren't you, it would be something else.

Perhaps in response to this letter of pain, Vivien decided to see Greene the day his tutoring ended. When he said goodbye to his charge and the family – 'a long pathetic farewell to mothers, aunts, great aunts, & grandfathers' – of Chestermans at Ashover Grange, he took a taxi to Chesterfield station.

Desperate to meet Vivien he caught an early train to Oxford and began at once another train letter describing his trip through the Black Country:

The Black Country's looking very beautiful this afternoon, great blast furnaces & fires & slag heaps, with the sun on them . . . I think, dark & mysterious like the Black Forest; one expects each chimney to be the one & only Dark Tower. But I have seen no Childe Roland yet, setting the slug horn dauntless to his lips.*

His excitement is that of a boy:

1.40. Leicester. Only a little more than an hour before Oxford . . . I've almost been to sleep. I kept on waking up during the night owing to excitement. At 5.30 there was a most wonderful sky, which I could see from where I lay in bed like a burning forest.

Darling, what fun it must be to build a bridge, a great steel bridge, with giant girders, like a God's meccano outfit.

Worried about being short of money, Greene thought of his friend, Kenneth Bell, the Balliol tutor: 'When I get to Oxford I shall have to rush round & borrow some money, because I've no cheques left, & the bank will be closed. Perhaps my tutor will be back.' Graham admired Kenneth Bell enormously:

---

* Browning's poem 'Childe Roland to the Dark Tower Came' with its final lines: 'I saw them and I knew them all. And yet/Dauntless the slug-horn to my lips I set,/ And blew. *Childe Roland to the Dark Tower Came.*' In his novel *A Gun for Sale* (1936), Greene has his detective Saunders refer to Browning's poem while he waits for the killer Raven: he repeats 'over to himself to pass the time the line of a poem learnt at school about a dark tower.'

I got a card from my tutor, Kenneth Bell, in France, offering to exert influence on practically every paper in the British Empire from the Scotsman to the Toronto Globe. But I refuse to go to Toronto. I might just as well go to China as there, as far as seeing you is concerned. Kenneth's a delightful individual. He accepts anything one does with immense enthusiasm, as though it were the one thing in the world, ideally suited. He bubbled over with joy at the idea of my being in the B.A.T. and now, directly he hears I've chucked it, and am going in for journalism, he sends an enthusiastic card, beginning 'Damn Tobacco and China' and offering his assistance in the new direction. I've never known a man I've admired more. Chucked up his Balliol fellowship, when war came, did extraordinarily well in the Artillery, although previously he'd had no scientific training, returns and is the most brilliant lecturer in Oxford on the Tudor period, full of ideas, swears like a Billingsgate fish porter, and married to a very fascinating, though not beautiful wife.★

Greene, who had arranged to meet Vivien opposite Wadham College at seven, arrived in Oxford early, took a taxi to Blackwell's where he had the driver stop, and left his train letter for Vivien without seeing her. But his evening with her must have been singularly satisfying for, two days later, writing from the Golden Cross Hotel at 8.45 a.m., he felt able to suggest a most novel form of engagement:

My darling love, thank you so much for the dear cinema note. It stayed under my pillow all through the night, & slept when I did, which wasn't very much . . . I wrote to you before the Capitol [the cinema] proposing a Marriage . . . can't we have an Engagement, which the World would not call an Engagement. I would not ask that that one in fifty chance should be increased. I would wait until I was settled & then ask you whether you'd marry me . . .

And the final lines of his letter show he was to go further:

here's a secret between us two. It's my turn to be shy now of speaking. I couldn't tell you aloud last night, even in the dark. Directly I know that I'm going to be settled somewhere for a few months on end, I'm going to get instruction & become a Catholic, if they'll have me.

★ In later years, Bell left his wife for a student. He lost his position at Balliol as a result. Later he became a Protestant minister. Sadly, he ended his own life.

PART 4

Conversion

16

In Search of a Career

So harshly has expectance been imposed
On my long need while those slow blank months passed.
— THOMAS HARDY

AFTER the meeting at the Golden Cross Hotel, Vivien agreed that
they should become engaged, though she made more restrictive
conditions. Greene was not to anticipate greater hopes of winning
her hand than an 80:1 chance; the engagement had to remain a secret
(only family being told), and the ring, when Graham had bought it
('Will you tell me what single stone you'd like best? I'll get it directly
I'm in pocket'), would not be worn in public. Plaintively, Greene
asked her: 'You'll wear [the ring] sometimes, won't you, when you
are alone with me?'[1]

We have no account of the response of Greene's family to the
engagement but a letter about it from Vivien's mother has survived.
Marion Dayrell was intelligent, forceful, even domineering, and she
had written novels ('a few rather poor ones under a pseudonym, but
her best book, *Maids of Honour*, under her own name', was how her
daughter described them). 'She left her husband in Africa,' Vivien
told me, 'worked for the War Office during the First World War
translating French, German, Swahili, Dutch and some other African
dialects likely to be used in German East Africa. She was very clever,
a good rider, adventurous. She was governess for a time to Rudyard
Kipling's children.'[2]

Mother and daughter had a passion for cats. She begins her letter
by addressing Vivien as 'My precious baby sugar-kitten', and ended
it, 'Your own whiskerspuss':

I do think it has been *sweet* of you to tell me about G. That you
did gives me an immense & fatuous pleasure because you cd. so
easily have said nothing & kept me in the dark. Darling pusskin I

not only feel flattered but honoured. I purr, being intensely gratified & rewarded for any small use I have ever been to you . . . Lots of mothers – even ever such delightful ones – would have been quite shut out. If anything could make me love you more, it is this kindness to an idiotic mother-cat who must have made so many mistakes in dealing with her adored kitten [the bite comes in what follows since her daughter was a convert and Vivien's mother only a reluctant believer] & who moreover, having no soul, is quite unworthy.

Darling little Viv – Graham's a poet & says things better, but he has not one millionth of the reason for loving you that I have & he never could have . . . Willie [her cat] is blissfully asleep on the rug & I suppose G. is blissfully re-living his afternoon with you (You two darling sillies really had *no* tea!).

Greene himself walked about in a dream: 'I went for a walk with Paddy [his dog] in a queer state of absolutely peaceful happiness in you . . . I got wet to the skin, but it didn't disturb my strange serenity.'[3]

Labouring under such love he would have agreed to anything Vivien might have demanded – that the sky was green, roses purple, the earth flat, or the moon's halo an ill omen. Even her discovering Negro spirituals was enough to bring about an excited response: 'Darling, we *have* got similarities! I love the Negro spirituals, most of all I think, "Swing Low Sweet Chariot," & next "Walking all over God's heaven."'

*

On 4 October 1925, at the age of twenty-one, Greene reached his legal majority. His father gave him a gold ring with a heraldic design on its surface, a griffin. He wore this on his left hand. When working for British Intelligence in Sierra Leone during the Second World War he used it as a seal for official and secret correspondence.

Asked by Vivien what present he wanted for his twenty-first, Greene answered with a long list:

Item.   As many stars [kisses] as can be compressed into the day.
Item.   Two lips – very lovely.
Item.   A voice that can put more loveliness into a few words than Kreisler into all of Bach.
Item.   Long & dark, mysterious, very beautiful hair – not too tidy, *please.*

Item. Two eyes like a pool in a magic wood, with the sun between the leaves lightening the green & mingling it with the gleam of silver birches.

Item. Two very small hands & two very small small feet, with ten fingers & ten toes like any mortal, but what fingers & what toes.

Item. Two legs lovelier than those of Mistinguette or Gaby Deslys, who lost King Manuel of Portugal his throne.

Item. Skin of a lovely & perfect white – or else of a lovely & novel brown.

Item. A lovelier & more precious home for my hand than I could ever find, though I lived for as long as the wandering Jew & sought for one all those years.[4]

But Greene also persuaded Vivien to come to Berkhamsted for his birthday and he described the family she would meet:

1 My father	(clever, rather sweet, but more sentimental even than I am, & I never was till I met you!)
2 My mother	(taller I think than yours. Perhaps that's why I didn't feel frightened of yours! Quite unterrifying though.)
3 My aunt	(the one I stay with at Battersea. Unmarried. Middle aged. My favourite aunt. Rather charming & very broadminded & up to date in her taste. You'll like her, I'm sure!)
4 My Oxford brother [Raymond]	(the one engaged to C. Inclined to be a little stiff & ram-roddish.)
5 My younger brother [Hugh]	(of whom I'm jealous already.)
6 My younger sister	(horribly tall for her age. Taller than you, I believe, but not old enough yet to be terrifying.)
7 Myself	

This was to be Vivien's first visit and, as Greene described it, nature was told of her impending arrival: 'We went for a walk through the beechwoods into Ashridge Park & I told every tree we passed, "Vivien's going to come & see you."' And when her arrival was delayed, he speaks of the beechwoods' growing impatience: 'They say, "We are spreading a carpet for your love's feet, but we cannot feel her tread." I feel conscience-stricken at having promised them these things.'[5]

Also, he felt able to dispense love with wild abandon: 'Give my love to Gladys Loveless, & to B[asil] B[lackwell] & to A.S.M[ott]. & to Hugh & to Markhouse & to Plumb & to Broad St & to each inmate of the Y.W.C.A. [where Vivien lived while working for Blackwell] & to the crossing sweeper, & to the man with the fruit cart & the top hat. And add all this love together, & multiply it by Infinity, & give the sum total to yourself.' And he made the following declaration:

> This is to certify that whereas the aforesaid Graham Greene has on this day, October 2nd, attained his legal majority & has thus become legal master of himself & his own actions, the aforesaid Graham Greene herewith states & declares that he surrenders himself entire, with no reservation, to be the property sole & freehold, of Miss Vivienne Dayrell, to do with as she may at any time think fit.
>
> Signed: – Graham Greene.
> Witness: Paddy [dog] – his mark

That month of October was to be a period of highs and lows and would eventually bring him to an acceptance of hard facts. Conscious of their youth he wrote: '& we won't let other people come in between us & make us behave, darling. We won't. The world belongs to the young, & we are going to teach it manners, & to speak only when it's spoken to.'

His imagined future success, outlined for Vivien's amusement, followed traditional lines: 'Darling, I can't be the Uncrowned King of Arabia, but I'll be The Right Honourable Graham Greene, youngest Conservative Prime Minister since Pitt, or Mr Graham Greene, O.M.* the successor of Thomas Hardy, or Sir Graham Greene, K.C.B. War Correspondent for the Times, & secret military adviser to the Emir of Afghanistan. Which would you prefer, dear heart? Any of them can be quite easily managed.'[6]

He had an idea that he would one day produce great work, and what he hoped to produce makes curious reading today:

---

* Mr Graham Greene was appointed to the Order of Merit by Queen Elizabeth on 10 February 1986.

My great works: The life of Prince Rupert.★
                         The Poetry of Christina Rossetti & that most
                         final & authoritative work.
                         The Carolians, in which of course will be incor-
                         porated the great essay on the Cavalier Spirit
                         in Religion.[7]

He was working hard on his novel: 'You see, if I can't tear up "The Episode", I'm determined to make you like it, before I've done with it.'[8] But vague notions of future achievement butter no parsnips. He could still be made to feel uncertain about the road he was travelling. Having at last read John Masefield's *Multitude & Solitude*, he regrets not having read it when he was fifteen as he would now have been a scientist: 'He proves with convincing power that writers are anachronisms . . . the thing which is of the greatest importance in any age, is the thing for which people die. So in the sixteenth century people died for religion, & in the seventeenth for constitutional government, & in the early nineteenth to a certain extent for literature. But now it's people like the radium man in France, & Professor Lefray who sacrifice themselves.'[9]

Although admitting that he would rather go on an Antarctic Expedition ('for that one must be either a millionaire or a naval officer or a scientist'),[10] he was now coming to accept that he must find a job, however prosaic, in the newspaper world. During September he had done some reviewing: 'I've got four novels from W[eekly] W[estminster] for review. . . it's a start & I'm getting a life of More from the Times Lit. Supp.' And late that month he visited the journalist 'Touchstone', whose advice was to make a tour of the provincial towns, as the provincial papers were clamouring for intelligent sub-editors, 'because they could never keep them, as after a short time they all shifted to the better paid job of leader writing.'[11] He settled on seeking employment as a sub-editor and threw himself into the search. He persuaded a friend to drop a line to Ramsay Muir, who he had heard was looking for a sub-editor willing to live in the provinces.

Impatient as ever, Greene wrote to Vivien the following day: 'I'm going to wait till the beginning of next week, & then, if I haven't heard from Muir, I shall take a trip to Birmingham, with a letter of

★ The most talented Royalist of the English Civil War, known by Royalists and Roundheads alike as the 'Mad Cavalier', the life and vitality of the Royalist cause, headstrong, brilliant and wilful, he won many battles – and lost many. His last years were spent conducting scientific experiments and he introduced mezzotint print-making into England, describing it to the Royal Society in 1662. He also invented an improved gunpowder.

introduction to the Editor of the Birmingham Daily Post, & try & take the offices by storm.'

The *Scotsman* also became a possibility: 'Sir John Findlay writes and says that they pay Union salaries from the beginning.' The *Scotsman* clearly attracted him, though in the margin of his letter to Vivien he fears parting from her: 'Edinburgh is so very far away.' He need not have worried. Later he wrote, 'I've just heard that there's nothing doing in that direction, & I've got to start the hunt all over again!'[12] But there was some consolation: 'My free lancing has begun to come in quicker. A proof from the Lit. Supp. of a short article called the "Growth of Truth on More & Gresham", & two proofs from the W.W., a short article on Stendhal, of whom I know nothing, & of the sonnet "Lord Love, when will you weary of this War?" We'll soon have the ring, darling, at this rate!'

Greene's next letter to Vivien hints why the *Scotsman* turned him down. In attempting to produce copy, he ran foul of certain (unstated) newspaper conventions of the time: 'I know that in all my work there are inclined to be scattered sentences, which the Isis informed me offends good taste, & the Scotsman says should be left in the smoking room!!! I know it, but I put them there of set purpose, to try & get the sort of effect of a leap from the ground – contrast in other words.'[13]

*

Greene went on his rapid tour of the North. Like Quixote charging at windmills, he attacked the provincial newspapers. He tried the *Yorkshire Post* and the *Bolton Journal*. 'The editor,' he told Vivien, 'Tillotson by name is a Balliol man & I have an introduction to him.'[14] 'WILL ME LUCK THIS AFTERNOON' he telegraphed her and Vivien did try to *will* Graham into a post.

He made an appointment to see Sir Charles Starmer, the great newspaper magnate of the day, for Greene was willing to beard any lion in any den if it helped win Vivien: 'I braved Sir Charles Starmer indeed dragged him out from a Westminster Gazette board meeting, & he's writing to the editors of [three of] his . . . provincial papers, The Northern Echo, The Sheffield Independent & The Birmingham Gazette.'

At the last minute he decided on a helter-skelter Birmingham visit: 'And from the [train] whistles we seem to be off', he wrote in his train letter to Vivien. 'I am told by the News of the World that Birmingham is the most immoral city in the world, which sounds exciting. I arrive before 8.'

Alas, Greene's northern journey 'to the most immoral city' didn't pay off: 'Birmingham didn't want me, darling. Poor Birmingham, they little know the treasure they have thrown away.' Yet there was hope, and it lay in Charles Starmer: 'if the Yorkshire Post fails, I can get training on The Nottingham Journal', another of Starmer's papers.[15] The trouble with Nottingham was that the *Journal* did not offer inexperienced sub-editors any salary and Greene desperately wanted independence from his parents.

He had already visited the London editor of the *Yorkshire Post* and felt the atmosphere was hopeful and he later received an invitation from its editor to return – 'if he's taking the trouble to interview me, it means he's willing to take someone'. After he had seen the editor, he announced, 'The Yorkshire Post may take me for three months probation', but Greene sounded a note of disappointment soon afterwards: 'I didn't much care for the editor of the Y.P. I felt absolutely no common ground.' Yet he was willing to go to the provinces 'in the smoke of Leeds & the nearly equal smoke of Nottingham'. Greene's youthful contempt for the third-ratedness of things provincial comes out in his next letter:

> I haven't heard yet from Leeds but I don't really mind whether I go there or to Nottingham. In a way I should prefer Nottingham. I should get much more attention there – a third rate paper, run by third class people & I should arrive under the aegis of the great Starmer. Also S. says in a tactful manner 'they might manage a small commencing salary, if you are going to assist the editor with contributions.' I think I should almost certainly get practice in leader writing, which I should not get at Leeds, & I have no intention of sticking finally to the editing side of journalism.[16]

At the last moment, Sir Charles Starmer, an endlessly friendly man, offered Greene leader writing on his Birmingham paper. In spite of Starmer's kindness, Greene made a controlled, rational decision to go to Nottingham, for Nottingham decided to take him on as a trainee sub-editor. He knew he needed experience as a sub-editor to find a place on the staff of *The Times*: 'I'm not going to endanger my future aims of The Times for a small salary in the hand', he wrote to Vivien. Once he had made a decision, Greene's concern was to do day-time, not night-time, sub-editing: 'Evening papering is useless for my purpose, as the whole technique is different . . . I pray it will be the morning, otherwise, as far as I can see, the whole business will have to start again. Journalism ought to be a fairly select profession, if everyone has as much trouble to get into it.'[17]

But 'evening papering' it had to be – that was the offer. At last, five months after he had graduated, Graham Greene made a start in the right direction.

17

Sub-editing in Nottingham

There was no dawn that day in Nottwich. Fog lay over
the city . . .

— GRAHAM GREENE

WHEN Greene left for Nottingham on 1 November 1925, the
train running past his old digs in Thorncliffe Road, he had a
strong desire to break down and weep. He felt concussed and half
out of his mind, for it was there he had often entertained Vivien and
seeing it slide past sharpened his sense of loss.

Ten years later his strong feeling of deprivation was to be reflected
in his thriller *A Gun for Sale*, (entitled *This Gun for Hire* in America),
when Raven, the hare-lipped killer on the run, catches the train to
Nottwich, and sees London recede, 'like a man watching something
he loves slide back from him out of his reach'.

Greene's letter to Vivien vividly describes his arrival at his new
home in Hamilton Road, Nottingham: 'The train was an hour late,
& it was raining & dark & the streets were almost unlighted, & the
taximan lost his way, & when I arrived I found it was not digs at all,
where I could be alone & hold you in a thought.'

The house in Hamilton Road turned out to be a boarding house,
which meant more communal living with two elderly and civilised
ladies '& an awful man, who had been at Oxford in 1914 for six
months & considered himself a University man, & whose mind is
the lowest cesspool of dirt I've ever come across.' Though he'd just
arrived, the old ladies, to make him feel welcome, invited him to
play cards, which they did until it was time for them to retire.
Graham found the latest intruder into his world as insufferable as the
bank clerk at the B.A.T.: 'the hearty proceeded to talk filth, which
I shouldn't have minded a bit a year ago, & it's so damned hard not
to follow suit, for fear of being considered a prig.'

The next day he was cheered by his first impressions of the editorial
office: 'The sun is shining, & I went along to the office this morning.

235

The editor wasn't in, but I saw the assistant editor, a young man, who was at Magdalen & he seemed an oasis in the desert. Extremely pleasant, & gave the somewhat heartening feeling that he was really glad to see me & have me there.' Moreover, he found the news editor to be 'a perfectly dear old man and frightfully kindly' and the other sub-editors 'cheerful friendly . . . with strong Notts. accents'.

Greene's working hours were from 5.30 p.m. until midnight – 'luckily Oxford got me used to bed at one', but on his first evening they let him off work early to break him in gently. Greene was soon deeply involved in the intricacies of his new job:

> The telegrams come in, & one has to go through them, filling in the missing words, & punctuating & where necessary correcting the grammar, & dividing into paras, & where possible cutting out a word here & there. If they are merely local news, one has to decide whether they are of sufficient value to go in.

The most amusing part, because it was rather like a cross-word puzzle, was doing the headlines:

> Each different type is called by a number. Leaving out the front page, there are eight different kinds. Each kind allows a different number of letters to the line, a space counting as a letter. The biggest type for the most important news & so on down. First one decides which type the particular news shall be allowed. Then one has to think out headlines to catch the eye, with the most interesting points in the news & with not more than the right number of letters. If one is very clever, one gets a lot of i's into the headline, & then one can cram in an extra letter. If one gets too many M's or W's, one can't have as many letters.

He found the technical aspect of sub-editing, and the speed with which the older sub-editors worked, deeply impressive. He 'took a quarter of an hour to correct a telegram of only a few lines', about the Prince of Wales saying goodbye to some emigrants:

> The worst part is the news which comes in from local agents in the towns round about in packets by trains. These have the same abbreviations as telegrams, very little punctuation, wd for would, & so on, & in the most ghastly handwriting, often in pencil.[1]

He was happy, finding the office 'frantically Dickensian', and scribbling to Vivien, 'disjointedly between divorce telegrams & violent assaults, & still more violent headings of my own devising', he catches for us the atmosphere of the place:

> We sit round a table together, with the News Editor . . . at the head, & snip & blue pencil & talk & smoke away, like a family party. And just before ten, someone goes out & buys two penny parcels of hot potato chips to eat, & the old bald headed Irishman, who does the Sporting page, puts on the kettle & makes tea. He's a dear, foul-mouthed perhaps, but in a Rabelaisian manner. Good solid earth, not slime, like the man in the boarding house. And then there's a huge fat man with rather long hair, who does the Angling notes, who wanders in about 10.30 & keeps everybody from working by telling endless tall fish stories.

And it seemed that even the secretarial staff were chosen on aesthetic grounds: 'There is a quite astonishing beauty chorus of secretaries of the "fluffy, chocolate box" kind.'

In his autobiography, Greene remembered the office building in Parliament Street: 'One entered . . . through a narrow stone Gothic door, stained with soot, which resembled the portal of a Pugin chapel, and the heads of Liberal statesmen stuck out above like gargoyles: on rainy days the nose of Gladstone dripped on my head as I came in.'[2] (It could not have been Gladstone's, but Palmerston's nose which dripped water on Greene's head.)

Such was Greene's initial happiness in the office that on one occasion, while correcting copy, he had an urge to break into song. His colleagues, he tells Vivien, would not have been surprised: 'Constant telegrams of Amazing and Startling Revelations have dried up the power of surprise. The old News Editor would have looked at me over his glasses and said, "Feeling cheerful, Son?", "Charley," who does the bigger divorces, would gently murmur, "Nottingham Gal got you?", "Leslie," Chief sub & Foreign News, would merely utter a loud base laugh, "John Albert," Parliamentary, would only grunt, and run his fingers through his hair, whilst my table companion, the little bald headed fat Irish Rabelais, Carleton, the Sports Page, would twinkle his pig eyes, and laugh.'

Also, he was appreciated, coming back very cheerful from the office when told he was picking things up well. Something of the effort Greene puts into a job shows in a letter to Vivien: 'I have to take in an awful lot of papers now, The Nottingham Journal to see if any of my [type]heads have been altered and how. The Westminster Gazette to try and get the atmosphere, and memorize the types, and compare their different values of the news. The Times for the same.'[3]

Although Greene soon began to see Nottingham as a place 'undisturbed by ambition',[4] it also made a strong impression on him which he recorded in *A Gun for Sale*:

There was no dawn that day in Nottwich. Fog lay over the city like a night sky with no stars. The air in the streets was clear. You have only to imagine that it was night. The first tram crawled out of its shed and took the steel track down towards the market. An old piece of newspaper blew up against the door of the Royal Theatre and flattened out. In the streets on the outskirts of Nottwich an old man plodded by with a pole tapping at the windows. The stationer's window in the High Street was full of Prayer Books and Bibles: a printed card remained among them, a relic of Armistice Day, like the old drab wreath of Haig poppies by the War Memorial: 'Look up, and swear by the slain of the war that you'll never forget' . . . the lit carriages drew slowly in past the cemetery . . . a smell of bad fish came in from the glue factory.[5]

There were two glue factories in Nottingham but the one which afflicted the passengers as they descended from the tram was probably Halls' Glue & Bone works, the Trentside Works in Holme Street. The smell, reaching Greene in his digs, was not forgotten.

But it was the fog that he remembered as lying over the city 'like a night sky with no stars,' and in *Journey Without Maps*, written simultaneously with *A Gun for Sale*, as lying 'heavy and black between the sun and the earth'.[6] Fog becomes an important narrative element in the novel. It helps to establish between the kidnapped (Anne Weaver) and kidnapper (Raven) an intimate relationship.[7] Because of it Raven is able to escape from the police – 'a cold damp yellow fog from the river, through which it would be easy, if it was thick enough, for a man to escape.'[8]

During his stay in Nottingham, one particular fog lasted two days.

A most marvellous fog here to-day [he wrote to Vivien]. It makes walking a thrilling adventure. I've never been in such a fog before in my life. If I stretch out my walking stick in front of me, the ferula is half lost in obscurity. Coming back I twice lost my way, & ran into a cyclist, to our mutual surprise. Stepping off a pavement to cross to the other side becomes a wild & fantastic adventure, like sailing into the Atlantic to find New York, with no chart or compass. Once where the breadth of the road was greater than the normal, I found myself back on the same pavement as I started, having slowly swerved in my course across the road.

He warned Vivien, 'If you never hear from me again, you will know that somewhere I am moving round in little plaintive circles, looking for a pavement.' Coming back from the office after midnight, the next day, Greene lost his way twice between the tram stop and his house, a distance of thirty yards.

After only two weeks, he made a move from the boarding house in Hamilton Road; he would have left earlier but for the fact that he did not want to upset his good landlady. The first excuse he gave was that he wanted a room to himself. The landlady promptly put her own sitting room at Greene's disposal without extra charge. He then told her that he would be bringing his dog Paddy from Berkhamsted and the trouble that would cause, but she countered that by stressing her love for dogs. 'She's awfully kind,' he wrote to Vivien, 'I don't know what to do?' The trouble lay of course in his dislike for the awful man with a mind like a cesspool:

> I can't very well explain that I don't like having meals at a table with other people, & that I intensely dislike some of her guests. The man is really quite unbearable. He's always asking what I think of the suit or the overcoat he's wearing, & then telling me the price. He has an inferiority complex. Yesterday he said, 'I like this boarding house. The ladies here are quite one's social equals,' & then turned with a sudden anxiety – 'Don't you think so?' I longed to say that I thought they were quite immeasurably his superiors. Terrible man.[9]

However, he found new digs at Ivy House* in All Saints Terrace, 'a grim grey row with a grim grey name',[10] but they were close to the park and only ten minutes' walk from his office. Full board was 35s. a week and included a sitting room of his own, which he described to Vivien as 'quite large & has bird wallpaper, the door has carved panels, leaves in the bottom ones & large figures with their names carved in parallelograms below of Diana & Ceres.'

Once winter set in, he became fed up with Nottingham: 'O blast the fog . . . I can't see a foot outside the window,' he complained to Vivien, 'Nottingham is horrid. Misty and with pavements deep in slush. I brought Paddy back from the vet. He rolled about in the slush and is looking cold . . .' But he was more troubled by Ivy House: 'Why baths are ever built for dwarfs I can't imagine – it's impossible to stretch in this one'; 'gramophone going on eternally in

---

* Although Ivy House appears in no street directory, it is almost certain that Greene lived at no. 2.

the next room', the shouting on the stairs at midnight, the late-
ness of meals. Moreover, he felt an evil influence in the house: 'I
haven't had a proper night's sleep since I came into it. I get to sleep
about 1, and wake up about 4, and then doze on and off till I give
up trying.'[11]

Nottingham and Ivy House were never forgotten and aspects of
them appear in a play and a number of his novels. Whenever he
needed to describe a disreputable house he returned to Ivy House: 'I
cannot invent,' he told V. S. Pritchett.[12] It appears in his play *The
Potting Shed* (1957), in his novels *A Gun for Sale* (1936), *Brighton Rock*
(1938), and *It's a Battlefield* (1934). In *A Gun for Sale*, it is All Saints
Road, 'two rows of small neo-Gothic houses lined up as carefully as
a company on parade',[13] and it is near the park, 'a place of dull
wilted trees and palings and gravel paths for perambulators.' Greene's
furnished rooms in All Saints Terrace did double duty in *A Gun for
Sale*, for he used them as both the digs of the chorus girl Anne Weaver
and the home of Acky, the defrocked priest.[14] In *Brighton Rock*, it is
the home of Lawyer Prewitt: 'Mr Prewitt's house was in a street
parallel to the railway, beyond the terminus . . . shaken by shunting
engines; the soot settled continuously on the glass . . .'[15]

The passageway he traversed daily from his sitting room to the
front door of Ivy House appears in *A Gun for Sale*:

> She stumbled backwards amongst the crowded litter of the little
> dark hall: he noted it all with hatred: the glass case with a stuffed
> pheasant, the moth-eaten head of a stag picked up at a country
> auction to act as a hat-stand, the black metal umbrella-holder
> painted with gold stars, the little pink glass shade over the gas-jet.[16]

It is also transferred to the Brighton of *Brighton Rock* when Pinkie
visits Brewer because he has not paid for protection:

> He looked with contempt down the narrow hall – the shell case
> converted into an umbrella-stand, the moth-eaten stag's head bear-
> ing on one horn a bowler hat, a steel helmet used for ferns.[17]

It is also part of Mrs Coney's house in *It's a Battlefield*.

Twelve years before he wrote *Brighton Rock*, Greene told Vivien
how he had to knock on the wall of his room in Ivy House to stop
another lodger playing his gramophone day and night; the walls were
'so thin you could hear the neighbour move behind the shelves like
a rat'. The experience is transferred to Lawyer Prewitt in *Brighton
Rock*:

'I beat on the wall.' He took a paper-weight off his desk and struck the wall twice: the music broke into a high oscillating wail and ceased. They could hear the neighbour move furiously behind the shelves. 'How now? A rat?' Mr Prewitt quoted. The house shook as a heavy engine pulled out. 'Polonius,' Mr Prewitt explained.[18]

Of his characters Greene writes that they were 'an amalgam of bits of real people' yet he asserts that he did not take people from real life. 'Real people are crowded out by imaginary ones . . . Real people are too limiting.'[19] Very true, but real people were necessary in the creation of fictional ones whether they attracted or repelled him. They forced their way into his imagination through the sheer pressure of his response to them and in that sense are 'fused by the heat of the unconscious'.

In *Ways of Escape* he writes: 'I like too the character of Acky, the unfrocked clergyman, and of his wife – the two old evil characters joined to each other by a selfless love.'[20] When asked in 1982, he could not recall the source of this bizarre couple who appear in the sometimes unreal world of *A Gun for Sale*, but they originated in Nottingham. Acky in *A Gun for Sale* and the crooked lawyer Prewitt in *Brighton Rock* have in common that they have both married and their wives have the same source – Greene's sour and short landlady, who appears in *It's a Battlefield* as Mrs Coney.

In *It's a Battlefield*, Greene describes Milly, the wife of a murdered policeman, as having small jet eyes. She 'gripped the edge of the table as though with an intolerable longing for a blow'. An incompetent woman, 'who drives the dust from one room to settle in another', she is very small: 'she only came half-way to his shoulder, grey and soiled and miserably tender' (*A Gun for Sale*). In *Brighton Rock*, Prewitt discusses his wife with the young gangster: 'Somebody in the basement slammed the floor beneath their feet. "What ho! old mole," Mr Prewitt said. 'The spouse – you've never met the spouse . . . Listen to the old mole down there. She's ruined me.'[21] Mrs Coney in *It's a Battlefield* is also a 'meek suspicious woman . . . Her spirit, like a mole, burrowed circuitously in darkness, emerging at unsuspected places.'[22] One further aspect mentioned in *A Gun for Sale* and *Brighton Rock* ties the two characters together and points to Greene's original model. When Acky's wife plucked at detective Mather, he smelt fish on her fingers. Lawyer Prewitt is at pains to tell Pinkie the kind of food his wife provides – 'tinned salmon, she has a passion for tinned salmon'.[23] Greene is describing his Nottingham landlady, the 'thin complaining widow', who also invariably gave him tinned salmon for high tea. He shared it with his dog Paddy, 'so that most days [the dog] was sick on the floor.'[24] This information is re-used in *The Potting Shed*: 'My landlady has a penchant for tinned salmon. My dog likes it, but it often makes him sick.'[25]

The landlady at Ivy House, All Saints Terrace, a Mrs Loney (how close the spelling is to widow Mrs Coney in *It's a Battlefield*), was by all accounts lazy – 'her gentlemen always clean their own shoes', she told Greene. She was also untidy (as Greene indicates in *It's a Battlefield*), watchful, and lived mostly in her basement where she was alert to the activities of her boarders. In *Brighton Rock* when Pinkie let himself out of Mr Prewitt's house, he looked down and 'met in the basement the hard suspicious gaze of Mr Prewitt's spouse; she had a duster in her hand and she watched him like a bitter enemy from her cave, under the foundations.'[26] Although Mrs Loney lived in the basement she sometimes came into the rooms she was letting, for on one occasion Greene came home unexpectedly to find her in his room writing a letter, and her habit of watching the world from her window is recorded in a letter which Greene wrote to Vivien in late February 1926. She asked his permission to use his ground floor window in order to watch, as she clearly could not do from her basement room, what was going on in her neighbour's house across the way:

> A man down the street was going to be taken to hospital. Dropsy and insanity and incurable. The ambulance at the door. My land-lady said with gusto that they'd find it difficult to get him on to the stretcher. She was very excited. She said she'd never seen anything like this before, and didn't want to miss it. She stood in the window jabbering for a quarter of an hour till they brought him out and the ambulance drove away, giving the most revolting details of his physical appearance with the dropsy.

Greene's only intimate companion during his four months in Nottingham was his dog Paddy, 'a rough-haired terrier with orange & brown bits' who yet called forth sympathy: 'I've never seen a dog which arouses so much promiscuous affection. The number of people who stop and pat him in the streets is extraordinary.'[27] Greene took him for a daily walk in a park where when you touched the leaves they left soot on the fingers. But his dog was in poor condition: 'I took him for a walk after Mass, he was extremely disobedient and I punished him – he was promptly sick. He's a nervy, neurotic beast.'[28] Greene's letters to Vivien are punctuated with references to Paddy's sickness. If he gets too excited he is sick; if he eats tinned salmon he is sick. On one occasion Paddy went down with catarrh, and Greene nursed him to sleep like a child. And during a very cold winter of 1925 and early 1926 they shuddered together in the cold: 'My handwriting's all awry, darling, but my hand is frozen stiff. It's still snowing steadily today. Poor Paddy is cold and miserable. The snow must be fearfully deep outside the town.'[29]

*

Greene's passion for the cinema continued unabated in Nottingham and was the means of escaping from his isolation. It was also cheap entertainment, for matinee seats in the stalls cost only fourpence. Each morning was spent writing a letter to Vivien and then he would do his daily stint of 500 words (on good days treble that number). In the afternoon he could escape to the cinema pretending, as he told Vivien, that she was with him in the darkness. The films were usually cheap and popular: 'Went to a most dramatic film yesterday afternoon *Smouldering Fires* with Pauline Frederick . . . This afternoon I'm going to Betty Balfour in *Satan's Sister*[30] . . . just been to a Cinema, very bad, called *The Wages of Virtue*.'[31] He is curiously priggish over *Spanish Love*: 'Last night I went to a terrible film . . .' It made him despair of the human race, 'the female portion of it especially'. He left the cinema before the film ended. He seems to have developed a hatred for Rudolf Valentino and Richard Cortez: 'One can imagine Novello as a matinee idol, because he really is extra-ordinarily good-looking, but Valentino and this man Cortez are simply gross fleshy animals, behaving like animals. But all the shop girls and stout matrons of England and America go and are thrilled.'[32]

Perhaps he was deliberately going overboard here, knowing that Vivien would applaud these sentiments. Indeed, she must have done so a day later, for we find Greene responding: 'That's exactly what I felt about Valentino & even more about Richard Cortez. I felt the female portion of mankind must be fearfully degraded to flock in crowds to get pleasure from . . . being embraced by him in proxy on the screen.' Yet he was perfectly happy with the simplicities of a swashbuckling hero: 'The new Douglas Fairbanks' *The Black Pirate*. I really begin to like Doug. He's such a refreshing change from the Cortez–Valentino lot. It was a really satisfactory film. Pirates & buried treasure & lots of fighting & ships & a princess held for ransom – altogether pleasant. It was a rather interesting experiment too, as it was all in colour, & much the most successful effect I've seen. It certainly emphasised the "gory" bits! It's really worth seeing.'

Greene was struck by the fact (as was his friend Joseph Macleod) that the cinema had certain advantages for a writer. In special circumstances it produced the right mood to do creative work: 'Cinemas have a peculiar effect. At Oxford if [Macleod] felt vaguely that he wanted to write something he would go to the cinema alone, and then go back to his digs and work at a story or something till 2 in the morning. Is it the concentrated emotion of lots of people? Because it doesn't work if one's not alone, for then one's withdrawn from the general audience and can scoff at the ridiculousness of the picture. It's all very curious.' He admitted that when he saw a film he liked alone, he came out into the street afterwards with his head in the clouds and the absolute certainty that, one day, he would write a good poem. Marvellous schemes flitted through his head: 'A 2,000 line verse poem founded on Browning's lines "The breathless fellow at the altar foot/Fresh from his murder, safe and sitting there".'[33] He was aware that this could not easily be part of a young woman's experience in 1926:

I suppose you never go to cinemas alone. It must be awfully curious, darling, to be a girl. I suppose one never goes to shows alone, or wanders about at night alone – unless one's disreputable. Curious and curiouser. The strange universal prison of the feminine. And you can't travel alone, suddenly pack a bag and go off somewhere. I *am* glad I'm not a girl . . . I should inevitably have fallen into vice by this time, the only means to excitement![34]

Although Greene owed a lot to Nottingham, not least for giving him his first experience of living in a seedy boarding house, his letters show that three weeks after his arrival he had become sufficiently restless and unhappy to begin seeking work in London, thus hoping to cut down what was to be in any case a short stay in the provinces. First he decided to approach *The Times* again: 'I shall point out', he wrote to Vivien, 'that though not exactly *very* experienced I am very much alive! One never knows. I always believe in taking a chance.'[35]

He went to London during the middle of January 1926 and stayed with his brother Raymond. On arriving, he deposited his bag and went out to eat. When he returned, he discovered his brother's sister-in-law had arrived for the night, so he had to make do with a couple of armchairs for a bed. That night he had a vivid dream, reflecting his uncertainty over Vivien's love which exacerbated his sense of hopelessness. He had little doubt that without a job in London at a first class newspaper, his career on no sure footing, he would have no chance of winning Vivien:

We were on a platform and you [Vivien] were going away, and you laughed in the most heartless manner at my misery, and I grew furious and you got cold and taunting and the train came in, and an awful looking bounder considerably older than yourself came along to the carriage door and started talking to you, and you were fearfully affectionate, and gave him your photo. And then I began really to hate you, and I pushed the man away, and took hold of you, by the shoulders and forced you to look at me. And you twisted yourself away, very white and contemptuous and said 'I won't have this. I'm sick of you.' So I got hold of you again and I wasn't furious, but I simply hated you. And I said that I'd make you understand how miserable I'd been for 9 months because of you. And you struggled and I hit you, and felt like hitting you. I hated you curiously enough all the more because I know you were not really sick of me, but were feeling perverse and in the mood for hurting me. And then I thought of a revenge far better. And I said 'I suppose you are going to marry that man?' And you smiled and said 'Yes, I certainly am.' And I let go of you and said 'Then I'm done with you and everything' and rushed away to shoot myself. Not through love of you, but through hate. Because I felt you'd never get over the thought of having made a Catholic kill himself. I woke up then, but the dream was so strong that though I knew it was a dream, the echo of the hate I'd felt drowned the real you. And I still felt that hatred.[36]

'It wasn't just a nightmare,' he explained to Vivien, 'it was evil in its vividness.'

Twenty years later, in *The Heart of the Matter* (1947), written when his marriage was disintegrating, Greene has his hero, Major Scobie, a convinced Catholic, consider the possibility of damning his soul for all eternity by committing suicide. Greene only dreamed of such an action; Scobie carries it out in an organised and cool manner.

In spite of his dream, Greene was excited to be back in London. His visit coincided with great blankets of snow: 'on the embankment . . . [I] can see for miles across endless snow covered fields'.[37] Undeterred by the weather, he tackled the magnate Sir Charles Starmer at the *Westminster Gazette*, once more sending his name in to him. No doubt Starmer was curious as to why Greene should be back in town after he had so recently sent him to the provinces:

I smiled disarmingly and said 'The bad penny' and he said rather disconcertingly 'Yes' and then added with a rather pathetic smile

'And what is it you want, *now*.' And I said with brazen impudence 'A sub-editorship on the *Westminster*.' And he looked rather taken aback and said 'But you only went to Nottingham in November.' So I pointed out that sub-editing was chiefly common sense, which was my strong point and that I'd picked Nottingham dry. And he laughed and rang up the News Editor and asked him to come down, which he did. And Starmer said 'This young man has been at Nottingham for a few weeks, and has come to me with the bold proposal that he should join our staff. Take him away and turn him inside out.'[38]

Greene reported happily to Vivien that he had been practically promised to be taken on for a month or two on probation: 'Cheek is victorious!!' It looked as if he had dug himself out of Nottingham at his very first try and he explained to Vivien that Hillyer, the News Editor, was helpful because he thought Greene must be a friend of Starmer and that Starmer was under the impression that Graham was a friend of his nephew – 'a complicated web'. What was being offered to him was an exciting prospect for a young man – 'a month with reporters, to see the battle, so to speak, from the ranks, and be sent to fires and murders . . . with some practice at leaders', so that Greene should be equipped all round.[39]

While in town he called on an ex-Balliol man, Maurice Gorham, who was then at the *Weekly Westminster*, and Gorham suggested that Graham should join an ex-student friend, Robin Turton, for a year in Hungary. Although intrigued by the idea, Greene was not going to leave Vivien at this stage.[40] He returned to Nottingham feeling that success would soon be his, but a week later he wrote to Vivien: 'Everything's gone wrong . . . I've heard nothing from the Westminster, but had a nasty knock this morning from the W[eekly] W[estminster].' He had received a letter from Gorham, sending back four poems they had already accepted and telling him there would be no more reviewing from them: ' "We *may* meet again under the auspices of Sir Charles Starmer, but as an independent paper we are closing down." '

Starmer, owner of the *Weekly Westminster* and the *Westminster Gazette*, with the failure of one of his papers, had his own troubles now and Greene's hopes were not realised. January 1926 passed without his hearing from the *Gazette*. In Nottingham, he was in the process of converting to Roman Catholicism, and his dislike of Nottingham returned: 'If I go on much longer I shall snap. I've tired of my chain and the stable. There's absolutely nothing worth doing in this beastly place. No excitement, no interest, nothing worth a halfpenny curse.'[41] But early in February there came a second chance of success:

> Things have been annoying. I went to the Times first and was told that Freeman never came till 12. Then I went to the Westminster and Hillyer said that the Union had blocked the scheme. But added politely that he thought I should be a first rate recruit for the paper etc. and that if there was any job going, which would allow him to edge me in sideways and evade the Union, he would do his best etc. Bunk! Then I went to the New Statesman and Mrs Vincent said that [Desmond] MacCarthy was away for the weekend and she rang up his home and they said they expected him back for dinner, so I've got to ring up the office at 4 and if he's dropped in during the afternoon, she'll fix up a meeting. Then I sent a wire to my landlady and rang you up, the one bright spot. And then I went back to the Times and waited till 12.35 and apparently if Freeman did not turn up till then, he wouldn't turn up till 3. So I shall be traipsing back soon, probably on a fruitless errand.

That night he had a most 'fearful nightmare':

> I dreamed I had been followed by a man, like a terribly coarsened and decadent De la Mare and at last I turned on him & in the fight got my thumb in his right eye and pressed and pressed, till – squish! I'd blinded him. Horrid, but exultant feeling. That disabled him for a time and gave me a start, but presently he was after me again, this time with a band of friends. And he was more horrible than ever, because besides his disfigured face, he had developed a hunchback. And I twisted and turned and doubled on my tracks and at last escaped.[42]

The headings in the letter below (9 February 1926) take on the character of descriptive chapters in a novel. Greene describes finding a place for lunch in a manner suggesting he was already seeking copy for his future thrillers:

> With my strange power (beware darling), of hitting on the shady, I went and had lunch at random and hit on a place of the most doubtful character, under the ground, beneath a most respectable hat shop, off the Strand! And then I came on here to the embankment . . . In front there's a most tantalising notice. Two intriguing lines of verse (one imagines religious, with a possible reference to the Last Day):

'A bell will be rung at closing time
Dogs must be led'

I wonder how it goes on. Is it a precious fragment, resurrected by the L.C.C., of some dead poet, who died perhaps of starvation and cold on the Embankment.

After lunch, he was back on his errand:

The Times – 3.15 p.m.

Dear love, here I am waiting. Send me luck please.

Chelsea Embankment – 6.35 p.m.

I was interrupted by someone coming and saying that Freeman was not coming to the office today. But I'm not going to be done, so I stay also. The one bright spot, dear heart, was the New Statesman. I saw MacCarthy, who was quite sweet and have taken away two books for review. One, heavy large and dull on the English Constitution for a short notice, and one amusing Auto-biography of an 11th Cent. French Abbot of the St Augustine type for a longish one. Then I went and had tea at Battersea [at the home of his aunt], and am hurriedly finishing off this letter where I used to come and write depressedly to you during the B.A.T. period. Darling, I love you so very, very much. I want to go on writing, but I can't, because I'm meeting someone.

And the following day he is writing at 10.30 a.m. from somewhere inside St James's Park:

Darling, has the Archbishop of Canterbury become a Catholic? Is there a 'Cabinet' meeting of the English Church to discuss a massacre of Catholics? A brace of hurrying bishops and a brace of deans have already passed me and there are more on the sky line, silhouetted against the damp mist and drizzle. It's very cold. I don't think I shall be able to write here for long.

What he longed for was to be a member of a club so that he could get out of the cold. He was pessimistic, for he felt that if *The Times* led to nothing it would not only be check but checkmate.

Leaving St James's Park, he popped into the waiting room at St Pancras Station for warmth and continued writing his saga to Vivien. He knew he had a long wait. It was just after 11 o'clock and the earliest he could see anyone at *The Times* was half past three; he also had to return to Nottingham that night. His efforts were, he suspected, to be fruitless for he had still not seen Freeman of *The Times*. Depression set in. 'O my love, is there anything more depressing than a General Waiting Room on a cold, drizzly day!! It's nearly 2.' Just waiting in those surroundings made him want to throw in the towel: 'I feel absolutely hopeless . . . If The Times has nothing definite to say, I shall have to try the provincial papers, Manchester, Leeds, and Glasgow, and if they fail me there's nothing left but abroad, and losing you . . .' Losing Vivien was the one prospect he just could not bear: 'Apart from you, I have no ambition, and there's nothing but you in life which is worth anything at all', were his last thoughts before he started again for *The Times*.

By 4.40 he had trudged back to St Pancras Station in the rain, as frustrated as ever, a frustration made greater because Vivien was at last in love with him, no doubt in part because he was becoming a Catholic for her sake: 'The Times was as vague as ever – "There'd be vacancies some time but –" Oh my dear, I wish you were here. You couldn't alter circumstances, but you'd be like a light in a dark room.' He also wished that she could be in Nottingham when he returned that night. The lack of justice in their situation struck him: 'It's not fair that we should have been made to love each other, if we aren't going to be allowed to marry.'

This letter was written in different places, as each event took place or soon afterwards. The letter is written as a novelist would write it and we are at the writer's elbow, witnesses to immediate events and his desperate reaction to them. He could see no escape and expresses his frustration in the terminology of a Luddite: 'I want to smash something. I want to get hold of a beautiful picture or a beautiful vase & break it.'[43]

*

His second attempt at job-hunting in London having failed, Greene's determination to fight diminished. On the train back to Nottingham he felt as if a wall was slowly being built, shutting Vivien away from him, and he wanted to hit out and smash through it – or else have the wall topple over on him. Suddenly, for the first time, in spite of his proclamations of love and desperate need to marry Vivien, he now writes that their relationship should end: 'I can't bear the thought of going on seeing you at intervals for short times for years on end. I'm not sure that it wouldn't be better to end it all at a stroke.' And then, thinking happily that they will soon see each other once more, he turns again to his doubts as to whether they should continue: '. . . should we? Wouldn't it only make it worse? . . . I don't know what to think or do. My brain's in a quagmire.'[44]

After a good night's sleep, his spirits revived, and he returned to seeking a place in journalism. After all, there were other newspapers of almost equal importance to *The Times*:

> I've got such a lot to do – trying to salvage the wreck I'm going to write to Montagu of the Manchester Guardian . . . and to Mann of the Yorkshire Post. Then I'll tackle the Birmingham Post again from a different angle, and write to my psycho-analyst, who used to know Robert Lynd, at least he showed him some of my work years ago. Lynd might supply an introduction to the Editor of the Daily News. I shall write to Kenneth [Bell] and ask him to try desperately to obtain intros. to the Telegraph and the Morning Post. These both pay as well as The Times. I shall also write to Browning, whom I knew at Balliol, who's a leader writer on The Glasgow Herald. I'll also ask Kenneth about the Toronto Globe, whether there is a chance in their London office.

Graham also wrote to Count Bernstorff (his contact during his student attempts at espionage) to see whether he could give him introductions to the *Daily Telegraph* and the *Morning Post*.

*

Seeking introductions here and seeking introductions there – this was to be the road to success. And if all else failed, he intended to make a third attempt on London, going the rounds if need be without introductions. He was still reluctant to become attached to a 'popular' newspaper, but if it had to be – well: 'I once had a riotous evening with Strube, the cartoonist of the [Daily] Express. I might look him up and get an intro. there. I once met the News Editor through my German stunt. The Express of course would be the last resort.'[45]

His urgency is indicated by the fact that after writing an unfinished six page letter to Vivien, he stopped to write to the *Guardian*, the *Yorkshire Post*, the *Glasgow Herald*, his college tutor Kenneth Bell and his psychoanalyst Kenneth Richmond, and then returned to complete his letter to Vivien.

Always there was the hope that someone somewhere might help him escape from being 'padlocked' in Nottingham.

Graham's friends rallied round: Kenneth Bell advised him that an acquaintance called Gillie was in Warsaw for the *Morning Post*; his friend Browning on the *Glasgow Herald* told him of a vacancy there as sub-editor; Richmond, his 'dear little analyst', wrote saying he had written to, and now heard from, Robert Lynd and that Greene must write to Lynd at the *Daily News*. Greene did so at once: 'I should like the D.N. better than any other papers except the three twopennies. Their politics always seem pleasantly sane, and they are excellent on the literary side.'[46] Whether he felt hopeful or not, he ended his letter with the words: 'I have given my landlady notice for the end of the month. It's no use my staying in Nottingham into March.'

What Greene remembered of Nottingham is highly selective – 'the elderly "boots" employed at the Black Dog Inn, the unemployed girls once in the lace trade, the trams rattling downhill through the goose market, the blackened Nottingham castle, the oldest pub in England and the haggard blue-haired prostitute who "haunted the corner by W. H. Smith's bookshop."' But what he chiefly recalled were his long months alone. Thirty years later, when writing his play *The Potting Shed* (1958), he found himself returning in spirit to those solitary days. He has it said of his hero, James Callifer: 'He used to go along the Trent when he had the dog. Or down to the goose market.' Also Greene recalled his sitting room in his note to Act Two:

This is the living-room of James Callifer's lodgings at Nottingham. The furniture is his landlady's, and could belong to nobody but a landlady: the bobbed fringes of the sage-green tablecloth, the sideboard with a mirror, the glass biscuit-box with a silver top, the Marcus Stone engravings.

Greene's feelings are further reflected in *A Gun For Sale* when his killer, Raven, standing beside the river in the rain and the dark, feels a 'dreadful sense of desolation'. It is a similar sense of desolation we find in a letter to Vivien: 'I went for a walk by the cold Trent, and sat under trees, from which leaves floated chillily and read some of the new Thomas Hardy [probably *Human Shows, Far Phantasies, Songs and Trifles* (1925)] and felt melancholy.'[47]

*

There was at least one well known novelist living in Nottingham, Cecil Roberts, recently editor of the *Nottingham Journal*. He recalled meeting Greene:

I . . . invited him to call. He proved to be a tall, gangling youth of twenty-one. He had recently published a book of verse, *Babbling April*, which he presented to me. As I thanked him . . . I said, 'I wonder if this is a presage. Young poets out of the cocoon often turn novelists – I have!' He shook his head, diffidently. He was shy at first. After all I was an ex-editor, the author of three published novels, and fairly well established. I suppose that in his eyes I represented success. I got him to talk, most intelligently, and after a pleasant hour he left.[48]

Roberts expressed a hope that they would meet again. They did not, and Roberts had it on his conscience that he was not more hospitable, for Greene 'must have been lonely, coming recently from the vivid life of a university and now living in grim lodgings in a provincial city.'[49]

Greene commented to his father about his visit to Roberts: 'I saw Mr R. on Friday & had supper & an amusing evening with him. An educated person in Nottingham is as precious & rare a find as jam in a wartime doughnut!'[50]

Greene's letters to Vivien from Nottingham were by no means uniformly sad. Along with the rest of the world, he found pleasure and solace in the gramophone and the popular songs of the day:

> I'm writing this little note to the strains of the Ukelele Lady, on my gramophone. Do you remember the song? The Trix Sisters sang it in that revue we saw in Oxford.

> The gramophone's playing 'I want to be happy, but I won't be happy' . . . It's fearfully distracting writing a letter with the gramophone going within a yard. It's singing 'Just tea for two, and two for tea.'

Living in the provinces in 1925 did have its pleasures. Live entertainment was still linked to the cinema: 'I went to a cinema, and the comic that came on first was one I'd seen in the Shaftesbury Pavilion, the last time I was waiting to meet you in London, and I wanted you more than ever.' Lunch could provide live entertainment: 'At 11.20 I departed [from you] rather sadly. And I had lunch at a restaurant, where there was a piano and a violin, and for a moment I felt I was at the George.'[51] 'I opened your letter & the little picture at the end caught my eye, & I read "O write & say you still love me a little when I'm semi-bobbed." And I said to myself, "She's been & gone & done it" & positively blanched.'[52]

It turned out to be a false alarm: 'Darling, it was a relief to find you hadn't gone to the barber's & got shingled or brindled or bobbed.' Greene nevertheless issued, two days later, a comic ultimatum: 'If you shingle, I shall grow a moustache . . . And in order to go with the moustache, I shall have to brush my hair back with loads of grease, pots and pots of scented stuff. And that will necessitate a pronounced waist and even stays [a corset], like Basil Murray . . . So you see the ruin to my character.'[53]

He had a strong sense of the melodramatic for, when looking out of his ground floor window and seeing strangers, he envisaged what could be a scene in a future thriller:

I think some of my shady political past – is it Irish Republicans, German Separatists or French Communists? – has found me out. Two villainous individuals have been patrolling in front of the house, looking in at the windows. I got up and stared out and they moved off. Now they are back, and have been joined by an official looking person in uniform. They've become quite brazen. The blue official has just peeped in at my window, and I heard him say 'This must be the house'. I feel like a character in John Buchan. And I haven't got my revolver, darling. What shall I do? This letter will probably be posted to you by a kind stranger, and it will be splashed with blood. They've been wandering round for seven minutes now. I wish I could play the piano. 'He was playing Debussy, when they came for him.' I feel like the man in Juno and the Paycock, who's expecting the Irregulars to come for him at any moment. Darling, they've rung the bell. Awful suspense. They've only inquired about the gas. Of course it may be a blind.★

Years later he would describe Nottingham as the farthest north he had ever made a home: 'I had fallen into a pocket out of life and out of time.'[54]

★ This comic scene finds a serious parallel in *A Gun for Sale* when Raven, searching for the imprisoned Anne Weaver in Acky's home, looks out of the window: 'His eye . . . noted a large rather clumsy-looking man in a soft hat chatting to a woman at the house opposite: another man came up the road and joined him and they strolled together out of sight. He recognised at once: the police . . . he could hear the faint whistling of the old man's breath somewhere near the foot of the stairs' (p. 96).

18

Thomas the Doubter

Doubt is part of all religion.
— ISAAC BASHEVIS SINGER

'I took the name of Thomas – after St Thomas the doubter and not
Thomas Aquinas – and then I went on to the *Nottingham Journal*
office and the football results and the evening of potato chips.'[1]
Greene's casual, unemotional style in describing a moment of great
importance, his acceptance into the Roman Catholic Church, is
typical. We do not need to rely solely on Greene's later statements
about this in *A Sort of Life*, recollected in tranquillity forty-five years
after the event. Letters written when he was undergoing instruction
before becoming a Roman Catholic give his more immediate response.

'Vivien was a Roman Catholic [he writes in *A Sort of Life*], but to
me religion went no deeper than the sentimental hymns in the school
chapel.'[2] Even if he had never met Vivien there was little chance that
Greene would have returned to the Protestantism of his father.
Protestant church-going had brought him, as a child, neither pleasure
nor a sense of belief, as we can see from a passage in the typescript
of *A Sort of Life* which was cut before publication:

Contacts with the Anglican beliefs of my family and school were
less happy. I had a habit of fainting at early morning chapel, unable
to draw sufficient breath through the fumes of black broadcloth
suits all around, and sometimes in the holidays – especially at
Christmas – my parents liked to attend an outlying church at
Potters End, where the rector was inclined . . . to recite the
interminable Anglican litany. Never had one's knees felt more the
agony of the bone, and the repeated prayer, 'We beseech Thee to
hear us O Lord,' would have been more heartfelt if one had believed
in any being at that moment more powerful than the rector himself
. . . I was confirmed at school, but only because it was expected

of me – the touch of the Bishop of St Albans' hand I found embarrassing, even though an older boy . . . urged on me the seriousness of the occasion.[3]

In *The Lawless Roads*, written after his conversion, he says that the Anglican church could not supply the same intimate symbols for heaven, 'only a big brass eagle, an organ voluntary, "Lord, Dismiss Us with Thy Blessing"'.[4] His conversion, he stresses in his autobiography, was due to the emptiness of life in Nottingham and to his sense of duty towards the woman he hoped to marry: 'Now it occurred to me, during the long empty mornings, that if I were to marry a Catholic I ought at least to learn the nature and limits of the beliefs she held. It was only fair, since she knew what I believed – in nothing supernatural. Besides, I thought, it would kill the time.'[5] Greene's honesty (whatever its consequences) is so pronounced it would be irresponsible to ignore these statements, even though made so many years after conversion. Killing time has been an important activity for him.

At University he did not go to church, understandably since he was an atheist. As we saw in Chapter 8, Lord Tranmire had never heard arguments in favour of atheism put forward better than by Greene, and 'The Improbable Tale of the Bishop of Canterbridge', published only a few months before he met Vivien, reveals an atheistical contempt for belief in God. In the early days of his love for Vivien, Greene made fun of her belief that humans have souls. He first denied he had one and then admitted that if he had, it was 'a small, dirty beast'.

But Greene did not have the character to be a permanent atheist, as Cockburn was probably aware when he advised Greene to convert if Vivien wouldn't marry him otherwise. 'You're the one that's superstitious, because I don't think it matters.' How right Cockburn was. Five months after meeting Vivien, Greene had his first religious dream – nightmare he called it:

Three of us, Cockburn, York-Lodge and myself were standing in a room, and at C's suggestion we were trying to do Black Magic. I scoffed but agreed to try for the excitement. We just stood and thought and suddenly I became very frightened and my mind became all dark save for little sparks of fire. And the sparks darted up more & more, & I grew into a frenzy with them & snatched a picture from the wall to dash on the ground. Then I glanced at it, & suddenly shoved it back on the wall, with a huge sense of escape, & woke up terrified.

It might be thought from this that Greene's arguments in favour of atheism were simply those of a young man pleased to play so effectively the devil's advocate, yet standing behind his powers of ratiocination were emotional fears which must have made him suitable material for conversion.

Also there has survived a short, humorous, undated manuscript poem by Greene written surely at the time he was contemplating entering the Catholic Church:

> Put out your right foot:
> Pray the shoe's tight:
> The C. of E.'s crumbling –
> Rome may be right.

We know from his numerous letters to Vivien that there was little he would not do to win her heart and clearly his decision to become a Catholic made an enormous impression on her:

                Oh
              G
                R
                  A
                    H
                      A
                        M!!!
How perfectly marvellous . . . Madly excited,

was her response. But how did he come to his decision?

On his second day in Nottingham he wrote to Vivien: 'Will you tell me what my moves should be in trying to become a Catholic? Do I just call at a priest's house & say "I want to be a Catholic"?'[6] But he realised he would have to take the first step himself. And his next letter shows that not only killing time, or being dutiful to Vivien, was the spur for his conversion: 'I admit the idea came to me, because of you. I do all the same feel I want to be a Catholic now, even a little apart from you. One does want fearfully hard, something fine & hard & certain, however uncomfortable, to catch hold of in the general flux.'[7]

'One day,' he recalls, 'I took Paddy for a walk to the sooty neo-Gothic Cathedral – it possessed for me a certain gloomy power because it represented the inconceivable and the incredible. There was a wooden box for inquiries and I dropped into it a note asking for instruction.'[8] In a letter to Vivien he speaks of having 'written at random to the Bishop's Guild here.'

Soon a Father Trollope responded but before meeting him Greene went to a Roman Catholic service and was deeply disappointed. He felt he could have no reverence for the pale young priest in the pulpit: 'He spoke & looked as though he had a very limited intellect . . . Oh dear, I'm afraid this is a very bad beginning for someone who wants to be a Catholic.'[9] Even when he met Father Trollope he had the harsh reservations of a critical young man whose sense of cultural superiority, in visiting inferior people in inferior provinces, was still strong: 'I was not struck by him. He was a little gross in appearance, & there was also a most trashy novel from Boots library, lying in his room.'[10]

Though he was sure he would not allow Father Trollope to shrug him off ('The priest will find it fearfully hard to snub me, darling. My answer to "Why do you want to be a Catholic?" is . . . "I can't tell whether I do want to be, until I've been instructed." He won't find any sentimental emotionalism to snub in me'),[11] he feared that the wrong person instructing him might prevent his becoming a Catholic:

I went to Mass this morning & came in for the Bishop's Visitation. You know, Personality seems to me to count an awful lot in belief. If the person, who upholds the doctrine, seems much too small for them, one doubts the doctrine. It's illogical of course. So Father Trollope makes me feel entirely un-Catholic. I felt an innate respect for the bishop this morning, & therefore for his faith. He'd got one of the most charming old faces I've seen, & at the same time a shrewd & intelligent one.

The bishop did not give a sermon but explained his own responsibilities, and gave lists of statistics about conversion, and mixed marriages, and duties. Greene, who has always been fascinated by statistics, found the speaker and the details impressive: 'it did show how extraordinarily thorough & businesslike the Church rules are. And that's a thing I had not realised before.'[12]

Suddenly, two days later, when he again turned up for instruction, his attitude towards Trollope changed, chiefly, one suspects, because he discovered Trollope's father knew a distant, though to him distasteful, member of the Greene family: 'I have quite changed my mind about Father Trollope. I like him very much. I like his careful avoidance of the slightest emotion or sentiment in his instruction.' The strange coincidence was that Dr Fry had been Trollope's father's greatest friend.[13] Trollope himself, originally a Protestant, made his conversion in spite of strong family opposition: 'Dr Fry, that former ogre of Berkhamsted, had persuaded his family, who lived in Lincoln under the shadow of the deanery, to oppose his conversion, and then he was driven further by some inner compulsion to the priesthood.'[14]

Gradually, Greene learned more about Trollope's background and his secret passion (which Greene shared) for acting. To Vivien he wrote, 'Father Trollope was on the London stage for ten years, before he became a Catholic.' In *A Sort of Life* he returned to his memory of the man:

> at the first sight he was all I detested most in my private image of the Church. A very tall and very fat man with big smooth jowls which looked as though they had never needed a razor, he resembled closely a character in one of those nineteenth-century paintings to be seen in art shops on the wrong side of Piccadilly – monks and cardinals enjoying their Friday abstinence by dismembering enormous lobsters and pouring great goblets of wine.[15]

In 1979, when Greene was shown a photograph of Father Trollope he was truly delighted that his descriptions tallied. There was in Greene's pale but mellowed blue eyes the gentleness of nostalgia for those Nottingham days and a love for Trollope himself.

In *Journey Without Maps*, Greene humorously records some of the strange places in which he received instruction:

> I was instructed in Catholicism, travelling here and there by tram into new country with the fat priest who had once been an actor. (It was one of his greatest sacrifices to be unable to see a play.) The tram clattered by the Post Office: 'Now we come to the Immaculate Conception'; past the cinema: 'Our Lady'; the theatre: a sad slanting look towards *The Private Secretary* (it was Christmas time).[16]

While he and Trollope may well have travelled by tram, and Trollope may have directed a 'sad slanting look' towards the theatre, it could not have been towards a poster advertising *The Private Secretary* for it was not playing in Nottingham during Christmas 1925.

Trollope was administrator of the Cathedral but was deeply dissatisfied with the thought of any future which could be represented as a success. He had not sacrificed enough and a few years after Greene left Nottingham he entered the Redemptionist Order: 'What had these monks, with an obligation to dwell in all their sermons and retreats on the reality of hell, in common with this stout cheerful man who loved the smell of greasepaint and the applause at a curtain-fall? Perhaps nothing except the desire to drown. A few years later he was dead of cancer.'[17] According to his obituary Trollope died when fifty-three, not of cancer, but of pneumonia while on a visit to London.* Greene was to say much later that Trollope's story carried a warning: 'See the danger of going too far . . . Be very careful. Keep well within your depth. There are dangerous currents out at sea which could sweep you anywhere . . .'[18]

The challenge of Trollope was 'the challenge of an inexplicable goodness'. But the struggle for Graham Greene's soul was long:

> My primary difficulty was to believe in a God at all. The date of the Gospels, the historical evidence for the existence of the man Jesus Christ: these were interesting subjects which came nowhere near the core of my disbelief. I didn't disbelieve in Christ – I disbelieved in God. If I were ever to be convinced in even the remote possibility of a supreme, omnipotent and omniscient power I realized that nothing afterwards could seem impossible.[19]

Greene fought Trollope's religious arguments with a dogmatic atheism – 'I fought and fought hard' – and he felt it a fight for personal survival. Greene's letters with their simultaneous assertions of belief and disbelief help to reveal his complex, ambiguous nature. Sometimes he simply hopes that he has found belief: 'I've suddenly realised that I *do* believe the Catholic faith. Rationally I've believed for some time, but only this evening imaginatively. I think the belief will stay. It's quite possible after all to believe it at this early stage, because the acceptance and belief in the Church as a guide includes faith in everything I've still got to be taught. I suddenly realised I believe at tea today . . . It's snowing again.'[20]

This was followed a few days later by a black mood when he hated life and God Himself:

> The only two methods I've had to fight emptiness I can't use, since I've loved you. I suppose in time I shall discover a new and proper

---

* A memoir written two years after his death fills in the details of Father Trollope's life on the London stage: 'His first engagement was with Ben Greet's Company, then touring in "The Sign of the Cross", in which he played first as a pagan, and then as a Christian, roared like a lion, and was eventually thrown to the lions. After a short time in London, playing small parts at the "Haymarket", he got his chance and made a name for himself. Strange to say, the part that brought him to the fore was that of a most awful "bounder", and when London managers had a part of that type to fill they always sent for him. He acted with Beerbohm Tree in "Business is Business", at His Majesty's, and in other plays, and also with Arthur Bourchier. In all he was on the stage ten years.'

way of doing it. Don't you ever wonder, in moods, now and again what the use of going on is? Religion doesn't answer it. One can believe in every point of the Catholic faith, and yet at times like this hate the initiator of it all, of life I mean. Justice can be just as hateful as injustice, more so often enough, because injustice puts us on a level with the wielder of it, whilst justice is more hateful because it emphasises our own inferiority.[21]

Six days later he had another go at the Almighty:

If we were shoved together in March, only to lose you in December or January or February, whatever the purpose, the means were extraordinarily cruel. If there's a God who does that sort of thing, he'd be pretty impossible to love. Infinite cleverness, all right, but not much of Infinite Mercy.[22]

Yet he was turning away from his parents' religion. At home for Christmas, he wrote firmly that he had gone to his last Anglican service: 'If anything would confirm me in Catholicism, it would be this morning. What a service, and what a sermon. The most awful sticky sentiment.'[23] And what attracted him as much as anything to Catholicism was the Church's belief in Hell: 'It gives something hard, non-sentimental and exciting' – a belief he no longer supports today.

At the end of the year, he assured Vivien he did 'believe . . . firmly for long periods' and also 'I have got a constant layer of Catholicism at the bottom of me now, because I feel up in arms directly I hear any argument against Catholics . . . I'm a good way on the road.' Indeed he was far too far down the slipway to go back.

Also, he was excited about the instruction itself:

We've finished the Papal Infallibility subject. Next time [Trollope's] taking the five cases, where the Protestants have argued he has shown fallibility. (Letter of 11 January 1926.)

I've just got up to Beatification and Canonisation in my instructions. (Letter of 14 January 1926.)

We did the Saints this morning . . . I asked him how much longer it would take, as I was probably leaving . . . He'll give me a note to a priest at The Oratory [in London], where he was instructed. (Letter of 19 January 1926.)

I've got to Mortal and Venial sins in instruction . . . no we haven't got to Marriage and Divorce yet. (Letter of 26 January 1926.)

Only just back . . . and very sleepy as I had to go and see Fr
Trollope after Benediction to try and cram in an instruction, and
I fell comfortably asleep in his room. Did I tell you he's giving me
a concentrated cram now, to finish me before I leave at the
beginning of March. (Letter of 8 February 1926.)

Greene paid rigorous regard to the rules. Writing to Vivien on 21
January he admitted his trials were to begin: 'I'm told that I've got
to begin to observe things, like Mass on Sundays and alas! Fridays.
My first meatless Friday tomorrow. I can't write, the gramophone
gets in the way.' He forgot to tell his landlady about his meatless
Friday – Greene must have thought she would not be sympathetic to
his impending conversion. He described the result to Vivien: 'With
great reluctance I was forced to give Paddy all the meat part of my
eggs & bacon.'

The priest was working against the clock. 'Father Trollope's just
managed to cram in the instruction in time . . . he's left one thing
(owing to lack of time) for you to instruct me about . . . the rosary
and its use', he wrote to Vivien on 27 February.

*

Graham Greene was as ready as he would ever be. He had no fear of
the judgment of others on his leaving the Protestant church or because
the dogmatic atheist was becoming a Catholic. Indeed, he probably
enjoyed the rumours. 'I got a letter from Macleod . . . he said he had
heard rumours exploding like little gunpowder caps over Oxford.'[24]
Also, he could be flippant when writing to his mother about his
impending entry into the Catholic Church:'I expect you have guessed
that I am embracing the Scarlet Woman.'[25] He had made his position
clear to his mother a month earlier. He was not, he assured her,
marrying into a Catholic family: 'V's people are not R.C.'s. She's a
convert. Mr & Mrs D[ayrell] are not divorced,but separated . . . he's
still farming in Rhodesia . . . his interests are confined to cattle . . .
Mrs D. apparently never cared for him particularly, but her family
told her that she was to have no more to do with him, so she promptly
ran away to Africa & married him!' And he felt the need to assure
Vivien that his family was not against *his* conversion: 'I hope you are
at rest about my people. I got a "sweet" letter from my father this
morning, wishing me happiness etc., all the more remarkable for the
fact that he practically never writes letters.'[26]

As the day approached he grew very nervous: 'that mixture of the
feelings before a dentist's and the excited feelings before making a
speech. I shall be glad when it's safely over.' His greatest fear was

his first general confession and the fact that another priest was to hear it: 'I'm awfully afraid that I may have the "mouldy" one to confess to. It's a drawback if one can't feel an instinctive respect for the man. Fr Trollope asked whether I'd like someone else to confess to. What will make it a bit more embarrassing is that I'm to have it in his room, and not in the formality of a box, before the reception ceremony begins.' In another letter the young convert admitted he was really quite frightened by Sunday's confession: 'I comfort myself by the thought that I shall be fleeing from Nottm . . . In three years of complete freedom it's difficult not to have collected a good deal of rather sordid muck.'[27]

In *A Sort of Life* Greene returns to the nature of that distant event:

The first General Confession, which precedes conditional baptism and which covers the whole of a man's previous life, is a humiliating ordeal . . . In the first Confession a convert really believes in his own promises. I carried mine down with me like heavy stones into an empty corridor of the Cathedral, dark already in the early afternoon, and the only witness of my baptism was a woman who had been dusting the chairs.*[28]

Writing on Thursday, the day before the ceremony, he expresses his spiritually elevated and passionate need for Vivien:

Coming back, I thought of you so hard that I felt I was bringing you from Oxford, and it was quite a disappointment to find the room empty when I got in. I'm longing so much for Saturday and Sunday AND Friday, dear love, dear only love for ever, dear heart's desire. I'm aching for you. I need you as much as any cripple might (do you remember what you said once?). After all, you are helping the lame soul to walk, aren't you? It's you who are the guardian.[29]

But his letters reveal a young man distressingly honest and anxious: 'The "ceremony" takes place at 3 tomorrow. I'm told it lasts a whole half hour! Dear! Dear! I haven't said anything about it, but don't think I'm going into it in the wrong spirit. I do take it seriously really.'[30] Vivien sent him a telegram which has not survived, though Greene described its arrival at All Saints Terrace: 'At about 7.10 I was just disappearing in a taxi to send off my trunk, when I saw, through the little window at the back, a telegraph boy get off at the

* The witness of his baptism was not a woman dusting the chairs but Stewart Wallis, an unofficial verger who helped around the cathedral.

gate. And when I got back three minutes ago, there was your telegram. My darling, thank you so much . . . you are so good to me, and it means an awful lot to me – your thoughts. I shall come to you very excitedly on Sunday night.'[31] Also Vivien sent him a small parcel with instructions not to open it until the morning of the ceremony:

> Darling, the little note was lovely. I put the parcel by my bed, and opened it directly I woke up. And I loved what you'd put inside the Missal.
>
> O heavens my watch has stopped. I must be off –

Ten years later, in *Journey Without Maps*, Greene recalled his first general confession and his baptism. What is striking always with Greene is his clinical observation of detail:

> The cathedral was a dark place full of inferior statues. I was baptized one foggy afternoon about four o'clock. I couldn't think of any names I particularly wanted, so I kept my old name. I was alone with the fat priest; it was all very quickly and formally done, while someone at a children's service muttered in another chapel. Then we shook hands and I went off to a salmon tea, the dog had been sick again on the mat. Before that I had made a general confession to another priest: it was like a life photographed as it came to mind, without any order, full of gaps, giving at best a general impression. I couldn't help feeling all the way to the newspaper office, past the Post Office, the Moroccan cafe, the ancient whore, that I had got somewhere new by way of memories I hadn't known I possessed. I had taken up the thread of life from very far back, from so far back as innocence.[32]

The remarkable calmness of his style gives equal weight to events of a diverse nature. His baptism is described in the same breath as salmon tea and the dog being sick. Incongruities are juxtaposed.

Forty-five years later Greene could remember very clearly the nature of his emotions as he walked away from the Cathedral:

> there was no joy in it at all, only a sombre apprehension. I had made the first move with a view to my future marriage, but now the land had given way under my feet and I was afraid of where the tide would take me . . . Suppose I discovered in myself what Father Trollope had once discovered, the desire to be a priest . . . At that moment it seemed by no means impossible.[33]

Looking back today, Greene is able to smile at the unreality of his fear but feels at the same time a sad nostalgia for it. He is aware that he lost more than he gained when the 'fear belonged irrevocably to the past'. Speaking of the humiliating ordeal of his first confession Greene shows how age (and the 'mass of memories and associations [which we] drag around with us like an over-full suitcase on our interminable journey') changes us and changed the hopeful young man joining the Catholic Church:

> Later we may become hardened to the formulas of confession and sceptical about ourselves: we may only half intend to keep the promises we make, until continual failure or the circumstances of our private life, finally make it impossible to make any promises at all and many of us abandon Confession and Communion to join the Foreign Legion of the Church and fight for a city of which we are no longer full citizens.[34]

Four months of Nottingham had been as much as Greene could bear, though in *A Sort of Life* he insists that he spent only three months there and was not unhappy. In his play *The Potting Shed*, James Callifer, remarkably similar in character to Greene, stays for five years in digs like his. Mr Corner questions the psychoanalyst as to what is wrong with James, for Corner can see no reason for Callifer's despair: 'But he's good at his job. Or he wouldn't have stayed five years on the *Journal*.'[35] Graham Greene, the young man with his way to make in the world, could not have stayed so long. His despair would have become intolerable. In Nottingham he often longed for suitable intellectual companionship. Writing to Vivien from Nottingham Park, in spite of the severe weather, in the middle of the afternoon of 15 February 1926, he admitted:

> O my dear, you can't know in Oxford, how one simply aches here for someone who's read Shelley and Keats, and who doesn't simply talk about ailments. Even the Magdalen man's chief topic is his landlady, who gets drunk every night, is on the verge of D.T.'s and once attacked his daughter with a hatchet.
>
> The half hour on Friday with the little Magdalen man is the only time during the week, when I speak to an educated person, and even we have no interests in common. I don't think I'm a prig, but it is rather ghastly. One sees absolutely no one here of one's own class. In the street, in the cafes, anywhere. It destroys democratic feelings at birth. Seeing you is like a leakage of air into a coffin.

Greene was not then democratically inclined. He found it difficult to communicate with and respond to the ordinary uneducated man in the street. Yet he did feel for others less fortunate than himself, as an unpublished and unknown poem, written in Nottingham during a spare moment from sub-editing, shows: 'I only see/Out in the streets where there's always rain/With cracked harmoniums the unemployed.'

A few days before he left he wrote to Vivien: 'It's awfully queer walking Nottm, and thinking I may never see it again after this week.' He then adds, what only a young man could: 'Four months is quite a large slice of existence.'

Greene never lived in Nottingham again and he did not wish to: 'This town makes one want a mental *and* physical bath every quarter of an hour', and he left without a job in spite of desperate attempts to find one. He would go to London and see what being armed with four months' experience as a sub-editor in the provinces would do for him. He left full of hope, and a sense of expectancy, for now he was a Catholic. His first letter to Vivien, after conversion, is entitled FIRST CATHOLIC LETTER, and his excitement is evident:

I've reached the station unnecessarily early, after a tempestuous departure. Doing up odd things. I couldn't get into my suitcase the brown paper parcels. Searching for string, discovering things in drawers. String breaking. Brown paper bursting. Gobbling an egg. Being dragged away by a too early taxi in the middle of a piece of toast. Marmalady . . . it's really becoming ridiculous – fantastic – stoopid – the way I fall more in love with you every day . . .

And his goodbye to Nottingham?

Ah! that's over . . . I'm wildly excited. The day is glorious, & I had to be extravagant & take a taxi from St Pancras, because of my many packages. And it was a fearfully long ride & the streets were lovely & grimy Nottingham was a hundred miles away . . . Thank God Nottingham's over. It's like coming back into real life again being here.[36]

19

Between the Tides

I was never particularly in love with life.
— GRAHAM GREENE

IN October 1925 Graham Greene had attained his majority but not his maturity and had certainly not fulfilled his ambitions, in spite of having eventually clearly defined them and pursuing them relentlessly and intelligently. He had, however, achieved some small victories and had obtained a good deal of valuable experience.

He was still limited in his response to classes of society other than his own and, even within his own family, given to expressions of cold-bloodedness. Yet he was astonishingly romantic and, withal, excessively shy. He was (and is) rigorously honest but it was an honesty not coupled with a comparable candour. Temperamentally given to enthusiasms of hope — useful in a convert — he turned to Catholicism for the wrong reason and he was (and is) susceptible to the attractions of the opposite sex. In love, especially when a competitive spirit was engendered by another entering the lists, Greene's passionate intensity was so aroused that he would raise the stakes, submit to, and argue in favour of, any condition of love's servitude, and persuade himself to believe even in a monastic marriage. In a showdown, Greene will gamble on life or death at a throw.

At this time he suffered from nightmares; had thoughts which, twenty years later, found their way into one of his finest novels; showed himself to have untutored but unquestioned mediumistic powers; and after intense activity had moments of such despair, followed by self-hatred, that inescapably we must conclude he carried within his breast a formidable desire for self-annihilation.

*

Of Greene's social conditioning he recalls, in the preface to *The Old School*, how his school despised elementary schoolboys, thinking them unwashed and willing to lie more readily than boys of a higher social class. This was due, he argues, to the school masters from whom he and others learnt their snobbery and the means to express it, though surely his mother played a part also. His enforced stepping out of his class in Nottingham caused him to emphasise his inherited class values. While later he was to reject them, there he accepted them without question.

Nevertheless, perhaps the process of change was beginning then, for we do notice the glimmerings of a social sense in his poem about what he saw in the streets of Nottingham – the cracked harmoniums, the eternal unemployed – but he had both to witness and experience poverty in the early 1930s before he could sympathise with, or even comprehend, the life of the poor in England. At this age, he finds it easier to be satirical at their expense. For example, he describes to Vivien two men in a park sitting down and talking to each other without having been introduced.

They began on their mutual ailments which necessitated them coming and sitting here in the sun and getting fresh air. One of them, an old man with a thick white beard, like a Tolstoy with a Nottingham accent, says, taking his pipe from his mouth 'Rest's the best thing'. He apparently lost his memory for four years. He doesn't seem to mind having got it back again. The other man's younger, about 50. He's just as cheerful. 'It's all the same whatever place one goes to. Just bricks'. And they haven't even got a distant hope of getting away, to the South Seas or somewhere. (3.30 p.m. The Park. 15 February 1926.)

Greene reports accurately working class speech patterns but does not catch the flavour and warmth of homespun wisdom ('It's all the same whatever place one goes to. Just bricks') and fails to see it as a way of dealing with impossible personal conditions. And the jibe, 'He doesn't seem to mind having got [his memory] back again', is unnecessary.

During his first attempt to find a job in London, he stayed at his brother Raymond's home. He arrived in London at ten at night, deposited his bag and, because he had not eaten, went to a cheap restaurant in Wilton Road. There he discovered a baritone who sang 'sadly and badly' and again the desire to speak satirically about the less cultured and less fortunate comes upon him. In song, it seems the baritone 'declared that he would meet his pilot face to face when he crossed the bar and then he laid him down with a will, and then he was one who marched breast forward and then the choir sang,

"Through the Night of Doubt and Sorrow".' Here the summary itself belittles the subject.

He was then (and still is) squeamish about too much intimacy with others. What Greene objected to in the lodger at Hamilton Road was understandably his obvious sexual vulgarity but he also disliked the man's 'most unpleasant craving for company'.[1] It was this aspect of character which Greene stressed when judging Vivien's father: 'Fearfully over-affectionate . . . Apparently when he returned from work he expected the whole family to rush out on to the *stoep* & embrace him, as though he'd been gone a year.'[2]

An example of his lack of sympathy is shown in the following:

I shall hear to-morrow whether my uncle's pulled through. Wednesday & Thursday were to be the days of fight. The doctors have been very non-committal on his chances. What annoys me most is that it should have come & spoilt my mother's holiday. It's the only one she gets away from the family . . . This sounds fearfully cold-blooded, but one can't feel very much for the person who's dying . . . except in the pain of the method chosen.[3]

His uncle did die: 'It's been so fearfully sudden. Alive & kicking last Saturday. He was rather brilliant & I think my favourite uncle [it was his Uncle Frank who made him, when a child, paper Chinese junks to sail in his bath], yet I don't feel much cut up. It must be pretty beastly for my mother, as he was her only brother, her other one died at about 20.'[4] But he showed enough religious concern to comment on how his uncle might be buried: 'I see from The Times that my uncle's funeral is at 11. tomorrow at Golders Green Crematorium. I wondered whether he'd be cremated. I can't think either he or my aunt had anything in the way of a religious belief.'[5]

One might suspect that a lack of a sympathetic identification with the plight of someone in his own family – a favourite uncle, too – facing death, would not augur well for Greene's future as a novelist.

Greene has, however, shown a continuing desire to go beyond the limited experiences of his class. He has gravitated towards the seedy, towards deeply-divided creatures and self-destructive heroes, towards middle class persons who have fallen from grace and live outside the bounds of family and society on the verge of despair. In this respect, we should not ignore his own sense of having fallen from grace. He observes the world seemingly without emotion, clinically in fact, and sometimes contemptuously, though as he registers his repugnance of what he sees, he often feels a guilt for his own irascible feelings. Given one's sense that he has little love for his fellow men in general (which does not exclude his strong sympathy for individuals) his novels sometimes seem a penance for this lack. His passionate inquisitiveness is undimmed even in old age. In an early unpublished play, 'A House of Reputation', the madam of a brothel asks his character why he visits it since he has a pretty wife; he answers, 'It's only this terrible curiosity.'

*

Greene also has a strong sense of the passage of time and we can see an example of this when he considers – his tone is not without a strain of bitterness – his first year with Vivien:

> With me that's a lot: Babbling April, and meeting you and falling in love and being turned down, and Finals and the B.A.T. and the Capitol and your getting a bit fond of me, and tutoring, and the Golden Cross and getting the reviewing jobs and sub-editing at Nottingham and becoming a Catholic and wouldn't it be theatrically effective for Fate, keeping to the Aristotle unities, to end with a breaking off, and perhaps run off to China as before. And by March 17 [when it would be exactly a year since they met] perhaps you'd be able to see it as a pleasant sentimental memory . . . If I was Fate I simply couldn't resist such an opportunity! and . . . they say that God is the great dramatist.[6]

Another aspect of Greene's character is his intense nervousness in face of lies, even when these are justified. We cannot understand Greene unless we accept this.

There is an occasion when a single lie caused him deep remorse. At the time he was writing his second novel, 'The Episode', and he sent Vivien a chapter which dealt with a character asking for his girlfriend's hand in marriage, only to be rejected. When Vivien read it, she was amazed to find fiction fact, discovering that what she was reading was an actual account of her own rejection of Greene on the canal at Wolvercote. When she objected, Greene denied he had used personal experience. He argued that he had made an outline of the scene before the Wolvercote rejection and therefore could not have had it in mind in any real sense. He had used the canal and the waves in the story, but he declared it was in every other respect totally different. And he went on to argue: 'Since the beginning of the world, people have said they will never marry and the way in which the girl in The Episode says it, is as different from the way in which you did, as my own feelings from those of the male in the story.'

He then went on to contrast Vivien's obvious sincerity in refusing him, with his character's mechanical utterances – 'Darling, I explain & explain & explain.'[7] But he was guilty, and later that day he felt he must write to Vivien once more to expunge his lie:

> It's no use. I wrote you a letter this morning explaining & explaining; & I went to a Cinema to try & forget all about it. But I can't. So I'll tell you the truth. *Every word* of that scene, the *idea* of it also, came *after* I said Goodbye in June. In January only the first page of the novel was written, & its planned continuation was entirely different. All the explanations I've made were lies.

His reason for lying was excuse enough – he was simply too afraid he would lose Vivien – but he had to tell her: 'I was feeling so miserable at going on trying to deceive you about that beastly scene.' And Greene was justified in his fear for there was competition for Vivien's hand, as we can tell from scattered comments throughout his letters to her.

On the occasion when Vivien received from Graham masses of flowers (see Chapter 13), she was disappointed because they were not from Mr 'X'. Who, we must ask, was Mr 'X'? During a later interview she said in passing that Mr 'X' was a certain Hugh. More was not forthcoming. My belief is that Mr 'X' was Hugh Chesterman, a children's novelist long since dead.

My own suspicions were first aroused by a note of unexplained acerbity in one of Greene's letters written from Ambervale in which he referred to his young pupil's grandfather. When I quoted the passage in Chapter 15, I deliberately left out a bracketed aside. Without the deletion it read: 'He manufactures all England's tape measures & his name (*he would have that nasty name*) is Chesterman' [my italics].

According to Sir Basil Blackwell, Vivien came to his firm 'in about 1920 and, in time, became assistant to Hugh Chesterman, then editing the *Merry-Go-Round* [a children's magazine].' Chesterman, though much older than Greene, published his first children's novel in 1926 (a year after Greene's first book of verse) and his last in 1946.

The importance of Chesterman's presence is that it allows us to compare Greene's experience of two loves which occurred within months of each other – those of Gwen Howell and Vivien. The nature of both experiences suggests an interesting psychological pattern, namely that, given certain circumstances – the sense of strong competition and the belief that there exists only a modicum of hope – Greene can be moved to an extraordinary determination to win.

In the case of Gwen Howell, two men were interested in her – her fiancé who was out of the country, and young Graham Greene – an uneven struggle. Yet there was hope for Greene. Gwen was having serious doubts about her returning fiancé (who 'had become like a stranger to her . . . once when she talked to me of her [future] marriage, she wept a little')[8] and any hope was a stimulus for Greene. But this situation took him to the dangerous edge (as his experiments with Russian roulette testify) as he struggled for Gwen's love. Could it be that Greene can only overcome shyness when the odds seem overwhelming and fight only when the situation seems an almost impossible one? And finally, was Vivien aware of the advantage of having another man in the wings? Did she know that it was especially when there was another competitor that Greene would be truly stirred? Probably it was simply that her love for Graham was uncertain.

As in the case of Gwen Howell, Greene was up against an older man, but now the situation was reversed, for it was Greene's turn to be unable to see his girlfriend daily; he was in Ashover, or Nottingham, or London, and Chesterman and Vivien worked together in Oxford. This must have heightened his imaginings of the possibilities and created a deep anxiety. Yet the terms he uses, at twenty-one ('cad', 'bounder'), to express his fears are the limiting terms of a schoolboy and, while later he excised them from his vocabulary, they indicate the standards of behaviour which he subscribed to at this time. 'Darling, I hate being all this way away, when that cad hurts you, if it *is* only for a little. It's not letters he wants. He wants to be physically and not metaphorically kicked. He'd be just the kind of bounder, who wouldn't in the least know what to do if someone hit him hard. He'd go off and complain to B[asil] B[lackwell]. What ought to be done to him on his wedding day is too "Rabelaisian" to write.'

It seems almost impossible to believe that the writer of this letter would one day become one of the finest novelists of his generation. What stands behind such language is popular late Victorian and Edwardian fiction; in such fictions the Englishman wins through because he is not a cad or a bounder. In another letter Greene calls Chesterman a 'damned swine' and in yet another he thinks, 'Hugh ought to be horsewhipped."[9]

In his battle to win Vivien, Greene makes great play with Chesterman's age: 'Darling, don't go off suddenly & marry some dotard of over thirty. All the modern psychologists demand an equality of age in marriage!!'[10]

A month later he is still driving the point home: 'went to a most dramatic film called *Smouldering Fires* . . . Excellent moral . . . Marry someone of your own age.' And his fear is real: 'O my dear, don't let Hugh carry you off from me.'[11]

And Greene recalled seeing *Little Nellie Kelly* with Vivien: 'I loved that. Walking up the Woodstock Road, for the first time, I learned, what I suspected, that Hugh wanted to marry you. That made me feel desperate . . . I had begun to love you an awful lot that night.'[12] Vivien would need no further proof of the link between love and Greene's competitive nature. *Little Nellie Kelly* was a play to raise the spectre of an older and more successful man competing for Vivien since George M. Cohan's story deals with a wealthy man throwing a party and showing a strong interest in the young heroine. Finally, Nellie decides she prefers the poor suitor, proving that love outweighs riches.

So the pattern of conflict, of being a competitor for love, is very much one aspect of Graham Greene's psychology of loving, and in such situations he becomes a powerful combative force. Joyfully he writes, 'I have dispatched my ultimatum to the world, & I won't have any interference by the League of Nations.'

> I will not let thee go.
> I hold thee by too many bands.
> Thou sayest 'Farewell,' & lo!
> I have thee by the hands
> And will not let thee go.[13]

Once he had met her and fallen in love, Greene put much of his energy into winning Vivien: 'My arms are round you, and how can I let go, even if all the clocks in the world start striking together.'[14]

He had his misgivings about doing this ('it's all wrong for love to be a monomania as it's been with me')[15] but couldn't help himself. Greene did not know how to handle Vivien, while she unwittingly played cat and mouse with him, which kept him at boiling point: 'It hurts a good deal when in one letter you seem to consider [marriage] as a possibility & then next day I'm almost certain to have a letter, which practically says "Never, never, never." '[16]

Moreover, another prospective candidate for love suddenly appeared – Harman Grisewood:

My dear Vivienne . . . I know nothing of what hours in the day claim your attention, so may I take the liberty (& the risk) of asking you to fix a time & date . . . Morning – Luncheon – afternoon tea, dinner theatre – any of these but *soon* & for as long as you can. I've got lots to talk to you about & this Fate that rearranges all our meetings must be overthrown. Harman.[17]

Vivien must have told Greene about Harman Grisewood, for fancifully he wrote: 'One day possibly centuries ahead, I shall see you again. Will you be white haired and stout, or boring and emaciated, or married to Grisewood?'[18] No doubt Vivien was taking note of her mother's advice, 'enjoy yourself and flirt hard'.[19]

A month after their semi-secret engagement, Vivien dropped a bombshell by suggesting they would be happiest as brother and sister. He answered soberly enough: 'I'm afraid it is not practicable. There is the material fact that Somerset House cannot make relations of non-relations.' Even Greene could not accept this suggestion: 'there is also . . . a limit of human endurance. And to be frank, apart altogether from practical obstacles, I shouldn't dare accept life on those conditions. A brother & sister don't have any privacy, or only scant crumbs of it, *& my love for you*, granted almost continual sight, & yet almost always other people between us . . . I would simply go mad . . .' Her letter, as he said, knocked him to the ropes, even though he was still trying to last out the round.[20]

*

Greene's time in Nottingham was coming to an end; he was receiving instruction to enter the Catholic Church but Vivien seems to have questioned the seriousness of his agreement to enter into a monastic marriage. One gathers that Vivien had talked over his promise of love without sex with her 'gaffer', Basil Blackwell. Greene tried to quiet Vivien's fears, first by admitting that anyone who did not know him might tell Vivien that he was a knave tricking her. Others who did know him might tell them that he was an infatuated fool and that he would repent his promise of such a marriage afterwards. Greene's answer to this argument was: 'I shall *know* they are wrong.' Denying he was an infatuated fool, he told Vivien that he had lived with the idea for five months and his mind had not wavered. He was categorical: 'I love you. I want your companionship. I want you to look after. I know that happiness is with you, and I am perfectly prepared to sacrifice one bit of one part of my love. I don't for one moment pretend that celibacy is a natural ideal for me, as it is for you. I'm not different from other men, but . . . who wouldn't pay a farthing to gain a pound?'

He dealt cleverly with Blackwell's assertions that such a marriage would be blasphemy, that physical consummation is a necessity; and that not more than one in a hundred could live without it:

Everyone knows that our scheme has been done by Catholics in the old days. The Virgin Mary was of course an exceptional case, but Joseph no one teaches was anything but an ordinary man, with the ordinary man's desires – in fact, there is the theory, which is not denied, that he had children by his first wife. And in the past this example was copied. If B.B. talks about 99/100 men, I should have to say that I was the 1/100, which would be ridiculous conceit. But I am not so cynical. I should say that wherever you find a man who loves his wife, until he dies in old age (and I believe that there are quite a number!) you've got someone who, if it had been asked of him, could have done what I'm willing to do. If B.B. makes physical consummation an absolute necessity to a man, he's going also to admit (which he'd be unwilling to do) that in a comparatively few years he'll no longer love Mrs B.B. because the physical side would not take long to satisfy, and if that is necessary to a man what's left when it's gone, but to run away with another woman? And yet people don't, and not all through cowardice or morality – but many because they still love their wife. Which means that it was not a *necessity* in the first place.[21]

Greene was in deadly earnest but as a practical ploy it could not be bettered. Chesterman would never have made a comparable offer.

*

Greene was undergoing great emotional stress, converting to Catholicism in part because he wanted Vivien. But also part of the attraction of his love letters is his use of hyperbole. He saw her as having miraculous qualities: 'My miracle worker . . . you've given trees shade, and the flowers scent, and the sun a gold it never had before.' He felt intensely his personal unworthiness – 'You are so wonderful, & I'm so paltry', 'Darling, I could worship *with* you, if you had your arms round me . . . when I see that Catholicism can produce something so fine all through.'

We have seen (Chapter 15) something of Greene's sense of personal unworthiness, and also (Chapter 17) when he was at a low ebb, his sense of being walled in or buried, even of being destroyed by walls falling in on him. Catholicism and Vivien provided a way of escaping from his personality problems. Thus Greene came to Catholicism because of his admiration of Vivien. Admiration is, however, too mild a word, for we have seen how his mind conjured up the idea of suicide by drowning at the moment when he felt he'd reached the summit of love: '& death comes and leaves eternally pictures on the mind . . . frozen in death, your head & eye & hair . . . and the mind

274

dwells on these eternally, knowing there is to be no awaking.' In becoming a convert Greene was simply following where Vivien led. His inner tension and strain alone would not have led him to conversion. It was to Vivien (and only to a lesser extent the Church) that he felt true loyalty.[22] He did not begin to think deeply about the Church, or feel the pull of its allegiance, until his visit to Mexico in 1937 to write about the Mexican government's persecution of priests and the Church.

*

There is a deep Celtic-like morbidity in Greene, and an unpublished poem written at this time has the quality of Hardy's graveyard verse:

> When this bright day
> shall end with night,
> and love and even you
> are fallen from sight;
>
> When, bone to bone in grappling earth,
> we lie
> our love beauty and our thoughts
> awry;
>
> shall this bone say to that bone,
> 'Who are you?'
> That bone answer this bone – 'At last
> I am you.'?

The English aspect might be said to lie in his interest in statistics:

> I always feel a bit more cheerful in the evening, because then, instead of another day to get through, it's another day got through, of the 17,500 odd, before I attain my three score years & ten! Isn't it a perfectly terrifying number? Statistics fascinate but horrify one. That's 25 and a quarter million minutes roughly.
>
> In 26,460 minutes, if you are punctual I shall be with you. Do be, darling, it would be awful to make it another ten – 26,469. One minute's gone.[23]

But the curious aspect of his morbidity lies in his concern with getting as quickly as possible to the end of life. And whenever he felt little chance of winning Vivien, his case hopeless – '[I] cling to so flimsy and crazy a hope' – mentally destructive tendencies predominate: 'Sometimes, the whole of my mind and my brain and even my body seems tired out with it, when you aren't with me. And I want to sleep and sleep and sleep, and forget all about you and everything.'[24]

When Vivien first met Greene, three different personalities must have been evident to her: the first what Greene described as 'the Oxford me', an undergraduate persona characterised by a devil-may-care, tongue-in-cheek delight in pricking Oxford pomposities, sometimes by the pose of insouciance; the second the richer, more ambiguous person described in this chapter; and the third hinted at in scattered references – the Hilary Trench personality.

Graham had already published a poem under the pseudonym of Hilary Trench ('If You Were Dead') written when he lost Gwen Howell to her intended.* His bitter mood is reflected also in a poem about Vivien (written at the height of a later despair).† It is difficult to discover all the ramifications of the 'Trench mood.' Notably, Greene hits out viciously at whoever is causing him deep distress, and his mockery is bitter and unpredictable. It is a mood he feared and he often stresses that Hilary Trench is dead and buried:

And . . . you need never be afraid of meeting H[ilary] T[rench] in our house [he declared to Vivien]. Poor devil, he can never come anywhere near you, even if he is alive, which he isn't. O it's no use writing. I've got to be with you to convince you that he's dead. He's been dying since March 17 [that is, the day they met].[25]

But he did not succeed in persuading Vivien that his secret personality would not return, though he deeply regretted the sudden assumption of this secret self. 'I don't know what comes over me at times & makes me write horridly to you. It's that Personal Evil you talked of I think that sends those ghastly dreams. And it whispers things & I get miserable & furious & then I hurt you.'[26]

After displaying to Vivien a mood of bitter raillery, his apology took the following form: 'I am so certain of my own innocence & H[ilary]'s death that I know you must have misunderstood.'[27] Nevertheless, the Hilary Trench personality – 'the stamp of one defect'[28] – usually made its appearance after deep anxiety had been prolonged to a point where Greene could stand it no longer, and this began before he met Vivien. Clearly Greene himself thought it a disturbing inheritance: 'Miserableness is like a small germ I've had inside me as long as I can remember. And sometimes it starts wriggling. And sometimes that wriggle coincides with a time when we are apart & there's some small misunderstanding on my side. And every time it's baulked . . .'[29]

* See page 153.   † See page 218.

In his youth his depressions assumed a terrible magnitude, and he was acutely aware of the symptoms (see Chapter 15). In his story, 'The End of the Party', the boy Francis is afraid of going to a party because 'they'll make [him] hide in the dark and [he's] afraid of the dark.' The boy knew he would scream and scream and scream. Greene recorded in his diary the occasion when James Joyce's daughter, later insane, said that if she were asked once more if she was Joyce's daughter, she would scream and scream and scream. She was then asked – and would not stop screaming.

On other occasions Greene's notion of Hilary Trench seems less severe and is more in line with seeking both an escape from intolerable restlessness and also new experiences to use for creative purposes: 'It seems ridiculous to think I can lop off a bit of me, which had been growing for two years in a month or two. And if I'm ungrateful to you, I'm ungrateful to H.T. too. It was no good writing about things, unless I experienced them first. Then I could never keep my depression long, because I could simply go off by myself in cheerful egoism, thinking of no one else . . . & come back with a huge joy & appetite at finding myself still alive. And even if I was out always for copy . . .'[30]

Using people (how does a creative writer avoid that?) troubled Vivien, and Greene, as the following note suggests: 'your joke about H.T. and his copy . . . hit on something that does hurt me, the feeling that when I publish verse I'm making money out of you.'

Greene's reactions (wishing a loved one dead; striking out in a letter in an intolerable fashion; dreaming of suicide *as a Catholic* deliberately to harm the person who discovers it) are to be seen now as methods of escaping from the grip of despair coupled with the feeling that unless something drastic is done madness might follow: and any action is preferable, including suicide. From this point of view his adventure with Russian roulette and later his incessant travelling to inaccessible and often dangerous places, is not simply the desire to test himself (the uninspired weakling on the playing fields of Berkhamsted becomes the inspired adventurer off them) but to escape from a depressed condition: '& the bubble gets bigger, & bigger & I want, oh God, how I want to be dead, or asleep or blind drunk . . . so that I can't think.'

Greene was, then and now, a man of strong contrasting moods and when his depressions were upon him, he might well have succeeded in taking his life, as some of his friends expected him to do. Michael Meyer, the biographer of Ibsen and Strindberg, talked to me about this depressive side of Greene:

I had never come across this black side of him until we went on our round-the-world trip together [in 1959] . . . but that can't be true because I remember Edward Sackville-West, and sitting with him in the billiard room . . . at the Savile Club. This would be in the early 50's. Anyway, we were talking about Graham and I said to Edward – he'd known Graham for years – 'What will Graham be like at such-and-such an age – 67 or 68?' and Edward said, 'Oh, he'll have committed suicide by then.'[31]

Greene himself admitted in a letter to Vivien: 'I was never particularly in love with life.' Even Greene imagery has a perverse quality to it in his letters. Speaking of coming to a decision on a certain course of action, he admits to being quite happy, 'rather in the same way as the consumptive is happy, who can number the number of days he has to live.'[32]

PART 5

London

20

The Times

The now, the here, through which all future plunges to the past.

— JAMES JOYCE

GRAHAM Greene arrived in London, thanking God that his time in Nottingham, where he had felt stranded on a muddy beach, miles from anywhere, was over.[1] The fogs and snows of Nottingham were replaced by spring sunshine, which he frequently mentioned in letters — 'The sun's shining hard into my room'[2] — and his lodgings in All Saints Terrace had been replaced by a good-sized bed-sitting room at 141 Albert Palace Mansions, Battersea Park. Even the land-ladies reflected the contrast. Mrs Coney, the sour widow in Nottingham, was superseded by Miss King, 'old & fat & ugly',[3] but also 'sweet', far from melancholy, untidy, exuberant and absent-minded. Articles of furniture disappeared from his room towards the end of a month to reappear a week later; she had put them in hock to overcome a temporary difficulty.[4] He wrote to his father to ask whether his mother could send him his deceased uncle's evening dress: 'Could . . . she send Uncle F.'s dinner jacket, trousers and waistcoat to me . . . I want to get alterations done & have them available for Friday night'[5] — a strange request.

He still had his two interdependent ambitions: to get a job, so that he would have enough money to marry Vivien, and though he had no definite expectations in London, there were possibilities. On 10 March he wrote to Vivien: 'do you think I should be justified in asking a question of most vital importance, if I could show 12 guineas a week — about £650 a year?' The concern with earning money was obsessive and in June he was writing, 'I want [marriage] fearfully. When put in terms of sordid cash, it seems ridiculously simple.'[6] On 19 July his calculations reveal some class distinctions, irritation and possibly the influence of Vivien's mother: 'I could marry a waitress

on £400, R[aymond, his brother] can marry C[harlotte] on £500 . . .
I can't marry *you* under £600!'

Quite suddenly, he did get a job, though after an initial disappointment. He arrived at Albert Palace Mansions to find a letter from the appointments manager of *The Times* saying he had been asked to recommend someone for an opening on a London weekly, and he thought this would suit Greene. Alas, the paper turned out to be the Methodist *Guardian* – the one weekly, as he wrote to Vivien, from *John Bull* to the *Spectator*, which was hardly suitable for a recent convert to Catholicism. But he was determined to find work and went to see Robert Lynd and afterwards the manager of the *Daily News*, Hugh Jones, with whom he hit it off – 'Not only his face but his voice was familiar' – and Jones promised to speak to his Night Editor,[7] whom Greene saw that night. 'He's the generalissimo of sub-editors,' he wrote to Vivien, but added, 'I hardly have hope yet though.'[8] But the next day he sent her the following telegram:

GOOD NEWS PLEASE BE PUNCTUAL DARLING 14367

The news was good indeed – he had been offered what he had been seeking all along, a post with *The Times*. A letter from the appointments manager majestically declared: 'You will join the sub-editorial staff of *The Times* on one month's trial as from tomorrow, March 10.' His salary was to be 'limited to a weekly sum of £5', and the letter ended loftily: 'If you show promise at the end of that period of being suitable your services will be retained.'[9] Greene wrote to his mother: 'The Times is really a marvellous piece of good fortune! My hours are 4 to 11, so I shall be in bed by midnight.'[10] And he also explained the reason for his change of fortune: 'Apparently the secret of why they are taking on an extra sub-editor in each department of The Times is that they are going to revert to the Northcliffe system of a five day week.' Referring to the allowance his father had been making him at Oxford and in Nottingham, and which he would no longer need, he wrote to Vivien: 'I had a sweet letter from my father yesterday. I suppose it must be cheering to increase your income by about £250 which he has done.'[11]

Greene's luck was not limited to his appointment with *The Times*. In a passage in the typescript of *A Sort of Life* which did not appear in the printed version, he records other offers. Apparently he had not only been accepted on trial as a sub-editor by *The Times* in the first week of March but also by the *Daily Telegraph* and the very next day by the *Daily Chronicle*. It was all due to his having offered himself to several papers at the same time: 'All the doors at which I had knocked in vain six months before flew open, simply because I had spent three [four] months on the *Nottingham Journal*.'[12] 'Who'd have believed a month ago', he wrote to Vivien, 'that I should be turning down as not good enough a trial on the Telegraph!!!'[13] On 1 April he wrote to her: 'It's very amusing but the London papers are almost running after me!!! I got a letter last night from the Daily News offering me a job! So I shall now have politely to refuse two papers!!!' It was the editor of *The Times*, Geoffrey Dawson, who, instead of rebuking him, advised him to 'turn down *The Telegraph*' and told him how to word 'his tactful rejection . . . without bringing in *The Times* who are on friendly terms with them'. There are two minor inaccuracies in the excised passage from *A Sort of Life* – it was not the *Daily Chronicle* but the *Daily News* which made him an offer and it was not the day after the *Telegraph* offer but a month later.

In any case, it was a remarkable business and a credit to his persistence and personality, for four months on the *Nottingham Journal* could surely not have brought about this state of affairs alone, and his referees could not have been too influential. They were Frank Roscoe of the *Education Outlook*, Kenneth Bell, his tutor at Balliol and F. F. Urquhart (Sligger), the Dean of Balliol. Only Urquhart's reference has survived in *The Times*'s archives and it is not impressive: 'H. G. Greene [is] one of our young men anxious to have an interview with you. I don't know him very well but he is certainly an able fellow with a very distinct gift ['gift' is crossed out and replaced by 'power'] of writing. I think too that he would be able to write quickly and effectively.' Certainly Kenneth Bell would have written most forcefully in Greene's favour. To Vivien, Greene suggested that his being a Catholic helped: 'Everything seems to be progressing, dear heart, since I became a Catholic – & I don't believe that it's only a coincidence'.*

Greene had such phenomenal persistence that he was bound to land a sub-editing job in London. Moreover, he intended writing in his spare time and in this way increasing his meagre earnings. Geoffrey Dawson told him during his interview that the best plan was for Greene to sub-edit and to write in his free hours, adding that most people didn't take advantage of their leisure. Reporting to Vivien, Greene added, 'I didn't point out that other people hadn't got the Motive.'[14]

On his very first day at *The Times* he began a campaign to earn an extra three guineas a week – a large sum in those days. 'In the pursuit

---

* In fact, on his application form, someone had written in capitals ROMAN CATHOLIC, though this was later scratched out.

of reviews,' he told Vivien, 'I've written to the Spectator, have got an intro to the Observer, & directly I have a free moment I shall go round & collect some more books from the New Statesman. It ought not to be hard to attain it, when I'm on the spot, & can go & seize books in person. I had another little cheque from the Lit. Supp. this morning.'[15]

There were disappointments in his search to find enough money on which to marry: 'I don't get my full salary for a year – then it's nine guineas a week (£492), & after another year it becomes ten a week (£546 a year). I shall sweat hard & try & pick up before the year's out, a job or jobs on weeklies to supply three guineas a week – because twelve guineas (£655 a year) would be worth considering.' Is it personal pique with the system that makes him offer Vivien an unexpected freedom if the right financial conditions are met by another?

> But, you do understand, don't you that I can't & don't expect you to tie yourself for that time – a year or eighteen months or even, God forbid, two years . . . if you ever feel the weeniest bit inclined to marry someone else, who's got the ready money – do it. Darling, money's a hateful thing . . .[16]

In June he was writing: 'Agreed that £50 a month is what we want. By either March or April I shall (touch wood) have £42 a month. And in the interval I've got to somehow make sure of that small difference! We *won't* be beaten.'[17]

Given his obsessive love for Vivien, it is interesting at this point to go back to that telegram he sent her – GOOD NEWS PLEASE BE PUNCTUAL DARLING 14367 – as it illustrates the side of his character which could be involved in secrecy in the middle of intense mental and physical activity – an extension of his broadcast directed secretly at Gwen Howell. The mixture is the same and suggests a man capable of and delighting in running at the same time the public life and the intensely private. The numerals 14367 are part of a love-code. Each number indicates the number of letters in a word, thus 143 stands for 'I love you' and 14367 for 'I love you always darling'. The purpose behind the code was not simply a matter of secrecy, but of economy. As he wrote to Vivien on 10 January 1926: 'How wonderful our code is. I was able to send you "I love you always darling" for 1d. That's the heart not getting in the way of the head.' Simple as it was, the code was not always easily understood and on one occasion he had to explain to Vivien that the numbers 7 and 5 stood for 'darling heart'. He used the code even on the back of envelopes (understood by the receiver though not by anyone else).

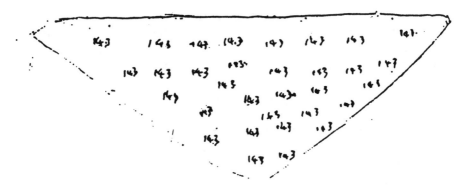

But their secret code went beyond numerals. On 17 February 1927 he wrote to her:

> Isn't it fine how a private code between us grows quite naturally & unintentionally – star [kiss] & leaf & so on. Soon we shall be able to have the most scandalous conversations in the most public place & no one be any the wiser. It opens endless possibilities of drawing-room games. Next time we are at Berkhamsted, at tea, surrounded by staid people, I shall make scandalous suggestions & express scandalous desires to you in a cold, collected fashion across the table, everyone will wonder why on earth you are blushing.

He was to make use of this notion of a secret code during the early part of the Second World War. When working for the Ministry of Information he wrote a story called 'The News in English', which appeared in June 1940. A slight story, it deals with an Englishman accused of being a traitor after being captured by the Germans. Like the famous Lord Haw-Haw (William Joyce), he read over German radio biased accounts of allied defeats and the success of German air-raids on Britain, but listening to these broadcasts his wife recognises that he was using a code to tell an entirely different story, attempting to give the British authorities valuable information. She goes to see a Colonel in the War Office to explain:

> If he was away from me and he telephoned 'The fact of the matter is' always meant, 'this is all lies, but take the initial letters which

follow . . .' Oh, Colonel, if you only knew the number of unhappy week-ends I've saved him from – because, you see, he could always telephone to me, even in front of his host.[18]

'I was happy on *The Times*,' wrote Greene in *A Sort of Life*, 'and I could have remained happy there for a lifetime', but he adds, significantly, 'if I had not in the end succeeded in publishing a novel.'[19] The basic urge of his talent was there underlying the present security of a job.

In the beginning he was contented: 'The Times is certainly pleasanter than the N[ottingham] J[ournal],' he wrote to Vivien. 'It's a change to be surrounded by University people. Though I feel rather like a junior who has found his way into the 6th by accident!'[20] It must have been a true comparison for him for he was younger than those he was working with. The usual age for journalists coming to London after experience in the provinces was twenty-four, and to Vivien he had written, 'if I do manage The Times at 21 and a half I shall have a good start.'[21] And to his mother, with some exaggeration: 'I feel terribly young with two or three exceptions of people about 24–25, everyone is going grey & slightly bald!'[22] The facilities alone were more attractive than those at the *Nottingham Journal* – no longer fish and chips in newspaper but a canteen. Joyfully he wrote to Vivien, 'at 8 we have a whole hour off for dinner & we either go out or have dinner in the Mess, or what's better the Canteen, where the workmen have it – very clean, nice white table cloths, flowers etc. & where it would be hard, owing to the limits of human appetites, to eat a dinner costing more than 1s.3d!! About 5 one can telephone down & have tea & cake brought up.'[23]

Everything Greene has written about this period suggests the pleasure of his years at *The Times* and the usefulness of the experience:

> It seemed to me only too likely that I would not survive the period of trial, but finally the leisurely life of the home subeditors . . . calmed my nerves and I began to realize I was as safe as though I had entered the Civil Service. No one on *The Times* was ever known to be sacked or to resign. I remember with pleasure – it was a symbol of the peaceful life – the slow burning fire in the sub-editors' room, the gentle thud of coals as they dropped one by one in the old black grate.[24]

Of his colleagues at *The Times* he admitted that no other group of men so planted themselves in his memory, nameless though they may have become: 'Perhaps this is always the case with a young man's first real job: the impression in the wax will never go quite so deep again.'[25]

The sub-editors worked on the first floor of the offices in Printing House Square where the editor, Geoffrey Dawson, had his room. He had an oval face 'which reminded one of Thomas Cranmer, large, dark, unfriendly eyes', but he had also a gift for immediately establishing a warm relationship.[26] Room 2 was the home sub-editors'; Room 3 the messenger boys'; Room 4 the Foreign Editor's. In Room 2 there were always ten to a dozen sub-editors at work, with one or two away each night. Apart from Greene, all but two are now dead.

The deputy chief sub-editor was Colonel Maude. He admired Greene as a young man, remembered him clearly and kept throughout his life a file on Greene's meteoric career. Greene describes him in *A Sort of Life* as 'a man of great courtesy, very tall and slim with a soft blond moustache' and when I met him at ninety-one he still stood tall and straight, his hair white, a beautifully mannered courteous man, friendly-eyed and shrewd: he talked excitedly of that period over half a century ago. In Room 2 there were Buxton, Gardiner and Jacob de Boinod. According to Maude, Boinod got a Rugger blue in spite of severe war injuries (he had a silver plate in his head). Without remembering his name, Greene recalls in *A Sort of Life* the youngest sub-editor, apart from himself, who was so fastidious he could eat nothing touched by human hand. In the canteen he would only take a cup of tea and Greene would tempt him with a tin of sardines. Greene connected his fastidiousness with his responsibility for the Court page. Leslie Smith, a contemporary of Greene, suggested this might have been a young man called Stokes who was known for his fastidiousness and curious feeding habits: 'He was plump & drank a lot of olive oil to keep him so – he thought it gave him 'presence'.[27]

Another survivor, G. L. Pearson, recalled arguments Greene had with Stokes: 'About that time, Greene was a rather new and very ardent Catholic, and one of his Room 2 colleagues curiously enough was an equally ardent and more bigoted Southern Irish Protestant. Naturally they argued that if he should happen to sub-edit material which had a pro-Protestant, or in the other case pro-Catholic, flavour, he would slash it ruthlessly.'[28] Stokes left *The Times* for the Church. Soon after Greene became a sub-editor, Pearson moved from Room 2 but he used to meet Greene in the canteen at supper and he recalled him as immature, 'an undergraduate flapping his wings rather than the young journalist.'[29] But Greene's keenness won him the friendship of his colleagues and he was quickly accepted.

They were all under the eye of the chief sub-editor, George

Anderson, who died in 1951 aged seventy-three. During his first week Greene hated him but before three years had passed he grew almost to love him: 'A small elderly Scotsman with a flushed face and a laconic humour, he drove a new subeditor hard with his sarcasm. Sometimes I almost fancied myself back at school again, and I was always glad when five-thirty came, for immediately the clock marked the hour when the pubs opened he would take his bowler hat from the coat-rack and disappear for thirty minutes to his favourite bar.'[30] Like Greene himself, Anderson's rather austere exterior hid, according to his obituary, a 'persistent shyness strangely blended with a real capacity for genial companionship.'[31] This hard-bitten Scots journalist was something of a martinet, but also a poet and an understanding man ready to encourage good writing. It pleased him that Greene, whenever there was a lull in Room 2, was always writing.[32]

It was a happy, busy, hopeful time for Greene – he liked his landlady and his sunny bed-sitter and the unexpected arrival of friends from his Oxford days: 'Yesterday, I dashed off to Charing X Rd. to try & trace a word of three letters for a Crossword for my mother, & when I got back I found Macleod & went & had lunch with him at the Blue Cockatoo, and then it was time for the office, & the reviews still to be done.'[33] It was work and play and freedom until early afternoon: 'I've got to write to the Litt. Supp. & do my minimum & have a shave & see a tailor & have lunch with Robert Scott'.[34] At night, when he had a free evening from *The Times*, he went to see musical revues: 'to Mr Pepys last night . . . a fragile imitation of [John] Gay without his guts and the 17th century laid on with a trowel. The girl who's succeeded Isabel Jeans as Nell Gwynne, was perfectly entrancing. And there was one song, sung in the puppet show in the last act, Henry VIII, his last wife, & a fortune teller, about his five previous wives . . . & all the chorus, which was simply glorious.'[35]

With seeing these revues comes a longing to escape from refined and proper behaviour:

My aunt 'treated' me to Riverside Nights. Mr Nigel Playfair trying to give an artistic revue & only succeeding in being too terribly 'refayned' . . . One longed thirstily for a little vulgarity . . . one yearned for the orchestra to leave off pseudo 18th century sugar & burst into jazz, & one ached for the cast to throw off 90% of their superfluous clothing, & start dancing uproariously with a great show of legs . . . But they never did. We gave a shout of joy when we came out into the vulgar blare of Hammersmith, & heard a party of drunks, singing with real spirit, & not with refinement, about 'the Ukelele Lady'.[36]

April saw an attempt on the life of the Italian Fascist leader Mussolini: 'Wasn't it fun about Mussolini?' he asked Vivien. 'But what a ghastly disgrace for Lord Ashbourne to have a sister who's as bad a shot as all that.'[37]

*

Greene's letters to Vivien show that outside the slow and secure hours at *The Times*, the frenzy of ambition and activity which were to win him Vivien went on – but there was still some uncertainty about her commitment to him. His love for her was the foundation on which he was building his future, but perhaps his ardent sexuality strengthened her reluctance to marry.

A 'train' letter to her, written as he returned from a weekend visit to Oxford, gives some indication of his state of mind. On the one hand he quotes lines from Rupert Brooke which presumably refer to one aspect of the weekend they had spent together: 'When two mouths thirsty each for each/find slaking/And agony's forgot & hushed the crying'. On the other hand, while he was writing this letter, he was afflicted by a severe attack of hay-fever (from which he suffered appallingly at this time), but he attributes the delay of the onset of this attack to Vivien's presence: 'I have just let off a sneeze & hay-fever is again taking sway. I should never have believed that I could have sat in grass in June & not suffered for it. I believe if one arm was tight round you it would be possible to put the other into a flower without feeling anything. I am now sneezing after nearly every other sentence!'

His passion for statistics is brought to bear on their love, its progress and, possibly, its difficulties: 'I've just been making hasty calculations. In one fortnight's honeymoon I should have more hours of you than the average six months now. Does that fill you with terror? It fills me with joy. It would be lovely to be able to squander hours much more easily than we dare minutes now.' And he plots the growing intensity of their love with historical markers (with perhaps an echo of Donne):

I love you more than I did last April at The Ship, more than last May at Malton, more than June at Blenheim, more than July on the thunder evening, more than August in the Capitol [cinema] or in the wood at Didcot, more than September at the Golden Cross, more than October in the backwoods, more than November at Nottingham, & December at Hampstead & January at Oxford [railway] platform, & February at Nottingham. And I know that in April I shall love you more even than at Berkhamsted in March.[38]

On the first anniversary of their meeting, in a letter dated precisely 17th March and written at 9.30, Greene recorded the fact that this time last year he did not know what Vivien looked like, knowing only that she existed: 'But in one hour from now she lodged herself in my thought, but the lodger now is a permanent tenant. In one hour my restlessness began.' He was 'blinded by the sun' of Vivien. He considers that he might save up and be able to buy a car but recalls that he would always want to travel with Vivien in taxis because 'You are wonderful in taxis . . . you were miraculously beautiful on the way to the theatre.' In what sense wonderful? Was Greene allowed to be somewhat sexually daring? This is doubtful since the letter's following sentence says only, 'the finger's still feeling proud & dazzled & distrait which you kissed suddenly in the theatre.'[39]

He wishes that he were a Theosophist so that by accepting the belief in reincarnation he might believe in the 'chances of a dozen lives' with her. In his dreams he would see Vivien with a look on her face which 'would have made St Anthony fall' or 'convert Brigham Young to monogamy', thus etherialising her into a kind of goddess of orthodox Christian marriage. On receiving a telegram from her, he would delay reading it until he had gone to bed and then read it by match-light and go to sleep on it. The words of her telegram were as a 'kind of light on the prow of the boat when we dive into the dark.'* Also before falling asleep he would think concentratedly of Vivien in Oxford and admit, 'I come to you every night, dear love, about midnight.'[40] He dreamt of finding his way to Vivien, asleep in her room: 'I'm kneeling by your bed, hoping that you'll wake up. I've given you two tentative stars but you've only wriggled a little. You are looking very lovely.' And he sees her again as the Sleeping Beauty in a letter which, for 1926, is rather daring since he is imagining a post marriage incident, which interestingly has a certain 'nursery' flavour to it and suggests they would occupy separate bedrooms:

---

* On this occasion he sent Vivien a stanza of religious verse written during a lull in Room 2:

> There was a woman watched her son hang dying,
> with the uprising of a hundred creeds,
> and centuries of chicanery & lying.
> She heard his long despair; she could not hear
> the shriek of trumpets & the din of deeds,
> saw but the cross, and even that not clear.

Darling, if we were married, sometimes perhaps I should find you awake when I came in, & we could sit & have bread & milk in front of the fire, you in your dressing gown & fluffy slippers, & you'd get drowsier & drowsier & presently you'd go fast asleep. And I should pick you up (& there'd be no protests, because you wouldn't know) & carry you into your room & put you into your bed. And in the morning you'd wake up & wonder whether you'd dreamed the bread & milk part!![41]

A performance of Shaw's *St Joan* suggests parallels with Vivien:

After every week end there are always two or three startlingly beautiful moments that I remember always, when the rest has become a blur of happiness. Like certain moments in St Joan – when she first unsheaths her sword in the court, & when she's deserted in the Cathedral, & the final curtain. I'm sorry always to drag in St Joan, but she always reminds me of you.★[42]

Often, there is an element of hyperbole in his wooing which again suggests the wit of Donne: 'I'm packing such a lot of love into this short letter, the envelope will bulge!' (undated letter); 'Darling, you are the most beautiful living thing there is now, not excluding tulips, race horses, irises, Alsatian wolfhounds, Isabel Jeans & cherry blossom' (11 May 1926); '. . . you seem to get more and more beautiful every day. It's quite frightening – as though the firmament might be no longer able to hold you & crack right across' (7 April 1926). The apotheosis is reached when he sees her as the person who has moulded him:

Except for the joint work of my people in producing me, you are much the most responsible person for the present me. You've chipped me about & added & taken away in the most wholesale & reckless fashion. I'm quite muddled myself not knowing what's me & what's you.[43]

Opposed to this adulation are some genuine fears that their relationship might break down because of Vivien's reluctance to marry and his own impatience for that consummation:

★ Thirty years later in 1957 Greene wrote the screenplay of *St Joan*. He tells how he came to do work on *St Joan* and his attitude towards it then: 'Preminger was insistent that I do the screenplay and I did have six weeks blank, so I acceded. Shaw is not a sacred name to me. I didn't mind adapting his work.' From the above letter we can see that, once, Shaw was a sacred name to him.

I just consider life some years hence with no you in it, & all this as a dim episode in the past. And that seems as impossible as imagining pigs flying. We've got too hopelessly mixed up with each other for anything short of death to untwist it all. Ergo if we are both alive we shall be together. Ergo since 1927 is the bounds of patience, somehow it's going to be managed. So prepare to be sacrificed on the altar of matrimony.[44]

In late March, when he had been with *The Times* only a month, she raised the spectre of her entering a convent. He told her firmly that her letter was frightening and made him terrified of loving her knowing she had such thoughts, and knowing also that he did not count a farthing: 'if you still have that at the back of your mind, it's not fair simply to keep it dark. I don't even see that it's right that love of God should swamp out all feeling for other people . . . I love you more than anything in the world or outside it, but if that made it impossible for me to love anything else I should consider that my love for you was to be squashed. If you are contemplating going into some religious body you ought to tell me so as to give me a chance of forcing myself out of love as quickly as possible.' In apology for this outburst he added, 'Dogs always snap when woken up suddenly',[45] and on the flap of an envelope he writes: 'It's almost pitch dark outside – a good setting for the most disagreeable letter I've ever written you!'

Part of the trouble was Vivien's fear of marriage, which he sensed: 'Then Christmas almost on top of us. The New Year, March – a decent salary for me & at last a ring for you (I shall feel you are really engaged to me then) & then I shall begin to keep a look out for a flat – & you'll begin to get frightened & trepidations.'[46] He also knew – or thought he did – the reason for her reluctance, which was the failure of her mother's disastrous runaway marriage. He tried to calm her fears on that score: 'Your mother's bad shot was taken with her eyes open, wasn't it? There was no disillusioning about it, as she was never in love with him, was she?'[47]

But Vivien's reluctance stemmed from a distaste for or reluctance to embark upon the sexual side of marriage. At the time of his conversion, as we have seen, Greene offered to enter into a unique form of marriage – a celibate one. Understandably, once he was properly engaged and once he felt he had at last made a fair start with his career, Greene began to marshal arguments in favour of the carnal side of marriage, of which Vivien had so real a fear. On 6 April Greene fired off a first salvo with a quotation from John Donne's 'Ecstasy' which has always seemed so ready-made for persuading reluctant lovers: 'Love's mysteries in souls do grow/But yet the body is his book.' They had been having an argument about material and spiritual love. Greene was now admitting that his love towards her was 50 per cent material and 50 per cent spiritual, and Vivien took fright, for earlier his feelings for her had been 70 per cent non-material. Greene dealt with that fear firmly:

It seems to me the two kinds are inextricably mixed up. When I kiss you, it would be very wrong to call it a mere kiss of spiritual affection, & it would be equally wrong to call it a mere material pleasure. The first works through the other. I don't think a love which did without those things would be a more spiritual one. It would be merely an unexpressed one. To misquote Browning 'Soul helps flesh no more than flesh helps soul' . . . all expression is more material than the thought. Just as the writing down of a poem is more material than just letting it run through the head. More material – not materialistic.

And I don't see that you've got much cause to be frightened. You've instilled into me just sufficient of a sense of decency to see that you run no risk – that is to say that I should *not* run off with anyone else, even if I got the chance!!! My peccadilloes, darling shall be kept in Paris.[48]

It is apparent that to the strain of sexual frustration (which was inevitable since Vivien considered a physical relationship before marriage out of the question) was added the fear that this problem might never be resolved – even after marriage. There is the possibility that only in Paris would he be able to indulge in sexual adventures, but in that material/spiritual argument about love he turned the tables easily – 'people put an accent of slight scorn on "physical", as if it's a transient & less thing than the other. When really it's a part of the other.'[49] And learning of Vivien's own thoughts which frightened her, he offers, among other things, insight into his own nature, and perhaps we can see here also the influence of Kenneth Richmond, his view that one should accept what one found within oneself and not be afraid of it:

Don't be frightened of the dark you. It's a very precious individual. I don't know if what frightens you is that you find sometimes things, feelings, happenings that don't seem connected with the mind. Is that it? If it is I'd argue that the part of the mind which one can watch working is the least valuable . . .

It's much easier for me because I've never had a fixed philosophy

& as long as I've been liable, so-to-speak, to such I've recognised the existence of the 'dark' side of myself & other people. And so when it comes it slips quietly into the place left for it. But you didn't leave the poor thing a space, arguing cynically that all people – or at least all women – married for a variety of sensible, practical reasons, & men from animality. When there's really no more connection with animality than the thin connection between an uneducated drunkard's lewd scribble on a patch of wall & a Velasquez.[50]

By August he put paid to the material/spiritual arguments of Vivien with one final dismissive assertion: 'There is only one creative instinct. I think the idea that physical marriage is debased and isn't spiritual in motive and feeling is simply prurient.'[51]

*

Though Greene was pleased to be working for *The Times*, his early restlessness sometimes returned. Just so long as he was snowed under with work he could control his feelings of hopelessness and despair but the work was not sufficiently fulfilling. Seeking an escape from this tedium, he began enquiries about learning to fly: 'I've heard from the Flying Club . . . The ordinary membership is three guineas & the 30/- an hour can include instruction. I really *am* rather thrilled at the idea of learning to fly. I feel it would be quite an original thing for a subeditor to do in his spare time.'[52] And he had plans of swooping down on Vivien at Oxford: 'When I can fly, I shall take out a club plane for an hour's flight from Edgware, & I shall wire to you to be at the meadows at 2.30 sharp, & I shall swoop down & you'll climb in with your suitcase & we'll fly back to London!!' But he had, also, a practical purpose as a letter to Vivien two days later shows:

There are some splendid photos of the Amazon in to-day's Times taken by the expedition which has been exploring the Amazon by air. The more I feel that there might be great opportunities for a journalist, who knew something about aeroplanes. The next twenty years will be full of that type of expedition – what with the Amazon, the Poles & New Guinea, & who knows that there might not be correspondencies going?[53]

Already he felt a prisoner in his occupation, love alone keeping this ever-restless man sane: 'Without you life seems to be made up of an endless sub-editing till death.' But history took its part in delaying

Graham's rising sense of tedium over sub-editing. On 3 May the General Strike began, and Greene played his small part in the front line.

21

The General Strike

Constitutional Government is being attacked.
— STANLEY BALDWIN

THE General Strike in Britain was literally a nine days' wonder. It began on 3 May 1926 and ended on the 12th. Writing in her diary two days after the strike, Beatrice Webb, reflecting that it had cost Britain tens of millions of pounds, commented that it had left 'other nations asking whether it was a baulked revolution or play-acting on a stupendous scale'. For some of the better off – students and young professional people – it was an exciting joke; for the poor it was a disaster; and for Britons generally it was a short, sharp conflict between the unions and the rest of society.

It began with the miners who, because of a decline in the economy, were threatened with wage cuts and longer working hours by the coal mine owners who were backed by the government. The Prime Minister's statement that 'all workers in this country have got to take reductions in wages' ensured the miners of support from other unions. The unions and the Labour Party believed that they could shut down the nation, and a government with no one to govern must cease to exist: 'If the [union] leaders . . . dinna let us doon we'll hae the Capitalists crawlin' on their bellies in a week', was not untypical preliminary rhetoric.[1] But the call to strike came precipitately and almost accidentally when the printers' union, Natsopa, attempted to prevent the publication by the *Daily Mail* of an editorial entitled 'For King and Country', which argued that an industrial dispute on a national scale was part of a revolutionary act intended to inflict suffering on the 'great mass of innocent persons in the community'. The printers saw this as an attack on the Labour side and struck. That was late on Sunday 2 May: on the following day the transport workers, the printing trade, iron and steel workers, metal, chemical and building workers came out.

296

But the strikers faced a well-prepared country, and if this General Strike was to be the dawn of revolution, Prime Minister Baldwin and his government were ready for it. Beforehand an Organisation for the Maintenance of Supplies (O.M.S.) had been set up. This was allegedly non-political and motivated only by patriotism, and so it was, but it was not the poor and unemployed who joined but the employed and comparatively prosperous. Placards posted throughout the country asking for volunteers to keep the coun ıy going – which meant replacing striking workers – brought a swarm of recruits lining up to become special constables, transport drivers, messengers and clerical workers, and they were mostly middle and upper class people, university students and professional men.

The Strike and its implications frightened the respectable classes and although it began peacefully, trouble was expected. Arnold Bennett, after lunching at the Reform Club, noted in his journal: 'Most people gloomy, but all uncompromising. General opinion that the fight would be short but violent. Bloodshed anticipated next week.'[2] The well-known journalist, Sir Philip Gibbs, forecast that: 'Before we are through, unless it is a quick finish, there is bound to be some outbreak of violence leading to stern and merciless suppression.'[3]

The government over-reacted. The battleships *Ramillies* and *Barham* were recalled from the Atlantic fleet; two battalions of infantry were landed at Liverpool and marched through the city with steel helmets and rifles; all Army and Navy leave was stopped; and Hyde Park, becoming a great food depot, had armoured cars guarding food trucks. In a wireless broadcast, the Home Secretary appealed 'to all who are fit and strong to offer their service as special constables', even though there were already 11,000 specials in London. By Friday he was appealing for more: 'I want 50,000 specials by Monday morning'; the appeal was couched in patriotic terms: 'Surely there must be another 30,000 men in London willing and eager to serve.' In the quadrangle of the Foreign Office in Whitehall, thousands formed up in fours, indeed 'willing and eager'.

*

The immediate effect of the cessation of most normal activities in London which struck many people on that first Tuesday morning, was 'a stillness which nobody had ever known before in English history'.[4] One observer stressed 'the breathless feeling of intense quietness', and Greene recalled in *A Sort of Life*: There was a wonderful absence of traffic, it was a beautiful hushed London that we were not to know again until the blitz.'[5] But enforced inaction also made him restless, as his letters to Vivien show. On the first day of the strike he wrote to her of the absurdity of staying in London if there was no job to be done: 'The Daily Mail has already stopped publication, & there'll be no papers after tomorrow, so that it seems utterly ridiculous that I've got to get stuck in London.' His instinct to seek out trouble-spots, to experience the situation at first hand and perhaps obtain copy, led him to continue: 'If there is nothing to do in London I've got a good mind to borrow a pack & go for a long week's walk. If I pass through Oxford, I'll call. It might be fun, if one could get enough trains to give one a start to go down to the Welsh or some other mining district.' By the following day his attitude had changed with changing events. As he recalled in *A Sort of Life*, 'there was the exciting sense of living on a frontier, close to violence. Armoured cars paraded the streets.'[6]

By the second day there was war in so far that violence broke out: mass pickets in the East End of London stopped and wrecked vehicles suspected of carrying goods; some vehicles were set alight and thrown into the river. On Thursday, the fourth day, there were further clashes in the East End and mounted police had to break up the crowds; in Camberwell some women laid their babies in front of commercial vehicles and when the vehicles drew up attacked them; at Middlesbrough a mob reputed to be 4,000 strong wrecked the goods and passenger stations and on the seventh day a train, the Flying Scotsman, was derailed at Cramlington.

Apart from this, however, Greene found himself in the 'front line', because the strikers had succeeded in bringing the publication of newspapers to a halt (which gave the new-fangled news broadcasts on 'the wireless' a chance to come into their own). There was an almost total blackout of newsprint, apart from the government-established (and quite unobjective) *British Gazette*, edited by Winston Churchill, and *The Times*. Greene was obviously not going to leave London in those circumstances.

Greene's letters to Vivien at this time are more revealing than his autobiography. He was concerned that the strike might prevent his letters reaching her, but mainly they reflect his excitement at the developments – putting a paper half its usual size to press at 10 p.m. before the men left on strike, expecting to go to the office that night only to be dismissed and going back home, then the excitement because the T.U.C. leaders went to Downing Street at 10 a.m., which suggested the strike might end – and then the non-delivery of his copy of *The Times*:

I went round to my newsagent to see why my Times hadn't come. Miss Friend had got hers from another newsagent. Mine was furious. He said there was going to be trouble for those that *had* distributed copies. His shop was crowded with sympathisers, unshaven toughs of Saklatvala's Battersea. Don't bite me, please. I can't help feeling a little excited. Claud [Cockburn] came round to the office last night & we went out to dinner. We could really imagine ourselves back in the Ruhr there was such a sense of sinister strain. I can't help wishing that there's a little bit of a civil war. Yesterday in Oxford I'd have betted ten to one against. Now I wouldn't bet more than 3-1 against.[7]

Shapurji Saklatvala was the Member of Parliament for Battersea where Greene lived, and the country's only Communist M.P. At a May Day rally in Hyde Park, he had called on the British Army and Navy to revolt: 'I want the army boys to revolt now and refuse to fight . . . they will be the real saviours of their homes and the workers . . . I want the army and navy really to protect the people instead of the rogues and thieves of the master classes.'[8]

At 4 p.m. on the second day, Greene was at the offices of *The Times* and at 4.30 was writing again to Vivien:

Having nothing else to do, I shall be able to talk to you. We are bringing out a single news sheet roneod. I don't know how it will be distributed. There were fights apparently yesterday. I'm feeling fearfully glad to be alive. Everything fearfully exciting. We are almost barricaded here. The front door closed & bolted, & the back guarded by innumerable people to prevent any but the staff getting in. Armoured cars passed down Fleet St last night for the East end, & the barracks in the King's Rd were full of field guns & bluejackets. And Saklatvala's under arrest & Yorkshire's on the edge of riot. Hurray!

Saklatvala was sentenced to two months' imprisonment.

Many people treated the General Strike as a bonus holiday. Greene discovered that his friend Claud Cockburn was taking time off and motoring down to Oxford, and although he would have liked to go with Cockburn and kept insisting there was nothing for him to do in London, it is clear from his letters that he was very busy. Almost alone among journalists, the staff of *The Times* continued working – and Greene, among others, was doing the work of the packers: 'We are going to go on printing news sheets. All the news to be crammed into 1600 words. I wish I was able to come down in that car tomorrow

The Life of Graham Greene

... And I wish I'd got my MSS here. I could get a good lot done. O Blast! They've just asked for volunteers to take the place of the packers who are on strike.'

Whenever danger subsided so did Greene's pleasure in the situation. Writing on the second day, he complained: 'Of course, there wasn't even excitement last night. We had 20 police to guard us, & the Union Men melted before them.' On the third day (5 May) he briefly wrote: 'Darling, I can't answer your letter now, I'm dog tired. I started work yesterday at 4.15 p.m. & finished this morning at 8 a.m. – 16 solid hours, just counting papers & putting them in piles. The whole staff, except the editorial's on strike, & we had to do everything. I'm going to go to bed now for a little while, before walking back for another night of it.'*

As the only newspaper being published, *The Times*, as it reported itself, became 'the very centre of fashion'. Members of Parliament and half the clubs in London, undergraduates and schoolboys offered their services. Volunteer motor-drivers included directors of banks and public companies. A Governor-elect put in some strenuous work as a packer.[9] There was precious little sub-editing needed to produce a single sheet and volunteers and editorial staff took on the business of lifting unending bundles of paper from the machines, transporting them to the publishing department, tying them into parcels, loading them into cars and being in fact general dogsbodies. The strain was considerable. Writing to Vivien, Greene said that 'if the 16 hour day continues for the next week, there'll be nothing left of The Times staff.'

On 5 May he wrote: 'There'll be trouble tonight, I think, from disappointed strikers. There was a very large crowd collecting on the Nine Elms side of [Vauxhall] bridge.'[10] The following day he wrote to Vivien:

Great triumph! Last night we got off a properly printed four page paper, with one machine working. The only paper in London to do it. The strikers are getting nasty though. Last night about 9.30 they set us on fire with the help of some petrol & a squirt, but we got it out all right, almost before the brigade arrived. We had a bit of trouble about 1:30 this morning. The police seem to have disappeared & we had to carry parcels of papers to private cars

* In *A Sort of Life* (p. 126) he explained: 'We had been up the whole previous night while the multigraph machines turned out the famous single sheet of May 5, 1926, Number 44263 ... price twopence ... the single sheet finally managed to include ... news of the strike, a weather report, broadcasting, sport, Stock Exchange, and a Court Page of five lines.'

lined up along Victoria St to carry them into the country, Oxford, Margate, Bournemouth, Dover etc. There was a bit of a scrimmage then. I didn't get hurt at all, but one man got a slight concussion from a blow on the head from his own parcel – they tipped him up & got hold of it – & another had his jaw cut & there were a number of bruises. Later the police arrived in greater force & they were held at a distance, but they'd already tampered with some of the cars.[11]

His account of the fire in his autobiography gives the atmosphere of *The Times*:

> The bell rang once, twice, three times. Someone asked with mild curiosity, 'A Fire?'. After a while the assistant chief subeditor, Colonel Maude, rose and moved with his usual elegant and leisurely gait into the corridor . . . when he returned to the room and sat down, it took quite a time to realize *The Times* – so he was telling us – had been set on fire.[12]

Colonel Maude recalled: 'I was walking towards *The Times* when two men I saw were peering in through the crack of the basement. I took no notice of them, but after we got in a fire broke out and the alarm bell went. Going out of the room I met Ackerman, the acting manager. He seemed perfectly amused and said casually, "The offices are afire." I snatched a fire extinguisher, I was young then, but when we got down into the basement there was only lots and lots of burnt paper in the machine room.'[13] The newspaper's own account of this historic fire is less bland: 'a great blaze of flame' roaring up 'to a height of nearly 30 feet'.[14]

The incident was reported by a *New York Times* correspondent, who witnessed it from an upper window of *The Times* and wrote of the assistant foreign editor getting 'into a furious fist fight with three or four strikers' sending 'smashing blows to his face and body'.[15] Greene's account is probably the more reliable – he was involved as one of *The Times*'s 'shock troops'. A photograph of the shock troops appeared in a book privately printed by *The Times*, providing a record of how the newspaper carried on during the strike while the rest of Fleet Street was shut down. Greene, among those photographed, looks very young and slightly impish. He sent a copy to Vivien and turned his looks to account: 'If I'm looking pensive in the photo it's probably because I'm thinking of you.'[16] The day after the fire he told her: 'We are trying to produce a five page paper tonight. But either there'll be no trouble at all or else last night's fire and scrimmage will be a mild opening. It's all very exciting.'[17]

The Graham Greene who was to identify later with the victims of society, had not yet surfaced. Not only was he a strike-breaker and one of *The Times*'s shock troops, he also became a special constable. In his autobiography he explains that he did this, 'More from curiosity than from any wish to support the Establishment', and this is no doubt true – it was an opportunity to explore another area of experience, but it was a superficial exploration and without any true understanding or sympathy on his part for the strikers. In the morning he would parade with 'a genuine policeman the length of Vauxhall Bridge.'[18] The two-man patrol 'always ceased at the south end, for beyond lay the enemy streets where groups of strikers stood outside the public houses.'

Vivien was a strong Conservative then and she seems to have suspected that Greene's sympathies lay with the wrong side, for on 7 May we find him defending himself: 'Darling, you talk as if I was Labour. I'm not. I'm really Conservative now – especially after Labour tried to burn us all.' But in the same letter he does make a criticism of Vivien's employer, Basil Blackwell – there was talk of his putting his staff on half pay during the strike: 'It's scandalous . . . you couldn't possibly live on half what you are getting now. That sort of thing makes me furious. Presumably some of the girls at B's, do depend on their salary. I feel more inclined to kick B.B. than any striker.' What did concern him about the strike as it affected *The Times* was 'that most [of the strikers] are our own men, who were awfully decent, cheerful & contented, when we had met in the canteen etc. They didn't want to strike, but now they've struck they've entirely changed, & of course no filth is bad enough to describe us and our parentage.' In his autobiography he recognises his own – and his own class's – ignorance at that time: 'A few years later my sympathies would have lain with them, but the great depression was still some years away: the middle-class had not yet been educated by the hunger-marchers.'[19]

*

Even before the strike ended, life began to return to normal and it was possible to go 'into the Tivoli and [hear] Paul Whiteman's Band. And they began playing "On Top of the World".' But his special constable duty continued, and he was now bored by it: 'The special constabling terribly dull so far. Victoria's a too respectable district. This morning from 10 a.m.–2 p.m. I was guarding (with others!) a petrol dump on the embankment by Vauxhall bridge. It's really extraordinarily tiring walking up & down fifty yards of road for four hours.'★[20]

On the day the strike broke, Greene was writing to Vivien: 'Apparently the betting in the City is 5-1 on the strike being over by Saturday. Oh it would be glorious – like a big hot bath after a long walk.' But it wasn't glorious. Life returned to normal without excitement or the prospect of danger. He had pulled his weight for *The Times* and *The Times* recognised this. Some of his colleagues had slipped away at 2 a.m. in the morning – who could blame them – but Greene had stuck it out and often saw the dawn rise. His three months' trial period had been made superfluous by the strike. He was accepted now and he received, as did others, a gift from the management of a silver match-box.

Colonel Maude told me that the inscription on each match-box was *Ictus meus utilis esto*. The significance of the Latin tag lay in the interpretation given to it: 'Let my strike be a useful one.' For the strikers it had been a disaster. Miners in the Northumberland and Durham coalfields had their wages reduced to levels lower than they had known for a decade. There was a bitter irony in their popular strike slogan: 'Not a penny off the pay: not a second on the day.'

The boredom of working on *The Times* – the daily tedium which now seemed to stretch into the future – returned:

> I'm going out to buy various necessities of life, & then I'm going for a walk, & then I'm going to have lunch, & then do a bit of work, & then go to the office & so ad infinitum, or rather for another sixty years according to my hand.† Only after another forty I suppose the office would drop out & a round of golf or a sleep at the Club would take its place. One of those cheering prospects one gets occasionally![21]

In July he spoke of unbearable monotony without Vivien and the mechanical routine he was following:

> Darling . . . it's wet & unsummery & miserable to-day, altogether suitable for a London that has no you in it. I must put on a macintosh & go out & buy some stamps. If I write to you any more I shall go depressing & pessimistic, because the ache's getting

---

★ 'I don't think I'm looking a wreck, darling!! I'm no longer doing very long hours. I turn up at office about 10 p.m., get away about 4.30 a.m., & *constabularise* 2 p.m.–6 p.m. Only two hours over the eight hour day.'

† If Greene had had his hand read as this seems to suggest, the prediction would seem to indicate that he would live until 1986.

bad. Things always seem so unbearably monotonous & routine-like when you aren't on the horizon. Even the time when one isn't at work goes by routine, letter, post office, Episode, lunch, bus, work.[22]

This sense of ennui has recurred throughout Greene's life. Of course, the missing factor in the Vivien years was Vivien: 'I dare say the dentist will fill up some of the time we are away from each other – I almost welcome him. This week with Joseph [Macleod], Christopher [Isherwood], dentist & an aunt, will fill up. It doesn't . . . stop the ache.'[23] Again in July he is having second thoughts about journalism: 'I suppose I must be off to the Times. I wonder, if I lose you, whether I shall ever stick at journalism. More than doubtful I think.'[24]

22

'The beastly Episode'

Writing is not a profession but a vocation of unhappiness.
— GEORGES SIMENON

IN February 1974, I was drinking with Graham Greene in a pub
in Piccadilly. Was he, I asked, still a Catholic? He thought he
probably was not. And later, on my asking him why he had taken
to writing, he answered that it had been an accident: 'There seemed
nothing else to do . . . It has become a habit and it's too late to change
now.'

There was no emotional charge behind either of these answers to
what were, after all, crucial questions. The diffidence of phrasing and
expression belied the fact that he was a controversial Catholic and a
very successful writer, just as his amiable, good-mannered surface
belied that tiny smile on his lips and his unflinching, though watery,
disturbingly calm blue eyes. 'Everybody in literary London in the
1940s *knew* Graham Greene,'[1] Walter Allen, the novelist and critic,
told me, as if there was nothing more to be known – or perhaps
nothing more that could be easily known?

As a shy person, Greene has an instinctive reticence, reinforced by
breeding and up-bringing and later deliberately developed into a
protective shield. It is an indication of the closeness of his relationship
with Vivien that at one time his trust in her allowed him to reveal
his most secret thoughts and ambitions – he could 'talk or write' to
her 'about things [he] could never do to any of [his] people'.[2] 'I blush
when I think of the things I tell you,' he confessed. 'Things, wants,
wishes and so on, that I'd be utterly ashamed of anyone else hearing.'[3]
Particularly, his confessions to Vivien show that rather than there
having been nothing else for him to do than be a writer, the desire
to be one was a secret passion with him: 'To other people I go to
tremendous lengths to convince them that I don't want to write, am
not interested in writing, am rather bored by poetry and so on. It's

a poor compliment to bore you with things I don't bore other people with.'[4] He described the nature of his passion: 'I wish I didn't have this ridiculous longing to publish things. I have always a futile and sentimental hunger to have at least a couple of volumes of verse and a couple of novels published, enough to force people to make some sort of an estimate of their value, if one was killed or something. It's ridiculous. It's not ambition in the proper sense. Only an utterly futile amount.'[5]

As well as asking her to burn his confession, he also indicated the further lengths he was prepared to go to to protect his secret ambition. When he was on the point of joining the B.A.T., he wrote: 'I do want to write well fearfully badly, & I don't mind telling *you* that. But rather than say anything to any of my family I'd go into the B.A.T. & depart to China.'[6]

His desire to write and publish had several stimuli, however. One was so as not to fall victim to the apparent contentment of his colleagues in Room 2 at *The Times* with their mundane and modest way of life – something which made him fear for his own future:

> *Mystery, darling.* Can you unravel it? How is it that all these sub-editors between 40 and 50 years old, earning if they are lucky 700 a year, seem perfectly happy – attending to their small garden at Streatham in their spare time, sending their children to school etc. &, I'm quite certain, feeling no acute disappointment with things. Cheerful thought.[7]

Hopefully he asked her: 'Do the people who *would* hate it [the lifestyle of his colleagues], always manage to avoid it & become automatically successful in one way or another?'[8]

Another fear arose from his mistaken belief that he did not have long to live, though he spoke humorously about this:

> Whilst on morbid subjects, it may be an inducement to you to marry me, to know that as long as I can remember I've had a certain instinct that I should be killed before I was thirty-two. I can't remember when I wasn't certain. Like the Apostolic Succession, it fades into the mists. So you wouldn't have such a terrible time. Safer really than with an old man of sixty who might live for over 20 years.[9]

If he had died before the age of thirty-two, he would have met his maker in 1936. Perhaps because of Vivien's response to this, the date of death was revised and included Vivien (though this could not have implied a suicide pact since the letter's tone was still humorous) when, writing of the strength his love would have twenty years on, he suddenly recalls: 'Oh, I forgot. We'd agreed to be dead by then.'[10] Responding to a further revision of the date of their dying he comments, significantly: 'Darling you know I don't promise to be killed or something in 1956. If I've succeeded in getting notorious by that time I don't suppose I should want to. So you'd have to go alone, darling, if you insisted on going.'

Most of this is play – he had given up Russian roulette because of his love for Vivien and he expresses no real desire for death during 1926 or, indeed, until after his marriage when depressions and thoughts of suicide did return – at least in the form of his risking death during future travels. But at this time he was certainly driven by the fear that he might die early without making a name as a writer: 'I can't afford to waste time. It does consciously lead me into making bad mistakes, because of a sense of hurry. Like publishing "Babbling April".' On the other hand, he felt that 'without that knowledge' (that he could not afford to waste time) he would never have written anything. The same sense of the need to hurry 'was fearfully vexing and delaying sometimes too. Because I want to finish the "Episode" and while I'm doing it I feel I ought to be getting on with a volume of verse, and with my pet biography, and with my blank verse play . . . They all get in each other's way in a sort of hustle.'[11]

A hustle it certainly was and driven by the demons, time and ambition, his life had a frenetic quality, physically and mentally. On the one hand, as the above remarks show, he was anxious to produce more works of different kinds, and he was attracted to writing about writers who seemed to have had similar difficulties to himself. The 'pet biography' he refers to is probably a life of the Irish poet, George Darley, which he had first considered in 1925. In 1929 his first substantial contribution to the *London Mercury* was an essay on Darley, reprinted in his *Collected Essays* forty years later. Darley wrote that underwater dirge: 'Wash him bloodless, smoothe him fair/Stretch his limbs and sleek his hair/Dingle-dong, the dead bells go/Mermen swing them to and fro.' And his *Nepenthe*, Greene thought, was one of the most remarkable poems of the nineteenth century. He wrote to Vivien from the sub-editors' room of the *Nottingham Journal* that Darley had 'such a bad stammer that he was afraid of meeting new people, an itch to write, & yet no real confidence in himself at all, so that he clung pathetically to the least praise. His letters are extraordinarily tragic. He suffered from fearful headaches, & intestinal illnesses of an undignified kind & died at about 50 [he committed suicide] . . . Time for hot chips, darling.' At this time, Greene was himself unconfident: 'I should find it easier to turn Latin into a crossword puzzle than into verse,' he wrote to his mother, 'I can't write verse nowadays.'

The difficulties of Darley were Greene's difficulties too, despite his prodigious efforts. There was the doubt of one's own abilities, for Darley wrote: 'You may ask could I not sustain myself on the strength of my own approbation? But it might be only my vanity, not my genius, that was strong', and Greene stressed: 'Darley was not a man with the courage to stand against silence. Attack might have made him aggressive, silence only made him question his own powers, the most fatal act an artist can commit.'[12]

The *fin de siècle* poet, John Davidson, also interested him as a subject of biography, and for similar reasons – 'his suicide at about fifty seems so extraordinary. As he'd got through so much, one would have imagined he'd have settled down to the rest. Besides a man who can write a long blank verse tragedy and call it "Smith" must have genius!'[13] But he discovered that Davidson had put an embargo on anyone writing his biography.

Perhaps with this model in mind, he considered reviving poetic drama by writing a blank verse play set in the sub-editors' room of a provincial newspaper: 'I shall report the ordinary conversation of various people here, with the slight metrical twist necessary, leaving it colloquial. The Irish Sports Subeditor will act the Elizabethan jester modernised, with modern "doubtful" stories substituted for the old type.'[14] An unlikely enterprise. Uncertainty about his ability and ultimate success must have turned his mind to Darley and Davidson. He admitted that about four times a year a mood comes upon him and he feels, 'with absolute certainty that some day I shall write something worthwhile', but then, 'I make up for the transient feeling by my certainty all the rest of the time that I never shall. I don't know why it comes on.'

'Genius is powerfully shy,' he wrote to Vivien and came to the conclusion that what he had was a 'hard working talent'[15], which brought him to stress the importance of the regular practice of his art; and though he was probably placing too great a value on her talents, he recommended this to her also: 'It's much more important that *you* should practise regularly. You *are* a genius, whatever you may say, and therefore it's of infinite importance that you should practise. Whether you want to or not. It ought to be a duty with you. Dear one, I shouldn't mind short letters to me if I felt that you were using that time writing.'[16]

He put his own advice into practice, forcing himself throughout 1926 to write each day, however busy he might be. Although in

March he 'gave warning' to Vivien that he would not 'write one single word on [their] wedding day & on the honeymoon',[17] we know that he did his daily stint on the day he was accepted into the Roman Catholic Church, and on 27 February 1926 he stopped in the middle of a letter to Vivien to write his minimum before lunch.

In his letters to her there are constant references to the number of words written and the quotas fulfilled or excelled: 'If only I could keep up my 500 minimum, which is not really exacting, I'd have the Episode done by June. If I can't get that published, I'll never have the energy to try again.'[18] 'I stayed in to supper & worked. I was very virtuous & did 1200 words of Episode & a review. I can't conceive of that time a year & a half ago, when I did 2000 of a shocker *every* day! I deserved the cramp I got!'[19] 'I've . . . worked this afternoon. It came fearfully slowly. It took me an hour & a half to do five hundred words, & then after tea I finished off the thousand in no time. Words came in a rush.'[20]

Many authors write more than 500 words a day, but with Greene his minimum was to become a duty and a daily discipline. His established habit of writing this number – not 501 or 499 – shows in his manuscripts where he has counted each word, and noted the total at the point at which he stopped. In July 1926, having written another 1,000 words of 'The Episode', he stopped 'right in the middle of the longed for murder'. 'Dearest old thing', he answered Vivien's query, 'No, the murder's wet, though quiet. A Johnnie stabbed in the back while working a Punch & Judy show.'[21]

That he should have been able to stop at an exciting climax suggests an astonishing emotional control – a tap turned off at will. Moreover he had, some four months earlier, determined on the murder and the point in the novel at which it would take place: 'There's going to be a rather nice scene in another 20,000 words where someone's stabbed in the back, while working a Punch and Judy show in the street.'[22] His reason for placing the murder at a Punch and Judy show was that, just before leaving Nottingham, he had stopped in the market place 'to watch Punch hang Jack Ketch . . . It gives a slight touch of ancientness to the too modern Nottingham.'[23]

Sometimes he terrified himself with a statistical account of a life-time of writing: 'I should work seven hours a day. After all one can't do it all through one's life. Terrifying thought, 500 words for another, say 40 years. 7,300,000 words, not allowing for leap years. Darling!! I *should* get a cramp! That's haunting me a little now, as yesterday my arm began to ache. I *do* want to finish the Episode before the next bout.'[24]

Such discipline and determination resulted in pressure and anxiety which is often revealed in his letters:

> To-day I've got to get all the way up to the Temple to lunch with George Whitman, who's up for a Law Exam. & after that I've got to see a tailor, & then it will be time for the office. And meanwhile there's the beastly Episode, & if I don't work on that, conscience will say 'How can you expect to win Vivienne, if you don't work for her?'
>
> It's already quarter to twelve, and I've got to telephone to somebody at 12, & I haven't touched the Episode yet, & how I'll get my thousand words done I don't know.[25]

Like the little girl who could not stop dancing in Hans Christian Andersen's story, 'The Red Shoes', Greene could not (and still cannot) stop writing and being active.★

From September 1925 to July 1926, 'The Episode' was a burden to Greene. He was 'sick to death of it', 'couldn't get on with it' – and yet his future hopes of success and of marrying Vivien had been invested in it. In his frustration he turned to ideas for other works and sent Vivien the first four chapters (which have long since disappeared) of a 'shocker' called 'Queen's Pawn', and he was planning another novel and some short stories:

> I'd start working again on that – Episode, but I've lost interest in it. I want to write a novel called 'The Gaudy Ship'. Do you know the Yeats poem called, I think, The [sic] Dream. A man dreams he's steering a boat along the edge of the sea with a dead man in it, & a crowd are running along the shore shouting & singing.
>
> > Though I'd my finger on my lip,
> > What could I but take up the song,
> > And running crowd & gaudy ship
> > Cried out the whole night long.
>
> I made a list about a month ago of plots for short stories, with their rough lengths, including one or two short sketches I'd got already done & it was enough for 30,000 words. Half a book.[26]

At the same time, fearing he was not a writer by nature, he took to comparing himself with two of his contemporaries: 'I met

---

★ Greene wrote to me on 20 January 1983: 'I feel guilty at continuing to be active. I have just come back from Panama, Nicaragua and Cuba . . . How are you going to keep up?'

Christopher Isherwood [Greene's cousin] in the Strand yesterday evening. He went down from Cambridge at the end of his second year, simply because he couldn't stand the place, & is now private secretary to some musician or other. He's one of those, whom I secretly envy, like Macleod, who have a fearfully strong urge to write.'[27]

Three weeks later he returned to the subject: 'I wish I was one of these people like Macleod & Isherwood who simply *had* to write. I've got the itch, but I practically never have the urge. With me it's a sort of echoed itch from adolescence, when *everyone* writes, & the echo will I hope die away completely in a year or two.'[28]

Sending Vivien a snippet from *The Times*, which he felt would have made a marvellous story if it hadn't happened in reality, he turns to his admired Conrad:

> Conrad would have made a marvellous thing of it. There's one mad religious-mania woman in The Golden Arrow [*sic*] – the best character in the book. *Conrad simply makes me wriggle up in my chair with envy*. The Blasted Pole! Think of a foreign sailor, who writes casually in a pot boiling essay, like this. He's talking of the work of sailors – 'And all that for no perceptible reward in the praise of man & the favour of gods – I mean the sea gods, an indigent, pitiless lot, who had nothing to offer to servants at their shrine but a ward in some hospital on shore or *a sudden wedding with death in a great uproar*, but with no gilding of fine words about it.' It's unfair that the man should write literature, when he's attempting journalism, when with most people it's a case of writing journalism when they are attempting literature.★[29]

As always, he somehow found time to read widely, as his monthly lists of his day-to-day reading show. He read the latest collection of Thomas Hardy's verse (Hardy still had two more years to live), *Human Shows, Far Phantasies, Songs & Trifles*: 'It's grown on me fearfully, that book. But he *does* write journalese, & I don't see why people should pretend that it's successful with him!'

Returning from a visit to Vivien in March 1926, he boarded a train and found himself in the same carriage as John Masefield and his family:

> In the carriage with me are Mr & Mrs Masefield & Judith Masefield! Judith Masefield's extraordinarily plain close to! Mrs is looking

---

★ Greene is quoting from the article 'Legends' which was left unfinished at Conrad's death. It appears in *Last Essays*.

vivacious. John is snoozing with folded hands. If *I'd just sold the film rights of Sard Harker for £10,000 I'd go first class*!! He looks utterly miserable & bullied, poor little man. Judith's studying typewritten scrolls, which look like lectures!

Mrs M. looks terribly ruthless, with very prominent chin, & a smile of satisfaction, as much as to say 'I've pushed little Johnnie into fame even though he didn't want it, & now I'm the wife of a famous man.'! . . .

I think Judith must be going to lecture on John's works. She glares at her papers, then looks up & stares through me & mumbles under her breath . . .

John is looking too intensely sad. He looks like an illustration for his own line that comes in Dauber [a poem], 'the long despair of doing nothing well.'[30]

A month later he was reading *Odtaa*, the latest Masefield: 'I've got *Odtaa* . . . not so good as *Sard Harker*. *Sard Harker* would have been the greatest adventure story in the language if it hadn't got the absurd ending.'[31]

It is obvious that at this time, not having yet found his own 'voice', he was reading other writers in order to find his way: 'If you want to read a Huxley, I've got a copy of Mortal Coils,' he wrote to Vivien, 'which has in it the best short story he's written, "The Tillotson Banquet." It's awfully fine, & shows a sort of sensitiveness & sympathy, which he very seldom has. And there's also quite a good one, about a man who's hanged for poisoning his wife, though he never did it at all. Rather terrifying – the awful piled up evidence, which did him in!'[32] Under Huxley's influence, he planned several short stories, assessing in advance their possible readership and even the number of words: 'I got my plot for "Figs in Lisbon" yesterday. It's fearfully Huxleian & unpleasant – "disagreeable" as my mother would say – but it's so subtly done that most people of the older generation won't see it, & simply be puzzled by the absence of point. That brings my short stories up to 35,000.'[33] But he adds, 'They'll never be written though.'

A pointer to the fact that he would find his own way lies in his intellectual assessment of other writers. He compares, for example, the incompatibles, Huxley and Rupert Brooke, and, by implication, draws out the common factor which was to influence him:

I've . . . been reading Huxley poems . . . It seems queer that he of all people in the world, should show so much the influence of Rupert Brooke. One would have thought that mentally they were miles apart. And yet I don't know. They both had the same joy in mixing up the beautiful and the disgusting on the same page.[34]

As always, there is Greene's determination, his unceasing activity, even though he is often unhopeful as to the outcome: 'I was sending out vain Mss all this morning, which will return later like pigeons to roost.' One was rejected by Sir John Squire, editor of the *London Mercury*: 'I got another polite personal note from the Squire yesterday. I suppose it's an advance on the printed rejections, but I'm getting tired of the elderly litterateur's encouragement of young promise!' 'I wish', he wrote, 'I could think of some other way of making money other than writing. I'm tired of trying that, & feeling lucky to get two quid a month!'[35]

Yet he was reviewing regularly for the *Glasgow Herald*: 'I'm being snowed under with books from the G.H. now. The spring season's beginning.' The *Herald* was delighted with his reviews – 'you are doing much to lighten the serious gloom of the literary page,' the editor wrote.[36] Greene was pleased, but sorry his reviews remained unsigned. Seeking a way out of his trap he decided to try journalism and mood pieces:

I made another good resolution this week, to do at least one journalese article a week. I've already done this week's & sent it to the Daily News, silly & facetious, called Re-Visiting Oxford, next week's will be sort of social chit-chat about poor Edith S. I don't mind trying to capitalise her! Even if I only get one in twenty accepted, it will be practice in journalism. After all one ought to be able to earn 2 pounds 2 shillings a week like that.[37]

To his mother he wrote: 'Did you see my chit-chat paragraphs on the Sitwells in the Woman's World of Tuesday's Evening Standard? My embarkation on yellow journalism.'[38]

'Poor Edith S' had made something of a stir and a spectacle of herself as a result of her concerts at the Chenil Galleries, when she read her poems into a loudspeaker called a Sengerphone to the music of William Walton. There seemed little relationship between poet and composer, and when the same concert was given at the Aeolian Hall in Bond Street the audience jeered and Noël Coward ostentatiously left. Later Coward impersonated Edith and her brothers as Hernia, Bog, and Sage Whittlebot.

It was not all work, though Greene was sometimes unhappy about wasting time:

A terrible thing happened this morning, darling. I was clearing off my Episode before writing to you (doing it first, because I know I should get too reckless & discontented to do it afterwards) when Macleod unexpectedly turned up. And we talked & then we went out to lunch & then we went to see the modern French paintings at the Tate, & then we drove through the Green Park & then round & round the statuary in front of Buckingham Palace, until we were both giddy & nearly collided with a lamp post & then I said firmly, 'Drive me to the Embankment near Blackfriars & put me down. I have a letter which I must write' . . . So now at last I can talk to you.[39]

In May 1926, he turned again to his rejected first novel 'Anthony Sant': 'Darling, I shall go out & post this & go for a bit of a walk & type out a Mss & then on with the Episode & try to do double quantity, as I did yesterday. I sent off the rehashed Anthony Sant to Heinemann a week ago in a vain hope. I think for one thing it's much too short. But they were the publishers that came nearest to taking the original version – it got as far as being read by Evans, the [managing] director.'[40] By the end of May, he seemed at last to be in control of his wayward second novel – 'double quantity of Episode this morning. A nice melodramatic incident, the last four or five pages on the dark staircase'[41] and two days later he was able to announce: 'She's on the straight . . . & ought to reach home by the end of next month. In the exhilaration of cleared ditches though she's getting too melodramatic.'[42] He was elated but yet at times faint of heart: 'If it's not taken I shall never have the energy to do another. I have a most certain feeling that like all the things I do it will fall between two stools, being neither bad enough nor good enough to publish.'[43]

By 28 July, Greene had finished 'The Episode', was ready to have it typed, and was keen to leave for a short break in Cornwall in order to begin some fresh short stories. He had had his first novel 'Anthony Sant' typed by Hunts, the Oxford typing agency, but when he finished his second novel he found a typist at *The Times* willing to type it in her spare time: 'I'm getting her to do a couple of copies of the Episode at about half the amount I'd have to pay Hunts.' His financial difficulties are revealed in a letter to his mother: 'Thanks most awfully for the offer of the raincoat, but I'd much rather buy it with the War Bond. You've bought me quite enough clothes lately. The greater part of The Times bonus had to go on typewriting – trying to write novels is an expensive gamble.'[44] To pay for the typing he borrowed £5 from his mother but insisted that it was a loan to be paid back at a rate of 10*s*. a week, and he insisted on this partly because of his fears that the book would be rejected: 'I feel it [will be] such a waste on your part, if I can't, as is only too likely, get the book taken.'

Forty-five years later, in *A Sort of Life*, recalling those early days, he hoped he repaid the loan: 'They were five wasted pounds, and I can only hope I paid her back.'*[45] Even though he had doubts about his novel being taken, he set about in typical fashion to give it a shove in the right direction. He was friendly with a City man who knew Geoffrey Faber, the publisher, and he had already decided on the publishers he would send the book to: 'I shall have an unassisted shot at Heinemann first; then Allen & Unwin, where Anthony Bertram, a friend of my brother, whom I met once, is principal reader, & lastly Faber. And God defend the right.'[46] But alas, God did not.

The reason why Greene had an unassisted shot at Heinemann was that, by this time, his literary agent, A. D. Peters, who had been enthusiastic about 'Anthony Sant', had rejected 'The Episode'. A passage in the typescript of *A Sort of Life*, not included in the published version, refers to this: 'A. D. Peters had learnt wisdom from his long and unsuccessful efforts to place my first novel and he returned this to me almost too promptly for politeness, writing that he saw no chance of finding it a publisher.'[47] But a letter to Vivien shows that Peters did not return Greene's manuscript too promptly (not in fact until 29 September), though it was returned: 'by a later post a returned Episode from Peters as he didn't think it publishable (which means, as he took a good deal of trouble over Anthony Sant that I'm becoming less publishable as I go on).'

The novel had unfortunate sources. One was Carlyle's *Life of John Sterling* – 'the only one of that great Scottish bore I have ever enjoyed' – which provided the setting for the novel. He was also influenced by Conrad's *The Arrow of Gold*. Themes of revolution and a Spanish background attracted him (as a schoolboy he had envied the fate of Wilfred Ewart, accidentally shot during the Pancho Villa rising in Mexico: 'it seemed a glamorous end in a glamorous country'). But the main weaknesses of the novel were the love affair derived not from life but from Conrad's Doña Rita ('that unbearable woman' as he was to describe her) and also the fact that, as a result of studying Percy Lubbock's *The Craft of Fiction*, he was paying too much attention to unity and point of view – 'I don't think [the

---

* He did. Three years later when his first published novel became a hit: 'Here is my debt to you. It was terribly useful. If I hadn't sent the previous Mss ['The Episode'] to Heinemann this one [*The Man Within*] wouldn't have had such a good show.' (Letter of 12 June 1929.)

hero] ever went nearer to Spain than Leicester Square . . . I called the novel rather drably The Episode, and that was all it proved to be.'[48]

After an initial acknowledgment of the receipt of the novel, the publishers mislaid the manuscript: 'It seemed', he wrote, 'as irrevocably lost as though I had dropped it into the coal-fire.'[49]

While he awaited a decision he went into 'a biographing mood' again, asking Vivien whether anyone had done a satisfactory life – a 'lay' life – of the Jesuit poet Southwell, who was executed in Elizabeth's reign. This biography was never written but he did not forget Southwell. Forty years later when he was honoured by the University of Hamburg and awarded the Shakespeare Prize, he censured Shakespeare and spoke up for Southwell. He argued that Shakespeare was the poet of the Establishment: he could speak of England as 'this little world, this blessed spot, this earth, this realm, this England', two years after his fellow poet, Southwell, had died on the scaffold. Greene commented, 'if only Shakespeare had shared Southwell's disloyalty we could have loved him better as a man.'

Still anxious to take to anything that would help him as a novelist he asked Vivien if she could write shorthand: 'I've always wanted to know it badly, so as to take down people's conversations in trains, but I've never been able to contemplate the fearful task of learning it!'

Six months went by, the new year came and further months followed before Greene plucked up courage to write to Heinemann. He told his mother, 'they've mislaid the wretched thing.' After eight months of waiting Charles Evans, head of the firm, wrote that he had two reports on the novel and had then intended to read it himself, 'but in the rush of work the intention got overlaid.'[50]

The bulky package came back quickly after that. At first, Greene was not too down-hearted. He felt that since the head of the firm had written to him it was an indication of how close the novel had come to being accepted, though a more likely explanation was that Evans felt the need to pacify an author whose manuscript had been mislaid. In any case, Greene decided that he would write one more novel and that, 'if the third book proved as unsuccessful as the others, [he] would abandon this ambition for ever.'[51]

Seeking excitement and probably also copy, he wrote to Vivien on 29 September 1926: 'Oh I have one thing to look forward to. A solicitor friend is letting me serve a writ on Monday. It's to a Co-respondent, a sailor, in a disreputable part of Shoreditch. A short while ago he cut the respondent's throat, & as the respondent's husband has to accompany me for purposes of identification, the chances I think are for excitement.'[52]

But it is doubtful whether he was able to keep that appointment, for fate took a hand in his life.

23

In Hospital and Suspected Epilepsy

'an Egyptian mummy . . . swathed in . . . bandages'
— GRAHAM GREENE

D URING September 1926 Greene had suffered recurrent stomach
pains, and, probably on 30 September, he consulted a doctor
who proved to be 'a dangerous man'. Greene described the event in
A Sort of Life:

> I had picked him at random as I wandered down a Battersea street
> troubled by a sharper stab of pain than usual. His brass plate caught
> my eye on a house not far from the railway viaduct. Smoke coated
> his panes, an aspidistra drooped on his window-sill, starved of
> tea-leaves, and his door vibrated gently as the trains emerged from
> Clapham Junction. The doctor opened the door himself, a young
> Hindu, and showed me into a dingy consulting room where he
> must have been waiting with eastern patience for the sick to seek
> him out.

The Hindu doctor judged his pulse (how do you judge a pulse
without taking it?), took his temperature, prodded where the pain
lay and gave him a bottle of already prepared medicine, charging six
shillings for the consultation and the bottle.[1] '. . . the Hindu doctor',
Greene wrote, 'stayed in my mind – a symbol of the shabby, the
inefficient and possibly the illegal, and he left his trace, with another
doctor, on some pages of *A Gun for Sale*'.[2] Greene turned his Hindu
into a Jew equally shifty and living clearly on the borders of the
criminal world, specialising, the passage suggests, in backstreet
abortions. We see Dr Yogel washing his hands in a fixed basin behind
a yellow desk and swivel chair, the poverty of his practice suggested
by the furnitureless room (apart from a kitchen chair, cabinet and

long couch); macabre indeed is the scene where Yogel sweats, though it is bitterly cold, his hand, holding a surgical knife, shaking as he prepares to operate on Raven's harelip. The light is bad but the Doctor replies, 'I'm used to it . . . I've a good eye.'[3]

Greene's first reaction was to write to his mother, playing down his illness as 'a slight attack of appendicitis . . . the doctor didn't want to advise an operation as it's quite slight', for he was well aware of the distress his mother had suffered earlier that year when her brother Frank had died of peritonitis. However, he also phoned his brother Raymond, then a houseman at Westminster Hospital who, as he told his mother, 'arranged a free examination tomorrow [1 October] with the Westminster surgeon & will see about getting me a bed in the public ward, probably next week . . . I've written to V[ivien] putting her off Saturday, as I don't think I'd better come down, lugging a heavy suitcase.'[4] Apart from the appendix he was feeling very fit, 'so there couldn't be a better time', he told his mother jocularly, 'for having the brute out'. It would seem that the idea of getting him into a public ward during the following week was not consistent with his state of health, for the day after his examination, on his birthday – 2 October – he wrote to Vivien, who had a horror of operations and was obviously deeply concerned about him:

> Your mind would be quite set at rest if you could see me lying like a large & lazy porpoise beneath unnecessary blankets, with a bored vacuity on my face, looking forward to the operation as a break in the monotony . . . Your lover for this side & tother side of eternity.[5]

The Times was sensitive in dealing with its young sub-editor's situation: the chief sub-editor sent down a young man from Room 2 to tell Greene that he was not to worry; he was promised six weeks' leave with pay and the cashier promised to post his salary to him each week; it was also promised that after the operation his colleagues would take turns to visit him.

He wrote daily to Vivien: on the day of his operation – 'I'm feeling rather like an Egyptian mummy being swathed in disinfecting bandages! The condemned man made a good breakfast . . . Only seven more hours before the scaffold.'[6] Since chloroform was to be used, he promised that he would go under thinking of her and he wrote her a poem, a poor piece, only a further indication of his romanticism and of his obsessional love for her. As the chloroform took effect, he tried to retain his vision of her, but finally lost it, and he made a vow: 'But if I lose you trampled in the route,/Let me sleep on forever & be true/Than wake to find I had forgotten you.'

The operation went without difficulty and two days later he was longing for the simple pleasures of life: 'I am feeling quite wellish & am longing for some sausages & mashed [potatoes] – which I shan't get';[7] he thanked Vivien for her prayers ('how I value your Masses'); he asked her forgiveness for not writing the day after the operation ('I only wrote a little letter on Tuesday & not at all on Wednesday. Forgive me . . . Anaesthetics, except plain gas, sometimes make me a bit illish').

If the poem is a disappointment, Greene's fanciful letter is touching as he explains how he will persuade the authorities to allow Vivien to visit him:

> I shall have to malinger & say 'I shall never get strong until I am fetched my heart's desire.' And they'll say 'What is his heart's desire?' & bring grapes & pears & oranges & other fruit. And I shall still malinger, saying 'I want my heart's desire'. And they'll fetch me books – Shelley, Landor, Burns, Bridges, Hardy & Robert Browning, but I shall shake my head & say 'I want my heart's desire'. And they'll go to Blackwell & say 'Can we borrow Vivien for a week, because we think that Graham will malinger until he has her'. And when I can speak again out of a very deep & beautiful content, I shall say, 'Why were you so long in finding my heart's desire?' And they'll say 'How could we guess you meant Vivien, when you asked merely for your heart's desire, because we know that she is also your body's desire & the desire of your mind & your lips & your eyes'. And I shall blink & say 'Yes, you are right I'm sorry. You see I didn't know you knew.'[8]

He longed for her embraces and admitted that he would not be able to use force for fear of breaking his stitches – and how comic it was 'being sewn up with brown cord like a sponge bag'.[9]

By the 14th of the month he had the twelve cross-stitches taken out and the following day he felt feeble for the first time. Eight days later (22 October 1926) the bandages were removed and he commented upon the result: 'I've cast off my bandages to-day, though my tummy looks rather like a Jacob's ladder, the place where the stitches were not having disappeared yet.' He then did a drawing of them:

Being in hospital did not stop him writing reviews for the *Glasgow*

Like this

Only larger & more symmetrical

Herald. He feared they might turn to someone else if he did not meet his deadlines. He complained that he was not reviewing well but then he was writing in pencil from his hospital bed. They were typed by Vivien and sent to Glasgow: 'I don't want to keep the G. H. waiting', he wrote to her, 'as I make about 10/- a week on them, which is not to be despised.'[10] Greene did not admire his work for the *Glasgow Herald*. After thanking Vivien for having typed 'all that review trash', he went on to tell her that he did not need carbons: 'I don't care to see again the fruits of a servile slavery to Mammon.' He need not have worried, for the *Glasgow Herald* soon decided to dispense with his services.

He had visits from his numerous aunts, his mother, Vivien (who had to obtain permission to be away from Blackwells), his brother Raymond, and his old cronies, friends made for life, those original members of the Mantichorean Club – Joseph Gordon Macleod, George Whitemore, Robert Scott, and Braine-Hartnell. All brought him grapes and Scott brought him a volume of Rimbaud's verse – Rimbaud except for about two poems struck him as 'dull & overrated. Not to be compared with my French idol Verlaine.'[11]

Recovering from what was thought to be a not too serious operation, he was soon observing the activities of the ward. Indeed on the day before the operation he told Vivien: 'There's a man here who says "What I do miss is my ole onions. Two or three I used to 'ave. Reglar. Every mornin'."' (3 October 1926). Three days afterwards he commented: 'A new patient has come in with such a mountainous wife. I'm glad I'm not considering the project of a hill of a woman: "A penny a pound for Juliet/Twopence a pound for Margaret/

Margaret was a queen/And only seventeen/So twopence a pound for Margaret/"'' (18 October 1926).

There was also a plucky old man of 75 who had been in hospital for ten months. He had had two operations for cancer and was very weak, but as Greene told Vivien, 'He'd upset your pessimistic views of matrimony . . . he's worrying to get home – they keep on fobbing him off with "perhaps next week"? . . . He'd got his wife on his mind, wanting to get back to her. She was as old as him. Born in the house next door . . . [they] were at school together & had been married fifty years. This was the first time they'd ever been long apart. She . . . hadn't been able to come & see him the last visiting day . . . He was afraid that she might die before he got back: "We've always wanted to go off in the same moment," he added. I thought of you then. Seventeen grandchildren though! How they did breed in the past' (19 October 1926). Then there was the emergency case – an 'arm crushed & pulled out of its socket . . . & all the right side crushed' (20 October 1926).

But the watcher was afraid of being watched and could not kiss the photograph of Vivien he had at his bedside – 'can't in a room with nearly a dozen alas' – and at night there was a light shining through the ward.

In his autobiography he remembered what he states was the first death in the ward, though in fact it was the second – an old man dying of cancer of the mouth, 'too old to join in the high jinks of the ward, the courtship of nurses, the teasings, the ticklings and the pinches,' and 'when the screens went up around his bed the silence in his corner was no deeper than it had always been.'[12] He saw this as 'inevitable fate', the death of 'a small boy with a broken leg' he described to Vivien as contingency. After an operation he appeared to be all right, 'Then about 8 the house surgeon on his round seemed to find his breathing almost non-existent. There was half an hour's rush & scurry round his bed with oxygen apparatuses, an undignified scrambling for the tail end of his life & he was gone.' But to him the terrible thing was the mother's reaction:

I've never seen any one with all their self-control gone before. She had to be supported in & she was calling out things at the top of her voice – what made it worse it was the sort of things people say on the cinema & which one had fondly imagined real life was free of – sentimental hackneyed things: 'Why did you go without saying good bye to your mother?' & 'Royston, Royston' (the ridiculous name seemed to make it worse) & 'What shall I do without him?' 'Sister, sister, don't tell me we're parted.' All in a sort of scream.

It was ghastly lying in bed listening to it. Then they half carried her out.

In *A Sort of Life*, he recalled how, in order to shut out the sound of the mother's cries, the patients in the ward 'lay with their ear-phones on, listening – there was nothing else for them to hear – to Children's Hour. All my companions but not myself. There is a splinter of ice in the heart of a writer. I watched and listened. This was something which one day I might need.'[13] This recollection of his attitude forty-five years after the incident is confirmed by his letter to Vivien at the time – the splinter of ice was certainly there, but so also a sense of disgust with himself:

> Are people who write entirely & absolutely selfish, darling? Even though in a way I hated it yesterday evening – one half of me was saying how lucky it was – added experience – & I kept on catching myself trying to memorise details – Sister's face, the faces of the other men in the ward. And I felt quite excited aesthetically. It made one rather disgusted with oneself. It really frightened me when the child went out & the old man was brought in for a delayed death. How haphazardly it seemed to happen.[14]

The conclusion of this incident survives in the typescript of *A Sort of Life* though Greene deleted it. 'When the parents had at last departed and the bed and the body had been wheeled away, the nurse began to clean with ether the other tables in the ward, rubbing away in a kind of fury as though she were effacing a memory, and the sick men one by one took off their ear-phones and lay quiet.'[15]

This incident must have occurred on the day he was admitted to hospital and was himself waiting for an operation, 3 October according to the date on his letter to Vivien, and suggests therefore considerable powers of detachment on his part at what must have been a worrying time. Yet his own attitude towards the death of those two, the young and the old, reveals his strange cast of mind:

> It wasn't the two arrivals who died I pitied. After all it's a thing we all want 40% of the time. Eighteen months ago I should have said 70%. What one disliked was the method – the scramble with oxygen pumps, the screaming woman – & particularly being present oneself. Not being used to it. It was rather weird to think that they were veritably having a devilishly nasty time in Purgatory while one was stretching oneself out to sleep, feeling glad that the fuss was over.[16]

His hospital experience was to be used seven years later in *It's a Battlefield* when he describes Conrad Drover slowly dying after having been knocked down by a car:

Then he was struck in the body and thrown a dozen yards and could not think: what has done this? nor wonder: why am I here? lying with his face over the pavement edge, watching the black water trickle down the gutter and fall through a grating, aware of pain and voices and pain, pain in the back and a worse pain in the jaw . . . he tried to scream, because pain was scratching now like little sharp finger-nails at his spine, and this time he heard . . . Pain was like a bird frantic for freedom, dashing from wall to wall of the imprisoning room; his brain was bruised with the beat of its wings . . .

'Better not move him; his back may be broken.' His hand touched the black water trickling in the gutter; he could see his own blood joining the water, flowing thickly off the pavement edge . . .

Big Ben struck the half-hour.* He was on a wheeled bed passing down long corridors, nurses walked the opposite way and stared at him and he tried to scream; he was in a small room and they held a little box in front of his face and he tried to scream. Then the pain became unbearable and he closed his eyes and opened them and Milly sat beside him and a metal flask hung above his head and a tube dropped saliva into his mouth and he felt no pain. The pain, he knew, was still there, but it was exhausted, it lay still and cramped in a corner, stiff with the bandages which confined him too; one pretended not to notice it; everyone walked softly on tiptoe not to wake it.

They had put screens round his bed, but through a gap he could see the wards, rows of men wearily sleeping, and a sister sitting reading at a table where one light burned . . .[17]

He never knew that he screamed in spite of his broken jaw; but with curious irrelevance, out of the darkness, after they had left him and his pulses had ceased beating and he was dead, consciousness returned for the fraction of a second, as if his brain had been a hopelessly shattered mirror, of which one piece caught a passing light. He saw and his brain recorded the sight: twelve men lying uneasily awake in the public ward with wireless headpieces clamped

---

* In letters written from his hospital bed, Greene often referred to Big Ben: 'It makes an awful noise in the night'; 'I lie & look at Big Ben so impatiently. It's saying 11 o'clock now – 30 hours & my love will be due.' (8 October 1926.)

across their ears, and a nurse reading under a lamp, and nobody beside his bed.[18]

Seeking the source of this accident is interesting because we can see how he is using his own, though secondary, experience. On 14 April 1926, he asked Vivien: 'Did you see about that bus accident in Piccadilly Circus? I came along about two minutes later, when the police were attending to the corpse.' Greene has amalgamated the bus accident with his own experience of hospital and with the death of an old man in hospital:

I'm afraid we're going to have another death in the ward to-day. An emergency case was brought in yesterday evening before they found the child was going out. An old man of about 76, who'd been in a motor accident, head fractured, one hand smashed & both legs. I don't think they expected him to last through the night. He's quite quiet though. I shall be glad to get away – it's all very morbid . . . The daughter of the old man's turned up & is sitting with him . . . They are bringing up the oxygen apparatus that means the end's near . . . They are putting up a screen now . . .

A little later

He's gone! Second death I've had the doubtful pleasure of seeing in a little over twelve hours. A high rate of mortality!

Greene had no doubt about how he wanted to go: 'I hope to goodness I don't die slowly & messily like that. I should like an aeroplane crash from 15,000 feet or a bullet, I think . . .'[19]

*

By the 19th Greene was allowed out of bed. 'Mr Greene will get up this afternoon', he overheard the doctor saying, and when he did get up his legs were like melted butter but he determined not to faint or to feel ill in order to be able to persuade the authorities that he was well enough to leave in three days' time on the Friday. In hospital he thought of places he could travel to and he had a sudden longing for Paris ('Naphtha flares going, the big arms of the Moulin Rouge whistling round . . . It will be so lovely being married to you dashing off to places with you with no conventions to stop it!').[20]

Greene left hospital on Friday 22 October – 'had breakfast out of bed &, an epoch-making occasion, had my first bath! And in a few hours I ought to be away.' He had arranged for Vivien to come to Berkhamsted and the very thought of that made him jump for joy:

'I want to stand up on my bed & stamp & beat my chest like a
baboon, & emit Zulu war-cries.' 'Please catch the trains safely', he
wrote, '& make the engine-drivers be punctual. Go & look at them
before the train starts, so that they know that they are carrying the
most beautiful & the most wonderful person in the world, & therefore
as the inevitable corollary the most adored by someone or other. No,
on second thoughts don't. They might go purposely slowly, so as
to have you as long as possible on the train (8.30, last day in hospital).'
He came home in style in a chauffeur-driven car, sent him by his
Uncle Eppy. He had been in hospital for three weeks.*

To convalesce, having still some time before his six weeks' leave of
absence from *The Times* was up, he decided to visit Brighton or Paris.
Even on the day he left for Brighton he had picked up a Bradshaw and
discovered that a train left from Victoria for Paris at 8 a.m., and was
again tempted, but Brighton it was to be. His father had given him a
late birthday and Christmas present in one – sufficient money for his
holiday. Vivien could not have gone with him to Brighton even if she
could have freed herself from her job: both her mother and her friend
Stella Weaver, wife of the librarian at Trinity (later President of Trinity)
watched hawk-like over Vivien's morals as the comment below
suggests. It also shows how advanced Greene's parents were: 'I don't
know what Stella would think of my mother. She's gone away for a
few days & before going she suggested you should come for the
week-end – fancy! all alone with me & my father!'[21]

During the train journey to Victoria it rained heavily and he had
fears of being bored to death. At Victoria he went on to Battersea to
search for his passport, 'because even if I go to B[righton] for to-night,
I might want to go across [to France] next day'. He broke the lock
of his trunk to find his passport but it was not there. Worst of all,
Jonathan Cape had returned his novel 'The Episode' – it rested
now on Evans and Heinemann. He went to Brighton and was, as
so often in his life, enchanted and excited by it. On his first night
there, he met an unusual man and his depression and despair left
him:

Have you ever dreamed of meeting the man who writes the love
lyrics for the Christmas crackers. Last night, about 10.30, sitting
in the dark in a shelter on the front, trying to light a cigarette &
waiting for something to happen, a being in a soft hat, spectacles
& a muffler materialised in the opposite corner. He had a sort of

* Two weeks after leaving hospital he learned that the walls of his stomach were
very thin. Thus his appendix had been in hourly danger of perforating.

echo of a forgotten twang in his voice, & darling, guess whom he claimed to be? 'Old Moore' – at least he'd done last year's Almanac. That was only one of the many incredible bits of life history I heard. He said he'd lived in California till the war, in which he'd lost £46,000 which were in German shipping. His father was Spanish & his mother 'Egyptian' & he said he could talk Romany. His father & mother were unmarried & he was brought up in a monastery & ran away. He was 65 & ate no artificial food, lived in a little flat by himself & baked his own loaves even! He said that since the war he'd made his living by lecturing & writing, but I didn't get his name. He claimed to be royal Romany – all in a slight American twang. Even though a consummate liar probably (though there were no material motives in his yarns), he was perfectly sweet.[22]

Twelve years later, in *Brighton Rock* this same shelter is where Hale is found dead – a piece of Brighton Rock having been pushed down his throat. And it is in *Brighton Rock* also that Cubitt, on the run from Pinkie, sits in a glass shelter staring out to sea. Like Greene he lights a cigarette and tries to share his cigarettes with an elderly gentleman wrapped in a heavy overcoat who is sharing the shelter: '"I don't smoke," the old gentleman said sharply and began to cough; a steady hack, hack, hack, towards the invisible sea.

'"A cold night," Cubitt said. The old gentleman swivelled his eyes on him like opera glasses and went on coughing . . . the vocal chords dry as straw. Somewhere out at sea a violin began to play: it was like a sea beast mourning and stretching towards the shore . . . The mist blew in, heavy compact drifts of it like ectoplasm.'[23]

Meanwhile in Oxford, Vivien, who painted and sketched well, had done a drawing of Eve & the Serpent and Greene was longing to see it.

After convalescing at Brighton, Greene returned to *The Times* and on his first day back (17 November) he fainted:

Will you [he wrote to Vivien] forgive this pencil because I'm lying on my bed? A most silly, stupid thing has happened. I do feel a damned fool. I turned up at the office, feeling quite fit at four o'clock & I went on feeling perfectly fit, until 7.45 when suddenly without warning I got a stab in the small of my back, which made me leap in my chair, much to the surprise of my neighbour. It passed, & I started going on with a telegram about a burst reservoir in Yorkshire. Then it came again like the very deuce. Beat any shooting tooth I've ever had. I felt twisted up inside, & things began going round. I thought this was silly & concentrated on you to steady myself. And to my surprise everyone's head was upside down looking at me, & I began to think that I was going to faint, until I realised that I was lying flat on the floor without a collar, & somebody holding my wrist & another person holding my head up. I've never felt such an utter fool before. Dr Wilson, the medical leader writer, came along & transported me to R[aymond]'s in his car, & I spent the night there. It's a fearful nuisance. I'm so afraid of losing standing by being told I've got to go back into the country. I'm tired to death of being semi-fit.[24]

Fifty years afterwards, Colonel Maude recalled: 'I remember Graham coming in one evening and promptly collapsing and fainting and we laid him out on the top of a "what-not", a two-decker affair . . . He was then as I remember very delicate, apart from the fact that he had fainted, he seemed to me to be pushing himself too hard, he wasn't strong in those days.'

As usual, Graham was circumspect about what he told his mother of his health: 'my first incursion back to work ended in disaster. I was "took ill" at the office & spent the night at R[aymond] & C[harlotte]'s. Nothing much.'[25] While he kept his fears to himself, something of a convalescent's irritation comes out in his letters: 'What an overrated, wet, beastly, contemptible, narrow, meagre place this country called – God save the mark – Great Britain is. Patriotism certainly is not enough. If I thought there was one spot in this decrepit and decaying land, where there was some sun, I'd take a week off and go to it.'[26] He just would not admit that he was sickly. Having presumably visited Vivien, he wrote on the train from Oxford to London: 'Fragile! Rot! Anyone would look a bit pulled about after an operation.'*[27] His method of keeping fit was to avoid Berkhamsted: 'I should be constantly reminded that I wasn't quite fit. Much the best way to get fit is to go completely away & forget the fact entirely.'

But on returning to Battersea, he found a telegram from Raymond advising him to go back to the hospital for a further examination and his mother wrote to him asking him to see his psychoanalyst, Kenneth

---

* In the train to London from Oxford he reported a conversation to Vivien which catches the flavour of the flapper of the 1920s: 'A mysterious female, who apparently knew me, got into the carriage coming down here, & said "Iole's having a coming-of-age dance on December 21st. Can you come?" I didn't know who she or Iole was, but I said brightly "Is she *really* coming of age? How fearfully exciting. I should love to come, only I'm afraid I shall probably be at work that day. Can I leave it open?" She said: "Oh do. I'll send you a proper invitation", & then we talked politics. I wonder who she – & Iole is – are!' (24 November 1926.)

Richmond, again. He was not then aware of 'the time-bomb' ticking in his mother's desk – Richmond's letter to his father of 1921, suggesting that his son suffered from epilepsy – which was soon to explode. In *A Sort of Life*, Greene compresses the events of the next few months, making a dramatic incident of the affair, but his letters suggest a more long-drawn-out period of doubt leading to a climax of anger and despair.

Puzzled by his mother's request, but pleased to be seeing Richmond again – a man whose influence in the publishing world might advance the fortunes of his unplaced novel – he visited him on 15 November 1926. Yet he had a feeling that his mother had some particular purpose in advising the visit. In his letter to Vivien of the previous day he refers only to Richmond's change of occupation: 'He's chucked his psychological work now & is managing in England a new & apparently very easy form of shorthand. I enclose a disguised advertisement about it he wrote in "The Observer" on Sunday. Apparently it's "going" fearfully well . . . in six weeks you are supposed to be able to attain the maximum of 130 words a minute.'[28] He discussed his novel with Richmond, who suggested a new title, *Goodnight Sweet Ladies*,★ but the main purpose of the visit – the revelation – is indicated in Greene's cryptic and frightening telegram to Vivien, sent after he left Richmond: 'I guarantee, darling, that there are no forceps inside me. I'll break gently to you the terrible news unfolded to me tomorrow.'[29] In his autobiography, he describes the visit, during which, presumably, links were suggested between his fainting in Room 2 and his fainting when undergoing treatment with Richmond when he was sixteen:

> I remembered how the specialist (Dr Riddick)† had questioned me about earlier attacks of fainting in the summer stuffiness of the school chapel. Many children, I told myself, went through such a phase.
> 'Doctor Riddick diagnosed epilepsy,' Richmond said.
> Epilepsy, cancer and leprosy – these are the three medical terms which rouse the greatest fear in the untutored, and at twenty-two one is unprepared for so final a judgement. Epilepsy, Richmond went on, could be inherited: I must consider the risk carefully before marriage, and he sought to comfort me by pointing out that Dostoievsky too had suffered from epilepsy. I couldn't think

★ The title is from *Hamlet* (Act IV, Scene 5).
† Actually, Dr Riddock.

of a reply. Dostoievsky was a dead Victorian writer, not a youth without a book to his name who had pledged himself to marry.[30]

His letter to Vivien on 26 November suggests a mind wildly trying to find an escape from an intolerable situation and seeking that escape in ideas for travel, coupled with the fear that he might never do this before he is middle-aged: 'How depressing time is. It goes so fearfully slowly in regard to seeing you again, & so beastly quick in regard to all the places one wants to see.' Then follows an incredibly miscellaneous list of desired places: 'New York, San Francisco, Edinburgh, the South Seas, Mexico City, Avignon, Peking & the Great Wall, Carcassonne, Exmoor, Sintra (for a second time), Peru & the Andes, the Pyrenees, Toledo, the Antarctic', and, Greene's eternal cry: 'Will one ever make enough money to have the time to see them before one gets stale & middle-aged . . . I want to see as many of them as you'd agree to – Edinburgh & the Antarctic I'm afraid would be alone – while we are both youngish. And all we shall probably have for years & years is a month. Perhaps till one retires after forty years sub-editing.'[31] He even considered fleeing the country on the strength of an overdraft.

Anxiety turned him in spirit away from writing: 'I wish that there was some other way of making money in one's spare time besides writing. I don't quite honestly believe that writing is my metier. I don't mean by that that I shan't make money by it. Of the novelists now writing, even of the good novelists, I don't think more than half a dozen are really suited.'[32] And then there was what he then saw (unseriously) as his real metier – spying. Unexpectedly he had heard again from Berlin and remembered his wonderful days of being a student spy: 'Berlin has suddenly started sending me a mysterious German review – financial & political – every week, which I can't read . . . I'm sure spying is my true spare-time pursuit. Would you marry a German spy? It would be sad to have to choose between you and my metier.'[33]

But his re-examination by Dr Turner and then by a Dr Abrahams for a second report – 'I am going to be examined by a Jew with a face like Disraeli',[34] he wrote to Vivien in the same letter – must have put his mind at rest since both doctors found him perfectly healthy, telling him that he was simply too inclined to hustle and to pressurise himself.

This must have seemed to be the end of the matter, but the time-bomb ticked on and for some reason on 18 January 1927, he was examined again by Dr Riddock. On this occasion Riddock repeated his suspicions and the shock to Greene was increased by the fact he now learnt, presumably from Riddock, that his parents had known of this diagnosis and lived with the terrible knowledge for five years. The time-bomb had certainly exploded.

Full of anguish, he was dumb-founded that his parents had been involved in such a cover-up, but forty years later he felt differently:

> Poor souls, I can sympathize with them now as I read the letters which were written to them on the same day by Richmond and Doctor Riddock. Doctor Riddock's was frightening, even in its moderation. 'The attacks to which he is occasionally subject are, I think, epileptic; but since he has lost consciousness in three only, there is a reasonably good chance that, with suitable treatment, the condition may be arrested.' The treatment seemed to consist of good walks and Keppler's Malt Extract. Richmond's letter was more encouraging, and my mother in pencil has pathetically under-lined all the optimistic phrases she could find, perhaps to comfort my father – 'quite likely to clear up completely' . . . 'no cause for alarm' – even the phrase about Dostoievsky is trotted out and surprisingly underlined.[35]

Richmond had also told Greene's parents that he and Dr Riddock agreed that 'Graham ought not to be told what is the matter in any terms that included the word epilepsy'.[36]

*

It is apparent that in the midst of his anxiety and confusion his main concern was the effect this revelation might have on his hopes of marrying Vivien, and acting with considerable unselfishness, instead of writing to her first with the appalling news, he wrote, presumably soon after the examination, to Stella Weaver, her friend and mentor. He felt that Vivien should have unbiased advice and a chance to withdraw. But on the same day, though probably later, he also wrote to Vivien explaining why he had done this: 'I thought it was best to let Stella do it, because for me it was difficult to give you unselfish advice. Dear heart. . . do pay attention to what Stella advises, however ghastly it is. If I don't write tomorrow, it will be because I don't want to sway you more than you'll be swayed anyway by your love. Somehow we've got to win happiness for you out of all this muddle.'[37]

On the following day, a bitterly cold one, sitting in the National Gallery, the only place where he knew he could keep warm, and exactly opposite the Vision of St Eustace, he wrote to Vivien:

> To-day the whole thing seems more incredible to me than yesterday. I don't believe for a moment that Riddock ever told my people that

331

I'd got slight epilepsy five years ago. He must have hugged the secret with Richmond. I can't help wondering whether he may not be a crank – he was a friend of R[ichmond] who is a crank, & it was R. who told my people to take me to him. The only cause was that between the ages of 14 and 16 I had several, perhaps four, fainting attacks. Large numbers of boys have them at that age – you've only got to attend a school chapel to know that – either through digestion troubles or through growing too quickly, which I certainly was doing. I shall make inquiries about Riddock. He admitted himself yesterday that he could find no traces of it in my family history, & that it was excessively unlikely that I myself should have recurrence of it. I'm trying to see my way in this muddle. If Riddock *is* right, it was simply criminal to have kept it hidden.[38]

He added:

I wonder if I've exaggerated things. I don't know. I'm waiting to hear what Stella says. On second thoughts I don't see there is much use in coming to Oxford. If I once had you in my arms, I'd damn the extra risks to your happiness with me. And that's not the right way to go about it. It's better to argue it all out in writing, I think. So I won't come. I think it would be fairer not to. Darling, darling, I love you and I only want to do what's best for your happiness. If Stella thinks that it adds too much to the chances of you marrying me not turning out well, we ought to throw it up. That sounds like Hell now, but it wouldn't in time, while if you married me & weren't happy, there'd be no escape for you.[39]

Until the matter was cleared up, Greene, who had been sending letters daily to Vivien for almost two years, stopped writing and advised Vivien to stop writing to him. Also, on the advice of his brother Raymond, he decided not to visit her, cancelling a visit already arranged on the spurious grounds that he had 'flu: 'If I'd come down, I couldn't have put you at ease about the situation, & as my brother said "both of you will be strained, not knowing whether it's the last time you'll meet as engaged people." Besides I considered then that the chances were about 2-1 on our being separated, in which case I thought it better that we shouldn't see each other again . . . That's why on Saturday I wrote about neither of us writing.' Greene's view was that if all turned out well, no harm would have been done, if ill the break-up would have begun gradually.[40]

Saturday looked very black: his friend Arthur Braine-Hartnell visited him and they went out together, which is often Greene's way of hiding from his troubles by a determined assault on the fleshpots of the town, striving for a false gaiety, trying by drink to put an end to thought. To Vivien he confessed:

On Saturday [night] far from sitting over a fire, preferring to coddle myself to your company, I set out to banish the idea of losing you, at any rate for one day. At 12.30, when myself & Arthur were bereft even from Lyons' All Night (no drinks being served after 12!), I lured the innocent Arthur on a search for a 'non-exclusive' club, & ended up at Jimmie's, where I danced. And by 3.30 was dancing quite intelligibly! I then rescued him from his vamp, & we walked home & smoked a last cigarette together on Albert Bridge at 4.30.[41]

One of the reasons for Greene's despair was the result of his seeking assistance from Father Christie* at Brompton Oratory (he calls him Father Talbot in *A Sort of Life*), to whom he had been passed on by Father Trollope.

My next thought was of an elderly priest, Father Talbot, of the Oratory . . . He was a man of very liberal views, and surely, I thought despairingly, he would have some answer to my greatest problem: that if I were epileptic, I must avoid having children. Surely there must be some cranny of canon law or moral theology that would contain a ruling for just such a case as mine.

He asked me to go out with him, and for the next hour we drove in a taxi, crossing and recrossing the same rectangle between the Brompton Road and Bayswater, just as we crossed and recrossed the same lines of argument. Under no circumstances at all was contraception permissible. 'The church forbids me to marry then?'

'Of course we don't forbid marriage.'

'Do you expect married people to live together without making love?'

'The Church expects you to trust God, that's all.'

Up and down, over and over, a useless embroidery – which made no pattern.

How differently he would have answered my question today, telling me, I have no doubt, to follow my conscience . . . Catholics

---

* Father Christie was at Brompton Oratory for almost fifty years and died in the 1930s. He was famous for being 'Prefect of the Little Oratory' (spiritual father for laymen associated with the Oratory). He was reputed to have received a great many converts into the Church. Christie's photograph suggests he was an unimaginative and cold man.

have sometimes accused me of making my clerical characters, Father Rank in *The Heart of the Matter* and Father James in *The Living Room*, fail unnecessarily before the human problems they were made to face. 'A real priest,' I have been told, 'would have had something further to say, he would have shown a deeper comprehension, he wouldn't have left the situation so unchanged.' But that is exactly what in those days, before John Roncalli was elected Pope, the priesthood was compelled to do. There was no failure in comprehension. Father Talbot was a man of the greatest human sympathy, but he had no solution for me at all. There was only one hard answer he could honestly give ('the Church knows all the rules,' as Father Rank said), while the meter of the taxi ticked away the repetitions of our fruitless argument. It was the Rock of Peter I was aware of in our long drive, and though it repulsed me, I couldn't help admiring its unyielding façade.[42]

There is a reflection of this dilemma in Greene's play, *The Living Room*, when Rose, who is in love with Michael Dennis but has also witnessed his wife's pain and is deeply troubled, begs her uncle, who is a priest, for help: 'She was just a name, that's all . . . and then she comes here and beats her fists on the table and cries in the chair . . . I've seen her touch his arm. Uncle, what am I to do? Tell me what to do, Father.' All that the priest can say is, 'You can pray.' And so Rose, bereft of assistance in her extreme need, commits suicide. Her uncle, Father James, later confesses: 'I said to God, "Put words into my mouth", but the words did not come.'
And to Michael, Father James has only one answer to give:

You're doing wrong to your wife, to Rose, to yourself . . . Go away. Don't see her, don't write to her, don't answer her letters if she writes to you. She'll have a terrible few weeks. So will you . . .
    Michael: And in the end. . . ?
James: We have to trust God. Everything will be all right.[43]

How close this is to what Father Christie said to Graham. Father James 'would only have had to touch her to give her peace.' Unquestionably, Greene saw Father Christie's strict following of canon law as spiritually crippling.
His letters to Vivien reveal nothing of his frustration and anxiety: 'I saw Fr Christie yesterday, but I had other and more urgent things to talk about & forgot the Confirmation. I shall be seeing him again soon & will remember next time.'[44] There is a certain tightness about this,

perhaps reflecting the dichotomy between Vivien's interest in the outward show of the Catholic Church and Greene's battle with its dogma.

In *A Sort of Life*, Greene tells us that after his baptism in Nottingham he added the name of Thomas the Doubter.[45] But he did not select such a name then, as we have seen. He delayed this until his confirmation, and given his deep perturbation over Father Christie's inability to help him in this crisis, it is surely understandable that he should have expressed his doubts by selecting such a name. The best indication of his personal distress comes in *A Sort of Life*, especially in the typescript which is fuller than the published version:

> Was the diagnosis right? With the hindsight of forty years, free from any recurrence, I don't believe it, but I believed it then. I remember next day standing on an Underground platform and trying to summon the will and the courage to jump. It was not my new Catholicism which restrained me. There was no theological despair in what I felt. I was simply tired out by the thought of starting a completely different future than the one I had planned. One in which I would be bound to my own company for life.

Time did prove the diagnosis wrong, but he believed it then, and an entry in his diary five years later (19 July 1932) shows that he had at least two further faintings. He had been reading E. H. Carr's life of Dostoievsky and he naturally took note of Dostoievsky's attacks of epilepsy. Carr stated that in common with some narcotic drugs and perhaps certain forms of recurrent insanity, epilepsy produces in its victim, at the moment prior to the attack, 'a sense of spiritual exaltation & triumph, a feeling of power to transcend the limits of the material world.' Greene's comment on this is: 'I am said to be mildly epileptic, but this was not my experience. My faintings are preceded always by physical revulsion, not physical pain however:* the last medically recognised fit was in 1929 when I was having a steel splinter taken out of my eye. I fainted (an epileptic seizure?) in 1930 during the hospital scene of the film "All Quiet on the Western Front".'

And then his fears were suddenly ended. His brother Raymond, now qualified, was sceptical of Dr Riddock's diagnosis. Moreover, Dr McNair Wilson of *The Times* stated that he had seen no symptoms of epilepsy. The nightmare was over and the rest of 1927, as he put it, had a clear field for good, and he had an idea for a special Christmas present for Vivien.

---

* But see pages 327–8

He asked her to send him a dummy – an imitation book with blank pages – from Blackwells and in it he transcribed the verses he had written since the publication of *Babbling April*. Thus Vivien would have a volume of verse written especially for her.[46] In his preface he wrote:

As one who has but a poor store to give and lacks the wealth to make his worship plain, throws down his mingled pile of sticks and stones . . . So do I throw these scattered verses down, some bad, some mediocre, best but fair, but all belonging to you and only you.

" ... Not tears I give, but all that he
Claspað in his arms — sweet charity;
All that he loved. to him I bring
For a close whispering ...."

de la Mare.

from letter. Jan 7. 1927.

"It is enough of honour for one lifetime
To have known you better than the rest have known."

It was a very private book, an assurance asserting that his love would never have an end. On the first page were quotations from his favourite poets; 'As common chests encasing wares of price' (Thomas Hardy); 'All measure and all language, I should pass/Should I tell what a miracle she was' (John Donne); and lovely lines from de la Mare: '. . . Not tears I give, but all that he/Clasped in his arms – sweet charity:/All that he loved, to him I bring/For a close whispering . . .' Beneath the de la Mare he placed a pressed flower. It is now brown with age – the stem is held in place by a taper of paper on which Greene wrote: 'It is enough of honour for one lifetime/To have known you better than the rest have known.' His plans for that winter were of walks with Vivien at Berkhamsted:

We will go the winter walk . . . It's best when the country's frozen, because otherwise it's fearfully muddy. It has a heavy & enjoyable melancholy like black treacle or Gray's Elegy. And then one comes in very hungry in the dusk, when the High St lamps are being lit, & there's a slight evening mist. And there's a big log fire blazing in the drawing room & plates & plates of rock buns and cups & cups of hot tea!

But just before Christmas, Greene had his pocket picked: 'Something awful's happened. I can't come to Oxford on Saturday . . . I've had £11 either lost, stolen or strayed . . . I'm literally penniless. I think my pocket was picked on the tube, when we were standing crushed together like sardines.'[47] That night he had a dream which suggests not only the intensity of his love but also his uncertainty about the future:

Last night I dreamed we were in a railway carriage on a long journey. I had wandered away along the corridor. We were passing through a foreign country towards the sea. We entered great mountain regions, & the guard suddenly came along & said that the danger was close at hand. I understood that he meant that we'd got to run the gauntlet of a volcanic eruption, & that there was a strong chance of us all being destroyed. I hurried back along the corridor to the carriage where you were because I wanted us to be killed together, if we were going to be killed, & not at opposite ends of the train, so that my spirit should have to waste no precious minutes of eternity in finding yours.

24

Marriage at Last

At least I have loved you;
   Though much went wrong,
This was good,
   This was strong.
            — SARAH TEASDALE

H IS illnesses over, Greene looked to 1927 as being 'a clear field
for good' and he wrote to Vivien in January: 'All I want is
work, work, work, so that I can marry you and take a slice of eternity
before my time.'[1] And reflecting on the failure of 'The Episode', he
deplored 'the awful waste of a year's time when I might have been
practising short articles & getting nearer to marrying you.' His failure
to find a publisher for 'The Episode' had to a surprising degree taken
away his writing confidence: 'I want to get out of this patch of
Sargasso Sea, where I'm too stuck even to write two lines of bad
verse.'[2] He was already thinking about other writing outlets: 'There
are two films I want very much to see in town – "The Lodger" at
the Marble Arch & "Hotel Imperial" at the Plaza. Apart from
marrying you, I think the most wonderful thing in the world would
be to write & produce a really first class film – something as good as
Manon Lescaut. Ooo!'[3]

He is constantly spurring himself on at this time: 'I've got large
imperial plans on which I've started. I'm chucking the novel
altogether as ballast. No more breakfasts in bed.' It is not certain
what the 'imperial plans' were, but they seem to have involved trying
to write for the *Saturday Review* and doing a script for a film studio:
'I've been dashing about town this morning picking up the threads
of my new scheme. Only they are being recalcitrant. Gerald Barry,
the editor of the *Saturday Review* isn't back from the country & I've
got to go there again to-morrow. This afternoon I'm going to talk
to Maxwell, managing director of British National Pictures, & then

this evening I'm going to see the first night of "Metropolis", Fritz Lang's new film.'⁴

Nothing came of these plans or of others – writing a play with Vivien, for example: 'Do think of a good plot for a play – shocker preferably. If we could write one together, there's a chance at the moment of getting it performed by "The Playroom Six". I say we. You'd have to do the writing. I find myself now incapable of writing anything other than Times English.'⁵ The following month, May 1927, he thought of writing short detective stories:

> Ooo darling, Methuen are offering two prizes of £250 & £150 & royalties for the best detective story (first one by the author) sent in by May, 1928. Judges: H. C. Bailey, A. A. Milne & Ronald Knox. We *must* go in – I thought of a plot – I'm afraid at Mass – which I thought was remarkably good, but now in the cold light of a railway carriage it seems a bit far fetched. I'm going to write up though for particulars. I've got an old Catholic priest in mind for the sake of Knox!★

But he lost confidence again and appealed to Vivien: 'Do help & win the £250 prize for a detective story. Help me invent deceptive clues. I've never tried a detective story.' His anxiety increased; he felt that his troubles came from lack of steady writing since October 1926 when he was in hospital. He again cried out for help: 'I'm getting restless interiorly. If only you'd help me with a plot for a detective story I might be able to settle down to work.'⁶ He felt at this time like a dose of Eno's that's lost its fizz: 'I can't work & I can't read.'⁷ He felt nostalgic for earlier days when he worked to a pattern: 'Last year until the Episode was finished, I got into a beautiful automatic swing and I want to get back to it.'⁸ On the following day he wrote to Vivien on the same subject: 'O dear, the morning's nearly gone & I haven't done a stroke of work yet, & I don't want to. I want to talk to you . . . Please when we are in the basket, make me work.'

*

'The Basket' was their code-name for their future home, probably having its origin in 'cat-basket', reflecting Vivien's attachment to cats. At long last, the date of their marriage had been decided, determined by the work rota in Room 2 at *The Times*. Sub-editors were allowed a month's holiday a year and when Greene was asked what dates he would prefer, he said that he did not want to take more

---

★ Greene's first published detective story 'Murder for the Wrong Reasons' appeared in *The Graphic* (5, 12 & 19 October 1929). It is the worst he ever wrote.

than two weeks in early summer because he needed a fortnight in October or November to get married. The response was: 'do try and manage October as Parliament won't be sitting and we'll have plenty of people to spare.'[9] This decision was come to in April 1927, but already during February and March there had been a search for a home (Vivien living at Oxford could not have had a lot to do with it) and plans were afoot for the wedding and honeymoon. Greene found cheap flats which were not attractive and pleasant places that were too expensive. There was a flat for £100 which they seriously considered in March but turned down because, in his precise way, Greene argued against it:

> we pay income tax & from Hampstead my tube fare, apart from any of yours, would come to somewhere about £18 a year more than Raymond's [his brother]. That, without the income tax, would cancel the difference between our income and theirs . . . Unless some stroke of luck comes my way & gives me a job as remunerative as the Glasgow Herald which would make just the financial difference, it seems to me, we shouldn't be able to afford anything more than Raymond and Charlotte are paying.[10]

He found a 'teeny flat' in Chelsea at a price they could afford – £82 – but there was no bath. At last, in March he found a home for them: 'When I saw the flat it was a lovely day & the sun was streaming into the bedroom – & the bathroom! I like having a bath in sunlight. I must say I'm awfully attracted by the constant hot water . . . This afternoon I'm going to agitate for my nine guineas!'[11] He approached *The Times* at once for this increase in salary because, as he explained to Vivien: 'it's no use being dreamy & poetical about money, I'm afraid, when we are as poor as we shall be. "Safety first" is the motto for keeping kittens on the financial side – though we'll live as dangerously & unprosaically as you like on all the other sides.'[12] The manager of *The Times* replied that he must be under a misunderstanding to expect so large an increase, but he did concede Greene another £2.

Greene was to move into their new home at the end of March, and a letter to Vivien, written before he left his bed-sitter at Miss King's house in Battersea, suggests one of the difficulties they had both experienced while he was in lodgings: 'I wish it was you [calling] and I should carry you in on my back so that Miss King would only hear one pair of feet if she was awake, & then when the "o'er-hasty sun" rose I'd let you out of the window like a sparrow.'[13]

He was helped with his removals by his friend from schooldays,

Eric Guest, who provided an extra trunk into which Greene put his typewriter, odd parcels and an eiderdown. He sent a telegram to Vivien in Oxford with their new address – 8 Heathcroft in Hampstead Way – and his first letter, both in his personal version of his address and his description of his first morning there, expresses his excitement and satisfaction:

> Our basket
> Somewhere about 8 a.m.
> In bed
> March 30, 1927. Wed.
>
> I was quite startled when I woke up this morning to the biggest & most expensive toy I've ever had to play with. But when I went & had a huge hot bath in our own bathroom, I felt fearfully excited.

It is clear that what he was luxuriating in, after months of lodgings, was the privacy and being able to organise his own life. For a week he took three baths a day – in Battersea he had used a shared bathroom which had an ancient geyser always, it seemed, on the point of exploding. And he was able, on hearing 'letters plip-plop in the box', without waiting to dry himself, to dash out to collect them: 'It was a lovely sensation not having to wait & put on a dressing gown for fear of scandalising Miss King.' Everything about the new flat excited him, from doing his own laundry and seeing about groceries to making his own breakfast, though he wasn't doing much cooking and seems to have been living on siege rations – milk and bread and butter for breakfast, milk and sardines for lunch and elevenpenny kippers and syrup roll in the evening.

He was looking forward to and planning for Vivien's first visit, though he warned her he had only a few sticks of furniture – 'there'll be nothing at all, but a bed & a chair & possibly a gas fire', but they would have 'a picnic supper. I'll buy a pie & tarts as you suggest. We shall have to wash up after tea, as I have only two plates. Ooo darling, I'm so excited.'[14]

'One lives in a sort of shadowgraph,' he told her in June, 'no one seems more than silhouettes compared with you, who are beautiful & vivid & real.' He was sure that the world would be a second rate sewer if she weren't in it. He made 'a bad social companion' in those days: 'I sit & think of you & think of you & think of you', and certainly at the family home in Berkhamsted at weekends, when he was separated from her, he would say nothing or pretend to be asleep as the drawl of voices talked the hours away, but behind his closed eyes she walked: 'I push the voices up & up until they only dimple the surface of hearing & then they are not heard at all & I can whisper to you in a silence how much I love you & want you & long for you & ache for you.'[15] He wanted to have her with him all his life, 'like a sort of philosopher's stone always to turn ugliness to beauty, yes, & if you had the chance, transform Hell into Heaven. I believe Satan if he ever dared to face you would find time turned backwards & revise the judgement of the fall.'[16]

Inevitably, he had the kind of doubts which afflict people on the threshold of marriage, but in his case they were heightened to an astonishing degree by emotional excitement and self-doubt:

> I wonder if you'll be really happy with me. Sometimes I think you are too fine for love, I mean human love. It must seem rather petty & futile when you are seeing 'things & people from the other side of the sun'. I'm afraid of spoiling your vision for you, of getting between you & what is really worthy of you. And if I do you'll dislike me intensely later . . . Sometimes it seems to me that marrying you is the biggest crime I could commit. It's sentimentality to pretend that love is enough, & that's all I'm giving you.[17]

And in an undated letter, amidst this 'fierce hunger to have you with me again', he admitted to 'veering between a wild longing for October' when they would marry and a desire to make time go slowly in order to put off the time 'when you'll feel – like other wives! – disappointed in it [your marriage] & me.' And in September he advises her to be prepared for the worst, 'because I know I shall be a pretty trying person to live with *continuously*.' Even Vivien caught the mood, for he replied to one of her letters: 'Dear, dear love, it's I who'll disappoint you, I'm afraid. You couldn't. Disappointment & you are a contradiction in terms.'[18] One of Vivien's fears was that Greene's enormous love (and events ultimately were to justify her fear) would not last. Greene answered her confidently: 'I shall love you always. Why not? One's fond of lots of people always – how much more then you? I shall love you always . . . I hate it when you are away. All rapture goes with you & one's left stranded, as it were, on mud. And I feel terribly cloddish & heavy & completely empty of the spirit of God that you bring with you. Come back to me & I'll soon make you believe again that I shall love you as long as life & if there's love after, afterwards.' He signed this epistle solemnly – 'your lover who *will* love you for eternity'.[19]

Opposed to his ardent desire, there was Vivien's fear of sex which she had until her marriage. Greene was probably right in believing that Vivien's mother had poisoned her mind about sex, 'with misrepresentations & exaggerations, so that you might never marry.'[20] Because of this and the celibate marriage Vivien had at first envisaged as the only possibility, he was still, very late in the day, trying to quieten her fears: 'Of course it's not wicked – that side of our love. It would be a half-hearted, horrid sort of affair without it. Dear love, dear heart, it won't grow too important. It can't be separated from all the other parts of love. When it's growing all the rest is growing too. And I've promised you that you'll never have more of it expressed than you yourself want.'

Following Richmond's treatment, Greene had continued to record his dreams, and as he came towards marriage, he had his share of nightmares:

We were in Turkey or somewhere & there'd been some sort of silly muddle & you had been certified absolutely by mistake as insane. That, by Turkish law, made you liable to arrest. Everyone knew it was a mistake, but red tape made it necessary to carry out the arrest, so they came along & arrested you to take you off for confinement in a Turkish warship. Somebody said cheerfully to the officer 'I suppose it will take a couple of years to get her released' & he said 'Oh no, one year ought to do it.' I felt desperate. We'd done all that could be done – sent to the British consul & started the processes of putting things right – but we were going to be separated for a year. They wouldn't even tell me where you'd be confined. Any letters of mine had to go through the officer & he thought you'd be allowed to write. I said 'She'll be looked after & entertained all right?' He said 'Oh well, of course, strictly she'd be never allowed outside her one room but a year's a long time. Perhaps she'll be allowed outside now & then.' I got more & more desperate & anxious & at last I had a brilliant idea & said 'Show me the warrant.' So he handed it over & they gave your address as Berkhamsted which they spelt Berkhamstead. So I said 'Look here you can't arrest her on this warrant. The spelling of this name's wrong.' Then there were great arguments & I stuck to it, & he grew doubtful & started telephoning to solicitors, & I argued & argued & put off the arrest minute by minute & woke up. And it was when I woke up, far more than in the dream, that I felt completely horrified at the thought of a year away from you, not knowing where you were or what was happening to you. And I lay & felt quite sick with horror although I was awake & knew it was a dream.[21]

343

Another dream finds them in a public park walking round the raised rim of a lake. Vivien deliberately falls in to test his love. Because he refuses to do a spectacular rescue, there is bitter silence between them. Then at the house they find a lot of drunken Germans with their mistresses and Greene has to clear them out. Then he rushes into a room bolting the door because a young man approaches with a revolver, and feeling Vivien is in danger makes him affectionate towards her again. The young man turns out to be a jealous rival and starts shooting through the door at the point where he imagines Greene is standing, but misses. Greene, standing on one side, an ancient revolver in his hand (with one charge), tells Vivien to open the door and let the rival in. Instead Vivien goes out and remonstrates with the man who lays aside his revolver and becomes amenable. Greene also lays aside his revolver and, as a gesture of trust, turns his back on the rival. The young man apologises for trying to kill Greene, an apology which he accepts. It seems that Vivien had acted in the young man's revue and he had imagined, since Vivien looked radiant the night before, that it was because she loved him and his revue, and it was a great shock to discover that she was instead in love with Greene.

All of this suggests a degree of uncertainty on his part regarding the fulfilment of his relationship with Vivien, and it would seem that the strain of unconsummated love took its toll of him: 'Remember that you have a ravenous wanting animal waiting in London who can't bear to be separated for too long & starts biting his own tail when he is.'[22] In his desperation he persuades himself that even when married he would not see enough of Vivien: 'what a devilish little I shall ever see of you, really no more than an endless succession of week-ends, as now. Because in the mornings as now, there'll be work as far as I'm concerned, only more need of it than ever. Breakfast to breakfast and weekend to weekend. And then at the end of life perhaps nothing at all and the whole of life wasted.'[23]

This was one mood ('I can see nothing but a waste of emptiness in front now') but its opposite also appeared when he compared his situation in 1927 with those of his contemporaries: 'I met Causton in Fleet St yesterday . . . he's working at Reuter's on awful night shifts at a rotten wage. And Scott's getting £160 in a dubious position with the Amalgamated Press, & Gorham – the ex-assistant editor of the W. W. – is sub-editing on a wretched broadcasting weekly. Gosh, I *am* lucky (touch wood!). But that luck is outweighed a million times by the luck of having you. That I wonder at every day of my life.'

'You'll always', he wrote to her, 'be the most important thing in life to me & the one thing it would be an utter terror to lose.'[24] Marriage to him was 'the biggest thing that can ever happen to me

. . . Even death becomes rather insignificant beside it.'[25] She was 'much more exciting than drunken republican innkeepers in Ireland, or directors of Krupps, or cabarets & communists in Paris or murder commissions in Heidelberg. You are far and away immeasurably the most exciting thing that's ever happened & more rapturous & expectant in feeling than when the curtain rose on St Joan.'[26] And he wished that he could 'go to sleep now [this was in June 1927] . . . & wake up only at the moment when you raise your veil.'[27]

*

On occasions that year, Greene's absorption with Vivien was distracted by family matters. His brother Raymond was having 'a rotten time with his throat' and had to have an operation followed by three months' speaking only when absolutely necessary and then in a whisper. Greene's younger brother Hugh was miserable during his first term at Berkhamsted as a boarder and his eldest brother Herbert's wife had had a serious operation. 'I seem the only one in luck,' Greene concluded, '& a luck that's never been equalled in the world before.'[28] He told Vivien, 'No man's ever been as lucky as I am, & no man, if he was Alexander & Shelley & Damien rolled into one, would be worthy of you.'[29]

It was also the year in which his father's long reign as Headmaster of Berkhamsted came to an end. He had been quite severely ill in the summer of 1926, and it was feared that he would have to retire early. He was suffering from diabetes, and his wife Marion was most attentive to his needs – there was a great love between them.[30]

Charles Greene's last Founder's Day before retirement was in June 1927, and Graham sent an account of it to *The Times*. It was entitled 'Tribute to the Headmaster of Berkhamsted' and recorded that Charles Greene was presented with a bound address expressing the school's loss and its gratitude for his friendship and help. His son's *bête noire*, Dr Fry, was there. In the evening there was a performance by the band of the Scots Guards in the Deans' Hall and an announcement was made that two windows would be placed in the School Chapel in Charles Greene's honour. Greene gave a farewell speech and admitted that 'his time had been so happy that if he had his life to live over again he would return to Berkhamsted.' Old Boys I have spoken to have to this day a touching memory of 'Charles' standing in the cloisters by the door of Deans' Hall with moist eyes, sadly shaking hands with nearly 600 boys as they filed out. In spite of his original intention to become a barrister, clearly Charles Greene loved the school where he had spent almost forty years.

No doubt Graham was moved by his father's retirement, but if so, there are no references to this in his letters to Vivien. What was uppermost in his mind was his longing for her – if only she could have left Oxford and visited Berkhamsted for this special occasion to show everyone 'that I was going to have the loveliest wife man ever had since the moon came down to Endymion'.

Charles Greene's retirement inevitably brought a move from the house that had been the centre of family life for so long. Marion and Charles Greene retired to Crowborough in Sussex, and this change affected Graham and made his relationship with Vivien even more important:

> I am so fearfully glad that I've got you now particularly. Because at the age I am now I should probably have dived off the deep end, & because now that Berkhamsted is so to speak going, & everyone is moving & changing & disappearing, I feel so extraordinarily lucky to have found something ten million times more valuable to take the place of beechwoods & associations . . . I do *literally* . . . thank God for you every night. You have been . . . an answer to prayer. I began to pray, I suppose for the first time for a good many years, that August & September when I was in Derbyshire & you in Italy & Oxford. You'd given me a one in forty chance . . . So – it seems queer because I was far from being a Catholic or really anything at all & it was only six months after the silly article in 'The Outlook' – I used to pray desperately nearly every night to Our Lady that I might win you.[31]

The need to win her: the struggle to succeed. 'It's extraordinary to think that the first part of a two & a half years' struggle is within six weeks of coming to an end,' he wrote at the end of August. 'How weird it will seem. Another struggle will never come to an end – that of keeping your love . . . Both struggles are joyful struggles, though I shall be glad when the first is over.'[32] Although his vision of this year had been at the beginning one of 'a clear field for good', 'work, work, work', it had turned out to be a year when he was *not* writing his third novel but concentrating his energies on marrying Vivien.

Not surprisingly, and perhaps a little bemused, while waiting for a train to London from Berkhamsted just before his father's retirement, he reflected, 'When I come home & see the masters, just as young or old, completely unchanged, doing the same things & thinking the same thoughts, I feel as if I've only left school about a year. Heavens, what a number of sensations and actions one does cram into five years.'

*

As the date of the wedding approached, Greene threw himself into the preparations and his choice of image in a letter to Vivien (2 August 1927) is instructive: 'I should like to have a sort of pedometer which would register the hours each day that I think of you. I'm sure they'd add up to 90% of when I was awake. And sometimes 90% of my sleep too.' Nothing was too insignificant for his attention:

Yesterday I (a) wrote four letters (b) sent out more invitations, (c) interviewed Gambil on the subject of the shelves (d) painted the shelves (e) knocked holes, according to your mother's directions, in the drainer, (f) called at the flat, (g) called at Bolding's about your plate glass, (h) called at Wilkinson's about the brass (i) had lunch with Scott (j) went & was fitted at my tailors' (k) went into the wilds of Camberwell & set Per Mundum in motion (l) visited the Canada Life Assurance (m) had dinner with Arthur.[33]

He had found a carpenter (presumably Garsubil) to make some shelves: 'An old deaf carpenter is eating his lunch in the sitting room & brooding over pieces of shelf. Occasionally he makes a deep aphorism, "Shelves is useful for books & things" & "Books is all this & that. No regular size, be they."' He had begun to collect a small store of tools for the house: 'I managed to get to Woolworth's and bought a. hammer, b. chisel, c. gimlet, d. bradawl, e. picture wire, f. eye hooks, g. paint, h. a new brush . . . i. a tin of Repolin, j. some emery paper, because the shelves which have arrived are very rough.'[34] But his mind was always on Vivien: 'I have nothing to say but I love you, & no ambition but to win you, & little idea of Paradise but to have you with me.'

By May he had a list of 63 wedding guests, but a month later it had gone up to 75 and he realised that, among others, he had forgotten to include his cousin, Christopher Isherwood. The wellknown organist Witaker Wilson was persuaded to play in the church and the banns were published:

I went to Golders Green this morning. The church isn't at all bad inside. The rector was away, & there was a very nice young priest there. I stayed behind & asked him about the banns. The rector had forgotten. However it's going to be done from next Sunday. He was very nice & told me things Father Valentine had never warned us about.[35]

Graham drafted the announcement for the wedding: 'Is this correct . . . darling! "A marriage has been arranged & will take place in

347

October between Graham Greene, third son of Mr C. H. Greene, headmaster of Berkhamsted School, & Mrs Greene, & Vivienne, only daughter of Mrs Dayrell-Browning, of Hampstead."' He added, 'I come first by custom, darling, not by choice!'*[36]

His imagination had begun to work on the two weeks' honeymoon in the south of France:

> O darling, I keep on thinking of our 'fortnight' and getting waves of impatience and excitement and an ache to make it real. I think – without exaggeration, don't you? – that we shall have an exciting time. All by ourselves in a foreign land – hundreds of miles from relations!! I think one will feel tempted to behave scandalously! No one who would recognize us anywhere near. One will be able to bathe and suddenly be affectionate in the middle of a breaker, go for a gentle stroll towards the Pyrenees and then sit down and rest and exchange thick clusters of stars [kisses] by the roadside and not have to think – 'we ought to be getting back. They'll be waiting dinner for us.' Linger until dusk and then go even slower back. O darling, it will be lovely tiptoeing into your room in the morning (will the sea be outside the window?) and waking you.†[37]

Suddenly, he remembered that Basil Blackwell, Vivien's employer, had advised Vivien not to regard marriage as an earthly Paradise, especially the honeymoon. Greene's comments are sharp: 'A fortnight as an earthly Paradise. I shouldn't think it could be with Mrs B.B.' From that unkind thought his imagination took off:

> But perhaps they only took three or four days – while I'd like to take three or four years of a honeymoon with you. O darling, please make the time till then go quickly. How glorious to be entirely marooned together – no social duties, no time-table, no artificial rules, no letters, no papers if we don't want them. I'll trust to you not to lose count of the days – otherwise I should return to the office and new faces, a few familiar ones with white hair, and they'd say 'Who are you?' and I'd say 'Graham Greene,' and they'd nod their heads like choice Chinese mandarins and say 'the name's familiar', and out of an ancient file 20 years' back, they'd find a piece of news on yellowing pages in a now unfamiliar type. And they'd say 'there was a sub-editor Graham Greene. I

---

* The announcement appeared in *The Times* in July unchanged but for the additional phrase after 'Hampstead' of 'and grand-daughter of Mr A. Green-Armytage of Bristol.' Vivien's father is rather pointedly not mentioned.

† We must assume that on their honeymoon they had separate bedrooms.

knew him a little. A nice promising boy. He disappeared as you see 20 years ago. The police couldn't trace him but he'd be a middle-aged man now and you can't be more than 23.' And I'd say 'But I am Graham Greene, and I've been on a fortnight's holiday with my love. She is called Vivienne and is more beautiful than anyone you have ever seen. Have I overstayed my leave?' And they will say sadly (because though they are married, they have met no one to make time pass unnoticed and have been aware of every year) 'By 20 years.'[38]

As early as February, Greene wrote that he 'could sit for ages dreaming of that railway journey, when the wedding's over, an empty carriage except for us, & the roar of the train & the quiet inside, & the slow realising of no goodbye at the end of the journey, & you close, wonderful & beautiful.'[39] He could dream of the announcement in *The Times* of their forthcoming wedding 'as a sort of symbol of certainty'[40] and delight in the fact that just before the wedding the telephone directory arrived: 'We are in it looking very important!' For the wedding, he bought spats ('I little thought that I would sink to spats') and all the while the plans for their honeymoon took shape:

> Please take care of yourself and if you have late nights have late mornings too. Mustn't tire yourself now – when you are very nearly almost a bride! O you will look beautiful, but almost as much I'm longing for the black taffeta dress on the Chesterfield and the slinky little coat in the train. O I shall love the little motor ride to Victoria. I should like to give you a star in Hampstead, another at Belsize Park, Camden town, Chalk Farm, and a huge one in Oxford St – but I suppose you'll keep me in my place. I get shivers of excitement. Isn't it incredible that you and I are going to be married in six weeks?'[41]

Greene gives the impression that he decided everything, for example, the amount of money that could be spent, and he handled all the details of the journey, a pointer to the fact that he would be able to work out in precise detail the logistics of his future adventurous travelling:

> I think we could have an awfully splendid honeymoon if we splash say £40–50, and we will. We'll never have another honeymoon so it's worth it. And we'll have a day in Paris if you like on our way back – *unless you'd rather have it on our way there.* Which? Could you let me know, in your letter? Which time would you be feeling

most lively and inclined for Paris. I don't care a hoot. We could either arrive in Paris Oct. 15. 9 p.m. and Sunday in Paris, leave Monday morning Oct. 17. 8.20 – Marseilles midnight. Cavalaire Tuesday Oct. 18 and leave Oct. 27 (Thursday), Avignon afternoon, leave about 9 Oct. 28, arrive Paris about 11 p.m. leave Saturday, Oct. 29, about 1 p.m., arrive at basket late for Supper, Oct. 29. Or we could have the whole 24 hours in Paris on our way back. Then we'd arrive at C. a day earlier (Oct. 17), leave a day earlier (October 26), arrive in Paris late on Oct. 27 and take the whole of 28 there.[42]

Spending the night in Paris had been Vivien's idea:

O I loved your description of us in Paris & the meteors. There'll be meteors all right in my heart if not in the sky that evening – & comets & shooting stars & even naphtha flares. It will be a queer, strange, wonderful, exciting, beautiful – rapturous dream. To wake up in the morning, sun through the window, train bells going, stretch sleepily, wonder where I am, remember suddenly that this is Paris – comic looking little men with beards & moustaches drinking coffee on the pavement underneath, talking gibberish – and then with a leap at the heart that my *wife* is fast asleep next door. And I should leap out of bed & jump into a bath & splash uproariously & chant minor & sentimental poetry by Rupert Brooke at the top of my voice & lose the soap & curse with mock fury & giggle & wonder whether you were awake & whether you'd be too shy to be affectionate & whether if you were you'd 'melt' in the train before we reached La Lavandou or wherever it was that evening.[43]

But if Greene shows an excess of juvenile romanticism, he was no juvenile when it came to keeping a record of the wedding presents they received:

Business first, dear heart. I have asked a Mrs Walde for a large green lacquer tray. I hope this doesn't conflict with Loulie. I have asked Raymond & Charlotte for a Staines coffee maker. Mrs Laws is sending us little ladles for soup or fruit. The Balfours' coffee set has arrived, but it was addressed to me, so you needn't trouble to write. I have heard from Cavalaire & they've kept the two rooms we want. Hugh is letting us spend up to ten shillings. Will you order the Dulac picture? Your mother says it's in a shilling number, not a 5/-, so 9/- can go to a frame. Aunt N[ono] is giving us a singing kettle for my birthday. Would you mind if we lunched with her & aunt M[aud] on Saturday? Could you? They want to see us before we become '*ooked*.'★44

A few days earlier he had received £5 from Sir Sidney Sitwell, his cousin and a relative of Edith Sitwell. Vivien's mother gave them a cigarette box made in wood that looked like a tortoise shell and when you lifted the lid it played Polish tunes – 'like a box out of Hans Andersen,' thought Greene. His younger sister Elisabeth gave table mats made by herself.

The largest present was from Uncle Edward, 'Eppy'. Edward Greene we have already met and it was his kindness on countless occasions which, one suspects, slightly nettled Graham and his family since he was the wealthy Greene. Edward sent Graham £50, a stupendous sum in 1927. 'Uncle Eppy's letter was so sweet & sentimental. I should have liked to have hugged him. He says "You shall have the car to take you to Victoria, a very appropriate name for a young man who has secured a bride like Vivien, far too good for him. No man is good enough for a bride on his wedding day – he can only pray to become so one day." '45 Money was terribly important to buy necessary furniture. His mother gave him £20, and they were banking on receiving a cheque from Stella and Reggie Weaver. Greene felt that with the money they ought to be able to furnish one whole room.

He continued, however, to be unhappy about the influence of Stella Weaver on Vivien, who had been taken out in pouring rain by Stella:

Stella is a selfish self-centered cad to take you out. You are being married in three weeks . . . Darling, for God's sake, don't be a weakling who'll do whatever S. or myself or your mother wants . . . If anything happened to you, I think I should commit what's supposed to be the one unforgiveable sin . . . I love you terribly, & I can't bear to see you taking risks of smashing up both our happiness for Stella's whim . . . I dread the idea of you going back to S's the week-end before the marriage. She'd take you out in a raging storm & keep you up late every night & you'd meekly comply. It's a dangerous habit to get into. I'll be only too quick to take advantage of compliance – so don't give me the chance.'46

There was more trouble with Stella Weaver before the wedding, as she refused to let her daughter be bridesmaid: 'If you want L. as

---

★ Hooked. A real cockney would more likely have said [h]itched.

bridesmaid you are going to have her as bridesmaid whatever . . .
[she] says' – but in fact Stella's daughter was not a bridesmaid. Vivien
had three bridesmaids – Greene's sister Elisabeth and the Misses
Marjorie and Betty Fry.

*

When a colleague at *The Times* went off on three weeks' holiday and
said to Greene, 'Oh, well, when I see you next, you'll be a married
man,' a 'thrill of excitement and anticipation' passed through him.[47]
He also quoted to Vivien the poem in *The Unknown Goddess* as exactly
expressing his disguised feelings on his wedding day: 'I shall look
perfectly calm, if anything calmer/than before, when we pass the
works of Messrs Hunt/ley & Palmer./And, while my heart will be
wild like a groom at his/wedding,/when the bride lifts her veil, I'll
merely mutter/"Reading"'.[48]

For himself he knew that on the day, however wild his heart, he
would be controlled by a consciousness of what he curiously called
'hoards of disapproving faces', and he quoted a poem on Stonehenge:
'They sit there forever on the dim/horizon of my mind, that
Stonehenge circle of elderly disapproving faces/Faces of the Uncles
& Schoolmasters who frowned on my youth.'

Perhaps he felt that he would always have to fight these disapproving faces, but there was one person he singled out for special comment; 'You must tell Stella to look cheerful and optimistic during
the ceremony. Think of turning round when it's over, drunk with
joy at having you at last, to see somewhere in a pew Stella with a
long, sad face . . .

He was living entirely for 15 October 1927: 'I'm going to light a
candle, turn out the gas, get into bed & have your stars the last thing
before I blow the candle out, & in the dark I shall dream that you are
close in my arms & your lips near.'[49]

Although he did not feel himself to be a good Catholic – 'It's hard
for someone like myself to realise the sacrament of Mass' – he allows
himself rhetorical exaggeration when thinking of the sacrament of
marriage 'when I see you lift your veil . . . the feeling [will] change
. . . to a holy & dark rapture.'[50] He saw their love in miraculous
terms: 'if you cut your finger, I should half expect one of my own
fingers to bleed . . . It's very nearly, I suppose, what the Church
calls "one flesh".' And he promoted Vivien to sainthood: 'I can
believe that miracles will be done at your grave. Only you should be
the patron saint of lovers & depose that nonentity St Valentine.'[51]
On occasions his emotion was so strong that he wrote of awakening
at 2.45 a.m. and imagining that he was visiting Vivien in her bedroom

and kneeling beside her bed under the crucifix and kissing her lips, and he added, 'you didn't wake up. I'm glad I've been in your room so that I can imagine it clearly.'[52] And he set out to be the apotheosis of husbands:

> It will be such fun doing odd jobs for you, turning on your bath water, cutting your bread, helping you tidy up, ringing up the butcher and the greengrocer, tucking you up in bed! What fun arranging holidays too with maps and timetables, sitting on the floor with them spread out. O we are going to be so happy![53]

He insisted in letters that Vivien would look marvellously lovely as a bride and he offered to try 'fearfully hard' to make her happy, not a compromising sort of 'quite' happy but the exact kind of happiness she wanted at any particular moment.[54] He was in seventh heaven – 'are you really & truly going to come and live with me & be me "ook"', and just before their marriage he wrote: 'In a fortnight (D.V.) we shall be driving along the edge of the Mediterranean at this hour', so he was precise to the last. He promised to love her more every year: 'How God knows, for every corner of me now is filled with the love & the want of you.' It is the sheer hyperbole of his letters that strikes one: 'You are the most wonderful event in my life & would be in any one's. October 15 will be a greater day than Cana, because all the water in the world will be turned into wine.'

SAINT MARY'S CATHOLIC CHURCH

Holly Place, N.W.3.

THE MARRIAGE OF
VIVIENNE DAYRELL-BROWNING
AND H. GRAHAM GREENE

at eleven o'clock on Saturday, October 15, MCMXXVII.

❧

*T*HE *Marriage Service will be followed by Mass, in which the Nuptial Blessing is given. The Mass is that appointed for the Feast of Saint Teresa, Carmelite. (Oct. 15.) The Civil Ceremony will take place in the sacristy after Mass, the congregation remaining in their places until the Bride and Bridegroom return down the aisle.*

❧

353

They were married at Saint Mary's Church in Holly Place, London N.W. The service began at eleven o'clock on Saturday, 15 October. Graham's elder brother Raymond was best man and his sister Elisabeth train-bearer. The *Morning Post*, under the heading 'Mr Graham Greene and Miss Dayrell-Browning' reported:

> The bride was attired in an ivory satin Florentine robe, draped with silver lace and cut with a square neck. The satin train was also trimmed with silver lace. A wreath of orange blossom and silver leaves secured her long tulle veil, and she carried a sheaf of Madonna lilies, tied with silver tissue. The train-bearer, Miss Elizabeth [*sic*] Greene, wore a rose-pink taffeta frock, trimmed with silver.[55]

The young train-bearer thought the service very long, never having attended a Roman Catholic wedding before. Looking back after fifty-six years, she remembered what impressed a child:

> I had to carry a little bag into which I had to put some coins handed to me by the bride or groom. Also a little bell was tinkled throughout the service which caused my small nephew John to hopefully think that a meal was in the offing – what funny things one remembers.[56]

The bride and groom left in Edward Greene's car for Victoria at 2 p.m. and were in Paris seven hours later where they spent their first night, travelling on to Marseilles the following day and staying at the Hotel Terminus. As Greene had planned they left Marseilles by motor coach, following the coastline of the Mediterranean on an exciting, hair-raising journey winding round precipices with sheer drops of several hundred feet down to rocks and the sea.

They stayed at Cavalaire in the only hotel on the beach and champagne was 2s.6d. a bottle. Greene thought it was the loveliest honeymoon anyone ever spent. They hired little flat-bottomed boats with transparent keels and, rowing into little bays and coves, explored the area. They sometimes bathed naked. They loved their rooms with the Mediterranean a few yards outside and the Maures mountains rising behind the hotel. The mimosa was in flower and they found a profusion of palms and pines and cacti. The hotel meals were an endless source of excitement.

Years later, Vivien recalled one strange incident. Her powerful mother had given her a letter on sex instruction which was sealed but which was to be handed by Vivien to Greene. He read it and promptly tore the letter up so that she never knew what her mother had written.[57]

On their return journey, they stopped at Avignon and spent the whole of Friday in Paris when life caught up with them again as they ran out of money. They found the *Times* office and Graham rooted out a friend called Lumley who cashed them a cheque. They crossed the Channel – it was very choppy – on a Saturday afternoon, and returned to 'the basket' to find that Vivien's mother had filled the flat with flowers, which they both found deeply touching.

They were back, married and living together in London, and life as a sub-editor stretched ahead.

November passed without much happening. As the end of 1927 approached, the weather in London became severe: 'We've been having an awful time. No hot water (pipe's frozen) & dirty water remaining permanently in the sink as the outside pipe . . . was frozen & the water couldn't run away.'[58] When there was a thaw and the hot water returned, the pipe burst in the roof and flooded their little kitchen. That night it rained and then froze – the result was 'ice on the roads, no buses, no milk or paper, because no cart could keep its wheels or man his feet.'[59]

They finished the year off by going to the show, 'One Damn Thing After Another', and Greene suggested to his mother that she should look out for a piece he had written for *The Times* in the unsigned Court page: 'If a Court page called "The First Pantomime" appears it's me!'[60]

PART 6

Battlefield

25

'Pussy' and 'Tiger' and
The Man Within

There are only three things to be done with a woman.
You can love her, you can suffer for her, or you can
turn her into literature.

— LAWRENCE DURRELL

'I was married and I was happy,' Greene wrote. 'In the evenings I worked at *The Times*, and in the mornings I worked on my third novel.'[1] It was an intense relationship between two very different personalities, and it was this closeness that impressed their friends and relatives.

Helga Guinness, Sir Hugh Greene's first wife, recalled, 'He called her pussy and she called him tiger,'[2] and perhaps their names for each other were appropriate. Graham's cousin, Ben, and his wife, looking back fifty years to Greene's and Vivien's courtship, thought the young couple had been 'too involved' with each other and that 'those sort of relationships do burn out'. They remembered that Greene and Vivien were always arm in arm, or touching each other, or 'going behind screens in a room and hiding their heads together'.[3]

The Greenes' need for physical closeness was confirmed by David Higham, Greene's literary agent. He visited them at their flat in Heathcroft during the early days of their marriage and they were 'terribly, terribly affectionate, a state of affairs which slightly ceased later, perhaps naturally, I don't know. There was a bit too much effusive affection in that flat, I thought. It was at Heathcroft that I remember the relationship best. I once said to my wife, "I can hardly get out of the place between the kisses."'[4]

According to Helga, Vivien was clever, 'but had no common sense. She was always an oddity in a way – especially in the clothes she wore. Odd in the sense that she didn't wear a watch, that she would cook by the sun (that is to say cook when it suited her). When driving a car she would say "to you" "to me", meaning "I'm turning left" or "I'm turning right".' She also was fascinated by Victorian dolls: 'They were to be found everywhere in the house, upstairs, downstairs, even in the loo.'[5] And commenting on Greene, Helga thought he had no common sense, though she granted he was very clever: 'He was not a logical man. Indeed neither of them was logical in this world. He was not logical about politics, he was not logical about his religion.'

The strength of Greene's obsession with Vivien is supported by Helga's comment: So far as Graham was concerned, while she was *it* she was *it* and black could be white.'[6]

The Greenes were often out and about. They went to Oxford in February 1928 for the Oxford Union Dramatic Society's production and in the same month had 'a lovely view of [General] Haig's funeral from the roof of Westminster Hospital', where Raymond was a doctor.[7] In March they had 'a bust', dining at the Florence and going to see Fred Astaire and his sister in *Funny Face* afterwards. Greene wrote to his mother: 'It was extraordinarily good & Leslie Henson incredibly funny. The Astaires as always superb.'[8] His letters to his mother at this time reflect his obsession with the cinema. In February they went to see Edna Best in *The Constant Nymph* and 'Anthony Asquith's film'. In September 1928 he advised his mother, 'If a film called The Fugitive Lover comes to Crowborough see it. It's excellent.'[9] He also advised her to see *The Informer* – 'a terribly good film', and said of the Russian film *The Last Days of St Petersburg*: 'It had been put on for a run without any particular advertisement at the obscure Scala up behind Goodge Street. We arrived a quarter of an hour before the time of showing to find a tremendous queue. None of Pudovkin's films has been shown before publicly, & one never knew that his fame had spread so generally.'[10]

In January 1929 he wrote: 'We've been doing a crowd of cinemas. On Saturday we went to Thou Shalt Not a French version of Thérèse Raquin [novel by Zola]. It deals with the remorse of a pair of lovers who after drowning the husband of the woman, finally kill themselves at the feet of the victim's mother . . . terribly moving in a gnomic & not pathetic fashion. We both felt quite shaken afterwards. It was the best film I've ever seen . . . This afternoon, my day off, we are going to The Patriot . . . The office is ravaged with flu. Two people in my room away & another on the verge.'[11]

He thought of joining the Amateur Film Society: 'It gives one an opportunity I believe of taking part in the production of films.'[12] He was also writing for *The Times* on films: 'On Sunday I did the Film

Society show for The Times – Rien Que Les Heures'; 'I've got another article on A Film Technique coming out on the Entertainments page.'[13] 'I don't know whether you saw a third film article of mine about Sounds and Silence on July 10.'[14] He was also reviewing: 'The Film Society last Sunday & last night the first play I've done – the new Edgar Wallace Reasons Unknown. I see they've given me a top & all in a large type, while Charles Morgan's notice of The Matriarch has gone down to the bottom! We had very good seats in the third row with a good view of Edgar Wallace. A criminal face! All the front two rows were filled with friends of his, terribly fleshy bookmakers with diamond studs & mistresses. It was great fun. I'd never been to a first night before.'[15]

*

In the mornings he was working on his third novel, 'Dear Sanity', eventually to be entitled The Man Within. It was to be his first published novel. He had many unfinished novels – 'Fanatic Arabia' (which begins in a bus station); a murder mystery which he thought of during Mass in May 1927 involving a murdered governess and a priest who deduced that a girl of twelve had committed the crime; a school novel about a boy blackmailing a housemaster who had protected him; a spy story entitled 'A Sense of Security'; and a fragment entitled The Other Side of the Border, published after the Second World War.[16] He had also written a short story called 'The Widow', published twenty years later as 'The Second Death' in Nineteen Stories, but The Man Within was to bring him fame.

It took him two years to write, two years of such a variety of activities and problems that it was something of an achievement for him to have completed it in that time. In A Sort of Life, he tells us that he began to plan it as he lay in the ward at the Westminster Hospital after his appendicectomy, that is in October 1926 – 'it began with a hunted man', the first of his many hunted heroes. Possibly, though, the notion of a hunted man as the initial inspiration for the novel came to him before he went into hospital when he was reviewing a book of poems by Wilfred Gibson, a popular poet of the time, for the Glasgow Herald. In his review he specifically referred to one poem which interested him whose subject was a prisoner being chased over a moor by men with rifles. And in writing to Vivien about Gibson's poem, he says: 'I can't get started on these beastly short stories and the worst of it is another novel's beginning to coagulate itself against my will.'[17] Certainly the strong sense in Gibson's poem of a feeling of freedom that comes when walking on the Downs is reflected in important chapters in the novel.

It is unlikely that he got much further than the idea of a man at bay, but while he was recuperating in hospital he read a history of smuggling, *The Smugglers*, by Lord Teignmouth and Charles G. Harper, and the 'coagulation began in earnest'. Excitedly he wrote to Vivien about the projected novel: 'It's all about smugglers round 1830 or 50. The first sentence is (roughly): "He came over the ridge of the downs at a weary jog trot and could almost have cried with relief at the sight of the wood below." '* But what ensured that it was not to be simply an historical novel 'all about smugglers' was a particular letter from *The Smugglers*: 'There's a gorgeous long cold-blooded letter by an anonymous informer to the Admiralty, after a fight in which a Customs Officer was killed. Which is lucky, because the "hero" of the novel has got to be an informer.'[18] The third element in the novel was surely the significance the hunted man and the betrayer had for him, in stimulating his imagination.

He told Vivien that he could not go further with the novel until he had 'been to Sussex and fixed up the scene and the scenery', and it could be that this urge, in spite of his dithering in November 1926 as to whether he should convalesce in Paris or Brighton, took him to Brighton. He knew Brighton and its surroundings well, had always been happy there as a child and relished the idea of exploring the Downs again. His first letter to Vivien from Brighton was written on 7 November and on the back of the hotel envelope (he was staying at 32 Regency Square which faces the West Pier) is a postscript: 'Been up on the Dyke and now walked down into Patcham and am having tea. Wonderful day and wonderful colours on the downs. One wood had four distinct colours – not shades. I wish you were here. Tomorrow if fine I shall train out to Hassocks in the middle of the downs. Feeling fearfully fit.'

While he was enjoying this period of physical convalescence he was very much mentally alive in terms of his projected novel. The following day provided him with the house his heroine Elizabeth would live in and where the novel would have its dramatic beginning and compulsive ending – though he seems also to have had in mind the possibility that he and Vivien might spend a holiday there:

The weather yesterday was lovely, and I had the most wonderful afternoon and evening that I've ever had apart from you. The colours on the downs were gorgeous and I covered endless backs of envelopes with snippets [for the novel]. As it got dusk I went

* He changed this very little when the book was published: 'He came over the top of the down as the last light failed and could almost have cried with relief at the sight of the wood below.' (*The Man Within*, p. 11.)

down into Patcham, a charming village, and found a cottage for
tea, and had hot homemade cakes by the light of an old lamp and
a great log fire. And wind and rain swept up outside. And I heard
the most wonderful, or it seemed to me then, conversation in the
passage outside. I had a sense of complete ecstasy. I wanted to
shout with joy. The cottage would be ideal to stay at. The widow
who keeps it has her own poultry, and being South African and
judging by her cakes she ought to be able to cook. And her charge
is 35/- a week in summer and 25/- a week in winter!!! Fifteen
minutes from Brighton by bus and right in the Downs! . . . I'm
afraid of seeing it all by daylight, after the wonderful last night
. . . Returning in the dark on the top of a bus – it had stopped
raining – I saw a train all sparks and flame – plunge through a
wood high up on the side of a Down.[19]

On the next day he writes of the South African widow as one 'who
sees the ghost of her husband in corners', and the heroine of the novel
is similarly conscious of the spirit of her recently deceased guardian,
and firmly believes that spirits rise again from the dead.

The 'scene and scenery' of the novel included the setting of
the middle chapters, the Assizes at Lewes. While his experience of
Assize courts was not great, he had, as we know, on several
occasions attended the Old Bailey when he was staying at his
psychiatrist's home in London, and in May 1927 he attended a court
session in the company of his friend Eric Guest. 'I went and
found Guest and strolled round the courts with him. The judges
are too ludicrously Dickensian for words. We haven't progressed
since the days of Jeffrys as far as the Lord Chief Justice is concerned.
He and Sherman and another judge were deciding some divorce
or paternity case. He sat like a small flat dissipated toad with his
chin on his belly, and every now and then exchanging a foul
joke and leer with Sherman and speaking in a soft sucking dove
voice.'[20]

These accounts of the beginning of the novel and the research for
it prefigure what was to become his established way of approaching
his material. Following the initial incident or situation which sparked
off his imagination, there would be careful and personal research of
the setting and also his note-taking, sparse but accurate – 'four distinct
colours – not shades'. Suggestions for characters would come from
people he met during his exploration of the chosen setting. And
important is the sense he gives of the experience of the travel involved
– riding on top of a bus, and the time it took from Brighton to
London. His setting and minor characters would be established by

these means, but he would in this instance look elsewhere for his major characters and his plot.

*

Between the research in Brighton in November 1926 and the completion of the novel in November 1928, he had had his period of illness and worry, had returned to work, found a flat for himself and Vivien, seen his father's retirement, married, and come back to London to a very full social and working life. In spite of this he pressed on with the novel. He wrote to his mother in February 1927 of how he 'longed to throw up hopeless ambition & go for walks instead.'[21] As late as March 1928 he was still researching the setting for the novel, as a postcard to his parents shows: 'Hope it will be fine for Lewes on Sat. We hope to walk over the Downs from Hassocks.' His need to go over the physical setting of a novel even when involved in writing the final version was already established.

Since he always wrote regularly to his mother, the fact that he did not write between 23 July and 21 September 1928 suggests that he was totally engrossed in the final stages of his novel, and this is confirmed in a letter of 27 September: 'I'm afraid I haven't written for years, but I've been frantically busy finishing off Dear Sanity. Yet another attempt on the publishers with at least the merits of no sickness.'[22] In November, the first anniversary of his marriage gone, he had the typescript of the novel in his hands, though it brought him no happiness: 'I'm beginning to go through Dear Sanity but having now read it at least six times it seems to me too incredibly purposeless for words. A mug's game!'[23] Nevertheless, he sent the typescript to both Heinemann and The Bodley Head. In his letter to Charles Evans at Heinemann, no doubt remembering their long delay over his previous mislaid manuscript and their subsequent rejection of it, he wrote: 'Dear Mr Evans, you will have forgotten who I am. I sent you a novel some 18 months ago called The Episode which you were kind enough to consider at some length and, I believe, read yourself.' And he expressed the hope that this, his latest attempt, 'may have scored an outer'. He was, however, resigned to another long delay and told his mother that the novel was 'unutterably bad'. There was some pleasure in not getting a quick decision for uncertainty was more easy to live with than the confirmation of another failure. In fact, he had to wait only ten days for a decision.

He recalls that one day during the winter of 1928 he was lying in bed suffering from a bad attack of flu and listening to the sounds of his wife washing up the breakfast things in the kitchen when –

The telephone rang in the sitting-room and my wife came in and told me, 'There's a Mr Evans wants to speak to you.' 'I don't know anyone called Evans,' I said. 'Tell him I'm in bed. Tell him I'm ill.' Suddenly a memory came back to me: Evans was the chairman of Heinemann's, and I ran to snatch the telephone. 'I've read your novel,' he said. 'We'd like to publish it. Would it be possible for you to look in here at eleven?' My flu was gone in that moment and never returned.[24]

Which was hardly surprising, given the events that followed, for Evans and his staff thought they had a best-seller on their hands. Grace Cranston, who worked for Heinemann in 1928, remembered well when *The Man Within* first arrived: 'It was the first promising book by a new author that came to us at the Windmill Press, and it was welcomed as an omen of good books to come . . . Leslie Cavender, then manager of the trade department here, and an excellent book man told us all to buy a copy of the first edition – "it's sure to appreciate in value". In fact, there was quite a bit of excitement about the book among the staff here.'[25]

Greene's excitement can be charted in his letters to his mother. On 7 January 1929 he wrote:

Great News! Doubleday, Doran & Co. have taken the book. £50 in advance of royalties & ten percent on all copies. They've promised me to send it to the Book Society of America . . . it sells about 80,000 copies straight away. It's coming out in England in May. Evans this morning read me a letter from Clemence Dane in which she said that she liked the book immensely & that I was 'a born writer' & she thought perhaps a born dramatist too, as there was a fine play to be got out of the novel! . . . We still haven't found a title. The M.S. is going to be sent to Tennyson Jesse as apparently she has a flair for such.[26]

The book was not to be published until after the general election in June. As late as March the title had not been decided on: '*Flight* has too much of a Lindbergh suggestion. My latest idea is *The Man Within* quotation from Sir Thomas Browne "There's another man within me that's angry with me." The voting is now between *The Man Within* (which both Evans and I now dislike as a hint of theology), *One Within* (Evans' suggestion) & *The Divided Heart* (mine).'

On 5 June 1929 Greene told his mother: 'There's a publicity para. in John O'London's this coming Saturday containing several inaccuracies for which I am not responsible', and he added: 'The editor of John O'London's (a terribly low brow paper but bought by masses) who has read it, predicts that "with ordinary luck it will be the publishing success of the late Spring season" . . . But I am earnestly pouring cold water on my hopes.'

The paragraph in *John O'London's Weekly* on 8 June 1929, in spite of some inaccuracies, obviously depended on information provided by Greene himself:

Messrs Heinemann have great expectations of a first novel which they are to publish in a few days' time. This is 'The Man Within', by Mr Graham Greene, a first cousin twice removed of Robert Louis Stevenson and Whyte-Melville.* Mr. Greene, who is only twenty-four years of age, seems to be a remarkable young man. He has barrel-organed through Hertfordshire, disguised as a tramp; tramped Ireland during the Republican 'troubles'; and worked for a tobacco firm, while publishing his verses and prose fantasies. After coming down from Oxford he became sub-editor on the Nottingham paper where Sir James Barrie began as a leader-writer and of which Mr. Cecil Roberts was at one time editor. Mr Greene was married two years ago – at the age of twenty-two. H.L.M.

'The plot thickens,' Greene wrote to his mother. 'More than 100 copies have been sent out to the big booksellers with a special letter. They [Heinemanns] are advertising as well in the trade papers – a full page advertisement in *The Publisher's Circular* this week.'[27] The plot thickened still further. The novel was a publishing success, selling 8,000 copies. Two editions were sold before publication and within six months it went into six impressions and was translated into German, Dutch, Norwegian, Danish and Swedish. On both sides of the Atlantic the story went out that a brilliant new literary star had been born, and the literary parties began two weeks before publication day: 'On Tuesday night we go to a party given by Doubleday, the Chairman of Doubleday & Doran, as well as Heinemann: Shy Youth will have to be my cue! I'm having my photograph taken next week at the firm's expense.'[28]

During that hot summer the parties continued and he met the writers of the day: 'lunch with my agent [David Higham] & met Storm Jameson'; 'On Thursday we've been invited to a party at one of the female portions of my agents' to meet the Somerville novelists,

---

* Major George Whyte-Melville, an authority on field sports, wrote novels on fox hunting and steeplechasing. He was killed in the hunting field in 1878.

Rose Macaulay, Margaret Kennedy [author of *The Constant Nymph*, best-seller in 1924]. Too terrifying' (undated letters). And they went to 'a terribly grand party at the American publishers the day before the publication, with people like the Duchess of Devonshire, Rudyard Kipling etc. floating about. We drank a lot of champagne & felt happy.'[29] Then there was the great banquet held by Doubleday and Heinemann – they were in uneasy partnership – at the Savoy Hotel: 'The party on Monday was fun,' he wrote. 'I was introduced to Arnold Bennett who was tipsy, Hugh Walpole, Miss Sackville-West, and Mary Borden. And other "great" figures who loomed round included Edgar Wallace, W. B. Maxwell, A. E. W. Mason & Maurice Baring! Bennett was sweet.'[30]

In August 1982 Greene said that he thought Bennett was the only great author he had met (though earlier he had said the same thing about H. G. Wells) and in his introduction to Margaret Lane's biography of Edgar Wallace he recalled that original meeting with Bennett, Walpole and Edgar Wallace, without mentioning that Bennett was tipsy: 'I found myself a junior guest, very much "a stranger and afraid" at a great publishers' do at the Savoy Hotel . . . Dinner at the long tables, set at right angles, seemed a kind of frozen geometry, but for a young man it was worse when the geometrical figure was eventually broken, and I found myself with my coffee seated beside Arnold Bennett, who, when a waiter gave me a glass of "something" . . . remarked sternly, "A serious writer does not drink liqueurs."' Bennett's comment doomed Greene, so far as liqueurs were concerned, to a lifetime's abstinence.

He also saw what he was certain was the first meeting between Edgar Wallace and Hugh Walpole – 'the giant of the circulating library and the giant of the cheap edition, the writer who wanted, vainly, to be distinguished and recognized and applauded as a literary figure, and the writer who wanted, vainly too, to have all the money he needed, not to bother about debts, to win the Derby every first Wednesday in June, and to escape, to escape from the knowledge of the world which perhaps the other would have given half his success to have really shared. I remember Walpole's patronizing gaze, his bald head inclined under the chandeliers like that of a bishop speaking with kindness to an unimportant member of his diocese. And the unimportant member? – he was so oblivious of the bishop's patronage that the other shrank into insignificance before the heavy confident body, the long challenging cigarette holder, the sense that this man cared not a fly-button for the other's world. They had nothing in common, not even an ambition. Even in those days I found myself on the side of Wallace.'[31]

A fortnight later he was again at the Savoy with his publisher and two favourite Heinemann authors, Michael Arlen, author of the best-seller, *The Green Hat* (1924), and Maurice Baring: 'Arlen wasn't nearly as bad as one would expect & Baring was sweet. Like one of P. G. Wodehouse's silly young men grown old and bald. Quite adorable.'[32] Meeting Arlen again for lunch a week later, Graham was now blasé enough to joke about it: 'Oh & next week I'm lunching to meet Michael Arlen. We brother best sellers, you know.'[33]

In an undated letter to his wife written from Heathcroft ('the basket' had now become 'the burrow') at 11.30 p.m. when she was asleep in bed, he describes a tea party that day at Charles Evans's home which was 'very nice. Strawberries & cream etc. under the trees. Everybody very amiable. . . Cunninghame Graham★ was there.' He also accepted a number of invitations: 'oh my dear I've been and gone and promised to [Clemence Dane] – "all butter" for a weekend'; 'Old Lowndes & his wife† were there. Mrs said she wanted to invite us to dinner . . . Mrs Doubleday very amiable.' He travelled back with Keith Winter, Barbara Noble (*The Years that Take the Best Away*) – 'too too country cousinish, lives at Brighton & Gillian Oliver (*The Broomscod Collar*) rather nice, staying at Golders Green. I've invited her to supper on Wednesday . . . I felt very seniorish as the last two knew nobody & their books had not been a success.'

Opinions on the novel were, almost without exception, commendatory – in some cases ecstatic. This view was understandable to Helga Guinness, her husband and the rest of the family, because: 'There was something special about [Graham], it was very difficult to know what it was, just that we thought so and indeed the family had always thought that he was a genius and this was a thought they had had right from his very early days when he was just a boy.' Hugh and Helga, while feeling that Greene was a genius, did not then think he

---

★ Cunninghame Graham (1852–1936) had an adventurous life, taught fencing as 'Professor Bontini' in Mexico City, punched cows in Texas, and was an aristocrat living – when he lived in Scotland at all – in the ancestral home of Gartmore. He was a socialist involved in the Trafalgar Square riots of 1887, and was an inveterate traveller who, like Graham Greene later, would set off for an outlandish place because it was difficult of access; hearing of the forbidden city in Morocco he set out for it disguised as a Turkish physician; he was a South American gaucho, a wonderful horseman, a rover, adventurer and grand eccentric. He was a friend of the great, especially of Hudson, Conrad and Bernard Shaw. He looked startlingly like the Spanish painter Velásquez.

† Mrs Belloc Lowndes (1867–1947) was the sister of Hilaire Belloc. She established herself as a writer of mystery stories with *The Lodger* (1913), a documented novel about Jack the Ripper.

would ever become famous and popular. They thought he would remain unappreciated by the general public: 'We thought *The Man Within* was a wonderful novel, very strange, very curious, and made him very different.'[34]

They were, of course, quite wrong. Greene was 'doomed' to reach success with his first published novel. The *Outlook and Independence* of New York called it 'probably the most original and possibly the strongest new talent of the year in English fiction, a remarkable study of the inward conflict of a dual nature.'[35] S. P. B. Mais, writing in the *Daily Telegraph*, thought it was a first novel of 'such perfect point and accomplishment that one trembled for the future of the young author.' The *Nation* was also concerned about the author's future in case this 'perfect adventure story of a psychological treasure might have led to the author's burning himself out in one trial'. The *Newsagent and Bookshelf* thought it was a wonderful story and strongly recommended it as a book to be introduced to customers who relied on a bookseller's judgment: 'They will be more than ever convinced that you are a good judge.' The Oxford journal, *Isis*, admitted that 'Oxford may or may not remember the author of this novel – not so long ago he was well known in Oxford journalism' – but considered that 'this book is a sufficiently forceful reminder.' The *Sunday Times* could find 'no flaw in this strangely fascinating book.' The *Sphere* published a photograph of the young author under the title 'A NEW STAR', and introduced him as: 'Mr Graham Greene, the author of *The Man Within* hailed upon this page by Mr Arnold Palmer as a novel of extreme brilliance.' The *Publisher's Circular* was certain that there would be 'a big demand for this book – in style original and powerful'.

A number of critics compared him with Robert Louis Stevenson: 'Mr Graham Greene writes with a distinction and a subtlety that Robert Louis Stevenson (of whom he is a cousin twice removed) would, we feel sure, have applauded' (*The Times*). The same point was made by the *Inverness Courier* while the *Daily Telegraph* spoke of the book as being impregnated with beauty, subtle in construction, in dramatic tension comparable with the best chapters of *Treasure Island*.

Writing from France to Robert Nichols in February 1930, Aldous Huxley asked: 'Have you read a novel called *The Man Within* by Graham Greene? I think it's most remarkable . . . Much better (between ourselves, for it's frightful heresy!) than Virginia [Woolf's] *To the Lighthouse* . . . It's the difference between something full and something empty; between a writer who has a close physical contact with reality and one who is a thousand miles away and only has a telescope to look, remotely, at the world.'[36] Such an assessment could perhaps have been made about Greene's first realistic novel, *Stamboul Train*, written three years later, but hardly about *The Man Within*.

There were more objective assessments. The *New York Times* considered that: 'Once he achieves . . . a less isolated and poetic approach to the inner workings of human character he will be a really significant novelist.' And J. B. Priestley, writing in the *Evening News*, while giving a meed of praise, rapped the author's knuckles. He saw the novel (justifiably, I believe) as an example of a plot which did not ring true. He thought the writing too mannered, the tale an ultra-romantic dream where reality never breaks in (though this surely is not true of the brilliant central chapters dealing with the trial at the Lewes Assizes) and he made a typical Priestley point: 'When we have put the book down, it is as if we had just walked out of a hot-house.' This criticism was to have an interesting sequel three years later on the publication of *Stamboul Train*.

Greene himself was to admit that if he had been a publisher's reader then, as he was to become later, he would unhesitatingly have turned down *The Man Within*, and his successful beginning as an author was due to the man who did *not* turn the novel down – Charles Evans. Originally an elementary school teacher, he had been in charge of Heinemann's modest educational list before becoming head of the firm after the death of Heinemann, and eighteen months later head of Doubleday after the death of Pawling. According to Cecil Roberts, the novelist, Evans's enthusiasm for *The Man Within* knew no bounds, and Roberts played a part in helping it along: 'One day when I called on Charles Evans I found him very excited by a new discovery. He gave me a proof copy of Greene's first novel . . . and sought my opinion. I read it. I thought it rather poor . . . but I wrote to Evans saying I thought it was good. I wished not to hurt him or his new author.'*

Evans was always kind to his new 'stars', as the literary agent David Higham wrote: 'Charles Evans had the air of a child almost, a certain simplicity, a naïvety of which he was never ashamed, and beneath all that a warm and genuine heart, a generous one, too. One day in 1929 a note came up to me in my office at C[urtis] B[rown]. It read (from memory): "The bearer of this note is a young author whose first novel I have just taken and who has, I believe, a consider-able future. He ought to have an agent and I should like that agent

---

* Roberts may have felt this in 1971 but he is on record, in a volume of his autobiography, *The Bright Twenties*, written one year previously, as publicly endorsing Evans's view about the new novel.

to be you." I rang reception at once. The young author who came up was Graham Greene.'[37]

Greene has said that nothing in a novelist's later life can equal the moment when a first book is accepted. Triumph is unalloyed by any future doubt. Yet in the office of the publisher Greene remained objectively observant, for he later recalled that the bald and lean Charles Evans's hands and legs were never still – 'he did everything, from shaking hands to ringing a bell, in quick jerks.'[38] As he came out of the Heinemann offices into Great Russell Street he was in a daze and, in the flush of success, felt that success is not slow but sudden.

*

It must seem to readers today that *The Man Within* is not recognisably a 'Greene' novel and indeed Greene himself, looking back, considers it the work of a stranger, of a very young, sentimental man, which now has no meaning for him whatsoever. He cannot understand the reason for its success still less his uncle Edward's comment at the time of publication that the book could only have been written by a Greene: 'I thought of the novel, the story of a hunted man, of smuggling and treachery, of murder and suicide and I wondered what on earth he was driving at. I wonder still.'[39] But surely Edward Greene was right. He might more accurately have said that only Graham Greene could have written it. Greene in his comment suggests the ingredients that made it a best-seller – and he might have added the saintly and betrayed heroine. It is obviously prentice work: the story is slight with much repetitive action, the setting and characters often unrealised and the dialogue sometimes maladroit. Apart from the middle chapters dealing with the Assize courts, the reader enters a romantic and unrealistic world populated by unlikely smugglers who show in their bearing and their aesthetic interests that they are of gentle birth.

Without interpreting the novel as autobiography one can say that its drive came from the various traumatic experiences Greene had before he reached the age of twenty-three and that it gathers those experiences together in a fictional form.

Andrews, the hero of the novel, betrays the smugglers' leader, Carlyon, whom he worships for his romantic and heroic nature, because he needs to escape from the life of smuggling which he hates. His reward is a life of fear. He worships Elizabeth for her courage, beauty and sanity, but he fails her also, so that she commits suicide to save herself from the smugglers while he dashes about the countryside looking for help – again because he is afraid to face the smugglers alone. The worship of heroism and purity, the selfish need to escape from dangerous and unpleasant situations even if it means betraying those one worships, the corrosive effects of fear and betrayal, the conflict between lust for and admiration of physical purity are the conflicts which torment Andrews and which lead him to suicide. At the end of the novel, when he is a captive, he steals back his own knife from the arresting officer: 'slowly his hand stole out unnoticed on an errand of supreme importance.'

Andrews's saviour in his flight from the people he has betrayed is Elizabeth. Her home on the Downs, 'this small warm room and its white occupant', is isolated and secure: 'But this is Paradise', says Andrews.[40] Andrews's love for Elizabeth becomes ecstatic and religious and the sexual side of their relationship is approached by Andrews with awe: 'I want to tell you now that I love you as I've never loved anyone or anything in the world before . . . I'll ask for you only when we're married and that as a favour which I don't deserve . . . You are holy.'[41]

Andrews's love for Elizabeth rather uncannily reflects Greene's love for Vivien in its devotion and worship. A few months before their marriage, Greene wrote to Vivien from Euston Station: 'Darling, it seems almost incredible that in less than an hour, I shall see you coming along a real pavement, tangible and beautiful and wise.' Just as Elizabeth's cottage was the secure home of a saintly person, so the first home of Greene and Vivien was to be 'Paradise'. He wrote to her: 'the basket's not at all itself without you because it only came into existence because of you and it's not fair to leave it without a creator, like Paradise bereft of God. I'm sorry if it's blasphemous, but one can't really be very blasphemous in praise of a saint, and I quite sincerely believe you are one.'[42] 'I want to live with you as long as you live and die with you when you die,' he told her. 'I've pursued you into the Church and I want to pursue you into eternity.'[43]

In *The Man Within*, Andrews watches through a keyhole while Elizabeth, in order to allay Carlyon's suspicions that Andrews may be in the cottage because there is a second cup on the table, claims it as her own and drinks from it. Andrews feels a wave of love and humility, and in spirit kneels to her. In a similar way, Greene praised Vivien because she once told a little lie on his behalf: 'when you ask "could I love you as much" after your mysterious misdeed . . . don't you see that . . . my whole feeling is a need to kiss your hands in reverence and worship . . . for *you* to tell a small untruth for me is a great thing.'[44] Greene admired Vivien's serenity, sanity and purity, the qualities Andrews admired in Elizabeth, and Greene, as did Andrews, expressed his love in terms of worship, for Vivien was 'all beauty and all mystery and all wonder', and his dream was that there would be, after the wedding, 'the slow realizing of no goodbye at the end of the journey and you . . . to be worshipped as holy with sacrament.'[45] In each case there is the sense of amazement at the possession of such a love: 'The face which [Andrews] raised to her was like that of one dazed and stunned by an unexampled good fortune.'[46]

Vivien came into Greene's life at a crucial time. He had a history of attempted suicides; he had had a devastating experience at school; he had undergone psychoanalysis; and his years as an undergraduate at Oxford had been largely without fixed purpose. He had had periods of excessive excitability which, when in a manic phase, made him hyperactive, highly energised and given to impulsive acts; he had had no anchor, apart from his ambition to be a writer, until he met Vivien Dayrell-Browning. It would seem, as with Andrews and his Elizabeth, that she was able, through her personality and religious conviction, to give him stability, to channel the energy, the excitability and the sexual drive, at least for a time. Because of his need for her he turned his attention to providing a home for them, earning money for them, and he followed her into the Roman Catholic Church, accepting its proscription of suicide – a mortal sin which would consign the sinner to hell for evermore. He was to face this acceptance in 1947 in his justly famous and precisely entitled *The Heart of the Matter*.

Andrews's entry into Elizabeth's secure world is an escape – a temporary escape – from the world of the smugglers: 'the sneers, the racket, that infernal sea, world without end.' 'Even in the middle of this fear and flight,' he tells her, 'you've given me more peace than I've known since I left school.'[47] Greene's need to 'escape' is an important part of his psychological make-up. He has been escaping since the age of thirteen when he ran away from school. We can take it back further to his very early escaping to the 'French' garden at St John's. He escaped from the British American Tobacco Company, among other reasons, because of the rough, uneducated nature of some of his colleagues; he escaped from Nottingham because of the provincial nature of its society. And the title of his memoirs is *Ways of Escape* (1980). Before and after his marriage to Vivien, Greene found it necessary to escape from her physically and spiritually at times, and this is reflected in *The Man Within*.

The trouble with Elizabeth, Andrews finds, is that in her there is 'a kind of mystery . . . a kind of sanctity which blurred and obscured his desire with love.' What Andrews discovers is that on occasions he needs a woman uncluttered by love. Thus once outside the secure boundary of Elizabeth's influence, in the town of Lewes, he descends to lechery when, as he puts it, 'the animal in him could ponder . . . beauty crudely and lustfully'. Greene has such a curiosity about all things in life, that it was inevitable that he would be attracted to profane love. He was always willing, especially after his treatment by the psychoanalyst, to try anything new, to seek out the unknown. He recognised the strong independence of the sexual appetite within him which led him to betray the spiritual Vivien as Andrews betrays Elizabeth.

Andrews believes he cannot love Elizabeth physically because of a fear that he will dirty her: 'how can I ever touch you without soiling you a little?'[48] and Greene felt Vivien to be too fine for human love, so that marrying could be construed as the biggest crime he could commit.[49] Andrews decides, after he has slept with the harlot Lucy, that he will seek out Elizabeth, and he dreams of taking her to London, gaining her love and marrying her – as Greene had recently married Vivien. Then comes the thought that even if he gained his desire, it would only be to soil her and cleanse himself: 'When I had been married to her for a month . . . I would be creeping out of the house on the sly to visit prostitutes.'[50]

Tooter Greene has said that, very early in Greene's marriage, and also before it, they used to go to London together:

> I remember very well the occasion when after we had been with a couple of girls, the next day was Sunday, and suddenly Graham said to me, 'I must go to confession before I go off to Spain.' Recently, when we met at Rule's restaurant in Maiden Lane, the whole Greene family met, some 19 of us, to celebrate Raymond Greene's 75th birthday, it was like old times – we talked about our sexual exploits of those days.[51]

In 1927 sex before marriage was frowned upon and yet the pressure on a young and highly-sexed Greene must at times have been so great that he would, Vivien being unobtainable sexually until after marriage, have capitulated to his desires. And Tooter's admission is proof that he – that they – did. There is other evidence. In his letters to Vivien at this time, Greene is circumspect but yet there are hints of his seeking elsewhere physical consolations: 'I don't know why but I want you more desperately than I've ever wanted you before. Perhaps because I've behaved less well this week.' And speaking of how Vivien is more efficacious 'than war or flood or earthquake or even a disreputable adventure', he goes on: 'It will be very hard not to misbehave on Saturday [he was not seeing Vivien that weekend] so as not to want you too badly. I *don't* mean drowning my sorrows in drink necessarily.'

The pressures of suppressed sexuality no doubt led to a number of encounters with prostitutes, amateur and professional. For Andrews there is something clean – before the event – in the simple bargaining: 'His leg felt the shape and touch of her thigh beneath the velvet . . . you can have me – tomorrow night . . . you've got me at a cheaper rate than any other man has done . . . Now feel here and here and here. Now give me your mouth.' But there is a strong reaction afterwards and a punishing sense of sin reflected in Andrews's attitude, 'he had capitulated at the first hungry wail his dirty, lusting body had uttered',[52] which reflects Greene's own reaction to sexual experiences as well as that of Andrews – the fear 'of going on soiling himself and repenting and soiling himself again'. Such was Greene's intensity of emotion that he often longed, like his hero Andrews, to be null and void. And just as Andrews after sex with Lucy feels the need for personal purification in order to get rid of his sense of shame and return to the pure Elizabeth, so Greene's purity of passion for Vivien was intensified after a jaunt to London.

The Man Within was not simply an historical novel about smugglers, hence Greene's decision about the title – the double drama of a man fighting within himself and without was pointed to by many reviewers, and it is likely that Sir Thomas Browne's statement: 'There's another man within me that's angry with me', originated in St Paul's statement in the *Epistle to the Romans*: 'I see another law in my members, warring against the law of my mind, and bringing me into captivity to the law of sin which is in my members.'

26

A False Start

We all want to be famous people, and the moment we
want to *be* something we are no longer free.
— KRISHNAMURTI

G REENE was now earning 10 guineas a week at *The Times* thanks
to the senior sub-editor, George Anderson, who had written to
the manager, Lints Smith, in March 1929 arguing that Greene deserved a rise: 'Though he came to Room 2 from Oxford quite
untrained, he learned quickly, and is now one of our best and
quickest sub-editors.'* Moreover, the fact that Greene had had a novel
published and one which was rapidly putting him into the best-seller
class must have had some influence.

During the vacation of the Court page editor, he was given the
responsibility of putting that page together – 'a deadly dull job with
heaps of scope for blunders' is how he described it to his mother, but
of course Greene was quick to see the advantages of such work: 'It
gives one experience of "making up" a page with the compositors,
arranging the items & so on, which is useful if one's ambitions run
journalistically, but mine do not.'¹ 'The other night [he wrote], our
too terrible assistant editor called me into his august presence . . . he
behaves like a caricature of a schoolmaster . . . He told me that I
"wielded a pretty pen," & why didn't I try my hand at some light
leaders. I just managed to refrain from saying that I had done my
best to cure "my pen" of being pretty.'²

There was another factor pressurising *The Times* to offer Greene
more promising work. The *Evening News* had approached him to
write an article for them but this would have infringed his contract
with *The Times*. He spoke to Barrington Ward, later to succeed
Geoffrey Dawson as editor, about this. An argument developed
between Barrington Ward and Lints Smith, who held the view that

* Had Anderson (conveniently?) forgotten about Greene's stint in Nottingham?

Greene should not be allowed to write for the *Evening News* since that paper and *The Times* were in commercial competition. The matter went up to the editor and Barrington Ward told Greene that the editor had decided to offer him new and different work. To his mother he wrote: 'I'm in suspense & excitement.'

But it came too late to affect Greene's future for he had already privately approached Charles Evans of Heinemann with what he called his 'Great Scheme' – understandable given the success of *The Man Within*. Putting the worst construction on his own action, as he often does, Greene describes in *A Sort of Life* how he wrote Evans a 'blackmailing letter' telling him that he must choose between *The Times* and novel writing for he could not do both; Greene clearly intended to leave *The Times*: 'Nothing has transpired yet with the Great Scheme', he wrote to his mother. 'I had a lovely lunch last week with Evans & Doran [of Doubleday and Doran] at the Savoy. But no word of business.'³ The reason for this, Greene surmised, was that while Evans wanted to free him from *The Times*, cautious old Doran wanted to wait and see how *The Man Within* did in America.

By 3 October the American reviews (all consistently good) had come in and Greene was put at once on a salary basis by Heinemann to tide him over and give him a chance to write full-time. He wrote to his mother: 'Evans . . . made me a definite offer of £650 a year in advance of royalties on The Man Within & the next two books for two years payable monthly after I cease other work.'⁴ He added: 'I've decided to accept it. There's a risk but not, I think, a big one.' He was to be proved wrong.

Approaching *The Times* with his resignation was difficult. He spoke first to his immediate chief, George Anderson, who told him that in a few more years he could be the correspondence editor – a job of which he had already had some temporary experience – and advised him that his future at *The Times* was promising, as indeed it was. He had been brought into personal contact with the editor himself: 'Closeted with the editor every afternoon at four o'clock I argued the merits of the letters and we decided which was to lead the page.'⁵ Greene felt exalted by the contact. He recalls to this day persuading the editor to accept a letter from the painter Walter Sickert which, because it looked as if it had been written with a matchstick, had offended Dawson's tidy mind.

Anderson's arguments did not dissuade him and though the night editor 'positively begged [him] to reconsider'⁶ Greene was determined to leave. For one thing, his book had already earned him £800 and had only recently appeared in America. With his usual succinct firmness he wrote to Lints Smith: 'my chief ambition lies in that direction. I have decided to accept [Heinemann's] offer.'[7] Yet his letter of resignation was not all firmness for he ended with the hope (it was a form of hedging his bets) that he would be able to 'retain some small connection with the paper by means of Court Page articles', adding that Mr Brumwell had been kind enough to suggest that he should occasionally try his hand at light leaders.[8]

Finally, the editor himself (a majestic figure in those days) tried to dissuade Greene from leaving – surely a measure of his success at *The Times*: 'Dawson . . . took the conversation urbanely into his own hands,' Greene wrote, 'he said he understood that I had written a novel, and he congratulated me on its success – his wife had demanded a copy from her circulating library. *The Times*, he assured me, would have no objection if I continued to write novels in my spare time. The art critic, Mr Charles Marriott, had done so for many years, and even the dramatic critic, Mr Charles Morgan, had published one or two. Indeed the time might have almost come to try me out with an occasional third leader.'[9] Something of the editor's irritation comes out in his final words. 'If his mind were really made up he could only say it was a rash and unfortunate decision.' Prophetic words!

Greene knew he had given his best to *The Times* and knew also what he had received in return. He was quite sure that there was no better career for a young novelist than to be for some years a sub-editor on 'a rather conservative newspaper': 'The hours from four till around midnight, give him plenty of time to do his own work in the morning when he is still fresh from sleep – let the office employ him during his hours of fatigue. He has the company of intelligent and agreeable men of greater experience than his own: he is not enclosed by himself in a small room tormented by the problems of expression; and, except for rare periods of rush, even his working hours leave him time for books and conversation (most of us brought a book to read between one piece of copy and another). Nor is the work monotonous . . . And while the young writer is spending these amusing and unexacting hours, he is learning lessons valuable to his own craft. He is removing the clichés of reporters; he is compressing a story to the minimum length possible without ruining its effect.'[10]

So often Greene gives us the impression that his actions are a bit of a lark and there was no emotional disturbance, but his wife's account of those days[11] gives us some notion of his anxiety while working for *The Times* and trying to write in his spare time: 'Graham felt that he could never be a novelist unless he gave his whole time – he simply could not do it. Working up to midnight and then coming back in the tube, resting and then writing a couple of hours and going back to *The Times*. I used to have sandwiches and a Thermos waiting for him when he came in every night. Tea or Horlicks, ham or salad sandwiches. It was too exhausting, he couldn't possibly work like that.'

A contemporary of his in Room 2, Leslie Smith, recalls that a good deal of *The Man Within* was written in Room 2: 'He actually began his career as a novelist in that room. I well remember our talking about it all. So he left Printing House Square & all his friends were delighted & relieved when there was no need for any looking back.'[12]

Douglas Jay, who joined *The Times* as a sub-editor on 21 October 1929 (the date of the Wall Street crash, and three months before Greene left) described Greene to me as he was then: 'He was good-looking, very distinctive looking. My main memory of him was that he had a worried look, and I used to glance at him particularly in the Tube and think "Is that just the cast of feature or is he really worrying terribly about something?" And to this day I never found the answer.'[13]

Perhaps the answer lay in his having given up a perfectly splendid job for an uncertain future. He was, no doubt, saving himself from dullness, and he was doing what many journalists on *The Times* longed to do, spreading his wings and flying elsewhere. No one had actually resigned before. Yet Greene was to discover that the next few years were to be extremely precarious, and that his editor was right, his was a rash and unfortunate decision. Looking back, forty years later, Greene, the least nostalgic of men, has a fond remembrance of his life as sub-editor: 'So I left the coal-grate and the faces under the green eyeshields, faces which remain as vivid to me now when the names of their owners are forgotten as those of close friends and women I have loved. In the years to come I was bitterly to regret my decision. I left *The Times* the author of a successful first novel. I thought I was a writer already and that the world was at my feet, but life wasn't like that. It was only a false start.'[14]

Graham Greene left *The Times* at the end of 1929. He spent the next fourteen months in London, living the life of a full-time writer at 8 Heathcroft, the 'love basket' – which was what it continued to be. A letter written on the third anniversary of his marriage gives an impressive indication that his love had not lessened:

This is a hasty scrawl before you come in. I love you infinitely more on Oct. 15, 1930 than on Oct. 15, 1927, 28, 29. I do hope you are still just as happy. My grumbles are for trivial things. Underneath them I'm ecstatically happy all the time because I'm married to you, beautiful miracle . . . Darling, darling, goodbye.

I'm afraid of you catching me writing & suspecting. I love you so.
Your lover always.

Surprisingly, the letter is unsigned. Perhaps he heard Vivien at the
door and had to hide his note.

Marriage initially mellowed Greene. And because, on his marriage,
relations with his parents entered a new phase, he felt the need to
acknowledge his debt to them: 'I'm very happy at present, and I
realise that a huge proportion of it I owe to you both. I hope I become
a success, if only so that all you've both done for me isn't wasted.
There comes a time when gratitude wells up to a height above flood
level, and as it's hard, owing to some kink in my nature, to speak it,
I have to write it.'[15]

He must have felt at this time that he was on the crest of a wave.
His first published novel was a runaway success and he was now
known as a writer and courted – the London *Evening News*, which
was publishing a series of interviews with clever young men and
women about what they expected from life, included Graham Greene.
Given his relative immaturity at twenty-five, his expectations 'after
sustained effort', were in part predictable: to be rich and successful
and have houses in London, Somerset and Rhodes. His personal
extravagances were to have his own private cinema and to walk the
Great Wall of China. But basically he returned to a negative desire
which reflected again his fundamental need – that his life should not
be dull, ordinary or mechanical. Looking at his life as it had developed
he recognised that all the happiest moments in the past seemed to
him to have been exciting and a little insecure – 'a sinister grouping
of figures at night in a back street of Essen under the occupation; an
aggressive crowd in an Irish village beyond a blown-up bridge . . .
the sense of a very tenuously held peace.'[16]

This of course would be eye-catching stuff in a newspaper interview, but it does reflect his recognition of his needs as a writer to
find his material in foreign and dangerous areas. He went on to set
a novel in Trier (*The Name of Action*) and Spain (*Rumour at Nightfall*)
but this was only a partial recognition of his needs. He also said
during the interview, again with insight, that success would mean
that he would have the leisure 'to become thoroughly acquainted
with such strange and slightly sinister suburbs as Brixton and
Streatham Hill'. What is also telling here, however, is the fact that
these 'suburbs' were 'strange and slightly sinister'. He is still looking
at life outside his class as something to be explored and therefore a
suitable subject for treatment in writing another best-seller. The
seedy sides of London and Brighton were to provide him with the

settings of *It's a Battlefield* and *Brighton Rock* – but not until several
years later. What he had to come to terms with was his mistaken
fascination with Joseph Conrad's *Arrow of Gold* – a romantic world
hopelessly barren for him. It took time before he recognised that he
had a sensitive nose for the odour of spiritual decay, for man's sense
of betrayal.

He began writing *The Name of Action* ten months before he was to
leave *The Times* and one month after the acceptance of *The Man
Within*. As usual he planned to visit the setting for his new novel and
wrote to his mother about taking a week in Trier in March to get
local colour,[17] but this did not come off. He was then living in
London as an up-and-coming novelist, no longer as an anonymous
sub-editor, and his time was so taken up with parties given by his
British and American publishers and his literary agent, having lunch
or dinner with a constant stream of new writers and taking an
increasingly professional interest in films and the making of films,
that he let slip the short holiday due him from *The Times*.

*

In August, he had a second chance to visit Trier but instead decided
on an Hellenic cruise. He thought it was a justifiable extravagance
and in excitement wrote to his mother to say he was sailing on 27
August on an Hellenic Club ship for a three weeks' cruise. His father,
who had often visited the Hellenes, was asked by Graham if he knew
some of the people who might be aboard the ship and was also
asked for a list of clothes he should pack: 'Dinner jacket not tails, I
imagine?'[18] Also a brown-coloured postcard has survived from
Athens which Greene sent to his senior colleague in Room 2 at *The
Times*, Colonel Maude. On one side was a picture of the Temple of
Theseus and on the other Greene had written, rather cryptically:
'One old stone after another. But really rather lovely. And a glorious
bathe in a hot clear emerald sea at Aegina. Very, very hot, but not
too ecclesiastical.'[19] But it was not simply a holiday, for during the
cruise he visited Constantinople, spending twenty-four hours
there. The brilliant last chapter of *Stamboul Train*, which he wrote
three years later, could not have been completed without this short
visit.

He was not to visit Trier until a month before he completed *The
Name of Action* and although, having spent only one night there, he
was again moved by its magic: 'It's the loveliest place I've ever been
to; I think it must have been my home in a previous incarnation'[20]
– his failure to renew his impressions of the town earlier was to be
fatal for the novel.

Characteristically, in order to complete *The Name of Action*, he took himself off in March 1930 to the King's Arms in Woodstock, Oxford, and finished it on the 23rd, though he fled elsewhere to do the revisions as there had been two deaths, as he told his mother, 'the landlord and his mother, in the last fortnight, and I saw a bat in the street this evening.'[21] He revised the novel in the home of his old landlady at Oxford, Mrs Higginson. By 5 April, the book was more or less finished.

In submitting the manuscript, he proposed to his publisher two uninspired titles, 'Falls the Shadow' and 'Heretics in Love'. Neither was satisfactory and it was left to Clemence Dane to provide the title: 'I've got the name of the book at last or rather C.D. got it: *The Name of Action* (". . . and lose the name of action". *Hamlet*).' The manuscript was dedicated to his wife and on the endpaper he wrote:

> For Vivienne
> Because of her increasing
> loveliness

followed by:

> 'Because the mountain grass
> Cannot but keep the form
> Where the mountain hare has lain'

And after writing,

> 'Manuscript of "The Name of
> Action" Begun March 1929;
> Finished July 1930
> published October 6, 1930'

he returned again to his wife:

> For Vivienne
> 'Thou art so true: that thought of thee suffice,
> To make dreams truth; and fables histories'

The novel completed, Greene was commissioned by the *Graphic* magazine, in which had appeared his 'Murder for the Wrong Reason', to visit Oberammergau, the village in the foothills of the Bavarian Alps, to write about its Passion Play, which had been produced by the villagers once every ten years since 1634 in fulfilment of a vow of thanksgiving for the end of the Black Death. The production is strictly amateur and the responsibility of the local villagers. Five thousand people attended that year (1930) with their hats, high heels, nasal voices and most of all umbrellas, for the performance took place in torrential rain: 'At the scene on Golgotha, Nature added what stage craft could not do . . . the sky darkened from bright sunlight, and as the body was being taken from the Cross, rain began . . . lashing into the covered inner stage, beating against the long white cerements and whirling the cloaks of the women watching at the foot of the Cross . . .'[22]

At Oberammergau he found a telegram waiting for him from his publisher Charles Evans: 'Your book magnificent. Congratulations.' 'So that's cheering,' he wrote laconically on a postcard to his mother. Forty years later, recalling the enthusiastic telegram, he asked, 'How could I tell how bad it really was? Evans must have known, but he was determined to keep it dark for the time. He had a reputation for discovering young writers, and he couldn't admit a mistake too quickly.'[23] Perhaps so, though publishers are human and make genuine mistakes, but still thinking of that telegram in his middle seventies, Greene was less condemnatory of his publisher: 'Perhaps he was as innocent and romantic as his author.'[24]

Between books, in spite of his trip to Oberammergau, Greene was very restless that summer. In June he was excited at the prospect of a visit to Iceland. He had approached the *Graphic* asking them to commission an article on that country, for Iceland was celebrating the millennium of its parliament, the *Althing*: 'I'm going to Iceland!!' he told his mother. 'Leave Leith in a steamer about the size of a channel boat on June 17. Arrive Reykjavik on June 24, and leave again on June 30.' Then he discovered he could not get a return passage in time for publication of his book, so his trip fell through.

In early July he saw Paul Robeson as Othello – 'he was very, very, good' – and he spent the following weekend with Clemence Dane at Axminster. Clemence Dane had, in the early 1920s, written plays which achieved long runs (in particular her near classic, *A Bill of Divorcement* and her ingenious reconstruction of the dramatist's life in *Will Shakespeare*), but more to the point she was, with others, involved in deciding on a novel for the monthly *Book Society* choice. She admired Greene and he, his eyes wide open, knew what he was doing spending the weekend with an attractive older woman: 'I hope she may induce the *Book Society* to do something for me.'

It was not to be: 'Alas! The *Book Society*, in spite of Clemence Dane, have not taken the book, so fame and fortune must wait awhile yet. I was *really* rather disappointed.'[25] If we take into account Graham's usually cautious tone when writing to his mother, it is probable that he had in fact suffered a deep disappointment over his novel's failure.

Then his brother Raymond, who was distraught because his first wife had recently left him, suggested they should go to Moscow together but the expense was too great. Instead, they settled for a trip to Burgundy, 'to Dijon, "the gastronomical centre of the world"'! We are going third class so as to have more money to spend on food and wine! The German Railways, to whom I wrote when we were thinking of Russia, have sent me a free pass to Königsberg in East Prussia, but as it's only for one it's not much use.'[26]

Just before his visit to Burgundy, he made a literary pilgrimage to Thomas Hardy country. Hardy had died two years before: 'We went over to Dorchester one day and bardolized, walking out to Stinsford Church (Mellstock) where Hardy is buried★ and to Bockhampton his birthplace, a tiny hidden village where a by-road comes to an end and fades out into moor.'[27]

*

Greene started his third novel, *Rumour at Nightfall*, on 5 September 1930.[28] He had a month's freedom to work on it without concern for the outcome of his second. Four days before the publication of *The Name of Action*, on 6 October, he wrote to his mother of their anticipated celebration: 'I look forward to the 6th too. V. and I are celebrating by having dinner at the Ivy and going to "Charlot's Revels". The book is nicely got up . . . Did you see the first advertisement in the Lit Supp. this morning?'

They were not to know they were celebrating a failure. According to Greene his novel sold barely 2,000 copies. Five days after publication, he confessed to his mother that he did not know how the book was going but admitted, 'the reviews are awful! The whole thing is pretty deadly depressing.' And the depression continued. By 20 October more reviews had come in: 'So far [he wrote to his mother] The Times is the only valuable review I've had . . . The Oxford Mail's is the most understanding . . . but it cuts no ice.' The trouble was that most reviewers compared *The Name of Action* unfavourably with *The Man Within* and at this time he had come to feel that *The Man Within* was more and more terrible. He admitted he was getting rather tired of kind friends who 'tell me they like this but of course they much prefer the other.' He was convinced that while his first was a moderately bad book, his second was a moderately good one. Even with his mother he argued against the view that his heroine Elizabeth in *The Man Within* was a success: 'I don't

---

★ Thomas Hardy's body was buried in Westminster Abbey; his heart in Stinsford Churchyard.

think she's a character at all, but a sentimental complex. But though I sez it as shouldn't I think Anna-Marie Demassener [heroine of *The Name of Action*] quite adorable.'[29]

In 1980, at the age of seventy-six, when he drove himself to re-read *The Name of Action*, he admitted that a few months afterwards he had forgotten what happened finally to his heroine – 'so little does she live or matter'. And of his hero, Oliver Chant, he admitted that he was 'only a daydream in the mind of a young romantic author, for it takes years of brooding and of guilt, of self-criticism and of self-justification, to clear from the eyes the haze of hopes and dreams and false ambitions.'[30] Almost a decade earlier he had had to conclude that not 'a single book of mine has failed to give me at least once a momentary illusion of success except *The Name of Action*.'[31]

In England, reviews of his novel were uniformly critical apart from that in *The Times Literary Supplement*, but even there the critic admitted that 'we are left with precisely the same impression of living in the peculiar, highly wrought world of our author's imagination rather than in any recognisable era of human life.' The *Bookman* thought the novel 'did not justify any salvo of cheers . . . a guileless tale, the narrative hollow and factitious'. The *New Statesman* set the seal on the novel's failure – 'his story is half in Cloud-cuckoo land and half in Ruritania and fits ill with his style.' The *Nation* and the *Athenaeum* praised the book (but who would wish to be so praised?): 'the warm chastity of pure Gothic with a little Byzantine to add wonder to our delight.' Evelyn Waugh's review (they were not friends then) was remarkable only because he reviewed the book under the title of *The Name of Reason*.

There was one unexpected fillip, though ultimately it came to nothing. Catherine Nesbitt, the actress, was excited about the dramatic possibilities of *The Name of Action*. Her husband, Cecil Ramage, a leading light of the OUDS, had roughed out a play, the dialogue mostly drawn from the book. Greene went to dinner with them:

> I liked him, and she was perfectly sweet. They seemed very fond of each other . . . She was very anxious to get the play put on & play Anna-Marie. He has, what seems to me, rather wild dreams of a cast. Ernest Milton as Kapper, and Cedric Hardwicke as the Dictator. She wants to get a Sunday night performance done by the Arts Theatre and then see if the bait catches. There the matter for the moment rests . . . I don't believe myself it will make a good enough play, and I think they are both too sanguine.[32]

He was later in *A Sort of Life* to recognise the difficulties involved in writing a second novel: 'the first is an adventure, the second is a duty'. More philosophically, after the success of *Stamboul Train* three years later, he wrote: 'A first novel is usually the result of many years' saturation; a second novel often uses a too immediate experience . . . The intensity of a first novel cannot be repeated; the novelist . . . must learn to set every precious scrap of personal experience where it will receive the greatest number of converging rays.'[33] In the same year, writing in the *Spectator* about the second novel of F. C. Boden whose first novel had been highly praised, he returned to the problem: 'he should not be unfairly judged by its successor. A first novel sometimes absorbs too much of a writer's vitality: he has not learnt to harbour his resources, and when it is a success he is driven to write another before he is ready.'[34] The failure of Greene's second novel had gone deep.

In spite of the bad reviews he pushed on with his third, *Rumour at Nightfall*, and since its setting was Spain he felt he must take some lessons in Spanish. 'The Spanish affair', he wrote to his mother, 'is rather comic. All in class with a blackboard! I haven't had time to do my homework and the class is tonight.'[35] His real mood, however, is revealed in a letter to his brother Hugh: 'I'm learning Spanish, not for any "slow sweet name's sake", but for the third novel of mental gloom.'[36]

In the midst of his depression over the reception of his second novel, he wrote a very moving story entitled, 'The End of the Party'. To his mother he admitted simply, 'I've got a very short story called "The End of the Party" (about hide & seek in the dark!) coming out some time in the [London] Mercury.'[37]

There were practical reasons for writing short stories – they took little time, and they did bring in needed currency. Earlier in 1930, he had sent a story entitled 'Proof Positive' to the *Manchester Guardian* for a Ghost Story competition and had won the first prize of ten guineas.

'The End of the Party' draws on his deepest emotions, being about a boy, Francis Morton, sensitive, vulnerable to criticism, afraid of the dark and the flight of bats, who dies from shock and fear when, during a game of hide-and-seek, he is touched suddenly in the dark. It is interesting that the girl whose contempt he fears is called Mabel Warren. The name is used again for the hard, sadistic, lesbian journalist in *Stamboul Train*.

'The End of the Party', having appeared in the *London Mercury* in January 1931, was later included by Edmund O'Brien in his collection of the best short stories of the year, but the editor of the *London*

Mercury, J. C. Squire, did not pay for the story until 24 June the following year and then only after Greene's agent threatened legal action.*

Financial pressures due to his small monthly sum from his publishers, his lack of success as a novelist and the high rental for 'the basket', resulted in the Greenes' renting out Heathcroft for £8 a week and seeking cheaper accommodation in the country.

The move had also been encouraged when Vivien read Adrian Bell's *Corduroy* (about the pleasures of living in the country), which had made a great impression on her: 'As we had to move and we had to go somewhere that was cheap, we went there' – 'there' being Chipping Campden which they had first visited in February 1931 to see a cottage, 'Little Orchard', owned by a friend which, Greene thought, 'sounded too good to be ignored'. It was a two-storeyed, stone-built, thatched cottage with a 'wildish garden', no electricity, oil lamps and a stove which, Vivien commented wryly, was called 'cook-and-heat': 'It did neither effectively. It all depended on the wind and I hadn't cooked at all before we married.'

* The *London Mercury*'s failure to pay their contributors became a scandal, righted somewhat by an action brought successfully in November 1932 by Miss Mackenzie against Squire and the magazine for non-payment.

27

Down and Out at
Chipping Campden

Life is short and so is money.
– BERTOLT BRECHT

THEY left London for Chipping Campden by train on 2 March
1931 in the company of a toy Pekinese, newly bought by Greene
for Vivien. They had seen one some months earlier, a puppy of
fourteen weeks with a beautiful smoky fur, belonging to Raymond's
wife, Charlotte (the Raymond Greenes were then living in Oxford
where Raymond had a medical practice), and this led Greene to buy
one. According to him, the puppy 'behaved like an angel on the
journey', though he observed, characteristically, that it was 'sleeping
uneasily and snoring a little.'[1] It was to have a short life and a rather
tragic end.

They had been ready at 7 a.m. for the furniture removers, but the
van was an hour late and in fact did not reach the cottage until
5.45 p.m., so that the unloading of the furniture had to be done by
the light of borrowed lamps. Moreover the curtains had not arrived
and the lino had not been laid. They gave up the idea of spending
the night there, boarded the dog out and went to an hotel. Greene
remembered mice running up and down in the wainscoting and the
dying coals in the grate 'fluttered like bats',[2] an image usually
indicating anxiety on his part. The next day Vivien got down to
staining the cottage floor with Greene crouched in a corner out of
the way, reading.

True they had substantially reduced their expenses by moving –
the cottage cost only £1 a week – but they had also dramatically
reduced their standard of living and quality of life.

Chipping Campden, some miles north of Oxford and situated in
the Cotswold Hills was a very old market town.* It was built of local

---

* Its name derives from Old English meaning a market town in a valley of camps.

388

stone, and even the public telephone box in the town square had the stone's colouring to make it blend in. There was a quality of stillness (which persists today), of light, the sound of church bells and the smell of jam-making, and inns with names like *Live and Let Live*.

The cottage, 'Little Orchard', was up a short street called Mud Lane, at the end of the High Street. At the bottom of Mud Lane was a pump, said to be haunted by the ghost of a dancing bear. During their first night in the cottage they discovered that the Aladdin paraffin lamps smoked when left alone for a few minutes and they spent a disturbed night. They missed the sound of traffic and were kept awake by the hooting of an owl in the darkness. Greene wrote to his mother, 'I have little news in this dim and distant spot', and their isolation clearly troubled him. He warned his mother that he might kidnap her to stay with them, though his plan was to live at Chipping Campden only one year and to buy a two-seater car and learn to drive (which he never did).

His letters to his mother suggest that Vivien liked Chipping Campden, or at any rate was making the best of it and moving into local society: 'V. is gradually entangled in rural activities'; 'V. plunged into a new experience, acting as judge of the fancy dress parade [at a local fête] . . . She's enjoying it so much that she hasn't come home yet – 9.45. p.m.'[3] But she found shopping in a country village confusing. She recorded in her diary: 'The fish shop sells china on one side and flies on the other. The best eggs come from Foster the paraffin man, the best strawberries from Keyle the coal merchant. Fruit and vegetables from Turners Garage. Papers and magazines from the ironmonger.'[4]

Their first visitor, Hugh Greene, must have had impressed upon him the primitiveness and isolation of the young couple's living conditions: 'We haven't too much room. If the divan bed hasn't come, do you mind the sofa? Also, there are a few wood lice, but we've nearly got them under.'[5] To his mother Greene wrote: 'Hugh and I did a long walk to Stow-in-the-Wold & I won more than 2/- off him at Rockaway . . . We were woke on the first night by hearing him being sick out of the window. We think it was the cider he had for supper after the railway journey. The Peke was being sick at about the same time as Hugh.'[6]

This letter was written on 28 April 1931, the day after he 'finished the new novel – the first version anyway . . . a long book, over 90,000 words' (his previous one had been just under 70,000). It had taken him seven months to reach this point. The novel was begun in September 1930 in London, but the pressure on him to produce a novel had led to his 'writing 24,000 words this month [April 1931] in spite of the move' – 'I've been working too hard,' he told his mother.

He thought of a singularly unsuitable title, *The Phantom in the Hair*, taken from an undistinguished poem by Coventry Patmore. By the time the proofs came to him in mid-August 1931 he still had not found a satisfactory title and, in some desperation, chose one previously put forward by his publisher for his preceding novel, a suggestion he had not then taken up – *Rumour at Nightfall*.

As a full-time writer, he took to going on long walks, possibly to work off his energy, no doubt to think of his work, and perhaps as a means of escape from work and the cramped conditions at 'Little Orchard'. He walked with Vivien, though she, being much shorter, must have had difficulty in keeping up with his long-legged strides:

> We used to go for tremendous walks, tremendous for me. Graham would work in the mornings in a pathetic little study, rather cold, upstairs . . . Then in the afternoon, he'd go for long walks and sometimes I'd go with him. He's a tremendous walker, and very fast. And I remember his . . . noting snow on a hill or a wonderful tree or something – and I wasn't responsive, and he bent down, and said, 'But you can't see over the hedge.'[7]

Sometimes Greene would go off on his long hops and Vivien would travel by bus or train to his destination, then they would spend the night together in a pub or small hotel and return.

He walked with his literary agent: 'Mrs Higham is coming down for the weekend a fortnight after Easter', he wrote to his mother, 'while I meet her husband at Bicester and we walk home spending a night on the way.'[8] But his favourite walking companion was always Hugh, though in later years it was mostly for visits to secondhand bookshops.* But he was also perfectly happy with his own company and gives the impression of being something of a Wordsworthian solitary. Whenever he had reached a point when he could not continue with a novel, or had completed one, he would go on a tramp: 'After Woodstock I went to Stow-on-the-Wold, a lovely barren little place. The next day I did a long stretch along the top of the Cotswolds of over 20 miles to Tewkesbury, and the next day I went down to Gloucester. I'm rapidly qualifying for the kind of village postman's record of mileage, not counting short strolls, I've walked 127 miles this month,' he told his mother.[9]

*

* Alas not now, since Sir Hugh died in 1987.

He had taken the risk of giving up a secure and promising career with *The Times*; the risk of accepting a salary from his publishers on the understanding that he would produce saleable novels; the risk, financially forced on him, of removing himself from the London literary scene and into the country. He was to take yet another but more inexplicable risk.

In 1930 he had begun writing the biography of John Wilmot, the second Earl of Rochester, who was born on 10 April 1647 and died at the age of thirty-three. Wilmot was a dissolute courtier at the Restoration court of Charles II, a lecher and a drunk, but also a poet who could treat himself and his world with satiric coolness and who helped to establish the tradition of English satiric verse and assisted Dryden in the writing of *Marriage-à-la-Mode*. He anticipated Swift in his 'Satyr Against Mankind' with its scathing denunciation of rationalism and optimism, contrasting human perfidy and the instinctive wisdom of the animal world. He wrote to his friend Henry Savile: 'Most human affairs are carried on at the same nonsensical rate which makes me . . . think it a fault to laugh at the monkey we have here, when I compare his condition with mankind.' He was to turn to Catholicism and make a death-bed repentance.

In a pencilled note to his mother on 24 September 1930, Greene wrote: 'I did a little work at the Bodleian on the Earl of Rochester.' He had started *Rumour at Nightfall* and was awaiting the publication of *The Name of Action*. In a letter to Hugh from the British Museum, undated, but probably written about November 15th, he said: 'I hope by Christmas that I shall be better off & able to give you two [presents] in one [it was Hugh's birthday]. You find me, as it were, deeply engaged working on my *magnum opus* "Strephon": The Life of the Second Earl of Rochester: – that is to say I am waiting in patience while half a dozen books of varying shades of indecency are brought to me. I've forgotten my ink so I can't go on with my third novel – now 1/7th done!'[10]

His commitment to the research involved was serious: even while he was revising the first draft of *Rumour at Nightfall* he was working on the biography. He wrote to Vivien from the British Museum in early June 1931, again waiting for books to be brought to him: 'I'm going to Le Million this evening, rewarding myself for several minor discoveries here this morning', and ended his short note: 'There are a pile of books coming down the aisle to me, so goodbye, darling angel.'

He was within walking distance (for him) from Chipping Campden to Rochester's birthplace and place of burial, and in the same June he set off: 'I went off walking Wednesday and Thursday, spending

Wednesday at Chipping Norton and visiting Spelsbury, where the Rochesters are buried and Adderbury where his country house remains.' He was following the route taken by the Parliamentary Army during the Civil War – 'over the final ridge of the Cotswolds, to Chipping Norton', and his personal experience of this journey appears in the opening of his biography – 'the level wash of fields . . . divided by grey walls, lapping round the small church and rising to the height of the gravestones in a foam of nettles before dwindling out against the black rise of Wychwood. A row of almshouses . . . an ancient stone shaped like a hawk in the middle of a field, innumerable heads of dandelions sparkling like points of dew in the sun – these are all that are likely to catch a traveller's attention. In the church vault the Rochester family is obscurely buried.'[11]

He visited Hinchingbrook House, home of the Earls of Sandwich, one of whom had married one of Rochester's daughters. 'A lovely house with a terrible Victorian front door; a beautiful garden terrace exactly as in Pepys' day.' He spent the night there and met the Earl: 'When I drove up two footmen and a butler to receive me, but no water laid on in the bedrooms. The Earl much younger than I'd expected – at any rate in appearance 50 at most; strong trace of Rochester blood in the extraordinarily heavy eyelids & rather protuberant eyes.'[12]

The proofs of *Rumour at Nightfall* arrived in August 1931, and he hurried through them, hoping that Heinemann would publish the novel in September, but it was to be October or November. Waiting, he worked on the Rochester biography, suffering from hay fever and asthma: 'It's very asthmatic this year, making it impossible to breathe deep,' he wrote to his mother. 'Could you let me have the names of those papers one burns at night?' But he worked on, doing his 500 words a day until he had finished the Rochester biography. It was to be rejected.

Long afterwards, in *A Sort of Life*, but still with a hint of bitterness he wrote: 'I had wasted time and effort on a life of Lord Rochester which Heinemann had without hesitation turned down, and I was too uncertain of myself to send it elsewhere.'[13] The biography, he concluded, was 'one of the follies which dot the landscapes of a novelist's life as much as an architect's.' But he was surely wrong. Of course it was quixotic to write it then, and it is difficult to judge why Greene at this crucial point in his life, as a comparatively unknown, comparatively unsuccessful novelist, should switch from the art of the novel to that of biography, which depends hugely on historical and literary research. Heinemann and Doubleday were waiting for a novel and the 'Great Scheme' had not been hatched for

Greene to become a biographer. The biography was not 'a folly' in terms of the quality of the work, in spite of being completed at a gallop. It is indeed an excellent short life, and when it was finally published forty-three years later in 1974, Greene made no substantial changes, keeping only those he would have made at proof stage in 1932. Moreover, the biography is a much more sophisticated and professional production than the three self-conscious novels he had written prior to it. There is nothing amateurish about it.

Why did Heinemann so summarily reject it? One reason must be that they already suspected that *Rumour at Nightfall* would be a failure and that they could do little with a biography from an author who had failed with his last two novels. They would also have been aware that, in those days, the general public might well have been scared off by Rochester's reputation as a pornographer. Nor would an academic audience be won over since the information Greene was able to provide on Rochester remained, inevitably, thin. There must also have been the fear that an action for obscenity might well have been brought against author and publishers, mild though the biography might seem to us now. He was warned about this by a friend he made at that time, John Hayward, editor of the *Penguin Book of Verse*, editorial director of *Book Collector* and editor of the Nonesuch *Rochester*, to whom he wrote from Campden on 12 October 1931, enthusiastic about his research: 'Did you look through the Sackville Papers in the Record Office? I was thinking of examining them. Do you know what old Lady Rochester's connection with Aylesbury was? I am interested as the father hid there after the failure of the "start".' (This was the failure of an insurrection against Cromwell, when Rochester's father, the first Earl, was forced to hide at Aylesbury, and then flee from an inn into the night leaving his baggage behind.) Hayward's advice to Greene was that he should bear in mind that if a charge of obscenity was brought against him over the Rochester biography, it might possibly be extended to include Hayward, whose text he had used, and his publishers.[14]

His friendship with Hayward developed only after the Second World War, but what we know of it reveals a very sympathetic aspect of Greene's character. In an article written on the death of John Hayward in 1965, he recalled their first meeting when Hayward, although a year younger than he, already had a reputation as a scholar, whereas Greene 'was established nowhere at all, yet he received me generously . . . I had no previous experience in writing a biography, and as a novelist I had as yet produced only three bad novels and one popular novel.'[15]

If his surviving first letter to Hayward approximately dates their meeting, he had not at that time even produced 'one popular novel', for *Rumour at Nightfall* (not to be popular) was still in proof stage and he was three months away from starting his 'one popular novel', *Stamboul Train*. But he must have greatly appreciated Hayward's friendship at a time when he had had failures, was living in the country, as poor as a church mouse, far away from London.

Hayward was physically ugly and badly crippled, but his condition only brought out a deep sympathy in Greene and a desire to defend him: 'That powerful head ugly? that twist of the half paralysed arm, as the agile hand seized a cup or procured itself a cigarette? the wicked intelligence of the eyes? A cripple, yes, but there are few men I can remember with greater vitality . . . I am sure no man in London in his day was a repository of more intimate confessions.'[16]

Because Hayward's only sexual satisfaction could be in the mind, Greene would send him 'dirty postcards' from every part of the world, recognising that there were 'few men with a greater appreciation of physical love'.[17] A typical example is a card which Greene sent in 1963, two years before Hayward's death. A shocked nurse and doctor are standing over an anaesthetised patient, the nurse with scissors in her hand: 'But Nurse,' says the doctor, 'I said remove his spectacles!'*

It is likely that scholastic, philosophical and literary drives, plus a fascination with Rochester's life and character, pushed him into writing this biography. It could also have been another way of escape from the writing of unsuccessful novels of the imaginative kind into the factual world of research, and from the monetary troubles and rustic life of Chipping Campden. Letters to Vivien when he was working in the British Museum suggest another way of escape – it was not all research.

One is dated simply 'Sat 5.30 The British Museum': 'I'm spending to-night with Tooter. He has a bed free and we are meeting at 6.30 for cocktails and a cinema. I do wish it was you and not him. I miss you so very, very much.' By Tuesday of the following week he had 'finished off the whole of the museum work, including Sodom. Quite fruitful. This afternoon I spent at the Record Office, a terrible place, enabling myself to see the Sackville Papers to-morrow morning.'

* In the following example the passage is treated as if it were a direct quotation from George Eliot's *The Mill on the Floss*: 'Mrs Glegg has doubtless the glossiest drawers and crispest brown curls in her drawers, as well as curls in various degrees of fuzzy laxness.'
We can see how cleverly Greene has turned the original into a salacious parody: 'Mrs Glegg had on her fuzziest front, and garments which appeared to have had a recent resurrection from rather a creasy form of burial; a costume selected with the high moral purpose of instilling perfect humility into Bessy and her children.'

Then he admits: 'I had a mild blind with Tooter on Saturday and on Sunday after Mass he drove me down to the Bridgewater Arms and we walked about round Ivinghoe. Then I went off to Battersea to Aunt N's. Last night I took her to Antoine's and the "Blue Express" afterwards. I wished all the time that it was you.'

*

Heinemann's rejection of his well-crafted biography must have been a terrible blow to the Greenes, but worse was to follow when the reviews of *Rumour at Nightfall* began to appear. The *New Statesman and Nation* said: 'Mr Graham Greene . . . has . . . a good story to tell. But he is so resolutely and laboriously romantic that one can believe scarcely a word he says. The (psychological) drama is dressed up in all the colours of carnival; the emotions of his characters are largely theatrical; he achieves definition of falsification.'[18] The American *The Nation* was puzzled: 'Mr Greene's mysticism, however, is so often akin to mystification that it is difficult to say just where the truth ends and the false begins.'[19]

There was not much difference in what the *New Republic* had to say on 27 April 1932: 'These characters stagger under the overwhelming weight of their own mental questionings and probings . . . Mr Greene's forte is his ability to cover places and objects with atmosphere laid on heavily, like paint', and the *Spectator*, the magazine for which Greene was later to do much of his best reviewing, commented that Mr Greene was, 'one of those authors who have something to say but whose turgidity prevents them from saying it'.[20]

The critics' response to *The Name of Action* and *Rumour at Nightfall* was justified. Both are juvenile novels of escape. In *The Name of Action* Greene is still inhabiting a boyhood world, reminiscent of Anthony Hope's romantic Ruritania. And his style lacks directness, being dogged by absurd images. In *The Name of Action*, 'a revolver drooped like a parched flower to the pavement.' In *Rumour at Nightfall*: 'The small drift of papers lay like winter between them, across the blown petals of the carpet.' Somewhere Greene has written, 'No one is born a bad writer', but if we had only these two novels we might be justified in thinking him mistaken. The trouble with *Rumour at Nightfall* is that it is worse than *The Name of Action*, the melodrama being pitched higher.

Many years later, in *Ways of Escape* (1980), he could himself look critically at the weaknesses of his early work: 'All is vague, shadowy, out of focus . . . There are far too many adjectives and too much explanation of motive, no trust in the reader's understanding and overlong description. The dialogue is ambiguous and . . . has to be explained to the reader. I find "he thought" ten times in ten pages.'[21]

In fact, he had not yet found his true vision and voice, but at the time he defended himself to his mother, 'Reviewers as usual are intent on blaming one for failing in doing something one has carefully and on purpose evaded.' Even if the result was bad he would appear to have had something in mind, with the action seen from the point of view of two characters who are fairly identical, and all readers of Conrad will recognise *his* influence again.

One reviewer, Frank Swinnerton, for whom Greene had little respect, nevertheless 'opened [his] eyes to [his] fool's progress . . . I knew the truth when I read it.'[22] That acknowledgment, however, came much later in *A Sort of Life*: the review was published in the *Evening News* on 20 November 1931.

Just before Swinnerton died he wrote: 'As to Graham Greene, I never met him: but have been told that he attributes to something I wrote a change in his manner of writing which has brought fame and fortune – not very gratefully, I fear.'[23] Swinnerton's assessment of the novel was clear-cut: 'Its setting is Carlist Spain; its characters are three in number; its story a simple triangle; and its mysteriousness infinite . . . Mr Greene's [characters] spend their time in hinting. You would think they concealed a difficult profundity . . . [Their] actions are . . . simple; their talk seems to belong to another world. It is the incongruity that baffles the reader. Not one of these people can give a plain answer to a plain question. Their tongues jump heavily into irrelevance. They are not so much evasive as gravely incomprehensible, even to one another.'

Greene was learning his lesson the hard way, and at a time when he was desperately short of money. In the middle of 1931, he told Hugh that his proposal of a walk together up the Moselle would be just unadulterated heaven, but he could not see how he could afford even a ten shilling excursion ticket to Southend. Near the end of the year he enclosed no present when sending Hugh birthday wishes, offering intead a choice: 'bread now, jam later. A. a book now up to the value of 10/6d or B. a cheque next month for £1.'

*

If 1931 was the worst year of Graham's life creatively and financially, what was it like for his brothers, Hugh, Herbert and Raymond?

Hugh was in his final year at Merton College, Oxford; Herbert, the black sheep of the family, truly a drifter unable to hold down any job for long, was living in Crowborough with (and on) his mother and retired father; but Raymond, three years Graham's senior, was reaching a pinnacle of popular fame.

From April to September 1931 Raymond Greene was hardly ever out of the news and his climb to fame could be followed in *The Times*. Raymond was a brilliant medical doctor but climbing was his life-long passion and that year, along with at least two other well known mountaineers, F. S. Smythe (an old Berkhamstedian and leader of the expedition) and Eric Shipton, set out to conquer the Himalayan mountain, Kamet. Raymond went as physician to the expedition and he also intended to carry out experiments on the effects on the human frame of low pressures and the lack of oxygen in high altitudes.

Curiously, there is little comment about Raymond's exploits in Greene's letters to his mother. In one undated letter (probably 13 September 1931) he does write of Raymond's success, and after Raymond's return he asked her to give him his love and congratulations: it is rather perfunctory and he makes no reference to the expedition during the months it was making headlines. His diary records that he skimmed through Smythe's book on the expedition for references to Raymond and noted that there were a lot of close-ups of him in the documentary film, but he must have felt strongly the contrast between his brother's success and what he saw as his own considerable failure: his Kamet, he must have felt, was insurmountable. And although they belonged to a close-knit family, Graham had always been closer to Hugh, feeling that Raymond was too snobbish, had too little time for the underdog, was too proper, too popular – and too successful. It cannot have helped that Raymond, after his latest success, returned to England from Paris by plane, an avant-garde thing to do then.

*

Greene recorded in his diary on 14 July 1932 that he had gone to a swimming baths that day, but expresses his dislike for the exercise because there is nothing to do but swim, but he goes on: 'Perhaps it dates back to what I suffered in the baths at school, not physical suffering . . . but mental, when I was alone, except for an older boy still, called Dunkerley, in being unable to swim.' His fear of being picked on extended into his adult years when he visited a circus at Chipping Campden with Vivien: 'There was only one other person in the ringside seats and I was a little oppressed with the fear of that unfeeling and unanswerable humour which makes the comic man so often pick out the conspicuous for his jokes. But we were left alone.'[24]

When Graham had returned to Berkhamsted after psychoanalysis his sense of competitiveness had increased, especially between Raymond and himself, and this seems to have in some degree directed the course of their lives:

I used to have an absurd competition complex with Raymond. Raymond used to write and publish in the School Magazine, and win school prizes for verse. So I had to write too, I never succeeded in winning any prizes for verse, but then . . . I began to make money on it, so I felt one up there.

R. had the same sense he confessed once, and stopped writing verse directly I began to get mine published, and his was much more promising. Then his new tack became adventure, and he became a first class mountaineer. That worried me, and so I started on my Irish and then my German stunt, and he parried with Aleister Crowley and Sicily . . . and then he got into the [Oxford University Mountaineering] Club and edited Oxford Mountaineering. I parried the last with the [Oxford] Outlook but his mountaineering was a thorn. You see I always had a sense that he might get killed doing it, and call me a very final 'blast' in the adventure line, so it was that, as well as boredom, that made me take up the revolver trick [Russian roulette]. It was very satisfactory the first time, though I felt in no end of a funk. I felt, even though he didn't know it, I'd got to a more exciting sensation than he ever had. But then, after I'd done it at pretty long intervals, five times, it was no longer fearfully exciting, and I felt the only fair way was to meet him on his own ground, and so last Easter vac. I'd meant to go up to the Lakes with him and begin to learn climbing, then just before that vac. came I met you, and I was no longer interested in the ridiculous competition . . . Of course it wasn't so consciously reasoned as this.[25]

Perhaps he was right, though the termination comes too pat as a compliment to Vivien at the beginning of their relationship. He told his mother, soon after Raymond's first wife had left him, that in his view Raymond was 'badly warped by his last years at school and it made him extraordinarily difficult', but when they went on holiday together to Burgundy, after the separation, he admitted that he had never before liked Raymond as much as on this trip but this was because the failure of his marriage 'had brought down his defences and he was himself'. His sympathy could go out to Raymond because he had been left on his own in Oxford to continue his medical practice in a town of knitting gossips: 'It's rotten for him to be left to have his bones picked by them and listen to the obscene whispers'.[26]

*

'In those days at Campden', Vivien recalled, 'we were very frightfully poor . . . I had pocket money 10 shillings a week and that was for clothes and stamps – everything. And Graham was getting more and more depressed for you see he was always in debt to his publisher and it was the debt he had himself willingly arranged. That was the terrible time, very depressing, the feeling that he was not making any headway and his books weren't selling.' Expenses had to be meticulously noted; the mantles for the paraffin lamps, for example, were very fragile and if broken cost half-a-crown each to replace: 'But it was a good period. It was before we had children and we were very wrapped up in each other, and struggled together . . . It was very idyllic in a way.'[27]

Their personal difficulties took place against the setting of the 'thread-bare thirties'[28] at the time of the great depression which began with the collapse of Wall Street in October 1929, and was repeated throughout the western world. This loss of confidence caused foreign funds to be withdrawn from European countries, including Britain – gold was leaving the country at a rate of £2 million a day.

To cope with the crisis a National Government was formed under the leadership of Ramsay MacDonald. On 11 September 1931, his Chancellor of the Exchequer, Philip Snowden, introduced an emergency bill, which, among other measures, included a 10 per cent cut in the pay of government employees, and in the dole for the unemployed. Snowden suspended the gold standard and at once the pound sterling found its true level at 70 per cent of its gold value. The results were an increase in unemployment and the creation of distressed areas with, in some cases, the whole population of some villages being on the dole.

Perhaps the fact that King George took a 10 per cent cut in his income inspired the conversation between Greene and a railway porter on Budget Day, 11 September 1931, which he recorded in a letter to his mother:

What an awful Budget! One really feels that someone ought to have been hanged on a lamp post. Dialogue with a porter at a minute country halt near here:
Porter: They do say as 'ow George [The King] may be going like Alphonso's gone. [In 1931, King Alfonso XIII left Spain rather than face civil war and street demonstrations.]
Self: O, well, I suppose he'll be quite glad to retire.
Porter: Ah, but where to?
Self: To his country house at Sandringham, perhaps.
Porter: (Mysteriously): Perhaps 'e'd go where 'is dog went.
Self: ?
Porter: Six feet under ground!

'Quite good for a country halt, is it not?'[29]

His mother's objections to the porter's remarks must have touched a sensitive nerve, for Greene's response, stemming no doubt from his own financial difficulties, was quite explosive:

No, I don't say that I agree with the porter. What I object to is the politicians' cant about patriotism. Both Conservatives and Socialists having by their ever criminal muddle landed us in a mess, they appeal to our patriotism to get them and ourselves out of it. I feel that floodlights should be turned on the once applauded quotation: 'Patriotism is not enough.' Economy too is not going to be more than a temporary expedient; these taxes will lead to less expenditure by people, less trade, and we shall be in a worse hole* than ever in two or three years. My only remedy is for all whose work can be done anywhere in the world to naturalise themselves as subjects of King Zog of Albania,† live five months a year only in England (so as not to be liable to income tax), four months in France (for the same reason) and three months in Germany! Thus escaping all direct taxation. It's time that we formed an Honourable Order of Rats to escape from this peculiarly useless, unaesthetic, disagreeably run and obviously sinking ship. Up with the flag of Albania and God save King Zog! One contemplates a choice of interesting and beautiful names – Rafechvitch Pzzchuygl or perhaps Thurchygl Ig. Of course one's *nom de plume* would be Graham Greene.[30]

The new government's increase in income tax must have increased Greene's anger, for, in Vivien's view, they were really 'terribly poor, certainly much poorer than anyone of our own social equality. The rent was £50 a year,'[31] though they could afford a servant, but this was traditional and no middle-class family then was without one, though it might mean going without certain essentials. Even so, they were forced to take the cheapest part-timer on the market – a certain Miss Greenall from a 'pathetic family', Vivien told me, 'illegitimate and the father lived with his daughters. Dreadful.'[32]

Down-at-heel though villages like Chipping Campden were, they were better able to survive the depression than town communities –

* In his excitement Greene made a spelling error – he wrote 'Whole' not 'hole'.

† Zog I was king of Albania, 1928–39. His personal name was Ahmed Bey Zogu. He was ousted by Mussolini, on the eve of the Second World War, and went into exile. He hoped to return after the war but a Communist regime was established under Enver Hoxha in 1945. Zog died in 1961.

they could at least grow their own vegetables. Vivien's journal kept during the summer of 1932 gives us an impression of village life:

> Greenall said this morning 'We had a long day yesterday. Up at four o'clock pea picking, then round to Mrs Huish and then here and then to Mrs H. again, and in the afternoon currant picking – two pots, that's 1/8d, and in the evening we did washing and then we filled up the copper and then we boiled blackcurrants for jam till 11 at night. There wasn't a bit of dinner in the house – not a scrap of bread, so we had to turn to, all of us.' Her father is a sweep, drawing unemployment pay, which is about to cease.

A gardener called Buckland when hungry would eat snails:

> 'Between Christmas and March I reckon on two or three feeds. You see that scum (tipping up the snail) well they feeds on that all winter and it gets hard as hard and after March they begin travelling. So if you cook 'em after Christmas the water they've been boiled in is green – o all green, and green as you could wish and that's all herbs you see – all good. That water's good for coughs, consumption too.'

Vivien continued in her journal: '*We* don't know how we shall live in a month's time: *they* don't know how they'll live in a week's time.' And her comments about class differences are shrewd:

> Greenall's brother is unemployed but somehow manages to keep a huge silver-plated motorbicycle wreathed with tubes when there isn't any food in the house; and we buy books instead of winter underclothes. It is a hold on life because luxuries are a sort of hostage to promise that the time will come when we won't be sick with worry over ways and means and rent and taxes and will have the peace of mind to enjoy them. Everything is clouded by a dull discomfort that changes imperceptibly into real pain.

As he became more successful, Greene's inherent vulnerability decreased and he became more certain of himself and more aloof. At Chipping Campden, and presumably throughout their courtship and marriage, Vivien, by her own account, tried to make him more relaxed and responsive. The Greenes were, she said, 'A very cool family. I never noticed any great affection between them. I can never imagine any child sitting on his mother's knee, being told a story or anything like that. They were not demonstrative . . . As a family they were awfully locked up and I think it was because they didn't have petting as children.' Vivien's strategy was to 'teach Graham everything about being demonstrative. Warm hugs of friendliness or blowing kisses or things like that.' It was she who invented their games, and their number code and the stars which proliferate their letters: 'Stars are kisses. White stars and red stars. A red star is much more passionate than a white one. The most passionate kiss on paper would be enormous with rays coming out and dark with ink.'

Because of her love of cats, Vivien brought them actively into their language: 'I've always used cat terminology. I've always been very devoted to the whole cat tribe so I'd sign myself Whiskerspuss, or Pussy, or Pusskins, or Puzzuck meaning wife. And Graham often called himself Tom or Tiger or Tyg, Tig, Wuff or even Wufth.'[33] One of his letters ends: 'Goodnight Pussina Minnow of Wuffles.'

Naturally, their Pekinese was drawn into this fantasy: 'When we were at Chipping Campden, I used to tie a letter to our Pekinese's collar – we called him Pekoe . . . because he was tea-coloured – and send it to Graham if I was in the garden and Graham in his study. Pekoe would turn up some time or other and sometimes there would be a toffee attached to his collar. There were other games.'

Some of these letters written in the spring of 1931 are still in Vivien's possession. One of hers, presumably written in the garden, reads:

Honoured Sir,

Just a short note as the Postman is waiting. I am well and longing for the return of my Husband from prison, from which I hope he will be released at the end of next month [from his study, presumably when he had completed his novel]. I can see his prison as I write – pleasant stone structure with one window open. Well, I miss him, love him very very much. I am getting Lord Sandwich* to frank this for me.

Your loving and obliged humble 'Ook
PER PEKOE POST

Written on the obverse and tucked into the dog's collar, Greene's reply was:

Honoured Madame,

In case you starve while your devoted husband is away I send you one toffee. Please suck it in memory of your devoted admirer.

* Lord Sandwich, 1718–92, was Postmaster General in 1768.

They ignored the name of their cottage at Chipping Campden and called it, between themselves, 'the Country basket' or 'Cat's Campden'. On her twenty-sixth birthday (1931), Greene gave his wife a first edition of one of his books and wrote her a letter at thirty minutes past midnight, no doubt when she was asleep, from the 'Cat's Basket':

> Lovely and adored Pussina Love-Cat, I do so love you and hope that you'll have a happy birthday. There ought to be piles of 'Orient pearls and Indian sand' heaped at your paws, scents from the south, raw gums from the West. But there is only a rather solid book with all my love and devotion.
>
> I love you so much – four times as much, he added with exactitude, as last week, recalling [what follows are four white stars. Presumably this note was also to be carried 'per Pekoe post']: The Peke has just been caught red-padded:

> One may speak of a First Edition
> at an exorbitant price,
> an ancient Pot (Phoenician),
> Performing Mice,★
> Or a Morning Star,
> a pedigree Colly,
> or a Ziegfeld Folly†
> (Naked or near,
> of a vintage year);
> What I prefer,
> when all is said,
> is the deep soft fur
> of a Cat in a double bed.

Although he must at that time have been deeply worried about his work and his prospects, according to Vivien they were happy. 'We had a gramophone which wound up. We had "Pacific 231" – a wonderful record it seemed to us then – a Pacific train engine. And one record, "Walk to the Paradise Garden", we played a good deal. It was very sweet and nice . . . it was that sort of atmosphere – very tender and happy and there was a good deal of intimacy, or as much',

---

★ The 'performing mouse' appeared one day in their kitchen cupboard, eating their breakfast cereal and staring at them completely without fear.

† Florenz Ziegfeld, 1869–1932, the American theatre manager, perfected the American revue spectacle. His *Follies*, based on the Folies Bergère, was established in 1907, an annual production until 1931. His name was synonymous with extravagant theatrical productions.

she added, 'as any writer, or come to that mathematician, or come to that any musician can have. There is always something he keeps back. I think any creative person has got to – where is the creation coming from unless it's something very deep inside themselves which they don't share with anyone?'

Vivien often returned, when talking to me of their life, to their use of cat language:

V.G.: You see I had to teach Graham to be frivolous and take things light-heartedly and I'm very fond of tigers, always have been and am still. I've a great scrapbook which I made of cutouts of tigers from newspapers. I belong to the Protection of Tigers League because now there are so few left in the world. I'm devoted to cats because they are the only people that we can meet so to speak socially. We can't meet tigers socially and the cats are the next best thing because they are the wildest of domesticated animals and the tiger is the least domesticated. It is the ultimate in the wildness and the non-human and mysterious.

N.S.: Is Graham the cat or the tiger?

V.G.: That is the extraordinary thing that has only just struck me – perhaps that was a quite unconscious understanding of his undomestic nature. That he was the wildest of creatures and the least domesticated. Our language was a kind of domesticating the undomesticated creature, but a pretty impossible task I think.[34]

Apart from walking to rid himself of tension and worry, like his father before him Greene took to chess. The Greenes became friends with Herbert Finberg, a convert to Catholicism. He had started the Alcuin Press in the High Street, Campden, doing fine printing, and was very musical. He would come in most nights and play chess with Greene, sometimes play gramophone records – the gramophone being wound up for every record – staying until midnight. Greene's 1932–33 diary often records Finberg's visits: 'played three games of chess after dinner with Benito.* Played very badly and lost all.'[35]

*

In spite of the influence on him of Swinnerton's review, the blast

---

* Finberg admired Benito Mussolini and Greene gave him his nickname. In 1932 Mussolini was still widely respected because he increased the efficiency of the Italians. After the invasion of Abyssinia, Mussolini's reputation abroad diminished.

of criticism directed at *Rumour at Nightfall*, and the fact that, the sales of his first novel reached 8,000 and those of his third only 1,200, Greene did not for some time recognise where he was going wrong. Reading Henry James's preface to *The Wings of the Dove*, in the bath one afternoon, he was so struck by one passage that he copied it into his diary. It says much for his percipience that he was able to extract a kernel from James's 'nut', but less for his percipience in that it almost confirmed him in the error of his ways. James's theory was that the writer (speaking of course for himself) should establish 'centres', points of view each commanding part of the main subject, so that they would create 'solid blocks of wrought material, squared to the sharp edge, as to have weight and mass and carrying power; to make for construction, that is, to conduce to effect and to provide for beauty.'

Greene seized on this concept, applying it to *Rumour at Nightfall*: 'Solid blocks – that was my aim in *Rumour at Nightfall*; I had sacrificed too much before to the single point of view. The fault of *Rumour* was the thinness of the final block, but I still think it was a fine attempt.'[36] He resolved that the next novel after *Stamboul Train* (then being written) would be accorded the 'solid block' technique. It was to be about a brother (a fraudulent medium) and his uncorrupted sister and there would be 'a solid block for the medium, a solid block for his lieutenant, and then a block again for the medium: the sister seen only through their eyes [shades of Eulelia, the heroine of *Rumour at Nightfall*] but she must share the honours fairly with her brother; indeed in the second part she must play him off the stage.'

Fascinated by the concept of these 'blocks' he rounded on *Stamboul Train* because of its lack of them: 'My dissatisfaction with the present [novel] is that it is not built at all in blocks; it is fluid.' He did not then recognise that this 'fluidity' was to be for him, to quote another Jamesian pronouncement, 'the very note and trick, the strange irregular rhythm of life, that is the attempt whose strenuous force keeps Fiction upon her feet.' It was not until well after the publication of *Stamboul Train*, when he was reviewing fiction in the *Spectator* and had become utterly opposed to novelists who wrote as he once did, that he commented: 'A few years later I would be attacking Charles Morgan, like a reformed rake, for the sin I had abandoned.'[37] And he records in *A Sort of Life* another important revelation: 'Discrimination in one's words is certainly required, but not love of one's words – that is a form of self-love, a fatal love which leads a young writer to . . . excesses.[38]

He says elsewhere that it takes 'years of brooding and of guilt, of self-criticism and of self-justification, to clear from the eyes the haze of hopes and dreams and false ambitions.' That is well said, but it did not take Graham Greene years – only months – to recognise what was wrong with his two failed novels. Discovering how he turned himself round makes a fascinating subject for an enquiry.

28

Stamboul Train/Orient Express

I have travelled so much because travel has enabled me
to arrive at unknown places within my clouded self.
— LAURENS VAN DER POST

S TAMBOUL TRAIN was a landmark in Graham Greene's career as a
novelist, for in writing it he discovered his true talent – his ability
to observe. Strangely, he has had some harsh things to say about this
novel, condemning it not only for its 'fluidity' and lack of 'blocks'
but also admitting that he has never been able to re-read it: 'The
pages are too laden by the anxieties of the time and the sense of
failure.' The latter comment is understandable, the former is not, for
he drew on some of his deepest pleasures as well as his despairs in
writing it. Taken altogether they helped him to produce a prototype,
ultimately to be perfected, for his later fiction.

The 'fluidity' of *Stamboul Train* derived naturally from the fact that
its setting was a train journey and there can be few things more fluid
than that. The railways were the most popular means of travel at the
time, and involved a sense of community with fellow passengers and
casual encounters with strangers that today's isolation in private cars
excludes. From his childhood, train journeys had been part of the
excitement of holidays and visits to relatives and were later to be a
significant aspect of his courtship of Vivien. Trains took him to her
and from her and some of his most brilliant and revealing letters to
her were written on trains. A train journey to visit her put him into
a time capsule when, in a closed environment, he could observe,
anonymously, his travelling companions and their eccentricities. Cut
off from his current problems he could extend his experience of other
people's lives, and have the excitement, the suspense, yet the surety
of meeting her at the end of the journey. A train journey, for him,
therefore, though not then recognised, involved all the necessary
ingredients of a novel: travel, adventure, suspense and final climax.
Train journeys reflected every aspect of life.

'The lunches I've most enjoyed', he wrote to Vivien, 'are the ones in the restaurant car coming to you. Looking out of the window, and watching the country fly past, and then a distant straight line of hedge, with telegraph poles above, like giraffes nibbling at the clouds, straight on and on towards Oxford.'[1] In January 1930, when he was in the middle of *Name of Action*, he took a train journey to Germany: 'Going I spent the night in the train between Ostend and Cologne. After Cologne, where I changed, the sun rose just as the train came alongside the Rhine, the water becoming the colour of this page. There was also a ruined castle on a hill at the exact psychological moment, the whole affair being too like a stage back cloth for words.'[2] In another train letter he writes: 'The man opposite me, who's just got in, is tearing his railway ticket into little tiny bits. Does he know what he's doing? What will happen at Willesden when the inspector comes round? . . . He's thrown the scraps of ticket under the seat. Is it an old one merely? He's very red in the face and elderly and picks his teeth with a safety pin. Perhaps he's going to have an apoplectic fit.'[3] And trains could have an image of luxury missing from his life then: 'On number one platform there was an express for Fishguard with a long restaurant car with beautiful shiny white linen and the glitter of glass. I wanted badly to be with you, off to catch the Fishguard–Waterford boat [to Ireland].' It is hardly surprising that one of Vivien's and Graham's favourite records was, as she said, Honegger's 'Pacific 231', with its insistent sound of the wheels of a train, which was the background to his writing of *Stamboul Train*.

But it was not until he had finished *Rumour at Nightfall* that the idea for a 'train' novel took shape. On 8 May 1931 he wrote to his mother: 'I've been bitten by a sudden desire for "furrin' parts" and have written to La Compagnie Internationale des Wagons Lits, saying that I am planning a novel for next year in which the whole of the action will take place on their Orient Express, Ostend to Constantinople, and will they let me have a return ticket for next month. It would be tremendous fun if they did.' Which suggests a good deal of enterprise and 'cheek' on his part. The Orient Express, which made its first trip in 1883, was looked upon, during its long life, as the 'King of Trains and the Train of Kings' and in the 1920s was christened 'The Magic Carpet of the East'. And it was unlikely that a fairly unknown novelist would be granted the privilege he was asking for: 'A German company', he wrote to his mother, 'would do it like a shot, but I'm doubtful of the French.'

He was right. The French explained that they were forbidden by their charter with the railway companies to give free passes. Since he could not afford to pay for the whole journey to Constantinople, he bought a third class ticket for the Orient Express to Cologne, or so he tells us in *Ways of Escape*: 'The reader will probably notice more details on this first stretch of the line than I had the confidence to include later, for as I sat at my third class window I made notes all through the daylight hours, and you may be sure the allotments outside Bruges were just where I placed them in April 1931.'[4] In support of this there is an undated letter to Vivien which describes a train journey to Cologne, bringing up the question of travelling third or second class:

We left Dover at 4 and got to Ostend at 7.30. The train doesn't go till 9.30. The sight of the third class carriages and the thought of a night journey made me go all of a heap. So I've come second! So much for my resolutions. But I *will* come back third.

Lovely coffee at Cologne and a lovely journey from there. The sunrise began just as the train came down to the Rhine and shone into the water and behind a great hill with a ruined castle on top . . . I had a peck of supper here and I've eaten all the jam rolls, but the chocolate I preserve till to-night. There was only about 30 people on the boat, and there are about five people in the train, none in my carriage, so far touch wood.[5]

Vivien had put up sandwiches for him, and in this way saved the expense of spending eight shillings on meals.

*

There were very strong pressures on him then to write a 'pot boiler' with the deliberate intention of appealing to the popular reading public, a novel which, with luck, might be made into a film.[6] He had a further six months on the Heinemann payroll, after which he would be on his own. By the time he began writing *Stamboul Train* on 2 January 1932, he had been thoroughly thumped by the critics, and had had his Rochester biography rejected, and while he was writing the novel further attacks were made on *Rumour at Nightfall* when it was published in America.

Something of his feelings at this time would seem to have contributed to the character of Dr Czinner in *Stamboul Train*, the first typical self-destructive, tormented character he created. Given his lack of success and his poverty he must have felt a stranger in his own country, as was Dr Czinner, and he was angry because of his poverty – 'someone ought to have been hanged on a lamp post!' What Dr Czinner saw as being wrong with society was what Greene saw as being wrong with British society in the 1930s and was what the socialists saw as being wrong. Czinner's criticisms reflect the clichés of the day heard in the Labour Party, in working men's clubs, in lecture halls and on street corners where the unemployed gathered: 'when the poor were starved and the rich were not happier for it; when the thief might be punished or rewarded with titles; when wheat was burned in Canada and coffee in Brazil, and the poor in his own country had no money for bread and froze to death in unheated rooms.'[7]

Knowing he is to be sentenced to death, Czinner makes a futile speech to which no one listens – the last testament of a good Communist:

> he became conscious of the artificiality of his words which did not bear witness to the great love and the great hate driving him on. Sad and beautiful faces, thin from bad food, old before their time, resigned to despair, passed through his mind; they were people he had known, whom he had attended and failed to save. The world was in chaos to leave so much nobility unused, while the great financiers and the soldiers prospered. He said, 'You are employed to bolster up an old world which is full of injustice and muddle . . . You are paid to defend the only system which would protect men like him. You put the small thief in prison, but the big thief lives in a palace.[8]

Czinner must have derived from Greene's beliefs at that time, for his diary shows that he was then reading the works of socialist philosophers: John Strachey's *The Coming Struggle for Power* and G. D. H. Cole's *The Intelligent Man's Guide Through World Chaos*. The diary also reveals that he was feeling particularly vulnerable then in a capitalist society and was seeking in socialism a solution to his personal problems.

On 12 June 1932, after he had completed a large part of *Stamboul Train*, he went to Oxford to see his two brothers. While there he learnt that Raymond had won a research fellowship and, with his usual watchfulness over his own motives, he questioned whether his great and genuine pleasure over this was quite so disinterested or was he taking it as a sign that good fortune had not quite deserted the Greene family?

The Oxford University Film Society, of which his brother Hugh was the first president, put on a showing of Feodor Ozep's *The Crime of Dmitri Karamazov*, which they went to see, and he was much taken with the female star, Anna Sten, and a gipsy song: 'Mellowed by beer, the beauty of Anna Sten and the ride of Dmitri to the gipsy inn and Grushenka's song brought tears to my eyes.' Because he suddenly saw Anna Sten as the type of heroine for his next novel, large portions of it came to him, and he felt happy. This must have been the last indication of his attachment to the romantic in fiction. After a party given by Hugh and the manager of the cinema following the film, he had a bad night, 'because I had talked foolishly to an undergraduate about the chances of a new Marxist party!'

Yet his 'bad night' could not have been too severe since the next day found him arguing with Raymond and Abernethy (Raymond's partner in the practice) about 'the capital levy and the Marxist state' and giving a good account of himself.

These were side issues in his struggle to become a successful novelist, which, though he perhaps did not recognise it then, meant that he had to turn from romanticism to realism, from being a fairly sloppy historical novelist to one able to write with force and point about his own times. The necessity to earn money was there, driving him towards the popular: but finding his individual voice took him into a more devious route.

His own account seems to be entirely wrong. He has argued in *A Sort of Life* that there was no spark of life in *The Name of Action* or *Rumour at Nightfall* because there was nothing of himself in them. He had been so determined not to write the typical autobiographical novels of a beginner that he had gone too far in the opposite direction. He had removed himself altogether: 'All that was left in the heavy pages of [*Rumour at Nightfall*] was the distorted ghost of Conrad.'[9]

But in fact Greene was the self-conscious, young, romantic hero of his early novels, the middle-class hero in style and standards – Andrews in *The Man Within*, Oliver Chant in *Name of Action* and Michael Crane in *Rumour at Nightfall*. There is too much self-love, too little self-criticism in these early portraits of pleasant, anguished young men built up from Greene's own notion of himself as a young man romantically caught in the toils of love.

Conrad is there of course – and the worst of Conrad – what Greene once called 'bastard Conradese tortuosity'. He would not again, in the guise of a young hero, give an indulgent and romantic account of himself.

*

Greene's journey towards his goal can be traced in his reviews for the *Spectator* which began, along with the start of *Stamboul Train*, in 1932: in them, bowling at (what had previously been his wicket) the other team's wicket, he works towards a conclusion about the kind of novel he must write.

The first appeared on 23 January 1932, a review of Norman

Collins's *The Facts of Fiction* of which only one phrase met with his approval – 'his [D. H. Lawrence's] books are essentially the expression of one rat in the trap' – a reflection of Greene's own feelings at that time. And when he writes of 'the horde of introspective novels which have enabled their authors to soliloquize on the particular slings and arrows offending them', he has his own early work in mind: 'These are novels of escape: delicious daydreams in which the writer is enabled to utter all his complaints and bafflements aloud . . . But Andrew Cather [hero of Conrad Aiken's *Great Circle*] is not a mask for the author.'[10] No character in *Stamboul Train* is a mask for its author either.

The necessity of the author's keeping his distance from his characters, not making the novel a vehicle for the projection of himself, is a recurrent theme in his reviews. Of a G. B. Stern novel he comments: 'Endless natural but unnecessary dialogue, one completely ridiculous incident; long natural descriptions which are not seen through the characters' eyes, nor are they of dramatic significance, simply the wallowing of the author in remembered scenes.' The emphasis comes down on objectivity and discipline. In his diary he wrote, 'An author should keep his own likings, whether for scenery or architecture or books, out of a story; he should avoid describing anything of which he is himself passionately fond, because he will be unable to subdue it to a character's view; the author will obtrude and take the [character's] elbow as obviously as if the first person were used.' He adds, 'Women are especially prone to this.'[11]

He expressed the same opinion, slightly differently but with the same firmness, a year and a half later when he was reviewing Yvonne Cloud's *Mediterranean Blues* and J. D. Beresford's *The Camberwell Miracle*. In the review, he rightly praises Miss Cloud and criticises Mr Beresford. He saw one of Miss Cloud's most admirable qualities as 'her detachment from her characters; she regards them all from the same distance.' Personal attachment by an author to one of his characters 'introduces into the reader's mind emotions ruinous to his receptivity'. He cites the example of Soames in Galsworthy's *The Forsyte Saga*: 'The reader's agreement, or failure to agree, with the author over the question whether Soames was nice to know became more important than the theme or the treatment of the whole book.' And Beresford had such admiration for the character of the faith-healer in his book that the novel became 'a dramatized essay on faith-healing, and his admiration had to be shared "against all probability" by every other character.'[12]

As in no previous novel of his, detachment operates in *Stamboul Train*: there is also a tightening of technique and style, a rejection of turgidity and a movement towards his later characteristics: brevity and an unromantic view of life. Suddenly, in his late twenties, he appears to have matured as a man and a novelist, and an extraordinary change in perspective has taken place. In *A Sort of Life* he offers no explanation for the change, only pointing to two disparate aspects of his nature that existed while he was writing *Rumour at Nightfall*, revealed on the one hand in its 'sentimental cardboard figures' of his fancy and on the other in the careful notes he was making in his diary about the people he met every day, 'between the muddy lane where [he] lived and the Live and Let Live Inn'. Yet he was 'content to pursue [his] romantic and derivative tale to its disastrous conclusion'.[13]

He is being wise after the event here, for by the time he began keeping his diary with its observations of those around him (it runs from 3 June 1932 to 13 August 1933) *Rumour at Nightfall* was published and *Stamboul Train* was well advanced. We can only conclude that failure was the spur that turned him from romanticism to a cynical realism in *Stamboul Train* and that turnabout later led to an equally cynical and realistic view of the life around him. Like Mabel Warren, that appalling female journalist in *Stamboul Train*, he takes up an unemotional, observational stance: 'There wasn't a suicide, a murdered woman, a raped child who had stirred her to the smallest emotion; she was an artist to examine critically, to watch, to listen; the tears were for paper.'[14] 'There is a splinter of ice in the heart of a writer,' he later wrote, 'I watched and listened'.[15] This is what he had at last taught himself to do.

*

There are still echoes of his own experiences. Dr Czinner obviously derived from one of the itinerant teachers his father was forced to employ during the war, 'facing a desert of pitch-pine desks, row on row of malicious faces', remembering 'the times when he had felt round his heart the . . . spurts of disguised laughter threatening his livelihood, for a master who could not keep order must eventually be dismissed'.[16] Czinner is given, also without emotional overtones, Greene's own religious experience – 'crouched in chapel at a service in which the living man had never believed, asking God with the breathing discordant multitude to dismiss him with His blessing'.*[17]

All kinds of scraps of his own experiences are put to use in this new, realistic novel (by using only scraps there was less pressure to draw on his whole nature as a character), for example Myatt carries examples of raisins from his commercial rivals and tests them compulsively (an echo from Greene's schooldays) and as Greene moved on his train journey from third to second class, so the chorus girl,

* See page 255.

Coral Musker, moves from third class to Myatt's first class compartment. She also, like Greene, had brought sandwiches with her to save 'about eight shillings';[18] and her experience of life in Nottingham is based on his – 'the electric signs flashing and changing over the theatre in Nottingham High Street . . . the passage of porters and paper-boys, recalled for a moment the goose market and to the memory of the market she clung.'[19]

One other influence helped to make *Stamboul Train* his first realistic novel – the cinema: his hope was that the film rights would be sold. After going through the typescript six times he concluded that it was 'too incredibly purposeless for words. A mug's game. I'd rather produce a film.' In his first article on film, published in *The Times* in 1928, he stated 'words are a clumsy, unmalleable material. Of the loveliest sonnet only the outline was formed in rapture, the rest had to be carved with toil', and he gives an example of the film's power by referring to the work of Erich von Stroheim in the 1923 film 'Greed': 'Erich von Stroheim . . . seized one image and conveyed infinitely more passion. The scene was a rainy day at a seaside "resort". The lovers were shown only as two backs, receding down a long breakwater, on each side a leaden sea and a lashing rain, which failed to disturb their complete self-absorption.'

In the same article Graham recalls an early 1923 Chaplin film (which Chaplin wrote and directed but did not appear in) where the characters are the images of despair and fatalism:

A girl, deserted by her lover, stands on a village platform at midnight waiting in vain. The Paris express, in which they were to have gone together, draws into the station, but we do not see the train. Only across her still face the shadows of the windows pass and then stay still. There are no tears, no sub-titles and no movement save of shadows.

His interest in films was professional – he wanted to learn. As early as 1928, as we have seen, he had joined a London Film Society in the hope of being able to take part in the production of films.[20] Films were his passion from an early age. He recalls seeing *Sophy of Kravonia*, his first film, at the age of twelve and retaining 'an enchanting vision of a flapping riding habit, an imperious switch, mountains, rebel guns rumbling across the keys of a single Brighton piano up the pass'.

In *Stamboul Train*, and more so in *It's a Battlefield*, he took up the technique of the camera with its ability to suggest emotion, character and drama, visually, economically, and to determine the pace of the drama. A 1949 story, 'All but Empty', refers to his habit of visiting the cinema in the afternoon when they were all but empty in order to watch critically the way a film was put together.

Almost any extract from *Stamboul Train* will show how Greene parallels the use of the camera. To take one at random:

> The fire-hole door opened and the blaze and the heat of the furnace for a moment emerged. The driver turned the regulator full open, and the footplate shook with the weight of the coaches. Presently the engine settled smoothly to its work, the driver brought the cut-off back, and the last of the sun came out as the train passed through Bruges, the regulator closed, coasting with little steam. The sunset lit up tall dripping walls, alleys with stagnant water radiant for a moment with liquid light. Somewhere within the dingy casing lay the ancient city, like a notorious jewel, too stared at, talked of, trafficked over. Then a wilderness of allotments opened through the steam, sometimes the monotony broken by tall ugly villas, facing every way, decorated with coloured tiles, which now absorbed the evening. The sparks from the express became visible, like hordes of scarlet beetles tempted into the air by night; they fell and smouldered by the track, touched leaves and twigs and cabbage-stalks and turned to soot. A girl riding a cart-horse lifted her face and laughed; on the bank beside the line a man and woman lay embraced. Then darkness fell outside and passengers through the glass could see only the transparent reflection of their own features.[21]

In 1951 Greene, reviewing Eric Ambler's *Judgment on Deltchev*, describes what the cinema had taught Ambler: 'The cinema has taught him speed and clarity, the revealing gesture. When he generalizes it is as though a camera were taking a panning shot and drawing evidence from face after face.'[22] This is what it also taught Greene. It is the influence of the cinema which led him to reduce the characters to two in order to highlight a scene. In his diary he writes: 'I think I've got some significance into the barn scene, I hope not too obviously, but I'm afraid it's not really strong enough to carry the whole book, which must remain a rather pointless adventure story.'[23]

This is the scene where Dr Czinner (is this a homophone for sinner?) is dying, his only companion the chorus girl Coral Musker. Almost fifty years later in *Ways of Escape* Greene explains what he was trying to do in such scenes.

He tells us that in those days he thought in terms of a key scene and that he would even chart its position on a sheet of paper before he began to write: '"Chapter 3. So-and-so comes alive." Often those scenes depended on the isolating of two characters – hiding in a railway shed in *Stamboul Train*, in an empty house in *A Gun For Sale*.' It was as though, he tells us, he wanted to escape from 'the vast liquidity of the novel and to play out the most important situation on a narrow stage', where he could direct every movement of his characters. 'A scene like that halts the progress of the novel with dramatic emphasis, just as in a film a close-up makes the moving picture momentarily pause.' He could watch himself following this method even in as late a novel as *The Comedians*, and though he had long ago abandoned using a sheet of paper, if he had used it he would have written 'Scene: Cemetery. Jones and Brown come alive.' The logical climax of the method appears in *The Honorary Consul*: 'where almost the whole story is contained in the hut in which the kidnappers have hidden their victim.'[24]

He had been working on *Stamboul Train* for about two and a half months when his publishers delivered a bombshell. His yearly sum of £650 from them was to be cut. He wrote to his mother: 'V. and I are going up to town for one night in order to be at an "Anti-Depression Party" given by Heinemann's and Doubleday's. It will be our last extravagance for some time, as from April until the delivery of the new MS. [*Stamboul Train*] I'm being cut to £400 a year.'[25] To his brother Hugh he had admitted how things were financially: 'Frankly, we are on the verge of bankruptcy, and we had someone to stay last week, whom we didn't want to see nearly as much as you, and we can't afford to put you up for four nights; we have been toying since we lost £250 a year to make p.g.'s [paying guests] the rule at 2/6d a night, but it's difficult. *Do come for two nights*, if you can manage to stay a day longer at Crowborough and go to R[aymond] a day earlier. One can manage two nights without increasing housekeeping.'[26]

Apart from writing daily, he joined Vivien in doing competitions in newspapers: 'Owing to the financial situation I have been bitten by the competition craze. I went in for an essay competition in the Everyman, prize a holiday to Leningrad.' Twenty days later, on 23 June 1932, he reported in his diary: 'No prize for me for Leningrad essay or for V. for Quebec essay.' He also failed to win £100 in a *Daily Mail* competition. Then he began to think seriously of finding an academic post abroad through the influence of Edmund Blunden.

Blunden visited him at Chipping Campden and Greene liked him immensely. They had a cold lunch: cold sausages and ham, bread and cheese, and beer, cider, parsnip and cowslip wine. Greene's friend Fred Hart, a retired naval commander, usually brought him cowslip wine and often took Vivien to antique shows (Vivien was a passionate collector in the making but unable, at this time, to buy). While Graham worked daily on his novel, the beautifully mannered old sailor would call for Vivien – 'Convinced', wrote Graham in his diary, 'more than ever that Fred Hart is in love with V., a trying position for an elderly, old-fashioned and terribly upright man.'

He found Blunden quiet, humble and shy and to his surprise discovered that Blunden's strongest urge was a desire to help people: 'He insisted on lending Hugh his fare to get a train back to Oxford: apropos of my fall in sales he said with complete ingenuousness: "I must see whether the Book Society can help you."' Moreover, he offered to write to Professor Sito in Tokyo on Greene's behalf to get him a job in case Heinemann ceased to support him financially after 1 August when the money was scheduled to stop.[27]

During the last financially depressing six months of 1932, his attacks of asthma became more frequent. On the first day of July he had a very bad night: 'High wind and rain. Woke up at 4.30 terribly asthmatic.' The following day his diary reads, 'Every night now I wake up in the early morning with asthma.'

To his mother on 3 July 1932 he wrote: 'My hay fever has been very bad; not so much in the eyes or nose as asthma. I slept well last night for about the first time for a week and it's a bit better today. I don't go out at all except to Mass. I've practically finished "Express", and am leaving the last few pages till my hay fever is better.'

*

His 'sea-change' from romanticism to realism had its reverberations in his married life, and we can begin to see this in his diary record of what he and Vivien did in Chipping Campden on Vivien's twenty-seventh birthday, which fell on a Bank Holiday. He describes their visit to the local swimming baths to watch rural celebrations – races, climbing up a greasy pole, and diving: 'All the Campden worthies looking on, and Mr Jones, the retired police inspector and local councillor, short, fat, straw-hatted, went round among the nubile, swelling forms with entrance lists and a pipe.' The scene reminded Graham of Aldous Huxley's *Crome Yellow*, in which the character Mrs Wimbush, based on the hostess Lady Ottoline Morrell, spent time watching through field glasses the villagers bathing in the lake in her park.

Later, over tea, birthday presents were given. Vivien received a Victorian mug, a necklace case from Graham's mother, a morning tea set and a beautiful papier-mâché blotter (which had belonged to Vivien's great aunt) from her own mother and from Graham a book on papier mâché – then all the rage. In the evening, in Victorian style,

Graham read aloud George Moore's *A Letter to Rome*. The last sentence of that day's entry ends on a sad note: 'We became a little embittered arguing about Aldous Huxley.'[28]

Obviously the subject of Huxley came up because Graham had been reminded of *Crome Yellow* while watching the swimmers in the baths. But why should they argue about him and could the argument throw light on our understanding of the change taking place in Graham during his last-ditch attempt to write a saleable novel?

In July 1979, Vivien recalled that argument and returned to the image of the splinter of ice in the heart:

> I remember him saying – we were talking about an Aldous Huxley book – and he said something about [Huxley's] wife would have been annoyed. I think she would have been right to be annoyed. Huxley described the death of his child from meningitis, how the eyes become all red, you know, terrible agony through the ears and brain, and Graham said, 'Oh I heard that his wife was absolutely outraged that he should describe all this.' But Graham felt that Huxley had obviously felt it very much and couldn't see why she should have been angry. I remember him approving that and saying 'Yes, that's quite right.'*
>
> He was originally warm and I could make him laugh, that sort of thing – but as he developed into a better novelist the splinter in his heart grew, he became icier. He said writers shouldn't marry and I dare say that's quite true.

From then on everything could be grist to the writer's mill. Nothing was to be sacred, all could be used, because all was in life. A decision of this kind must inevitably bring about a moving away from middle-class taboos for the sake of creation. He knew he would need to surrender himself to actions, judged by his parents' standards, as irresponsible. And it was Greene's allegiance to his art that took him far beyond the restrictive bounds into which he was born. Most writers in their thoughts, actions and writings have to go beyond the

---

* The description of the death of a child by meningitis is in *Point Counter Point*. The detail is graphic – deafness, severe dilation of the pupils, one side of the face paralysed in a crooked grin, the incessant clockwork regularity of the child's screams, and the final violent convulsions before death. Yet it was not his own child that Huxley was describing but that of a dear friend, Lady Naomi Mitchison. The Huxley critic, Kerpal Singh, recalled Lady Naomi saying to him: 'That child was my child, our eldest. We were most upset . . . but I don't believe Aldous did it with the intention to hurt.'

limits of their own class or fail. Graham Greene's face now, in his mid-eighties, is that of one who has seen too much, but perhaps most of all it is the face of one who has been on close terms with his own thoughts, both those that refine and those that corrupt.

In 1935, reviewing Mrs Conrad's book on the life of her husband Joseph Conrad, Greene returned to the argument he had had with Vivien over Aldous Huxley: 'The trouble is that a writer's home, just as much as the world outside, is his raw material. His wife's or a child's sickness.'[29] Necessarily, Greene made use of his own real life and the lives of those close to him (though suitably modified, changed or expanded so as to allow him to retain the secrecy of his sources – and Greene has a developed taste for secrecy) because such material was essential to his fiction.

Necessarily he needed to widen his horizons, and gain knowledge of a larger cross-section of society, a knowledge on which the success of *Stamboul Train* depends. Thus he gradually began to travel in a direction that was to take him far beyond Vivien's settled, middle-class and conventional world, a journey she could not take. His seeking out of the seedy, the sordid, the sexual and the deviant took him in many directions, as his diary shows:

A hot day. In the High Street the workmen remaking the road all stopped work for several minutes to watch a very small Pekinese being raped by a fox terrier. Released after the first *coup*, she flirted her tail and ran coquettishly down the street. When I came out of the bank, work was still interrupted. A black terrier was making a third and was being warned off by the successful lover. There was an air of content on the Pekinese's face. Later I met them again outside the post office. A second *coup* was in progress, and the black terrier was watching. Several very small boys watched and laughed with some secrecy . . . It was the same Pekinese . . . I saw inspected a few days ago by a collie. The collie had to lie down flat on the pavement so as to be able to sniff at her tail.[30]

Eight months later it was two cats:

Returning I saw two cats copulating close to the front door; I have never seen a cat copulating publicly like a dog. Five minutes later I looked out of the window and they were still at it. The female cat with its eyes half closed, giving little whistles of satisfaction, but she became conscious of my stare and broke away and fled to a distant corner where they were soon at it again.[31]

Lafourcade's biography of the poet Swinburne brought to Greene's attention Swinburne's 'sadistic vices', and interested him in the whipping establishment in the Euston Road the poet used to frequent: 'I must remember to look up at the Bodleian "The Whippingham Papers", published anonymously in 1888', he noted.[32] And on being told by Nina Hamnett that a statue of Ezra Pound by Gaudier-Brzeska was refused by the museums because it was in the form of a sexual organ and that it then stood in a back garden in Kensington, he made a note to write to his friend Jim Ede (author of the recently published book, *Savage Messiah*) 'asking its provenance'.[33]

*

The ups and downs in bringing *Stamboul Train* to a conclusion put him under great nervous strain. On 11 June he is cheered and writes in his diary with his usual precision, '1000 words & finished the Subotica chapter. 69,000 odd completed & only one short chapter to go.' 'There's good stuff here' – and he was right.

The next day he spent at Oxford visiting both his brothers, Raymond and Hugh. When he returned to 'Little Orchard', though very tired, he read aloud to Vivien the last part of the Subotica chapter and was depressed by it. He felt he had failed to lift it out of the rank of good thrillers. He was depressed too about the next book he had to write and the chances of Heinemann continuing their contract. Depression continued. Two days later he wrote: 'Very depressed about my work and the future.' The following day (16 June) brought an income tax demand for £60. He had only £30 left in the bank. He was driven in desperation to work and went through the first three parts of the novel for the third time in typescript. The end of the fourth part, which he had tried in vain to rewrite the previous day, came to him. He decided on two possible outcomes for the novel: 'Coral must have a heart attack, which Miss Warren [the lesbian journalist] absorbed in her triumph does not recognise; the other ending with Coral living and going back with Miss W. is a little too factitiously cynical.' But it was this second version that Greene decided to use. His diary entry for the end of June was, 'Very depressed all day with nothing to read.'

On 10 July 1933, he records writing 1,000 words despite a tiring morning in Oxford spent 'in waiting at various points for V . . . My nerves horribly on edge.'

As Greene summoned up his creative energies for the short but fundamental last chapter of *Stamboul Train*, entitled 'Constantinople', he had a curious dream which he found 'half encouraging' and yet he was depressed by it. He dreamt of receiving a copy of a new book from

Heinemann written by himself but printed on bad paper and badly bound with a bad title: 'I opened it and had the sense of strong, firm writing better than anything I had ever done, and was tormented at the thought of its format standing in the way of it being reviewed or read.'

Five days later, while still struggling with the conclusion of *Stamboul Train* and some two weeks away from finishing the novel, he recorded (28 June 1932), 'V. went off walking to Snowshill with Fred Hart and I had tea alone', and he read a few essays in G. K. Chesterton's *Sidelights* but they 'clattered like old machinery' and made him want something deep, quiet and mysterious, so he returned to a novel he had vowed never to read again – Joseph Conrad's *Heart of Darkness*: 'It makes one despair of the book I am finishing, of any book I am now likely to write, but at the same time filled me with longing to write finely. Ideas stirred sluggishly at the bottom of my mind, but not ideas for the novel I had set myself to do after "Express" is finished. I want more than ever to read Heuser's "Inner Journey", hoping for something of this dark pregnant kind.'[34]

On 7 July 1932, his diary records that he read 'to V.' all that he had completed of the Constantinople chapter: 'It read well . . . Ideas for the completion stir.'

What follows is not exactly kept to in the novel but the tone of the ending of the novel is exactly caught:

> The theatre Myatt visits should be near the railway station. In an interval he should suddenly be faced by some phrase, some look, which shows him the inevitability of his marriage to Janet Pardoe [previously companion of Mabel Warren]. It is time for the last train from Subotica. He gives the past one chance over the future, the future wins and he's uncertain whether he is glad or sorry.[35]

Yet he did not rush to complete the novel because he was expecting his literary agent in Chipping Campden: 'I'm waiting to finish "Express" until I hear from David Higham on the subject of Constantinople.' This is a curious diary entry, and when I asked him about it, he wrote: 'I don't know why I wanted to speak to David Higham about Constantinople . . . perhaps I wondered whether he could arrange something which would enable me to visit Constantinople before finishing the book. As it was I had to do it without any knowledge.'[36]

Obviously Higham was not able to arrange anything. But Greene did very well. Having no experience of Stamboul and its station in the old part of Constantinople where his characters were due to end their journey, he switched to the arrival of tourists and travellers, among them his characters Myatt, Janet Pardoe and Savory, at an international hotel 'which has sunk a little in the world'. Myatt takes Janet Pardoe to the more fashionable Pera Palace for dinner and then to a cabaret at the Petits Champs 'near the British Embassy', on the European side of the town. References to places obviously of interest to the tourist are not inappropriate in this novel about travellers – the Blue Mosque, lined with twenty-one thousand blue tiles, the Roman cistern, the fishing boats in the Golden Horn flashing 'like pocket torches'. That familiarity with the native life of his settings, which was to become his trade-mark, came later. But he found one book which helped him to create the background of the city: 'Received from Corbual [?] Libraries *Constantinople: Settings & Traits* by H. G. Dwight. Lovely photographs of Constantinople. It will help me with the theatre and the scenes at evening',[37] and there are references in Dwight's book to St Sophia, the Fire Tower and the long stretch of water up the western side of the Golden Horn, the Pera Palace and the Petits Champs, but not much more.

Perhaps a more important source for him was John Dos Passos's *Orient Express*, which is not a 'train travel book', though it begins with travellers leaving the Channel boat at Ostend, going through customs, having their passports stamped and then boarding the Orient Express: 'I can read the bronze letters on the wet side of the sleeping car . . .' writes Dos Passos. 'A gust of wet air slaps me in the face . . . bringing a smell of varnish and axlegrease.'[38] The weather at Ostend for Greene was also wet, but he did not need to rely on Dos Passos here – he had had his own experience: 'If you're writing of a thing you want to see it with your eyes. You don't want to discuss it with somebody else.'[39] But it is possible that an influence lies in the idea of a novel set on the Orient Express (and *Stamboul Train* was to be entitled *Orient Express* in America)★ and there would seem to be an influence in the scene in the novel in the Petits Champs with its crowded tables, which Myatt and Janet Pardoe visit – a Frenchwoman prances on the stage singing a song about 'Ma Tante', and afterwards a man turns cartwheels and then a troupe of British girls in shorts, called the Dunn Babies, dance and sing, 'Come up here', which encourages some English sailors to clap and one of them to begin pushing his way to the stage between the tables. Turks sit unmoved drinking coffee. Dos Passos stayed at the famous Pera Palace Hotel, visited the Petits Champs, but also a restaurant in the Taxim Garden where he saw an international vaudeville taking place on a stage among the trees:

★ Greene constantly refers to his novel in his diary as *The Express*.

First a Russian lady waves a green handkerchief in a peasant dance
. . . Then two extraordinarily tough English girls in socks and
jumpers . . . One of them croons in a curious bored and jerky
manner as they go through the steps and kicking that shocked
country parsons at the Gaiety when Queen Victoria was a girl.
Then came Greek acrobats . . . a Frenchwoman in black with
operatic arms . . . sings the mad scene from 'Lucia' . . . People
move about the gardens . . . jokes are passed, drinks poured. Three
girls . . . dart into a side path followed by three Italian sailors . . .
youngsters in white suits . . . Elderly Turkish gentlemen . . .
sitting so quiet.[40]

Perhaps this description helped Greene create his Istanbul.

*

Stamboul Train was finished on 17 July. He revised the last chapter
and then went off to London for a break without having submitted
the manuscript to his publishers, perhaps because he was still unsure
of his work. He told Hugh he was going up to town for a day of
business, but it must have been two days, since he wrote an account
of his visit to his mother on 23 July telling her that he had seen, from
the pit of the theatre, *Musical Chairs* and, on the following morning
Tallulah Bankhead in a film called *Thunder Below*, which 'proved to
be pure drivel . . . Do forgive this writing & incoherence 76,000
words in eight months plays havoc with the muscles!'

It was obviously not only a visit for a 'day of business', and because
some passages in his diary for those two days have been torn out, a
certain mystery surrounds them. The first entry for 21 July is: 'Went
to the Herb Shop in North Audley Street & got presents for V.
Looked in at Selfridge's Book Remainders; left bag at Hemming &
Hemming's, had supper (cold lamb & new potatoes & peas, black
currant tart & cream) at Stone's [Chop Shop which was opposite the
Criterion Theatre] with half a pint of Old Burton.' Given the state
of his finances this would be cheap. H. E. Bates recalls in his autobiography being taken to lunch by Greene in 1933, at a place he
had found which was both cheap and excellent: 'that splendidly
Edwardian pub in the heart of London's theatre-land, all brass and
red plush and mirrors and beer engines and snug corners, *The
Salisbury* in St Martin's Lane. Graham, as impecunious as I was, had
discovered with delight that for one-and-ninepence you could get
soup, a large plate of boiled or roast beef, roast lamb or pork, some
sort of pudding or cheese with perfectly magnificent celery. It was
all excellent.'[41]

A second diary entry is missing after his reference to seeing *Musical Chairs*. After seeing *Thunder Below* he had a cocktail at Oddenino's which was in Regent Street; took a bus up Fleet Street to look at the new *Daily Express* offices – 'all black steel and glass'; walked over Waterloo Bridge to a bookshop, but drew a blank; went to another bookshop looking for Edel's *The Prefaces of Henry James* and drew a blank again; had a salmon sandwich and a cup of coffee; picked up his bag from Hemming and Hemming's and reached the motor-coach station with ten minutes to spare. The bus was late arriving at Oxford and he missed his train to Chipping Campden. He went on by bus to Cross Hands: 'My suitcase was light, the late sun picked lovely colours from the great panorama of sky & I was glad to be on the way back to V. with presents I felt sure she would like. The walk flashed by, I bought a bottle of cider at the Volunteer [Inn] to quench my thirst. I felt so happy that even the income tax & rates demand among my letters made no difference.'[42] But what was Greene hiding when he tore out of his diary two entries about his London outing?

*

By 29 July he felt he had done all he could on *Stamboul Train*, but not before revising yet again the first two parts of the novel. On that day he went for a walk: 'I wanted to give V. an empty home to enable her to read through "The Express", I took sandwiches & walked into Evesham the long way (9 miles). I got in at 11.20 & had a pint & a half of beer at the Crown Vaults. Talked to a man in a kind of naval officer's cap (he is employed in the river steamers) . . . Took a bus to Broadway and walked home eating sandwiches on the way.' As usual, at the end of a month, Greene listed his achievements for the period in his diary – 'written 2,200 words of "The Express", and heavily revised it; 1,000 words of "Brandon's Acre" [a novel which has disappeared from Greene's memory; nothing of it survives] did a 750 word review for the Spectator, and so earned £5.' The last day of July was the last day he could expect money from Heinemann, the £450 a year guarantee had ended. He sent in the manuscript of 'The Express' on 4 August. Financially he was at the end of his tether. He wrote in his diary: 'Is my position at its worst? Although I have been given till Sep. 15 to pay the remainder of my income tax, I am to all intents minus about £30 with no guarantee of any money or employment after this month.'[43]

His publisher wrote immediately on receipt of his manuscript: 'Heard from Charles Evans that he would try to read the novel during the week-end. I pray to God that his verdict may be favourable.' On the following day, Sunday 7 August, he and Vivien went to Mass and on returning found on the lawn the daughters of Colonel Bender-Turner, Comfort and Mary, and Rupert Hart-Davis. 'They had walked over from Blockley in tennis shoes and we drank parsnip wine and talked.' Greene was much taken by the company, not least because Rupert Hart-Davis was secretary of the Book Society. Greene reports that 'under the influence of sun and parsnip wine he promised to do his best for me.' Hart-Davis kept his promise.

Greene was without a novel to write. He had worked hard at 'Brandon's Acre' but it petered out. By the middle of August he was at a loose end. He wrote the blurb for his 'Express' novel – and how intelligently Greene summed up his own work – and sent it off. He went for long walks, one of them away from the Cotswolds into Warwickshire. Whatever happened on that occasion – surely something quite minor – he nevertheless felt the need to tear out of his diary half a page.

Also in August the playwright Ronald Mackenzie, author of *Musical Chairs*, was killed in a car accident in France. Greene recorded in his diary: 'Apart from Noël Coward [Mackenzie was] the only dramatist in England with signs of distinction. So fate helps the cinema to destroy the stage, God bless it.' At once he began writing a play entitled 'The Editor Regrets' but noted in his diary: 'I do not expect to finish it',[44] which he did not. He played chess nightly with Benito and one night he went to Benito's to hear Beethoven's *Benedictus* and a song of Brahms, but he ended his diary entry with the note: 'Very depressed about our financial position.'

Greene has always lived on his nerves and his boredom could get to screaming point, according to his wife. His escape was either to go off somewhere or to work.[45] An indication of his almost uncontrollable despair was his totally uncharacteristic losing of his temper with their servant, Nellie Greenall: 'My temper badly upset by finding a piece of trickery on the daily maid's part to get paid extra time for work which should have been done in her regular time. The cheating in pence of people in so bad a financial way as we infuriated me.'[46]

He could not stand any longer the strain of not knowing what his future was to be and he wrote to his publisher thirteen days after sending *Stamboul Train*, asking for a decision. He wrote in his diary: 'The suspense is becoming terrible.'[47]

29

The Book Society and
the J. B. Priestley Affair

*In nature there are neither rewards nor punishments –
there are consequences.*

— ROBERT G. INGERSOLL

W HILE he was waiting for Charles Evans of Heinemann to
respond to his letter, Greene had a visit from a rich Edinburgh
man with whom he had made friends a year earlier when he was
visiting the de Selincourts – he was 'a sweet, cultured and most ugly
Catholic Jew' and he had built 'a most lovely church for Canon
Grey.'[1] His name was André Raffalovitch and he arrived at Chipping
Campden with Canon Grey. One wonders how Greene felt at that
moment since Raffalovitch was the probable source for Eckman in
Stamboul Train, an old Jew who, like Raffalovitch, was a convert to
Christianity and kept 'a chained Bible by his lavatory seat . . . it
advertised to every man and woman who dined in his flat Mr
Eckman's Christianity.'[2]

After his guests left, he went to bed oppressed by what decision
the next day might bring from Heinemann's. He was near breaking
point from anxiety.[3]

*

The next day, directly he was called, he went downstairs and there
'sure enough was a letter from Heinemann's':

I took it half way upstairs & opened it with fingers which really
trembled. I was astonished by the sentences I read: they were too
good, I thought, to be true, & then, O God, what a lightening of
heart. Charles Evans wrote: 'I have read "The Orient Express"
with very much pleasure. It is beyond doubt the best book, as a
whole, which you have written so far, although there is no single

part of it comes up to the best part of "The Man Within". I think it will increase your reputation & everybody will find it easier to read than the last book, for the story is quite enthralling. I wish you could have found a way of bringing that scoundrel Grunlich to justice. This may seem a naïve remark from a blasé old novel reader such as I am, but it will show you that your people have got hold of me.' Although the financial question had still to be decided, I felt so relieved and happy that I went into the church and thanked God.[4]

As he admitted in a further note in his diary: 'The failure of Rumour at Nightfall, the turning down of Rochester, had given me such a conviction that I had proved of no value as a writer that the praise in the letter raised my spirits extraordinarily. Hope was re-born, & a new theme for a novel, more in key with the "Express" than the Spiritualist one [the unfinished 'Brandon's Acre'] leapt to birth.' This was to be *It's a Battlefield*.

Next day reaction set in. What kind of contract would Heinemann's now offer him, given that up to that point his novels had incurred only debts and financially he was at rock bottom? His diary reveals his anxiety:

August 20:
>A reaction from yesterday's relief. Will Heinemann keep me for another year at the same rate as now?

August 24:
>Still no word from Heinemann. I am getting anxious again.

August 25:
>Still nothing from Heinemann.

August 26:
>No news from H. I began to map out the next novel . . . Planning to go for a week to Crowborough from the 1st. This would enable us to get up to town with 5/- half day excursion tickets and me to see Heinemann if necessary.

August 30:
>I woke at about 7 as the postman arrived and went downstairs for the fateful letter which proved a damp squib, Charles Evans merely writing that he had been discussing a new arrangement with Miss Leonard and naming an hour on Thursday for me to see him.

'One ominous day,' as he describes it in *A Sort of Life*,[5] he and Vivien took excursion tickets from Crowborough to London – he to discuss his future with Charles Evans and Doubleday's representative, Mary Leonard, Vivien to do some shopping. He had sandwiches and a Guinness at the Leicester Lounge and then visited a News Cinema (in those days they showed continuous newsreels) and then went on to Heinemann's. 'With Miss Leonard [later Mrs Pritchett], Charles Evans sat on my case,' he wrote in his diary.[6] He recalled that there was some sympathy from Evans but none at all from Miss Leonard. According to *A Sort of Life* she was that day 'a dragon indeed:'

> The interview with Evans and Mary Pritchett proceeded on its dreary course: accounts showing the disastrous sales of the last two books were before them: the typescript of *Stamboul Train* lay on the desk beside the accounts – the third book in the three-year contract which had now come to an end. No further advances would be due to me until another novel was completed. I waited hopelessly while an argument went on between Evans and Mary Pritchett and then the meeting was quickly brought to a close. Heinemann, Evans said, would continue to pay me my three hundred pounds for one more year, but Doubleday would promise nothing beyond two further monthly payments, and in the mean-while they would study the new manuscript. There were several conditions attached even to these payments – another contract for two books with all losses to be recovered by the publishers before any further royalties were paid.[7]

In fact the situation was worse than this since Doubleday made no promise of two further monthly payments then, and the opinion was that there appeared to be little hope of *Stamboul Train* becoming a Book Society Choice because Greene had introduced a lesbian character.[8] He admits in his diary that during the interview he felt close to tears as he realised he might have to write two more novels with no payment for them whatsoever.

The interview over, according to his diary, he 'went up and down Bond Street looking at the whores, had tea at the St James's tea rooms and went to Victoria to meet V. and catch the bus to Crowborough'. But Miss Leonard did write, renewing the financial arrangement for two months while his American publishers considered the possibili-ties of *Stamboul Train*. Graham's diary entry on this occasion has a very Greeneian image: 'Suspense began again like an aching tooth, so that I must be always doing something, going for a walk, blackberrying, playing games, strolling into Crowborough for no real reason, going to a sale.'⁹

'During the following two months, while I was still receiving payment from Doubleday,' he writes in *A Sort of Life*, 'I had to find a job at all costs anywhere. Our country peace was over, and the nights held little sleep.'[10]

Barrington Ward, at *The Times*, 'a cold complacent man, prematurely bald', gave him 'a frozen response', payment for his temerity in leaving the paper in the first place. He tried 'for half-time jobs on Sunday papers with no success'. The editor of the *Catholic Herald* treated him as a cat would a mouse, receiving him first with 'humiliating condescension', then recalling him to say that with his three novels and experience with *The Times* he was too good for the job of sub-editor with them and would never settle down – 'perhaps,' Greene reflected, 'he hadn't liked my name appearing in the same number of the *Spectator* with his own [he had been strategical correspondent]. I had too much pride and too little spirit left to ask him to return my railway fare, and since then I have taken a biased view of Catholic journalism and Catholic humanity.'[11] He felt 'the desolate isolation of defeat, like a casualty left behind and forgotten', but he was cheered by the arrival on 12 September of an old Berkhamstedian called Ratcliffe (whom he had hardly seen since their schooldays) who brought with him a Norwegian poet, Nordahl Grieg, whose brother was publishing *The Man Within* in Oslo, because of its success.

The unexpected arrival of that Norwegian poet, an admirer of his, down that muddy Gloucestershire lane at such a time of depression, was: 'Unaccountable and dreamlike and oddly encouraging. Like the appearance of three crows on a gate he was an omen.'[12] Hearing of Graham's straitened circumstances, he suggested that he should try for a lectureship in Norway (though Greene thought this would not be possible for him), and gave a fascinating picture of Oslo, a town surrounded by forests, the great stoves in the houses, the rather stupid Norwegians drinking heavily, but blindly admiring England. Graham thought that life in Norway would be ideal, 'with its personal freedom, no prudery to react from', and, as he stressed in his diary, something he was not receiving from Heinemann, 'kindly, cultured relations between publisher and writer',[13] for the lack of which he never forgave them.

The Norwegian project came to nothing, but the friendship was kept up through occasional letters and three further meetings. Greene describes Nordahl Grieg's position as a writer in Norway as 'somewhat the same . . . as Saint-Exupéry in France and Stig Dagerman in Sweden – that flavour of promise just fulfilled which comes from an early and mysterious death. Even his death was to prove legendary, so that none will be able to say with any certainty "In this place he died." He was shot down in an air raid over Berlin in 1943.'[14]

Nine days later Greene and Vivien were travelling again to London by bus. It was a Saturday and since the City was deserted at weekends, apart from tourists, it was unlikely that he had gone on business. As usual Vivien went off shopping. Graham's aunt Nora, realising their financial plight, had given Vivien ten shillings. Greene records in his diary: 'With typical tenderness and sacrifice, she insisted on my taking 3/6d to buy a book with. I bought "Daisy Miller", had sandwiches at a pub behind the Palace Theatre, a Guinness at another pub, & strolled about looking for whoever, non existent on a Saturday afternoon, save the dregs of the profession.'

Vivien went home by train but Graham went via Oxford by bus. At Chipping Norton, the lights came on, even though the late sun still shone, and in the High Street he saw a girl from the King's Arms, 'who was so kind the night I was there with Higham and whom I in vain tried to seduce.' Nearly a year had passed since he had seen her and he had forgotten that she was so pretty. He walked to Moreton but was fifteen minutes late for the train and ran back to the High Street for the bus. He was put down at Cross Hands and walked home: 'A beautiful orange sunset over Broadway & lemon-shaped moon glowing above Batsford woods. It was nearly dark and the bats were out when I came into the Watney Lane and the lights in the cottages filled me with content.'[15]

*

The proofs of *Stamboul Train* arrived on 17 September and Greene worked on them for the next ten days, but he was depressed by what he saw as the sentimentality and banality of the novel, what he called its 'staring unreality'. Then he heard from Mary Leonard that 'Hugh Walpole was "delighted" with *Stamboul Train*' – a simple message, but with important implications, for Walpole was not only a writer of best-sellers in the 1930s, but also chairman of the Book Society. The Society, established in 1928, was the brain-child of Arnold Bennett, who enlisted the support of Frere-Reeves (later known simply as Frere), a director of Heinemann who was to replace Charles Evans as Managing Director. Frere asked Walpole if he would agree to be chairman of the Society and Walpole replied that he was 'proud to be asked'.[16] He also said he would love to have a finger in the 'Book of the Month suggestion'. The committee of the Book Society (which had a 10,000 membership) selected one particular book each month, which guaranteed a large sale for the chosen author.

Walpole formed a committee made up of Professor Gordon, and the writers Clemence Dane, Sylvia Lynd, and J. B. Priestley, who was a friend of his. Priestley left the committee early in 1932 and his place was taken by Edmund Blunden. So that, of the committee, the chairman admired *Stamboul Train*, Edmund Blunden was a close friend of Hugh Greene and had met Graham, Clemence Dane had done her best to get *The Name of Action* chosen earlier, and the secretary, Rupert Hart-Davis, was also a friend of Graham. Hart-Davis wrote to tell him there was 'hope that *Stamboul Train* will be the December choice of the Book Society'. J. B. Priestley, no longer able to influence the committee's decision, was to review *Stamboul Train* harshly.

Greene had himself, earlier, taken a sceptical look at the Book Society's choices. Reviewing Casanova's life and Lieutenant Maglic's account of his escape from an Italian prison, which he preferred, he commented: 'But Time is as arbitrary in its choice as the Book Society, and Lieutenant Maglic's story will probably be forgotten at the end of the publishing season. Casanova has been chosen.'[17] And he thought little of another of their choices, Margaret Irwin's *Royal Flush*: 'The past swims into the characters' minds just at the wrong time when the present would really be absorbing.'[18] Nevertheless he did not object to *Stamboul Train* being a possible choice, since the suggestion had already stimulated Doubleday into agreeing future pay arrangements with Heinemann for him.

On 27 September 1932 he wrote in his diary: 'Frere-Reeves hopeful of the Book Society, but I do not dare hope, or rather I hope but do not believe in the actuality of the hope.' There is, though, a happier note in his diary entries, or a more relaxed one: 'V. went over to Stratford. Made myself for the first time bacon and eggs. Did proofs.'[19]

On 7 October 1932, when the Book Society committee was in session, he visited London again, recording in his diary:

Caught the 7.15 to London. Went to Hemming & Hemming's and took a room. Went to the Observer and saw the assistant editor, who promised to bear me in mind when there should be a vacancy on the staff. Found it difficult to forget, but more difficult to hope for anything, that the Book Society might be meeting . . . a sandwich lunch at the Leicester Lounge . . . bus back & to Heinemann's where the atmosphere was very changed from my last visit; once again a favourite author, I had tea with Charlie Evans & heard that the Book Society was in session. Frere-Reeves rang up but found they were meeting in Walpole's [what follows is indecipherable but probably reads 'Walpole's flat'] no news could be got. Went down . . .

The rest of this entry has been torn out, so that we do not know where he 'went down' to, but a second entry curiously for the same date begins:

> . . . then went back to Hemming's to see if there was a message. A telegram in the rack at once caught my eye. I opened it and the first word I saw was 'Congratulations'. It was Rupert telling me that "Stamboul Train" had been chosen for December. I have seldom been more happy than that evening but I behaved with an odd dream-like sobriety – went and had dinner with a bottle of beer at Good Housekeeping, walked about London dreamily for half an hour, finished a poem of which the first two verses had been written about a year before and had a gin and ginger in a pub in Piccadilly while I wrote it down, and then went to the film Mädchen in Uniform, afterwards quietly to bed.

The poem, entitled 'Family Portrait', and very reminiscent of Hardy's 'The Family Face', he sent to the *Spectator*. It was not accepted.

The next day he tramped London from nine in the morning looking for celebratory presents for Vivien and in Church Street found an eighteenth-century whist counter set and a Victorian flower book. He also rang up Rupert Hart-Davis and arranged lunch at Mary Borden's flat. The meeting between Greene and Rupert Hart-Davis must have been very interesting, with many things to be talked over, and some indication of what was discussed is suggested in a letter Greene later wrote to Hugh:

> I was interested to hear about Blunden. But his story doesn't coincide at all, at all, with what Rupert told me of the meeting. According to him Walpole, [Clemence] Dane, [Sylvia] Lynd were firm for it; Gordon strongly opposed it and said it would offend their readers, and then Blunden spoke up rather weakly and said he admired the quality of the writing, but could quite see what Gordon meant. There was a moment of wavering then, but a vote was taken before it had time to grow.[20]

The dedication of *Stamboul Train* is: 'For Vivien with all my love', but the typescript has this dedication: 'For Rupert Hart-Davis/This White Elephant/in affection and gratitude/from Graham Greene.'

After lunch with Hart-Davis, he went to Praed Street and found a second-hand copy of Edith Wharton's *Hudson River Bracketed* – his gift to himself – and a little Victorian notebook for Vivien. The last line of his diary for 8 October was: 'Home & told the great news.'

Speaking of this time, Vivien recalled that with their grant from Heinemann being stopped, or worse, all losses on previous books being deducted, it was a very hard life indeed at Chipping Campden, so that the idea of getting this prize – the Book of the Month – seemed absolutely marvellous. 'I remember Graham being tremendously elated – one of the few times I've seen him really excited and joyful. He was not often elated, no.'[21]

For the next fifty days Greene wrote reviews but did nothing on what he called his Opus V (*It's A Battlefield*). It seemed he couldn't get started. He was, of course, as he records in his diary, 'very tired, after the reaction from constant anxiety.'[22] He was as usual reading widely and perhaps reading with his next book in mind, since it was about a workers' meeting getting out of hand and the murder of a policeman by a gentle bus driver. His wife had bought him Henry James's *Princess Casamassima*, a novel about anarchists and aristocrats in London. He writes in his diary, 14 October: 'Finished "The Princess C." the last sixty pages or so superbly dramatic – the discovery of the body with the wonderful Jacobean phrase – "something dark, something ambiguous, something outstretched".' We have already noted that he was reading G. D. H. Cole's *An Intelligent Man's Guide Through World Chaos*, 'a brilliant and lucid account of an economic situation – from the Socialist standpoint which is the one I wish to understand', he wrote in his diary. He received an unexpected income-tax demand and admits in his diary that he would have been sent 'frantic' if it had not been for the hope the Book Society had raised in him. He had an overdraft at the bank then of £20.

After the excitement of the Book Society meeting, Greene found it impossible to work at Chipping Campden. He planted forty-five wallflowers in the garden; he cleaned with petrol the greasy covers of the Edith Wharton book he had bought. He was in a very nervous state which he described in his diary for 25 October: 'Woke with my nerves wretched. Have been sleeping badly of late. The noise of mice in the thatch, the flutter of moths against the glass, are enough to wake me & keep me awake terrified. V. went into Cheltenham to shop & have her hair waved. I bought Cenasprin & after lunch my nerves rawer than ever from the stupid, stubborn, disobedient behaviour of the dog, took two [tablets] and lay down on my bed & read & slept.'

The next day the nerves in his mouth were so 'wretched' he decided to see a dentist. The dentist did a temporary filling in one tooth but put his general condition down to neuralgia, yet Greene recorded: 'Whatever it was, it was more active than ever this evening, keeping my nerves stretched.' He tried in vain to read J. B. Priestley's novel *Faraway* – 'a piece of sheer impertinence even to his public, so padded and slackly written and childishly constructed.' He did not know that he was occupying J. B. Priestley's mind a great deal at that time and that Priestley would be taking action against him very soon.

On 3 November their Pekinese dog had two fits and by the evening two more. He was foaming through locked jaws and snapping at the air. Greene felt that this was the end.

He gave the dog a bromide and then telephoned the vet to take Pekoe away to destroy him. Greene records his feelings in his diary: 'The bromide worked quickly and he sat and dozed on my knee in the attitude of a Trafalgar square lion, till the vet came. All the hour of waiting I could have cried. The dog's sleep gave me the opportunity to whisper; I could not have talked aloud without my voice breaking. I have always hated sentimentality over dogs and now I am ashamed of my own. V. carried him quite quiet to the vet's car and he went calmly and we back in the dark to a peculiarly empty cottage. We couldn't eat or sit there and went to Audrey's.'[23]

The next day was miserable; they both remembered all the dog's endearing qualities – his begging with waving paws, his frantic rolls on the floor at the word 'die', his cavorting, ball in mouth, and his tremulous whimper when one returned to him after a few hours' absence. Greene was glad the vet had come the same night: 'We could never have parted with a calm Pekoe this morning.'

Incredibly, he was accosted the following day in the square by the local policeman, Sergeant Tonks. The following conversation ensued:

'I was going to come and see you, sir, and ask whether you have a licence for your dog.'

I lamented with upraised hands, 'Alas, Sergeant, the dog is no more. It had to be destroyed. So sad. We are so miserable.'

A long pause and a glance out of his black beady eyes.

'Did you have one, sir?'

'Oh, I've destroyed everything. I don't want to be reminded of the brute. Basket, brushes, everything.'

He moved his enormous bulk away, with a disgusted glance.

'So ends', Greene recorded in his diary, 'a successful 15/- fraud on the government, but I would much rather have Pekoe back.'

434

He was still not writing and still not sleeping: 'Feeling very tired and a little strange. I haven't slept solidly for a week now.' And he was still not writing his new novel. Benito was coming in most nights to play chess: 'Benito came in the evening and beat me twice at chess and kept me up till nearly one arguing about socialism, which resulted for me in a very bad night.' On 27 November, a Sunday, he went to early Mass with Vivien and in the morning made notes for a review for the *Oxford Magazine* of the work of three poets, Lawrence, Blunden and Auden. He records, apparently casually, in his diary that *Stamboul Train* was to appear on 1 December with the Book Society lunch to follow on 2 December. But three days before publication he wrote in his diary: 'My God: I don't know whether to laugh or cry. A wire from Charles [Evans] at 11 to ring him up immediately. I do so. J. B. Priestley threatens to bring a libel action if Stamboul Train is published.'[24] Vivien recalled the arrival of Charles Evans's telegram and Greene going to the telephone box in the square to phone him, since they had no telephone in the house, with no expectation of the bombshell that was to explode, of Greene nearly fainting in the telephone box on being told what was happening, of their fears of a libel suit, payment of damages, etc.: 'It was a dreadful time. Very frightening.' Apparently Priestley had read a review copy of the novel which had been sent to the *Evening Standard*, and had concluded that the popular novelist, Mr Savory, in the novel was based on him.

Speaking to Charles Evans from the phone box in the square at eleven o'clock, Greene suggested that Heinemann should fight the libel action, but Evans made it clear that if they were to lose one of their authors they would much prefer to lose Greene than Priestley. It was laid down that Greene had to share the cost of the changes Priestley required and the changes had to be made immediately from the public telephone box, without time for reflection. After a discussion Evans said that he would talk the changes over with Priestley and that Graham should phone him again at 3.30 p.m. What a despairing time, in the interval, Greene must have spent. Back promptly at the telephone box, he learnt that Priestley wanted references to Dickens, to a pipe, to blunt fingers, to come out. Priestley also objected to the comment, 'sold a hundred thousand copies. Two hundred characters.' An undistinguished piece of dialogue, 'You believe in Dickens, Chaucer, Charles Reade, that sort of thing', had to be altered with 'Shakespeare' inserted instead of 'Dickens'. 'It was almost', wrote Greene afterwards,[25] 'as though Mr Priestley were defending Dickens rather than himself.' Graham wrote to Hugh:

STAMBOUL TRAIN is not appearing till the 8th. On Monday Priestley appeared at Heinemann's and said that if it was published as it stood he would bring an action for libel. He remained adamant and I had a frantic day on the phone arranging for alterations. 1300 copies were all printed and bound and they all have to be unstitched and some pages printed over again.

Yours in exhaustion.

A letter to his mother was more careful – disturbed but not too disturbed: 'I spent all yesterday on the telephone to Heinemann's. Fearful contretemps and all. Priestley had been in and said that if the book was published as it stood, he would bring an action for libel! His family had all recognised him in it, and the fact that neither his publishers nor his friends on the Book Society seemed to have spotted him, did not make him waver . . . Altogether while it has its funny side, yesterday was almost too frantic and exciting. Of course the book doesn't have to be reprinted. They can unsew it and reprint the necessary pages but still . . .'[26] In fact twenty pages had to be reprinted. In his diary he comments that he could have laughed if all his hopes did not rest on *Stamboul Train*, but the experience must have been excoriating what with the shock, the libel threat, Heinemann's attitude to him, the costs involved in making the changes, the delay in publication and certainly the humiliation of having to deal with the situation on the spot, 'the spot' being a public telephone box.

Greene was to deny strongly that Priestley was the model for Savory: 'I had never met Mr Priestley and had been unable to read *The Good Companions* which had brought him immense popularity three years before.'[27] In *Ways of Escape* he repeats that he had never met Priestley, even though one might have anticipated that he would have had some contact with Heinemann's premier author.

Just before leaving London for Chipping Campden, Graham wrote to his mother in an undated letter: 'Did you hear about Heinemann's wonderful "Columbus" party to say fond farewell to J. B. Priestley who is off to America. It was last Monday and altogether lovely. There was about 240 people and champagne flowed continuously, without check, from 4.30, at any rate until we left at about 1.45. By 1. all the waiters were tipsy! It must have cost hundreds of pounds. Lovely refreshments. We enjoyed ourselves immensely.'

It seems likely that the guest of honour would be present, and that therefore Greene would at least have seen him from a distance. Also, he must have heard and read a great deal about Priestley – a letter has survived in which he speaks of Arnot Robertson complaining loudly at a party about Priestley. And although he may not have been able to read Priestley's enormously successful *Good Companions*, we know he had read *Faraway* and held it in contempt. In *Ways of Escape*, moreover, he gives the reasons for Priestley's taking the character of Savory as a portrait of himself: 'I had described Savory as a popular novelist in the manner of Dickens, and Priestley had recently published . . . his novel *The Good Companions*, which led some reviewers to compare him with Dickens',[28] which is why Priestley wanted the Dickens reference taken out.

It would be very natural, at that time, when his promise as a writer seemed to have fizzled out and when his financial problems were great, that Greene should have felt a twinge of jealousy for the Yorkshireman who was such a success without having, in Greene's eyes, any talent, and that he should see him as a target for satire. He records in his diary on 29 June 1932 that he is going through *Stamboul Train* and slightly touching up Mr Savory and adding cockney touches. And he was to argue that for Mr Savory he had had the socialist politician, J. H. Thomas, in mind, 'when I gave him a touch of the cockney', and in giving him a pipe he had in mind Stanley Baldwin, twice Prime Minister then and to have a third term of office. But there is a remark in Greene's diary, so crossed out that it could be deciphered only with difficulty, that suggests he was taking a calculated risk: 'my policy of course is to be perfectly indiscreet'.

Greene was also under the impression that Priestley's friends on the Book Society committee had not recognised him in Mr Savory, though again this is doubtful. Priestley would not have threatened his own publishers (as well as Greene) with a libel case and Heinemann would not have reacted so strongly had there not been some consensus of opinion that Priestley had a case. Indeed, Hugh Walpole, Chairman of the Book Society, would have been very sensitive to such a situation since two years earlier he had found himself being satirised in the character of Alroy Kear in Somerset Maugham's *Cakes and Ale*. According to his diary he: 'Read on with increasing horror. Unmistakable portrait of myself. Never slept.'[29] He phoned his friend Priestley about it and, though Priestley had already spoken to Charles Evans about the similarities, he was able to save Walpole's face by means of a letter from Maugham to himself denying Alroy Kear was based on Walpole, though it was known that he was and Walpole himself knew it. Walpole was not the kind of person to embark on a libel suit, but Priestley, the robust Yorkshireman, was.

*

Uniquely, *Stamboul Train* had not been published before the Book Society lunch honouring its author took place, and Greene is under the impression that he did not attend anyway, but his diary and an undated letter to his mother show that he did and that in spite of the four previous very trying days he was able to cope with it. On 2 December, he and Vivien caught the 7.15 train to London and went to the Regent Palace Hotel, Greene and Vivien soon separating. As usual Graham sold copies of books he had reviewed to Foyle's, this time for 35/-. He then went down Charing Cross Road buying 'two Juveniles [?] for V.' and James's *Roderick Hudson* for himself. Next he went into a news cinema for half an hour, had a quick double whisky and took a taxi to the Park Lane Hotel where the Book Society lunch was being held:

> A huge gathering. Authors & committee sat at the top table so that the members could watch them eat. I was between Mazo de la Roche,* a simple middle aged woman, and Sir Robert Donald, owner of Everyman, a simple elderly man with whom I talked chiefly politics. Professor Gordon, Priestley, Charles Morgan and Walpole spoke. A dull lunch but a certain exaltation in the crowded room, about 400 people.[30]

He wrote to his mother immediately afterwards: 'The dismembered book comes out on Thursday; a week late. Ironically I had to drink the toast to Literature coupled with the name of Mr J. B. Priestley on Friday. I didn't see him except when he rose to speak. It was a gigantic lunch . . . We all had to sit in a row to be stared at by the members. The same atmosphere as the Zoo at feeding time.'[31] The report of the lunch in *The Times* shows that Priestley had Priestley-type things to say – that the standard of reviewing was higher than twenty years ago; that the quality of the writing today was such that reviewers were 'compelled by sheer conscience to praise many more books'; that the present age would probably lack outstanding figures in literature but also had 'a great body of people capable of producing good literature.'[32]

The Priestley affair must have proved to Greene once again how vulnerable he was. Having worked so hard to produce a best-seller, having achieved a coveted award, fate (slightly assisted perhaps by himself) had dashed the cup of success from his lips. His application for a post at Chulalungkorn University, Bangkok, had gone astray

---

* Mazo de la Roche (1885–1961) Canadian novelist who wrote *Jalna* (1927), the first of a series of novels about the Whiteoak family. *Whiteoaks* (1929) was successfully dramatised.

and on 4 January he wrote letters to Kenneth Bell and the famous Sligger, asking for testimonials. That same night he had a dream which gives us some notion of the upset caused by the Priestley business: 'Terribly worried over finances. Feeling tired out. Went to bed at 9.30 & had my first really long night's sleep for months. Dreamed I was in prison. My dreams during the last four weeks have continually reflected crime. One night I dreamed that I had murdered Priestley & was arrested at the Times Book Club & taken away in a Black Maria.'[33]

Greene had his revenge on Priestley through his reviews. Writing of Priestley's undistinguished novel of 1933, *Albert Goes Through* with Lady Eleanor Smith's *Christmas Tree*, he allows Priestley to come out ahead, but in such a way as to belittle both: 'Mr Priestley's gentle satire of the cinema is hardly original; one remembers Mr Elmer Rice's very much more finished *Purdau*; but it is intended for a less sophisticated public. If these novelists feel bound to put on paper caps at Christmas or dress as Santa Claus to amuse their public, I prefer Mr. Priestley's way to Lady Eleanor Smith's.'[34]

And when in his well known autobiography *Midnight on the Desert* Priestley speaks of 'tap-tapping' away at it, 'in the rain and fog of London Streets', and while he is sitting in the desert, curtains drawn, to dull the bright sunlight, Greene dismisses him as follows:

'Tap-tap away': the sound of a typewriter is mesmeric, and I can well believe that a great part of Mr Priestley's work is done under its spell. The huge vague cosmic words pour out: 'cold hell,' 'eternal zero,' 'freezing universe,' 'flashes of lightning into the inmost recesses of the human heart.' Nothing (in spite of the reviewers who call him a reporter) is vividly or exactly rendered: '. . . there are miracles of fire in the sky. Night uncovers two million more stars than you have ever seen before; and the planets are not points but globes.' Tap, tap, tap, out it pours from the machine: graceless sentences: (It is one of Mr Priestley's illusions that he has a 'professional trick of rather easy and pleasant exposition'). Tap, tap, tap: too fast for the elementary courtesy of quoting a contemporary poet correctly: too fast for grace or exactitude: too fast, much too fast for ideas.[35]

A year later, writing on the popular novel, Greene lumps Walpole, Brett Young and Priestley together: 'We are aware of rather crude minds representing no more of contemporary life than is to be got in a holiday snapshot.'[36] The same year, 1938, when *Brighton Rock* appeared, he was still shooting Priestley down, but not so that

Priestley could take him to court, with a reference to 'a well-known popular author [displaying] his plump too famous face in the window of the Royal Albion [Hotel]'.[37] Up to the Second World War Greene was still having a go at Priestley. Admitting that his novel, *Let the People Sing*, was written to appeal to an enormous, mixed audience, he concedes that it would therefore be unfair to complain that the effects are broad, the sentiment lush, and the theme far from subtle – 'if it were not that all his novels seem to have fulfilled the same condition'. As for Priestley's dialogue, its chief function is to cover the paper with so many hundred words – 'long, loose, repetitive, it is tied to the character like the balloons in a caricature, by certain easily recognisable characteristics, which have long ceased to bear any relationship to real people.'[38]

Greene's dislike of Priestley suddenly evaporated after the evacuation of British troops from Dunkirk during the Second World War. At this crucial point in the struggle against Hitler when Britain was up against it and Hitler's army had swept through France, J. B. Priestley came, it was thought by many, to the rescue of the British at this low, disastrous moment of their lives. He began what were to be his famous Sunday evening 'postscripts' on radio, following the nine o'clock news when millions listened. Britain needed the Priestley voice and the Priestley stolidity and Graham Greene made full recompense in his acknowledgment of this in a review entitled 'A Lost Leader':

There were many of us who, before war made such disagreements seem trivial, regarded Mr Priestley with some venom. We felt that as a novelist he represented a false attitude to the crumbling, untidy, depressing world; that he had clothed himself in the rags of a Victorian tradition. He was continually speaking for England and we very much doubted whether *The Good Companions* or *Let the People Sing* represented England at all. Then, after the disaster of Dunkirk, he became a voice: a slow, roughened voice without the French polish of the usual B.B.C. speaker; we had been driven off the Continent of Europe with a shattering loss of men and material: in a few weeks we had watched the enemy obtain what he had failed to win previously after four years of war,* and the voice on Wednesday, June 5th, began to lead the way out of despair: 'Now that it's over, and we can look back on it, doesn't it seem to you to have an inevitable air about it – as if we had turned a page in the history of Britain and seen a chapter headed "Dunkirk"?'

* Presumably during the First World War, 1914–18.

440

Priestley became, Greene tells us, in the months following Dunkirk, a leader second only to Churchill:

> We shall never know how much this country owed to Mr Priestley last summer, but at a time when many writers showed unmistakable signs of panic, Mr Priestley took the lead. When the war is over we may argue again about his merits as a novelist: for those dangerous months, when the Gestapo arrived in Paris, he was unmistakably a great man.[39]

Graham Greene was to learn later in his career how dangerous the libel laws of those days could be to a writer. At least Priestley acted in good faith, but later Greene was to be faced with other libel suits which had little justification.

He recalls that a friend of his was once approached by a solicitor's clerk at the door of his flat with a copy of a novel wherein his friend's name appeared, suggesting that he should institute proceedings. In those days publishers had little zest for fighting: 'They were always prepared to cut their losses and make a small settlement.'[40] Greene was fortunate at the time of publication of *Stamboul Train*, for there was an American girl who could have taken him to court and 'to the cleaners'. In the novel Janet Pardoe is kept by the lesbian journalist Mabel Warren. In 1932 lesbianism was not to be spoken of. He must have been relieved to receive an uncomplaining letter from a 'woman somewhere in Pennsylvania', he told his mother, 'saying that her name is Janet Pardoe: "Am considered rather attractive, as was your character, but, hope not the empty-headed, self-centered, parasitical person your Janet was." '

*

The delayed *Stamboul Train* appeared in the bookshops on 8 December. That day, Vivien gave Graham a recording of Delius's *Walk to the Paradise Garden* which, now that they no longer needed to play on the gramophone Honegger's *Pacific 231*, became their favourite. Then the reviews began to pour in. There was an excellent one in the *Spectator* from L. A. G. Strong (whom Greene was to replace as the fiction reviewer in the following year). Strong had been a friend and an admirer for many years. The *Observer* spoke well of Greene, indeed, in *The Times Literary Supplement* advertisement, under the heading 'LAST MINUTE Choice of Christmas Books', we are told that 'The *Observer* predicts "wide success" for the new novel by the author of *The Man Within*'. The review was written by Gerald Gould, a maker (and breaker) then of reputations, and while

441

the review pleased Greene he noted in his diary: 'a grudging and patronising review'. He was ecstatic about a review in *Time & Tide* which he thought (wrongly) was written by Aldous Huxley: 'To my joy and surprise a glowing review by Aldous Huxley (under the name of Francis Iles).'[41] His spirits were down the next day, but then rose in the afternoon on reading an excellent review by Kate O'Brien in the *Referee*. On 23 December he admits to good reviews pouring in and adds 'the only really bad ones Priestley & Compton Mackenzie'.

But his novel received severe criticism from certain members of the Book Society itself. He and Vivien were staying in London in a flat belonging to Mary Borden. He had invited his agent David Higham and Rupert Hart-Davis to dinner. Rupert told him that a good many copies of *Stamboul Train* were coming back to the Book Society from members. One lady wrote: 'Are none of your members pure in heart?' and another, 'This may be like life, but if it is, I don't want to read about it.'[42] These letters were supported by a review which appeared prematurely in the *Liverpool Post* on 1 December: 'This is an episode which, even if it has any relation to truth, which I doubt, is quite gratuitous in its frankness. Why do novelists indulge in this sort of stuff?' In 1980 an old lady recalled reading *Stamboul Train* on its publication: 'It was a Book Society choice. I thought it was the dirtiest book I had ever read. If you compare it with the modern books – it is quite clean!!'*

By 1930 standards (though not by today's) Greene's novel was sexually explicit and it was this aspect which troubled Professor Gordon, who thought it would offend Book Society readers. And of course there are many scenes of sex, or approaching sex, in the novel: Myatt walking along the corridor of the train observes a man, 'who shared [Coral Musker's] seat, put his hand cautiously on her ankle and moved it very slowly up towards her knee',[43] while she slept; Myatt's dream recalls a previous experience of being with his friend Isaacs in his Bentley, and the seeking of girls, 'shopgirls offering themselves dangerously for a drink at the inn, a fast ride, and the fun of the thing; on the other side of the road, in the dark, on a few seats, the prostitutes sat, shapeless and shabby and old, with their backs to the sandy slopes and the thorn bushes, waiting for a man old and dumb and blind enough to offer them ten shillings.'[44] And in his dream, Myatt sees Coral Musker who wants him, a Jew, and the 'short barbarous enjoyment in the stubble';[45] and poor Coral Musker with her simple, inherited working-class philosophy:

---

* Greene's aunt, Miss Helen Greene, disapproved of *Stamboul Train*, telling Muriel Bradbrook, former Mistress of Girton College, that she felt the need to banish her nephew's photo from her sitting room to a bedroom.

'There's only one thing a man wants' – knowing that 'one never got anything for nothing. Novelists like Ruby M. Ayres might say that chastity was worth more than rubies, but the truth was it was priced at a fur coat or thereabouts.'[46]

But it was probably Miss Warren's passion for Janet Pardoe which disturbed many readers in the 1930s. Mabel Warren with her 'coarse hair, red lips, and obstinately masculine and discordant voice'; ageing, plain Miss Warren, infatuated by Janet who was slim, dark and beautiful. Janet is fed and clothed by Mabel but later, when Mabel sees that she is going to lose her, she begins to look for a possible substitute in Coral Musker: 'Coral in pyjamas mixing a cocktail, Coral asleep in the redecorated and rejuvenated flat.' Perhaps also it was not only the sexual aspects but the cynical nature of most of the characters that caused revulsion.

In the last few lines of the novel, Mr Stein's niece, Janet Pardoe, and Myatt are seen dining together and watching a stage show. Momentarily, Myatt thinks of Coral Musker, a virgin until he had slept with her on the Orient Express, but her face eludes him: 'She was fair, she was thin, but he could not remember her features.'

> Myatt saw Mr Stein pressing his way between the tables, pipe in hand . . . He knew that he only had to lean forward now to ask [Janet] to marry him and he would have arranged far more than his domestic future; he would have bought Mr Stein's business at Mr Stein's figure, and Mr Stein would have a nephew on the board and be satisfied . . . Mr Stein waved his pipe again . . . Myatt said, 'Don't go back to her [Miss Warren]. Stay with me.' . . . She nodded and their hands moved together. He wondered whether Mr Stein had the contract in his pocket.[47]

By Greene's standards his book was not overtly sexual. What would have seemed much more sensual to him would have been a passage from Guy de Maupassant which he transferred to his diary:

> Reading Maupassant's short stories in translation. Some delicious little sexual morsels. Enjoyed particularly 'The Window' where the hero lifted up the petticoat of the lady he is courting & kisses her buttock mistaking her for her maid, leaning out of a window. 'With infinite caution I took hold of the two edges of the petticoat & lifted it quickly. Immediately I recognised, round, fresh, plump and smooth, my mistress's secret face . . .'[48]

Six months previously, the circus had come to Chipping Campden, and Greene, writing of the popularity with low comedians of jokes about the bum, went on to say, 'yet in the case of women it can be the most beautiful & alluring part'.[49]

*

In *Ways of Escape*, Greene writes of the courage and understanding of his wife, 'who never complained of this dangerous cul-de-sac into which I had led her from the safe easy highroad we had been travelling while I remained on *The Times*',[50] but it would seem that the move to Chipping Campden, together with his newly-developed view of the novelist's right – and need – to use his own and others' experience more ruthlessly, sowed the seeds of the break-up of their marriage. They had the ideal Hansel and Gretel existence he had wanted – love in a cottage, what his character Andrews in *The Man Within* had prayed for – a sanctuary, a home (the Cat's basket), isolated, secure. But the reality was an isolated and very rural cottage in an unstimulating environment, far from London, the literary centre; reality was uncomfortable living and smoking paraffin lamps; and their security depended on his efforts and things were going wrong with his plans. Close contact with Vivien in those circumstances seemed to reduce his reverence for her. She was perhaps no longer 'all beauty and all mystery and all wonder'.

30

1933

Writing criticism is to writing fiction as hugging the
shore is to sailing in the open sea.

                                   – JOHN UPDIKE

O N 30 September 1932, while Greene's youngest brother Hugh
was still at University, and his eldest, Herbert, was as usual
out of work, Greene was being shown in the Heinemann offices the
evidence of the disastrous sales of his last two books and told there
would be no further advances and no royalties on further books until
all losses had been recovered. Only the second eldest, Raymond,
seemed on the verge of successfully hunting 'the white stag Fame'
for he was already involved in the preparations for the 1933 Everest
expedition, of which he was to be chief medical officer.

The leader was Ruttledge, but the team of fourteen included men
with whom Raymond had climbed Mount Kamet in 1931: '[F. S.]
Smythe, Binnie and [Eric] Shipton are coming too,' he wrote to his
mother, 'so we still have a Kamet clique.' In spite of working long
hours as a general medical practitioner, Raymond was doing much
physiological work in preparation for Everest, using himself as a
guinea pig in the study of man's acclimatisation to altitude. He
consulted leading physiologists, Haldane, Douglas and Priestley, and
spent many hours in a low-pressure chamber at Oxford, suffering
agonising earache and some days of deafness when a careless
technician 'crashed' him from a simulated 20,000 feet to earth in
a few seconds. He concluded, as a result of his experiments, that no
climber should ascend more than a thousand feet a day and that
there should be a proper acclimatisation stop at each camp. He was
also designing lightweight oxygen equipment. 'Perhaps,' he wrote
to his mother, 'it [the Expedition] will yet save the situation for the
whole family.'

The year 1933, in which his brother Raymond tackled Everest,
was important for Graham too. It had its depressions and financial

difficulties, but it also saw the birth of a first child; above all, it was a time when Greene made significant experiments as a novelist.

January began mildly. By the middle of the month the weather had radically changed, though its harshness did not stop Greene working and walking, as entries in his diary reveal: 'A thin layer of snow when we got up, and a dim yellow light all morning. The sky very heavy with snow . . . Flu very bad, all over the village' (17 January); '500 words after early Mass. Went for a walk after lunch with Tooter but was driven back by a heavy storm' (19 February); '500 words. We had an early lunch and then I went for a ten mile walk, up to the Cross Hands, along the Five Mile Way, down into Blockley and home. On the ridge of the Five Mile Way a snow storm blew up. It was quite terrifying, as the land on either side of the ridge was blotted out by fine grey snow, while the storm raced up behind. But after blinding minutes it was gone, the sun shining, and a blue clear sky. Passed the lake in Northwick Park where Mrs Keiton drowned herself the other day, walking out from one of the council houses in Broad Campden after dark on one of the bitterest nights of a cold month' (21 February).

It was also a year which saw the deaths of a number of famous writers: on 22 January that of the Irish writer George Moore, though his death was not as tragic to Greene as had been those of Conrad (1924), Hardy (1928) and Lawrence (1930); but he noted on 29 January 1933, 'George Saintsbury dead. Galsworthy seriously ill. A big clearance this fluy frosty winter of the old men of letters.'

On 13 January a young man of nineteen, Nigel Dennis, who occasionally visited Chipping Campden where his step-father kept the Noel Arms, called on the Greenes. He was later to become a promising novelist and distinguished reviewer, but at that time was selling women's tweeds and living in a boarding house in Earl's Court where there was also a Russian Admiral and his daughter, a ballet dancer who sold chocolates at the theatre, and a landlady who had known George Moore twenty-five years earlier in Dublin.[1] On the occasion of Greene's seventy-fifth birthday in 1979, Dennis, looking back to his 1933 visit,[2] remembered that 'up the garden walk, came a telegraph boy. The message he brought, in lettering that is still in my mind's eye, was from the *Spectator*: Mr Greene was told that six books were being held for him to review. They would be sent immediately, if he had no objection. I have no idea what happened next. I was dumbfounded which is why the memory has persisted. First, there was the astonishing discovery that a publication should *want* a reviewer (begging letters to literary editors were all I knew about). Second, there was a request for agreement by the reviewer – surely an astonishing courtesy? Third, and most astonishing of all, there was the promise of six books. I could hardly credit such an immense number.' And Nigel Dennis concluded that 'though [he] had read two of Mr Greene's novels, [he] now recognised his stature for the first time.'

Certainly the invitation from Peter Fleming, brother of Ian Fleming and literary editor of the *Spectator*, to review for them (L. A. G. Strong, their usual fiction reviewer, was ill) was an indication of his growing stature in the literary world. He had begun to review for the journal regularly, and two weeks later he was asked whether he would be prepared to review fiction twice a month: 'a new arrangement was being contemplated. This would mean £75 to £130 a year.'[3] 'It's more or less decided now but still a secret', he confided to his mother, 'that I shall do the fiction review once a fortnight at 5 guineas a time with a six months contract. It will be a great help – and there's a possibility that I may also be given the job of film critic at 2 guineas a week.'[4] Greene was to share the fiction reviewing with William Plomer and Bonamy Dobrée. Moreover, *Stamboul Train* was selling well. Charles Evans wrote to him on 6 January that 14,074 copies had been sold – one hundred per day had been sold ever since Christmas. Twenty days later he heard from his friend, Benito (who had been visiting Heinemann's), that the sales had passed the 16,000 mark: 'A wave of prosperity seems to be lifting us up,' he concluded.[5]

Yet his diary does not reflect a sense of success – quite the contrary and for a number of reasons. For one thing, although *Stamboul Train* was selling well, he felt he was facing financial disaster. His records of his earnings show that even when he was reviewing regularly for the *Spectator*, he earned hardly enough to keep the wolf from the door.

Figures for the first six months of 1933 show that during February he wrote 1,900 words of reviews yet earned only £6-6-0. Even this was a great improvement on the previous year when during the months of November and December, he had earned from his reviewing £1-7-0 and £2-14-0 respectively. In March 1933 he earned £1-8-0 and when he began writing two important reviews per month in April his earnings leapt to £15-12-0. For the following three months earnings stayed at 10 guineas, but given his publishers' revised conditions this was not enough. It is not surprising that he should again have begun looking for other sources of income, for more certain jobs than freelance writing.

On 19 January Greene went to London: 'Saw Ernest Manton, news editor of the *Sunday Times*, about a job. He wasn't hopeful. Saw Charles Evans: *Stamboul Train* was doing well, the 15000 turned.

Saw Miss Leonard and tried to see Allen Lane. Decided to apply for Burma [presumably for a post at the University of Rangoon].'⁶ On 23 January he took time off from the novel to send in another application for a job: 'After lunch Captain Cox drove us into Stratford to post my application by air mail to Siam [application for a university post in Bangkok].' Unquestionably Greene felt himself on the margin of failure and his nerves were stretched by the agony of never feeling secure. On 17 March, he wrote:

> £10 from Ivor Nicholson for the James essay; I sent it to the bank for my deposit account; after three years of 5d in it, I have now £17.11.11, £7.11.6 from my surrendered life policy.

Yet he was regularly and successfully reviewing for the *Spectator* until the early 1940s and was a film critic for them from July 1935. In 1940 he succeeded H. E. Bates as literary editor when Bates left for the war, and was himself succeeded by W. J. Turner in 1942. But he was neither aggressive nor conceited: Charles Seaton, librarian at the *Spectator*, wrote in 1977: 'So far as his persona at the office is concerned he is remembered as a "tall, shy figure who got on with his job quietly and without fuss".'

If Graham Greene was well liked at the *Spectator* offices, the editor Wilson Harris was not. H. E. Bates recalled that he appeared to have about as much humanity as a clothes prop. He once told him a slightly risqué joke which was received in frozen silence, 'that would have greeted an incident of indecent exposure in the House of Lords':

> Aloof, cold, ascetic, distant, Wilson Harris appeared to be . . . a kind of bloodless public school headmaster . . . I used to enter his study armed with proofs, books or articles like a small boy tremblingly ready to apologise that he had failed to finish his impositions, do his Latin prep. or unravel the diabolical mysteries of his trigonometry. In consequence I never felt anything but very, very small, very, very inferior, very, very unhappy.⁷

Nor was much love lost between Graham Greene and Wilson Harris. Something of this is shown in his division of the editor's name between two insignificant characters (still living on memories of their minor public school), Wilson and Harris in *The Heart of the Matter*. Greene later recalled their relationship: 'Wilson Harris disliked me very much. He objected to the poems I published . . . He took books away from my office to read at the weekends and I noticed they were always called *Married Love** or some such title.'[8] And Greene makes the point that while his wife drove an ambulance during the blitz Wilson Harris slept out of London to avoid the air-raids. In *The Ministry of Fear*, a Mr Newey has a walk-on part and he also has to get back every evening to Welwyn before the raids start. But by this time, Graham Greene the prankster was beginning to come out of his shell. On the occasion of the 150th anniversary of the *Spectator*, Geoffrey Wheatcroft recalled that not everyone liked Mr Harris: 'When Mr Graham Greene was literary editor he showed his disdain for the editor on his birthday. His present to Harris was what was then known as a rubber article stuffed with Smarties.'

*

In spite of his success as a reviewer he was having trouble with *It's a Battlefield* which, from its conception in the middle of August 1932 to its completion on 4 August 1933, was beset by difficulties in the writing and in his own circumstances. The manuscript of the novel shows that he did not begin writing it until 13 September. Part of the initial difficulty was that he was distracted by hearing that various film companies were interested in *Stamboul Train* and with hopes that his financial troubles might be at an end. Excitedly he wrote to his mother: 'Basil Dean is reading S.T. on the way to New York, another company R.K.O. are interested, and now I hear that there are hopes in New York of the richest company of all, except perhaps Paramount, Metro-Goldwyn-Mayer. There really seems a chance of big money from this book.'[9]

He wrote this after he had returned from his first Spanish holiday, which he took after *Stamboul Train* became the Book Society choice. He stayed at the Hotel Alfonso in Seville and then at the Hotel Atlantica in Cadiz. He visited Toledo, Avila, Gredos, 'a mountain inn 4000 feet up with big log fires'. Within hours of his arrival in Madrid, he went to his first bull fight: 'There were six bulls killed and the first I enjoyed. During the second I suddenly thought I'd faint but I held on.'

He records in his diary: 'Impossible to work during these excitements.'[10] In the month of October 1932 he wrote only 1,000 words of *It's a Battlefield*. In November even this number was reduced – he did no more in thirty days than he normally did in one – 500 words. December was distinctly better. On 5 December, just days before the publication of *Stamboul Train*, he started *It's a Battlefield*

---

* Marie C. Stopes (1880–1958), pioneer advocate of birth control, wrote *Married Love* in 1918. It caused a storm of controversy.

once again: '500 words sweated out for Opus V', and it began to
come more easily once his novel was published, on one occasion
reaching a daily total of 900 words. January was a crucial month:
altogether he wrote that month 8,500 words; the struggle was often
desperate.

By 20 January he was very low. At first it seemed he was depressed
by a minor matter: 'Greenall [the help] ruins my shoes in knocking
a nail down.' But his depression had a more significant source than
a broken shoe: 'No interest in my novel, but 500 words padded
out. Thoroughly stale.' Later that day he began reading Margaret
Kennedy's *A Long Time Ago*: 'a brilliantly able lightweight novel
with an excellent idea. As easy to read as a soufflé is easy to eat. How
I envy her air of ease.'[11] For three days he did his regular stint of 500
words but by 26 January he had to miss another day. He walked to
Evesham, taking his lunch with him. There he got a copy of Anthony
Powell's *Venusberg*: 'a mildly amusing, rather tiresome book in the
Evelyn Waugh manner – caricature and understatement without
Waugh's narrative power.' On the last day of a cold January he
recorded in his diary, '500 difficult stillborn, unsatisfactory words'.
He struggled on, but when it was hopeless he went for a long walk,
sometimes on his own, sometimes with Vivien: 'Took a day off
work, and V. and I went by train to Adelstrop and then walked to
the Rollick Stones. Snow still on the uplands. Ate our lunch under
a hedge.'[12]

He kept on working during January, February and March. March
was particularly difficult – he wrote no more than 4,500 words that
month (normally he would write 4,500 words in 9 days). On 9 March
he writes in his diary: 'An extreme reluctance to work, but hammered
out 500.' He missed the following day but things were little better
on 11 March: '500 words ground out.' A week later he records: 'The
brain absolutely dead, impossible to write, so I shall give myself a
few days holiday.' He gave himself two days, did a further 500 words
but the following day he was writing: '500 very unsatisfactory words.
It's no good. I've got to have a holiday.'[13] Vivien and he went to
London, but before going, they received a telegram from Frere
Reeves asking whether he would take at least £150 for serial rights
in *Stamboul Train* from *Pearson's Weekly*: 'God,' he wrote in his
diary, 'that it may come off; I don't dare believe it.' And Greene
was right not to believe it. Frere Reeves overstretched himself by
asking Pearson's to raise their offer. Instead they turned the novel
down.

In spite of this, it was not the feeling that he was failing financially
that was preventing him writing easily. *Stamboul Train* was selling

well in the United States: 'Heard that Orient Express had sold 4,300 odd by the day of publication.'[14] He had had high hopes for some time that the book would be sold to a film company, and negotiations through his agent in America were still going on. It was simply that 'Opus V' was being written according to a new conception.

Even during April he was still fighting staleness. On 3 April he commits his feelings to his diary: 'Feeling depressed by the book and thoroughly stale. I think I shall have to cancel the last 2 or 3,000 and start Part II differently.' The following day he 'did more revisions of typescript and was a little encouraged. It's not bad: the shape will emerge. I shall scrap the 2,000 words or so of prison scene with which I was closing Part II and shall start straight away with Mr Surrogate.'

Suddenly on 25 April he found a way to break out and tap his reserves, coming up unexpectedly with whatever inspiration was lying dormant. He stopped his habit of long years of writing his stint in the early morning. 'Quite unable to work during the morning', he wrote in his diary on 25 April, 'but did 500 in the afternoon.' In no time at all he had pushed the number of daily words to 750 and then later to 1,000, all done after tea: 'I've decided to try working after tea for a change, and it certainly worked well again today – 750 words, after a walk in the afternoon with Peggy [a dog belonging to Fred Hart which the Greenes were looking after while Hart was travelling] down the Nightingale Woods.'[15]

*

Greene knew that in starting *It's a Battlefield* he had embarked on what looked like a self-destructive path; he needed desperately to produce a successful novel, yet had no illusions that this book would prove commercial: 'My passbook increases the financial worry, nor does Opus V look like being a popular book.'[16] He had a genuine contempt for best-sellers, including his own successful *Stamboul Train*, which his diaries and reviews reflect. But they also show that, in spite of worries and difficulties, this was a seminal period for his future work. He was trying to understand his purpose in writing this novel and was searching for the technique which would bring success. At the same time his private struggle with *It's a Battlefield* affected his views of other authors. His concern was with the technical problems involved in writing a novel rather than with theory.

On 25 July 1932, he and Vivien went to Moreton, where his agent was holidaying. They had lunch with the Highams and Mary Borden: 'She has the prettiest American voice I have ever heard and lovely eyes.' Over lunch Greene argued uselessly against a novel, *Nymph Errant*: 'No one, with the blessed exception of V. seemed to have the slightest feeling for the technical problems of a novel; a novel in their eyes can be written anyhow (referring of course to method and not to style) so long as it "gets across", but I cannot understand how it can "get across" to an educated person if it is written "anyhow".'[17]

David Higham had written a play at this time, later produced at the Gate Theatre, and he wanted Greene's comments: 'I have never read anything flatter or more muddled,' he wrote in his diary. 'The characters proceeded from one mental state to another in jumps, and all the space between was left in the author's mind unimpressed. And, oh the cigarette smoking and the badinage and the endless dialogue with no relation to the theme, though God knows what the theme was.'[18]

Greene was concerned about how the point of view in a novel was to be presented, and he copied into his diary a quotation from *The Popular Novel in England, 1770–1800*, referring to the sentimental eighteenth-century novel: 'What these authors aimed at – at least the best of them – was delicacy and variety of emotional hue.' 'It seems to me,' he commented, 'that this (with delicacy left out) is my method in "The Express" where I had to surrender point of view.'[19] In a sense he was to surrender point of view in *It's a Battlefield* as well.

Since he was dealing with contemporary events in *It's a Battlefield*, he was interested in methods of introducing them in a novel. He criticised the working-class novelist, James Barke, because his crude treatment of current affairs shatters the novel, which is an expression of extreme class consciousness; though his hatred for the upper classes, Greene concedes, gives 'a fine vitality to the portrait of the coal-owner'. But the weakness of writing with political bias is that it so often results in 'speeches on dead problems and martyrdom for dead causes', as in Upton Sinclair's *Manassas*.[20] Looking further, he concludes that even minor German novelists seem to possess the skill of letting contemporary affairs into their novels without sacrificing a pattern,[21] while he is aware that 'most artists who deal with contemporary life deal with it as political partisans.'[22]

So, in the same review, he turns to Anton Chekhov, whose work he was reading at the time, for a definition of what a writer of fiction is; 'Fiction is called artistic because it draws life as it actually is . . . a writer is not a confectioner, not a cosmetician, not an entertainer; he is a man bound, under contract, by his awareness of his duty and his conscience.' Having established the artist's contract to duty and conscience, he turns to Chekhov again for a judgment on the question of bias, political or otherwise:

You are right in demanding that an artist should take a conscious attitude to his work, but you confuse two conceptions: *the solution of a question and the correct setting of a question.* The latter alone is obligatory for the artist. In *Anna Karenina* and in *Onyeguin* not a single problem is solved, but they satisfy completely because all the problems are set correctly.

The artist, therefore, is not to provide solutions, but to present the human problem, objectively, in its correct setting; a world which is not manipulated by the writer, 'is not to be altered with moral fables', and it is 'beyond the novelist's scope to offer a remedy. He must have the habit of noting the world, not offering a cure.'[23] Greene's passion for technique is specifically revealed in another *Spectator* review where he argues that: 'The failure of so many contemporary novelists is a failure to stay the course. Two or three books raise hopes which are never fulfilled because the author seems to have lacked the interest in the technicalities of his art that can alone prevent the mind dulling, the imagination losing power. Nothing else can enable an author to approach each new book with sustained intellectual excitement.'[24]

Greene was aware that most writers who see themselves as entertainers have two crippling disadvantages: 'stories written purely for entertainment are almost invariably dull'; and 'all the fountains are coloured, all the mirrors are distorting, all the voices speak through megaphones, and the rifles in all the shooting booths are wrongly sighted.'[25] Because the writer as entertainer has as his aim flattery and excitement, his stories are often so packed with violent incident that there is no room left for anything but simplified and sentimentalised characters. The truth is that there is no truth, but the mind 'persistently demands in a story something it can recognize as truth'.[26]

Neither did Greene believe that the writer should be bent on mere political impartiality at the cost of truth. Speaking of Rearden Conner's novel, *Shake Hands With The Devil*, which dealt with the Irish Revolution at its harshest phase, he notices that 'an atrocity committed by English troops has to be carefully balanced by an atrocity committed by Irish irregulars . . . This is propaganda against fanaticism, not an impartial presentation of fanatics.'[27]

His strongest criticism was reserved for the 'popular novelists', two of whom, Warwick Deeping and A. J. Cronin (medical doctors who had turned to novel writing), attracted his most contemptuous attention. He comments on Deeping's *Two Black Sheep*: 'The style is sometimes illiterate, sometimes comically involved ("Taxis and private cars made of the night a bowl of black glass that was shivered upon the pavement of progress"); and the metaphors and similes are often delightfully grotesque as when Mr Deeping describes "a pile of cloud glowing like a bosom".'[28] Cronin he sees both as 'a perfect example' and 'an awful example' of the popular novelist. The guarantee to the reader of his novels is that: 'There will be nothing to shock, nothing to disturb you, nothing to give you ideas.' And so we have the missionary seduced by a loose woman, the boxer with a seductive Irish voice, a sardonic, embittered doctor won back to hope in life by the love of a good woman. Literary phrases run riot: 'Slowly before their eyes the day languished as with love, swooning towards the arms of the dark'; silence is 'lingering yet chaste', principal characters have 'visions which words cannot formulate' but their physical appearance is minutely described – 'chiselled' features, 'strong' teeth, sometimes 'firm' teeth, sometimes 'perfect' teeth, almost always 'white' teeth; they 'hiss' words, their eyes 'blaze'. Such writers are said to have a narrative gift but it is 'difficult to understand how a narrative gift can ever be said to exist apart from any merit of style, story or character.'[29]

Such popular writers often avoid the awful necessity of finding the precise words to describe emotion. Reviewing Francis Brett Young, he quotes him as writing: 'It is impossible to paint the tortures of jealousy and of humiliation that she endured' and Greene concludes that if he finds it impossible to describe the chief emotion of his character, 'I cannot see why the story should have been attempted at all.'[30]

We can see very plainly where Greene stands and what, since he considered his first three novels failures, he has come to believe, and even what he is trying to do in *It's a Battlefield*. Dealing with Hans Carossa, who had made a reputation as an autobiographer and had then turned novelist, Greene suggests Carossa failed because in a novel he had to do what he had never before done – that is to invent relationships which have no existence outside the author's brain. He admits that the characters are emotionally real to the author, 'but he cannot find the descriptions, the dialogue, the intonations which will make them real to others.'[31]

What stylistically he was after was a prose bare and lucid, and without obvious literary echoes, not an imitation of but a development of eighteenth-century prose, giving a cool look at the world in the 1930s. What Greene says of Edith Wharton's stories, collected under the title *Human Nature*, almost exactly applies to the new professional Greene: 'her study, and her attitude, admirably maintained, is cool, aloof, a little withering. Human nature, in fact, does not come well out of the ordeal of being closely regarded by so shrewd and unsympathetic a critic.'[32] This is the voice of the man who wrote *It's a Battlefield*.

His approval of Julian Green's *The Strange River* suggests what his own standards are: 'The tone of the book is immediately and unerringly struck', and later, comparing Green with others, he admits: 'I cannot help preferring that firm line which Mr Julian Green draws round his subject, a line which is never crossed even by the thoughts of his characters.'[33]

3 1

It's a Battlefield

Almost an act of self-destruction.
        – GRAHAM GREENE

I N spite of his denigration of the popular novel and his determination
not to produce one, the account he sent to Mary Pritchett, now
his agent in America, of *It's a Battlefield* suggests that the novel had
all the ingredients of a best-selling thriller. The novel was unfinished
then and he was perhaps trying to help her to sell the book:

> It is, roughly speaking, a panoramic novel of London. The central
> point is the bus driver condemned to death for the murder of a
> policeman at a political meeting, and the effect on his wife &
> brother & their relationship. But from this central point the story
> radiates out to all the people affected, so that there are scenes at
> Scotland Yard, with the Flying Squad at the capture of a murderer
> near Euston, at a match factory in Battersea, at a café in Little
> Compton Street, at a literary party, at a bishop's palace [this last
> is no longer in the novel], at a political meeting, at an insurance
> office, at a newspaper office.[1]

However, what he goes on to say suggests that the thriller elements
were controlled by a serious creative design, though his hope still is
that the novel will sell well: 'but the story continually returns to its
central points – the condemned cell & the home of the condemned
man. I'm afraid this gives a rather confused idea, but the book is
really quite closely shaped & patterned. The treatment is mainly
ironic & objective, but becomes a little more subjective as the story
works inward to those central points. It is not gloomy (!), except in
places; some of it is definitely comic. On the whole it is remarkably
clean! & I should think would be serialisable.'
    Mary Pritchett on 6 May 1933 responded as gently as she could: 'I
like the part of the new book which you have sent me tremendously

– it is good writing, and a good story . . . Your writing is so good that certain kinds of readers will not appreciate it until you have become noted! . . . It seems to me the book has only one thing which makes it less certain of success than *Stamboul Train*, and that is that so far the sombre predominates.'

In his diary (19 August 1932) Greene writes that the novel was to describe: 'a large inclusive picture of a city which should use my experience as much as my imagination, the connecting link . . . the conviction of a man for the murder of a policeman. Is it politic to hang him? and the detectives go out through the city listening.' The experience that went into the making of the novel was not his intimate, personal experience, except perhaps for his dreams; but on a subconscious level, it was responsible for the 'sombre' predominating.

A major source from his 'literary' experience, which influenced the conception, characterisation, movement, even at times the style of the novel, was the writer he so much admired but tried to avoid as a model. His diary shows that some three weeks before the inspiration for the novel came to him, he had been re-reading Joseph Conrad's *The Secret Agent*. The 'large inclusive picture of a city' must have derived from that novel. Conrad wrote in his Preface: 'Then the vision of an enormous town presented itself.' The city in both novels was London, and while the attitude to it was individual to each writer, there are many parallels between the two novels. It is surely significant that Greene's hero is called Conrad Drover.

Conrad's *The Secret Agent* centred on an anarchistic bomb plot and drew characters ranging from the upper classes – the Lady Patroness, the Assistant Commissioner of Police, the Home Secretary and his private secretary – to the seedy, lower-class Verlocs. The basis of *It's a Battlefield* was the dispersal by police of a Communist demonstration during which a policeman was accidentally killed, and it also ranges over society from an Assistant Commissioner of Police, an over-worked Cabinet Minister and his private secretary, a patroness, Lady Caroline, to the lower-class Drovers and Kay Rimmer, a worker in a match factory.

The main theme of the novel was to be 'the injustice of men's justice', and the subject, which he says, significantly, was 'the fruit of anxiety-ridden weeks', was suggested by a dream.[2] The dreams which were to be of creative value to him in writing *It's a Battlefield* stemmed from private anxieties. In them he committed murder, was to be imprisoned for the crime and had difficulty in disposing of the body, and the dreams appear to have reflected a deeply felt guilt over the course he had taken with his career: 'the dangerous cul-de-sac'[3] into which he had led his wife by leaving his steady job on *The Times*.

The first of these dreams occurred in June 1932, even before he had completed *Stamboul Train*: 'Dreamed last night that I was being sent to prison for five years and woke depressed with the farewell to V. & the thought that she would be over 30 when we would live with each other again.'[4] On 4 January 1933, on an evening when he was terribly worried about his finances, he had gone to bed early, at 9.30 p.m. This was the night that he dreamt he had murdered J. B. Priestley and was taken away in a Black Maria. His diary continues: 'This dream did not worry me. A worse dream was that I had murdered someone and deposited his body in a suitcase at a railway cloak room. I wanted to get it away again before it began to smell.'

This he combined with a poem he had written in his diary on 21 November 1932 about a murdered woman dealing with it from the clinical police point of view:

> This the analysis of blood-stain –
> 　'on woollen beret of a common make';
> the experts complain
> 　that the fingers left no mark
>
> On the park chair
> 　or the young breast;
> microscopic stare
> 　at uncertain past,
>
> Grass inspected, note-book entry,
> 　'torn bodice and lace';
> Over the body the solitary sentry
> 　of her certain peace.

The result was an episode in the novel in which the Assistant Commissioner of Police goes with the Superintendent to arrest the 'body in the trunk' murderer – a mad member of the Salvation Army. The body was that of a prostitute and had been found in a trunk at Paddington Station. Although Greene did some meticulous research for this novel, the 'trunk murder' derives solely from his dreams – there was no such murder, as far as *The Times* records, until June 1934 (his novel was published in February) when, under the headline 'WOMAN'S BODY IN A TRUNK', a special correspondent reported: 'The discovery of the dismembered body of a woman in a trunk in the left luggage office at Brighton Railway Station last night caused the local police without delay to call in the aid of Scotland Yard. Inside was the body of a woman of between 40 and 45 years of age and about 5ft 2in in height. The head, arms and legs were missing.'

However, although this event was extraordinarily well done in the novel, Greene decided that it did not fit in with its theme, 'the injustice of men's justice,' and he cut the scene out when revising the book for a paperback edition in 1940. Later he realised that 'Without the mad murderer of the Salvation Army, the battlefield of the title lacked the sense of violence and confusion. The metaphor became a political and not an ironic one.'[5]

*

His aim to present 'a large inclusive picture of a city' must have caused him some worry – how could he make it inclusive given the limits of his experience? How could he deal with characters, such as those of the working-class, of whom he had had limited experience? He had in *Stamboul Train* dealt with a melodramatic assortment of people – a chorus girl, a Jewish businessman, a female journalist, a revolutionary, a colonel in the secret police, a house-breaker. But his aim now was realism, not melodrama.

The physical setting of the novel – the city of London – would have presented no problem. He knew London, was fascinated by it, had lived in Battersea before his marriage and visited his aunt Nono there while writing the novel. There is a detail and authenticity to the characters in that setting. It is not only Conrad Drover who crosses Battersea Bridge, for behind him stands Graham who many times made this journey: 'the trams came screeching like a finger drawn on glass up the curve of Battersea Bridge and down into the ill-lighted network of streets beyond; on the water the gulls floated asleep.'[6]

On a visit to Milly Drover, his sister-in-law, Conrad sees a police boat on the river: 'A police boat went gently down the stream, burning a red light, and disturbed a sleeping gull which beat up through the rain to the level of the bus windows, then sank again on rigid wings into the dark and the silence, while the sheets of rain fell between.'[7] Six years previously, Greene wrote to Vivien from Battersea, 'The river's lovely at that time [about midnight]. Chelsea Bridge, with the light of the police boat creeping fearfully quietly along the edge. You can't see the boat at all only the light, until it's right up underneath you, and then you just get one glimpse of two mysterious muffled figures sitting very stiff like Egyptian Kings in the stern & then it's gone again. Absolutely no noise, but the stir in the water.'[8] This was at the time of the General Strike and Graham was working early and late and saw London at all hours; 'I'm beginning to know London at dawn very well. It's an attractive time.'[9]

Greene then was clearly going back over the full range of his experiences in Battersea, and the description of violence in the novel when police dispersed the Communist demonstration which led to the accidental murder of a policeman may come, in part, from Graham's experiences as a special constable during the Strike.

Milly Drover explains that her husband accidentally killed the policeman to prevent him clubbing her:

> 'The policeman was going to hit me,' she said. 'Everyone was excited.' She began to shake all over as if she were again in the centre of the mob near Hyde Park Corner . . .
>
> The crowd turned and ran as the mounted police came down the Row with drawn staves. The man by the Achilles statue struck out with his banner at two policemen who pulled him to the ground and twisted his arms behind his back. He shouted for help, but the crowd was fighting to get away from the wedge of police who were driving them towards the gates. The great green plains of the Park were dotted with shabby men running away.
>
> 'They won't do anything for him,' Milly said, flinching again at the raised truncheon and the fear of a pain which never came. The policeman was on his knees bleeding into the turf and crying and gasping, and the crowd was suddenly very far away and the three of them were alone with the grass and a park chair and a sense of disaster. The policeman's face was wet with tears.[10]

But contemporary with his writing of the novel there were many demonstrations, some organised by the Communist Party who were rapidly attracting recruits from the poverty-stricken unemployed. The most spectacular was the Hunger March of 1932 when 3,000 people set out from the provinces to walk to London, supported on their way by field kitchens and cobblers to mend their boots. The Glasgow contingent took five weeks to reach London. They then joined in Hyde Park a further 100,000 and violent confrontations with the police were inevitable.

The Times reported that: 'Both mounted and foot police made baton charges . . . In Hyde Park . . . there were at least 100 mounted police . . . they helped substantially the large force of foot police who were striving to keep the vast crowd within bounds . . . with drawn batons mounted men charged and repeatedly swept all before them as they went up and down. Chief Inspector Oger and a special constable were badly injured and a passerby hurt.'[11]

Whether or not Greene witnessed this event, he certainly witnessed a demonstration in London organised by Sir Oswald Mosley, leading the British Union of Fascists: 'Mosley had organized a provocative procession of his black-shirts through the East End with its strongly Jewish population . . . I went along to watch; I wanted to see what would happen. The crowd panicked and tried to escape from the batons. I really did panic then, by contagion, I suppose.'[12]

By having a policeman not simply injured but killed, Greene provides the keystone for his plot and theme, and by the policeman dying with 'his face wet with tears' he increases the pathos and maintains an even-handed stance. Yet we cannot doubt where Greene's sympathies lay. There was a general feeling at the time that by becoming active in a political party one could do something about the terrible social conditions, which perhaps accounts for Greene's growing interest in politics. In his diary on 11 August 1933, a week after finishing his novel, he wrote: 'Joined the I.L.P. My political progress has been rather curved.' He was referring to the fact that he had canvassed for the Conservatives in Oxford in 1923; was close to the Liberals in 1924; joined the Communists in 1925 – though that was a joke membership; had been a special constable during the General Strike, and had now become a member of the Independent Labour Party – more extreme than the modest Labour Party. He told his mother that he had begun to establish a branch of the I.L.P. in Oxford and that the Party Chairman, Jimmy Maxton, a gifted orator who thought the Labour Party thoroughly counter-revolutionary, was going to speak at the opening meeting.

*

Two areas of the novel required deliberate seeking out of information: the prison scenes and the match factory scenes. On 7 October 1932 when he was in London to learn of the Book Society Award, Greene recorded in his diary: 'Went to Wormwood Scrubs and saw over the prison. In great white letters on the walls, staring out over a flat common ringed with railway lines, the words "Youth Fight or Starve" & the Communist hammer and sickle.'

On 3 December he visited a second prison for copy: 'Took a bus out to Wandsworth Prison to inspect the terrain for Opus V.' He also visited a match factory: 'V[ivien] went up to town for the day. I went into Gloucester & saw over Moreland's Match factory for use in Opus V. The noise of engines, too loud for anyone to speak, gave me a headache after one hour: the employees work from 7.30 to 5 for a five day week, on a minimum of 30/- for girls. Wormwood Scrubs was infinitely preferable.'[13]

Deliberately in the novel he emphasised the similarity between

prison and factory conditions for the inmates, the fictional match
factory portrayed as being worse (unless, of course, you were in a
condemned cell). Both were governed on the 'Block' system of
Wormwood Scrubs. People were moved from one block to another
to give credit for good behaviour. As the chief warden of the prison
explains: 'That's Block A. The new prisoners all go there. If they
behave themselves they get shifted to . . . Block B. Block C . . .
that's the highest grade. Of course if there's any complaint against
them, they get shifted down. It's just like a school.'

And at the match factory, the manager explains: 'that's Block A.
The new employees go there for the simplest processes. Then if they
work well they move to Block B, and so to Block C. Everyone in
Block C is a skilled employee. Any serious mistake and they are
moved back to Block B.' In both cases Block C has privileges
including better food.

What impressed Greene at the match factory was the noise of the
machines which made communication impossible, the long hours of
work, the discomfort and the danger of injuries: 'Kay Rimmer moved
a hand to the left, a hand to the right, pressed down her foot, and
winked her left eye. The girl opposite winked twice. Between the
spitting of the machines, before the stair [carrying the matches] could
move a foot away, the message passed. "Hunting tonight?" "No,
the curse [menstrual period]." '[14]

He describes factory injuries: 'A finger sliced off so cleanly at the
knuckle that it might never have been, a foot crushed between
opposed revolving wheels. "It never hurt her. She suffered nothing
. . . So brave. She chatted all the way, carried on the stretcher to the
operating-room." '[15] Greene had indirect experience of a finger being
sliced: 'Extraordinary the fortitude of the poor', he wrote in his diary
on 12 November 1932, 'Greenall, our maid, tells us this morning
that yesterday chopping wood she practically took off the top of her
finger. I was in the house, but thank God she didn't call to me. She
put her head between her knees to prevent her fainting & then ran to
the district nurse who was out, so that she went to the tobacconists
to have her finger done up by Mrs Thornton.'

*

On 28 August 1932 Greene had further inspiration for the novel: 'In
church, as usual, the new novel grew in the mind, a new character,
a psychological complexity, a splendid second climax, the Commissioner's walk through the London streets, followed and conscious
of being followed, and the end of the pursuit on Lady Ottoline's
doorstep.' There are two interesting developments here – the 'psycho-

logical complexity', which we shall come to later, and the introduction of people Greene knew as models for his characters.

On 1 March 1933 Greene records in his diary that he has passed the sticky patch in the novel for the moment and that he is sailing in easy waters. Then he adds: 'The Commissioner is developing into the best & most important character in the book; he'll have to have the last word & not Drover.'

Some aspects of Greene's Assistant Commissioner are derived from Conrad's Assistant Commissioner, but Greene claimed that his uncle, Sir Graham Greene, who visited him at Chipping Campden while he was at work on the novel, was a source for the Assistant Commissioner, especially in lending 'a little of his stiff inhibited bachelor integrity' to the character.

Greene's cousin, Felix, like the rest of his family, held his uncle in high regard. He recalled that even during the Second World War, Sir Graham (and he was born in January 1857) still went to important meetings of the Committee of Imperial Defence:

> He would come down periodically, every week from Harston to go to this meeting and I one day came down with him. He had always walked from King's Cross to 10 Downing Street, which is a long way, and this old man, still very alive, a bit lined, always walked in a particular way through the streets and on this occasion it had been after a bombing raid and there'd been an unexploded bomb in the street which he normally goes down. There was a policeman at each end to prevent people from going down there. When we came up to the policeman, all he did was to do this, a little gesture because he had this sort of air of authority and the policeman stepped aside and we walked through hoping the damned thing wouldn't go off while we walked. But he had that absolute certainty of his own authority, the gesture slightly pushing the policeman aside as if he had the authority to go through. He was an absolute gentleman, the best kind of Civil Service chap.[16]

Surely we recognise in this account Graham's Assistant Commissioner, as we find him in the first scene of the novel walking from his office to Berkeley Restaurant, down Northumberland Avenue, round Trafalgar Square where 'the buses roar up Parliament Street and swing in a great circle', and a policeman at the corner of the avenue recognises him and salutes.

At the age of eighty-nine, Sir Graham Greene fell under a tube train owing to failing eyesight. He rolled between the rails as a train was approaching and it passed over him. Raymond Greene recalled that his uncle had once commented: 'It was most interesting. I had never before seen the underside of an electric train.' He was ninety-three when he died. Tooter Greene said:

> Raymond and I were Trustees and in his Will he insisted that he wished to be buried at sea. He was a dry old stick but he got on well with Churchill and though it took him forty years after he had left the Admiralty to die, yet the Navy made a great fuss of him at the end of his life. I can still recall his burial at sea, it was a most moving occasion: great ships in the harbour hooting; men standing on deck saluting as the destroyer *Finisterre* with Raymond and myself put out to sea from Portsmouth with the urn. Each ship dipped its flag to half-mast. On the *Implacable* the whole ship's company lined up at the salute.
>
> We went about twelve miles out beyond the Nab Light, and after a short funeral service, the urn was tipped over the side to the tune of the Last Post. Everything was very relaxed once we began to return, but I remember weeping, it was a splendid and most moving occasion.[17]

In his Introduction to *It's a Battlefield*, Greene not only acknowledges his uncle as a source, but mentions that he was 'aware of Lady Ottoline Morrell in the background of Lady Caroline'. Lady Caroline, having been given the details by Mr Surrogate about Drover's crime and imminent execution, and because of her 'passion to help', tries to intercede for the condemned man and fails. Behind this brief portrait lies a detailed knowledge of Lady Ottoline Morrell.

She was renowned for her patronage of writers, artists, scholars and poets, especially those who were up-and-coming. She described herself to Virginia Woolf as having 'an absurd overdose of "kindness".'[18] It stemmed from her recognition that she lacked a creative talent, and as a result, was 'a magnet for egotists'.[19] To her friend, Robert Gathorne-Hardy, she wrote: 'It is so humiliating that one is so uncreative. Perhaps in another existence I may be able to.'[20]

She was startling in appearance and dress, had a nasal voice, a neighing laugh, was physically ugly to some, yet she had a short affair with the painter Augustus John, Middleton Murry came under her spell, and the philosopher Bertrand Russell fell deeply in love with her, though that was in 1909 when her hair was golden – it was generally red but was sometimes dyed purple.[21]

Lady Ottoline was famous for her parties attended by leading, or promising, writers and politicians – among them Bertrand Russell, Virginia Woolf, Clive Bell, Henry James, Max Beerbohm, W. B.

Yeats, Lytton Strachey, D. H. and Frieda Lawrence, John Middleton Murry and Katherine Mansfield and prime ministers Asquith and Ramsay MacDonald. She suddenly appeared in Greene's life in October 1930, though he had seen her before when he was a student at Oxford: 'There was a painted old woman I used to see occasionally wandering about Oxford, rather a revolting spectacle. I used to wonder who she was. Now she's suddenly cropped up in the form of Lady Ottoline Morrell and invited us to tea. It appears that Aldous Huxley recommended her to read *The Man Within*.' Just before they moved from Chipping Campden, Greene and Vivien went to a number of Lady Ottoline's regular Thursday parties at number 10 Gower Street (the home of Lady Caroline Bury in *It's a Battlefield*) and at one of these met a writer they admired, Aldous Huxley.

Vivien recalled a visit Lady Ottoline made to Chipping Campden: 'She did look very strange. I think even now she would look very strange. There was always a crowd of small boys following her. And she came all that way, I suppose from Garsington [manor] then. I remember her coming in and I had a little girl in that day to help and she opened the door and seeing Lady Ottoline she screamed – gave a sort of yelp because Lady Ottoline was very, very tall and dressed that day entirely in white with a very large hat with large white feathers, and her husband was with her and they stayed for tea. And, this was a very sweet and touching thing, Philip Morrell took the saucer poured his tea into it and blew on it to cool it and she was so unaffected.'[22]

Many writers portrayed Lady Ottoline in their work, in particular Aldous Huxley and D. H. Lawrence. Huxley's characters were unpleasant – as Mrs Wimbush in *Crome Yellow* and Mrs Aldwinkle in *Those Barren Leaves*; Lawrence's was cruel – as Hermione in *Women in Love*. Lady Ottoline recalled that the ghastly portrait of herself haunted her thoughts and horrified her.

If Lady Ottoline was doomed to be translated into several fictitious look-alikes, each one bearing the distinctive imprint of its creator, Greene's portrait of her reflects, in Caroline Bury, the best characteristics as well as the eccentricities of Ottoline. And while Caroline Bury has Lady Ottoline's 'overdose of kindness', with her desire to help and her reputation as a hostess she also reflects Greene's experience of Ottoline, who is the source of important scenes and plot connections, and she contributes to the theme of the novel. When she tries to prevent the execution of Drover, the Assistant Commissioner reflects about his old friend: 'She had never, he believed, received anything from anyone . . . she had given and given, time and money and nerves, "You are very brave," he concluded.'

He tells her, linking her with the theme of the novel: 'The truth is, nobody cares about anything but his own troubles. Everybody's too busy fighting his own little battle to think of the next man. Except you, Caroline.'[23] And he thinks, 'it's lucky she has got Faith, whatever she means by it, she'd got nothing else: an ageing haggard woman in a dark room crowded with the relics of a taste which had been enthusiastic, never impeccable.'[24]

Greene is even kind about Lady Ottoline's appearance, for Caroline Bury's 'haggard sunken face would have had its beauty recognized at once on an ancient fresco or an Eastern tomb.'[25]

Greene's precise but generous portrait of Lady Ottoline must stem from his gratitude for her praise and attempts to help him at a difficult time. On 19 November 1931 he had written to her: 'I seemed doomed to please no one after "The Man Within". It [*Rumour at Nightfall*] has been out nearly three weeks and has received only three reviews. The Lit. Supp. which has always before been both kind and prompt remains grimly silent: one does not expect anything from "The Observer" but "The Sunday Times" seems to have abandoned me. After praising extravagantly my first book, it never reviewed my second at all and looks like ignoring this one. Altogether I am feeling depressed. Books are a labour to write and a hell to publish; why does one do it? The grim spectre of a return to journalism looms on the horizon.'

It was at this time that Lady Ottoline wrote to him praising the novel, which must have meant a great deal, especially since, three days later, Swinnerton did his hatchet job on the book. Two months earlier he had sought her help in obtaining an introduction to the editor of *The Sunday Times*: 'I'm anxious to get some work on a weekly paper to make up for a fall in royalties', and her help would certainly have been forthcoming. When he had finished his Rochester book, it was to her he confided that he had sent it off to his old tutor at Balliol to be vetted for historical blunders. He told her also of his hopes for the Rochester book which was rejected: 'I believe it's coming out in April. It's not the book it ought to have been, as I was writing against time.' Yes, Graham was kind, but surely if anyone deserved a gentle portrait it was Lady Ottoline Morrell.

*

It is the left-wing intellectual Mr Surrogate who, in the novel, asks Lady Caroline to approach someone in authority to try to prevent Drover being hanged, and Greene writes in his Introduction: 'my idea of Middleton Murry, whom I did not personally know, was responsible in small part for Mr Surrogate.' Again Greene was probably indebted to Lady Ottoline for some insight into the nature of the relationship between Murry and his wife Katherine Mansfield. This relationship is suggested in Surrogate's with his dead wife to whom 'during a long, faithful and unhappy marriage they had exposed each other . . . with a complete lack of reticence.'

There was also a reservoir of gossip and hearsay about Murry and his wife to be drawn on – they appeared, after all, as Burlap and his wife in Aldous Huxley's *Point Counter Point* – and reference to Murry appears in Greene's diary on 2 August 1932. Friends of his had come to 'Little Orchard' for tea and scandalous tales of Middleton Murry were recounted. When Murry was publishing his late wife's letters; Lady Ottoline had sent him a letter which Katherine Mansfield had written to her, and later discovered he had inserted passages reflecting on himself which were not in the original.

The gossip must have been deep since Greene writes with surprising accuracy about Murry/Surrogate, a man he 'did not personally know', though in transmuting Murry and his wife Katherine Mansfield to Surrogate and his wife (and after all a 'surrogate' is a 'substitute'), Katherine becomes an artist, not a writer.

Murry had a mania for public confessions, especially in the magazines, though the confessions were often geared to what he considered was expedient, and he constantly blackened his own character. 'I suppose his instinct is to absolve himself in these bleatings', wrote Virginia Woolf, 'and so get permission for more sins.'[26] And this is fundamental to Surrogate whose 'inability to conceal anything had humiliated him so often that he had needed to form a philosophy of humiliation, to found his career on self-exposure. "Be humble that you may be exalted," and from the depth of humility he would spring refreshed to the height of pride.'[27]

The intimacies of Murry's married life are also reflected in those of the Surrogates. Middleton Murry ate the soul out of Katherine yet she knew his nature well; that his 'very frankness' was 'a falsity'.[28] Certainly he admitted to being her inferior in many ways – she had to take the 'active male role and he became the passive female'.[29] Surrogate complains to Caroline Bury that his wife 'did not respect his manhood', but when Katherine Mansfield died, Murry turned that tough, outspoken, sexually promiscuous woman into a different character, enshrined and made perfect – as Aldous Huxley wrote of Burlap: 'When Susan died Burlap exploited the grief he felt, or at any rate loudly said he felt, in a more than usually painful series of always painfully personal articles which were the secret of his success as a journalist.'[30] While extolling his perfect love for his late wife, Murry had an affair with Frieda Lawrence. And so Surrogate, with the aim of seducing Kay Rimmer, the factory worker, takes her to his home and shows her the bedroom in which hangs his late wife's portrait, she gasps with pleasure at the semi-circular bed, the silk bedspread and rose hangings, but says of his wife: 'How you must have loved her', and 'for a moment Mr Surrogate longed to tell the truth, that it [the portrait] was hung there as an atonement for his dislike, as a satisfaction for his humility, because of its reminder of the one woman who had never failed to see through him.'[31]

*

The 'new character' in the novel, 'the psychological complexity', is Conrad Drover. He comes from a working-class home, wins a scholarship and works his way up alone to his present success, but he has two problems. He is devoted to his brother, grieving for what is happening to him, and he is in love with his brother's wife. On the other hand, so far as his career is concerned, he is conscious of his vulnerability and without any confidence: 'People had promoted him when he had expected dismissal; they had praised him when he had expected blame.' His job is to see to the running of the office and to keep the clerks in order, but among them is the nephew of the managing director, 'who was learning the business from the bottom. He wore a light suit and a public-school tie . . . The young man stared back insolently. He smelt of money.' Troubled by his brother's situation, Conrad Drover reflects that he cannot give way even for a moment since the manager might 'begin to mistrust him, his figures and his discipline; he might decide that it was time to try the director's nephew. Conrad was quite certain that one day that would happen.'[32] The two 'heroes', Conrad and the Assistant Commissioner, are therefore poles apart – one certain of his status and place in society, the other in the shifting sands of the lower classes. But Graham's inspiration for the character of Conrad derived in part from his own situation – his own sense of insecurity, and his fears of a diminishing income.

At the time he was influenced by a Hans Fallada novel which he reviewed for the *Spectator*: 'Finished *Little Man What Now* with intense respect,' he recorded in his diary. 'It disturbed me so much that in my sleep I argued furiously against the convention which pays one man in a business £10,000 and a clerk in the same business £150 for the same hours of work. I remember that I took Sidney Sitwell as my example, arguing with [mother] and Aunt Nono.'*[33] In his review he wrote: 'Everything that gives pleasure costs money. If you

* Sitwell, related to the literary Sitwells, had, at one time, courted Greene's aunt.

want a little country air – money. If you want to hear a little music – money. It all costs money; nothing can be had without money . . . There are chapters which pluck the nerves with the agony of those who are insecure.'[34]

If Greene has not changed politically since writing *Stamboul Train* – 'You put the small thief in prison, but the big thief lives in a palace' – he has strengthened in his convictions. Condor, the journalist in *It's a Battlefield*, comments, 'They hanged this man and pardoned that; one embezzler was in prison, but other men of the same kind were sent to Parliament . . . [and] it was not systematic enough to be called injustice.'[35] Lady Caroline Bury expresses the same sense of injustice and sympathy for the down-trodden in the 1930s: 'Do you believe in the way the country is organized? Do you believe that wages should run from thirty shillings a week to fifteen thousand a year, that a manual labourer should be paid less than a man who works with his brains? They are both indispensable, they both work the same hours, they are both dog-tired at the end of their day. Do you think I've the right to leave two hundred thousand pounds to anyone I like?'[36] Greene's experiences of extreme financial insecurity had finally put paid to any lingering Conservatism.

Conrad Drover's feelings of injustice, uncertainty and frustration drive him to futile decisions and actions. He buys a rusty revolver from a pawn-broker and his obsession with buying a gun is fed by Milly Drover's comment, 'You'd be no use with a gun'; he has thoughts of the people he might shoot – the manager of his firm and a plump man laughing outside the Berkeley Hotel along with a smiling, yellow-faced man – the private secretary and the Assistant Commissioner. They are amused at the sight of 'a pram on a taxi' (Greene had eight years earlier seen such a sight), but the amusement here came on the day Conrad's brother was condemned to death and as a result, Conrad becomes increasingly obsessed and neurotic. He follows the Assistant Commissioner to Lady Caroline's house and fires at him – but the rusty trigger did not move – in any case the gun was loaded with blanks. He is struck by a car and thrown a dozen yards. In agony, he is taken to hospital, his body broken, and dies.

In imaginatively re-creating Conrad Drover's last hours Greene returns to aspects of his own experience in Westminster Hospital, though the irony is Greene's own. Conrad dies uselessly while his brother is reprieved.

32

'The skeletons of
other people's people'

Sin is the writer's element.
— FRANÇOIS MAURIAC

WITHIN the territory of *It's a Battlefield* falls the area of sexual
relationships; Greene's treatment of these, marital and non-
marital, would seem to reflect his own problems at this time. The
Surrogates' marriage was a failure, the Drovers' marriage has lasted
five years: 'I know they were happy,' says Kay Rimmer. 'They were
so dull together, they couldn't be anything else but happy.' Surrogate
finds some consolation with Kay, who is happily promiscuous. And
Conrad Drover sleeps with his sister-in-law, her husband being in
prison. Sexual relationships in the novel fail when they are based on
love; lust makes everything simple, 'It was only love that complicated
the act.' This problem concerned Greene at the time.

On 28 November 1932 his diary shows that he was considering
the question, not which was best – wife or lover – but which was
best – lover or prostitute? He crossed out the word 'prostitute' and
replaced it with 'grue': 'It is the grue's responsibility to satisfy, but
the lover has to be satisfied. There is something to be said in favour
of the affair with a paid companion.' Greene's diary at this time
reveals that he had already put this conclusion into practice though
his love for Vivien had not diminished. His next novel, *England Made
Me*, is dedicated to Vivien, 'with ten years love 1925–1935'.

Nevertheless, he did lust after other women. He records in his
diary, on 30 July 1932, going on a long walk with Hugh and seeing
two American girls who were staying at the Coach and Horses in
Chipping Campden – 'one of them small, dark, well-dressed, slight
enough to show her lovely rump, beautiful small hands; she raised
my lust extraordinarily'. Later on the same day he strolled out with
Vivien before supper, 'hoping in vain to see the American girls at C.

470

Horses'. On the night of 2 August he dreamed 'strangely, of Gwen Howell, whom I loved with such unreasoning passion in 1924–25.' Two days later, driving out with Captain and Mrs Cox, Vivien, Nigel Dennis and his sixteen-year-old niece, to Warwick and then to Stratford, he was attracted by the sight of bathers in 'alluring costumes cut to the small of the back, three delightful beach pyjamas, and one lovely fair-haired girl punting a paralysed man coolly and gracefully up the river: against a strong tide but without strain.' 'Perhaps', he adds, 'the sight of all the exposed bodies was the cause of my dreaming of Annette and my using her in the "Italian manner"?'[1]

Annette appears to be one of two girls he was irregularly involved with, the other being a prostitute he refers to as 'O'. For Annette, or 'A' as he sometimes calls her, he seems to have had some feeling. The first reference to her in his diary is on 6 July 1932 when he was working on the last chapter of *Stamboul Train*: 'Annette comes to mind often with the stirrings of lust.' But their relationship had begun much earlier, after he had been in Chipping Campden about seven months and when *Rumour at Nightfall* was completed and he was researching the Rochester biography in the British Museum, for on 15 March 1932, he records in his diary that after having gone to the Bond Street Bureau to look for a kitten for his wife, no doubt to console her after the death of their Pekinese, he went after lunch 'to A's, but to my disappointment A. was in bed. Stayed and talked for three quarters of an hour and drank Liebfraumilch which I had brought with me. Toasted an 18 months acquaintance.'

The entries in his diary for 7 October are curious. That was the day on which he went to London to discover whether or not he had won the Book Society Award. Two separate pages cover the events of the same day giving two different versions. In one he goes quietly to bed. The second version begins as the first – 'Caught 7.15 to London' – but adds that he telegraphed 'A' to expect him at 6.15. After he heard from Frere Reeves at Heinemann's that the Book Society meeting was in progress at Walpole's house, we know no more, since the rest of the page is torn out of the diary. Perhaps the evening of that day was spent less quietly than the first version suggests.

Throughout the writing of *It's a Battlefield* it would seem that on business trips to London he would visit Annette or, more rarely, 'O'. On 12 March 1933 he risks sending a letter to 'A' by way of his favourite cousin: 'Wrote to Tooter enclosing a note to A mentioning a possible time for meeting on Wednesday.' Three weeks later, after lunch at Antoine's, he 'went to A. where I stayed an hour'. The writing which follows is indecipherable, but one fact to be noted is that he always visits 'A' at her home and then leaves – he does not take her to Antoine's for lunch – perhaps he could not have afforded it. This was the day he at last bought Vivien a sweet long-haired tabby kitten in Bond Street: 'Caught the 6.5 home, the kitten in a cardboard box. Let her out for the amusement of a family in the carriage and then found it difficult to get her back in the box. I had enlarged one of the holes too much, so that she kept on forcing her head through the lid. Also a stink filled the carriage as she relieved herself in the box.'[2]

Relying on short notes in his diary, with passages scribbled over or torn out, it is difficult to assess the importance of his relationship with Annette, though it is significant that he ends with a fear that he might have lost her. On 24 May he attended his mother-in-law's cremation and: 'Afterwards went down to Piccadilly and met in Brunswick St. 'O' and visited 2687 Regent, a very fine but very empty façade.' On 12 July he called again on A to whom he had earlier sent a telegram warning her of his arrival: 'bought a lovely papier-mâché tea caddy for V's birthday . . . then to a pub and then to A's. No answer. Went and had another drink and returned: no answer. Went to Imhof's [a gramophone record shop] to try and get a record of "Invitation au Voyage" but couldn't get the one I wanted. Took a taxi and returned to A's. A woman in the flat opposite said A had gone to a nursing home: I suppose for the stone.'[3] On 2 August, after visiting the Swedish Travel Bureau, he 'saw Anna Sten in "The Tempest" went to Cook's to see about passport. Walked hither and thither. In Bond Street met O. whom I'd been hoping to see. Definitely unsatisfactory.'[4]

Conrad Drover's love for Milly Drover goes back to before the time she married his brother. Drover spends the night at his sister-in-law's house, making up a bed for himself downstairs: 'He put two chairs together and arranged a sheet and two blankets.' Afterwards hearing Milly and Kay talking, he thinks, 'How simple [Kay] seemed to make it . . . how simple this going to bed. It was only love which complicated the act.'[5] Later Conrad accepts Milly's invitation to her bed. For some aspects of this incident, Greene was drawing on his own experience, going back to his days in Nottingham when during a visit to London in January 1926, he stayed at the home of Raymond and Charlotte. Since there was only one spare bed, occupied by Charlotte's sister, Greene had to spend the night of 18 January 1926 on a bed made up of two armchairs – as Conrad Drover had done. Drover's thought that, 'He felt no guilt at all; this did not harm his brother',[6] could have applied in the circumstances.

But in spite of diary entries or passages of illicit love in his novels we must not conclude that Greene's love for Vivien had faltered. On a picnic with the Coxes on 12 July 1932, he records: 'V & I were separated from the others and walked very happily alone together by the stream.'[7] Vivien's importance comes out in all sorts of small ways: 'Home to Campden, an empty blank feeling house without V.'[8] Then on the occasion of Vivien's going off to Oxford for a few days, he records a visit to Captain Cox and seeing a rare pamphlet – only twenty copies then extant – written by Mark Twain in Elizabethan English and purporting to be a conversation between Queen Elizabeth, Shakespeare, Raleigh and Bacon and others – 'several pages of gross lavatory humour' (which Greene always objected to) but he adds that it is a remarkable example of underground literature. On returning home, his last entry in his diary is, 'Found a postcard from V. in my bed. She is the sweetest and best person imaginable.'[9] Shortly after that there were some important events – Vivien became pregnant and both her parents died suddenly.

*

Neither Vivien nor Greene wanted children and tried to avoid having them. Vivien has said that if she had had no children she would not have missed them. 'You know, if it happened, it was God's will.' And we know something of Greene's feelings before Vivien became pregnant, in his description of a couple he saw round Enstone: 'we passed a double bicycle, a girl and a young man in khaki shorts, with a kind of pram attached with a baby in it. My heart warmed to them for their courage. They were not going to be kept under by a child.'[10]

Greene's cousin, Countess Strachwitz, put it more strongly: 'They didn't want children. For years they said they were never going to have children. They were going to just live for each other. Even when their eldest one was expected, they were very distressed about it, and even thought of having it adopted. But once it was born they didn't.'

We can follow their feelings about the pregnancy through Greene's diary. It begins with an outing of a couple of days to London on 25 March 1933, when he and Vivien stayed at the Kenilworth Hotel. Failing to get a boat to Greenwich from Westminster Pier, they travelled there by bus, 'a long squalid drive'. On returning to town, they went to see *Kamet Conquered* – 'A lot of close-ups of Raymond'. On the following day they went to the Victoria and Albert Museum, had tea and supper at the Kenilworth and then went to see Eddie Cantor in *The Kid from Spain*. His final comment is – 'an orgiastic night', and he obviously feared the consequences. On 7 April, the day after he had bought the kitten for his wife, he comments: 'Funny how I feel even a minute kitten as an intrusion and a responsibility until I get used to her. Her very smallness is painful to me.' By 15 April he had become 'very anxious lest V. should have begun child'. He expressed his anxiety again the following day and on 17 April writes: 'V. still late. I've got to prepare myself now, just as we've got straight with hope of a prosperous year, for a baby. I feel hopeless.' The following day he came back to the same subject: 'V. has obviously dropped her month and next month will decide if there's to be a baby. I can't bear the idea of her suffering, and any child will be an intrusion. I'm trying to resign myself to it and not to let V. see that I'm worried.'

On the 21st he found a female doctor, Dr Turner, who saw Vivien: 'It looks as if it's going to be a baby. Thank God V. seems quite happy about it, and I pretend to be. I don't think V. is pretending.' On the same day he was asked by Peter Fleming of the *Spectator* to do a 40,000 word biography of Thomas Chatterton, the boy poet who killed himself with arsenic when eighteen. The money would have been welcome at that point, 'God knows I shall need the £40 offered in advance of royalties', but he wrote in his diary, 'Alas! I can't accept; Chatterton is too dead a subject.' Nevertheless, he went to the Oxford Union Library next day to read up on Chatterton but this only confirmed his decision. To his mother he wrote that 'it went badly against the grain to have to refuse. But I couldn't [do it]. Such an abysmally dull dog.' He added that there was no more news except the arrival of 'a form to fill in from "Who's Who"!'[11]

Later that month he recorded in his diary: 'V. heard that her mother had fallen down and broken her leg, and so plans to go to the nursing home to-morrow' (25 April). What Vivien found at the nursing home was her mother sitting up in bed, waving a telegram and saying, exultantly, 'I'm a widow, I'm a widow!' – such jubilation at the death of a husband, but Marion Dayrell-Browning was a remarkable woman. Her husband had had an affair with a factory girl; she had left him – an unusual thing to do in those days. Her correspondence with her daughter gives a vivid insight into her personality. Admitting that she cared only for her two children, she wrote:

I cared for *nothing* else . . . now the things I wanted so much are all coming to me and I'm *free* – best of all and independent. Whew – that awful caged feeling I had with S.B. like being in a small dark room . . . I've locked up the drawer in my mind where every memory of it is only too damn clear & try to start at Oct. 30, 1915 when I burst the door & left him.

Telling her daughter that she has sent her a frock, she adds: 'I feel sure you'll like it – good style and material though simple (like me!) washes and will not fray – wear guaranteed!'[12]

Ironically, her relief at her husband's death was to be short-lived. She had, apparently, been 'jumping on to or off a bus and broke her hip or leg and was badly treated and got embolism' and on her second visit, Vivien found her mother in a lot of pain and saying, 'Why should it happen to me?' Vivien had not told her mother she was pregnant: 'I didn't tell her. I thought she would be annoyed and I was a little frightened of her. She was very efficient indeed.'[13] She and Vivien were not really good friends because Vivien found her bossy and she had forced Vivien as a girl to break off completely with her father. Vivien never forgave her for that: 'My mother made me when I was 15 write this extremely unkind letter to him. He wrote to me from Rhodesia [where he died alone] and she made me write a letter [rejecting him]. It was a dreadful thing to have done, dreadful, dreadful, dreadful . . .'[14]

At this point, an unexpected piece of luck came to the Greenes which enabled them to take a holiday in Wales to improve Vivien's health for the ordeal of giving birth. Mary Pritchett had sold the *Orient Express* to Twentieth Century Fox.* In his diary, 2 May 1933, he records: 'A lovely & exciting day. A cheque for £1,738.3.8d from New York for the film rights. I felt quite dazed all morning. It meant security for the first time since I left *The Times*.' Vivien and Greene went for a whole morning's walk: they 'had seldom been so happy. If she has a child we can well afford it now. We went over Dover's Hill to Weston & then by footpath to Aston and home through the Nightingale Woods' and they finished up having lunch at the King's Arms.

They travelled by train, taking the 9.1 to Cheltenham ('V. felt very sick in train') and then a through train to Swansea, arriving at 1.59 and being met by a car which took them to Honton and a 'sea beach, a house right on the sand. There was no road to it and the suitcase had to be carried along the top of the sandhills.'[15] After tea, they scrambled happily among the rocks, but on returning to the house found two telegrams had arrived simultaneously. Greene opened them in the wrong order. The first one reported that Vivien's mother was dead; the second that she was seriously ill.†

He writes in his diary of Vivien's reaction: 'Vivien, terribly broken,

---

* Fox Film corporation bought *Orient Express* outright from Greene for $7,500.

† Greene in his autobiography, *A Sort of Life*, tells us that when he was in Sierra Leone (during the war), running an office of the secret service, he also received two telegrams in the wrong order – the first telling him of his father's death, the second of his father's serious illness.

a horrible high cry. Got her up to her bed and telephoned to the nursing home and from them got the telephone number of her doctor uncle, Vivien. At last got through to him. A clot of blood had gone to the brain from the leg. Cremation Thursday. I told him Vivien was pregnant and asked him to write and dissuade her from going up to town. I knew it was no good trying to dissuade her for the moment. She calmed down a little and had supper and went to bed early and slept.' The following day, Uncle Vivien's letter arrived and set Vivien off crying again. Greene now got the local doctor to tell her that it would be silly for her to go to the funeral. Vivien at last was persuaded and Greene went in her place.

The cremation made a strong impression on him, and, as usual when an experience is new, he was hypersensitive to his surroundings and sharply alert:

Back to the crematorium where I met Vivien [brother of deceased] Bob [another brother] Tinty, Toto & Pat. A very pretty girl from the Hampstead Flat [where Vivien's mother had lived]. An atmosphere of high spirits roused by Bob who was laughing heartily a great deal of the time; in the place itself an air of heartless sentimentality, gardens and flowers and columbariums and 20 funerals a day and a man shouting along the piazza, 'Any more for the 4.30'. A very short cut service presented by an old emaciated vulture–like clergyman who recited the same preposterous address to the mourners as he does 20 times a day; an air of irreligion posing as undogmatic Christianity. The coffin laid on a moving shelf and at the appropriate words a decorative door opens, one hears the roar of the furnace; the coffin rather grimly, because in appearance of its own volition, slides through the door and the door closes behind it. Bob's comment on the whole affair, 'Like shelling peas'. Scientific efficiency behind the façade of mechanical sentimentality. A uniformed man later insisted on showing the women the columbarium and the ashes of Pavlova [the Russian ballerina cremated in 1931], obviously after a tip. He also came ingratiatingly over to Bob, Vivien, Paul, Pat and I, but Bob drove him off: 'Go away. We're busy.' At the end of the service the emaciated vulture shook hands with Tinty and Toto who were in the front row. The undertaker's man told Pat that hospitals would not take wreaths and the vulture immediately descended in a flutter of surplice. 'Perhaps you would like me to have them for my war memorial.' Imagine. The wreaths of 20 funerals a day.[16]

Greene was to make creative use of this cremation in his next novel, *England Made Me*, also in *Brighton Rock*, and in *The End of the Affair* (1951).

In *The End of the Affair*, Greene has his hero Bendrix arrive too late at the Golders Green crematorium (which was where Mrs Marion Dayrell-Browning was cremated) for Sarah's cremation. 'The crematorium tower was smoking, and the water lay in half-frozen puddles on the gravel walks. A lot of strangers came by – from a previous cremation, I supposed: they had the brisk cheerful air of people who have left a dull party and can now "go on" . . . As we reached the chapel everyone was leaving . . . I had an odd conventional stab of grief – I hadn't after all "seen the last" of Sarah, and I thought dully, so it was her smoke that was blowing over the suburban gardens . . . I went to the door of the chapel and looked in. The runway to the furnace was empty for the moment, but as the old wreaths were being carried out, new ones were being carried in.'[17]

*

Just before the arrival of the cheque from Twentieth Century Fox, Vivien had visited Oxford to seek a flat, for the regular book reviewing was beginning to give them confidence that they could leave the depths of the country. Vivien found a possible flat in Banbury Road for £85 a year inclusive and she took an option for a week, but once the largest cheque Greene had ever received arrived, the estate agent took them to see more expensive modern flats in Woodstock Close: 'Can't get used', he wrote in his diary, 'to the idea of our being well off and able to afford £150.' He described it in detail to his mother, and even the lift and the refrigerator were of special interest to him:

It's a top, third floor flat, outside there's an electric lift. Beautifully light. Tradesmen come up a kind of fire escape at the back to the kitchen door, and there's also a service lift . . . One large bedroom, one large drawing room, one room for dining room and study. A nice sized kitchen with a little electric refrigerator installed. A lovely bathroom with a square bath with black glass sides. Constant hot water. Hot towel rail. Heated linen cupboard. And along the hall a lovely let in cupboard with great sliding doors . . . Nobody has had the flat before us, so that it is speckless. Beautiful unstained oak doors and staircase. Fascinating windows which are hinged so that they can be cleaned from inside.[18]

As early as February, when a thaw set in and when the sun was out and the stream behind 'Little Orchard' was rushing down, Vivien and Graham had walked down to the railway station and back and he confides in his diary that if he went to Oxford he would miss the country: 'the quiet aesthetic pleasure of merely walking down the High Street to the chemist's; it is not an active aesthetic pleasure now, except on more than usually lovely days, but a complete absence of anything ugly, noisy or hurried to offend.'[19]

One of the last things Greene did before he left Chipping Campden was to respond to a letter from Walter Greenwood, author of *Love on the Dole*. He had reviewed Greenwood's novel in the *Spectator* on 30 June 1930 and praised it strongly. *Love on the Dole* made a tremendous impact as a record of the life of the unemployed in the 1930s: 'Several novels have been written lately on unemployment with hatred as the driving force: the occasion has made the novelist. But *Love on the Dole* is not a tract; it is a novel beautifully constructed by a born novelist . . . Mr Greenwood writes with vivid clarity; a gesture, a turn of speech, a cough, and the whole man lives. Judged by the highest standard, this is an impressive, a deeply moving book.'

As soon as Greene had read the novel and before his review appeared, he wrote to congratulate the author. Greenwood quickly wrote back: 'Heard from Walter Greenwood', he wrote in his diary, '. . . a pathetic letter referring to the hard life he had had, his broken engagement, etc. Living now on 30/- a week wages at Salford. Glad I had written.'[20] The following day he wrote to Naomi Mitchison asking whether something might not be done for Greenwood through the Authors' Society.

The last days in Chipping Campden came. Printed cards notifying friends and relatives and others of their move had already been sent out:

Mr & Mrs Graham Greene
have moved to
9 Woodstock Close
Woodstock Road
Oxford
Telephone: Summertown 58173

from Little Orchard
Campden, Glos.

On 22 June Vivien left for Oxford to be ready to receive the removers and Greene stayed to supervise them at the Chipping Campden end. But later that day he went to a literary party in London given by Mrs Belloc Lowndes. He did not enjoy it: 'Everybody sitting at little gold tables with only tea to drink; as soon as one had a sip one moved on. First had a terrible American woman whose name I didn't catch; was talked to for a long while about someone's books – her accent was incomprehensible; I thought we were talking about Cabell [James Branch Cabell] but it turned out in the end to be Garnett [David Garnett].* Charles and Dwye Evans turned up and Charles Morgan. Dwye said: "I haven't read the paper. Who got the Hawthornden [literary prize] yesterday?" No one of us knew. Presently Morgan said dryly: "As a matter of fact I did."' In the previous year, having read a new novel by Ford Madox Ford, Greene had written in his diary: 'Finished Ford's Novel. What a book. A "lovely" book from the technical point of view; his complicated time juggling better than Conrad's. One is inclined to exclaim "genius", but the critics will not; they all go hunting the safe, literary stylists like Charles Morgan, who have no originality to speak of but a pretty style, dead as last year's leaves. But Ford's is as full of life as a flea.'†[21]

After the party he had supper, 'and wandered dubiously about and went to Paddington early in the morning not getting back to Campden until 3 in the morning.' It was his last night in Chipping Campden: 'walked up from the station in bright moonlight, one light beaming in Station road, Campden at its loveliest. Audrey Cox put her head out of the window and said goodnight.'

He was up at eight next morning and started for Oxford. On Sunday, 25 June they moved into the new flat. It must have been a busy day for him, especially since Vivien was pregnant, yet he found time to do a four hundred word review for *John O'London's Weekly* and on the following day he was back to work on *It's a Battlefield*: 'A lot of re-shuffling of the novel. Cut out 2,000 words of prison interpolations. Cut out 400 of Communist meeting and wrote about 500 in. Wrote a completely new scene for the Commissioner.' Wherever Graham Greene lives he will sit down and write – that is his way of settling into a new environment.

*

The Greenes had been living in their new home in Oxford for five weeks when, on 4 August, Graham quietly recorded in his diary the

---

* In the book, *The Third Man*, Graham Greene's hero, Holly Martins, at a literary lecture for the Cultural Institute, to which he is mistakenly invited to lecture though he is only an unsuccessful writer of Westerns who has never seen a cowboy, naturally praises Zane Grey, the most successful writer of cowboy stories. The master of ceremonies quickly corrects him thinking he could only mean the eighteenth-century poet Gray. Perhaps the notion of such an error comes from the confusion reported above.

† During 1962 and 1963, Greene edited four volumes of Ford Madox Ford for The Bodley Head and wrote an introduction to volumes one and three. 'No one in our century', he writes, 'except James has been more attentive to the craft of letters.'

completion of *It's a Battlefield*, eight days in advance of his estimated time of completion: 'Finished my book, 67,500 words.' He did not find an appropriate title until late on into the book, a title, that is, which would embody the view of society he was trying to portray. That view developed from his personal experience, the trivial event of the delivery of the morning newspaper being delayed: 'Yesterday,' he recorded in his diary as early as 18 June 1932, 'the papers didn't arrive till about 10.30. The reason is in this morning's paper: a bad accident to the L[ondon] M[idland] and S[cottish] express between Crewe & Birmingham; 3 dead, 52 seriously injured. The effect on us, delayed papers, might be compared to the last & faintest ring a stone makes thrown into the pond. The first & clearest ring is death and physical pain: the next mental pain. Our ring is slight discomfort and irritation.' This vision of human life as a series of concentric circles of experience ranging from the tragic to the trivial and linked only by an accidental and brief 'knock-on' effect is the origin of his vision for *It's a Battlefield* which he was to begin three months later. The inner circles of death and physical and mental pain are those of the Drovers, Conrad, Jim and Milly. The outer circle belongs to the journalist Condor and the Assistant Commissioner, doing his duty and untouched by personal tragedy.

Such a vision of society required an appropriate technique, as Greene was aware. T. S. Eliot in 'The Love Song of J. Alfred Prufrock' had found his own solution, leaping from one subject and scene to the next. But this technique in a novel can be too abrupt, breaking up rather than blending together, as we see on page 85 (the first page of section 3) when in rapid succession we have a few lines on Mr Surrogate, then on the match factory, then on Condor the journalist.

On 13 January 1933, having written what he called the 'Mr Surrogate scene', he records in his diary that he suddenly thought of 'a new piece of carpentry: 'The simultaneity of the various shots [note the film imagery] to be emphasized by interpolated shots of the prison which all run straight on, though interrupted by the larger scenes. This to be carried on throughout the book, except when dealing with "Inner Circle".' And in effect this is what he did, the longer 'shots' of the Drover family's tragedy bringing out their pathos and ineffectuality, the shorter 'shots' of those removed from the tragedy emphasising their concern with expedience and personal success, throwing the Drovers' situation into greater tragic relief.

Structurally, the novel *is* a circle, beginning and ending with the outer boundary of the vortex, the detached stability of the Assistant

Commissioner, holding it together. There are no divisions into chapters, only five sections following each other without any formal separation.

The conviction that what he was portraying was a battlefield came as late as 1 July 1933, when he jettisoned the provisional titles of 'Opus V' and 'A New Novel': 'Almost decided on *It's a Battlefield* as a title with a beautifully suitable quotation from Kinglake's *Crimea*'. The quotation was apt since Kinglake saw the Crimean battlefield as a number of small, isolated circles:

> In so far as the battlefield presented itself to the bare eyesight of men, it had no entirety, no length, no breadth, no depth, no size, no shape, and was made up of nothing except small numberless circlets commensurate with such ranges of vision as the mist might allow at each spot . . . In such conditions, each separate gathering of English soldiery went on fighting its own little battle in happy and advantageous ignorance of the general state of the action; nay, even very often in ignorance of the fact that any great conflict was raging'.★

The idea of life as a battlefield in which individuals, ignorant of the extent of the whole war, fought their own separate battles, is the metaphor which embodies the theme of the novel, but the Kinglake quotation was found too late to have been the inspiration for this theme.

Out of the difficulties of writing this experimental novel, the characteristic Greene novel was to come, but his notion of what the modern novel should be was strengthened, after he had finished *It's a Battlefield*, by reviewing a story called *The Gates of Hell*.[22] It was a spy story, of the kind he was to excel in – *The Confidential Agent* (1939) and *The Ministry of Fear* (1943). Two quotations from *The Gates of Hell* present the basic Greene concept of life. The author is describing what he calls 'the Black Front':

> . . . a front that is within and around us. We live in dry trenches, camp shoulder to shoulder, but in front of us lie all the Dragons – the pleasures of the flesh, the tendency to compromise, and tepidity, materialism, liberalism, deification of the State, nationalism, individualism, superman-snobbery; in a word, all the philosophical and political illusions that we have been fighting wildly and confusedly for two thousand years.

★ A. W. Kinglake (1809–91). His *History of the War in the Crimea*, in 8 volumes, was written over a period of 25 years.

In particular, the passage which follows has an authentic Greeneian ring:

> The enemy is encamped not only in front of us, but within us, so that our battle-front is doubled . . . And the saddest part of it is that we are all merely a fragment of a sector of the infinite firing-line; we never see the shots; somewhere or other we find ourselves placed in the firing-line; we battle for a few decades; and then in some way or other we go down under the fire.

How close this is to *It's a Battlefield*: 'we are all merely a fragment of a sector of the infinite firing line'. How close to the philosophy and structure of the distinctive Greene novel.

*

There is an interesting postscript to *It's a Battlefield*. In 1968, an unknown Malian writer, one Yambo Ouologuem, wrote a novel entitled *Le Devoir de Violence*. It won the Prix Renaudot and was described as a 'horrifying saga of violence, degradation, cannibalism and eroticism'. Moreover it was acclaimed throughout the European and English-speaking world. It was translated by a distinguished translator into English and entitled *Bound to Violence*. On 12 March 1972, Robert MacDonald, an admirer of the novels of Graham Greene, and also a student of recent African literature, was struck by the similarities between certain pages of *Bound to Violence* and pages of Greene's *It's a Battlefield*. He contacted Greene and wrote an article about Yambo (referred to on one occasion by Greene as 'Little Black Yambo') asserting that he had simply lifted the scene between Surrogate and Kay Rimmer in Surrogate's house and Africanised the details, Surrogate becoming Chevalier, the Administrator, and Kay Awa, the magnificent black woman, being shown round his home, shown his bedroom, the books he has written, the portrait of his dead wife. Apart from the introduction of a verandah and such details as oil lamps, the scene is identical to that in *It's a Battlefield*. Later in his novel, Yambo inserted unchanged Greene's description of the injured Conrad Drover's sufferings.

Greene was more amused than angry. The *Bookseller* wrote: 'It is understood that Graham Greene has no intention of making a battle-field of the matter.' In the United States, where Harcourt Brace Jovanovich were in the process of bringing out a paperback edition of *Bound to Violence*, William Jovanovich, who said cancellation costs would be about $10,000, was quite firm. He determined that the book would not be reprinted in any form and he also determined that all existing copies in their possession would be destroyed. The *New York Times* quoted him as saying: 'Even if Mr Greene were to say that he just wants an acknowledgement, we would still go ahead and destroy the copies . . . If I cannot warrant it, I cannot publish it.' So Greene did not take any legal action, but Mr Alan Hill, chairman of Heinemann Educational Books, received a telephone call from Graham Greene about it when the news of the 'borrowings' reached him. He said: 'Greene came on the telephone to me. There was a dry, old-paper feel about his voice. You could almost tear it.'

No doubt it became a skeleton in Yambo's cupboard or, as Greene wrote in another context, 'the skeletons of other people's people'.

33

England Made Me – and the Black Sheep of the Family

In life the loser's score is always zero.
– W. H. AUDEN

'DIRECTLY this book's finished,' Greene told Mary Pritchett, 'I'm off to Sweden for three weeks.' This was no idle statement and did not refer to a holiday trip. It is an indication of Greene's restlessness, physical and mental, of his creative energy and his need to plan ahead; he had already decided that 'the next book was going to be divided between London and Stockholm'. London as a setting is no surprise, but Stockholm is – he had never been there. Why Stockholm?

The answer lies in a review he wrote for the *Spectator* in March 1933 of the biography of 'the Match King', 'the Napoleon of finance', the Swede Ivar Kreuger. Kreuger controlled three-quarters of the world's match trade, which sounds incongruous but was very lucrative. He juggled with astronomical figures, lending large sums to governments in exchange for monopolistic concessions – $75 million to the French, $125 million to the German government. He was a great man, 'and presently he is a little less than ordinary, lying on his bed with a bullet through the heart.'[1] His forgeries, discovered after his suicide, were, like everything else he did, massive. Four months after this review, Greene wrote in his diary: 'Almost decided on going to Stockholm next month as Kreuger will probably be model for one of the principal characters in next novel.*[2] (It is an odd coincidence that he was writing about a match factory in *It's a Battlefield*.)

Shortly before he and Vivien moved to Oxford, while on a short

---

* Greene's first title in his diary for *England Made Me* was 'Brother and Sister'.

484

visit to London, Greene went to the Swedish Agency to enquire about a holiday in Sweden (16 June). He also began seeking introductions to people who could show him round Stockholm. He approached David Higham about this, and he also wrote to Mary Pritchett: 'You don't know anyone nice in Stockholm I suppose whom I could go and see? I'm going by myself so I shall get horribly bored.' David Higham certainly did his best at a garden party arranged by Heinemann's in Kingswood on 12 July, which was well-attended. R. B. Cunninghame Graham and Lord Dunsany were there, and so was Louis Golding, whom Greene (in his student days) had persuaded to contribute to the *Oxford Outlook* ('Louis Golding, talking continuously about his own books'). The novelist L. P. Hartley was 'sitting in an immaculate overcoat in the warm sun, quiet, affected, exaggeratedly Balliol; a Russian American with a square yellow face like a Chinese lion-dog and a little white sun hat advised: "When you've got nothing, just sit still. Something turns up. I landed at Harbin with 13 dollars and I spent 12 dollars on a cable. I didn't worry. I just sat still." . . . At the cocktails Arnot Robertson, shrill, malicious, amusing, bawdy: presently became involved with Theodora Benson and her Askwith partner. By this time I was a little drunk and presently they drove me back to London just in time to catch the 7.35 to Oxford.'

During the party he was introduced by David Higham to the novelist Elizabeth Sprigge, 'about 30, cool, remote, handsome', so that she might give him introductions in Scandinavia as she was well able to do. He was 'paralysed; having just written a bad review of her latest novel', which was about to appear in the *Spectator* – he had written to his mother of the 'terrible lot of Heinemann novels for review lately – all tripe'. Elizabeth Sprigge's novel, *The Old Man Dies*, was interesting because the main character was presented through the conversation of relatives, but he found her style 'irritatingly chatty; the characters discuss at great length for the benefit of the reader what they themselves know already' and worse still, the novel depended for its success on dialogue and 'dialogue is what she is least able to write'.

Next day, sober and having assessed the situation, he wrote to Elizabeth Sprigge accusing himself of 'moral cowardice in not confessing the review' and asking her to do no more about the introductions.[3] Matters did not end there. In the same review he had criticised Beatrice Kean Seymour's *Daughter to Philip* for being very long, very shapeless, very unfinished. In his opinion, at least two hundred pages and half a dozen characters could have been cut out, and the novel was unwritten: 'It has not passed the stage of conception; it has not been criticised and refined and worked over.' Beatrice

Kean Seymour complained about the review to Charles Evans of Heinemann, who took the astonishing view that Greene should not review books he could not praise, and David Higham advised him not to review the latest by J. B. Priestley, another Heinemann author, since his contract for *It's a Battlefield* had not yet been signed. He gave way over the Priestley novel, but he did not give up over Sweden and introductions: 'I've got to the last chapter of *It's a Battlefield*,' he told his mother, 'and it looks as if I shall be free about 12th [August]. I wish Hugh could get a job fixed . . . and come with me. I've got a lot of introductions in Stockholm and Copenhagen.' He wrote to Hugh in the same vein, but Hugh had no job and no money, and even Greene's enticing information that 'the Gotha Canal Company are letting me have a free ticket, excluding food', had no effect.

Greene of course wanted a travelling companion, but he was also concerned about his brother who was going through a bad patch. He had taken his final examinations at Oxford that month: 'Hugh very pleased and excited by his viva which was a very short and complimentary one,' Greene noted; 'his hopes of a first dangerously soaring.'[4] His instinct had been right. 'Poor Hugh,' he wrote on 28 July, 'he got a second. He'll be terribly disappointed',[5] and to Hugh he wrote: 'It would have been a superhuman feat to have got a first as well as run the Film Society, but that doesn't make it less maddening.'

Rather like Graham, Hugh had let other things get in the way of his studies. He switched from Classics to English Literature after making friends with Edmund Blunden, Fellow and Tutor in English Literature (in his view one of the better decisions of his life), and had hopes of becoming a don. But he became President of the Oxford Film Society and led a fast life which included an affair with the 'beautiful, frail' wife of the manager of the Electra Cinema where the Film Society congregated on Sunday evenings. She was, alas, to die of consumption, but the manager did not seem to object to the affair, having, according to Hugh, other fish to fry. It was, however, to become somewhat public, when the commissionaire at the Electra 'strode one evening into the crowded George bar where [he] was waiting for her, snapped to attention, saluted and bellowed in his best parade ground voice, "Mrs Roberts will be twenty minutes late, sir." '[6]

A 1932 letter to Greene includes a poem which indicates Hugh's mood at the time: 'There are lips and laughter, where the lamps are Right/And lifting feet that ripple into rhyme/What do you do alone above the soil?/What do you do? I plough [university slang for failing exams].' So two brilliant brothers achieved seconds.

Undeterred and needing to get away when his novel was finished, Greene suggested an alternative to Hugh – a week in Burgundy – and 'if we do Burgundy, you must be prepared, passport and all, to leave with about 12 hours' notice.' Probably Greene was recalling the visit the two of them had made to Burgundy two years earlier during which he had played a prank. As Hugh explained: 'we were in an old fashioned third class carriage with the partition between the carriages only going half way up, and as I remember it there was somebody with his elbow and his hand laid out on the partition fast asleep in the next carriage, and just before we got out at the station, Graham very quietly fitted a French-letter on one of his fingers.'[7] But obviously Burgundy would not have suited Greene's purpose.

*

Greene eventually had his way. He and Hugh were to go to Sweden and, characteristically, he began organising down to the most minute detail. By that time Vivien was five months pregnant and it was arranged that she should stay with his mother: 'I shall dispatch V. from London to you "with care" on Tuesday, 15 [August] . . . You'll make her take exercise won't you?' Thanking his mother for taking Vivien he adds, 'She's anxious to be taught how to knit' – for obvious reasons. His mother was given their itinerary: 'Hugh and I leave at 6.20 pm on the 16th. We get to Gothenburg on the 18th at 7.am and I plan to stay the night there. Then the next day we catch the Canal Boat at 10.am (the 19th) and go gently up the Canal: one gets out and goes for walks at the locks; arrive at Stockholm bang opposite the Town Hall on the 21st at 6.pm.' Greene intended to spend five days in Stockholm and then push on to the island of Gothland to Visby, a mediaeval town with several miles of old wall still standing and five ruined cathedrals, then on to Copenhagen. He anticipated being home by 7 September.

As a traveller, not only did he note meticulously that their arrival at Stockholm would be 'bang opposite the Town Hall on the 21st at 6.pm', but also, with Hugh's financial problems in mind, he advised that he should get Sweden and Denmark added to his passport at once and 'while he's about it, if I were he, I should add to his application every country in Europe he can think of: each application for an addition costs 1/-, but you can have as many countries as you like added at one time for that 1/-.' Moreover, 'It may possibly get quite cold by the end of the month [August] – one forgets Stockholm is about as far north as the very tip of Scotland, so I shall take some warm underclothes.' 'One' might forget but Graham Greene never,

487

though he was wrong about the need for the warm underclothes. 'August is not the best time of year to see Stockholm for the first time – what with the heat and the humidity', he recalled in *Ways of Escape*.

He was particularly glad to have Hugh with him as otherwise he would have had to fall back on the Schellings as companions, described by his aunt Helen, not very promisingly, as 'two jolly girls' – he would so much have preferred 'two morbid girls'. However, they were to provide some interest. Writing to Vivien from the Strand Hotel, Gothenburg, on 18 August, about meeting them, he avoided mentioning anything that might cause jealousy: 'As for the "jolly girls" – Ursula, the younger, very healthy and managing and girl-girlish. She was on the look out for us at the barrier at Victoria [Station] and pounced; there was no avoiding them. The elder sister is quite tolerable but with a bad skin. They've just departed with their mother in a car . . . This is a nice room with a panorama of docks and liners fifty yards away. I'd rather have chaos.'[8]

But he wrote in *Ways of Escape*: 'I remember that my brother and I carried on a harmless flirtation with two English visitors of sixteen and twenty; we went for walks in separate pairs when the boat stopped at a lock, and once, for some inexplicable reason, considerable alarm arose because my brother and the younger girl had not returned to the little liner at the proper time, and the mother – an intellectual lady who frequently won literary competitions in the Liberal weekly *Time and Tide* – was convinced that both had been drowned in the canal.'[9] The elder girl was to make a small contribution to *England Made Me* in the character of Loo, the Coventry girl on holiday with her parents who has an encounter with the scapegoat hero, Anthony: 'One evening in Stockholm, on the borders of the lake, my companion of the canal slapped my face in almost the same circumstances as those in which Loo slapped Anthony's in my story, for I had told her that I believed she was a virgin. Afterwards we sat decorously enough in Skansen, Stockholm's park, among the grey rocks and the silver trees. (Her reaction was the only characteristic she had in common with Loo.)' Thirty-five years later, one of the girls, presumably the one who slapped his face, wrote to him: 'Can't imagine what prompted me to write to you after half the biblical span of life.' She had little to say about their original meeting: 'We met about thirty-five years ago in Sweden – I was the girl who wouldn't dance a bacchante with you. I always regretted it afterwards. I wonder if you still love Delius's "Walk to the Paradise Garden"?'

What Greene remembered of his visit to Sweden was the 'speckless miniature liner' which brought his brother and him up the canal from

Gothenburg to Stockholm, which he hoped would be the setting for his novel; he remembered walking in the soft summer brilliance of midnight and the silver of the birches going by, almost within reach of his hands, and the chickens pecking on the bank.[10]

What Hugh recalled, apart from wandering off with the younger sister and her mother fearing that they had both been drowned, was 'the wonderful sight of those locks coming straight down the mountainside'.

Details which did not appear in the novel, but which fill out Graham and Hugh's experiences, appear in an article which Greene wrote for the *Spectator*. The following passage shows how socially sensitive he has become, how he is reflecting on the hidden violence of a so-called pacifist:

> But in Stockholm, the moon glinted on the sentry's bayonet parading on the palace terrace; and at midday a beating of drums and flashing of swords and prancing of chargers as the royal guard changes. Our little country, our little country, the Swedish lawyer and the Swedish publisher kept repeating with sentimental humility and a deep hidden arrogance. (In Oslo they said, our small country, our small country, meaning the latest census result, the extent of the herring fisheries.)
>
> In his formal house, where every piece of furniture was like a child in a charity school, well-scrubbed, in place, at attention, the Swedish pacifist supported war between races. He grew excited at the thought of Russia, spoke of the glory of a war of extermination: poison gas, germs, aerial bombardment, savouring the words; after the schnaps and the beer and the wine (Skoll, with the glass held at the fourth button of the waistcoat, while the charity children stood stiffly around) and the glasses of punch and three whiskies and sodas, he became vehement about women, ears back, eyes popping: no woman has character . . . made to be the mates of men . . .

And there was the terrible insensitivity of a Swedish publisher:

> The publisher with the military carriage and the bristling red moustache said, If the Socialists really came to power, I should be the first to take up arms. I do not, of course, believe in God, but if our Church was threatened, I should be the first . . . He said, We haven't any need of Socialism here. I will show you how the workmen live. Poor, but so clean, so contented. He thrust his way into strangers' cottages, leant in at their windows, opened their

doors, displayed their bare rooms. The young man out of work with the fine starved features played an accordion for us, as we stood in the one room he shared with his mother. You see, Red Moustache said, speaking through the music, he has been unemployed for three years, the State gives them just enough to live on, but it is all so clean, they are so contented. He threw a krona on the table, and the young man played on, paying no attention. He rapped the krona on the table, and the young man nodded and went on playing and paid him no attention.[11]

Such, including 'the extreme formality of one dinner' they attended at Saltsjoba, was the sum of his experiences. 'I am amazed now', he wrote in *Ways of Escape*, 'at my temerity in laying the scene of a novel in a city of which I knew so little.' But, as we shall see, the novel did not depend solely on that brief visit and the biography of 'the Match King'.

They were home on 7 September and the following month Greene received, unexpectedly, an invitation from the managing director of Chatto and Windus, Ian Parsons, to join their publishing house. Obviously, this pleased Greene, and he must have given it some thought, but decided that he could not accept. If he had been living in London, he would have leapt at it, knowing that he could have 'gone on gently with [his] own work of an evening', but he could not leave Oxford just then with six months of the lease on their flat to run, so that he would have to spend each evening getting home and as his wife was having a baby in December, he felt rather tied.

Not one to miss an opportunity, however, and with family loyalties influencing him, he tried to interest Parsons in Hugh, and his letter suggests a further reason why he himself might have rejected the invitation:

> You spoke of an apprentice job being the one really vacant. I don't know if it would be any good putting in a word for a brother of mine who has just gone down from Oxford and is anxious to get into a publisher's? He was at a German university for a time and speaks German well. At Oxford he took a second in Honour Mods. and just missed a first in English. Edmund Blunden was his tutor and speaks highly of his work. His name is Hugh Carleton Greene, and his home is Incents, Crowborough, Sussex. But I daresay you've got dozens of apprentices to choose from.

Parsons was willing to see Hugh – 'I'm sure we shall like him and very much hope that it may be possible to offer him something', but all they offered him, since he was without experience, was a nominal salary of £100 a year for the first six months and after probation a gradual progress to £300. In any case, the interview did not go well; Hugh was afflicted with extreme shyness and no offer of a job was made, probably, given Hugh's future career, a fortunate decision.*

*

Graham Greene began writing *England Made Me*, according to the manuscript, on 16 November 1933. His instinct in settling on Ivar Kreuger as a key figure in the novel (he becomes the corrupt financier, Krogh) was sound as was his determination to visit Stockholm which provided him with the appropriate setting for his theme – the corruption that arises, in his view at the time, from the inherent failure of capitalism, a socio-political and contemporary theme, following on appropriately from *It's a Battlefield*: 'the economic background of the thirties and that sense of capitalism staggering from crisis to crisis.'[12] But this is cerebral. What he is really concerned with is the effect of childhood on the mature man, and this takes him back again to his own childhood, in an indirect way. The contemporary political scene is less significant than his own and his family's experiences and relationships, and Berkhamsted School.

England Made Me, an ironic title, refers to the forming of a certain type of character not so much by England, as by the English public school. In the novel, Kate, who is the twin of Anthony the no-good hero, arouses her brother's interest in moving to Stockholm only when, responding to his enquiry, 'And there'll be pickings for yours truly?' she answers, 'Yes there'll be pickings.'[13]

Both Anthony Farrant and the incredibly seedy journalist Minty, that powerful minor figure who runs away with parts of the novel, are in their respective ways grotesques who owe their twisted characters to their schooldays. Neither can rid himself of the indelible stamp of his public school, but there are differences. Minty is an old Harrovian – the 'school and he were joined by a painful reluctant coition' and as a consequence of this love-hate relationship he has, in spite of jettisoning the public school ethic, retained a loyalty to the outward symbols. He uses school phrases, respects the school tie and organises in Stockholm Harrovian dinners to raise funds for the school.

Anthony Farrant, though he has also rejected the ethic, in spite of failure, deception and fraud, has retained the veneer that was produced

---

* In 1969 Chatto and Windus joined up with Jonathan Cape and Hugh's eldest son Graham Carleton Greene became joint Chairman of the group.

491

by his public school – useful in keeping one's head above water. He has his one good suit and a confident manner and has 'promoted himself' by sporting, not the tie of his minor public school, but an Harrovian tie. Minty immediately recognises Anthony's deception: 'And he imagines he can sport a Harrow tie and get away with it.'[14] However seedy and discredited one becomes, the school pride lives on.*

Why did Greene, in his novels of the 1930s and 1940s, round on the educational system that had produced him and condemn its values? In part it must have been a reaction to his own experiences of school which were followed by his personal struggles to make a living, but his verbal and public condemnation was sparked off by two books. In a *Spectator* review, written long before the conception of *England Made Me*, he wrote: '*Gentleman – the Regiment* is an embarrassing book. What begins as a satire on the dead traditions of the Army . . . develops into a school-boy's daydream of Honour, Love, Back to the Wall . . . it is [hard] to sympathise with the naïve emotionalism of what follows. It recalls school speech days (The School . . . Honour of . . . The School), housemasters' perorations (The House . . . Honour of . . . The House).'[15]

Then in July 1933, he read Robert Graves's autobiography which had been published in 1929: 'Began with immense pleasure Graves' *Goodbye to All That*, which I had not read before: full of the right kind of anecdote, ones which set the creative instinct going.' Immediately, he had the subject for a novel – though one never to be written: 'What a subject for a slightly Kafka novel: the schoolboy who had skeleton keys made for all the rooms in the school and would steal down at night and turn them upside down. In the headmaster's study he even found a memo for his own expulsion and brought it back.'[16] It is interesting that, as the son of a headmaster, his sympathies are on the side of the anarchic pupil, and in the same diary entry he goes on: 'I want to propose a symposium to a publisher. "The Old School", studies of the horror of the public school by about ten prominent young authors with the schools mentioned by name', an idea which he followed up, writing to Mary Pritchett that the book would be 'a symposium of essays, called ironically The Old School – various distinguished authors telling candidly the horrors of their schools. Among others I have Harold Nicolson, Richard Hughes,

---

* Minty, living in seedy Stockholm lodgings 'watched by a spider under a tooth glass', appears late in the novel. He still retains a schoolboy phrase, among others, 'Oh, Holy Cnut' which might well refer to King Canute or Cnut. However, since it is often on Minty's lips and used as an expletive, it may also be a private joke of Graham's, an anagram of Holy Cunt.

Arnot Robertson, Elizabeth Bowen, Theodora Benson, William Plomer.'

The Old School was published in 1934 and, writing of Berkhamsted in the final chapter, Greene considers what is involved in the public school idea of 'Honour':

> As a training for life indeed the school was not more efficient than other public schools. It taught a moral standard quite out of keeping with adult manners. Mr Auden's essay reminded me that we too had the silly, but for our supervisors convenient, tradition of owning up. A hypocritical tradition, for who in later life 'owns up' to all his petty illegalities? I remember a junior house-master addressing the assembled boys at length on the subject of Honour; the occasion was quite typical. A dirty and unmarked gym shoe had been left in the changing-room, and he called on the boy to 'own up'. The boy, being more adult than the master, naturally did nothing of the kind. But the Honour of the whole house was at stake and the whole house was punished, an implicit encouragement to us to discover and lynch the offender. I cannot see any moral distinction between a rope for a negro and a knotted towel for a boy.[17]

The basic theme of *England Made Me* has been worked out here – the condemnation of an out-dated code of behaviour intended to prepare an individual for life in a hard world which is demonstrated by trivial incidents in an enclosed and protected community. Minty embodies the theme in its extreme manifestation, but Anthony Farrant is more convincing, no doubt because he was based on personal knowledge. In *Ways of Escape*, Greene tells us that he was quite satisfied with his portrait of Anthony: 'Hadn't I lived with him closely over many years? He was an idealized portrait of my eldest brother, Herbert.'[18]

If we separate the model from the character, we can understand what Greene meant by idealisation. Greene's condemnation of the public school, his contrast between principles taught and worldly practice, probably drew strength from a very personal emotion, a feeling that Herbert, the black sheep, had, in spite of his disasters, initially at least, been the recipient of much sympathy and assistance from his parents. The stringent devotion to work, the determination to be successful and independent which was Graham's creed, had been cunningly avoided by Herbert.

We also have to take into account a second portrait of Herbert, called on this occasion not Anthony but Hands, which appears in an abandoned novel, part of which was published in 'Penguin New Writing' in 1947. In his Introduction to the unfinished *Across the Border*, he states that he probably wrote it in 1937, but it is likely that it was written after his return from Liberia when he was also writing *Journey Without Maps*, and felt that after trying Herbert out successfully in *England Made Me* he might as well try him out again more realistically.

*

Greene's portrait of Anthony Farrant is of someone charming but entirely untrustworthy, characteristics which are underlined by the imagery: 'Congratulate me, he seemed to be saying, and his humorous friendly shifty eyes raked her like the headlamps of a second-hand car which had been painted and polished to deceive . . . But when he turned, his smile explained everything; he carried it always with him as a leper carried his bell; it was a perpetual warning that he was not to be trusted.'[19] Anthony is dishonest but not dishonest enough; he has a child's cunning in a world of cunning men; he has a habit of sending cables to his father, from distant places in the world: '"I have resigned" from Shanghai, "I have resigned" from Bangkok, "I have resigned" from Aden, creeping remorselessly nearer. His father had believed to the end the literal truth of those cables . . . But Kate had always known too much; to her these messages conveyed – "Sacked. I am sacked."' The truth is that he can't open his mouth without lying. But he is a man of ideas and schemes. He buys three hundred bags of spoilt tea for a song and sells them at the full rate. He had a plan to buy up old library novels and sell them in country villages, an idea for a shop which would pack and post Christmas parcels and one for a patent hand warmer (a stick of burning charcoal in the hollow handle of an umbrella). He is a skilled story-teller, adapting the same story to suit different audiences. There was the incident of the killing of an Indian minister when he 'told the fellows at the club how I was on the pavement when the coolie threw the bomb. A cart had broken down and the Minister's car pulled up and the coolie threw the bomb, but of course, I hadn't seen it, I'd only heard the noise over the roofs and seen the screens tremble . . . they [the fellows at the club] paid for three whiskies and we played cards and I won over two pounds before Major Wilber came in, who knew I had not been there.'[20]

Later, in Stockholm, his sister Kate comes upon him telling the same story to a girl (who has fallen for him): '"And then the bomb exploded," he was saying. "The coolie simply dropped it at his own feet. They picked him up in bits all over the city . . . My voice had frightened him." . . . "And the Minister?" a girl's voice said. "Not a scratch."'[21]

He is utterly feckless about money, but he never sponged – only accumulated debts which were never paid: 'What do you mean? I'm not going to sponge', and he sincerely believed he had never sponged. 'He had borrowed, of course; his debts to relatives must by now have almost reached the thousand mark; but they remained debts not gifts, one day, when a scheme of his succeeded, to be repaid.'[22]

Hands, in *Across the Border*, has also had a life of 'lost jobs . . . borrowed money . . . accumulated failures', and he has the same need to have an audience to listen to his extravagant, dishonest stories:

'Africa,' Hands said. 'The West Coast.'
'And when are you off?'
'It's not fixed definitely.'
'Those will be wild parts?'
'Oh,' Hands said, 'there's ivory, of course. And diamonds. Gold – You have to have men with you you can trust – in an emergency.'
. . . He had an audience at last: in the inner room he could just see the girl's face listening. It wasn't a pretty face, and it wasn't very young. He would have liked something a bit better, but it was an audience . . . as he started on the long fake tale he felt happy and ready for anything because no one here knew of the lost jobs and the borrowed money and the accumulated failures. The whole world was at his feet . . .[23]

Hands has much less appeal than Anthony, less charm, less spontaneity, is more calculating, and is closer to Graham's brother Herbert. He is seen returning to Berkhamsted, called Denton in the story – which reflects obvious aspects of Berkhamsted Graham used again and again in his stories – to meet his father, obviously based on Charles Greene. In the train, Hands is considering how he can explain one more failure to his father: '"I've been getting in touch with various companies" – a hint of mystery and importance.' . . . '"I've made contacts," Hands said . . . "Are they interested – I mean have they any vacancies?" "This isn't going to be a job of that kind," Hands said. "This is going to be more – " the dream grew as he talked – "more of an administrative job, men under me. It's what I've always wanted you know . . ."'[24] Anthony, Hands and Herbert all 'bore the knobs, excrescences, fungi of a dozen careers',[25] but Hands and Herbert drank, and Hands tries to hide this from his father:

'You've had a tiring day. Shall I get out a little burgundy?'
'Oh, no,' Hands said. 'I'm in training.'

495

'Harvest burgundy won't hurt you.'

'No, really. I'm not drinking.' He sighed at the cabbage and a very faint smell of whisky percolated through the room. He smelt it himself: it infuriated him. How could a fellow succeed with such a father? Smelling his breath, grudging the taxi, disbelieving. He said stubbornly: 'You know – what I've always needed is – well, to show I can lead men.'[26]

Sir Cecil Parrott, Graham's contemporary at Berkhamsted, recalled that 'Herbert was a drunk and often had to be carried home every night and a coach was specially kept for him to take him home.' In later years, when he was an alcoholic, he was perfectly frank about it. The journalist, Olga Franklin, interviewed Herbert Greene some eight years before he died: 'Herb was very tall, good-looking like the Brothers, but conscious that he was at least an inch shorter than Graham, and very much shorter than "Little Hugh"* . . . Herbert said he was now an alcoholic and he felt sorry if it embarrassed his brothers. He had no wish to embarrass Graham or Little Hughie or anyone else, but he was whisky-dependent now . . . It was impossible not to like Herbert and feel sympathy because of his honesty, frankness and simple acceptance of himself as "the family failure" . . . Herbert was not entirely without the family charm, talent and there was an absence of bitterness which was appealing despite his complaints.'[27]

Probably Herbert's first post was in Santos, Brazil, where a firm of coffee merchants was run by Edward Greene. It was natural that Edward would be willing to find a place for Charles's son. He was given a chance. Tooter Greene briefly presented the facts of Herbert's career in Brazil:

He was a drunk and he was irresponsible where money was concerned. He got a job in Brazil through the assistance of my father but he couldn't be trusted and had to go. I think he got a girl in the family way there. Later when he got another job in Argentina, his boat stopped at Santos and he brought the whole of the passengers to my father's home and we had to entertain. Also, he signed chits around the town to show that he was a big man, and again my father had to pay the bill.[28]

Felix Greene, Tooter's younger brother, while having a soft spot for Herbert, admitted, 'He was financially utterly untrustworthy, he gambled and got everyone else gambling.'[29]

* Sir Hugh Greene was 6 ft 6 in. Their cousin Ben Greene was 6 ft 8 in.

Letters written by Graham to Vivien before his marriage, and to his mother, show how disturbed, bitter and even savage Greene felt towards Herbert. To Vivien on 24 February 1926, in the early days of courtship, he wrote:

I had a letter from my eldest brother the other day. I wish he wouldn't choose me as his confidant, as he always does. I can see he's going to do something foolish. The man's an utter bounder. The fact that he's been practically living on his people for the last nearly thirty years doesn't seem to prey on him in the least. With him one has the continual choice of breaking his confidence, or watching, without doing anything, fresh trouble for my people looming on the horizon. I thought and genuinely hoped (I think he's driven most of his family that far) that something might finish him in Argentina. I know it's a horrid thing to say, but if he'd had the self respect of a louse he'd have done himself in by this time.

Three weeks later he wrote: 'My eldest brother's "broken out" again. His is a case where I can't help feeling that suicide far from being sinful would be meritorious. It's fearfully depressing and hopeless for my people.'[30]

Immediately after this, Herbert went out to a job in Rhodesia. He went out to one job but had to find another and back came an optimistic telegram. To Vivien, Greene wrote: 'Herbert has said to Audrey [Herbert's future wife] "Good job" – the firm he went out to had sold up; and they've had a long cable which is in code and they have to wait till my uncle gets back from London, who knows the business code. So I hope to goodness he's settled.'[31] The good new job turned out to be with Lloyd's but lasted only two months:

Herbert's started again. Cables home that the Lloyd's job has 'come to an end' and money needed. Poor Audrey was really hoping to be going out in a month or so. I wish to goodness he'd shoot himself – if he'd got any self-respect whatever he would – after all he's not a Catholic – there'd be no sense of sin in it, and therefore no sin to him. But I suppose he hasn't the pluck for that. I think in his case the sin is in not shooting himself. I think my people are getting simply desperate about him. If I was my father, I should simply send him nothing and let him get something or starve. Only I suppose he'd borrow enough money from some fool and get home. Killing would be no murder in his case![32]

And there is a letter, written to Vivien some time in 1926, in which Greene argues, on the basis of his knowledge of Herbert, that parents would only want to keep twenty per cent of those born and that if parents had the same power as the artist has over his pictures, they would destroy the rest. He admitted that an individual was not a picture: 'Though practically every week there's a case of a mother who's arrested for killing her baby. The creative instinct was there, but the result wasn't wanted.'

Perhaps because of the trouble created by Herbert, at this point, 1935, the time of *The Old School* and *England Made Me*, he became warmly supportive of his father. He saw him now as a progressive headmaster. In *The Old School* he writes as follows:

> I am thinking of my own school. I do not believe that it is family pride which makes me admire the head master's achievement (he is my father). He was an admirably progressive head master, never more so than in his later years at the school. A great many of the reforms which the progressive schools still regard as daring innovations could be found working smoothly at Berkhamsted. The masters were allowed an unusually free hand if they wished to experiment. An enthusiast was even allowed to start a system of self-government. It failed (you cannot be a socialist in a capitalist state), but he was given time and sympathy for his experiment. I remember with gratitude the admirable chamber concerts . . . Discipline was as humane as you could find anywhere outside a progressive school. Only house-masters were allowed to cane, neither prefects nor form-masters. It was not a really satisfactory school for sadists; only two sadistic masters come back to mind, and one of them was so openly sadistic, so cheerful a debauchee, that one could not grudge him his pleasure. Boys, like whores, prefer a man who enjoys shamelessly what he is about.
>
> But my father retired, a young man was appointed, and it was the young man who preferred to follow the older tradition. More time was given to games and less to work, physical training ceased to be a serious part of the curriculum, prefects were given the right to cane.[33]

Perhaps his father's increasing helplessness and sickness was another reason why Greene began to see him in a new light. In his diary for 28 March 1933, Greene writes: 'Cheered a good deal with Da sitting in the garden.' During his visit to Stockholm he wrote the following card to his mother: 'I'm terribly sorry of Da's affliction, remembering Henry James's letters of suffering; he had it about the same age.'[34]

This could mean that Charles Greene was then suffering from shingles, angina or diabetes – this last he certainly suffered from. In *A Sort of Life*, Greene writes of his father: 'In his last years he had diabetes and always beside her place at table there stood a weighing-machine to measure his diet, and it was she [Greene's mother] who daily gave him his injections of insulin.'[35] And certainly what made Graham speak so venomously against his brother Herbert at this time was the sense that his father and mother, but especially his father, were being overwhelmed by Herbert's fecklessness, his irresponsibility and his sheer dishonesty. To Vivien he wrote:

> It's rather gloomy being at home. More trouble about H. It's knocked my father up physically. He's got to see a specialist on Saturday. I shouldn't be in the least surprised if that bounder literally killed him. I shall do my best to give him a thin time if he ever gets back to England. It makes one feel positively murderous to see a useless idiot like him killing someone who's worth a million times more than him.

The sheer nobility and simplicity and unworldliness of Graham's father comes out in both *England Made Me* and *Across the Border*. When Kate speaks of leaving England and of her father's remarks about Anthony, we must wonder if these reflect those made by Charles Greene to Graham about Herbert: '"I wish Anthony were with you." He said I must be careful, there would be temptations. But he had never been tempted, he didn't know what the word meant . . . He had a profound trust in human nature. But be chaste, prudent, pay your debts, and do not love immoderately.'[36] It is put more strongly in the abandoned novel *Across the Border*:

> But Mr Hands wasn't listening . . . his old tired grey face had peculiar nobility. For nearly seventy years he had been believing in human nature, against every evidence . . . He was a Liberal, he thought men could govern themselves if they were left alone to it, that wealth did not corrupt and that statesmen loved their country. All that had marked his face until it was a kind of image of what he believed the world to be. But it was breaking up now . . . his son had begun to come – regularly – home with his excuses and breezy anecdotes and unjustified contempt.[37]

Then suddenly there seemed hope for Herbert in Rhodesia. His father must have provided financial assistance; a tobacco farm became a possibility late in 1926, and the following year he returned home to marry Audrey: 'Audrey seemed very well and cheerful,' writes Greene to his future wife. 'She sails on Thursday. She must have a good deal of courage really – and she hasn't seen him for about a year. One would have thought she'd have cooled a bit.'[38]

Felix Greene, then nineteen, visited Herbert in Rhodesia in 1928, and of course Herbert had come unstuck again. Felix remembered him kindly: '. . . long talks with him in his place in Rhodesia.' It was Felix's view that Herbert had really been 'shipped out there as in the old days they would ship out the black sheep they don't want around. He's a trouble, send him off.'

According to Herbert's wife, the tobacco farm collapsed, so they moved nearer to Salisbury (now Harare) and started next, with further financial help from home, a chicken farm, but all the chickens died of TB. As Felix commented: 'Yes. He was one of the unfortunates in this world.'

Herbert was charming and crooked, having what Greene called, in another context, depraved innocence. Postcards and telegrams would arrive at the home of his parents in Crowborough – he had resigned; honour had really been involved (exactly as in the case of Anthony and Hands); he really could not explain that.

There are one or two other interesting aspects of the 'Herbert' figure. According to Kate Farrant, her brother Anthony likes his girls common and in his digs she smells the scent of an older woman on his pillow and finds the photograph of another girl who has now left him, signed, 'With Love from Annette'. In 1930s' slang, he explains: 'She was the goods, Kate . . . She hasn't been here for a long time now. I haven't had any money, and the kid's got to live. God knows where she is now. She's left her digs. I tried there yesterday.'[39]

Graham has told us in *Ways of Escape* that he had shared many of Anthony's experiences and gives us one short example: 'I had known Annette, the young tart whom Anthony loved. I had walked up those forbidding stairs and found with the same emotion the notices.'[40] So we have an autobiographical sequence in *England Made Me*:

When I pushed the button no bell rang, and the light on the landing had been disconnected. The wall was covered with pencil notes: 'See you later', 'Off to the baker's', 'Leave the beer outside the door', 'Off for the week-end', 'No milk this morning'. There was hardly one patch of whitewash unwritten upon and the messages were all of them scratched out. Only one remained uncancelled, it looked months old, but it might have been new, for it said: 'Gone out. Be back at 12.30, dear', and I had written her a post-card saying that I would be coming at half-past twelve. So I waited, sitting there on the stone stairs for two hours, in front of the top flat and nobody came up.[41]

Greene here fills out the details of the relationship with Annette in a way that his diary, with its secretive brevity, does not. However, Anthony's unsuccessful wait for Annette certainly reflects Greene's own unsuccessful, and more anxious wait: 'to A's. No answer. Went and had another drink and returned: no answer. Went to Imhof's . . . took a taxi and returned to A's.' Not getting an answer, he remarks later in his diary: 'I hope A is not finally lost.'

Greene's Berkhamsted School experiences also play an important part in the novel – the stone stairs, the hated cubicles, the noisy nights which are recorded in his autobiography and in his unpublished first novel, 'Anthony Sant', reappear in *England Made Me*:

Pale-green dormitory walls and the cracked bell ringing for tea, my face bandaged and I listening to the feet on the stone stairs going down to tea. I could hear how many waited by the matron's room for eggs marked on the shell with their names in indelible pencil, and the cracked bell ringing again before the boot-boy put his hand on the clapper. And then silence, like heaven . . .

Feet on the stone stairs, running, scrambling, pushing, up to the dormitory . . . and the room full and the prefects turning out the lights. Not a moment of quiet even at night, for always someone talks in his sleep the other side of the wooden partition. I lay sweating gently unable to sleep, forgetting the pain under my eye, waiting for the thrown sponge, the rustle of curtains, the hand plucking at my bed-clothes, the giggles, the slap of bare feet on the wooden boards . . .

Voices whispering in the dormitory: 'Someone has left a vest in the changing-room. Honour of the House,' running the gauntlet of the knotted towels, noise over the roof-tops, paper screens trembling, spoilt tea, shooting in the streets, 'honour of the firm.'[42]

The details are similar, the situation the same, in the novel and in *The Old School* – in one case a vest, in the other a gym shoe left in the changing room, the involvement of the Honour of the House and running the gauntlet of knotted towels.

Central also is Anthony's running away from school, slipping out with his clothes under his dressing-gown, his walk of freedom, meeting in a barn his sister, who sends him back to school and regrets sending him back, 'to conform, to pick up the conventions, the manners of all the rest. He tried to break away and I sent him back.'[43]

She tries to make up for it by finding him a job in Stockholm. In varying degrees, Anthony Farrant, Hands, Herbert and Graham were all failures of the system – in the system's terms.

Hands is an unusual name, but there was, in Greene's day, a master at Berkhamsted called Hands. The indefatigable schoolboy diarist, J. B. Wilson, made the following entries:

> June 12. Hands 100 lines for forgetting to put my cubicle straight.
> June 16. 250 lines in French for Hands, the tick.
> July 8. Sit at side table in dining room for a week. Hands. I don't know what it was for.

Hands sometimes appears in the diary as 'Hoof' or 'Hands the Hoof'. The April 1919 edition of the *Berkhamstedian* reported in the column 'School News': 'We regret the absence of H. S. Hands, Esq. who is away owing to illness.' The event was recorded by J. B. Wilson:

> January 20, 1919: Hoof was sacked by Charles [Greene] last Thursday, what for I don't know and Scribbens is in a most frightful row, part of which is that Little B [nickname for head of the house, Mr Herbert] in clearing out Hands' room – the dirty little swine – read a letter which Scribbens had written to Hoof in the holiday. Scribs had written in the hols discussing Little B. This the tick took to Charles and there was a hell of a row. Hoof has been absent since Wednesday and has I believe gone home today. I don't know what's up with him. As far as I know he's only got a scab on account of which he told us not to rag Harold.

It is impossible to get to the source of this storm in a teacup after so many years, except for Hands's special relationship with a Scribbens and a boy called Harold. Possibly there were suspicions of a homosexual group, and Little B and Charles Greene thought they might have a dangerous situation there. If Greene was recalling this event in using the name Hands, it must only have been that he saw Hands, like Herbert, as a loser.

*

In the novel, the Herbert figure is killed off. Anthony is drowned through an accident in mist but there is a strong suspicion that he was in fact drowned by Krogh's henchman, Hall. The notion of a drowning which might have been suicide was probably in Greene's mind as early as 1925 when he wrote to his mother: 'Did I tell you of my other excitement about a week ago, seeing a body carried up out of the Thames as I was crossing Albert Bridge? All very dramatic, deep dusk, the two lights burning on the little quay below the bridge and a couple of policemen carrying the covered stretcher across to the embankment steps.'

The details of Anthony's cremation suggest that Greene had in mind his mother-in-law's cremation: 'Minty stood at the door, took the names, noted the wreaths . . . The coffin slid smoothly along its runway beneath the angular crucifix. The doors opened to receive it; the flapping of the flames was picked up by the microphone beside the altar and dispersed through the great bleak building. Minty crossed himself: they might just as well have left the body in the water. He had a horror of this death by fire.'[44]

*

Characteristically, Greene wrote to Hugh, then in Berlin, on 26 November 1934: 'I was frantically busy, finishing The Shipwrecked [a discarded title for *England Made Me* which was used for an American edition], doing a short story which is supposed to be coming out in a limited edition, and getting ready for Liberia. Now there's a slight calm before the storm.' But there wasn't. Vivien was coming towards the end of her pregnancy.

In the earlier days of the pregnancy, Greene had referred to the expected child as 'the amoeba'. He had planned to try to cross Lapland by reindeer with his friend Nils, though Nils became ill and this was called off, but Nils and his wife were willing to adopt 'the amoeba'. As time went on, his attitude changed. On 15 October 1933, he sent Vivien earrings and addressed the envelope:

> For My Most Darling
>   Broody Queen
>   on the 6th anniversary [of their marriage]
>   with all the love in
>   the world.

And going back to his earliest love letters, he drew a white star, their mutual sign for a loving kiss –

Christmas Day fell on a Monday in 1933. On Christmas Eve, Greene went to Midnight Mass and on Christmas Day, Vivien cooked the turkey. There was ice on the canal but it was gently thawing and, Greene recalls, 'making a noise like dry straw'. All the barges collected together for Christmas at one lock and the children rolled tin motor cars from Woolworths down the gang planks. The Greenes opened their presents at tea-time. They had books from publishers – an anthology of Elizabethan prose, a limited signed edition of Maugham's short stories, a collected edition of Edward Marsh's *La Fontaine*, a limited and signed Masefield. Vivien gave her husband a 1686 edition of Thomas Flatman, a poet and painter of miniatures. Presents for Vivien were mostly connected with the forthcoming birth – a beautifully worked cot cover and a handsome pram cover among other things. What touched her most was the fact that their morning maid came all the way over from Kidlington and left a present for her outside the front door.

Vivien gave birth to a daughter, Lucy Caroline, on 28 December 1933. It was a terrible experience and one which she recalled vividly forty-six years later:

> It was like a train running slowly into the buffers. You can see the accident from afar and then the birth comes. In those days no one told you. Lucy was born in that horrible Radcliffe Hospital in Oxford. The Campden period was over, and Graham was just beginning to do well and we had moved to Woodstock Road. It was very bad anyway. In those days they didn't look at you beforehand. Lucy was a really bad birth. It was very bad and they were very unfriendly, horrible nurses. They didn't look at you, they didn't weigh you or take your blood pressure. I think I saw the doctor twice before I had her and I was extremely ignorant. I remember asking, 'Will it hurt much?' and he said, 'We'll see.' That was Dr Shurrock. It certainly did hurt. Chloroform, after a long, long time – 28 hours was quite enough. The gas and air went wrong. It had to be a caesarean and they were so brutal about the stitches. I remember that awful head nurse or sister coming to me and saying, 'Oh this room smells' and flinging open the window, and I said, 'I can't do anything about it – I can't get up.' And she came up and leant over me and said, 'Don't you talk to me like that!' It was terrifying.

Though the child was born at 8.40 p.m. and weighed 7 lbs 11 oz., Graham was not allowed to see Vivien until the following evening. He walked back from the Radcliffe to Woodstock Close, tears pouring down his face (as he told Vivien afterwards) because of the pain she had suffered and the condition she was in.

Lucy Caroline Greene was baptised according to Roman Catholic rites on 27 January 1934, dressed in the christening robe which had been used in the Greene family since the days of Graham Greene's grandmother and is still in use: 'it would be safest', Greene advised his mother, 'if you sent it [the robe] to me, and I should not undo the parcel until it was required.'[45] On 27 January he wrote to her:

The christening went off all right, Lucy protesting at each thing done to her, but not setting up a continuous howl. A much more elaborate ceremony than the Anglican; salt in the mouth (she didn't mind this a bit), oil on each shoulder, on the back of the neck and the forehead, and of course, water over the head. She also had to catch hold of the stole and at one point a lighted candle!

PART 7

Liberia to North Side

EETS SUSPECTEL
'S MYSTERY ILLI

U.S.
Joi
W

Fr.

An
Amer.
World
of
ter

s
s
to
Re
to
f

W
tha
sors
nec.
Sen

D
to
tic
th
tic
cei
C

g's
ets
ys-
the
.
), of
oad,
pital
sus-
om-

girl
New
nd
nt
er
ut

Miss Barbara Greene and her cousin, Mr. G. Greene, the novelist, who have left London on an exploration trip to Liberia, the African negro republic

34

Champagne and Fate

How narrow is the line which separates an adventure
from an ordeal.

— HAROLD NICOLSON

GREENE's journey through Liberia was the first of his exploratory
journeys into distant, dangerous, little-known places in search
of adventure, experience and inspiration for a book. Not only was
this trip extremely dangerous, it was his first trip out of Europe, and
he made it with his twenty-three-year-old cousin, Barbara Greene.
The adventure, he wrote later, in these circumstances, was 'to say
the least, rash'.[1]

In his customary way, he had begun early to obtain information
and introductions but he had failed to find a travelling companion.
'It all happened', his young cousin blandly tells us, 'after a wedding':
'"Why don't you come to Liberia with me?" I was asked by my
cousin Graham, and, having just had a glass or two of champagne,
it seemed a remarkably easy thing to do. I agreed at once. It sounded
fun. Liberia, wherever it was, had a jaunty sound about it. Liberia!
The more I said it to myself the more I liked it . . . Yes, of course I
would go to Liberia.'[2]

Afterwards, the party atmosphere gone, both of them had misgivings: 'My invitation to her', Greene admitted, 'can only be excused
because I had drunk too much champagne at my brother Hugh's
wedding and I never expected her to accept.'[3] When the effect of the
champagne wore off he panicked and sent his cousin a League of
Nations account of the conditions in Liberia, hoping to discourage
her. She regretted her decision because she was enjoying herself very
much in London, but she felt sure her father would forbid her to go.
However, when she told him what she had agreed to, his response
was, 'At last one of my daughters is showing a little initiative.' The
'champagne decision' was to be held to, and for Barbara Greene it
was to be fun. She set out for the Liberian jungle with no more

509

seriousness than if she were going off on a weekend hike, with little planning or calculation – but that was what a wealthy debutante of the 1930s felt able to do and did. She was young and zany and up to any lark. The fun for her began when she gave an interview to a *News Chronicle* reporter which led to dramatic headlines:

BEAUTY OF 23 SETS OUT FOR CANNIBAL LAND
COUSIN AS ONLY COMPANION
TO BLAZE WHITE TRAIL IN THE JUNGLE
SLAVERY AND DISEASE

The report went on:

A girl leaves London today to explore a wild country where no white man has ever trod before – the depths of the hinterland of Liberia (the Negro Republic of Africa) a land of cannibalism and witchcraft. This is her debut as an explorer. 'I'm ashamed to confess I've never been on so much as a caravan trip before,' Miss Greene told me yesterday in her Chelsea flat.[4]

Greene knew nothing of this and for him 'fun' had nothing to do with the expedition. Later, when asked why he went to Liberia he wrote, 'like Everest, it was there.' Not a satisfactory reason, though the fact that he equated Liberia with Everest might indicate the competitive direction of his thoughts, given his brother Raymond's heroic failure to climb that mountain the previous year.

There were other reasons, not least his longing to escape from the pressure of writing. To Hugh he wrote: '[I'd] rather get bubonic plague than write another novel for a year.'[5] No doubt also he wanted to escape the tasks of fatherhood. There was now a baby in the house and a wife inevitably caught up with mothering. But if he felt the intense need to escape from the writing of fiction, he had to write something – he had a family to support. More important, he had the financial backing of his publisher: 'Charles Evans is enthusiastic over Liberia', he excitedly told Hugh 'and has offered to pay all my expenses in advance.'[6] There was another factor: travel books by young authors who made 'uncomfortable journeys in search of bizarre material' (Peter Fleming to Brazil and Manchuria, Evelyn Waugh to British Guiana and Abyssinia) were popular.[7]

Liberia would certainly provide him with the dangerous, the unknown and the bizarre. The Republic originated in 1822 when an American philanthropic society bought land in Liberia from native chiefs and established a settlement there for freed American slaves with its capital at Monrovia. Eventually, as a Republic, it had a constitution based on that of the United States and descendants of the slaves became the ruling class. They already had, or adopted, English names and spoke English, according to Barbara, with a strong American accent.

Preparing for his journey, Greene learnt from the League of Nations report and the British Blue Book of May 1934 that the diseases in the interior were elephantiasis, leprosy, yaws, malaria, hookworm, schistosomiasis and dysentery; the President was privately exporting slaves to Fernando Po;[8] and a black mercenary called Colonel Davis, carrying out a savage campaign, had burnt 41 villages and killed 140 men, women and children; his troops had surrounded villages and poured volleys into the huts; the charred remains of six children were reported after the departure of his troops.

Other considerations pointed him to Liberia rather than to other parts of Africa and a clue to one of these was provided by the reporter for the *News Chronicle*. It seems that Sir John Harris, Parliamentary Secretary to the Anti-Slavery and Aborigines Protection Society, had been giving the young explorers advice before they set out, and he had some notions of the dangers ahead: 'They are going into the hinterland farther than any white man had gone before . . . The negro tribes, which have been savagely oppressed, may welcome them – but you can never tell.' Harris also gives a hint of a special mission: 'I should think they ought to get through, and their information if they do will be very valuable.' So it would appear that Greene would be seeking information about present oppressions, including slavery, for the Anti-Slavery Society. Barbara Greene (now Countess Strachwitz) in 1976 admitted that though she never knew whether Graham wrote a report about slavery, he did have a commission of some sort, 'that gave him the idea of going there'.

If there was a commission, it seems to have been somewhat secret. There is no reference to it in the minutes of the committee meetings of the Anti-Slavery Society. However, Sir John Harris did report, rather cryptically, to his committee on 6 December 1934 that he and Lady Simon 'had had an interview with Mr Graham Greene who was going out to Liberia early in the New Year with the object of writing a book. They were endeavouring to secure introductions for Mr Greene from the Foreign Office and the Colonial Office, to the British Consul at Monrovia and to the Governor of Sierra Leone. The publication of the book would involve the Society in no financial responsibility.'

Greene was able to talk to C. H. Buxton who had just returned from Liberia, but he himself had no experience of travelling through jungle – and he had no reliable map. He wrote to his brother: 'The whole trip gets more and more fantastic every day . . . I have to take out cases of food and a book I've read on Sierra Leone says cheerfully that several Europeans have recently gone across the border [into Liberia] but none of them have returned! This, of course, is not to be repeated to the family.'[9] At last he had managed to get 'a fairly large scale map; most of it blank white with dotted lines showing the probable course of rivers!' He also managed to get an American military map, though it showed whole areas left blank except for the word 'Cannibals'. Something of the initial distaste for the journey appears on the outside flap of the envelope of the November letter he sent to Hugh: 'Proposed title for Liberian book: "You Can Keep Africa".' But he had to go and, as with many future foreign journeys, it was an essential step into a new existence. Greene would certainly not be looking to the journey for any 'fun'. Besides he had the responsibility for a young woman's safety.

Their journey began on 4 January 1935 at Euston Station where they caught the 6.5 p.m. train and sat down immediately to what sounds like typical train fare – pieces of damp white fish. According to Barbara they were both shy people, and one wonders what they found to talk about, with Greene's thoughts no doubt engrossed with what might lie ahead. They spent the night at the vast Liverpool Adelphi Hotel which looks down over the shopping and commercial centre of the city towards the River Mersey and the docks. Greene described the Adelphi as having been 'designed without aesthetic taste but with the right ideas about comfort and a genuine idea of magnificence!' The next morning, a cold January day, they embarked at the Prince's Stage: 'The black steamers knocking about in the yellow Mersey, under a sky so low that they seemed to touch it with their funnels . . . the grey mildness, shading away into black at every pretext.'[10]

Along with its account of their journey, the *News Chronicle* published a photograph of the cousins walking up the gangway of the cargo boat, the *David Livingstone*, a photograph which is striking, not because Greene is following his cousin and wearing a mackintosh, but because he looks desperately unhappy. He has recalled that he was furious over the interview Barbara had given to the *News Chronicle*. The reason for his anger, perhaps, was that he felt the interview might have cost him Harris's support; this can be inferred from a letter Sir John wrote to Vivien (no doubt in response to one of Vivien's pouring oil on troubled waters), a copy of which is in the archives of the Anti-Slavery Society: 'Frankly, I was sorry to see the interview, for I was afraid it might do harm,' wrote Harris.

'However, unless something unusual happens, Liberia won't see the *News Chronicle.*'

Harris had been immensely kind to the young novelist, and understandably Greene would not want to lose his patronage. He had talked to the Colonial Secretary, and to the British Foreign Secretary, Sir John Simon, to try to smooth Greene's way at least through the British colony of Sierra Leone. He also gave Greene an introduction to the native chief at Cape Palmas. But more than this was involved.

Light-heartedly, Greene had written to his brother about other possible spin-offs from his relationship with Harris – an amazing result of the trip might be offers of a variety of jobs from the most august to the most farcical – 'adoption by old Harris as his successor as Parliamentary Secretary to the Anti-Slavery Society . . . I have to be stared at and my private life examined by a committee of philanthropists . . . On Wed. I have tea with Lady Simon.' It was no idle fantasy, for he wrote to his mother: 'Sir John Harris is so taken by me that he wants me to come in as his assistant when I get back and in three years succeed him, but I don't think it's really my sort of job . . .'

The journey, with its dangers, discomforts and trials, was to be well-documented. Both cousins kept diaries, each published an account, and Greene's letters to his mother give a further dimension. He eventually concluded that Barbara proved 'as good a companion as the circumstances allowed, and I shudder to think of the quarrels I would have had with a companion of the same sex after exhaustion had set in, all the arguments, and indecisions . . . My cousin left all decisions to me and never criticized me when I made the wrong one, and because of the difference of sex we were both forced to control our irritated nerves.'[11] Barbara wrote that his brain frightened her. It was sharp and clear and cruel. She admired him for being always unsentimental, but noted, 'always remember to rely on yourself . . . If you are in a sticky place he will be so interested in noting your reactions that he will probably forget to rescue you.'[12] Although he tore down her cherished ideals so that she had to rebuild them, she also concluded he was the best companion one could have had on such a trip – and she was to learn far more than he expected.

*

The sea voyage at least was relaxing, the other passengers interesting, and there were some hilarious moments. In chapter 2 of *Journey Without Maps*, Greene wrote: 'My cousin and I had five fellow-passengers in the cargo ship, two shipping agents, a traveller for an engineering firm, a doctor on his way to the Coast with anti-yellow fever serum and a woman joining her husband at Bathurst.' Three days out, in the Bay of Biscay, he wrote to his mother, 'Rather sick the second day and the sea getting up again now, but the Bay perfectly smooth . . . The other passengers very nice.' He gave additional information: the commercial on his way to Nigeria was very fat, the young woman joining her husband very dull and the Elder Dempster agents very North Country.

Greene liked the skipper and the fat agent, a drunk with the stamina of a bull, whom he calls Younger in his travel book, but whose real name was Holt. There were some boisterous drinking parties on board and at Las Palmas the Greenes went ashore with 'Younger' and Phil who was the ship's third officer. They all had a wild party at a dance hall:

> [Younger's] inevitable expression, 'You saucy little sausage', could be heard throughout all the rooms, his progress was one long slap and tickle and free drink. The manager followed him around with bills he wouldn't pay and Phil brought up the rear . . . afraid there would be trouble . . . Every now and again to keep the manager quiet Phil paid a bill and the manager tore it up and dropped it on the floor and wrote another. Then Younger stole the woman belonging to a man with a guitar . . . the manager wrote a bill, and Phil plucked at Younger's sleeve and said, 'Go steady, old man. Go steady.' A madman came up and threatened Younger, but Younger didn't understand, didn't care anyway . . . He sat on a chair playing pat-paw with his stout black bitch; sometimes he made a pass at her mouth, but she avoided that, nudging with her elbow, pushing forward her empty glass while the manager wrote out another bill.[13]

The terse entries in Greene's diary confirm this extraordinary account: 'Holt runs riot. The language of slaps, the way the tart kept control of him, got drink after drink and always fended off her face. Lavish expenditure at the bar followed by refusal to pay the bill. You saucy old sausage. The third officer's protest . . . The man with the banjo and the madman.'[14] Barbara also recalled the madman, 'drunk and with curiously twitching limbs, was walking round the room from table to table, screaming out all kinds of threats.'[15] They returned to the ship in a rowing boat at 12.30 a.m. with a helplessly drunk and unconscious Younger.

Next day there was an indication of the other side of things – of the nature of the land they were approaching. Greene wrote to his mother that they had 'passed through what is known as the Elder

Dempster graveyard, because of the people . . . who catch fever there on the way home, the day was most curious and delicious: warm, damp with a strong smell of seaweed everywhere and haze over the sea.' Barbara recorded that many ports were closed to them because of yellow fever. At Bathurst, a quarantined town, they dropped off the 'frightened, repressed little woman who had never before left Liverpool . . . to join a husband she had not seen since her honeymoon'.

*

The Freetown *Weekly News* reported on 26 January 1935 that there had arrived on Saturday last by the *David Livingstone* from England, 'Mr Graham Greene, one of the distinguished authors in London, who is on his way to Liberia. Mr Greene intends to write a book on his travels and proposes to travel to Monrovia overland from Kanri Lahun [Kailahun].' The African newspaper tells us that he was for some time connected with one of the leading journals in London, and that Miss Greene, his cousin and travelling companion, 'is an accomplished Lady', followed by the expressed presumption (news to Barbara) that she would play an important part as a typist in the preparation of her cousin's book.

For Greene, Freetown was 'an impression of heat and damp' and a mist which 'streamed along the lower streets and lay over the roofs like smoke'.[16] It was his first contact with a British colony, an outpost of the Empire which his father and the masters at school had praised: 'Freetown. An intense seediness. Europeans had withdrawn to the hill. All shabbiness an English responsibility, the only colour native,' he records in his diary. 'The fish lying ten deep on the ground; Cabins standing in thick plantations.' This reaction – the condemnation of the whites: 'England had planted this town . . . Everything ugly . . . was European';[17] the romantic view of the natives – 'if there was anything beautiful in the place it was native: the little stalls of the fruit-sellers which went up after dark at the street corners, lit by candles; the native women rolling home magnificently from church on a Sunday morning . . . the lovely roll of the thighs, the swing of the great shoulders',[18] was not unusual in first encountering the culture shock of a colonial settlement; indeed it was predictable in a man predisposed to anti-colonialism by his Independent Labour Party affiliations.

Greene's views were supported by highly selective details – the peeling Remembrance Day posters, tin roofs, broken windows, the Anglican Cathedral of 'laterite bricks and tin with a square tower' and – part of the fraud – the Norman church built in the nineteenth century, and the vultures – 'birds one turns away from at the Zoo with dusty feathers and horrible tiny heads sitting on the roofs, crouching in the gardens, like turkeys, seven out of my bedroom window'.

His diary confirms a swing from white to native: 'Kru Town. Long hanging breasts', which becomes 'breasts falling in flat bronze folds' in his travel book, and to his eyes they seem more beautiful than the 'small rounded immature European breasts'.[19] This, for Greene, remained a quintessential aspect of Africa and when a year or two later he reviewed a film which attempted to portray the white civilisation of the coast by means of a picturesque market and a native hospital, he stressed the need for a different set of images: 'Tin roofs . . . broken windows, long dreary bars and ants on the floor, vultures pecking like turkeys in arid back gardens.'[20]

Characteristically, his interest was in the unsuccessful as opposed to the career men, the colonial officers, the kind who came from just such a school as his own – the rulers. He could sympathise with the whites at the sharp end of the stick, whom he found drinking in the City Bar: 'Worms and malaria, even without yellow fever, are enough to cloud life in "the healthiest place along the Coast". These men in the City Bar, prospectors, shipping agents, merchants, engineers, had to reproduce English conditions if they were to be happy at all. They weren't the real rulers; they were out to make money; and there was no hypocrisy in their attitude towards "the bloody blacks".'[21]

He returned to this topic many times. As late as 1968 he wrote of the City Bar failures who 'knew more of Africa than the successes who were waiting to get transferred to a smarter colony and were careful to take no risks with their personal file.'[22] These latter, 'the real rulers, came out for a few years, had a long leave every eighteen months, gave garden parties, were supposed to be there for the good of the ruled. It was these men who had so much to answer for.'[23]

The City Bar men were those who had stayed put into 'the beginnings of old age . . . The dream which had brought them to Africa was still alive: it didn't depend on carefully mounting the ladder of a career.'[24] 'One came home and wrote a book,' he guiltily admitted, 'leaving the condemned behind . . . eking out a miserable living in little tropical towns.'[25]

Moreover, the City Bar men gave Greene an insight into human purpose and behaviour which was to influence his future work. He would seek a significance and a virtue in the sordid. His long-standing friend, A. S. Frere, who succeeded Charles Evans as head of Heinemann, admired Greene, but had a strong impression of his difference from other people. 'If you read the opening of *The Power and the Glory*', he said, 'and all that heat and squalor that he enjoys – I don't think he's interested in the softer human emotions. The things that come first, good food, good drink and comfortable sleep – Graham is never interested in these.'[26] Barbara Greene extends this assessment of her cousin: 'Apart from three or four people he was really fond of, I felt that the rest of humanity was to him like a heap of insects that he liked to examine, as a scientist might examine his specimens, coldly and clearly.' But she adds, 'He was always polite.'[27]

*

The *Weekly News* reported on their activities during their stay: 'Mr Greene and Miss Greene had the pleasure of meeting several European ladies and gentlemen and had a jolly drive to Lumley Beach and other interesting places worth seeing. Mr Greene hopes on the homeward voyage D.V. to meet with as many Africans as possible. They left on Wednesday morning by the Bo train.'

What the reporter did not know was that during those few days it was essential that the Greenes acquired more information about their journey, yet it seemed impossible to come by any that was reliable. Barbara commented: 'Graham had never done anything like this before . . . It was, in fact, not in his line . . . For some reason he had a permanently shaky hand, so I hoped we would not meet any wild beasts on our trip. I had never shot anything in my life, and my cousin would undoubtedly miss anything he aimed at. Physically, he did not look strong. He seemed somewhat vague and unpractical, and later I was continually astonished at his efficiency and attention to every little detail.'[28]

He had indeed tried to arrange everything in advance. When they came on shore they were met by an elderly Kruman who had received a cable from London asking him to be there. 'My name', he said, 'is Mr D.' 'He knew the Republic well', writes Greene, and describes a visit to Mr D's home in Krutown – 'one of the few parts of Freetown with any beauty'. Barbara, who accompanied him, described Mr D as 'a very black gentleman who, for some reason . . . had been banished from Liberia'. She recalled being bitten by insects. Mr D did his best, but could not be sure 'to a matter of ten miles' where the places were on the route he was recommending they should take.

To go up country they needed carriers and servants. Apart from provisions, one had to take furniture and cooking utensils. Greene thought this had been arranged through a man he calls Jimmie Daker (probably not his real name, though the diary gives no other), but Daker had forgotten to do it: 'He was vague, charming, lost, and a little drunk.' Fortunately, at a cocktail party, they met the irresistibly attractive 'Daddy', who, although drunk, drove them round

Freetown erratically while subjecting them to an interrogation which brought home their inadequacy:

> Had [they] ever been in Africa before? Had [they] ever been on trek? What on earth made [them] choose to go There? . . . Had [they] any idea of what [they] were up against? Had [they] any reliable maps? Had [they] any boys? Had [they] let the D.C.'s [District Commissioners] up the line know of [their] coming and engaged rest-houses? No, [Greene] hadn't known it was necessary. When [they] crossed the border, how were [they] going to sleep? In native huts. Had [they] ever considered what a native hut meant? The rats, the lice, the bugs.[29]

He concluded, nearly weeping over the wheel, that they were 'poor innocents' (and they were!) and, drawing on his twenty-five years' experience of Freetown, he next turned up early at their hotel with the best boys in Freetown outside waiting for orders. Greene confessed that, as the boys stared at him from the bottom of the hotel steps, he did not know what to say to them. Barbara recorded that nervously he addressed them in rather literary English. There was Amedoo, the head boy, who was also to look after Graham, 'grey-faced and expressionless, holding his fez to his chest'; 'Souri, the cook, a very old, toothless man, in a long white robe'; Laminah, who was to look after Barbara, 'very young, in shorts and a little white jacket . . . with a knitted woollen cap on his head crowned by a scarlet bobble.' 'I couldn't have imagined then', Greene wrote, 'the affection I would come to feel for them . . . Our relationship was to be almost as intimate as a love affair.'[30]

Returning to Sierra Leone as a British Intelligence agent six years later, Greene sought out Laminah, no longer the little boy in shorts and a woollen cap with a scarlet bobble – 'War had brought him prosperity and dignity.' Greene had searched in vain for Amedoo and when he asked Laminah about him he broke into peals of laughter: 'Old cook, he all right, but Amedoo he under ground.'

*

They left Freetown on the narrow gauge railway for Pendembu just in time, as Greene noted in his diary: 'In the train to Bo [halfway to Pendembu] heard that day we left, Freetown was put into quarantine, a case of yellow fever among the whites [actually a young man*

---

* This was a Mr Henry Owen Lipscombe. He was, according to the local newspaper, supervisor of schools. His wife had arrived in the Colony only a month earlier. He was thirty-five.

from the educational department]. Attempts to stop arrival of aero-planes.' It was a slow journey, taking two days to cover 250 miles, and Greene and his cousin had never been so hot and damp – 'if we pulled down the blinds in the small dusty compartment, we shut out all the air; if we raised them, the sun scorched the wicker, the wooden floor, drenched hands and knees in sweat.'[31] As they travelled, Greene noticed that the price of oranges dropped from six a penny to fifteen a penny at Bo, and also at every station – and the train stopped at every station – 'women pressed up along the line, their great black nipples like the centre point of a target.'[32] They stopped for the night at Bo, and were met by the District Commissioner's messenger, Sergeant Penny Carlyle, who took them to a rest house, squashed a beetle under his toes, clicked his bare heels, and dismissed himself.[33] Greene was struck by the egrets, 'like thin snow-white ducks with yellow beaks', the total absence of vultures, the PZ stores which sold everything – clothes, food, ironware, and also advertised a '50 & 50 cure for gonorrhoea', and again the naked breasts of the black women. Later, he would tire of naked bodies and feel he had lived for years with nothing but cows, but at first he was fascinated, watching the children taking their milk standing – 'they ran to the breasts in pairs like lambs, pulling at the teats.'[34]

At Bo, in spite of cockroaches larger than black beetles in the bathroom of the rest house, the dry, tasteless chicken, the hurricane lamps providing the only light, Greene felt happier: 'It was as if I had left something I distrusted behind.'[35] This he put down to the fact that they had left the Colony of Sierra Leone and were in the Protectorate, presumably implying a loosening of the white man's control and a closer proximity to the true Africa. The white men up-country, he noticed, did not talk of 'bloody blacks' or laugh at them or patronise them. He suggests the reason for this was that the Englishmen up-country were dealing with 'real' natives, not Creoles, and that the real native was someone to love and admire. And he makes an important point. The white man knew about some things, but the natives knew about other things – 'one's gun was only an improvement on their poisoned spear, and unless one was a doctor, one had less chance of curing a snake-bite than they.' Moreover, the Englishmen up country were a finer, subtler type than those on the Coast, 'they cared for something in their country other than its externals, they couldn't build their English corner with a few tin roofs and peeling posters and drinks at the bar.'[36]

Another messenger met them next day at the station at Pendembu with a lorry and the paramount chief of the area, small and bow-legged, who spoke no English. Greene had an incomprehensible conversation with him. They were taken on to Kailahun, on the border with French Guinea, the local natives fleeing at the sight and sound of their unfamiliar vehicle, and were put up at the rest house. There were only two white men in the village – the District Commissioner who held the dangerous post (Greene recorded in his diary that three of his predecessors had died mysteriously, and Barbara was pleased to see that he 'had all my cousin's books in a row on his bookshelf'), and a Scottish engineer who was building a bridge.

As the Greenes were drinking warm cocktails with the D.C., a third white man strolled into the bungalow wearing dirty trousers and a singlet, his head shaven and with a black tuft of beard. The D.C. immediately took him to be a Liberian messenger who was reported to be in the area having been sent to guide the Greenes on the next stage of their journey. Consequently, he was not asked to sit down or offered a drink but was given instructions to show the Greenes the way to Bolahun and the Holy Cross mission in two days' time. The man agreed to this, saying that he had just come from there. When, eventually, he was asked whether he was the Liberian messenger, he said that he was not. He was German, had come from Liberia and was returning there and simply wanted a bed.

The bland, enigmatic German appeared next day in a clean shirt, a pair of fawn trousers, a round white topee and carrying an ivory-headed stick and a long cigarette-holder. According to Greene's diary, his name was Heydoern, and he was profoundly struck by the man and his reticence. Greene, a total amateur in jungle travel, tried to elicit information:

> Had he ever been to Africa before he came out to the Republic two years ago? No never. Hadn't he found things difficult? No, he said with a tiny smile, it had all been very simple. Would one have trouble with the Customs at the frontier? Well, of course, it was possible; he himself had no trouble, but they knew him. Should one bribe them? That was one of the questions he didn't answer, putting it aside, smiling gently, tipping the ash off his cigarette on to the beaten earth of the floor. The cockchafers buzzed in and out and he sat with lowered head smoking. No, he wouldn't have another biscuit.[37]

But he did tell them that the Liberian Commissioner at Bolahun was a scoundrel; that he could make things unpleasant; that a permit of residence was necessary, and then Heydoern 'walked briskly away, twirling his ivory-headed stick'. It was not until they were a further week on their journey, had crossed the border and were going full-out on their trek that, during a stroll, Heydoern explained why he was in that part of the world. He had spent some years wandering about from village to village, learning old customs and the various dialects.[38] He was gathering material for a dissertation at Berlin University and hoped to make a grammar of the various languages.[39]

Greene was beginning to learn the ways of the country, sending a letter a day's journey ahead of them to the mission at Bolahun in Liberia by messenger, and sending a runner by night, with a fill of paraffin for his lamp, a dagger hanging over his shoulder as he ran out into the dark bush, and the letter stuck in a cleft stick.[40] But by 26 January 1935, when the Greenes really began their safari, Graham had to come to grips with the country he was travelling through; he had to become a leader, dealing with all kinds of difficulties and unexpected events. It was a twenty-mile trek from Kailahun to the mission in Liberia to which they were going. He had ordered two lorries to pick up Barbara, himself and the German at seven o'clock, but only one turned up, 'and it was an hour and a quarter late.' He was vexed by the delay – looking ahead, and taking into account possible delays at the Customs post, he was hoping to reach the mission before dark.

It was his first encounter, as a man of precise and orderly habits, with 'the idea that time, as a measured and recorded period, had been left behind on the coast . . . watches couldn't stand the climate. Sooner or later they stopped.' He was still thinking in European terms, confident that he could plan his journey according to a time-table, thinking that they were going from Bolahun to the capital, Monrovia, and that they would be there in a fortnight, with no idea that in four weeks' time they would be more or less lost in the middle of Liberia. He did not have the money for such a long journey. The problems came upon him in many different ways, in terms of real difficulties and dangers and images, all forcing him to take command, to become the leader he had never wanted to be (or thought he could be) at school.

He was later to conclude that his anxiety about timetables and destinations was that of an 'unpractised traveller'. He 'got used to not caring a damn, just walking and staying put when I had walked far enough, at some village of which I didn't know the name, to letting myself drift in Africa.'

Logistical problems faced him at Biedu where, for the first time, he saw 'the full extent' of their luggage spread out down the centre of the village: 'six boxes of food, the two beds and chairs and mosquito-nets, three suitcases, a tent we were never to use, two boxes of miscellaneous things, a bath, a bundle of blankets, a folding table, a money-box [the money was all silver coins, though he discovered that those with Queen Victoria's head were unacceptable since she was dead], a hammock.' He was shamed by the fact that each of his servants carried only a small flat suitcase, and he knew that a German botanist had made a ten-day trek without a hammock, without provisions, without even a bed or mosquito nets – 'he slept on native beds, ate native food', but he also died of dysentery.

At Biedu, he decided he must take on twenty-five carriers – a District Officer never travelled with fewer even on a short journey and the Greenes were going into unknown territory. Moreover, four carriers would be needed for Barbara's hammock. Graham decided to walk and so save 7s.6d. on a larger hammock with six carriers. That thorn in his flesh, the experienced Heydoern, usually travelled on a chair slung on poles and doubted whether, with only one hammock, the Greenes would reach Bolahun before night. He could not conceive of white people walking and scrambling along with the men. The carriers were asking 1s.6d. each and though Greene knew they were poor he also knew that Heydoern paid only 6d., and so he beat them down to 1s.3d.

The three travellers faced a journey of twenty miles to the Holy Cross mission, run by American Episcopalian monks at Bolahun, and it involved crossing the border into Liberia.

A typical day's march was eight miles. Greene was to average twelve miles a day over the next four weeks. On starting, he gave orders to the carriers, feeling like a subaltern facing his platoon for the first time. He could not believe that twenty-five men would obey when he commanded, 'Set in motion': 'I stood back and watched them with . . . an absurd sense of pride.' They were like a long mechanical toy striding out of the village. The German, in his chair, went ahead of Graham's column,[41] Graham walked and Barbara followed in the hammock. At first the track was wide and then it narrowed into a path through elephant grass. The first stream crossed, they were among woods and clearings and woods again. In his diary Graham records: 'Started after German. B[arbara] in hammock. A good deal of elephant grass, bridges made out of tree trunks.'[42]

*

They arrived at the Liberian frontier about midday – three or four huts, a few riflemen in scarlet fezzes with a gold device, the Liberian flag (a star and stripes), and a little man with a black moustache and a yellow skin and a worn topee who came out into the clearing and greeted them.[43]

In his diary Greene reveals more anxiety than he shows in *Journey*

Without Maps: 'Smoked with one customs man and tried to be agreeable. German passed through. Had to sign 8 forms . . . Entirely in their power. Left my invoice and £4.10.0 in guarantee. Had heard of our coming. Denied having any weapon and ammunition. Both hidden in money box under shoes.'[44] A child brought specially to see white skins screamed in fright. They were pleased to enter the Republic but they had not seen the last of that customs officer.

The next day, when they had already arrived at the mission at Bolahun, he sent a soldier to demand a further £6.10s. Greene could ill afford the money and sent the soldier back empty-handed, but the customs officer himself came, 'borne in a hammock, the long rough path from Foya with four carriers and a couple of soldiers . . . He swaggered across the verandah, a little sour, mean, avaricious figure, grinning and friendly and furious and determined. He got his money, drank two glasses of whisky, smoked two cigarettes; there was nothing one could do about it; it was impossible to bribe an official who probably took a lion's share anyway of what he exacted.'[45] In any case, Greene noted in his diary, he was: 'Scared lest he should follow me and see the automatic in the money box.'[46]

They left Foya at the hottest time of the day, just after midday, and climbed steeply, yet they enjoyed the first day's trek in the Republic. They were on the edge of the immense forest which covers Liberia to within a few miles of the coast.

Barbara Greene recalls her cousin walking on in front at a tremendous speed. It was the habit Greene started from day one and it was carried on until much later when he fell ill. They never walked together, though Barbara could use the hammock for only five or ten minutes each hour – apparently to save money on the carriers (in any case it was very uncomfortable). Greene recorded in his diary: 'This is a long trek . . . B's hammock broke at one point. Had to hoist it over about 4 streams. Appallingly hot . . . the fruit the men ate. Their cheerfulness and running conversation. Final race with the dark.'[47] Later Barbara had to walk all the time. They walked hour after hour, the bush thick enough to block out every view. Barbara confided: 'I did not notice the trees or the plants. If we went through any villages I did not see them.'[48] The ground was steep and difficult and sometimes they had to scramble on all fours. Greene wrote: 'Over the worst part, the precipitous rocky paths down and up.'[49]

Away from the luxury of her Chelsea flat and on her first trip through jungle, walking and scrambling on the hot, mountainous, enclosed track, it is not surprising that Barbara should be under such strain that she did not notice the villages she passed through. In contrast, Graham's vigilance never faltered: 'However tired I became of the seven hour trek through the untidy and unbeautiful forest, I never wearied of the villages in which I spent the night,' he wrote,[50] and he had absorbed their typical geography, layout and interiors – even coming to an understanding of the community life: the villages (in the Banda territory) made up of circular huts with pointed thatched roofs and set on the hilltops 'on several levels like medieval towns'; the paths to them dropped down to the stream where 'the villagers came to wash their clothes and bathe and rose abruptly up a wider beaten track out of the shade to a silhouette of pointed huts against the midday glare.' Each had 'its palaver hut and forge, the burning ember carried round at dark [to light the individual fires], the cows and goats standing between the huts, the little groves of banana trees like clusters of tall green feathers.' The fire in the middle of each hut, he noted, kept out mosquitoes, fleas, bugs and cockroaches – but not the rats.

He saw the villages as 'small, courageous' communities 'barely existing above a desert of trees, hemmed in by a sun too fierce to work under and a darkness filled with evil spirits'; 'love', he concluded, 'was an arm around the neck, a cramped embrace in the smoke, wealth a little pile of palm-nuts . . . religion a few stones in the centre of the village where the dead chiefs lay . . . a man in a mask with raffia skirts dancing at burials.'[51] 'This', he wrote, 'never varied, only their kindness to strangers, the extent of their poverty and the immediacy of their terrors.' They were tender to each other and to their children, 'they never revealed the rasped nerves of the European poor in shrill speech or sudden blows.' They had 'a standard of courtesy.' He even came to admire his carriers and to accept their smell.

Though white 'twisters' claimed that a 'black boy will always do you down', he never found any dishonesty in his boys or the carriers or the natives in the interior, 'Only gentleness, kindness, an honesty which one would not have found, or dared to assume was there, in Europe.'[52] He was astonished by the fact that he was travelling through unpoliced country with twenty-five men who knew that his money box contained what would be a fortune to them in silver which they could easily have stolen and disappeared with into the bush, but they never did.

On the last dark and wearying trek to the mission, he remembered Souri, the old cook, in his long white Mohammedan robes flitting ahead and carrying a trussed chicken, the smoke from fires blowing across the narrow paths between huts and 'the little flames . . . the African equivalent of the lights behind red blinds in English villages'.[53]

The last village before the mission was Mosambolahun, nearly two hundred huts packed together on a thimble of rock, standing in its own pagan dirt, the Christian garden village of Bolahun in the cleared plain below. The chief of Mosambolahun himself came to them in a swaying hammock with a noisy group of men. Ninety years old – he was the puppet of younger men – 'he quivered and shook and smiled . . . He was swept away again by his impatient hammock-bearers, waving his dried old hand, smiling gently, curiously, quizzically . . .' He had over two hundred wives; the same ones were sold to him over and over again and he was too old to keep count.

Even when they reached Bolahun village there was a further walk of two more miles to the mission.

Both Greenes record their utter exhaustion and that of their carriers when they reached the Holy Cross Mission. In his diary Greene wrote, 'Carriers entering faint fallen on ground: plummy smell', their loads dumped outside the long bungalow, Barbara sunk on the steps, 'only the white eyeballs of the carriers were visible where they squatted silent on the verandah.'[54] Greene was now in a mood to see good everywhere. Listening to the low murmur of Benediction inside the church, and watching the priests, white robes stirring in the cold hill wind as they came out, Greene felt that 'the sound of the Latin represented a better civilization than the tin shacks of the English port, better than anything [he] had seen in Sierra Leone';[55] he was for the first time unashamed by the comparison between white and black – the mission 'at least wasn't commercial. One couldn't put it higher than this, that the little group of priests and nuns had a standard of gentleness and honesty equal to the native standard. Whether what they brought with them in the shape of a crucified God was superior to the local fetish worship had to be the subject of future speculation.'[56]

The boys unpacked their things in an empty room in the rest house and set out their wooden table and chairs and opened some tins for their supper – while they drank bottled water feverishly[57] and took their quinine.[58] A case of whisky was opened and Greene went out to seek a Dutch gold prospector in his tent to invite him to bring his soda and have a drink. Greene calls him Van Gogh, though the diary shows that his name was De Groot, but he was sweating with fever: 'He was bad, very bad: he had spent a lifetime in the tropics, but nine months in the Republic had got him down.'[59] Barbara, who had 'never known before what it was to be quite so weary', crept on to her hard camp bed and fell fast asleep.

On the following day, 27 January 1935, their first at the mission, they were relaxed, without anxiety, unaware of the difficulties that lay ahead. They were struck by the extraordinary Sabbath peace of that garden village: 'It was . . . unmistakably Sunday. A herdsman drove out his goats among absurdly Biblical rocks, a bell went for early service, and I saw five nuns going down in single file to the village through the banana plantations in veils and white sun–helmets carrying prayer-books.'[60] A photograph taken on that first morning has survived, on the back of which Greene has written: 'Biblical scene outside the Rest House, Holy Cross Mission, Bolahun.' Greene invited the nuns to have 'chop' (dinner) with them – 'girlish excitement', he records in his diary. Also he noted the excitement of an old black woman on seeing a white woman who was not a nun: 'old woman came leaping across beating her arms in the air with excitement at the sight of B[arbara]. Wanted to shake hands. So did all the children. A touch of the lips and then a simultaneous licking of the thumb and first finger.'[61] Nevertheless, there was sickness and disease at the mission as Barbara Greene records: 'Everywhere the natives . . . walking about with smallpox, yaws, elephantiasis, and covered with venereal sores. A horrible sight, which we saw in every village we stayed at.'[62] No wonder that the mission concentrated on teaching the elementary rules of hygiene and on healing bodies. Greene's servant Amedoo went down with lung trouble and 'lay on the doctor's couch dumb with terror'.[63]

Characteristically, Greene was observant of everything around him. At Benediction in the ugly tin-roofed church he noted two young converts: 'A tiny piccaninny wearing nothing but a short transparent shirt scratched and prayed, lifting his shirt above his shoulders to scratch his loins better; a one-armed boy knelt below a hideous varnished picture (He had fallen from a palm tree gathering nuts, had broken his arm and feeling its limp uselessness had taken a knife and cut it off at the elbow).'[64] They went to Tailahun, the next village, to see funeral ceremonies and took photographs:

Christianity and paganism both marked the dead man's grave, for there was a rough cross stuck on the mound to propitiate the God whom the old chief had accepted on his deathbed, while in a pit close by, following a pagan rite, sat eight wives, naked, except for a loin-cloth. Other women were smearing them with clay; it was rubbed even into their hair. The majority were old and hideous anyway, but now the pale colour of the pit in which they sat, they looked as if they had been torn half-decomposed from the ground. They had lost with their colour their mark of race and might have been women of any nation who had been buried and dug up again.[65]

They stayed at the mission a week. To Jimmy Daker in Freetown the Greenes were 'poor innocents'. Father Parsell, still living at Bolahun at the age of eighty-two, recently spoke of the two travellers as 'babes in the wood' without 'a clue' of what they were getting into.[66] And this was true – how could it be otherwise? However, they assiduously studied manuscript maps of the Western Province drawn up by Dutch prospectors seeking gold, had consultations with the German linguist Heydoern and finally decided on a different (and longer) route.

After Bolahun, Greene and Heydoern parted, never to see each other again. Heydoern was indeed a rare man, a German scholar at ease in the jungle and able to speak the local languages – Mende, some Buzie and even a few words of Pelle. Twenty years later, Heydoern came back into Greene's life in a curious way, or at least his memory did. Greene was in a hotel room in Cracow drinking with a Polish novelist and talking cautiously in Stalinist Poland. Both novelists were taken aback by a knock on their door, thinking it might be the secret police. Extraordinarily, it turned out to be a German who introduced himself to Greene with the words: 'You knew my brother in Liberia . . . he walked with you to Bolahun.' Greene searched his mind and remembered the reticent mysterious and scholarly German. He asked his whereabouts and was told that Heydoern had been killed in 1943 on the Russian front.

*

Bolahun was a village Barbara called 'a kind of Garden City', with its cheap oranges, mangoes and bananas. What Greene remembered was the swooping flights of small, bright rice-birds, the fragile yellow cotton flowers, 'butterflies, palms, goats and rocks and great straight silver cotton trees', 'the graceful walking women with baskets on their heads'.[67] It was a friendly mission with its spartan but clean rest house, where on that last night there was dancing on the verandah. Amedoo had recovered as had De Groot who came over for a cup of tea, 'pale as a ghost under his bleached gold stubble . . . he treated the natives with a harsh lack of consideration one would never have guessed existed behind the horn-rimmed glasses.'[68]

'It wasn't so good when the dancers went,' Greene recalled. Barbara had been bitten all over by insects and he had a rash over his back and arms. After dinner, he went to the last pail-closet ('the wooden seat . . . swarming with ants') he would see before the end of his journey in Monrovia. It was a luxury, as was the rest house. It would be native huts after that, with rats, worms and fevers. This last night was to be a grim presage of the future. Their boys now included

Mark, whom Greene describes as 'slightly touched' but who was a Christian and spoke some English. Mark needed their two lamps while washing up the dinner things, and Graham and Barbara sat 'in the waning light' of their two electric torches. Large horseflies, cockroaches, beetles, cockchafers and moths invaded the place; 'big spiders dashed up and down the wall, the [water] filter in the corner slowly and regularly dripped, a tom-tom was beating somewhere.'[69] He was at last driven to bed by a great black moth the size of a small bat.[70]

Greene's mind must have been going over their journey. On the following day he would indeed embark on a journey without maps, and we can interpret that phrase in a number of ways.

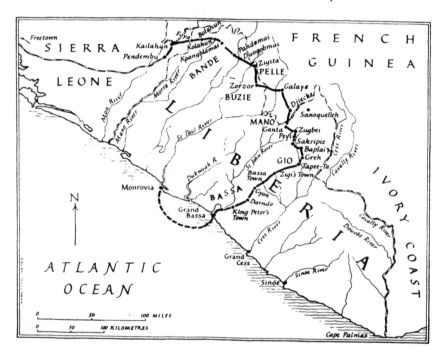

In the strictly geographical sense, he was about to enter an unmapped area of Liberia. People in Sierra Leone did not travel inland. They went off by sea or air. In Monrovia, the capital of Liberia, few people, whether Liberian or European, had travelled more than 30 miles inland. The Fathers had been kind, finding 26 carriers who would go with the party all the way to Monrovia and cashing Greene's cheque for £40 in small silver, but they could not advise on the journey ahead. There was the possibility of a route to Sinoe and Mana Kru by way of the northern border to Ganta, where they hoped to find the medical missionary, Dr Harley, who might help them to work out a route to the coast. The German doctor at the mission knew only of Kpangblamai, Duogobmai and a long march to Nicoboozu and then to Zigita. Dutch prospectors' maps did not go far. The only certain route seemed to be Sir Alfred Sharpe's, but to follow it, one had to rely on rumour and hearsay.

Then there were the cultural maps. What we might call 'the disease maps', he had copies of before leaving England, but the cultural maps had to be absorbed gradually, in a process of confrontation, first as the tourist, more or less insulated from the places he was travelling through, then as the independent adventurous traveller and then as the white man forced by an intimate contact with an unknown civilisation to adopt colonial attitudes in order to survive and to accept that he must bargain, command and live uncomfortably while depending on the natives. The next stage, for Greene, was an encounter with the black ruling class. From his point of view, they were all journeys without maps. And there was the final map – a totally new one, which was the mental, physical and psychological one – again, his personal map. And he was to push himself to the limit, physically and mentally.

Although in his travel book Greene gives details of his problems and fears, it is from his diary, in which he describes his dreams, that we can judge the true extent of the pressure he was under at this point: 'Dreamed I'd got home again and played with V. Missed and loved her a great deal.' He fell asleep and 'woke missing her' and then after further sleep woke up again 'wanting V quite desperately'. It is no wonder that, after his return to England and when he had completed his travel book, Graham, in dedicating the book to his wife, added that beautiful quotation from William Plomer's 'Visiting the Caves': 'I carry you like a passport everywhere.' Close to the references to his wife, he wrote in small print the following:

Woke up at 4 cold & had to put on a vest. Dreamed also that there was a case of yellow fever and we were put in quarantine. Found one of The Times' night staff burning this diary in case it carried infection. All my family about. Furious to the point of tears.

Dreamed that I was present at the assassination of the President of Liberia. He was shot in his carriage by one of the drummers I saw at Tailahun. Tried to send the news to The Times.

Mark, who wakened Greene at five o'clock on the following morning, had impressed him, 'though he is ugly and smelly'.[71] Mark spoke and wrote English after a fashion and had made a supreme effort to be taken on for the rest of the trek. Greene kept in his diary Mark's letter of application to him:

> Sir. In honour to ask you that I am willingly to go with you down Monrovia please kindly I beg you and Miss or Madam.
>
> Because your love me so dearly I don't want you must live me here again, and more over I am too little to take a load. I will be assisting the hammock till we reach. Me and the headman. Please sir dont live me here again. I was fearing to tell you last night please master, good master and good servant. I am yours ever friend
>
> Mark.

It was to be a great adventure for Mark who had never seen the sea or a ship or a brick house.

35

Whisky and Epsom Salts

You cannot create experience. You must undergo it.
– ALBERT CAMUS

AT 7 a.m., Barbara set off in the hammock with a light heart, 'A long line of us', she wrote in her book, *Land Benighted*, 'winding down the road . . . The sweat streamed down [the carriers'] backs. They carried their heavy packs on their heads, and worked hard for their three shillings a week.'[1] Graham left half an hour later, setting himself his usual gruelling pace and catching up with them in less than an hour.

They made very good progress, reaching their first stop, Kolahun, in two hours; because of the President's recent visit to the area the trees on each side of the road had been cut down. When the sun broke through the heavy morning mist there would be no shade, and this made Graham anxious to press on to Kolahun where they were to have their first encounter with a representative of the Liberian ruling class. They were not looking forward to their obligatory visit to the District Commissioner, D.C. Reeves, to whom they each had to pay two pounds in order to obtain permits of residence. He was a Vai, a Mohammedan who hated Christians, white men, and the English language.[2] Also, he had a reputation for cruelty. It was believed that on capturing some Mandingo traders smuggling goods over the border from French territory, he had them shut up in a hut and burnt to death. The nuns at the Holy Mission had seen him passing rapidly in a hammock, his messengers whipping the carriers.

Greene waited for him in the compound of his house – superior because of its two storeys: 'Everything was still . . . A gramophone was playing, and Miss Josephine Baker's voice drifted across the compound with an amusing and sophisticated melancholy. It made everything for the moment rather unreal: the carriers sitting in the dust, the quiet drift of huts, the forest edging up over the horizon became no more than a backcloth for a lovely unclothed cabaret figure.'[3] It was not a cabaret figure who appeared, of course, but Mr Reeves, coming from behind some curtains dressed in a scarlet fez and a long native robe, with black Victorian side-whiskers, and thick grey skin.

Greene's description of Reeves as a character in a Parisian revue plays down any sense of danger, but there must have been some threat in this initial meeting. Reeves 'gave an effect, more Oriental than African, of cruelty and sensuality: he was gross, impassive and corrupt.'[4] The situation could have turned nasty.

However, Greene's forward planning turned out to be useful. He had written, according to his diary, what he calls a flowery letter to the President of Liberia, and the President, far from having left the area, was staying in Reeves's house and Greene was to have an interview with him. As the two Greenes waited, a black officer changed the gramophone record, and then a young woman came in. She was the loveliest thing he saw in Liberia and he could not keep his eyes off her. He wanted somehow to express the pleasure the sight of her gave in the 'empty sun-cracked place.'[5]

Even Barbara conceded that she was beautiful, with dreamy black eyes that brought to mind stories of the *Thousand and One Nights*. She wore European dress, looked more Chinese than African, and had a quality of deep repose. She did not speak a word, only taking up a pack of cards and shuffling them. He was to see her once more at the end of the journey, in Monrovia, standing on the President's balcony watching the Krus demonstrate their loyalty below, and she remained for Greene 'the kind of vivid memory which draws one back to a place, even after many years'.[6]

Greene was conscious that he was meeting the President of the country dressed in shirt and shorts, a water-bottle at his side, and covered in the dust collected on the way. He remembered all the stories he had heard of how Liberian rulers liked to keep a white man waiting and might demand that he be suitably clothed for the interview. Moreover, Greene expected to meet a thug similar to District Commissioner Reeves, or perhaps like the black mercenary, Colonel Davis.

But then President Barclay – who Greene had dreamed the night before had been assassinated – walked into the room.* To Barbara he looked 'as if he had just left the Fifty Shilling Tailors', and Greene described him in his diary as 'a mulatto type wearing a dark suit, a cheap striped shirt and striped tie', but both were impressed by his

---

* President Barclay lived for another twenty years, dying of cancer in 1955.

affable manner, and rhetoric. He talked to them for an hour, reluctant to relinquish them: 'it was not easy to stem the rolling tide of the President's hopes, the roads, the aeroplanes, the motor-cars.'[7] 'He was a politician in the Tammany Hall manner, but he was something new on the Coast. He might be out to play his own game, but he was going to play it with unexampled vigour.' He told them that his power was greater than the American President's since, once elected, he was 'boss of the whole show'.[8]

Eventually, and no doubt delicately, Greene had to end the interview. They had a four and a half hours' march to the next village, Kpanglamai, to which he had sent Mark and Amah on ahead to tell the chieftain of the white man's arrival and his need for a hut and food for 30 men, and he wanted to reach it before nightfall.

They were now travelling along the northern border of Liberia, trekking generally one hundred feet above sea level over broken ground and scrambling up hills, crossing the great Mano river over a bridge of twisted creepers. Sir Alfred Sharpe admitted that he had never been in any part of Africa where the going was so bad, yet Greene enjoyed those earlier days of the march – the swallow-tailed butterflies swarming at the water courses – 'Everything was new, the villages with the women pounding rice, the cluster of stones where the chiefs were buried, the cows rubbing their horns along the huts, the taste of warm, boiled and filtered water in the dried mouth.'[9]

In those early days he walked in high excitement, and faster than his carriers or his cousin, with a sense that he was going deeper and deeper into unknown Liberia. That first week was 'a dash', and his hammock men kept up with his gruelling pace and thus 'an evasive half-relationship developed from shared oranges, the rests at the water courses',[10] where they drank out of the empty meat tins they carefully preserved and Greene from his bottle.

Towards the end of the worst heat of the day they saw Kpangblamai and Mark running to greet them with 'plenty, plenty fine house' – and it was their finest lodging in a native village in Liberia. Greene describes it as 'a small stable with two stalls and a verandah . . . The walls [incongruously] were papered thickly with old advertisements and photographs out of illustrated papers, most of them German or American. Over a chair made out of an old packing-case . . . beautiful women showed their teeth brushed with Chlorodone, handsome men displayed their ready-made suitings, somebody wondered why she wasn't a social success, and a man in uniform denounced a clause of the Treaty of Versailles.'[11]

Thus the headlines of the 1930s, commercial and political, were preserved (as in formalin) deep in the Liberian jungle and provided, in the narrow clearing of a simple African village, the brightness of our limited civilisation. Greene and his cousin were to sleep that night on platforms of beaten earth spread with matting.

The villagers were overpoweringly hospitable, presenting them with three gourds of palm wine, a basin full of bad eggs and a chicken, and treating them like royalty. Like royalty they had to endure the discomforts of being shown everything – weavers at work, a man cutting leather sheaths for daggers, a native smithy where they made blades, a woman boiling leaves to make dye, a devil dance. The devil, from a women's society, swayed forward swinging a great raffia bustle, nodding its black mask. Finally there was the gift of a kid which escaped and had to be chased and brought back and tethered. In spite of having had no rest after their march, they had the royal necessity to keep their faces fixed in bright, cheerful masks.

Feeling weak and ill and unable to face food, Barbara went to bed leaving Graham to escape to a very English meal alone – sardines on toast, a steaming hot steak and kidney pudding, an omelette washed down with whisky and orange. But halfway through the second course the old chief in tea gown and turban arrived with an orchestra that played tinkling music – the old chief eventually slipping away into the moonless night carrying his chair.

Two things the Greenes learnt at this stop. One was that it was not necessary to 'dash', that is, return gift for gift, but only to 'dash' at the end of the stay. The other was that the presents they had brought with them from England – knives, and 'housewives' – were useless. The natives made better knives, had nothing to sew, and preferred gifts of money to enable them to pay their taxes.

It was their first night in a native hut and for privacy's sake they kept the door shut, but it was also their first experience of the terrors of the heat, which was like a blanket over the face, choking one. It was, Greene recorded in his diary, like the heat of a furnace.

*

He decided to follow the German doctor's advice and make for Dagomai: the trouble was that nobody had heard of it – not the chieftain or his headman (absolute inseparables 'like the higher and the lower nature').[12] To the chieftain's son, Greene kept on repeating 'Dagomai, Dagomai' and at last the chief spoke of a place called Duogobmai, which to Greene's unskilled ears seemed nearly right, and he decided to make for it – a bad mistake on his part. His determination to reach Duogobmai next day led to dissension among the carriers, mostly fuelled by a carrier called Alfred, complaining, 'Too far . . . too far', to the other carriers who had not yet become a team and were full of jealousy and suspicion, so that the 'oily, smart, ingratiating, mutinous'[13] trouble-maker had good material to work on. Throughout the next eight-hour journey, with Graham travelling fast ahead, the carriers followed slowly with Alfred telling them it was too far to Duogobmai. Unfortunately, it turned out that Alfred was right. Without knowing it, Greene was travelling to the wrong village. That day was to be an exhausting trial of wills between him and Alfred and the carriers.

After two hours they reached a village, Pandemai, which Greene had arranged they should reach the day before, but had then sent a message – which had obviously not arrived – cancelling this arrangement. As a result, the chief was surly, but he was also in the hands of a hard-faced black missionary who was always laughing as if to say, ' "I'm only a black and you are a white, you are always laughing at me" . . . with a bitter humility which didn't . . . disguise the hardness and meanness below it.' Afraid that the carriers, if they once put down their loads, would cause trouble, he decided to go straight through the village, his refusal to stay being accepted by the missionary 'as one more sign that he was despised'.[14]

Although the missionary told him that Duogobmai was six hours away, Greene would not be delayed, and, working on the premise that 'a black always exaggerated', pledged himself that Duogobmai was only five hours away, and like the proverbial mad dog of an Englishman, he led his party on, stalking ahead of the carriers and Barbara as the midday heat struck up from the dry ground and beat 'down on one's helmet so that for moments at a time it was cooler to raise it and take the full sun on the skull.'[15]

On this portion of the journey, he observed 'great yellow tenements, twelve feet high' built by ants who drove in swarms across the path and the guerilla ants 'who whipped at one singly through the air and fastened their pincers in the skin . . . their nip was like the cut of a knife'. He concluded that the ants were the real owners and rulers of the bush, not the men in the villages and certainly not the few white men who had left in little cleared spaces beside the path abandoned gold-workings: 'a deep hole the size of a coffin, a few decaying wooden struts above a well of stagnant water.'[16]

Eventually, struck with inertia under the vertical sun, he waited in a village for his party to catch up, watching the old men drowsing, blinking and scratching, a woman lying 'in a patch of shade on her face in the dust', sleeping. 'A long time passed . . . It was too hot to be really curious about anyone.'

When Barbara, the carriers and Alfred arrived, the latter stirring things up and gathering evidence from the villagers as to how far

Duogobmai was, there was much palaver and, faced with an incipient revolt, Greene felt the blacks were humbugging him, until his servant Laminah whispered, 'Amedoo's feet very bad', but added, 'Amedoo go on. He say he no humbug.'[17] Thus he discovered that 'one of the curious things about a black servant [is] the way in which he included loyalty in his service and there was no trait of cowardice in their loyalty, no admission that the richer is the better man.'

Greene stubbornly went on, allowing only short rests. At one point a man with a few words of English followed him, saying they would never reach Duogobmai before dark – and they did not.

The Loffa river had to be crossed by a seventy-year-old hammock bridge of knotted creeper swinging down from a platform fifteen feet in the air. 'Sometimes the creepers had given way', and, 'the whole bridge swung like a rope ladder'.[18] According to Greene's diary the actual struts (on which one stepped) were about a foot wide. A good many were broken. On that bridge he caught up with Mark and Amah whom he had sent off at five that morning to reach Duogobmai and warn the chief that they would need food and board for the night. He had been walking for eight hours, they for twelve: Mark was 'completely exhausted, clutching a chicken', but Amah, a Mandingo, physically a fine specimen, was still fresh, and amused that Greene had caught up with them.

After the bridge, Duogobmai came in sight as the dusk was falling, a line of blackened huts at the top of a long red clay slope: 'A strange pink light welled out of the air, touching the tall termite mounds which stood along the path. It gave the whole landscape, the ant heaps and the red clay and the black huts of Duogobmai on the hill-top camp, a curious Martian air. Men ran out of the huts and looked down at [them] climbing up out of the dusk and the forest.'[19]

There was no moon and the smouldering torches of the blacks moving between the huts 'lit only wretchedness and dirt'. He was anxious about his cousin, wondering whether she had managed to cross the long, hammock bridge in the dark, avoiding the gaps where the creepers had given way. She arrived about forty minutes later with a sullen pack of worn-out men to find him sitting on a box, dozing.

The majority of the carriers had decided not to cross the river Loffa until next day, because it was too dark to use the bridge, so that the Greenes were without beds, mosquito nets, lamps, torches, food and the essential water filter. However, they were given green palm wine which tasted like sour barley water and for which Greene was developing a taste; Amedoo slung up their hammocks; and the two Greenes stumbled out into the jungle to relieve themselves. It was pitch black except for the light of fireflies and they struck endless matches, making water in the dry, pitted ground.[20]

It was, as he recorded in his diary, their worst night yet, but he began to come to terms with the situation and suddenly felt curiously happy and carefree: 'One couldn't, I was sure, get lower than Duogobmai. I had been afraid of the primitive, had wanted it broken gently, but here it came on us in a breath, as we stumbled up through the dung and the cramped and stinking huts to our lampless sleeping place among rats. It was the worst one need fear, and it was bearable because it was inescapable.'[21]

But to a degree it was escapable. Vande, his headman, had persuaded the carriers to cross the river and so they did have beds and mosquito nets, food and a filter after all. They sat on a box, too tired to talk, too tired to eat, except for a cup of soup which tasted heavenly. The carriers were too tired to grumble. They sat round the lamps and had their chop: 'I heard vitality come slowly back to them and Alfred sowing dissension.' When the carriers' lamp went out the rats came 'all together, falling heavily down the wall like water'.

In an undated letter from Liberia, Barbara wrote of her experience of sleeping in native huts: 'I sat up all night in a state of fear & horror. It was not a case of one rat or two rats but literally *swarms* of rats. My suitcase was broken so that it didn't close properly & next morning my clothes were chewed into great big holes. Then there were bats overhead & every imaginable thing ready to bite us . . . fleas & bugs that became friendly with me that night and haven't left me since.' But her sense of humour came through in the next line: 'I've never had such faithful friends in my life.'[22] Greene lay awake listening to the 'vermin cascading down the walls, racing over boxes'. He discovered that nothing could be left out for the rats would eat anything, shirts, stockings, hair-brushes, the laces in one's shoes.

And after all they had come to the wrong village, one that had never seen a white face so that they were a constant source of interest. The oldest man said he didn't want a 'dash' he only wanted to sit and watch the white man writing, drinking, coughing, wiping the sweat from his face.[23] And the village was shifty and mean: 'A woman goes round scraping up the cow and goat dung with her hands, children with skin disease, whelping bitches and little puppies . . . among the food Souri is cooking for us in the dust outside a hut.' Even the village beauty had smeared and whitened breasts which hung in flat pouches to her waist, which caused Greene to consider for how short a period of their lives most people can be seen naked with any pleasure. Barbara Greene wrote of the village: 'There was an atmosphere of decay everywhere . . . Even the children were like horrid old men, and their wicked little faces grinned at us. I felt that if we stayed in this village much longer we, too, would deteriorate and go bad, the atmosphere of degeneration was so strong . . . I kept looking at Graham to see if I could see any change beginning in him . . . I thought I might see that shameful, shameless look creep into his eyes. I half expected his face to alter, and his body to become diseased and horrible like those around us. The unlovely nakedness pressing so close to me filled me with repulsion.'[24]

But the carriers demanded a day's rest and Greene thought it wise to agree; so both Greenes took the opportunity to spend the morning writing up their diaries under the intent stare of the villagers. Graham tried to get drunk, but the spirit ran out in sweat almost as quickly as he drank it.

At least they got rid of the trouble-maker, Alfred. 'Alfred goes home with a dash,' Greene wrote in his diary, and he was replaced by an impressive singer whose voice could be heard 'down the trail proposing the line of an impromptu song, which the carriers took up', the songs ridiculing the moods and manners of their employers and informing the inhabitants of the villages they passed through about their journey.[25]

*

'In Duogobmai the atmosphere had been sordid and degenerate. In Nicoboozu it was happy and charming, and . . . in Zigita, even in the light of morning, it was evil,' Barbara wrote in *Land Benighted*.

Nicoboozu was an artistic centre where the blacksmith beat out little silver arrows for the women's hair and twisted silver bracelets and anklets from 'old Napoleon coins brought from French Guinea'; the men wore 'primitive signet rings' and 'the weavers were busy' and there was 'an air of happiness about the place'.[26] Graham bought two rings and gave one to Barbara; Laminah bought a magnificent robe for ten shillings for his father, and Amedoo, bargaining for a robe and being advised by the seller that his master would advance the money, replied: 'I be bad man if I ask master for big money . . . I get small coppers from master, but master can't afford to give me big money.' They had been provided with very good, honest servants. Laminah, when Barbara was bargaining for something, would advise, 'No buy, Missis. Dat man plenty big humbug. No good sword.'[27]

In Nicoboozu the women walked through the village with 'glowing wood from the smithy . . . to light the fires . . . All round . . . were the sounds of tinkling harps . . . There was a moon and a native village . . . there were two white people watching and having their arms stroked from time to time' as a sign of approval.[28] There was also a dance by 'emaciated old women slapping their pitted buttocks in a kind of Charleston; but they were cheerful and happy and we were happy too . . . and we drank warm boiled water with whisky and the juice of limes.'[29] Their cook, Souri, made them an enormous omelette and Amedoo, Laminah and Mark served them with the greatest dignity and care. With the little huts shining in the moonlight around them, Barbara began to feel the overwhelming magic of Africa, and sitting in the dark there, at that moment she wanted nothing more. Graham wrote that 'the timelessness, the irresponsibility, the freedom of Africa' began to touch them at last.[30] It was one of their happiest moments together and one of the last times they could talk completely naturally together. The other side of the coin was that they had to adapt to the strains of the journey: 'Graham . . . would sometimes become rather obstinate, hanging on to some small, unimportant point like a dog to a bone. But we never quarrelled . . . We knew . . . it was the ghastly damp heat that was lowering our vitality, and we would smile at one another and think, "We won't talk about that again." Politics was the first thing to go . . . One subject after another would be put away, left on one side, marked carefully "Not wanted during voyage", till gradually practically nothing remained on the last day or two of our trip except the enthralling subject of food.'[31] But in Nicoboozu that was a possibility they had not even considered.

Apart from the difficulties of travelling without maps and finding accommodation in native villages, Greene was put into the position of one of his boyhood fictional heroes – having, in spite of his shyness and inexperience, to deal with a party of native carriers in a country of which he did not know not only the geography but also the customs. He had to become a white leader of black men overnight. He must have drawn to some extent on his public school and Balliol experiences, being used to that effortless sense of knowing how to behave, the courteousness in the face of any difficulty. He had also the physical determination and ability to push on. Fortunately, he did not distrust and despise the natives. Barbara wrote:

Graham, from the beginning, treated them exactly as if they were white men from our own country. He talked to them quite naturally and they liked him. They knew where they were with him, and apart from their everlasting cries of 'Too far,' they did everything he wanted them to do. His method of conversation was far from simple, and he used long, complicated phrases. I do not believe that the men ever understood him, but after a while they began to get some dim idea of what he was driving at. After the day's trek they would like to lie round him, and joke and laugh, while he would smile kindly upon them.

His position became that of a benevolent white father:

> Once away from their own country the men depended so much on us. They knew they were going to Monrovia, but what or where Monrovia was they had no idea. But with child-like simplicity they handed all responsibilities over to my cousin, quite sure that he would look after them and see that they came to no harm.[32]

Every evening the carriers came to him, pointing out their hurts 'with the utmost confidence that he could make them well again', though the Greenes had left their medical supplies behind in the last minute rush and had only Epsom salts, boric acid and iodine. With them he treated sore throats, venereal sores, yaws and even a leper who came to them at Zigita to be healed, dumbly holding out his rotting hands. 'I gave him', wrote Greene, 'a few tablets of boric acid to dissolve and bathe his hands with.'[33] 'The man took it with shining eyes. He turned and went away with a firm step. It meant at least one day of happiness for him,' Barbara wrote.[34]

*

The trek to Zigita was short (a mere five and a half hours) but extremely tough. This, the largest town of the Buzie tribe, was one of the highest points in Liberia, nearly two thousand feet up and reached by forest paths so steep that they were both almost on hands and knees scrambling over rocks and boulders, climbing up and up.[35] So steep and yet there was thick bush on either side of them, the high trees joining in an archway over their heads. Barbara felt it hard to breathe and she recalls that it felt as if someone was hammering iron nails into her throat.[36]

Zigita was also reputedly the home of evil spirits, the centre of Buzie sorcery: on nights of storm, lightning ran along the top of the encircling hills in a green flame and the inhabitants lived under the shadow of sorcerers. The Greenes were to be affected by that atmosphere of evil and magic.

They were accommodated in a rest house with two rooms and a verandah, but only their bedrooms were free from the intrusion of the carriers wanting medicine and sleeping in corners. More worrying was the villagers' fear of the Big Bush Devil. While the Greenes were drinking whisky and lime, a stranger came in with a command from the Big Bush Devil not to be out that night or to look through a window since the Devil would be dancing through the village. The warning reached the carriers gathered in the cookhouse and 'suddenly all the voices were turned low like lamp flames'.[37] They were warned that if the white people disobeyed the Bush Devil's order, the carriers would be poisoned – and Zigita women learnt the secrets of poisoning in bush school.

In spite of their servant Laminah's warning that, if they looked at the Devil, 'Massa go blind. Missis go blind', the Greenes had to go out into the night to relieve themselves at the edge of the forest, and afterwards, in the rest house, they lifted their screens to look out, but saw nothing; yet they had, that night, 'almost believed in strange supernatural things'. In his diary, Greene quotes Saki: 'When once you have taken the Impossible into your calculations its possibilities become practically limitless.'

Next day a storm burst and there was a vertical wall of water all day, the guard outside the Devil's house waving the storm away with a black elephant-hair fan – there was no sound from the carriers, no dancing or singing – thirty of them were crushed into a small hut. At night rats like large cats rampaged in Greene's hut so that he could not sleep.

Greene concluded that there was certainly something bad about Zigita. 'I never felt quite well again until I reached the Coast. It was not that I believed in the devil's power so much as in the power of my own mind. The suggestion of malice and evil here was so great that I could imagine it influencing my mind until I half believed, and a half-belief can be strong enough to affect the health.'[38] From that last evening at Zigita Greene's health began to suffer, and for the rest of the trip and for some time after he returned to England, he was, according to Barbara, unwell.[39]

Incredibly, given the country they had covered and their diverse experiences, only five weeks had passed since they left London.

They left Zigita in a mist so heavy that they could not see twenty yards ahead, but then, when the sun had sucked up the mist, they had all the ferocity of the African sun on a shadeless road. It sickened Greene even through his sun helmet.

They were heading for a Lutheran mission at Zorzor, and a messenger sent ahead met them with the promise of accommodation. The mission proved to be dirty and desolate, with a lady missionary living alone who inspired Barbara's single harsh description in her book: 'A large white lump, like bread before it is put in the oven to be baked.' She felt that if she pressed her she would sink in and the dent would remain. 'Someone had put two black currants into the dough for eyes, and her mouth was an old strip of orange peel.'[40]

She was a Mrs Curran, though Greene calls her Croup in his book, and she had been left to cope when her husband was drowned and the other missionary had gone off his head. She had been alone there, without seeing another white face, for six months and she was quite strange. She kept a cobra in her garden, fed it a chicken a day, and said to the Greenes, 'I'd have sent you an invite to dinner but I'm going home in six months.' She was desperately lonely.

As usual at a stop, Greene was faced with the problem of which way to go next. He felt that if he could reach Ganta and Dr Harley (a famous authority, incidentally, on Bush Devils), he would be given accurate advice on the rest of the journey. Mrs Curran advised them to cut across the corner of French Guinea to Ganta, making a first stay at Bamakama. Only gradually did Greene realise that this very fat woman had always travelled in a hammock with eighteen carriers and could not remember the names of any villages she had passed through. Her guide said that Bamakama was two days ahead and the shortest way was by Jbaiay, and in order to please his carriers, Greene decided to take the shortest way.

There were no rats that last night in Zorzor, but there were cockroaches – like large blood blisters against the wall. What Greene was chiefly to remember about Liberia was cockroaches eating their clothes, rats on the floor, dust in the throat, jiggers under the nails and ants building their conical buildings or fastening on the flesh.

Then the carriers, deciding that he was planning to take them too far on the next day, led them astray to another village, whose name they never knew. In a note in her diary, Barbara writes: 'he is convinced that the carriers are leading us out of our way, so that we shall not be able to reach Bamakama tonight. I am angry. Graham is angry. And . . . the carriers are all furious too.'[41] The village was in French Guinea and that was all they knew. The carriers kept apart from them and talked in high angry voices. Just before sundown, when Graham was sponging himself down in a tin bath, his personal servant Amedoo came into the hut. Greene compares him to Jeeves advising Bertie Wooster – it was a strain living up to Amedoo's standards of loyalty, honesty and complete reliability. He put the situation in a nutshell: 'The labourers say they want more money. Massa say no.' Greene had a strike on his hands.

He lingered in the bath and then the carriers approached and there was a long argument. Greene knew he was exploiting them, as other white masters had. He also knew that he could not go on without them. If he paid them off then, he could not afford to take on new carriers; if he cut the journey short and made for Monrovia, his money would still not last. Barbara watched the palaver, which lasted a long time, and though she could not hear what was going on she knew that the 'carriers were growling and muttering at Graham. He looked calm, but some of his gestures were nervous . . . Suddenly I could see him decide to . . . bluff. He waved his hand. "All right," he seemed to say, "go home. Come for your money later and then go away." And he turned as if everything were now at an end.'[42]

What he had actually said to the mutineers was: 'Tell them they can go home. I'll give them their pay, but they won't get any dash, I'll take new carriers here.' And his bluff worked. Barbara recorded: 'There was a moment's pause, and sudden sheepish grins spread over the faces of our men. That was going too far. They did not want to leave us . . . smiling and laughing they forgot the whole argument and were as friendly as ever.'[43] Greene was banking on the fact that if they stayed together for another two weeks they would be in a country as strange to them as it was to him. He knew there was a tribe, about a week ahead, reputed to be still practising cannibalism, and the carriers clearly would not want to be paid off there.

To celebrate the return to the fold the carriers wanted to kill the kid which a chief had given to Greene in Kpangblamai. It was a time to conciliate and Graham agreed, not expecting an immediate slaughter: at once they held the little kid down on the ground by its legs 'like a crucified child, the knife across the throat and the screams through the flow of blood. The kid took a long time dying.'[44] In his diary he records, 'music and dancing till late' by the carriers.

Apart from his travel book, his journey through Liberia produced one short story, 'A Chance for Mr Lever', published in the *London Mercury* in January 1936, which mirrors closely Greene's experience, even to the final confrontation with the carriers:

Then his boy was beside him again. He whispered urgently to Mr Lever through the mosquito-net, 'Massa, the labourers say they go home.'

'Go home?' Mr Lever asked wearily; he had heard it so often before. 'Why do they want to go home? What is it now?' but he didn't really want to hear the latest squabble: that the Bande men were never sent to carry water because the headman was a Bande, that someone had stolen an empty treacle tin and sold it in the village . . . that someone wasn't made to carry a proper load, that the next day's journey was 'too far.' He said, 'Tell 'em they can go home. I'll pay them off in the morning. But they won't get any dash. They'd have got a good dash if they'd stayed.' He was certain it was just another try-on; he wasn't as green as all that.[45]

In Mr Lever's case they did leave him.

On the following day, Barbara got lost. Graham had started at 7 a.m. The ground was rough and Barbara fell behind in country that changed from hills and forest to a plateau covered with elephant grass twice the height of a man, stretching northwards towards the Mountains of Kong. When there were many paths, the carriers would lay a small branch across the path to be followed, but Barbara's carriers missed the branch, and her party scrambled on through rough tracks with trunks of trees across them until they reached a deserted village, which she thought might have been stricken by some decimating disease. Suddenly the path disappeared and they faced an impenetrable wall of jungle.

Though she felt Graham had disappeared completely, she did not panic. She had to go back and, ignoring the complaints of her carriers – it was her turn to deal with an incipient revolt – she smiled, told the headman, 'I go on', turned on her heels and went back, and she won her battle – the carriers followed.

By a piece of luck she met an old man who knew Bamakama, the village they had been heading for, who led them, unceasingly, over streams and along wider paths, the carriers suddenly happy, yelling all together in the hope that Greene's carriers would hear them, and finally they were brought to a broad river, St Paul – and their shouts were answered from the opposite bank by Greene and his men. He had been on the point of departure because darkness was falling. Barbara and her carriers crossed the great river on a flat raft, pulling themselves over by means of creepers. There was great excitement and relief at joining up again.

The trek did not end there. After some food, they marched through elephant grass for four hours to a decayed rest house, full of bugs, in Bamakama, where they drank tea and an army of flies settled on their faces and their pet monkey sat in a corner and moaned like a child. Greene concluded, 'There is only one thing to do here. Get drunk!' and while he was doing so more trouble broke out among the men over water-carrying, as he describes in 'A Chance for Mr Lever'. Barbara recorded his response. 'In his new mood Graham went out. He listened majestically for a few minutes. Then he gave his verdict firmly . . . "Palaver finished." Then (swaying, oh so slightly) he walked away. It was a superb performance. We were all astonished. The men had no more to say.'[46]

But physically and mentally, Greene was reaching the end of his tether. His continuous problem is reflected in his short story: 'the way you travelled in the Republic was to write down a list of names and trust that someone in the villages you passed would understand and know the route. But they always said "Too far." Good fellowship wilted before the phrase.'[47]

The chief of Bamakama, a man of action, strapped on his sword and set off as their guide at a smart pace, and in three hours they reached Galaye, a town with old mud walls, which pleased the carriers probably because the girls here were a great deal more forward with strangers than Greene had seen in any previous village. He remembered watching one girl in particular, who, as darkness fell and the drums and harps and rattles were taken out, joined the carriers in their dances. In his book Greene writes of 'a stamping and thrusting out of the elbows and buttocks, a caricature of sexuality';[48] in his diary 'the buttocks thrust out instead of the belly. Does this represent the appeal of the different sexual position?'

Greene was struck by their dancing which went on for hours, 'a close hot circle before our hut'. He felt that it was the moon that worked on their spirits: 'The carriers were aware of the moon with an intimacy from which we were excluded.'[49] But there was a tremendous ugliness also:

> the most grotesque of the dancers was a moron dwarf. They dropped him into the ring with a couple of piccaninnies of three years old who were as tall as he, and he swayed a great inflated head, like a blister a pin would burst, to the beat of the rattle, and then howled and wept to be released.[50]

That night, at the end of ten days of continuous trekking, they were faced with another invasion by rats. As soon as they had put out the lamps, the rats rushed down the walls.

The indications are that the journey was becoming a nightmare. Ganta seemed to recede rather than come closer, and there was the continual getting up in darkness, the hurried breakfast, the long trek through a forest which seemed to him to be dead: 'a green wilderness . . . an endless back garden of tangled weeds; they didn't seem to be growing round us so much as dying.'

His thoughts were turning homewards. He wrote in his diary: 'Longing to be there [at Ganta] and start south for home. The trek's already wearisome . . . Thought of walking in England, lunch at pubs, the Cotswolds. The same dense untidy scenery grows dull.' And the day before he recorded that he missed Vivien very badly – 'and . . . Lucy [his daughter]'. Listening that night to the music, the beat of a rattle, he wanted flowers and dew and scent: 'It was hard to believe they existed in the same world and that there were emotions of tenderness and regret that couldn't be expressed with a harp, a drum and a rattle, buttocks and black teats.'[51]

They went on, this time following the Galaye chief through the forest, scorched by the sun and cutting a clearing with swords to make a shade. At an unnamed village the chief welcomed them with gourds of wine for the carriers and Greene shook hands with him before realising that he was a leper, his hand covered with white sores.

At another village a procession arrived of a chief in a closed hammock who was preceded by an old man with a sporting gun over his shoulder and a boy blowing a bugle. The chief, wearing an old white topee, a Fair Isle jumper, breeches and braces, a belt and gaiters and little white gloves, invited them to visit him at Djecki, which they did the following day after a two-hour journey. They found the chief sitting on the floor with his wives and daughters, the latter being some of the prettiest women Greene had seen in Africa.

The chief provided a bottle of French white wine and Greene a bottle of whisky, and they drank out of a common mug. Barbara began to feel the atmosphere was only of sex and drunkenness and Greene, in his diary, refers to the chief's favourite and beautiful daughter, to the ogling, the wine, the smoke, the increasing friendliness with someone one can't speak to: 'Her thigh under the tight cloth about her waist was like the soft furry rump of a kitten; she had lovely breasts: she was quite clean, much cleaner than we were. The chief wanted us to stay the night, and I began to wonder how far his hospitality might go.'[52]

They drank for a further two hours in the heat of day but did not stay overnight, Greene being worried because the village schoolmaster wanted them to see the French Commissioner, when they had no permit to be on French colonial soil. Moreover they discovered that the monsoons were starting early and they could be stranded if they did not press on, and Barbara wanted to get away from the attentions of the chief, whose daughter had told her at intervals: 'My fadder says you very fine woman.' 'The chief', she wrote, 'seemed ready to buy me from Graham, but we did not stay to hear what I was really worth.'

Eventually, leaving the route followed by earlier travellers, they crossed the forty-foot-wide St John's river in a dug-out canoe, and entered Liberia again. The carriers were happy, in spite of the fact that they were in the territory of the Manos who still practised ritual cannibalism, though they ate only strangers, not men from their own tribe. Mark exclaimed, 'Back in our own land!' and the carriers sang and ran at twice their usual speed.[53]

*

Their meeting with Dr Harley, the Methodist medical missionary in Ganta, was to be an upsetting experience.

Although the Harleys welcomed them, they both felt that the atmosphere was not right – the Harleys were not happy. Barbara remembered that Mrs Harley, with a face like chalk, wearing a white dress, invited them for supper and then relapsed into silence. Greene recorded, 'Harley a dead-tired man and his wife washed out . . . Two yellow-faced self-possessed young boys.' On the second evening, as Greene wrote in his diary, they 'Went up to Harley's for chop. Not feeling too well. Another grim evening.'

There were several reasons for the prevailing sense of unhappiness. To begin with, they had arrived on what would have been the birthday of the Harleys' third child, who had died from swallowing quinine tablets from a bottle.* Moreover, Harley was a man 'with a body and nerves worn threadbare by ten years' unselfish work, cutting away the pus from the huge swollen genitals, injecting for yaws, anointing for craw-craw, injecting two hundred natives a week for venereal disease.' He also seemed to have a persecution complex, expecting death at any moment. Barbara wrote: 'After supper Dr Harley talked to us, putting aside his private sorrows and playing, gallantly, the part of host. Every now and then his head would sink down between his hands in an effort to remember what he was talking about. And sometimes he would get up quickly and open the door to see if anyone were listening. They were after him, he said. His boys thought that he knew too much. One day they would kill him. He expected it all the time . . .'[54]

Dr Harley expected death because of his knowledge of the native secret societies who sought out special victims, the ritual need being on such occasions to take from the victim the heart, palms of the hands and the skin of the forehead. The Greenes were shown Harley's secret collection of 'grotesquely horrible devils' masks', the very holding of which could warrant a man's death.

The Greenes arrived tired at Ganta and Graham was on the verge of a fever. What troubled both of them was Dr Harley's insistence that white men should not walk too far in that area. He told them that they had just sent 'a man home dead who had walked up from Monrovia without a hammock: another white had died a few days before of dysentery . . . Death seemed rather close.'[55] He warned Graham that he was walking too fast, too far, without sufficient resting times – sheer madness in that climate.

---

* This supper with the Harleys must have been on 14 February 1935 since their deceased son was born on 14 February, according to Methodist records.

Though the possessor of dangerous secrets, Dr Harley did not in the event die mysteriously, but lived on until 1966. He was called by many 'Methodism's Albert Schweitzer', and was compared with the famous Dr Livingstone. Establishing himself at Ganta in 1925, he did not leave Liberia until 1960, but there was clearly some evidence to support Greene's observation that Harley had 'body and nerves worn threadbare', for his record card, housed in the Methodist headquarters in New York, shows that in March 1933 he was suffering from exhaustion and was forced to take emergency leave. No doubt this was due in part to the death of his child the previous year.

It was in Ganta that Barbara began to worry about Greene's health. He developed a twitching of the nerve over the right eye: 'When he felt particularly unwell it would twitch incessantly, and I watched it with horror. It fascinated me, and I would find my eyes fixed upon it till I was almost unable to look anywhere else . . . I was definitely frightened.' What Barbara was frightened about was that in a day or two they would be away from Dr Harley and she would be alone with 'the twitching nerve' and she understood nothing about nursing. She was aware that illness in the bush often meant death. She watched him put spoonfuls of Epsom Salts in his tea, his face grey, and was aware also that only his tremendous willpower was giving him 'his burning vitality'.[56]

Greene's diary tells us little about his condition; perhaps it was the beginnings of dysentery: 'Tum out of order again. Still rather flattened by the muggy heat.'

They left Ganta on 17 February, but Greene was determined to be true to himself and follow the unmapped paths to Grand Bassa on the coast, a route unknown to white men, though known to Mandingo traders, and arduous because of the heavy bush. He was determined not to make straight for Monrovia.[57]

The journey began with guilt. The carrier Babu, who had been always dependable, had to be left because he was sick. Knowing that if he gave Babu a good dash, the other carriers would go sick and demand the same, he pretended to be angry with Babu and gave him a small dash. He felt guilty, but the journey had to go on, though the loss of Babu meant that just when he felt, for the first time, he might need to use a hammock, he had to leave his hammock behind.

At Zugbei, they at last did what Greene had long wished to do – turned south. At their stopping place a carrier called Siafa asked him to treat a venereal sore which he had had on his face for three years, yet had not shown to Dr Harley, who could have given him an injection. It had to be dressed daily. That night Greene recorded in his diary that he 'dosed himself with Epsom [Salts]. Had to get up in the night. Bright moonlight. Absolute quiet. Goats wandering between the huts. Every door and window closed.'

Afterwards they travelled into the thick bush, seeing monkeys, baboons, the pad marks of leopards, and bushmen – naked except for loin-cloths, carrying bows and steel-tipped arrows, their bodies cicatrised – and a man carrying a folding chair on his head and on top of it a black felt hat.

They stopped at Peyi, a very poor village where nearly everyone was old, suffering from goitre and venereal sores, and where little groups of women were delousing each other's heads. But they were offered a clean hut and although the carriers were given only one bucket of rice, yet under a full moon, 'they bore no malice . . . the moon and its deep green light made them happy'. They shared their small meal with the chief and the 'village was full of song and laughter and running feet'. As a European who had lost touch with the influence of the moon, Greene could only envy them. The lunar influence to the civilised, he reflected, meant 'self-conscious emotion, crooners and little sentimental songs of lust and separation; at best a cerebral worked-up excitement'.[58]

Greene noted in his diary: 'Every movement we make is closely watched. If one puts on glasses, if one cleans one's glasses, if one takes something from a pocket . . . two days growth with idea of a small beard.'[59]

The Greenes, the first whites to be travelling this route, caused much excitement: 'Children screamed when they saw us . . . Even the women we met in the bush away from their homes would give a horrified moan and dart away into the forest. In the villages . . . the natives . . . yelled with excitement, cutting off big branches from the trees and running along beside us. Sometimes they would dance, and our carriers with them, doing quite complicated steps with the heavy weights on their heads.'[60]

To see a white man was amazing but to see a white woman was greater reason for rejoicing. A short note in Greene's diary, '[went] by various villages where there was generally great outcry round B', is developed in Barbara's own book: 'In one place the men of the village made me get into my hammock, and four strong men picked it up and rushed me round and round at a tremendous pace, shouting with joy, till Amadu and Laminah drew their swords and flew at the men with such a ferocious expression on their faces that they dropped my hammock and fled.'[61]

*

At Sakripie, they met with civilisation again. It was a bustling town with wide, clean streets and stores, and a middle-aged Mandingo trader in a scarlet fez, called Steve Dunbar, insisted on buying their chairs and table and bed when they reached Monrovia – though they did not see him again. The paramount chief lived there with his fifty-five wives. At sunset they were presented with the vision of two devils on stilts, twenty feet high and in black masks and black witches' hats and striped pyjamas, stepping over walls and sitting on roofs.

In spite of Greene's efforts, the chief did not provide food for their carriers, and the next day he upbraided the chief in English – though neither the chief nor the carriers understood, it pleased the carriers: 'I cursed him,' Greene writes. 'I was very Imperialistic, very prefectorial, as I told him a chief must be judged by his discipline, that he ought not to allow his headman to disobey him.' Barbara recorded: 'Graham did not get up, and the carriers stood round in a ring. Slowly, with many biting expressions . . . that no one except myself understood, Graham delivered his lecture. The effect on our men was miraculous. They loved it.'[62]

The road to Baplai took five hard hours. They had to be carried over much of the road, since the storms had turned the paths into swamps, and they had to avoid the guinea-worm which makes its way through 'any sore in the foot, going up as far as the knee'. When the foot was put in water afterwards the worm spewed 'its eggs into the water through the sore'. In the absence of a doctor, one had to 'find its end like a thread of cotton and wind it out in a long unbroken length round a match-stick.'[63]

Baplai was another 'low'. The Grio tribe, as he noted in his diary, were a 'scoundrelly looking lot of bushmen', naked except for loin-cloths and so thin that he expected to see the bones through the venereal sores. Mr Nelson, the tax-gatherer, was yellow with disease and was squeezing money from the villagers living on the edge of subsistence. Once the villagers understood that Greene was not a government official their mood changed, and the chieftain brought their carriers the best food they had had on the whole journey – fourteen bowls of chop and three of meat scraps, together with palm wine. Greene's headman was quite drunk long before dark and Greene himself got a little drunk and wandered round the village, 'listening to the laughter and the music among the little glowing fires and thinking that, after all, the whole journey was worthwhile'. Waxing philosophical, he thought that 'it did reawaken a kind of hope in human nature. If one could get back to this bareness, simplicity, instinctive friendliness, feeling rather than thought, and start again . . .'[64]

Yaws, venereal sores and guinea-worms had been forgotten, and a young black Catholic, Victor Prosser, head teacher of Tapee-Ta mission school, asked Barbara many geographical and historical questions, such as, 'Was it true that Queen Elizabeth was a Protestant, and Mary Queen of Scots a Catholic like himself? Where did the Thames rise? Was London on the Tiber as well as the Thames?' They joined him singing 'God Save the King' and 'Onward, Christian Soldiers' as they 'picked their way through the Liberian jungle'.[65]

They went on through Greh, a primitive village, with a very sick Laminah who had to be carried, to signs of progress in the shape of a wide, exposed road of white soil, the glare from which blinded them, to Tapee-Ta where they unexpectedly met the President's special agent, Colonel Elwood Davis, the American black mercenary, leader of the Liberian force and known as the Dictator of Grand Bassa. In the British Blue Book he had been accused of being responsible for atrocities against the Kru people – the skewering of children on his soldiers' bayonets, the burning alive of women imprisoned in native huts. Amedoo feared that this 'wicked man' would make trouble for Massa.

T. ELWOOD DAVIS., K. C. S. A.,

(*Colonel Liberian Army.*)

Special Agent Of The President of Liberia,

Greene left his carriers outside the District Commissioner's compound – an impressive place with groups of bungalows behind a stockade, well guarded and with the Liberian flag flying – and they lay down, as Barbara recorded, as if their bones were rotting. Graham, dirty, absurd in his stained shorts, stockings falling over his ankles, and wearing a pith helmet, went in to find a centre of military and diplomatic activity. The verandah was crowded with blacks who had 'just finished lunch and were smoking cigars and drinking coffee . . . clerks kept on delivering messages and running briskly off again, sentries saluted . . . and . . . supercilious diplomatic gentlemen leant over the verandah and studied with well-bred curiosity the dusty arrival' – Graham Greene.

The District Commissioner was 'a middle-aged man with a yellow face, Victorian side-whiskers' and bad teeth. His name was Words-worth, and he had Graham and Barbara housed in the paramount chief's home, 'a palatial building of four rooms and a cookhouse', where Greene sank exhausted into a wooden chair. Greene bargained for rice for his carriers, and finally was promised a few moments only with Colonel Davis, the Dictator of Grand Bassa, though this developed in fact into several hours. There was something attractive about him. He had personality and carried himself with a military swagger, was well dressed, and had a small pointed beard.[66]

In 1940 Greene, at the height of the blitz, recalled that remarkable man. After speaking of the atrocities connected with his name, he admitted: 'He was a Scoutmaster and he talked emotionally about his old mother and got rather drunk on my whisky. He was bizarre and gullible and unaccountable: his atmosphere was that of deep forest . . . and an injustice as wayward as generosity.'[67]

Davis's career had been remarkable. He had once been a private in the American army, probably as a medical orderly, had served in Pershing's disastrous Mexican expedition and later seen service in the Philippines. He had landed in Monrovia without any medical degree, but was soon appointed medical officer of health and worked his way up in Liberian politics. He told Graham and Barbara many exciting stories, so tinged with melodrama that they were almost unbelievable but for the tone of them, the general goodwill, and the confidence with which they were told. He gave the Greenes an account of his activities to show that, rather than having perpetrated atrocities, he had been a benefactor to the women and children he had been accused of burning alive.[68]

But the small prison standing next to the bungalow they stayed in was a reminder to the Greenes that all was not civilised in Liberia. The prison was a small dark hut with tiny portholes for windows: 'Each port-hole, the size of a man's head, represented a cell. The prisoners within, men and women, were tied by ropes to a stick which was laid crosswise against the port-hole outside. There were two or three men who were driven out to work each morning, two skinny old women who carried in the food and water, their ropes coiled round their waists, an old man who was allowed to lie outside on a mat tied to one of the posts which supported the thatch. In a dark cavernous entrance, where the whitewash stopped, a few warders used to lounge all through the day shouting and squabbling and sometimes diving, club in hand, into one of the tiny cells. The old prisoner was a half-wit; I saw one of the warders beating him with his club to make him move to the tin basin in which he had to wash, but he didn't seem to feel the blows. Life to him was narrowed into a few very simple, very pale sensations, of warmth on his mat in the sun and cold in his cell, for Tapee-Ta at night was very cold.'[69]

They did not see Colonel Davis on their last night there as, in spite of having stated that there was no yellow fever in Liberia, he went down with a bad attack. Quartermaster Wordsworth, the brother of the District Commissioner, whose lustrous eyes and correspondence with Greene indicated his fascination and love for this white man, entertained them on his last evening. In what was almost their last conversation, he commented on the fact that the Buzie people had a wonderful cure for venereal disease: 'You tie a rope round your waist' – though he had never tried it. 'I guess you white people aren't troubled with venereal disease,' he said, wistfully. He intercepted Graham that night as he was going into the forest to relieve himself, and said that there was 'a very good closet behind the Colonel's bungalow with a wooden seat', but in the circumstances, Greene preferred the forest.[70]

*

Greene was now definitely ill with a fever coming on. His urge was to get out of Liberia and return home. In his diary he wrote: 'Longing too much for V. If only there was a wireless station before Monrovia. The worst is being out of touch, not being able to say how much I think of her, and how dearly I love her. I want to be off, off, off. Going for a walk before lunch, I planned to take an aeroplane from Liverpool. Sudden dread that there might be bad news at M[onrovia] that she might be ill or unhappy.'

His diary shows that he was retiring to bed, completely exhausted. Barbara felt that Graham had caught some 'strange internal disease. He felt sick, and yet he was hungry all the time, and I wondered what was the right treatment for him. We had so little medicine with us, and were forced to put our entire trust in Epsom Salts.'[71]

Their next stop was Zigi's Town. Afterwards he could not remember much of that: '8 and a half hours solid trek.' His temperature was up and he went to bed.[72] His one thought then was getting to the coast at Grand Bassa, still a week to ten days away: 'it seemed like heaven. There would be another white man there; the sea in front instead of bush; there might be beer to drink.'[73] But as soon as he began to walk to Zigi's Town at 6.45 a.m. he felt sick. He needed a hammock, but that had been left at Ganta. Perhaps Dr Harley's opinion was justified – fever was the result of a white man travelling too far each day.

He was profoundly exhausted – never in his life had he been so exhausted, and always before them was the impenetrable forest. His diary entries become extremely brief. Just outside Zigi's Town, there was a stream trickling down a slope. He noted: 'Ducks on a pond', and the unexpected English scene made him want to sit down, but he could not – there were always decisions to be made. At last he took more Epsom Salts and twenty grains of quinine, wrapped himself in a blanket and lay down under a mosquito net.

He knew he had fever and remembered De Groot and his fever, 'the sweat on his golden stubble'. In his diary he wrote, 'Thunderstorm. Want to get back to V. desperately. Shadow on the mosquito net, the dim hurricane lamp, the empty whisky bottle on the chop box.' Barbara's account of that night gives a vivid description of Graham's condition and an insight into her response to it.

Graham was tottering as we got to Zigi's town; he was staggering as though he was a little drunk. He could get no rest from the carriers while he was up, for they came to him as usual with all their troubles, but I managed to persuade him to go to bed. I took his temperature and it was very high. I gave him plenty of whisky and Epsom salts, and covered him with blankets, hoping that I was doing the right thing.

She had supper by herself while the thunder roared; and the boys served her with grave faces. The same thought was in all their minds. Graham would die. She never doubted it for a minute. He looked like a dead man already. The stormy atmosphere made her head ache and the men quarrelsome. She could hear them snapping at each other, but she left them alone.

She took Graham's temperature again, and it had gone up. She felt quite calm at the thought of Graham's death. To her own horror she felt unemotional about it. Her mind kept telling her that she was really very upset, but actually she was so tired she was incapable of feeling anything. She worked out quietly how she would have her cousin buried, how she would go down to the coast, to whom she would send telegrams.

Only one thing worried her. Graham was a Catholic, and into her weary brain came the thought that she ought to burn candles for him if he died. She was horribly upset, for they had no candles. She felt vaguely that his soul would find no peace if she could not do that for him.[74] To cheer herself up, she smoked an extra cigarette after supper and tried to write up her diary, and although she was tired she was still feeling fit. She found the village pleasant and friendly, Laminah and Mark walking behind her as she went through the village, making her understand that whatever happened they would protect the

Greenes to the end of the journey. She realised again what valuable and loyal friends their boys were.

Before going to bed she had another look at Graham who was in a restless doze, muttering to himself and soaked in perspiration. 'I went to my room,' she wrote, '. . . but did not dare to sleep very much in case my cousin should call out. Outside the rains descended and the thunder roared.' Next morning, she went into her cousin's room 'expecting to see him either delirious or gasping out his last few breaths'. To her amazement, he was up and dressed, though he looked terrible. A kind of horrid death's head grinned at her. His cheeks had sunk in, there were thick black smudges under his eyes, and his scrubby beard added to his seedy effect. His expression, however, was more normal, for the uncanny harsh light that had glowed in his eyes the day before had disappeared. She took his temperature and it was very subnormal.

> 'We must go on quickly,' he said. 'I'm all right again.'
> 'Won't you rest just one day?' I asked.
> 'No,' said Graham impatiently. 'We must get down to the coast.'
> The coast. My cousin was craving to get down to the coast as a pilgrim might crave to get to a holy city.[75]

Greene discovered that night that he had a passionate interest in living: 'I had always assumed before . . . that death was desirable. It seemed that night an important discovery. It was like a conversion . . . I should have known that conversions don't last, or if they last at all it is only as a little sediment at the bottom of the brain.'[76] Some of his own experience is used in 'A Chance for Mr Lever' in which the narrator, with an eighteenth-century cynicism, comments that, 'The story might very well have encouraged my faith in that loving omniscience if it had not been shaken by personal knowledge of the drab empty forest through which Mr Lever now went so merrily, where it is impossible to believe in any spiritual life, in anything outside the nature dying round you, the shrivelling of the weeds.' Mr Lever, seeing Davidson die, now knows the nonsense of the 'Solemnity of Death: death wasn't solemn; it was a lemon-yellow skin and a black vomit.'[77]

*

Their next stop was to be Bassa Town and, reluctantly, Greene hired two extra carriers so that he might travel in a hammock, but he felt that he was thus treating the carriers as animals. 'One heard the hammock strings grinding on the pole and saw the shoulder muscles strain under the weight', and so he walked two hours and then rested ten minutes in the hammock.

At Bassa Town he noticed evidence of 'civilization' in a young prostitute rushing to meet them who 'hung around all day posturing with her thighs and hips suggestively. Naked to the waist, she was conscious of her nakedness; she knew that breasts had a significance to the white man they didn't have to the native. There couldn't be any doubt that she had known whites before.'[78] Greene is vague as to whom she was posturing at but Barbara Greene is quite clear about the matter: 'A young girl, an obvious little prostitute, hovered round and postured in front of Graham. She was a beautiful little creature . . . my cousin was beyond noticing anything.'[79]

That night, sweating between blankets in a fever, Graham recorded in his diary: 'Last tin of biscuits, last tin of milk, last piece of bread', and added a message to his wife: 'Dear, dearest love. I love you so. Ten years ago next month [since Graham first saw Vivien]. The first anniversary that we've been apart since we married, but I've never, never loved you more dearly or more longingly and deeply than on this silly trip. I'm so hopefully longing at this moment (8.20 p.m.), to be with you again. I've thought of you so much.'[80]

On 27 February, after an eight-hour trek, they reached Gyon: 'Inhospitable,' he recorded. 'More than 3 hours before we could get into houses . . . One spoonful of whisky in tea found to be excellent restorative. Dog tired.' They were down to their last half-bottle of whisky which they now rationed out in teaspoonfuls.

Next day, in a place Greene thought was called Darndo, he met the ugliest Liberian he had seen and felt a deep affection for him. He wore dirty pyjamas, his face was yellow, his few teeth decaying and he had a glass eye, but he brought them chairs to sit on and large bitter oranges and limes – the first fresh fruit they had seen for weeks – and arranged a hut for them. He came to believe that Greene was a member of the British Royal Family. He was a tax collector. Greene gave him a dozen pages out of his notebook which he used to write a report on a member of the British Royal Family he had found wandering through Liberia.

That night a sick man dragged himself across the coffee beans spread out to dry to ask Greene for some white man's medicine to cure his gonorrhoea. It was, as Barbara records, the last straw – Graham turned green and went off to bed without supper. The rain came down in a solid wall.

Another two days' trek would bring them to King Peter's Town, and they heard in advance that only a day's further marching to Harlingsville would lead them to a truck which, if permission were granted, could take them down a new road to Grand Bassa. The carriers had never seen a truck before, but had heard of its magic: 'We sat and grinned at each other, blacks and whites, closer in this happiness than we had been all through the trek.' In their relief of spirit there was no longer any need to control the temper, and to the carriers' joy Greene broke out with a flow of obscenity he had not known was at his command at a guide who refused to guide. 'This was the greatest happiness of all: to feel that restraint was no longer necessary.'[81]

Greene sent a note by messenger to the only white man living in Grand Bassa, the manager of the PZ store, asking if the truck could meet them: 'The messenger stuck the note into a cleft stick, and with some of the last of our oil in his lamp set off to walk to Grand Bassa all night through the forest . . . the little lantern bobbing away from us between the trees.'[82] Greene was determined to press on until he reached Grand Bassa, but fortunately some five miles on from King Peter's Town they reached a Seventh Day Adventist mission, arriving there on a Saturday, with the bell ringing for church. The mission was a cluster of white buildings on a hilltop, and the German missionary took them in where his wife, an old-fashioned German Hausfrau, welcomed them with gingerbread and iced fruit drinks; and 'little paper serviettes to wipe their roughened fingers'.

Barbara was almost moved to tears by this meeting. The woman put her hand softly on Barbara's head and said, 'Mein armes Kind' (My poor child), a phrase Barbara's German mother had used to her as a child when she felt sad. Barbara, realising that they had almost reached the end of their memorable journey, wanted more than anything to be petted and spoilt and made a fuss of, but Graham only wanted to get out of the jungle and into Monrovia.

Although the German missionary doubted that the truck would meet them, it did. After another long trek, they came out of the jungle into open country – a grassy path and long, rolling downs – and expected to see the sea. For Graham it was like breathing again, but Barbara felt unsheltered and shy as if she had suddenly cast off her clothes.[83] They found the truck waiting. 'It was wonderful,' Barbara recalled, 'like waking up as a very small child on Christmas morning and finding that Father Christmas *really had* been.' She was dumb with joy and wonder.

Even Greene's more phlegmatic personality was deeply touched. He wanted to laugh and shout and cry. It was the end – the end of the worst daily boredom, of the worst fear and the worst exhaustion he had known. They had been walking, almost without missing a day, for four weeks and had covered three hundred and fifty miles through dense jungle. Starting out as 'poor innocents', they had proved themselves as explorers and after one short truck ride they would have reached Grand Bassa.

Greene recalled how the carriers, on seeing their first truck, drew back in dread and hid their faces in the banks, then according to Barbara they examined it from every side, chattering like magpies. It took them some time to understand that the truck would carry them and all the equipment they had hoisted throughout the journey, without any physical effort on their part. For Greene the journey which had begun with the stink of petrol ended with the same smell. For Barbara, the drive in the old truck, as it rattled along, carrying thirty-two human beings, was one of the most utterly satisfying experiences she had ever had. For the carriers, it was a mystery. Greene's diary records briefly: 'found lorry waiting, and so joyously down to G.B., the P.Z. stores and iced beer.' The iced beer they had longed for throughout the trip had at last come to them. It was 2 March.

In the courtyard of the store, close to the beach with the surf breaking beyond, Greene paid off the carriers, feeling 'sorry for the end of something which was unlikely ever to happen again. One was never likely to live for long in company so simple and uncorrupted.' Their eyes 'were full of excitement and wonder at Grand Bassa'; they had never seen so many stores, the sea, a motor-lorry. Unfortunately, they did not know the way back to their homes. The manager of the PZ store advised them not to follow the beach to Monrovia in order to get in touch with the Holy Cross Mission – it was 'the most dangerous road in all Liberia to travellers, because its people [had] been touched by civilization, [had] learnt to steal and lie and kill'.[84] They should go away quickly – they were 'too innocent to be safe in the town as long as they had money. They would be robbed and the police would take away all they had with many fictitious fines and taxes.' As Barbara recorded, 'The men looked bewildered, for they felt lost now without Graham, who had been their father for so long.'[85] And that night Greene heard their drunken singing and shouts brought on by drinking cane juice, much less gentle than the palm wine they were accustomed to – 'This was crude spirit and crude coastal drunkenness.' Greene could hear the police coming up 'to get their pickings' and Vande, Graham's headman, and Amah were 'being persuaded towards the wooden [police] station'. Greene 'thought of Vande in the dark urging the carriers over the long gaping swaying bridge at Duogobmai.' But Greene's response is curiously negative. He does not go out and try to rescue Vande and Amah from the police or somehow help them in their return up country, instead he writes off-centre, refusing to deal with the problem at hand now that the journey is over: 'We were all of us back in the hands of adolescence, and I thought rebelliously: I am glad, for here is iced beer and a wireless set which will pick up the Empire programme from Daventry, and after all it is home, in the sense that we have been taught to know home, where we will soon forget the finer taste, the finer pleasure, the finer terror on which we might have built.'[86]

But it is easy to speak from one's armchair of what someone in Liberia should do or should not do. When I followed in Greene's footsteps (visiting many of the stone age villages he visited) just before the coup that swept the then President to his death in 1980, I was aware of being in the most corrupt of countries where the police asked for bribes with a machine gun at the ready. Greene, at the end of his historic journey, had no money left to offer the police a bribe. Nothing else would have had the remotest chance of helping Vande and his carriers.

*

By an unexpected stroke of luck, the Greenes were not kept waiting a week with their servants, Amedoo and Laminah, for a Dutch cargo boat. The next morning, Barbara was awakened by Laminah saying, 'Missis get up. Plenty fine boat. Go quick, quick, quick to Monrovia.'[87] The PZ store manager, Shuttleworth, had discovered that a launch was leaving at 7 a.m. on her maiden voyage to Monrovia.

Greene's diary gives a description of it: '30 foot long launch bought for £18, repaired for £25. Two second hand automobile engines, Dodge and Studebaker, had been installed.' It was already carrying 150 black opposition politicians bound for a presidential election in Monrovia, who justifiably shouted that there was no room for the Greenes and their servants, and Mr Shuttleworth tried to dissuade the Greenes from embarking, but they were squeezed on board. The launch tilted one way and another with the fear of her passengers, until the captain, a fat Kru in hat and singlet, shouted that anyone who moved would be put in irons, and, blowing on a little whistle, he put off and they slid away from the yellow sand of the African shore, the dark green forest they had walked through and the tin shacks of Grand Bassa.

The voyage was to be as dangerous and as unpredictable and humorous as their long walk. They sailed 60 miles – seven and a half hours of lurching slowly over the flat, scorching, African sea in the company of black politicians, drinking bottle after bottle of cane juice, roaring drunk but forced to stillness – when they moved, the boat keeled over and the captain roared and threatened anyone who moved would be put in irons. The presence of Greene as the only white man on board convinced the politicians that the British were behind their party. A sudden crash, suggesting they had gone over a rock, brought panic, but it was just one of their party passing out, his head hitting the deck. Watching the 'frieze of black heads', Greene was aware that 'five hundred yards away, the yellow African beach slid unchangingly by without a sign of human occupation.'[88]

At last, the politicians slept almost to a man and woke almost to a man when, late in the afternoon, the promontory that shelters Monrovia, the capital of Liberia, came in sight. They put on their ties and waistcoats, ready to embrace the reception committee that was waving and cheering on the small jetty.

*

The Greenes stayed in Monrovia only nine days, but it seemed an unending time. 'Liberia,' Graham wrote, 'whether to the diplomat or to the storekeeper, was about the deadest of all ends; there was really nothing but drink and the wireless, and of the two the drink was preferable.'[89] In Monrovia there were only thirty whites – Poles, Germans, Dutch, Americans, Italians, French, English and a single Hungarian, store-keepers, gold smugglers, shipping agents and consuls, who went down regularly with fever – eight of them in the nine days the Greenes were there, according to Graham, nine according to Barbara. During their stay, 'Once a week they played a little tennis at the British Legation or had a game of billiards, and once a week, too, the older men of the white colony shot with a pistol at bottles perched above the beach at the edge of the British Legation ground. That custom had been going on for years, every Saturday evening until the light was too bad to see.'[90] In his diary Greene recorded: 'Had tea at bishop's home and then went to Yapp's [I assume Yapp to be the British Consul at the British Legation]. Iced cocktails and champagne for dinner. Talked till 1. Tiddly.'[91] In a letter to his mother, written on British Legation stationery, he speaks of the luxurious legation and of having 'lashings of drink'.

Both Greenes were bored – a natural reaction after their tremendous journey through the Liberian forests. Monrovia was a damp squib by comparison, and their urge was to be home. Every now and then there would be a rumour that a boat was expected, but a few hours later it would be denied. Barbara recalls that her cousin's manners in this situation were better than hers – he did not show his boredom so much, but his diary entries are terse, the one dealing with their departure on 12 March being as brief as a telegram: 'Caught the *Macgregor Laird.*'

According to Barbara she went straight to her cabin and fell asleep, waking only when they reached Freetown, but this seems unlikely since the cargo ship took four days to reach Freetown. Barbara writes of their boys, Amedoo and Laminah, 'hovering round us, ready to serve us to the last minute. They seemed heartbroken at the thought that we would have to part with them at Freetown; we were so used to one another now and knew each other's little ways.'[92] Greene does not mention this parting. He records his reflections about returning to 'civilization': 'How happy I had thought I should be, while I was struggling down to Grand Bassa, back in *my* world . . . Of course I was happy, I told myself, opening the bathroom door, examining again a real water-closet, studying the menu at lunch, while out of the port-hole Cape Mount slid away, Liberia slid away . . . One had been scared and sick and one was well again, in the world to which one belonged.'[93] But he also remembered the squalor of Kru town, the huts at Duogobmai, the devil's servant fanning away the storm – 'all gathered together behind the white line of the bar no European steamer ever crossed.'

The differences between the two Greenes are revealed through their preoccupations on board ship. Barbara was aware of the dreariness of the journey, the condition of her clothes and of how unemotional and without immediate hope she felt on returning to England: 'The days – indescribably dreary – passed by like a slow-motion picture. Soon we left behind the burning sunshine and plunged into storms and fogs. My only warm dress was filthy, the rats had eaten my stockings, and my mackintosh was torn beyond repair. I found I was tired of being dirty, and all day long I shivered with cold. I was incapable somehow of looking forward to the future with any excitement.'[94]

Her cousin, relieved now of the daily responsibilities of that exhausting trek, observed those around him: 'The captain leant over the rail, old and dissatisfied, complaining of his men: "Boil the whole bloody lot of the men in the ship together and you wouldn't make an ordinary seaman"; he was looking back – to the age of sail.'[95] In his diary, Greene described the first mate, who eyed him like an enemy: 'The tipsy half-wit mate . . . "I'd send my master's ticket to the Board of Trade & tell them to wipe their bloody arses with it . . . My dear friend."' At Freetown guests came on board and they all drank themselves free from Africa and the captain stuck his fingers down his throat, brought up his drink and was dead sober again, and the ship went out of harbour, out of Africa.

*

Barbara and Graham arrived in England, their small cargo vessel landing at Dover, on a bitterly cold April morning: 'After the blinding sunlight on the sand beyond the bar, after the long push of the Atlantic sea, the lights of Dover burning at four in the morning, a cold April mist coming out from shore with the tender.'[96]

According to Barbara they were turned promptly off the ship and they sat on their boxes in the customs house, silent and depressed, waiting for an official to come and let them through. It was in Dover that the two cousins parted, Graham going into Dover where he was staying, and Barbara waiting for a train to take her to London, the rain pouring down, the wind whistling round her, feeling lonely in the world. Then a railway porter took pity on her and offered her coffee beside a hot fire. The African journey, taken on so casually over a glass of champagne at Hugh Greene's wedding, ended with coffee with a friendly porter.

What did Greene do in Dover? A note on the last page of his diary, probably a draft of a telegram sent to his wife, reads simply: '*Macgregor Laird* arrives Dover. Wire ship where find you. Want suit overcoat.' In a letter (28 October 1986), Vivien recalls that she met her husband in an hotel and not on the ship or wharf and that they went home together. 'Out of mischief' she bought a blonde wig (her hair was black then) 'to surprise him'. A pleasant surprise, no doubt, after the black hair he had seen so much of during the past three months.

*

Was that all? Did the journey with Barbara and its experiences end in wind and rain and a cold, empty customs house? It would seem so, but in fact it was the beginning of another journey.

*

On his return, Greene began an exploration of his true motives for going to Liberia which continued for many years, and although in a review of 1952 he commented, 'Men have always tried to rationalise their irrational acts . . . explanations . . . are as unconvincing as last night's supper as the cause of our fantastic dreams',[97] he was still seeking reasons. He equates the writer with the explorer: 'Is it that the explorer has the same creative sickness as the writer . . . and that to fill in the map, as to fill in the character or features of a human being, requires the urge to surrender and self-destruction?' Basically therefore, there is the need to be a 'farer', as in the stanza from Auden's poem printed at the beginning of *Journey Without Maps*, in which the 'fearer' suggests that the 'farer' will 'discover the lacking/ Your footsteps feel from granite to grass.' The 'farer's reply is,

"Yours never will."' The journey has to be made, the dangers encountered, the map filled in. And in the same review of 1952 he argues that West Africa, more than any other part of the continent, has cast a strong spell on Englishmen, not least for those very aspects that inspire fear – 'the mists, the mangrove swamps, the malaria, the black water and yellow fever of the Coast'.

But more than fear was involved in his journey, and in his purpose and experience he perhaps comes closest to Joseph Conrad's experience in the Congo – there are many parallels between his journey in Liberia and Conrad's 'Heart of Darkness'. Both were writers seeking new experiences; both urgently needed to make some money – Conrad by becoming master of a Congo river-steamer, Greene by writing a travel book. Each had an urge based on an ideal: Conrad's recollection of his childhood fascination with the map of Africa and the great explorers; Greene's desire to experience real 'seediness, not the seediness he knew from the outside' (the sky-signs in Leicester Square, the 'tarts' in Bond Street) but a more interesting variety. 'There seemed to be a seediness about [Liberia] that you couldn't get to the same extent elsewhere and seediness has a very deep appeal.'[98] They both started their journeys with confrontations with bureaucracy, Conrad in the headquarters of the S.A.B. in Brussels, 'the sepulchral city', Greene with the Anti-Slavery Society and the Liberian consulate in London, and both made journeys of ever growing discomfort, fear and eventually illness. Both experienced more than they had bargained for – an insight into what Conrad called 'the fascination of the abomination', a confrontation with the primitive.

Conrad himself felt the attraction of the dirt, disease, barbarity and primitiveness of Africa, so that he could not condemn entirely Kurtz, the man who succumbed to the fascination; and Greene could find some sympathy for the Liberian politicians who had not succumbed: 'I could not be quite fair to them, coming . . . from an interior where there was a greater simplicity, an older more natural culture, and traditions of honesty and hospitality . . . It seemed to me that they, almost as much as oneself, had lost touch with the true primitive source. It was not their fault. Two hundred years of American servitude separated them from Africa.'[99]

Greene, in spite of his experiences – the old man being beaten with a club outside the prison at Tapee-Ta, the naked, clay-covered widows at Tailahun, the 'wooden-toothed devil swaying his raffia skirts between the huts' – retained a belief in primitive virtues and saw the evils as 'like the images in a dream to stand for something of importance to myself'.[100]

He did not want to stay in Africa; he had no yearning for a mindless sensuality, but the deep appeal of the seedy was due to the fact that it is nearer to the beginnings of human development – 'it hasn't reached so far away as the smart, the new, the chic, the cerebral' – and also, 'it is only when one has appreciated such a beginning, its terrors as well as its placidity, the power as well as the gentleness, that the pity for what we have done with ourselves is driven more forcibly home.'[101]

It is possible that Greene's desire to go to Africa, to find out the worst, to reach rock bottom and to seek out the primitive, was inspired by his reading, immediately before his journey, the novel, *The Inner Journey*, by Kurt Heuser. The young hero, Jeronimo, seeks to escape his past and also expresses a fascination with the 'true native' of Africa and he sees Africa in terms similar to those of Greene. In the urban world we grow unhappier and 'what ails us is nothing else than our continuous submission to chaos, because our deepest desire is to submit . . . the same impulse that makes us yearn for release and death, in our weak moments . . . the will to self-destruction . . .' And Greene points out in a 1952 review that both Mary Kingsley and Mungo Park went to Africa to seek death, and Mungo Park found it. This desire for self-destruction, in spite of a powerful desire to succeed as a writer, is part of the paradox of Graham Greene. He has a strong desire – it is still with him – to take a leap into the unknown, a journey in the dark, this last being his original title for *Journey Without Maps*.

There was, however, a further dimension to his journey: a Freudian journey back to one's beginnings, but 'a more costly, less easy method, calling for physical as well as mental strength'.[102] On a subconscious level it was a retreat from civilisation in a search for the 'ancestral threads which still exist in our unconscious minds'. Only through experiencing the primitive as the French novelist Céline described it, 'Hidden away in all this flowering forest of twisted vegetation, a few decimated tribes of natives squatted among fleas and flies, crushed by taboos and eating nothing at all but rotten tapioca', could one escape from the rationality of civilised man. As Greene wrote: 'when one sees to what unhappiness, to what peril of extinction centuries of cerebration have brought us, one sometimes has a curiosity to discover if one can, from what we have come to recall at which point we went astray.'[103] From this experience follows his description of one of the first sounds he heard on his return to England – 'the wail of a child [in a tenement] too young to speak, too young to have learned what the dark may conceal in the way of lust and murder, crying for no intelligible reason but because it still possessed the ancestral fear, the devil was dancing in its sleep'.[104]

Praising a documentary on Abyssinia in a 1935 film review, he ended with these firm words – which could have been written by Greene only after his Liberian experience: the film 'leaves you with a vivid sense of something very old, very dusty, very cruel, but something dignified in its dirt and popular in its tyranny and perhaps more worth preserving than the bright slick streamlined civilization which threatens it . . .'[105]

Journey Without Maps was published on 11 May 1936. A year and a half later, the book was withdrawn because of a libel case and remained out of print for almost a decade. Greene wrote to his brother Hugh about it:

> The other fly in the ointment is a libel action. I don't know whether you remember the drunk party at Freetown in Journey Without Maps. I called the drunk, whose real name was quite different, Pa Oakley. It now turns out that there is a Dr P. D. Oakley, head of the Sierra Leone Medical Service. The book's been withdrawn (luckily all but 200 copies have been sold), writs have been served, and he's out for damages! Anxious days.[106]

By 1946, Greene had himself become a publisher at Eyre and Spottiswoode and he rescued his travel book. To Louise Callendar of Heinemann he wrote: 'After the libel action from the Sierra Leone Doctor the book was withdrawn and has never been in print since. My own view is that it would be only equitable for you to surrender the rights back to me personally, in which case I should probably give a licence for three years to either Pan Books or Penguin.'[107] He sold to Pan Books.

When Peter Fleming came to review *Journey Without Maps* in the *Spectator*, he struck the right note in describing Greene's account of his journey; he speaks of his 'unillusioned honesty which stamps all his impressions' and, comparing him with Ernest Hemingway (whose *Green Hills of Africa* appeared in 1935), he speaks of both authors seeking Africa as 'fugitives from western civilization'; and while he admits that 'that note of disgust which pervades all [Greene's] writings sounds . . . all the time in our ears', yet he feels that in Greene's descriptions of the interior we are looking through his eyes, 'whereas in the other book we are always being forced to look into Mr Hemingway's'.[108]

*

At the beginning of *Journey Without Maps* Greene gives a quotation from Oliver Wendell Holmes describing an individual's life as a child's dissected map which, if we lived long enough, we could reassemble so that our life was 'intelligently laid out before' us. To some degree, the continent was an important piece in the jigsaw of the map of his life – or rather several pieces, as a letter to his cousin Barbara in 1975 suggests:

> By God! I think you are right. 40 years. I would have loved to split a bottle with you – preferably not champagne – it should be whisky with warm filtered water & squeezed limes.
>
> To me too that trip has been very important – it started a love of Africa which has never quite left me & that led to Freetown in the war, & Kenya & the Mau Mau afterwards, & the Congo & the Cameroons when I stumbled on Yvonne. Altogether a trip which altered life.[109]

36

14 North Side

Knowledge can be acquired only by hard work.
— W. SOMERSET MAUGHAM

A LTHOUGH on his return to England Greene must have been debilitated by the journey and the fever, he almost immediately began to reorganise his life. He was faced with the fact that he and his family were living on uncertain royalties from his novels. In an effort to find some permanent income he again approached his former employer, *The Times*. He was now an established book reviewer, had had his fourth novel, *Stamboul Train*, made into a film, had his sixth novel in press and had branched out as a traveller and explorer. But it would seem that *The Times* demanded an apology for his defection. He wrote to his mother: 'The Times plan will not, I think, come off; it necessitates a letter on my part which I don't feel inclined to write saying that I see now I was mistaken in leaving them.'[1] He was not likely to grovel in this way.

However, he did feel that he needed to leave Oxford and live in London, the centre of the publishing world, and he went to look at flats and houses at Clapham Common. 'I was terribly struck by the place,' he wrote to his mother, 'most beautiful, of the Hampstead period, with lovely air and nice shops and only about twelve minutes from Leicester Square by tube and close to Aunt N[ora].' He went to see Derek Verschoyle's sister. She and her husband had bought 'a most beautiful Queen Anne house in a lovely row opposite the common and done it up absolutely like a museum piece; the most beautifully decorated house I've ever been in.'[2] The Robertsons (the owners) wanted to let the house furnished from the end of July as Mr Robertson had given up a business job in town in order to become a master at Sherborne. The rent was £5 a week, quite a substantial sum in 1935, and beyond Greene's means, but Mrs Robertson was so taken with him that she promised that, if he could get rid of his flat in Oxford and if she had found no suitable tenant, she would let him have the house for the same rent he was paying at Oxford. And it turned out that way.

He had decided on the house without Vivien's help, but when, arriving with Lucy and the luggage, she first saw No. 14 North Side, she was delighted with his choice:

> It was almost entirely panelled throughout – mostly pale grey, except the bedroom and the front sitting room. There was a big square entrance hall of stone . . . there was a room where we kept china and things in. The kitchen and an adjoining room were semi-basement and a door from the kitchen (glass) led into a small garden, part paved, quickly turned into a sand pit and garden slide. And then there was this wonderful staircase which is called a flying staircase. Someone said the flying staircase might be by Vauban but this seems unlikely.* On the first floor there was a drawing room (pale grey panelling) and I got stripes – cherry and white – for the chairs and sofa. I had some papier mâché tables. And then the front was a sort of living room, sitting room and very pretty. The curtains were pale green with lilies of the valley on them. It was very elegant. Most of the rooms had shutters and window seats. And then, on that landing, there was a room for the maid and a bathroom. And the nursery. Oh, yes, and then next to the nursery was the night nursery. That's it.[3]

Lady Read, the wife of Herbert Read, described it as 'a most enchanting house – like a Mozart opera – with the double step.'

Greene wrote to his mother: 'The whole appearance of Clapham Common is lovely, like a wide green plateau on a hilltop above Battersea, with the common stretching out of sight in one direction, and on three sides surrounded by little country-like shops and Queen Anne houses, a pond and in the middle of the Common, the 18th century church to which the Clapham set belonged. The house was built in 1730 and was used by Macaulay's father as a school for black children.'[4]

Something of his pride in the house is shown when, in 1938, having decided that his American publishers, Doubleday, were not selling enough copies of his books and he moved to Viking, he invited his contact with them, director Ben Hubsch, at that time staying at 55

---

* Le Prestre de Vauban (15 May 1633–30 March 1707) was the military engineer who revolutionised the art of siegecraft and defensive fortifications. He also invented the socket bayonet and introduced ricochet gunfire.

Jermyn Street, to a party at his home. He sent Hubsch the following neat sketch and accurate directions (though printed the handwriting is recognisably Vivien's) as to how to find 14 North Side – and reminding him to wear a black tie!

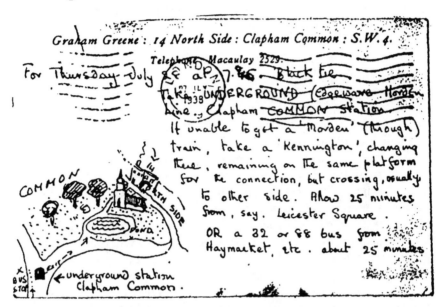

Number 14 North Side was to play a significant part in their lives. It was to be the last house they lived in together and it was to be destroyed by a bomb during the blitz on London in the Second World War. J. Maclaren-Ross recalled walking one day off Clapham Common with a friend in 1956 and his companion pointed to a gutted ruin with a façade of blackened brick and said, 'That used to be a Queen Anne house before the blitz. Beautiful place I believe. It belonged to Graham Greene.' 'I know,' replied Maclaren-Ross, no doubt with some satisfaction, 'I lunched there once. In 1938', and his friend was suitably impressed.

The bombing of that house was to be used creatively by Greene in two works – first in his novel *The End of the Affair*, and then in a curious and bizarre short story, 'The Destructors', about a gang of boys who pull down, brick by brick, a Queen Anne house.

Now settled in London, he pressed on with his career on several fronts. Having contacted a lecture agency, in May he gave a lecture at the League of Nations' Union lunch club. It went off well and some well known writers came to hear him. He told his mother, 'Rose Macaulay was at my table & Winifred Holtby introduced herself.' He also gave a short but important lecture to the Anti-Slavery

Society, who were anxious to hear his account of conditions in Liberia as letters in their files from Sir John Harris to Greene and to his father reveal. One letter states that the Society had left open the date of their annual general meeting until they knew when Greene would return. That they should do so when two personages of political eminence, Lord Lugard and the Maharaja of Nepal, were scheduled to speak, gives an indication of the importance to them of Greene's journey to Liberia and the information about slavery they anticipated he would bring back.

The meeting was arranged for 18 June at Caxton Hall, Westminster, and despité his parents' keenness to attend, Greene, who is never happy about lecturing, dissuaded his father and told his mother that the affair would not be amusing. If it was not amusing, his lecture was shrewd. He began with honeyed words about his supporters in the Society, telling them that the first thing that Barclay, the President of Liberia, had said when they met in the interior was, 'Do you know Lady Simon and a man called Sir John Harris?'

The greater part of his speech was given over to describing the difficulties of his journey and a consideration as to whether conditions of slavery existed there. He explained the fact that deep in the interior there is no restraint of law and that the law-givers are the supreme breakers of the law. He concentrated on District Commissioner Reeves, in charge of the district near the border of Sierra Leone.

Greene also told the story of the infamous Colonel Davis, the man responsible for the atrocities on the Kru coast, whom he found holding an enquiry into alleged cruelties of others at Tapee-Ta: 'One was naturally surprised, therefore, to find Colonel Davis still in a position of authority, the facts [of the atrocities] having been proved to the last degree.' Greene is all too human here. Either he had thought again about the Kru atrocities and come to the conclusion that Davis was guilty, as had been stated in the British Blue Book, or he was paying lip-service to the views of Simon and Harris, or simply felt that he could no longer sustain the view, strongly expressed in his diary after meeting the 'Dictator of Grand Bassa' at Tapee-Ta, that Davis was not guilty. After all, he was back in England and away from the influence of that powerful, exhilarating American mercenary.

But Greene did put forward his firm criticism of the half-educated, the so-called 'civilised' blacks of the coast – the term 'civilised' could be applied in Liberia only to those who 'could write their own name and read it when it is written', as opposed to those natives of the interior, a courageous, honest people who on a short acquaintance made one 'absurdly fond of them'. Greene stressed that those villagers with their own industries – dyeing, weaving, making of knives, making of scabbards – did not need 'either the semi-European civilization of the coast, or even the complete white civilization such as we have known it lately'.

For some time after his return from Liberia, Greene reviewed whatever came up about West Africa, and he had not been back much more than a week when Gorer's *Africa Dances* appeared. Immediately Greene took the offensive over what he considered Gorer's irresponsible assertion of 'sex-obsessed missionaries': 'For every sex-obsessed missionary you will find half a dozen who are trained anthropologists studying native customs with more authority than Mr Gorer possesses.'[5] The following year a book written by two men and called *Unknown Liberia* came to Greene's notice. He wrote to his mother: 'I've just been reviewing a book for the Spectator . . . a most fishy production, full of obvious lies, photographs stolen from other books, a strong suspicion that they never really went into the interior or made the journey at all.'[6] When Greene made this apparent in his review he drew further attention to it by means of the title to the review, 'Two Tall Travellers'.[7]

His letters to his mother, to Hugh, and to literary agents, his articles, book and film reviews, after he had established himself in London, all reveal a growing sense of confidence, and one wonders whether this was not in part due to the fact that he had, in Liberia, experienced what few of his contemporaries in London had experienced: he had undertaken a journey into the unknown, come close to the primitive origins of mankind, journeyed without maps and had, like those who had survived the horrors of the First World War, come through – by means of his own determination and grit. Certainly, he now had a surge of creative energy which was nothing short of phenomenal.

In the two months after his return, he corrected the proofs of *England Made Me*, wrote a story entitled 'The Bear Fell Free', worked on *Journey Without Maps* and tried his hand at a 'shocker' – *A Gun for Sale* (*This Gun for Hire* in America). He wrote another short story, 'The Jubilee', and completed 'The Basement Room', which he had begun on board ship to escape the tedium of the return from Liberia. The *News Chronicle*, he told his mother, had 'commissioned a five-day serial (£50) [The Basement Room] and I'm just finishing it'. 'The Bear Fell Free' was 'supposed to have come out on Monday'. 'Did you see', he asked her, 'the review in the Lit Supp? England Made Me comes out on June 17.' He even acted as a judge of short stories at the annual Eisteddfod of the City of London Literary Institute. And there was much social activity:

On the 25th, we had dinner with Rupert and Comfort [Hart-Davis], on Sunday we went to a wearing party at Highams, on Monday we had lunch with Arnot Robertson, yesterday I had lunch with Winifred Holtby, on Thursday we are having lunch with Ede at the Tate and are giving a sherry party (Antonia White is coming: I haven't met her yet). And so it goes on. In spite of it all, I'm getting a tremendous amount of work done.[8]

In a postscript he added, 'Lucy now crawls about at a terrific speed.' Incredibly, as early as 1935, someone gave a lecture, the first of many, on his work: 'On the 24th, my French agent', he wrote to his mother, 'came to dinner and gave me a cheque for serial rights of "Stamboul Train" (apparently the lecture on me is being given in the Sorbonne!).'[9]

His short story, 'The Bear Fell Free' is a sport, experimental and brittle in style with much use of interior monologue; its theme is betrayal, but this time of a man by a woman, based on the type of 1930s woman he was probably beginning to meet. It also seems to have some slight reflections of his own experiences. The hero, Tony Farrell, after five sherries accepts a dare to fly across the Atlantic. Farrell, like Anthony Farrant in *England Made Me* (both characters probably based on Herbert Greene), has about him the sweet smell of failure, and the dare ends in his death. The teddy bear mascot which his girlfriend Jane had thrown into the rear of the tiny plane falls free before the plane crashes, and Jane tells Tony's friend, Carter, 'Yes, I gave him the teddy bear. We were crazy about each other . . . Yes, I was terribly sad, but after all, Mr Carter, it's better than the suspense', and she invites Carter to return the bear to her, having in mind a desire to meet him and, presumably putting down the phone (this is not clear because of the story's technique), she runs naked back to bed, laughing, adorable: 'That was Carter, darling. You remember him at the party. All ex-officer. I've got such a lech for him, darling.'

This story was published in book form by Grayson Books. Grayson himself chose stories by twelve authors (a story a book) whom he saw as likely to become famous – among them H. E. Bates, H. A. Manhood, James Hanley, Arthur Calder-Marshall, T. F. Powys and Sean O'Faolain. The books were signed volumes and beautifully produced. In those days it was possible to make a profit on limited editions – 285 signed and numbered and 250 offered for sale at 10s.6d. each. They are now collectors' items.

The story 'The Jubilee' shows Greene writing with an eye to catching the public's interest through a contemporary event. On 6 May 1935, the Silver Jubilee of King George V's accession to the throne was celebrated. By 1935 the depression had begun to ease and King George was suddenly taken to the hearts of the British people. Everywhere Jubilee committees sprang up to organise local celebrations and to hang out lively banners across streets, to decorate lamp-posts and public buildings. At night the Houses of Parliament, St Paul's Cathedral and Buckingham Palace were floodlit and every house had its Union Jack and coloured streamers. On the 6th, the Royal Family drove in state to St Paul's to attend a Thanksgiving Service. London was crammed with visitors, and there was a tremendous crowd of people outside the Palace cheering endlessly and waiting for the King to come out on the balcony.

That night Trafalgar Square was packed with tipsy revellers singing First World War songs, 'Tipperary', 'There's a Long, Long Trail A-winding' and 'Keep the Home Fires Burning'. The celebration was, of course, commercially exploited. Everything was called Jubilee; there were Jubilee dresses, Jubilee hats, and especially Jubilee stamps (the King was a keen philatelist).

One must assume that Greene's story was written with the May Jubilee★ in mind and that it was called 'The Jubilee' for the same reason that dresses and hats were. Yet in spite of the commercial opportunism it is recognisably by Graham Greene. Greene is willing to seize a chance, but not to write a pot-boiler. 'The Jubilee' was not his only work influenced by this contemporary event. The novel, called in manuscript 'The Shipwrecked', received a different name: 'I've changed the title of the novel,' he wrote to his mother, 'to *England Made Me* to fit the Jubilee.'

*

The hero of 'The Jubilee', the fastidious, ageing gigolo, Mr Chalfont, living in a small bed-sitting room off Shepherd's Market, had not, with the rest of London, blown whistles or thrown paper ribbons, or danced to harmoniums in the street. He had stayed locked away in his room in case he met people he had known in better days. When he does go into the London streets looking for game (women of a certain age attracted to tall, well-preserved gentlemen), he is careful to hide his poverty: 'He had learned to hold his hand so that one frayed patch on his sleeve didn't show, and the rather exclusive club tie, freshly ironed, might have been bought that morning.'

Entering a pub, he is unexpectedly 'picked up' by Amy, not at all his kind, but a vulgar, outspoken, ex-prostitute who, unlike Mr

---

★ In Greene's collection, *Twenty-One Stories*, 'The Jubilee' is dated 1936. This should not trouble us. For no obvious reason, Greene often dates his activities and his stories wrongly. He is generally out a year and sometimes two.

Chalfont, had made a killing during the Jubilee. She had opened a spurious tourist bureau, had provided 'private' entertainment and made £5,000. Mr Chalfont's day is over. The world has moved on. To succeed you need to be vulgar and uneducated – the old school tie is no longer enough and Amy could say: 'It was really my jubilee . . . I saw . . . how I could extend my business. I opened at Brighton too. I cleaned up England in a way of speaking.'

It is this tough, down to earth manner, no airs and graces, eye on the main chance new type whom the old colonials, or those who pretend to such a background, now have to rely on. Amy leads Mr Chalfont out of the pub to have her fun: 'Cheer up, my dear . . . a girl likes a cheerful face.' And suddenly she becomes raucous and merry, slapping Mr Chalfont on his back, pinching his arm: 'Let's have a little Jubilee spirit, dear.'

Thus was the vulgar Amy born, to reappear more fully developed in *Brighton Rock* three years later as the inimitable, big-breasted, good sport, Ida Arnold.

*

It must have been a tremendous fillip for Greene when the *News Chronicle* commissioned a five-day serial of 'The Basement Room' – one of his finest stories which was later made into a successful film, *The Fallen Idol*, the screenplay done by himself. While 'The Jubilee' dealt with the impact of the new world on the old, 'The Basement Room' was derived from the theme of lost childhood. It features the green baize door, always for Greene the means of entry into unknown, alien and feared worlds, the world of searing experiences. What lies beyond the baize door (in an embassy) is the basement room inhabited by the butler Baines and his wife. The boy Philip Lane, left in their care while his parents are abroad, begins there his premature initiation into the adult world, with a growing recognition of the manipulative nature of adults, of the nature of evil, when he enters that room: 'Philip Lane went downstairs and pushed at the baize door; . . . he set foot for the first time on the stairs to the basement. Again he had the sense: this is life. All his seven nursery years vibrated, with the strange, the new experience . . . He was apprehensive, but he was happier than he had ever been. Everything was more important than before.' Baines becomes the boy's hero – he is devoted to him and fascinated by the stories of his experiences in West Africa. While Baines is of the uneducated classes, his attitude towards the blacks in the interior (in 1935 it was common to call blacks 'niggers') is identical to Greene's and Greene is making use of observations recorded in *Journey Without Maps*:

'Did you ever shoot a nigger?'
'I never had any call to shoot,' Baines said. 'Of course I carried a
gun. But you didn't need to treat them bad. That just made
them stupid.' 'Why,' Baines said, bowing his thin grey hair with
embarrassment over the ginger pop, 'I loved some of those damned
niggers. I couldn't help loving them. There they'd be laughing,
holding hands; they liked to touch each other; it made them feel
fine to know the other fellow was round.'

Baines, boasting to Philip on the top of a bus, after a visit to the zoo, says:

'I said don't let me see you touch that black again.' Baines had led
a man's life; everyone on top of the bus pricked their ears up when
he told Philip all about it.
    'Would you have shot him?' Philip asked, and Baines put his
head back and tilted his dark respectable man-servant's hat to a
better angle as the bus swerved round the artillery memorial.[10]

But young Philip has a deep fear of Mrs Baines's voice; 'like the voice
in a nightmare when the small Price light has guttered in the saucer
and the curtains move; it was sharp and shrill and full of malice . . .
she was darkness when the night-light went out in a draught; she
was the frozen blocks of earth he had seen one winter in a graveyard
when someone said, "They need an electric drill".'* The devastating
effect that the adult world has upon the boy, his inability to understand adult manoeuvring and to keep their confusing secrets, leads
him, innocently, to betray his hero, with the result that sixty years
later, nearing the end of his life, he has nothing to show because he
must avoid preserving 'the memory of Mrs Baines's malicious voice
saying good night, her soft determined footfalls on the stairs to the
basement, going down, going down.'[11]

*

At this time his correspondence with his mother, brother Hugh and
his literary agent, indicates the determination of his second onslaught
on London; it entailed much entertaining and being entertained. He
records: 'Rupert and Comfort Hart-Davis came to dinner one night

* Philip's unexpected analogy is based on an experience of Greene's in Chipping
Campden. He noted in his diary on 18 January 1933: '13 days of hard frost. Coming
up the hill by the Church I saw a funeral breaking up in the churchyard. I had seen it in
the village, an old woman, Mrs Greene, was making a very stately exit with a double
row of bearers and two cars following. Terrible weather for gravediggers – the ground
hard enough for an electric drill for six inches down.'

to meet Antonia White, and Paul Willert, a young publisher and his wife, another night, and Hamish Hamilton . . . They were all entranced by the house.'[12] Earlier that week he had lunched with Hamish Hamilton; an offer was made to Greene in connection with a publishing scheme but the offer was not good enough. The next night he was off to a party at Antonia White's and days later he was going to an 'intimate' supper at Herbert Read's to meet T. S. Eliot: 'This is rather terrifying like having dinner alone with Henry James.'[13] Forty-five years later he recollected it in *Ways of Escape* as being 'like receiving an invitation from Coleridge – "Wordsworth is coming, but no one else."' Then his old school friend and later London Magistrate, Eric Guest, and his wife came to have sherry. Almost simultaneously Greene was off to have tea with Violet Hunt, who was pleased with a review he had done of Jessie Conrad's reminiscences of her husband Joseph Conrad.[14]

Violet Hunt had lived with Ford Madox Hueffer (later Ford) and was the daughter of W. A. Hunt, one of the pre-Raphaelite group of painters and a member of the Rossetti circle. She had been educated with the daughters of William Morris and Burne-Jones and, giving up the study of art, had written successful books including a volume of gossipy memoirs. She was seventy-one when Greene met her: 'A very strange wandering old lady living in a house stacked with pre-Raphaelite objects,' he wrote to his mother. 'She had thought I was a female novelist writing under a pseudonym! She used to come to Clapham Common when she was a child to parties . . . and had met Charles Reade [author of *The Cloister and the Hearth* (1814–84)] at one of them. A lot of scandal . . . about Ford Madox Hueffer. I don't know how one's had time to meet anyone what with films, reviews and reading M.S. and writing the two books.'[15]

'Reading M.S.' was the correcting of *England Made Me* which was published on 17 June 1935. And he found the time to write some literary criticism: 'Bonamy Dobrée has asked me to write a chapter on Fielding & Sterne for a book he's editing next year for Cassell.' This appeared in a volume entitled *From Anne to Victoria* in 1937.

*

It was in 1935 that David Higham and Lawrence Pollinger left the Curtis Brown literary agency to form their own agency with Nancy Pearn – Pearn, Pollinger and Higham – and Greene moved to them. He was interested in earning money between novels and his plan, while writing *Journey Without Maps*, was to get certain sections in prime condition and publish them in advance in magazines, just as he hoped to publish short stories in this way before collecting them into a book.

His letters to his agents reveal him as being cool, clinical and business-like, keeping them up to scratch, and he had something of the Trollope mentality, writing to his mother in August that, given his tight discipline of writing a set number of words a day, he would complete the two books he was working on by a set date: 'I've been frantically busy . . . it looks as if I shall have both Liberia and the shocker [*A Gun for Sale*] finished by Christmas.' He adds: 'Then I can start the novel for the autumn.' This presumably was *Brighton Rock* which was published in 1938 – his first major pre-war novel.

All was not success, however. By August 1935 he had sent a section of his travel book, entitled 'Liberian Masks', to Curtis Brown, with photographs. These were sent on to Nancy Pearn who was responsible for placing material with magazines in the new agency. Her first letter was not encouraging: '"Liberian Masks" declined by the Geographical Magazine . . . I am now holding this for the other chapters in order to show this as a whole to "Nash's" or some other suitable medium for use as extracts . . . They returned at the same time the story "A Chance for Mr Lever" which by the way has been declined by "Nash's" and "The Strand". This therefore, we are planning to offer in other directions.'

In reply, Greene told Nancy that the 'Mr Lever' story could no longer be offered since his first collection of stories, called *The Basement Room*, after the title story, was being brought out by Cresset Press in the autumn. 'Mr Lever' does appear in Greene's first collection. It needed to, as he had collected only eight stories.

The collection made little impact on the general public. *The Times Literary Supplement* reviewed it in a paragraph, commenting that Greene's first three stories about children touched on larger worlds than their limited experience could cope with, and that he showed skill and variety 'turning . . . from Pimlico nursery to Paris revolution, and from Liberian jungle to a psychic lecturer'. But the anonymous writer felt the need to balance his praise with a slight smack of the wrist: 'Intimations of deeper emotions become apparent now and again, but fail to enforce themselves.'[16]

It was a contributor to the *Spectator* who spoke best about Greene's 'intimation of deeper emotions': 'Mr Greene is able, especially in the title story, to catch in a few pages more of truth as it flies than some novelists catch in a lifetime.'[17]

It must have seemed to Greene, by the end of 1935, that success was far off. Not only did his first collection of stories fall flat, but his June novel, *England Made Me*, did not do well – and never has. *The Times Literary Supplement* suggested, with justification, that the hero, Anthony Farrant, was the fruit of his public school training in his moral and intellectual emptiness, his automatic and protective charm – criticism of the 'old school tie' attitude to life is implicit all through.[18] William Plomer in the *Spectator* took up the same point: 'Mr Greene lays emphasis . . . on the importance of the often damaging influence of his school on a man's nature.'[19]

Greene's school friend, Peter Quennell, reviewed it in the *New Statesman and Nation*. While telling us that it was the portrait of a cad who 'sponges, tells lies, seduces girls, loses innumerable jobs, wears school colours to which he is not entitled', Quennell found a more 'unamiable trait – [he] talks an argot that proves a sad strain on the reader's patience'. What troubled Quennell was that Anthony Farrant spoke of his clothes as 'glad rags'. He wrongly predicted that the novel would be a popular success.

The sales in America were catastrophic – only 930 copies – and they were not very much better in England. Heinemann, naturally, thought that it should be remaindered (which it was in 1939). Not one to take such a suggestion lying down, Greene wrote to his agent listing the sales figures, pitiful though they were, for the past eighteen months.

Period ending	30. 6.37 . . . 400 copies sold.
" "	31.12.37 . . . 150 copies sold.
" "	30. 6.38 . . . 240 copies sold.

He pointed out that it had seemed to sell better in the first half of 1938 than in the second half of 1937. That it was still wriggling and that therefore an enquiry might be in order.[20]

Nor could the sales of his collection of short stories, *The Basement Room*, have been large and the reviews were too few to have attracted a substantial readership; but because the *News Chronicle* had serialised 'The Basement Room', it wasn't long before he was asking Nancy Pearn to try to interest the newspaper in a further story. She thought that it was a little too early for the paper to run another one by him, but she did suggest he should work one out in synopsis form, and in her letter of 14 October 1935, stressed that she 'should *very* much like some new short stories' from him.

Their correspondence reveals some of the excitement of his life then, his continual striving to write and place his work. His response to her request and the *News Chronicle*'s apparent interest, reflects the intense creative activity of his life. He admitted he was putting all his energies into finishing the Liberian book and the thriller by Christmas; that he had not sent her pieces out of the travel book because he was only now (20 October 1935) getting the first wedge of typescript properly revised; that he would think of a story for the *News Chronicle*;

and he admitted there was a story which she could take over but which had already gone out to two magazines – Greene's writing life was ever complicated:

> I wonder if you'd take over a short story . . . now resting in the office of the Listener. Ackerley [assistant literary editor, later literary editor of the *Listener*] wrote to me & asked me for something & as I had just finished this story, called 'The Innocent', I sent it to him. Now weeks go by without any sign of life. As he had invited a contribution I think he should have come to a quicker decision. I had also sent a copy to The Mercury; Scott James had asked me to do an article & I sent this instead, but he insisted on the article & the story still reposes there. Could you inquire of Ackerley? I dare say if the worst came to the worst it would suit Time & Tide.[21]

With so much on hand Greene might well have let the suggestion of providing a synopsis for the *News Chronicle* sleep awhile. Not so. The day after promising to think about a story he produced a synopsis called 'Miss Mitton in Moscow' and coupled it with the astonishing idea that he should leave for Moscow, almost immediately, his urgent deadlines for his two books notwithstanding: 'Here is the synopsis of a 10,000 word story for the News Chronicle. If they feel inclined to commission it, could you hurry up their decision, as I want to get in the background and the satirical description of the tourists, as it were, on the spot. In other words, will they make up their minds so that I can book a seat for Moscow to leave in ten days!'[22]

It is strange that on the suggestion of a commission for a serial Greene was willing to drop everything and go to Moscow. It could not be because the synopsis promised a brilliant story, yet he was prepared to follow his star to Moscow, chasing after background for a story about a bored, disillusioned journalist meeting up with an old lady's naïvety and excitement in visiting Moscow for the first time; of how her absurdities become a topic of conversation; of how he has to help her out of the country ahead of the other tourists as she had tried the Moscow authorities too much; only to discover, when he finds himself to be a central figure in an advertised Soviet Trial that Miss Mitton was a dye expert and had carried out a smart piece of commercial espionage.

The literary editor of the *News Chronicle* liked the synopsis and asked to see the first instalment, which Nancy Pearn thought encouraging, but this was not sufficient for Greene: 'I explained it was dependent on a definite decision within ten days. The boat's sailed now & there's not another till the spring. Besides it's a costly business & I wouldn't take the trip without a definite commission. So we'll have to wait for another story to come to mind.'[23]

It would seem that Greene had an ulterior motive in his haste to get the commission, and depart, by ship, within ten days. A hint of it lies in the editor's comment that she thought that when he returned from Moscow he would have got another idea for a story, for his whole plan is similar to his previous plans for travelling abroad – to get a commission to help pay his way so that he could get first-hand experience of one of the world's trouble spots. In this case he might have foreseen a novel, not a short story, coming out of the famous purge trials in Moscow in which leading communists accused themselves of treason without being guilty and were promptly executed.

'The Innocent' was rejected by the *Listener*, the *Mercury* (though they asked Greene if he would like to call in to discuss the possibility generally of his writing future articles and stories for them), and the *Fortnightly Review*, and so Greene suggested to Nancy Pearn that it should go next to the literary editor of *Time and Tide*, whom he described rather snobbishly as 'our old friend from the coalfields . . . they ought to pay five guineas'. They did not. He was sorry, he wrote to Nancy, that the story was causing her so much trouble: 'I thought it was one of those sweetly pretty tales which would find a home easily.' The year was coming to an end and Nancy Pearn invited him to call on her: 'There are several things we might well discuss in the near future, I feel, such as the tendencies in the various markets which you might care to follow up.' Greene had certainly found himself a devoted literary agent.

*

Greene kept his promise to complete his books: *Journey Without Maps* was finished just before the end of the year; *A Gun for Sale* ran over his target date by a few days. 'Now today', he wrote to his agent on 4 January 1936, 'I've finished my thriller and can look round a little.'

'Looking round a little' is a deceptive phrase, untypical of Greene with his energy, ambition, and tendency to depression and boredom. As late as April 1936 he wrote to his mother that he had 'been buried in that rather empty supine between books, with two books in proof and nothing to write'.[24] And in spite of his attempt to get off to Moscow for material, he obviously did not want to start another novel so soon; yet he had to support his family, and so he threw himself into finding outlets for other forms of writing. Nancy Pearn suggested that he write the occasional editorial piece for *Time and Tide*'s column 'Notes on the Way'. This he did – 'It's quite well paid, isn't it?' he enquired of Nancy.

He quickly produced a second synopsis of a story entitled *Return Home*: 'Here's a synopsis and 2,000 words to try out on the News Chronicle', he wrote, adding that she could not say that he did not work hard these days. Nancy Pearn agreed that he was working hard but had her reservations about the synopsis – 'negroes in black republican settings! I wonder if that may not be testing your "popular" editor too far.'[25] And she was right, but let him down lightly: 'There have been many changes and upsets down at the News Chronicle recently and I rather doubt the likelihood of getting any new stuff through with them at the moment.'

In January he came into conflict with R. J. Minney, the managing editor of the *Sunday Referee*, over what he saw as an issue of injustice. Minney had commissioned a Sunday gossip article from him, which he then rejected. Graham wrote to Nancy:

I sent him a perfectly good one which he now returns and wants re-written, keeping off books altogether: this wasn't specified in his original letter. I really haven't the time or the inclination to write another article: the payment is seven guineas and he's had seven guineas worth of work. I don't feel that for me the Referee is an important market, therefore I should like to insist on payment for my work. He can print the article or not as he chooses.

He pointed out to Nancy, sending her the commissioning letter, that Minney had sent him examples of recent contributions and asked him to touch on five or six topics in the article. He had also been advertising the forthcoming article every Sunday. He *had* touched on five topics – 'anonymous letters, small town atmosphere, the BBC, women novelists, and a ms. from India'.* Why then would Minney not pay?

Minney's argument was that while each paragraph was about a different subject, 'they were yet all connected with novels, and in such a way as to make it too purely personal in application'. Greene's attitude to Minney was not personal:

I'm not cross or offended. He wrote quite nicely and I liked his book about Hollywood! Only it simply wouldn't be economic for

* This last item must refer to his receiving the manuscript of R. K. Narayan's first novel and the beginning of his admiration for, and assistance to, this novelist.

a slow writer like myself to spend any more days on the article. I simply can't afford it. It's business.[26]

Minney was adamant. He was not paying Greene for that article. But he did temper his response by saying that he would be willing to wait a considerable time for revised copy; that he was hoping Greene would be able to co-operate on further work – 'he's glad you like his book and he likes yours and all that', wrote Nancy. At this point Greene gave up: 'All right. I surrender. I'll do him something which doesn't so much as mention a book or an author. Only I can't name a date. A lot of work seems to be flowing in.'[27]

He was indeed busy. On 20 January 1936, King George V died and three days later Greene had a patriotic article published in *The Times* about the King's lying in state in Westminster Hall: 'The white plumed soldiers, the tall candles burning at every corner, the Crown, the cross, the empty throne do not disguise the fact that he is closer now to his people than he has ever been, closer even than on Christmas Day when his deep, rather husky voice made him familiar to millions. This is his dock and this is his trial, and it is the ordinary man now who judges him – the city clerk, the unemployed workman, the woman from the suburbs – who will pass round the catafalque. Their silence and grief are his acquittal.'[28]

On 28 January, the day of the King's funeral, Greene observed, no doubt from the window of his study overlooking Clapham Common, a rather different event which he recorded in his diary begun as soon as *A Gun for Sale* was finished:

Dark and drenching rain: a couple on the Common: the man respectably dressed: holding themselves mouth to mouth, bodies pressed together, the man holding the girl with one hand, an umbrella over them both with the other. This was romantic pathos, but you could tell from the attitude, the prolongation, the pressure, real carnality.

This was the writer's observation at work, as it was in the first entry in this diary:

Jan. 4 Returning late from town by tube, I sat opposite a fat prosperous man of the shopkeeping class. He had pretence lilies of the valley in his button hole. When the train stopped at a station he let out a piercing whistle, like a police whistle and then was quite still and expressionless again. A look of subdued horror on the faces of the other passengers who after one startled glance looked away from him. A distinct atmosphere of apprehension at the next stop in case he whistled again.

The next entry, undated but given a title, 'A Nymph in the Hedge', returns to his own experiences. It is an account of a dream he had in which a doctor he consulted 'made a curious whistle that brought me dizzily to my knees and let off a little fart from a test tube. He said, "You have a nymph in the hedge" . . . The nymph in the hedge to my mind seemed to represent a small naked baby – a foundling . . . and I suspected him of wanting to impose some by-blow [bastard] of his own on me by trickery . . . But I was worried in case this strange baby should harm Lucy.'

On 29 March he records: 'From a scientific film show at the Film Socy, one gathers that the earthworm rather than man or the higher animals enjoys the greatest sexual satisfaction. Coition lasts for a whole hour and as the worm is hermaphroditic, the flow of semen proceeds from both partners during that time.'

Nancy Pearn continued to forward his interests: 'Why not, if you find you are now in the vein, write another story with the big magazine markets in view? I am thinking of "The Strand" primarily.'[29] She had also succeeded in placing a short story in the *Daily Mail* which Greene was contributing to a collection to be published by Hutchinson: 'delighted about the successful outcome with the Daily Mail. Herewith the cheque. The early Hutchinson date made it impossible to fit the story into any of the monthlies, while it was too long for most of the weeklies. In fact, there was really only one hope for it – with "Passing Show" [a weekly magazine]. And there we have met with luck, glory be! for they will be able to fit it in just in time before the book comes out, so there will be an extra fifteen guineas to come on this additional sale.'

Greene replied with thanks for getting him the *Mail* and for working such marvels with the story: 'I'll try my hand at another some time, but [referring to the bitterly cold weather in London during February 1936] I can't think in this cold.'

By the middle of March Nancy felt she had brought off something rather special, and that just after having spent an evening at Greene's home at Clapham Common: 'Here's fun – following so closely too on our merry meeting the other evening: "The Argosy [a fiction magazine] have spotted your story "The Basement Room" from the volume, and we are going to be able to collect Eighteen guineas from them for Second British Serial Rights . . . I told you I felt that the omens were all for a big short story push – and now you see! How soon shall we receive the first of the many destined for "The Strand"?'

Greene responded on a domestic note: 'What good news. It will pay for the curtains, a new ceiling and lino for the new nursery'*[30], which indicates how far eighteen guineas once used to go.

At the end of March, Nancy learnt that still further changes had taken place at the *News Chronicle* and that the new man handling the fiction side was an admirer of Graham Greene. Greene came up with the thoughts for a tale 'about a Night Motor Coach which might swell out to ten thousand. I expect I could let you have a first instalment in the next week or two.' Greene wrote this on the last day of March. And in line with his urge to do things at once, if not before, he wrote to Nancy the following day, 1 April: 'At least you ought to praise my promptness this time. Here is a summary and first instalment. Do you think you could persuade the News Chronicle to be a little quicker this time in their decision? One loses interest when one is held up for weeks.' Greene added a postscript – 'It's a damned good story.' And Nancy responded, 'I do – and it is!'

But the decision did not come quickly from the *News Chronicle* and when it came it was a refusal: 'I have just extracted a decision from the News Chronicle', wrote Nancy, 'on "In the Night Coach." The man there who had particularly admired "The Basement Room", says he frankly does not see this as a five-day serial at all, owing to its relative lack of action . . . Dost think that it could be turned into a straight-action story of "The Strand" variety?'[31]

Greene replied the following day (9 May) that he was quite glad about the rejection by the *News Chronicle* as he had already incorporated the whole thing in a new novel he had begun. This novel, given the unlikely title of 'Fanatic Arabia', was to be another unfinished project, perhaps because, as he admitted to his mother, it was 'with great reluctance' that he began it; perhaps because the admiring editor of the *News Chronicle* had rejected it; perhaps because the editor knew what he was talking about. A portion of the novel has survived and is in the archives in Austin, Texas. It begins with a night coach trip to Nottingham and is without sparkle.

Nevertheless, Greene went on location looking for material. On 20 April, after a holiday in Devon, he wrote to his mother, 'when I get home I have to go up north to Nottingham and York by one of those night motor coaches as the new novel begins that way!'

The most interesting insights into his life at this time come from his letters to his mother. Both he and Hugh, in their letters to her, give, understandably, their immediate personal responses to their experiences in their individual efforts to succeed. Greene wrote to her an

---

* Vivien was again pregnant.

account of an editorial dinner put on by the *Spectator* to honour its contributors:

> We sat at six tables. . . . Rose Macaulay on one side, and a nice retired soldier and authority on Abyssinia called Athil on the other. Peter Fleming, a big stiff called Sir Frederick Whyte, a rather silly old man, Beach Thomas who made a speech appealing quite seriously for more sentimentality in the paper, and a very nice gentle creature who was Empire Marketing Board and started Grierson's [film] unit and is now B.B.C., Sir Stephen Tallents. The editor [Wilson Harris] made a long and rather dull speech saying that he wanted the policy of the paper throughout to be left centre. J. A. Spender made a nostalgic speech. The Dean of St Paul's a gentle amusing speech. Sir Bernard Pares a pathetic, old-time Liberal speech. Mrs Williams-Ellis a very trying fluent motherly speech – flinging me a big bouquet! . . . a lot of nice people scattered round: Rupert [Hart-Davis] and Monica Redlich and A. L. Rowse and H. E. Bates and Herbert Read . . .
>
> Journey Without Maps failed to make the Book Society – too much sex, they said – though they've given it first recommendation for May [it actually was not published until 11 May and failed to make the Book Society]. In America the thriller is coming out first in the early summer. [*This Gun for Hire* came out in June and appeared in Britain in July.]

He then told his mother about the Henry James chapter he had written for the English Novelists' Series – a survey of the Novel by Twenty Contemporary Novelists and edited by his friend Derek Verschoyle, which came out in April; the story which Hutchinsons were bringing out and which his agent had quickly sold to *Passing Show*, and the fact that 'The Basement Room' story had been sold again, this time to *Argosy* – 'that story will have made me nearly £70'. He then played his trump card to his mother as to the way he was climbing: 'Altogether I'm having a hand in four books this year as well as my own two!'[32]

On 1 May Greene writes to his mother that the publisher Collins had asked him to write a book about Oxford: 'I think for financial reasons I may have to do it.' But he was wrong for a tremendous windfall was ahead: 'Great excitement,' he wrote to her on 14 May 1936. 'Cable came last night from Mary Leonard, New York, who has been trying to sell film rights of "A Gun for Sale", "Closing for twelve thousand [dollars] whoops." ' So the novel was sold to Paramount pictures even before it had appeared in either Britain or America.

There had been straws in the wind that it might be very successful. On 28 January he had written to Hugh of the 'great enthusiasm on

Heinemann's part for the shocker', repeating this on 4 March, and writing also of the future birth of his second child. He had written in an earlier undated letter, 'expect you've heard about the increase in *our* family', which Hugh apparently had not understood, for in the next letter he writes; 'The addition is an infant in September! I'm trusting to the thriller to pay for it. There seems to be huge enthusiasm about it (the thriller I mean) at Heinemann's and Doubleday!' The possibility of *A Gun for Sale* being made into a film was on the cards as early as 19 May, when he wrote to Hugh: 'Basil Dean wants to see me about a possible play in my thriller and cables to do with film rights come regularly across the Atlantic.'

But while Greene was jubilant, and even when writing to Hugh on 11 June about the birth of *his* son Graham Carleton:* 'A thousand congratulations. Everyone we know seems to be having infants this month', he did show a strange parsimoniousness: 'I didn't answer your last letter as I thought I'd wait and save a 2½ penny stamp. It's no good being extravagant over stamps just because one has sold a film.'

---

* Hugh and Helga asked Greene whether 'Graham' was on offer and he replied that the name would be free because all his children would be called after Saints.

37

The Pleasure Dome

... all those Empires and Odeons of a luxury
and extravagance which we shall never see again.
— GRAHAM GREENE

G REENE's long fascination with the cinema aroused in him extremes of emotional response and a deeply critical attitude
towards films, their makers and those who appeared in them. It also
involved him in the process of film-making – adapting work for the
screen, producing (*Calendar of the Year*, May 1936),[1] writing scripts,
working on sets, meeting the famous of the industry. It also gave
him an escape from writing novels and greater success, at that time,
than writing fiction. Although he had written to Hugh in January
1936[2] that there had never been a time when he had written so much
(and this applied to the rest of the year also), his success had not been
great: *England Made Me*, a failure; 'Fanatic Arabia' abortive; short
stories and reviews not bringing in much money. His greatest
financial successes had been the films of *Stamboul Train* and *A Gun
for Sale*. Moreover, through reviewing films he developed an
understanding of the technique of the film and serious views on
its significance as a popular art form. The more films he reviewed,
the more certain he was that the wrong people were making
them.

He began reviewing films in the middle of 1935, he says in *Ways
of Escape*, as a result of circumstances rather similar to those which
started him on his journey to Liberia. The idea came at a party, 'after
the dangerous third Martini', and since he was talking to the Literary
Editor of the *Spectator*, he took the opportunity to point out that the
magazine had hitherto neglected the cinema and suggested that he
should do something to fill the gap. He anticipated that the reviewing
would last two or three weeks and might be fun, but Derek
Verschoyle held him in high regard as a book reviewer and as a
result he began a four and a half year stint of film reviewing which

ended only in March 1940, six months into the Second World War: 'I can hardly believe in that life of the distant thirties now . . . How, I find myself wondering, could I possibly have written all those film reviews? And yet I remember opening the envelopes, which contained the gilded cards of invitation for the morning press performances (mornings when I should have been struggling with other work), with a sense of curiosity and anticipation.'[3]

His very first review, appearing on 5 July 1935, set the tone of what was to follow. In it he had a go not only at film executives but also at the whole ethos of the modern world. The film was *The Bride of Frankenstein*, based on 'Poor harmless Mary Shelley's novel, *Frankenstein*'. For him, Mary Shelley's dream 'that she was watched by pale, yellow, speculative eyes between the curtains of her bed', which was the inspiration for her novel, that 'one genuine moment of horror . . . vanished long ago, and there is nothing in *The Bride of Frankenstein* . . . to scare a child'. Her dream only 'set in motion a vast machinery of bogus horror, a wilderness of cardboard sets, of mouthing actors, of sound systems and trick shots and yes men.' The result was 'not Mrs Shelley's dream, but the dream of a committee of film executives who wanted to go one better than Mrs Shelley and let Frankenstein create a second monster.' It was 'a pompous, badly acted film, full of absurd anachronisms and inconsistencies.' Furthermore, in his opinion, the modern world was threatened by the 'bright, slick, stream-lined civilization . . . the whole tone of a time whose popular art is on the level of *The Bride of Frankenstein*.'

He attacked, in his *Spectator* reviews, in his article in the *Fortnightly* (April 1936), in his reviews in the short-lived *Night and Day* (July–December 1937), and in his contribution, 'Subjects and Stories', to Charles Davy's book, *Footnotes to the Film* (1937), almost every aspect of film-making of the time. Philip French, the film critic, has described his criticism as being 'among the most ferocious I've ever come across'.[4] The 'holy cows' of the screen came under his scrutiny. In reviewing *Anna Karenina*, with Greta Garbo playing Anna, he commented that no one in Hollywood knew what to do with Garbo, 'her awkward ungainly body, her hollow face strong and rough as an Epstein cast'; and, after praising 'the melancholy grandeur of her voice', 'watch her among a crowd of other actresses in the mazurka, she is stiff, awkward, bony, rather grotesque among the graceful bodies, the lovely shoulders.'[5] This criticism so disturbed one reader that he sent Greene an anonymous picture postcard with the message, 'If you are the best critic on films that the *Spectator* can raise, I am sorry for the *Spectator*'s readers. Perhaps you are a woman and not a man. *Quién sabe*. It is as a beautiful woman that men love Greta

Garbo. To nearly every man she is a lovely woman – free figure & carriage. You must be abnormal and "Cretin".'[6]

Marlene Dietrich was also criticised: 'The great abstractions come whistling hoarsely out in Miss Dietrich's stylized, weary, and monotonous whisper, among the hideous Technicolor flowers, the yellow cratered desert like Gruyère cheese, the beige faces.'[7] He had sympathy with Robert Donat who had to act without a partner as: 'Miss Dietrich never acts. She lends her too beautiful body: she consents to pose: she is the marble motive for heroisms and sacrifices: as for acting – that is merely the word for what goes on all round her: she leaves it to her servants.'[8]

Mae West came off better as she had a personality 'so outrageously suggestive to the middle-aged' (which Greene was not) that he admitted he was completely uncritical: 'I enjoy every one of her films [he was reviewing *Klondyke Annie*] aware all the time, whether the scene be the Bowery, the Klondyke, Texas or a New York drawing-room, of that bowler-hatted brigade gathered invisibly like seraphs about her stout matronly figure.'[9] Yet he was somewhat critical in reviewing her next film, *Go West, Young Man*, when he wrote of 'the Edwardian bust, the piled peroxided hair, the seductive and reeling motions reminiscent of an overfed python', and as for the story it is 'incredibly tedious, as slow and wobbling in its pace as Miss West's famous walk . . . seldom have so many feet of film been expended on a mere dirty look'.[10] He was unfair to Madeleine Carrol: 'She has what must be, to all but the most blindly devoted keepers, the less endearing traits of a young elephant . . . we cannot help wondering whether Mr Dick Powell with his little moustache and his laving hands, has the stamina to withstand her more-than-lifesize embrace. Handsome in a big way, given to intense proboscine whispers, she lends an impression of weight to every action.'[11] Jean Harlow's last film (the famous platinum blonde did not live to see it) received a poor notice – Greene is rarely sentimental: 'Tough and conscienceless, containing one admirable scene of carnal comedy . . . *Saratoga* is one of Miss Harlow's better films, though there is no sign that her acting would ever have progressed beyond the scope of the restless shoulders and the protuberant breasts: her technique was the gangster's technique – she toted a breast like a man totes a gun.'[12]

Famous male actors meet with the same fate. Charles Laughton, whom Greene admired and praised, is yet damned for his part in *Rembrandt* because it gives 'Charles Laughton a chance to show his remarkable powers as a "ham" actor – the very best ham . . .'[13] Of John Lodge, the principal actor in *The Tenth Man* (a title which

Greene himself used for a novel, lost in the 1940s, and discovered and published in 1985), he wrote in the *Spectator* at the end of 1936, that he suffered 'from a kind of lockjaw, an inability to move the tight muscle of his mouth, to do anything but glare with the dumbness and glossiness of an injured seal', and Herbert Marshall had an 'Old English sheep dog manner . . . the damp muzzle of a healthy British dog'.[14]

In an article in the *Fortnightly* (April 1936), 'The Middle-Brow Film,' he attacks Alexander Korda (who was later to become a very special friend) because he must only be a great publicist since he had 'put over so many undistinguished and positively bad films as if they were a succession of masterpieces'. Though having criticised him in this article he was not too severe in reviews. He speaks of 'the childlike eyes of the great film executives' and of the many film magnates not being able to think of a serious message – mild enough criticism. Greene also shot down Alfred Hitchcock – his films amuse, they do not excite. They give a momentary impression of great liveliness, that's all. He's tricky not imaginative, though he granted that some of Hitchcock's tricks were good – the scream of the charwoman finding the murdered woman cut to the shriek of the Flying Scotsman rushing North.

What he found particularly abhorrent was the sensational and blatant advertising publicity, in a word, the ballyhoo:

> Dog, I suppose, ought not to eat dog, otherwise I should be inclined to cast a malicious eye towards my fellow film-reviewers who have gone into such curious Gothic attitudes of reverence before what must be one of the worst films of the year, *The Dark Angel*, writing of 'classic tragedy' and the 'great' acting of Miss Merle Oberon. It is the ballyhoo, of course, which has done it: the advance gossip and the advertisements, the crowds outside the cinema on the opening night, the carefully drilled curiosity as to what Mr Sam Goldwyn had done to Miss Oberon's eyebrows . . .[15]

He had had personal experience of the 'ballyhoo'. When he landed at Tenerife with his cousin Barbara, on their way to Liberia, the cinema there was showing the film *Orient Express* which was loosely based on his novel *Stamboul Train*: 'The direction', he wrote in *Journey Without Maps*, 'was incompetent, the photography undistinguished, the story sentimental . . . By what was unchanged I could judge and condemn my own novel: I could see clearly what was cheap and banal enough to fit the cheap banal film.'[16] But it was being 'sold':

'*Two Youthful Hearts in the Grip of Intrigue. Fleeing from Life. Cheated? Crashing Across Europe. Wheels of Fate.*' The press book stated:

> The real Orient Express runs across Europe from Belgium to Constantinople. Therefore, you will go wrong if you interpret the word 'Orient' to indicate something of a Chinese or Japanese nature. There is enough material of other kinds to arrange a lively colourful ballyhoo, as you will see as soon as you turn to the exploitation pages . . .

The press book also suggested a 'date tie-up' offering a set of three stills – 'Norman Foster explaining the sex life of a date to Heather Angel,* passing dates to Heather Angel and Heather Angel buying dates from the car window . . . Every city has high-class food shops which feature fancy packages of dates. Tie-in with one of these for window-displays . . . have a demonstration of date products, the many uses of dates, etc . . . Don't underestimate the value of a real smart window fixed up with date products and the three stills . . . Buy a package of delicious dates, and take "The Orient Express" for Constantinople, a most thrilling and satisfying evening's entertainment at the Rialto Theatre.' And: 'Do You Know That: Heather Angel's pet kitten Penang had to have its claws clipped because it insisted on sharpening them on the legs of expensive tables; That the pet economy of Heather Angel is buying washable gloves and laundering them herself.'[17] Enough material, as the press book put it, 'to arrange a lively colourful ballyhoo'.

He found much to criticise in American films – Love, Country, Ambition – the great fake emotions (*Marie Walewska*), the concentrated atmosphere of young innocence (*Girls' Dormitory*). Reviewing the film version of Parnell's life he commented that the 'fictional screen has never really got beyond wish-fulfilment dreams, and the only interest this week is in seeing the kind of wish-fulfilment the big film executives enjoy'[18] – Parnell's adultery with Mrs O'Shea can't really be revealed: '. . . anything secretive . . . anything a little bit lecherous in the story has been eliminated. No illegitimate children, no assignations in seaside hotels under assumed names, no furtive vigils at Waterloo Station . . . how clean a film magnate's wish-fulfilments are, how virginal and high-minded the tawdry

* The name Heather Angel sounds like one made up for the purposes of Hollywood. She was born in Oxford, Heather Grace Angel, the daughter of a Christ Church chemistry don, and was popular with cinema audiences in the 1930s. In 1970 she witnessed the fatal stabbing of her third husband by a prowler at their home at Montecito, California. She died in January 1987, aged 77.

pathetic human past becomes when the Mayers and Goldwyns turn the magic ring.'[19] 'It needs some stamina to be a film reviewer', he concluded in the *Spectator*, 14 August 1936, in a review of a Bing Crosby film. Occasionally, he concedes, 'a film of truth and tragic value gets somehow out of Hollywood and on to the screen. Nobody can explain it – perhaps a stage needs using, all the big executives are in conference over the latest Mamoulian "masterpiece"* – Jehovah is asleep . . .'[20]

A feeling which comes through these reviews is that behind his criticism of American films lies an implicit criticism of American life and standards in general – a suggestion that he was already becoming anti-American. This comes out strongly in his review of *The Road Back*, a film based on a novel by Remarque about starvation, revolution and family tragedies:

It's an awful film, one big Mother's Day, celebrated by American youth, plump, adolescent faces with breaking sissy voices. Voices which began to break in the trenches – remembering the kid sister or watching a companion die . . . We've lived through a lot in that time, but not through war, revolution, starvation – but through 'Can you turn me a little so I can see you go down the road?' and the young fleshy face is turned away from the dying friend to hide the drip of tears . . . Like Buchman† boys starved of confession they break out on the moral front – 'There's one more battle to be fought. I must find myself.' And always all the time, the breaking voices, the unformed unlined faces and the well-fed bodies of American youth, clean-limbed prize-cattle mooing into the microphone. They call it an all-star cast and that always means there isn't a single player of any distinction to be picked out of the herd.

It might be funny if it wasn't horrifying. This is America seeing the world in its own image. There is a scene in which the returned soldiers all go back to their school. Sitting in uniform on the benches they are addressed by the Headmaster; they start their lessons again where they left off . . . what it really emphasizes is the eternal adolescence of the American mind, to which . . . morality means keeping Mother's Day and looking after the kid sister's purity.[21]

---

* Rouben Mamoulian, an American film and stage director.
† The American Dr Frank Buchman founded the movement of Moral Rearmament . . . It advocated the regeneration of society by 'complete honesty, purity, and love', the members seeking divine guidance in all their meetings for mutual encouragement and their sharing in their confession of failures.

Greene's belief in the 'eternal adolescence' of Americans must have remained dormant in his mind for twenty years, for surely the quiet American, Pyle, has this specific characteristic in the novel of the same name. Greene's strong and bitter dislike of certain aspects of American life and culture, which must have stemmed from seeing countless American movies, even colours his impression of Americans on the streets of London: 'One came daunted out of the cinema and there, strolling up the Haymarket, dressed up in blue uniforms with little forage-caps and medals clinking, were the American Legionaries, arm in arm with women dressed just the same – all guide-books, glasses and military salutes: caps marked Santa Anna and Minnesota: hair – what there was of it – grey, but the same adolescent features, plump, smug, sentimental, ready for the easy tear and the hearty laugh and the fraternity yell. What use in pretending that with these allies it was ever possible to fight for civilization? For Mother's Day, yes, for anti-vivisection and humanitarianism, the pet dog and the home fire, for the co-ed college and the campus. Civilization would shock them: eyes on the guide book for safety, they pass it quickly as if it were a nude in a national collection.'[22]

The British cinema did not escape whipping either: 'Nothing, a novice might think, could be easier than to catch reality with a camera, and yet this shy bird evades almost every English director . . . Bad casting, bad story construction, uncertain editing: these are the three main faults of English films.' He was reviewing, in February 1937, the British film *Sensation*. Two months later dealing with *Dark Journey* he began: 'Abandon life all you who enter here: the pedestrian unreality of most Denham pictures lies over this spy drama.' Above all else, Greene wants 'no tiresome "message", but a belief in the importance of a human activity truthfully reported'.[23]

Yet he does praise. He praises Luise Rainer's performance in *The Good Earth* – 'the stupid stuck-out lips, the scared, uncalculating and humble gaze, convey all the peasant's fear of hope . . . the character she presents . . . carries the film: the awful pathos of the wedding walk . . . at the heels of the bridegroom she has never seen, the scrabbling in the ditch for the peach stone he has spat out (from it a tree may grow); toiling heavy with child in the fields to save the harvest from the hurricane . . . in the long drought taking the knife to the ox her husband fears to kill.'

He notices not only acting ability but also the director's sharp notion of visual images which will best represent the drought – 'like clear exact epithets the images stab home: the plough jammed in the rocky soil, the vultures on the kid's carcase, the dark sullen stare of the starved child.'[24]

What Greene *did* admire was 'the brilliant eye' for surface life to be found in documentary films, and he reviewed them while other critics ignored them. In his first review, as well as dealing with *The Bride of Frankenstein*, he praised a documentary on Abyssinia:

> . . . the best film in London . . . the finest travel film I have seen . . . explained in an admirably plain commentary. Here is the last medieval State in all its squalor (the flies swarming round the eyes and nostrils as though they were so much exposed meat in a butcher's shop), its dignity (the white-robed noblemen flowing into the capital followed by their armed retainers, the caged symbolic lions, and the Lion of Judah himself, his dark cramped dignity, his air of a thousand years of breeding), its democratic justice (the little courts by the roadside, on the railway track; the debtor and creditor chained together; the murderer led off to execution by the relatives of the murdered).[25]

He consistently praised the documentaries of John Grierson and Basil Wright, but in his 'Footnotes to the Film' article he struck out at the documentary pioneer Robert Flaherty's *Man of Aran*, comparing it unfavourably with *Hortobagy*, a Hungarian documentary about horses. *Man of Aran* was a glaring example of 'arty' cinema – 'how affected and wearisome were those figures against the skyline, how meaningless that magnificent photography of storm after storm.' He was particularly concerned about the truthfulness of the documentary: 'The inhabitants [of Aran] had to be taught shark-hunting in order to supply Mr Flaherty with a dramatic sequence', but *Hortobagy* 'did . . . attempt to show life truthfully: those wild herds tossing across the enormous plain . . . the leaping of the stallions, the foaling of the mares shown with meticulous candour, did leave the impression that we were seeing, as far as was humanly possible, life as it is.'[26]

For this reason he was highly critical of the Marquis de la Falaise's travel film about Indo-China. He much preferred Smythe's *Kamet*, a plain statement about the climb of Mount Kamet, and *Song of Ceylon*, directed by Basil Wright, who was 'content to accept the limitations of ignorance, of a European mind'. He seriously doubted the Marquis's claim that his close-ups of tigers were genuine, particularly since one sequence was of a man being attacked by a tiger – 'the Marquis with eighteenth-century imperturbability must have continued to shoot his film within a few feet of the struggle. How are we to help doubting either his accuracy or his humanity? And the little well-shaven gentleman in shorts and topee emerging from that fever-ridden swamp has all the appearance of a kindly man.'[27]

This review appeared on 17 April and on 26 April Greene wrote in his diary: 'Received a letter (anonymous) from High Wycombe addressed to me as Film Critic at the Spectator. This contained a piece of notepaper covered with human shit. Now my last article – on "Kliou the Tiger" – could have offended no one but the Marquis de la Falaise, the producer.' Thirty years later, in Paris at a dinner, Graham sat opposite the Marquis and was charmed by his conversation. 'I longed to ask him the truth, but I was daunted by the furniture.'[28]

He objected strongly to foreigners being brought in to make films about Britain. He thought it typical of the British film industry, whose leading showman was Mr Alexander Korda, that M. Clair 'should be brought to this country to direct a Scottish film full of what must be to him rather incomprehensible jokes about whisky and bagpipes'.[29]

Fire Over England was even more ironically treated: 'Herr Pommer, the German producer, and William K. Howard, the American director, of Mr Korda's great national Coronation-year picture of Elizabethan England have done one remarkable thing: they have caught the very spirit of an English public school mistress's vision of history . . . Miss [Flora] Robson [who played the part of Queen Elizabeth] catches the very accent and manner of an adored headmistress . . .' It is not so much Korda who comes in for criticism as A. E. W. Mason, from whose novel the film was made, and the writer of the screenplay, Clemence Dane, author of *Will Shakespeare* and the woman who supported Greene's admittedly poor novel, *The Name of Action*, for the Book Society choice, and also *Stamboul Train*. Greene is a hard, unswerving man where his ideals and beliefs are concerned. 'It is not, I am sure, Miss Robson's fault,' he writes; 'she has only too faithfully carried out the suggestions of the script . . . From neither of these authors [Dane and Mason] do we expect a very penetrating or realistic study of the Queen.'[30] And on a nationalist note, though also a creative one, he speaks out about the disturbing influence of foreigners making English films:

The artist belongs to the cave: he is national: and the men through whom he must transmit his idea, in whose company he must retain the integrity of his conception, are – very frequently – foreign. In what can with technical accuracy be termed an English company you may have an Hungarian producer assisted by an Hungarian art director and an Hungarian scenario editor. Among its directors there may be Frenchmen, Hungarians, Germans, and Americans. The language is strange to them, the ideas are strange: little wonder that the characters are slowly smoothed out of existence, the English corners rubbed away. The public – you may say – has been reached by something, and they'll be reached again next week and the week after by so many thousand feet of celluloid; they haven't been reached by an idea: that has died on the way, somewhere in the central-heated office, at a conference, among the foreign accents.[31]

William Hazlitt's comment on the performance of the lecturer Mackintosh could well be applied to Greene's film reviewing: 'The havoc was amazing, the desolation was complete.' But his criticism was consistently brilliant, often cruel, and generally justified. And he did work towards a philosophy of what the film should be. In his article 'Subjects and Stories' he stated that what he wanted was a film that reflected Chekhov's view of what a play should present – 'life as it is and life as it ought to be'. Only films which come up to this standard will provide poetic cinema and that is the only form worth considering, the only kind of film fulfilling the proper function of the cinema. He condemned the popular playwrights of the day, St John Ervine and Dodie Smith for example, as having no sense of life as it is lived. If they have some dim idea of a better life it is visualised in terms of sexual or financial happiness. This also applied to the popular novelists – Hugh Walpole, Brett Young, J. B. Priestley – 'representing no more of contemporary life than is to be got out of a holiday snapshot'.

Writing this essay in the third week of February 1937, Greene turned to the list of films then to be seen in London. He quotes a number of the representative plots, of which one, that of *Magnificent Obsession*, is not untypical in its absurdity: 'a woman loses her eyesight when a drunken young plutocrat smashes his car! The young man turns over a new leaf, studies medicine, becomes the greatest eye surgeon of his day in time to cure and marry the girl while both are young.'

Yet, however absurd these examples of bad films, it was the film which had the most to offer creatively – a vast audience: 'What a chance there is for the creative artist, one persists in believing, to produce for an audience incomparably greater than all the "popular" novelists combined . . . a genuinely vulgar art . . . The novelist may write for a few thousand readers, but the film artist *must* work for millions. To truly work for the millions, then the art had to be vulgar in the same sense of being popular as a dance tune.'

Greene is not thinking of stooping down to the masses. In contrast it should be an honour: 'It should be [the film-maker's] distinction and pride that he has a public whose needs have never been met since the closing of the theatres by Cromwell.'[32]

For Greene, the film executive has it wrong. He thinks of the trivialities of the 'popular' play and 'popular' novel of a limited middle-class audience, of the tired businessman and the female reader. These are private responses, but 'a popular response is not the sum of private excitements, but mass feeling, mass excitement, the Wembley roar.' The Elizabethan stage had provided action which 'arouses as communal a response as bear-baiting'. The film executive's caveat, that 'people want to be taken out of themselves', is answered by Greene, 'people are taken out of themselves at Wembley'. Greene's view was that an excited audience is never depressed and that, 'if you excite your audience first, you can put over what you will of horror, suffering, truth.'

There was a snag – the Board of Censors forbade any controversial subject on the screen. Yet this was not all bad: 'We are saved from the merely topical by our absurd censorship.' And we are driven back to the 'blood', the thriller.

Coming from the middle classes of England Greene is yet determined to reject middle-class recipes: 'There never has been a school of popular English blood. We have been damned from the start by middle-class virtues, by gentlemen cracksmen and stolen plans and Mr Wu's. We have to go farther back than this, dive below the polite level, to something nearer to the common life.'

The first need is to return to a more popular drama, even if it is in the simplest terms of blood on a garage floor (he quotes from *Macbeth* – 'There lay Duncan laced in his golden blood'), 'the scream of cars in flight, all the old excitements at their simplest and most sure-fire, then we can begin – secretly, with low cunning – to develop our poetic drama . . . Our characters can develop from the level of *The Spanish Tragedy* towards a subtler, more thoughtful level.'

Some such development, Greene argues, is shown in the work of the German director Fritz Lang: his thriller *The Spy*, 'has no human values at all, only a brilliant eye for the surface of life and the power of physical excitement – but the human, the poetic value has to be introduced by means, not of words – that is the way of the stage' – but by means of poetic use of imagery and incident. In Greene's view this is to be found, for example, in the 1936 Russian film *We From Kronstadt*, and he gives examples of this power to suggest human values by poetic, visual images: a 'sooty tree drooping on the huge rocky Kronstadt walls above a bench where a sailor and woman embrace, against the dark tide'; 'the gulls sweeping and coursing above the cliffs where the Red prisoners are lined up for their death by drowning, the camera moving from the heavy rocks round their necks to the movement of the light, white wings'; 'every poetic image [is] chosen for its contrasting value, to represent peace and normal human values under the heroics and the wartime patriotism.' 'The object of the film', he wrote, 'should be the translation of thought back into images. America has made the mistake of translating it into action.'[33]

So we can say that at least up to August 1936 Greene held high hopes of the value of writing for the cinema. But a year later, when he had written his brilliant article, 'Film Lunch', for *Night and Day* with its clever put-down of Louis B. Mayer, head of Metro-Goldwyn-Mayer, Greene was suffering from some disillusionment. Moreover, he had made some enemies among the film magnates by his unrelenting (and acid) comments about all the slop and slush that he was forced to view and judge. Near the end of 'Film Lunch' he speaks of the scriptwriter's job on films as 'the novelist's Irish sweep: money for no thought, for the banal situation and the inhuman romance; money for forgetting how people live: money for "Sid-down, won't yer" and "I love, I love, I love," endlessly repeated. Inside the voice [of Mayer] goes on "God . . . I pray . . ." and the writers, a little stuffed and a little boozed, lean back and dream of the hundred pounds a week – and all that's asked in return the dried imagination and the dead pen.'

Greene himself was to be one of those writers who were to serve a hungry screen, and no doubt, like others at the lunch 'a little stuffed and a little boozed'. He learnt of the situation at first hand.

*

Ironically, his fierce criticism of the film world turned its interest to him. As early as 28 January 1936, he wrote to Hugh: 'I'm getting deep into films, so deep that Grierson sounded me the other day on whether I should be interested in a producing job.' Perhaps with his tongue (slightly) in his cheek, he added: 'I hope he is picturing me as the head of the proposed BBC Film Unit. I'm on a kind of advisory committee on television as it is. Altogether I seem to have cut into the racket at the right angle. Last night we were at quite an amusing party given for Lotte Reiniger [German animator, well known for her silhouette cartoons] with a programme of trick films.'[34] He was making friends in the film world and friends among the directors he most admired: 'I'm dining with Basil Wright of the G.P.O. unit on Thursday.'[35]

By 9 May Greene was producing *Calendar of the Year*, and by the third week of May he reported to his brother Hugh: 'Did I tell you Cavalcanti wants me to do a film with him; Basil Dean proposed a collaboration on a Galsworthy, and I'm producing at the G.P.O.' He then expresses a desire to escape from writing through the film opportunities: 'I have hopes of being able to retire from writing altogether.'

The film Cavalcanti wanted to do with Greene must be *Went the Day Well?*, based on Greene's short story, 'The Lieutenant Died Last'. It was long in appearing, some six years after this letter was written.★ The Basil Dean collaboration (*Twenty-One Days*) was based on Galsworthy's story 'The First and Last', and appeared three years later in 1939. At this time also, he became involved with a story of his own devising made into a film called *The Green Cockatoo*. In *Ways of Escape* he recalled how it happened. Perhaps because he had persistently attacked the films made by Alexander Korda, Korda became curious to meet his enemy and asked Greene's agent to bring him to Denham Film Studios.

A letter suggests that he visited Korda in May 1936. Cheekily, he writes to his mother, 'In about a fortnight I hope I'm going to do a tour of the film studios with John Grierson, asking Korda etc. embarrassing questions.' But that visit was delayed until November, and before the meeting he reviewed (4 September 1936) Korda's film of H. G. Wells's story, *The Man Who Could Work Miracles*. He criticised both Wells and Korda. Greene stressed that in this film 'a few immortals and great conspiracies are tacked . . . to the early short story. The result is pretentious and mildly entertaining.' In asking rhetorically what remains of Mr Wells's idea, Greene admitted, 'the answer is muddle, a rather too Wellsian muddle.'[36]

He went on: 'The direction and the production are shocking. That is not Mr Wells's fault. And it may not be altogether the fault of Mr Lothar Mendes, the director, for the slowness, vulgarity, over-emphasis are typical of Mr Korda's productions.' He also attacks Korda (but clears Wells) for the deplorable miscasting: 'Mr Korda, a publicity man of genius, who has not yet revealed a talent for the films, casts his pictures with little regard for anything but gossip paragraphs.' As for the film, Greene's last paragraph adds the final insult: 'sometimes fake poetry, sometimes unsuccessful comedy, sometimes farce, sometimes sociological discussion, without a spark of creative talent or a trace of film ability.'

★ 'The Lieutenant Died Last' appeared in *Collier's*, 29 June 1940. The earliest reference to the story is when Greene sent a copy to his British agent in April. The story is about an invasion of a British village by a small contingent of German troops disguised as British armed forces. If Greene was writing this in 1936, then his story must have been futuristic and an example of his mediumistic powers.

H. G. Wells read the review in the *Spectator*, and Greene wrote breathlessly to his mother: 'Last night, I had a letter from Wells. He asked me whether I'd have dinner with him. He said he'd liked my notice of The Man Who Could Work Miracles: "But you've still got to meet your Korda. We'll say no more about the damned disgraceful thing. But I'd like to meet you. You'd be good for me." Rather sweet way to take my review.' Greene met Wells and also Wells's mistress, Baroness Budberg, whom Wells loved so deeply, who had been Maxim Gorky's mistress. When asked recently who was the most important writer he had met, Greene answered without pause, 'H. G. Wells'.

Greene did meet Korda in November and he recalled his meeting in *Ways of Escape*:

> when we were alone he asked if I had any film story in mind. I had none, so I began to improvise a thriller – early morning on Platform 1 at Paddington, the platform empty, except for one man who is waiting for the last train from Wales. From below his raincoat, a trickle of blood forms a pool on the platform.
>
> 'Yes? And then?'
>
> 'It would take too long to tell you the whole plot – and the idea needs a lot more working out.'[37]

So *The Green Cockatoo* was born and Greene left half an hour later to work for eight weeks on what seemed then an extravagant salary – 'and the worst and least successful of Korda's productions thus began.'[38] Greene's letter to his mother about this (18 November 1936) shows his excitement on meeting 'the great Korda'. His manner is different from the tough, critical, even superior stance of his reviews:

> I thought you'd be amused to hear what had happened with Korda. I went down on Friday and saw the business manager and a very nice Scotch-American Menzies, who is to direct a series of thrillers. I went down again on Saturday and had lunch at the studios (wonderful buildings with stages as big as cathedrals). Then yesterday I went down again with my agent and saw the great Korda and an arrangement was reached. The first day I'd invented a shocker idea for them which they liked immensely and they want if possible to have a character who will run through a whole series. Anyway in three weeks I have to elaborate the idea and turn it in. For this they pay £175 whether they use it or not. If they use it, they employ me on the film for four weeks at £125 a week. At the end of that time they can call on my services for six months at

£125 a week. They insisted on tying me up over a further period, so the following year they could then call on my services for six months at £175 a week, and the next year for six months at £225 a week. They can sell me to Hollywood or elsewhere during that time splitting the gain in salary 50-50. These figures sound astronomical, and of course, only £175 is certain, but these further arrangements were their own idea. It's all very exciting.

A month later, he is filming at Denham and very happy. The day after Christmas Day 1936, he writes to Hugh: 'I'm thick in scenario. Medium Shots and Insert Shots and Flash Backs and the rest of the racket. Korda, I'm glad to say, has given up the Robey idea and seems to be leaving us alone. Casting is proving very difficult. Menzies finds lovely people with appallingly tough faces, but when they open their mouths they all have Oxford accents.'

*

In the middle of September 1936 Nancy Pearn was still slogging away trying to place Greene in better-paying magazine slots, and her letter about the latest opening needs to be quoted in full:

Knowing my Nash's I made sure that the editor saw your most deliciously diverting review of the Beverley Nichols book.★ This added to other factors, leads him now to say that he would like to see you soon in Nash's, and haven't you some suggestions you would care to put up. Now would you like to meet this editor, and if so I would arrange it straight away. It would be undutiful and unbecoming not to stress the fact that this is far and away the best paying medium for articles which, although they have, of course, to be framed rather differently than for the Reviews, are nevertheless in the main on a fairly serious type of subject.

Greene certainly hoped to find a place in *Nash's*. In an undated letter to his mother he writes: 'My agent has sold my Korda film story [probably *The Green Cockatoo*] to *Nash's* as a short story for £250. All it needs is about a day's work with a secretary, altering it from

---

★ In his review, Graham pretends Beverley Nichols is a lady: 'A middle-aged and maiden lady, so I picture the author, connected in some way with the church: I would hazard a guess that she housekeeps for her brother . . . She is not married, I am sure, for she finds the sight of men's sleeping apparel oddly disturbing: "It was almost indecent, the way he took out pyjamas and shook them . . ."' To his mother, he wrote, quietening her fears: 'The B.N. review had no repercussions except fan mail praising it (unusual for a review).' Letter of 8 September 1936.

its film form.' But Greene was too busy to do such a day's work. He had turned in to Basil Dean his adaptation of John Galsworthy's story: 'I expect we shall argue about it this coming week and then I'll have to set to work on the shooting script, a thing I've never done before. Every camera angle has to be described, each angle being a scene, an average film having about 550 scenes. A long business. I find it very tiring, as you have to visualise exactly the whole time, not merely what the person is doing, but from what angle you watch him doing it.'

We do not have Greene's judgment of his 'first' script in 1937, but over twenty years later, in 1958, he felt his script (actually his second) was a terrible affair and typical in one way of the cinema world. Greene's problem was that he had to adapt John Galsworthy's story ('a sensational tale of a murderer who killed himself and an innocent man who was hanged for the suicide's crime') and he found himself in an impossible strait-jacket: 'If the story had any force at all, it lay in its extreme sensationalism, but as the sensation was impossible under the rules of the British Board of Film Censors, who forbade suicide and forbade a failure of English justice, there was little of Galsworthy's plot left when I had finished. This unfortunate first effort was suffered with good-humoured nonchalance by Laurence Olivier and Vivien Leigh.'[39]

But perhaps their nonchalance stemmed from another source. According to Basil Dean, the two 'lovers' in the film, Leigh and Olivier, had actually fallen in love with each other in real life: 'By the second or third day's shooting I knew I was in for a difficult time, for Vivien and Larry were in the first stages of their love affair, destined to bring joy and suffering to both, and to raise Larry to full maturity as one of our greatest actors. Their joyous awareness of each other took the form of much laughter and giggling on the set; it was impossible for them to take the film seriously.'[40]

An important scene in the film was set in Number One Court of the Old Bailey. Vincent Korda, Alexander's brother, had spent a week building it and the production manager had 'peopled it with barristers, solicitors, ushers, police witnesses and members of the curious public.'[41] All was ready and a satisfactory opening shot was taken in the afternoon, but then Dean was instructed by Alexander Korda to take the set down in the evening. As Dean discovered, there was method in Korda's madness. The shooting schedules were being deliberately rearranged so that Leigh and Olivier could go to Denmark for a week to play together in *Hamlet* in the courtyard in Elsinore, a production arranged by the Danish Tourist Board. Korda was determined to make Vivien Leigh a star. Not content with rearranging schedules Korda directed an additional sequence, 'to inject a more Continental atmosphere', and changed the working title *The First and the Last* to *Twenty-One Days*.

Poor Dean had much to complain about (and he does in his autobiography). He was not asked to see either the 'rough cut' or the finished picture. It was, to quote Greene about other work produced at Denham, 'the usual Denham mouse'. It was not immediately released but was kept in Korda's vaults, having its trade show in April 1939 and only being released a year later, by which time *Gone with the Wind* had made Vivien Leigh a household name.

When it was released, Greene, with that even-handedness of his, his criticism equally as sharp for his own work as for others, pelted justifiable stones at it:

> Galsworthy's story . . . was peculiarly unsuited for film adaptation, as its whole point lay in a double suicide (forbidden by the censor), a burned confession, and an innocent man's conviction for murder (forbidden by the great public). For the rather dubious merits of the original the adaptors have substituted incredible coincidences and banal situations. Slow, wordy, unbearably sentimental, the picture reels awkwardly towards the only suicide the censorship allowed – and that, I find with some astonishment, has been cut out. I wish I could tell the extraordinary story that lies behind this shelved and resurrected picture, a story involving a theme-song, and a bottle of whisky, and camels in Wales . . . Meanwhile, let one guilty man, at any rate, stand in the dock, swearing never, never to do it again . . .[42]

No doubt it was for Greene also a disillusioning experience and certainly, a year later, the enthusiasm seems to have died, for that was the time of his article 'Film Lunch'. He himself was now one of that group writing for the screen 'and all that's asked in return the dried imagination and the dead pen'. Greene, commenting much later on the novelist working for the cinema, writes: 'a writer should not be employed by anyone but himself. If you are using words in one craft, it is impossible not to corrupt them by employing them in another medium under direction.'[43]

Ahead were fine film scripts by Greene and fine films – but they were indeed ahead and released after the Second World War – *Brighton Rock* (1947); *The Fallen Idol* (1948) and *The Third Man* (1949). There, part of the pleasure and part of the success was due to the close working partnership Graham Greene had with the director Carol Reed.

Basil Dean's remarks, and those in Sykes's life of Evelyn Waugh, treat Alexander Korda with some contempt – and so did Greene before he knew him well. The Korda and Greene friendship was to develop though, and Greene came to have the deepest trust in him, even turning to him on one occasion when he felt suicidal: 'So . . . began our friendship which endured and deepened till his death, in spite of my reviews which remained unfavourable,' writes Greene in *Ways of Escape*. 'There was never a man who bore less malice, and I think of him with affection – even love – as the only film producer I have ever known with whom I could spend days and nights of conversation without so much as mentioning the cinema.'[44]

38

Night and Day

There is no test of literary merit except survival.
— GEORGE ORWELL

I N a diary begun on 26 December 1936,★ Greene records that on 29 December he 'ran into Arthur Calder-Marshall and lunched with him at a pub by Leicester Square station'. Arthur Calder-Marshall in 1977 recalled that his impression of Greene then was of a very successful writer: 'It is all so long ago, memories are indistinct. But I remember the house he was living in at Clapham Common North, with the beautiful Adam staircase. To the struggling author subsisting in digs on £5 a week, the Greene establishment appeared the pinnacle of affluence. Here was the Established Writer . . .'[1]

Appearances can be deceptive. No doubt Greene had been involved with what Basil Dean called 'those Alice-in-Wonderland studios at Denham, Bucks, surrounded by hurrying crowds of actors and technicians, all with the confident look of security in their eyes and the jingle of coins in their pockets',[2] but he had also been through a very stressful time in 1936 on a personal and professional level.

He was anxious about his wife, who was expecting a second baby in September. Replying to his brother Hugh's suggestion that they might have a walking holiday together, he wrote: 'I think I might manage a short holiday in October, but it's difficult to promise and I think it would have to be the end of the month . . . everything is in the air. I want to see Vivien safely and comfortably home. Spain might be exciting.' And referring to Vivien's ordeal over the birth of Lucy he wrote: 'Vivien is full of envy for the ease and celerity with which Helga has produced. She had an awful time. They tried a new kind of anaesthetiser on her which broke down.'[3]

In July he had begun to think of another 'entertainment', which

---

★ Dated incorrectly by Greene as 26 December 1937.

was to become *Brighton Rock* (1938), to follow *A Gun for Sale*, and, incredibly, as early as May 1936 he was considering another travel book, based this time in Mexico and dealing with the Mexican Revolution and the Catholic Church. This was to lead to *The Lawless Roads* (1939) and his masterpiece, *The Power and the Glory* (1940). In the same month he had an idea for what he called a 'silly book' – one which also involved travel and Evelyn Waugh. His idea was that he and Waugh should do a race round the world, an idea derived from Jules Verne's *Around the World in Eighty Days*, and he immediately began seeking a publisher for a book about the journey: 'A young man in Heinemann's was grieved by our idea; he thought it vulgar,' he wrote to Hugh on a postcard picturing the Spread Eagle Hotel, Midhurst, 'but Theodora Benson's anxious to get Gollancz in on it.* If you look at the map somewhere in Afghanistan offers three various routes.' On 30 July he wrote to Hugh: 'The Silly Book may yet come off. Evelyn Waugh went back to Abyssinia yesterday on an Italian troop ship, but Theodora wrote to him before he went and I got him on the phone, and he's quite open to discuss the book when he comes back in September.'

Indeed Waugh seemed interested. On his arrival in Rome he wrote to Greene from the Grand Hotel de Russie: 'I am afraid I did not make much sense on the telephone yesterday. I had gone to bed very late & tipsy, got up early & still tipsy, was packing for an indefinite trip to Africa, and not in the best shape for talking business.' Waugh saw possibilities in Greene's plan: 'I think that it should be a race not in time but economy. Each competitor to start with no luggage and a limited sum – say £100 – and the one who arrives with most cash in hand to get a prize.' He suggested at least five competitors and offered Robert Byron's name as a possible candidate. Warming to the subject he added: 'In fact it might be open to anyone who cares to put up his own stake – three or four professional tourists like ourselves to get paid for. Why not in November? Don't answer until October as I have no address.'[4] The idea came to nothing: another way of escape had been blocked.

The pressures built up as Vivien came to the end of her pregnancy. Greene's mother, to relieve the burden, took Lucy over until after the happy event, as the following note written in August shows: 'There's no chance now I'm afraid of having Bear [Lucy's nickname]

---

* If the journey had taken place Theodora Benson would have given Greene a run for his money for she was tough and outspoken and had written about her journeys – *Chip, chip, my little horse: the story of an hair-holiday* (1934) and *The Unambitious Journey* (1935). Many of her books were written in collaboration with Betty Askwith.

back till the end of the month, I mean the end of Sept. We miss her a great deal.' In the same letter he speaks of a rash of boils that invaded his face: 'My run-downess culminated about a week ago in a poisoned face, which swelled up in a most embarrassing way. Painful too, like continuous tooth-ache. The day before yesterday I couldn't stand it any longer and had a cut made by a doctor, and yesterday and today a good deal of the poison has been coming out. I think the swelling will be a lot down tomorrow, and I find I can get my toothbrush round this morning.'[5]

Two days later he writes to Hugh: 'I'm having a wretched time at the present with a poisoned face. I lurk in my tent, only creeping out after dark.'[6] A week later he speaks of Vivien's pregnancy: 'We had a false alarm yesterday morning, but now the amoeba seems to have settled down for the winter.' In the last sentence of the letter his two concerns come together in one sentence: 'I shall be very glad when V's safely through things and when my face is presentable again. I can't shave, but haven't yet reached the stage of looking as if I'm growing a beard. It makes seeing people very difficult.'[7]

Just how painful his condition was he explains to his brother: 'These bloody boils have been going on for more than two months, four days in seven painfully, & one has no certain feeling that one day they will stop. At the moment I have them on me, all just broken – the lips, the thigh & the scrotum – so they've ceased to hurt.' This same letter records that he met Alfred Hitchcock, who was in the process of turning Conrad's novel *The Secret Agent* into the film *Sabotage*: 'I had to see Hitchcock, the other day . . . A silly harmless clown. I shuddered at the things he told me he was doing to Conrad's Secret Agent.'

Moreover, he had decided to change his American publishers: 'I have broken with Doubledays more or less, & have tried to buy back from them, without success, Journey Without Maps, which Viking Press offered to take on. They, the V.P., are going to have my next book anyway, though D's keep on sending anxious cables.'

His lunches and his meetings with writers went on as usual: 'I had a painful Purgatorial lunch yesterday with [Geoffrey] Grigson, [Stephen] Spender & Rosamund Lehmann, my mind clouded with aspirins. I hadn't met S. before: he struck one as having too much human kindness. A little soft.'

Earlier Greene had written of Grigson to his mother: 'The assistant editor, literary, of the M[orning] P[ost] is the young avant garde critic, Geoffrey Grigson, a fierce and dangerous creature. I haven't met him, but over the telephone the other day he claimed to be a distant cousin. He said he thought it was through a Holt Wilson connection, his father being an H.W. first cousin?'[8]

And he recorded that, during his lunch with Arthur Calder-Marshall in December, Langdon Davies was in the same pub, 'about to return to the Spanish Civil War to take moving pictures on sixteen millimetre film which he finally hopes to enlarge for public showing. L.D. one of those extreme leftwingers who give the impression of a lack of intellectual hardness at the centre. Spender another. They are very pleased with violence and ruthlessness theoretically, but with them it is less a rational policy than a sentimental reaction to their own softness.'

On 13 September Greene's son Francis was born without difficulty. In 1979 Vivien described the birth of her second child at Dr Pink's in Greenwich: 'That was marvellous – he was so kind, nine hours or so, Francis was born at two minutes to six in the morning and I had started at about nine the evening before and everybody was very supportive. All the nurses were young New Zealanders; all dressed in white, even white shoes and stockings, and so sympathetic. I remember Dr Pink saying "You've done it all by yourself", instead of forceps and stitches and the rest of it. The nurse brushed my hair – it was a most marvellous thing to be lying there, flat again and exhausted, and she brushed my hair very gently away from my face. And then they brought this little bundle in, smelling delicious, violets and everything. Graham was very supportive. He was very distressed about the first birth but the other was very successful. He'd grown a beard because he had either been abroad or was going abroad, or for some reason anyway he had a beard.' Vivien must have forgotten his boils.

In his letter to Hugh on 31 October Greene recorded: 'The baby is crying & I have ten books accumulated for review & this damned thriller [*Brighton Rock*] to write.'

By the middle of November his boils had disappeared and by 26 December 1936 he was able to tell Hugh that he had been offered the literary editorship of the new weekly magazine, *Night and Day*, which Chatto and Windus were launching in the spring of 1937 under the managing directorship of Ian Parsons, senior director at Chatto. He wrote to his mother, 'I may have to decide between Mexico & the literary editorship of a new paper – if it gets all its finances by Christmas. A horrid decision. I'd much rather have Mexico, but the L.E. would be worth £600 a year. I have to decide between buying this house or leaving next year: the lease won't be renewed.'

He decided to take up the *Night and Day* offer so long as Korda did not exercise his option, and he added, 'If it wasn't for the libel action [over *Journey Without Maps*] we'd be feeling on a prosperity wave.' He had done the responsible thing – taken the bird in the hand, though it was not what he desired. As early as August that year he had written to his mother with the Mexican book in mind, 'D.V. I shall be going off in January. I shall go via New York to pick up introductions and information.' Instead, in December 1936 he was writing to Hugh to ask how his wife, Helga, was enjoying New York and regretting an opportunity lost and an adventure missed: 'O dear, I'd hoped to be there this winter.'

*

Nevertheless, in spite of disappointment, Greene threw himself into the job of being literary editor of what was to be a short-lived, but unique magazine. Ian Parsons described him as 'a model literary editor, hard working, completely conscientious, and with such a large circle of gifted literary friends that not only the book pages, but many of the features were of an exceptionally high order.'9

Greene approached Evelyn Waugh, seeing him as dramatic critic of the magazine, but Waugh proved not an easy fish to catch. From St James, Piccadilly, he wrote in a rather laid-back manner: 'I thought that at the moment you would be racing Theodora Benson across the Gobi desert. It is nice of you to think of me in connection with your new paper & I like the idea of dramatic criticism. The trouble is that I can't bind myself to be in London every week. Could you find a second chap to do it, irregularly, turn & turn about with me . . . How does that suit you?'10 He also tried to determine the payment he would receive: 'I will give you a contract to do 25 criticisms a year at £250.' He ended on a sombre note: 'I remember being approached in 1929 by a London New Yorker that never materialized. Is yours soundly backed?'11

Along the bottom of this page of Waugh's letter Greene has written –

> Osbert
> Lancaster.
> Isherwood.
> Waugh.

– presumably the first three writers he turned to for contributions. Waugh switched from drama to fiction, perhaps because *Night and Day* would not pay £10 a review and reviewing fiction had an added advantage: 'Yes, the pay is rather disappointing', he wrote, 'but I'm getting spliced & want as many regular jobs as I can get. Six guineas a week will be worth it (a) if this was the understanding that it would be raised to ten if the paper became a success. (b) I could have, either to keep or sell, all the review books. That is to say you'd circularize to publishers saying you are a new weekly, etc., that I was doing the book page & that books were to be sent direct to me. This would save trouble in selection, all to my library and supplement the wages very considerably. Is that o.k.?'

It was not 'o.k.', but Evelyn Waugh was not willing to let go on this: 'I am sure you will realise that the English New Yorker is a purely commercial proposition – not like the Tablet [Catholic newspaper] for which we are both willing to work for joke wages. My suggestion was for an *average* of £2 a week in books. I quite see that some weeks this would be difficult. You can then make it up when there is a spate. You say the review books are worth £800 a year, so I don't see the difficulty. But if your boss [John Marks] won't agree to this, I'm afraid that it simply isn't worth my while.'

Greene finally brought Waugh into the *Night and Day* corral, Waugh conceding, 'Yes, I see the difficulty. I had no conception that the output of new books was so big. If you can promise to supplement the six guineas wage with an average of £2 weekly in selling value of books (half price non-fiction: one third fiction) that will be perfectly o.k. I quite see that the literary editor must decide what books are given chief notice.'

The additional £2 from the sale of books brought Waugh's wage to £8, double the payment of other contributors. He was worth it and we can see something of his liveliness when he later opted not to review a popular Francis Brett Young novel, probably *They See a Country*. To Greene he wrote: 'There's nothing to take hold of in Brett Young – just flabby longwinded stuff. Not enough character to attack. A cushion not a bubble to prick.'[12] Waugh's letter ended with the query, 'When do you come out?'

The magazine came out on 30 June 1937. Greene wrote to Charles Evans of Heinemann, 'you'll be receiving an invitation to a party at the Dorchester on the 30th to celebrate the first number of Night and Day.' There was a guest list of celebrities, each of whom was presented with a copy of the first weekly issue with its brilliant cover drawn by Feliks Topolski. A. P. Herbert, on this occasion, made the public address.

*

Early that June Greene became involved for a short time in the Spanish Civil War. Basically it was a conflict between Catholicism and atheism – churches were gutted, 12 bishops, 4,184 priests, 2,365 monks and about 300 nuns died. George Orwell recorded that 'almost

every church [in Barcelona] had been gutted and its images burnt',
and Hugh Thomas tells us that the ears of priests were often passed
round – monks had their eardrums perforated by rosary beads being
forced into them, the mother of two Jesuit priests had a rosary forced
down her throat, 800 people were thrown down a mine shaft. The
cry was: 'Do you still believe in this God who never speaks and who
does not defend himself even when his images and temples are
burned? Admit that God does not exist and that you priests . . .
deceive the people.'[13] From Hitler's Germany on Franco's behalf,
planes bombed Spanish towns.

There was great pressure from the left-wing on young writers in
Britain to join the Republican forces in Spain. In June 1937, at the
time Greene was involved in the first issue of *Night and Day*, the *Left
Review* sent out a questionnaire to writers and poets: 'This is the
question we are asking you: Are you for, or against, the legal
Government and the people of Republican Spain? Are you for, or
against, Franco and Fascism?' The results were published in a booklet
entitled *Authors Take Sides*. The poets Auden, Spender, and C. Day
Lewis supported the Republicans. C. Day Lewis's poem, 'First Hymn
to Lenin', provided the slogan: 'Evolution the dance, revolution the
steps', and Auden wrote in his poem, 'Spain', 'Death? Very well, I
accept, for I am your choice, your decision. Yes, I am Spain'; and
he, with two thousand other young men, joined the International
Brigade against Franco, and many died. The Spanish poet Lorca
was shot by Nationalist partisans. Alan Jenkins, then twenty-three,
unemployed and living in Soho, wrote: 'Soho was full of young
writers and out-of-work film extras who were asking each other:
"Have you seen Tony? He's been *under fire*." And then: "Are *you*
going? Why not – are you a Trotskyist or something?"'[14]

Personal pressure was certainly put on Greene. In a review of
Authors Take Sides, Anthony Powell asked: 'Where is . . . Mr Graham
Greene?', and later Valentine Cunningham wrote: 'One would like
to know whether Graham Greene, a leftist Catholic who wrote the
not unsympathetic *The Confidential Agent* (1939) about Spain, was
asked [by the *Left Review*] and refused to respond, or responded too
cagily for the compiler's pleasure.' A week after the Powell review,
Greene responded in an article in the *Spectator* by setting side by side
Tennyson's and his friend Hallam's visit to Spain during the rash and
unsuccessful conspiracy of General Torrijos and other Spanish exiles
against the restored Bourbon monarch, Ferdinand, and the florid
rhetoric of *Authors Take Sides*. Tennyson and Hallam were out to be
amused (though a companion of theirs was shot by a firing-squad)
but they did at least cross the Pyrénées, and he concludes, 'the

dilettante tone [of Hallam] has charm after the sweeping statements, the safe marble gestures, the self-importance [of *Authors Take Sides*]: "I stand with the People and Government of Spain." '

This was only one aspect of his view of the Spanish Civil War. In a letter of 14 January 1987, he writes that one reason he did not respond to the questionnaire was that, although he was against Franco, he was not 100 per cent for the Republicans, chiefly because of their brutality and the murder of nuns. But he did side with the Basques. The rebel General Mola threatened to raze their province, Vizcaya, to the ground if submission was not immediate and began bombing the defenceless town of Durango. The Nationalists blockaded the port of Bilbao, but a certain British Captain, 'Captain Roberts', went in with his merchant ship, the *Seven Seas Spray*, 'the captain and his daughter standing on the bridge, the hungry people of Bilbao massed excitedly on the quayside and cried, "Long live the British Sailors!" '[15] But the historic Basque city of Guernica was bombed and strafed by the Germans every twenty minutes, incendiary bombs were dropped and the fleeing population was machine-gunned.

Greene's sympathy for the Basques lay in the fact that while they were on the side of the Republicans they were not fighting for a Communist or anarchist state, for they were Catholics and their army was attended by 82 priests who would celebrate Mass and be present at the last moments of the dying. Arthur Calder-Marshall felt that as a Catholic convert Greene faced a different quandary from that of Evelyn Waugh whose sympathies lay with Franco, as an enemy of Communism. Greene's sense of right and wrong lay with the Popular Front movement, but as a Catholic he had to side with the Catholics, and when General Mola's troops surrounded Bilbao, he tried to get there: 'A restlessness set in then which has never been quite allayed: a desire to be a spectator of history, history in which I was concerned myself.'

His intention was to make a broadcast about the besieged Basques, flying in from Toulouse to Bilbao, and presumably backed by the B.B.C., who must be the 'they' in the following: 'After they'd sent me hurtling down to Toulouse at a few hours notice, I found myself stuck.' This is from an undated letter to his mother. His own account of the event forty years later is as follows: 'I carried a letter of recommendation from the Basque Delegation in London to a small café owner in Toulouse who had been breaking the blockade of Bilbao with a two-seater plane. I found him shaving in a corner of his café at six in the morning and handed him the Delegation's dignified letter sealed with scarlet wax, but no amount of official sealing wax would induce him to fly his plane again into Bilbao – Franco's guns on his last flight had proved themselves too accurate for his comfort.'[16] But Greene's letter to his mother suggests that what prevented him flying into Bilbao was the limited time he had at his disposal: 'Their aeroplane had been taken over by the Spanish Govt. and I should have had to wait at least a week while another one was bought in London and sent to Bayonne. As I expect to start work on the new magazine in a week, it was no good waiting.'

In any case, what had been described as Bilbao's defences – 'a ring of iron' – had their weaknesses betrayed by the man who had planned them, Major Goicoechea. The Basques' leader, Colonel Vidal, was a failure: 'His battalions did not know where he was. He did not know where his battalions were', George Steer wrote of the fall of Bilbao on 19 June 1937. The result was a rout. Apart from Greene, only two other writers, Mauriac and Maritain, both Catholics, supported the Basques – the Vatican did not.

But if Greene did not reach Spain, ironically his eldest brother, the black sheep of the family, did. On 16 January 1938 Greene wrote to Hugh: 'Did you see Herbert's front page news story in the Daily Worker, Dec. 22, "I was a Secret Agent of Japan"?' He told Hugh that it was Claud Cockburn who wrote the article for Herbert and what made Greene jubilant was that Herbert, who had for years borrowed from his own family, was paid nothing for the article by Cockburn, who also succeeded in borrowing five shillings from Herbert. The headlines to the article: 'I WAS IN THE PAY OF JAPAN: A SECRET AGENT TELLS HIS STORY TO THE DAILY WORKER', have more bite than the story itself, though Herbert does appear to have got himself on the payroll of the Japanese naval intelligence which was operating secretly in London.

He had approached the Japanese in 1934 and no doubt played on the fact that he had contacts – it must have embarrassed his uncle, Sir Graham Greene, to have had it stated in his nephew's article that he was for years one of the highest officials of the British Admiralty. Herbert's con appears to have been successful – he had carefully planned meetings with a Captain Oka who went by the code name 'Arthur' in England, and having emphasised his dislike of Americans and his important contacts, he persuaded Captain Oka, in the Japanese Club in Cavendish Square, to take him on his unofficial staff, with an outfit allowance of £200 and payment of £50 a month. His claim that his information (imaginary) came from 'a retired commander in the Navy, now unfortunately dead' obviously gave Captain Oka some doubts and Oka wrote on 19 December 1934 that 'any information without the source from which it came is really of no value at all.'

The article was intended to provide publicity for Herbert's book, *Secret Agent in Spain*, for he apparently was also taken on as a spy by the rebel side, and told his story because he was double-crossed during his second journey there. He tells a good yarn and appears to have spent his spare time in the Florida Hotel in Madrid with well known journalists – Henry Buckley of the *Daily Telegraph*, Sefton Delmer of the *Daily Express*. He tells us that he had been warned by 'a very high official [most likely his uncle], seated in a small room in the British Admiralty over-looking the Horse Guards Parade: "Greene, if you are not more careful you will some day find yourself in the Thames."'

Many years later Hugh Greene said that he thought Herbert simply supplied the Japanese with information on naval matters which he gleaned from technical magazines – which they could have picked up themselves. But he did get himself into M.I.5 files. During the war, Hugh was approached by a friend in M.I.5. They met in the Nell Gwynn pub in the Strand and he was shown some burnt bits of paper. A bomb on one of their buildings had destroyed some of their files and they were trying to reconstruct such burnt pieces of paper. One of them referred to a Mr Herbert Greene and his connection with the Japanese. Hugh told him that he thought Herbert had done some very harmless work for the Japanese.

Herbert, Hugh said, was 'a bit of a crook and he was clever enough to know that he could get away with letting the Japanese have material which had already been published'.[17] Probably what Greene wrote of *Unknown Liberia* – 'a very fishy production, full of obvious lies', applies also to Herbert's book, but Herbert was important to Graham not only as the source of Anthony Farrant in *England Made Me*, but as the vacuum-cleaner salesman in *Our Man in Havana* who successfully cons British Intelligence into paying him for drawings of parts of vacuum cleaners supposed to be connected with military installations.

Herbert begins the *Secret Agent in Spain*: 'This is not a story of violent adventure; it happens to be true. I could easily tell you of how I blew up munition dumps, captured University City and escaped on the morning of my execution from St Anton Prison.' Herbert could indeed have done this.

But unquestionably Herbert did visit Spain and was thought to be a spy, according to Claud Cockburn. Claud was friendly with Ernest Hemingway at the time of the battle for Madrid and on one occasion Hemingway pointed to a tall man with glasses and said he was going to shoot the man, for he had discovered that he was a spy for the other side. Claud looked closely and then turned to Hemingway saying, 'Don't shoot him, he's my headmaster's eldest son.'

*

After three months, *Night and Day* published a selection of readers' letters entitled *Pen Pricks and Praise for Night and Day*. The editors had honestly looked for genuine rejections – 'I might say frightfully weak, old chap. Cheer up, it may catch on, God knows queerer things have happened'; 'Jokes *very* poor, illustration rotten . . . Give us real humour . . . or in my opinion – early demise.' Others could and did praise it as 'badly needed in Great Britain. It is very intelligent.' It was also light, frivolous, holding little sacred, even itself. Reading all the issues now from 1 July to 23 December 1937 is a joy, and not for nostalgic reasons either. Articles and illustrations are of an exceptionally high standard. Of course, since there were no sacred cows it was bound to be a disturbing magazine.[18]

Essentially, it was flippant, outrageous and, at a time when, leading up to the Second World War, there was increasing political polarisation, its policy, as expressed by Patrick Ransome, was 'a strictly non-Party one, and any political article must depend entirely on its wit to secure inclusion'. Thus John Marks, the editor, rejecting a poem by William Douglas Home, explained that he felt that 'if it appeared with the rest of the magazine – which is essentially flippant – it might run the risk of being misunderstood by our readers'.[19] Witty and satirical, it appealed to the sophisticated and discriminating, and realising this the editors tried to turn this limitation of sales into an advantage: 'Discriminating people who subscribe to NIGHT AND DAY as from the first number will have something to boast to their grandchildren about – assuming, of course, that discriminating people *have* grandchildren. We're not sure about this.' In the first issue the editors, stating who would review books, theatre and film, said, 'For the rest, a wealth of talent, some of it anonymous, some of it not, invigilates over a mad world, annotating its absurdities as they come to light.'

Credit must go to Greene as Literary Editor for bringing into the magazine some of the most talented of the time, many of them not then well known: 'is there any paper which can rival our roll of honour?' he asked in 1985. 'It reads like the death of a whole literary generation: Evelyn Waugh, Elizabeth Bowen, Herbert Read, William Empson, Nicolas Bentley, John Betjeman, Cyril Connolly, Stevie Smith, A. J. A. Symons, John Hayward, Hugh Kingsmill, William Plomer.'[20] He could have added Peter Fleming (a better writer than his younger brother Ian), Christopher Hollis, Antonia White, Gerald Kersh, Christopher Isherwood and Malcolm Muggeridge.

Greene played his part in invigilating over a mad world by turning upside down his contributors' talents. T. O. Beachcroft, the short story writer, was put to writing on amateur athletics; the novelist from the Northern Transvaal, William Plomer, then living in London, wrote on All-in wrestling, seeing it in terms of a theatrical performance and noting that, 'the sudden geranium flow of blood . . . makes a face more luminous than grease-paint can'; the poet Louis MacNeice, writing about the Kennel Club, described Afghan hounds as 'baboons dressed up in pyjamas', a chihuahua as 'an insect in a comic strip' and Alsatians as abominations; the novelist and critic, Walter Allen, set himself up, as he put it, 'as the soccer expert with an article on Aston Villa, tracing its origins to the bible class of Aston Villa Wesleyan Chapel, Birmingham'.[21] William Empson, perhaps the greatest academic of his day, wrote on 'Learning Chinese' (which he had done very successfully): 'I made a curious discovery in turning over Giles's dictionary . . . that the character for the male organ is a combination of signs meaning the Imploring Corpse, or the Corpse in Pain.'

Greene was rash enough to approach the art critic Herbert Read (Professor of Fine Arts at Edinburgh University from 1931 to 1933 and then editor of the prestigious *Burlington Magazine*) to step outside his discipline and write for *Night and Day* regular reviews of detective stories. Read promptly accepted, sending in as his first contribution a dismissive criticism of Dorothy L. Sayers's *Busman's Honeymoon* and following with a review of Peter Cheyney which was a criticism of Cheyney's style, written as a parody of it: 'His hero is Lemmy Caution, G-man, the toughest guy in the fiction racket who . . . don't at all disdain the dames. "There's something fascinatin' about 'em. They got rhythm. They got technique – and how!" There are two janes in this little story – Henrietta and Paulette. They've both got what it takes – and then a bundle!'

There was a growing friendship between Read and Greene at this time. Lady Read has described Greene as 'a precocious schoolboy with tremendous depths . . . and these are the depths one doesn't enquire into . . . he has always remained exactly the same – casual and amusing and rather shy. He must have been quite different from my husband but they talked the same language and were amused about the same things. They were always amused by the literary in London – they both loved almost anything funny. They laughed a lot together. They were both very free men – they were nobody's slave and nobody's fool either. They always enjoyed each other's company.'[22] Read celebrated their friendship with an odd little verse written in red ink:

> Shall it be Graham or be Greene?
> There's nothing betwixt or between.
> Shall it be Graham or be Greene?
> Neither is Christian or intime,
> But one is milk the other cream.
> So Graham let it be, not Greene.

The non-biased political but witty approach of *Night and Day* can be seen in a number of reviews and articles. Evelyn Waugh had a go at the young Arthur Calder-Marshall's book, *The Changing Scene*: 'Mr Calder-Marshall is still in his twenties, but this does not prevent him from describing in the most cocksure manner the social conditions of the pre-war era . . . he talks of proletarian fiction as though it were the very recent discovery of a few of his friends. He does not seem to have learned that all the great stories of the world are proletarian: has he ever heard of *Piers Plowman* or the *Pilgrim's Progress*, or of the enormous, various and opulent folk-lore'; and after taking Calder-Marshall to task over his belief that rich Lords are blood parasites and newspapers and cinemas tools of exploitation, Waugh adds a compassionate note: 'One other thought I would commend to Mr Calder-Marshall. He must not despair of growing up . . . the opinions of the young are not necessarily the opinions of the future.' Evelyn Waugh himself was then only thirty-four.

Russian Communist leaders were dealt with in the same manner. Nigel Balchin, whose fame with *The Small Back Room* and *Mine Own Executioner* was yet to come, in an article called 'Trotsky or Notsky', wrote that Trotsky returning to Russia 'still disguised as a Communist', created the Red Army. 'This, clearly, was a masterstroke. For he must have seen, with his uncanny foresight, that a strong Red Army would frighten the life out of Germany, bring about Fascism there, and so provide him with somebody to plot with and somebody to offer the Ukraine to.'[23]

On the other hand, Elizabeth Bowen, the drama critic, whom Greene once described as having 'a fine, restless, tricky talent, occasionally superbly successful', strongly recommended A. S. J. Tessimond's anti-capitalist *Song of the City* and the *Aristocrates* whose theme was the 'building up [in prisoners in the Gulag camps] of a new morale, and the breaking down of that individualistic spirit that makes a man Man's enemy'. Both were performed at the Unity Theatre. A further sign of even-handedness appeared in P. Y. Betts's

'The Snob's Guide to Good Form' which ended on the following note: 'To sum up – break as many rules as you like, but be sure to find out first which rules it is good form to break. This is the whole art of being a Snob.'[24]

Foremost among the artists who worked for the magazine was Feliks Topolski, and *Night and Day* put his remarkable talent on the map. He had come from Poland two years earlier to London to cover the Jubilee. He has recalled his immediate success:

> I was very spoilt because I had early success in Poland . . . they were pushing me to come to London and they started to push me as an artist, with me relaxing and following girls, and not being able to say a word in English. They were rushing about announcing what a genius had arrived here, and indeed, within that year of 1935, within a few months, a book was published of my drawings, an exhibition was held, and simply there was no way of not noticing me. My work was all over the place.

Ian Parsons brought him into *Night and Day*, 'a man who became a friend and was involved in the whole structure of *Night and Day*'. His brilliant drawings, without exception, presented the Polish artist's view of the absurd preoccupations and social life of the British upper class, preserving typical gestures and situations so that they freshly reveal the 1930s to us – gentlemen at the races, at the ballet, in the foyer (a woman's face once caught never to be forgotten), in a satirical light. As was stated in the magazine: 'Feliks Topolski . . . is conducting a little regular field-work in these islands and . . . lays bare, as with a scalpel, the essential whatever-it-is of Britain's most cherished institutions.'

The magazine's appeal was to the educated and sophisticated. Hugh Kingsmill and Malcolm Muggeridge, for example, embarked on a series of Literary Pilgrimages, signing their brilliant accounts 'H.K.' and 'M.M.'. The tone was of two friends visiting literary sites and the discussions that ensued.

In Paris they sought out a Madame Blanchet, elderly, grey-haired and serene and thought they detected 'a suggestion of Wordsworth in her brows and eyes', not surprisingly because she was his great-great-granddaughter, coming in line from his illegitimate daughter, Caroline, who was the result of his affair with Annette Vallon. They recalled how Wordsworth returned to France with his sister to tell Annette that he was going to be married and walked by the sea with the nine-year-old daughter he had never seen before, commemorating the event in a sonnet: 'Dear Child! dear Girl! that walkest with me here', but making no mention of the fact that Annette had been left to bring up the child, 'through the grim years of the French Revolution and the First Empire'. They noted that in documents the French rarely got his name right – he was Mr Williams, Wortsworth, Williams Wordsworth, and M. Williams, and on her death Annette was registered as 'Marie Anne Vallon, known as Williams'. They concluded that Wordsworth 'had not the candour to cut his moral losses; the deserter became a prig, the deserted kept her kindliness and courage.'

*

At the end of October, the magazine's fourth month of publication, Greene's review of the nine-year-old star Shirley Temple's film, *Wee Willie Winkie*, appeared in *Night and Day*. It was a forceful piece and was to have traumatic consequences for *Night and Day* and for himself. In the *Spectator*, in May 1936, he had already praised her appearance in *The Littlest Rebel*: 'I had not seen Miss Temple before . . . as I expected there was the usual sentimental exploitation of childhood, but I had not expected the tremendous energy which her rivals certainly lacked.'[25] On 7 August that year he reviewed *Captain January*, and was already re-assessing the child star in terms of her surprising maturity: 'Shirley Temple acts and dances with immense vigour and assurance, but some of her popularity seems to rest on a coquetry quite as mature as Miss [Claudette] Colbert's and on an oddly precocious body as voluptuous in grey flannel trousers as Miss Dietrich's.'

This theme was developed in his review of *Wee Willie Winkie*:

Miss Shirley Temple's case, though, has peculiar interest: infancy with her is a disguise, her appeal is more secret and more adult. Already two years ago she was a fancy little piece (real childhood, I think, went out after *The Littlest Rebel*). In *Captain January* she wore trousers with the mature suggestiveness of a Dietrich: her neat and well-developed rump twisted in the tap-dance: her eyes had a sidelong searching coquetry. Now in *Wee Willie Winkie*, wearing short kilts, she is a complete totsy. Watch her swaggering stride across the Indian barrack-square: hear the gasp of excited expectation from her antique audience when the sergeant's palm is raised: watch the way she measures a man with agile studio eyes, with dimpled depravity. Adult emotions of love and grief glissade across the mask of childhood, a childhood skin-deep.

It is clever, but it cannot last. Her admirers – middle-aged men and clergymen – respond to her dubious coquetry, to the sight of her well-shaped and desirable little body, packed with enormous vitality, only because the safety curtain of story and dialogue drops between their intelligence and their desire.

If anyone had cause for complaint it was her admirers, castigated here as 'middle-aged men and clergymen' and also as her gasping 'antique audience'. Greene's review did not appear in America, but stories printed suggested that Greene believed Shirley Temple was a midget with a seven-year-old child of her own. Perhaps this is one reason why Twentieth Century Fox decided on a libel action. [26]

Too late, *Night and Day* became extremely careful. John Marks, returning a proof to Stevie Smith, told her that the character Montague Cohen in her poem had an original living in Golders Green. She changed the name of the place to 'Bottle Green'. And Greene gave a caution to Evelyn Waugh, who replied: 'Very sorry you scented libel. The chap is a confessed thief so I don't know what he can complain of. If you'll let me have it back I will soften the phraseology. I think that kind of work needs snubbing . . . What ho S. Temple!' Recalling that time a year later on 24 September when Prime Minister Chamberlain was having his second meeting with Hitler, Greene put the libel case into perspective – 'last year the Shirley Temple libel action – and possible ruin – seemed unimportant because Lucy was ill.' [27]

The libel case did not appear before the King's Bench until 22 March 1938, by which time *Night and Day* had produced its last issue (23 December 1937) and Graham was almost at the end of his epic Mexican journey through the swamps of Tabasco and the mountainous region of Chiapas, but the case caused a stir. It was recorded in *The Times* Law Reports:

> *Libel on Miss Shirley Temple: 'A Gross Outrage'*
> Temple and Others v. Night and Day Magazine,
> Limited and Others
> *Before the* Lord Chief Justice

Sir Patrick Hastings appeared for the plaintiffs and after describing the plaintiff as a child of nine years with a world-wide reputation as an artist in films, Hastings went on to speak damagingly about the review and cleverly made the occasion more sinister by refusing to read it out fully in court:

> In his view it was one of the most horrible libels that one could well imagine. Obviously he would not read it all – it was better

that he should not – but a glance at the statement of claim, where a poster was set out, was quite sufficient to show the nature of the libel written about this child.

Of course, it is better to hint than to show and it seems to have worked wonders on the Lord Chief Justice. Hastings went on: 'This beastly publication was written, and it was right to say that every respectable distributor in London refused to be a party to selling it [this was true of W. H. Smith & Sons only]. Notwithstanding that, the magazine company with the object no doubt of increasing the sale, proceeded to advertise the fact that it had been banned.'

Of course, every publication must take advantage of the possibility of increasing sales, but the fact is that the distinguished King's Counsel, D. N. Pritt, had advised *Night and Day* (wrongly as it turned out) that in his opinion the article was not libellous. Relying on the barrister's verdict, *Night and Day* naturally publicised the article during the week that the issue in question was on sale.

There were, ultimately, apologies all round; even Greene was forced through the magazine's counsel to apologise. To Elizabeth Bowen, Graham wrote from Mexico: 'I found a cable waiting for me in Mexico City asking me to apologise to that bitch Shirley Temple.' Their counsel, Valentine Holmes, ate humble pie – deepest apology to Miss Temple for the pain not caused but which would most certainly have been caused to her by the article if she read it. Everyone seemed to rat on Greene – 'There was no justification for the criticism of the film, which was one which anybody could take their children to see . . . So far as the publishers of the magazine were concerned, they had not seen the article before publication and the printers "welcomed the opportunity of making any amends in their power".' And Godfrey Winn, a popular writer for women's magazines, put in his threepennyworth. He thought the review 'a queer one, because it was not a criticism of Shirley's clever acting at all, but one which introduced potential audience reactions – reactions which were entirely alien to Shirley's lovable and innocent humour'.

One has to say that this was mild of Godfrey Winn since Greene had very unfavourably reviewed a film about a day in the life of Winn, setting it against a documentary about the Hurdanos, 'Spanish people inbred, diseased, forgotten' while Mr Winn wakened 'prettily to order, kissing his dog [the famous Mr Sponge] upon the pillow', getting into his car, ('some flowers and a kiss from his mother'), kneeling by a bed to be introduced as 'Uncle Godfrey' to the new-born baby of one of his readers: 'What message for these ['the goitred and moron and hunger-tortured faces' of the Hurdanos] from Uncle

Godfrey?' wrote Greene, 'the eyes look out at us so innocently, so candidly, so doggily, they might be the eyes of the famous Mr Sponge.'*[28]

The Lord Chief Justice, Lord Hewart, clearly incensed by the article, took a hard line. He spoke from the bench:

> His Lordship – Who is the author of this article?
> Mr Holmes [for the defendant] – Mr Graham Greene.
> His Lordship – Is he within the jurisdiction?
> Mr Holmes – I am afraid I do not know, my Lord . . .
> His Lordship – Can you tell me where Mr Greene is?
> Mr Mathew [for the co-defendant] – I have no information on the subject.
> His Lordship – This libel is simply a gross outrage, and I will take care to see that suitable attention is directed to it.

Greene later recalled that he kept on his bathroom wall, until a bomb removed the wall, the statement of claim, 'that I had accused Twentieth Century Fox of "procuring" Miss Temple "for immoral purposes".' Lord Hewart sent the papers in the case to the Director of Public Prosecutions, so that ever since Greene has been traceable in the files of Scotland Yard, and he might have been prosecuted for criminal libel. From the Hotel Canada in Mexico City he wrote on 22 April 1938, 'it looks as if I shall be arrested when I land if the L.C.J.'s bite is as bad as his bark.' His publisher was so worried that he offered to send money for his upkeep so that he need not return to England until things had quietened down. Greene, ever willing to take a risk, took the next cargo boat home.

He had written to Hugh in January 1938, the month after *Night and Day* had foundered: 'I'm glad you agree about S.T. [She] is going to cost me about £250 if I'm lucky', but his critical judgment was not swayed by his anger, for he added, 'But see Captain January. That's her great film.'[29] He was not lucky. Twentieth Century Fox were awarded £3,500 in damages, £500 of which was to be paid by Greene – a sum roughly equivalent to £15,000 today and a considerable amount for him to find at that time.

*

There was a further charge against Greene, suggested by Victoria Glendinning while writing the life of Elizabeth Bowen. She sent the

---

* Godfrey Winn's 'Sincerity Page' in the *Daily Mirror* often seemed to discerning readers to be largely about his little dog, Mr Sponge.

draft of her account of the libel case to Greene for his approval: '*Night and Day* was ruined by a libel action brought against Graham Greene on account of an article about Shirley Temple.' In reply he wrote: 'For your information *Night and Day* was not really ruined by the libel action. Unfortunately the charge for advertisements was far too high for the circulation and it was in financial difficulties. In fact, the Number containing the so-called libel sold better than any other issue.' Though Greene then admits that 'in the search for money the case may have had a certain influence. Probably the paper would have had to have closed anyway.'

In spite of its brilliant talent, the magazine did not catch on. It was, perhaps, too much like the *New Yorker* although as the weeks passed on it seemed to develop a character of its own. But it was very much a London orientated magazine – though attempts were in the offing to advertise it in Manchester and Birmingham, it was unlikely to have succeeded in the provinces. And it did seem clannish with its articles by 'in boys' for other 'in boys', and its hopes to appeal to 'discriminating' people were not fulfilled – presumably there were not sufficient of them willing to spend 6*d.* a week for the pleasure.

At the end of August 75,000 leaflets were printed offering a trial three-month subscription for only five shillings, but the magazine was losing money to the tune of £200 a week. A month before the Shirley Temple review appeared, the company felt that, given this situation, they probably could not continue beyond Christmas, and two days after the review, before there had been any adverse reaction to it, Ian Parsons announced at a General Meeting that the Board thought that 'publication could not be effectively continued unless a large amount of fresh capital was procured'. Evelyn Waugh noted in his diary on 18 November: 'Greene rang up to say that *Night and Day* is on its last legs; would I put them into touch with [Viscount] Evan Tredegar, whom I barely know, to help them raise capital. They must indeed be in a bad way.'[30]

Contributors were asked to take less than their promised four guineas and Theodora Benson agreed to accept three guineas for 'Rise and Fall' (an ominous title in the circumstances) as it was 'shorter and lousier than the things you gave me four guineas for'.[31] Waugh was not willing to take less: 'I received your telegram this morning after the enclosed article had been written. As it had been definitely commissioned . . . I am afraid I must hold you to your offer, whether you print it or not.'

Just before his death, Ian Parsons expressed the belief that the libel case brought the magazine down: 'The paper had had a hard struggle to survive but had just begun to turn the corner in terms of circulation and I think would have survived with the addition of some offered further capital from certain shareholders, had not this blow struck us.'[32] But, alas, in December, though they needed £8,000 more capital to continue, only £3,000 conditional offers had come in. Perhaps the libel case proved the last straw – as Ian Parsons wrote: 'Of course, one cannot accept further capital with an unsettled libel action on one's hands, and as you can imagine it took many weeks of parleying between London and Hollywood before we knew how much the whole thing was going to cost us. Sad end of story. The shareholders lost their money and the staff their jobs.'[33]

Night and Day paid comparatively small damages of £3,500, but the legal costs amounted to another £1,500, 'enough to make the Company insolvent'.

According to the critic John Atkins such was the ferocity of Greene's attacks on the American film industry in the *Spectator* and *Night and Day* that it collectively ganged up on him and was waiting for him to go too far: 'One false step and they would move heaven, earth . . . to put an end to it . . . He would certainly go too far, if not next week, then the week after', and he did so in reviewing *Wee Willie Winkie*.[34] Ian Parsons in his 1976 letter suggested as much: 'I seem to have heard that the film people pursued a vindictive action against Graham personally, as the author of the article, or tried to.' Greene put forward a less sensational view: 'He [Atkins] is completely wrong in saying that there was any ganging up against [me] . . . 20th Century Fox went beyond the limits for an ordinary action for libel by writing to an editor and trying to get [my] criticisms stopped in future.'[35] The editor in question was Derek Verschoyle of the *Spectator*. But, from a letter written to Hugh a month after *Night and Day*'s demise we can see how nasty that film company had become: 'The Fox people went round to Gaumont-British to try and get them to withdraw all tickets [free tickets to see previews] from me, thus breaking me as a critic, but G.B. told them to go to hell.' Something of his hidden anger and determination over this affair comes out as he completes the sentence with: 'and I'm popping up in the Spectator again in the Spring and, my God, won't I go gunning.'[36]

He did go gunning when he returned from Mexico. The first Twentieth Century Fox film reviewed by him was *Sally, Irene and Mary* rightly dismissed in a paragraph. But he saw red when on 5 August 1938 he had to review another Fox film, this time supposedly based on his cousin Robert Louis Stevenson's famous novel, *Kidnapped*:

I doubt if the summer will show a worse film than *Kidnapped*; the only fun you are likely to get from it is speculation, speculation on the astonishing ignorance of film-makers who claim to know what the public wants. The public will certainly not want this *Kidnapped*, where all the adventures which made them read the book have been omitted. Is it even honest to bring in Stevenson's name? . . . Apart from the title and the circumstances of David Balfour's kidnapping, there is practically nothing of the original story here. Alan Breck's character, with its cunning and vanity, is not so much altered as lost – he is shouting over and over again, 'To Edinburgh' or 'The Redcoats': he is only a set of teeth like those exhibited in the windows of cheap dentists . . . As for the girl with her great dewy eyes, her dimples and her tartan and her kissing mouth, she represents, I suppose, the love interest – as if there wasn't love enough in the original story to wither these wistful caresses and misunderstandings and virginal pursuits.

Graham had not retreated in face of the enemy and of course the enemy was not the American film industry as such. If Greene waged a vendetta at all it was against the worst aspects of Hollywood. Those films he could praise, he praised.

39

Brighton Rock

In art, we shed our sicknesses.
— JOSEPH CONRAD

W HEN in 1953 Martin Shuttleworth and Simon Raven interviewed Greene for the *Paris Review*, they came with some
preconceptions and a blunt approach. He was then living in a first
floor flat at the bottom of St James's Street, London, which seemed
to arouse their suspicions as much as did the surrounding area – 'black
with smartness, the Rolls-Royces and the bowler hats of the men are
black, the court shoes and the correct suits of the women are black
– not the sort of area in which one expects to find a novelist.' (Today
it is black with taxi cabs only.) The flat also troubled them, with its
snugness, its books, great padded armchairs: no suggestion of an
obsession or anything out of the ordinary – not even the Henry
Moore pastel, 'for so many people have Henry Moores these days' –
except perhaps for 'a collection of seventy-four different miniature
whisky bottles, ranged on top of a bookcase'.

What worried his interviewers most was that he seemed to be so
much happier than they had expected and the whole atmosphere (and
the whisky bottles) seemed to be the production 'of something much
more positive than that very limited optimum of happiness' that he had
described in *The Power and the Glory*: 'The world is all much of a piece;
it is engaged everywhere in the same subterranean struggle . . . there
is no peace anywhere where there is life; but there are quiet and active
sectors of the line.' And the contrast between his setting and that of so
many of his novels was marked. They quoted the suicidal Scobie in
The Heart of the Matter: 'Point me out the happy man and I will show
you either egotism, selfishness, evil or else an absolute ignorance.'

And so they suggested that his ruling passion, what they described
as his 'absorption with failure, pursuit and poverty', was simply a
fabrication on his part. His response was, 'I think that you have

misjudged me and my consistency. This flat, my way of life – these are simply my hole in the ground.' 'A moderately comfortable hole.' 'Shall we leave it at that?'

But they pressed him further: 'many of your most memorable characters, Raven for instance, are from low life. Have you ever had any experience of low life?' 'No . . . I have never known [poverty],' he responded, honestly. 'I was "short" yes, in the sense that I had to be careful for the first eight years of my adult life, but I have never been any closer.'[1] One wonders whether, in interviewing Shakespeare, they would have questioned him on his experience of living in a Scottish castle, fighting on the battlefield at Agincourt, stabbing an old man by mistake through an arras or – intentionally – a king, or being thrown out by his daughters in his old age. They were not acknowledging the writer's ability to research his fictional world carefully and the sympathetic interchange that can take place between his emotion and experience and that of his characters even though the circumstances are different; and that he can project the pattern of his obsessions – which was the case when Greene came to write *Brighton Rock* – into the life of fictional characters. Such critics fail to acknowledge the oddity and variety of this novel's origins, and the pathways down which it was to take Greene.

*

Brighton Rock was intended to be another successful thriller. Greene wrote to his mother in August 1936, when *A Gun for Sale* had been on the bookstalls for a month: 'A Gun seems to have been doing pretty well. I'm trying to follow up with another thriller, scene set at Brighton.' Certainly he was planning to deal with areas of human life that he did not 'know', the working and criminal class life of Brighton, the race-course gang feuds, the world of the Ravens and Pinkies.

But he had the curiosity and the desire to learn about people outside his own class, 'to discover what lies behind the dark, thick leaf of the aspidistra that guards like an exotic fungus the vulnerable gap between the lace curtains', and he was exact in his observations and had a great respect for the smallest detail. This was a real desire poetically expressed in the *Evening News* in 1930 as 'the hope that life would leave me ears . . . leave me eyes – "This wonder and this white/ Astonishment of sight".'

His strong voyeuristic streak was his first means of access to the experience of others. 'The disreputable geography of London is a fascinating study,' he wrote to Vivien (probably in August 1926), about his intention to explore unsavoury streets: 'It is funny how things run in streets. Half the blackmail or swindling cases live in Gerrard Street . . . a quite openly avaricious street in the usual way. But if *I* was a swindler I'd live in St John's Wood . . . not in a street which everyone knows is disreputable. In the same way the more violent criminals seem inclined to hang out in Charlotte Street. Then there's Bouverie Street . . . That, according to [Herbert], holds the pub where the Sabini gang have their headquarters. Quite likely that's true. He used to run up against weird people.'

One notices that he is already trying to think like a criminal, in an amateur way, and imagining himself linked up with the criminal world, as an earlier letter to Vivien shows: 'I must tell you of the incident that befell me yesterday afternoon, of the drunken jockey, who would be straight with me as long as I was straight with him which remark forced me out of mere joy in Buchanism to give him a false name and address, on his parting shake of the hand, and his straight it is, Mr Gough. We shall meet again. And my fear now that the Sabini gang will be on my steps since the horrid realisation that he was not drunk at all. If I am found with my throat cut call the police to enquire of Jockey Caley, Greenery Cottage, Park Lane, Newmarket!!'[2]

He appears to have been given a hot tip, because he adds humorously: 'In Friday morning's paper look at the Gatwick races. If a horse called Owen wins or gets a place, expect the news of my murder. If not, we'll meet again! Of course, I might get off with a dislocated jaw or a broken nose. Could you love me 2 inches with a broken nose?'

When Maclaren-Ross visited Greene at 14 North Side to discuss his adaptation for radio of *A Gun for Sale*, the question came up as to why Raven should speak in a Jewish manner. Raven was not Jewish, but Greene insisted that he would have a voice like that. 'He told me that when he worked for Korda, he had been taken round various clubs in the King's Cross area by a cameraman with underworld connections, and it was there that he had heard voices of the type he meant. "In one place the regulars only drank milk. It was owned by a great fat homosexual known as the Giant Pander . . . but the customers weren't queer. Very tough looking, razor scars and all that, but quiet. Very quiet. I asked if the milk was laced with brandy or anything, but they said no. Straight milk. Made it much more sinister I thought."'[3] And no doubt Greene got the idea of his boy criminal Pinkie drinking only milk from this.

As he began *Brighton Rock* in July 1936, he was still seeking the 'low life'. To his agent he wrote: 'I see the B.B.C. are running a series called From Darkness to Dawn. Hugh Ross Williamson did the first –

a night in a prison cell. Any chance of gate crashing into this lot? What I should like to do would be simply Central London, Piccadilly etc., the Corner House, the cabmen's shelters, the dingier clubs – like Smokey Joe's – between 2 & 6 say.'[4] *Brighton Rock* was to take him much further than this kind of research.

*

There are several layers to *Brighton Rock*. To begin with it was grounded in the town and the Brighton races, and the geography of Brighton does not, any more than does its human activity as portrayed in the novel, 'in part belong to an imaginary geographical region', as Graham Greene claimed. He knew Brighton well, no town at that time having had such a hold on his affections, and he kept close to its topography as he did to the topography of London in *It's a Battlefield*. But, vague as Henry James in tracing the sources of his material, he credits his fictional Brighton to the pressures of his fictional characters: 'Why did I exclude so much of the Brighton I really knew from this imaginary Brighton? I had every intention of describing it, but it was as though my characters had taken the Brighton *I* knew into their own consciousness and transformed the whole picture (I have never again felt so much the victim of my own inventions.)'[5] He came to use only those aspects of the city which were essential to his story.

He writes in *Ways of Escape*: 'The Brighton race gangs were to all intents quashed forever as a serious menace at Lewes Assizes a little before the date of my novel.' Now the Lewes case was reported in the *Brighton Argus* on 29 July 1936 (and in the London papers also) and immediately he wrote to Hugh: 'I've got to go to Brighton Races on either Aug. 4, 5, or 6. Mrs Frere-Reeves who was going to take me, can't manage the dates. I wonder if you and Helga feel inclined for a day of low sport on any of those days. I warn you that I shall want to spend my time in the lowest enclosure.'[6] The sense of realism, the excitement and drama of the scene at the races in the novel must derive from the author's visit to the races at that time, and his close observation of what was happening. The crowds 'stood packed deep on the tops of the trams rocking down to the Aquarium, they surged like some natural and irrational migration of insects up and down the front; the negro wearing a bright striped tie sat on a bench in the Pavilion garden and smoked a cigar.' Because black people in England were such a rarity then, it was natural that local working-class children would stop play, stare at him, and back slowly away. And Greene could well have seen a blind band playing drums and trumpets, walking in the gutter, scraping the sides of their shoes along the edge, just such a band as Pinkie met when he pushed the leader out of the way, swearing at him softly: 'the whole band hearing their leader move, shifted uneasily a foot into the roadway and stood there stranded . . . like barques becalmed on a huge and landless Atlantic. Then they edged back feeling for the landfall of the pavement.'[7] Graham pleads guilty in *Ways of Escape* 'to manufacturing this Brighton of mine',[8] but the St Dunstan's Home for blinded ex-servicemen stands on the coast two miles east of Brighton.

There are the public school grounds where the crowds milled past and where: 'the girls trooped solemnly out to hockey . . . through the wrought-iron main gates they could see the plebeian procession . . . plodding up the down, kicking up the dust, eating buns out of paper bags . . . up the steep hill came the crammed taxicabs – a seat for anyone at ninepence a time . . . It was as if the whole road moved upwards like an Underground staircase in the dusty sunlight, a creaking, shouting, jostling crowd of cars moving with it. The junior girls took to their heels like ponies racing on the turf . . . as if this were a day on which life for many people reached a kind of climax. The odds on Black Boy had shortened.'[9]

Greene must have had in mind here Roedean, which he would have passed on his way to the races, still standing today unchanged, and while no horse called Black Boy was running during the possible dates of Greene's visit, the local newspapers reported that a Blue Boy won the Balcombe stakes two months earlier in June 1936 at Brighton. In the novel, Hale, before he is murdered by Pinkie's mob, advises the barmaid, Ida, to bet on Black Boy – which wins. Blue Boy won at 10-1 and Ida put £25 on Black Boy at that price.

Like Pinkie and Spicer (whom Pinkie is later to murder), Graham and Hugh must have heard 'The loudspeakers on the vans', advising them 'whom to put their money with', and Graham's eyes, with that 'alert watchful quality, the eyeballs slightly bloodshot',[10] must have observed gypsy children chasing 'a rabbit with cries across the trampled chalk'. Like Pinkie they would have gone through the tunnel under the course and come up into 'the light and the short grey grass sloping down by the bungalow houses to the sea. Old bookies' tickets rotting into the chalk: "Barker for the Odds", a smug smiling nonconformist face printed in yellow: "Don't Worry I Pay", and old tote tickets among the stunted plantains.' And they would have gone 'through the wire fence into the half-crown [the cheapest] enclosure.'[11]

Then there is the case of Lobby Lud – an essential part of the plot. Lobby Lud was a made-up name for a man who worked for the popular liberal newspaper of that time, the *News Chronicle*. As a sales gimmick during August, Lobby Lud wandered round Brighton and through the holiday crowds, as the *News Chronicle* stated:

Following his Bank Holiday custom Lobby will be at Brighton today. Study his picture above and when you spot him show him your copy of today's *News Chronicle* and say:
    'You are Mr Lobby Lud, I claim the "News Chronicle" prize [of £10].'
Lobby is of medium height and has grey eyes and dark complexion. He leaves a number of clue cards worth 10s. each.
    Here is today's programme:
11 a.m. to 11.15 a.m. – At Brighton Station and proceed via Queen's Road, Clock Tower and West Street to Promenade.
11.15 a.m. to 11.45 a.m. – To West Pier.
11.45 a.m. to 12.15 p.m. – Along promenade between the Piers, passing Savoy Cinema just after noon.
12.15 p.m. to 12.45 p.m. – Within 100 yards of Palace Pier.
12.45 p.m. to 1. p.m. – On the Aquarium Sun Terrace.
1. p.m. to 2. p.m. – Lunch near Castle Square.
2. p.m. to 3. p.m. – If still undetected Lobby will proceed via North Street, Queen's Road to Brighton Station.

The next day, Tuesday 4 August 1936, the day Greene visited the Brighton Races, appeared the following account in the *News Chronicle*: 'At Forte's Cafe, opposite the pier [Lobby writes], I cooled myself with an ice cream and left a card under the ashtray on my table. By the Memorial a man with the "go-to-win fever" in his eyes bore down on me and finished a hectic run. He was Mr Herbert Gayler.'

The significance of this advertising gimmick for the novel was that it provided Greene with an occupation for his character Hale who, under the pseudonym Kolley Kibber,* represented the *Messenger* newspaper in Brighton on a Whitsun Bank Holiday as their mystery man: 'Advertised on every *Messenger* poster: "Kolley Kibber in Brighton today." In his pocket he had a packet of cards to distribute in hidden places along his route; those who found them would receive ten shillings from the *Messenger*, but the big prize was reserved for whoever challenged Hale in the proper form of words and with a copy of the *Messenger* in his hand: "You are Mr Kolley Kibber. I claim the *Daily Messenger* prize."' (*Brighton Rock*, p. 5.)

* Professor Cedric Watts has suggested that the pseudonym Kolley Kibber is adapted from the eighteenth-century actor-manager and Poet Laureate Colley Cibber (1671–1757).

And Kolley Kibber/Hale also had to stick closely to a programme: 'from ten till eleven Queen's Road and Castle Square, from eleven till twelve the Aquarium and Palace Pier, twelve till one the front between the Old Ship and West Pier, back for lunch between one and two in any restaurant he chose round the Castle Square, and after that he had to make his way all down the parade to the West Pier and then to the station by the Hove streets. These were the limits of his absurd and widely advertised sentry-go.'[12]

Hale's wanderings can be traced on the map of Brighton and Greene's descriptions of streets and buildings are precise. For example, while he is walking along the front, Hale turns into a pub where he first meets Ida: 'Somewhere out of sight a woman was singing, "When I came up from Brighton by train": a rich Guinness voice, a voice from a public bar. Hale turned into the private saloon and watched her big blown charms across two bars and through a glass partition.'[13] This pub is unnamed in the novel, but it was probably based on the 'Star and Garter', known locally as 'Dr Brighton's'. The ground floor lay-out resembled that in the novel and it would have been possible for someone, like Ida, to sing in one bar and be heard, and seen, in the adjoining bar.

Greene made use of the Lobby Lud situation very skilfully, by binding it into the plot in a way that increased the tension of the novel, for Hale 'knew, before he had been in Brighton three hours, that they [Pinkie's gang] meant to murder him', because he had grassed on Pinkie's boss, Kite, which led to Kite's murder.

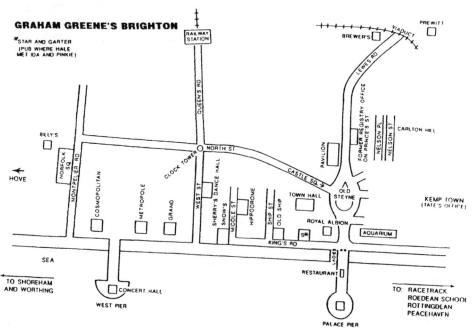

He realises that since his movements have been advertised in the *Daily Messenger* Pinkie's gang can keep track of him – he is in a trap. As he passes the Grand Hotel, twenty yards away was Cubitt, one of Pinkie's mob, keeping a check on him. He manages to establish contact with Ida, the singer in the bar, in order to protect himself. She makes him feel secure, but as they drive in a taxi to the Palace Pier, he knows that Pinkie is following in his old 1925 Morris car. Ida wants to go to the Aquarium and Black Rock – 'There's always something new on the Palace Pier' – but at the turnstile she leaves him to go to the ladies' lavatory and it is at the turnstile that he is picked up by Pinkie's mob – just opposite Forte's Cafe where Lobby Lud cooled himself with an ice cream.

Later in the novel, Pinkie's 'assistant', Spicer, in order to see whether the police will begin a reconstruction of Hale's kidnapping, goes back to the scene, and if today you were to take up the same position you would see what Spicer then saw: 'He took up his stand between the turnstile of the pier and the ladies' lavatory. There weren't many people about: He could spot the bogies [police] easily enough – if they came. Over there was the Royal Albion; he could see all the way up the Grand Parade to Old Steyne; the pale green domes of the Pavilion floated above the dusty trees; he could see anyone in the hot empty mid-week afternoon who went down below the Aquarium, the white deck ready for dancing, to the little covered arcade where the cheap shops stood between the sea and the stone wall, selling Brighton rock.'[14]

Old Steyne (sometimes spelt Old Steine) is still there and is one of the main central areas of the town, a cluster of roads and gardens running from the Royal Albion Hotel past the Royal Pavilion. The various hotels described in the novel add an extra interest. And what Hale observed, the drinking of cocktails, in the Grand Hotel must have been observed by Greene: Through Pinkie's eyes we see the Royal Albion and the Cosmopolitan: 'a well-known popular author displayed his plump too famous face in the window of the Royal Albion, staring out to sea.'[15] The Royal Albion is a distinguished hotel which attracted writers – Oscar Wilde in the 1890s and Greene often went there to write when he had a writer's block or wanted to finish a novel.

For the original of the Cosmopolitan, where women with bright brass hair and ermined coats have their heads close together like parrots and where the gangster Colleoni lived, we have to look elsewhere. Again the view of the hotel is Greene's filtered through Pinkie, who watches 'young men arriving in huge motoring coats accompanied by small tinted creatures, who rang like expensive glass when touched but [were] as sharp and tough as tin.' Colleoni asks Pinkie what happened to Kite:

'*You* won't want to hear the details. It wouldn't have happened if
we hadn't been crossed. A journalist thought he could put one
over on us.'

'What journalist's that?'

'You oughter read the inquests,' the Boy said.

Colleoni, totally undisturbed by Pinkie's threat, comments: 'Napoleon the Third used to have this room . . . and Eugenie.'[16] This
suggests that Greene had the Bedford Hotel in mind as a model for
the Cosmopolitan, for it was there that Charles Dickens wrote
Dombey and Son; and where Louis Napoleon, Napoleon III, stayed.

Brighton Greene knew, but not the gang life and he probably had
to 'fake' some of this. As he confessed in *Ways of Escape*: 'I had spent
only one night in the company of someone who could have belonged
to Pinkie's gang – a man from the Wandsworth dog-tracks whose
face had been carved because he was suspected of grassing to the
bogies after a killing at the stadium.'[17]

*

The bare facts of the tale seem to go back to his time with Korda
when Greene improvised a plot which led to the script of *The Green
Cockatoo* (originally called *Four Dark Hours*) in which Eileen, a young
West-country girl visiting London for the first time, accidentally
meets Dave Connor, who has just been stabbed at the railway station
by race-course gangsters he has double-crossed – his blood dripping
down on to the platform. This is developed in *A Gun for Sale* where
a gang leader called Kite tried to 'bump off' the leader of Raven's
gang and had his throat cut as he got out of a railway carriage: 'I cut
his throat', says Raven, 'and the others held him up till we were all
through the barrier in a bunch. Then we dropped him by the bookstall
and did a bolt.'[18] This is the situation in *Brighton Rock* where Hale
grasses on Kite (original leader of Pinkie's race gang whom Pinkie
looked on as a father) to the gangster Colleoni – who arranged his
death, which also takes place in a railway station – St Pancras. And
so Pinkie decided Hale had to be killed.

The kidnapping of Hale derives from the kidnapping of a man on
Brighton front in broad daylight, 'in the thirties'. He was found on
the Downs dead, as Greene records in *Ways of Escape*.* But the idea
of basing the novel on a race gang feud came from the Lewes Assize
case and certainly one incident – the attack on Pinkie and Spicer by

* The man was Ernest Friend Smith, aged 67. The incident happened in Madeira
Drive; not in the thirties but in April 1928. He was attacked by three men, thrown
into a car, taken to the Downs, battered and robbed. He died weeks later.

Colleoni's mob – derives from that case. The actual attack was made by sixteen men on Alfred Solomon, a bookmaker, and his clerk, Mark Frater. Solomon was struck several blows on the head and ran away but Frater was held and attacked with a hatchet and kicked. The attack was ended by the arrival of the police. In the same way, Pinkie and Spicer are attacked – but by men carrying razors. Spicer goes down and Pinkie is kicked and slashed and the arrival of the police ends the attack – Pinkie running away. The account in the *Brighton Argus* (29 July 1936) records the name of the leader of the attacking gang as Spinks, known as Spinky, and it is possible that Greene derived the name Pinkie from this.

Nevertheless, Greene asserted that 'there were no living models for these gangsters'. He also says that 'there was no living model for the barmaid, Ida, who so obstinately refused to come alive,'[19] but it could be that Mae West was the model – he had reviewed one of her films in the *Spectator* before he had begun writing *Brighton Rock*:

'Ah'm an Occidental wooman, in an Awriental mood.' The big-busted carnivorous creature in tight white sequins sits as firmly and inscrutably for inspection as the fat tattooed women in the pleasure arcades. The husky voice drones, the plump jewelled fingers pluck, the eyes slant, and immediately we are in the familiar atmosphere . . . the friendly, smoky, alcoholic atmosphere of a Private Bar, hung with advertisements for Guinness.[20]

Ida of course drinks only Guinness, sings songs in what Greene calls 'a rich Guinness voice' as Hale watches her big blown charms across two bars. 'She wasn't old, somewhere in the late thirties or the early forties . . . she was only a little drunk in a friendly accommodating way. You thought of sucking babies when you looked at her, but if she'd borne them she hadn't let them pull her down: she took care of herself. Her lipstick told you that, the confidence of her big body.' The next sentence Greene invented but it smacks of a Mae West witticism: 'She was well-covered, but she wasn't careless; she kept her lines for those who cared for lines.'[21] Ida is pleasure-seeking: 'She was cheery, she was healthy, she could get a bit lit with the best of them. She liked a good time, her big breasts bore their carnality frankly down the Old Steyne, but you had only to look at her to know that you could rely on her. She wouldn't tell tales to your wife, she wouldn't remind you next morning of what you wanted to forget.'[22]

If we accept that Mae West is Greene's model then the parallels are many. Hale invites Ida to have a meal with him but she plays to her audience, as well as to Hale, with Mae West posturing:

'Where shall we go, Sir Horace? To the Old Ship?'

'Yes,' Hale said. 'If you like the Old Ship.'

'Hear that,' she told them in all the bars . . . her own half dozen cronies. 'This gentleman's invited me to the Old Ship,' she said in a mock-refined voice. 'Tomorrow I shall be delighted, but today I have a prior engagement at the Dirty Dog.'[23]

Mae West's description of herself as 'a girl who lost her reputation but never missed it' could be said of Ida, and their philosophies are similar: 'It's better to be looked over than overlooked' (Mae West). And just as Greene ultimately changed his opinion of Mae West so also Ida is seen as a perpetually friendly but superficial person whom no man can satisfy, as his description of her when she has won on the races and can afford to take Phil Corkery to the Cosmopolitan for a dirty weekend shows:

> Then she got up slowly and began to undress. She never believed in wearing much: it wasn't any time at all before she was exposed in the long mirror: a body firm and bulky: a proper handful. She stood on a deep soft rug, surrounded by gilt frames and red velvet hangings, and a dozen common and popular phrases bloomed in her mind – 'A Night of Love', 'You Only Live Once', and the rest. She bore the same relation to passion as a peepshow. She sucked the chocolate between her teeth and smiled, her plump toes working in the rug, waiting for Mr Corkery – just a great big blossoming surprise.[24]

The image of the gull which is used at different important moments to suggest the true nature of a person, in this case to underscore the predatory nature of Ida, ends the chapter, 'A gull swooped screaming down to a dead crab beaten and broken against the iron foundation of the pier. It was the time of near-darkness and of the evening mist from the Channel and of love.'[25] Yet it is Ida who is the avenger figure in the novel, searching out Pinkie after Hale has been killed by having a stick of Brighton rock thrust down his throat.

The strangest aspect of the novel, however, is the development of the religious theme which changed it from a story about gang warfare into a struggle between good and evil set against a representative background of human society. As Arthur Calder-Marshall put it:

> *Brighton Rock* was sparked off by the fights between the Brighton Race gangs. But the theme, the conflict between the two moral worlds, that of Good and Evil and Right and Wrong, was not

inherent in the plot as given by research. It was a working out of a conflict in Graham's nature, which was posed acutely by the political situation in the 1930's. Pinkie's Credo in Unum Satanum (a phrase no Pinkie in real life would have coined) seems to me to have been based upon Graham's own pre-conversion experience of evil. If Satan exists, God must.[26]

Pinkie, therefore, did not need to be based on any gangster known to Greene because he is a character from a morality play – a tortured soul – just as his girl-friend is the ultimate representation of innocence totally outside the arena of evil. We have seen how Greene, very early in life, through the influence of Carter and of Visconti in *The Viper of Milan*, came to accept that evil is not necessarily something which comes with age and experience. It exists, it is there at any age, and he had not forgotten his experience of it, and thus also the oddity of Pinkie's extreme youth is not an oddity to Greene. References to dividers in the story point back to Greene's experience, each time in a context of sadism.

When Pinkie is slashed with a razor on the racecourse by Colleoni's men, he is 'filled with horror and astonishment as if one of the bullied brats at school had stabbed first with the dividers'.[27] Though earlier, when Pinkie is playing with Spicer like a cat with a mouse, treating him well, buying a glass of beer, insisting that he enjoy himself – ' "You're a fine fellow, Spicer", the Boy said, squeezing his arm . . . "Go on", the Boy said, "have a good time while you can." '[28] – the Boy is seen by Greene as being 'like a cruel child who hides the dividers behind him [as] he put his hand with spurious affection on Spicer's arm', and all the time we know that he intends to murder Spicer. He even enjoys the pleasures of the *double entendre*:

> 'I don't mind telling you. I'm going to make it up with Colleoni . . .'
> 'I'm all for peace,' Spicer said. 'I always have been.'
> The Boy grinned through the broken windscreen at the long disorder of cars. 'That's what I'm going to arrange,' he said.
> 'A peace that lasts,' Spicer said.
> 'No one's going to break this peace,' the Boy said.[29]

Pinkie's schooling was not, of course, the same as Carter's – it was the rough schooling of the extremely poor of the 1930s and was probably based on a film Greene reviewed in *Night and Day* on 14 October 1937 (when his novel was still uncompleted), *Children at School*: 'A small child hurries down a dreary concrete passage . . .

Cracks in the ceiling and the beams, damp on the walls, hideous Gothic exteriors of out-of-date schools, spiked railings, narrow windows, scarred cracked playgrounds of ancient concrete . . . the wire dustbin, the chipped basin, the hideous lavatory-seat and the grinding of trains behind the school-yard.' It was at just such a school that Pinkie bullied at his desk and in the concrete playground. Significantly, too, it is in that review that Greene first uses the phrase, to describe the school's conditions, '. . . hell too lies about us in our infancy'. The phrase obviously seemed appropriate to Pinkie, for when, at the end of Part Two, the police Inspector advises him to leave Brighton – 'you're too young to run a racket if you ask me' – although Pinkie grins as he leaves the charge room, there 'was poison in his veins . . . he had been insulted. He was going to show the world. They thought because he was only seventeen . . . he jerked his narrow shoulders back at the memory that he'd killed his man, and these bogies who thought they were clever weren't clever enough to discover that. He trailed the clouds of his own glory after him: hell lay about him in his infancy. He was ready for more deaths.'[30]

Greene returned to the phrase in the Prologue to *The Lawless Roads* when, in discussing cruelty at his school, citing the three persons he knew there who had a genuine quality of evil, he ends the paragraph: 'Hell lay about them in their infancy.' The phrase is, of course, a sardonic reversal of a passage in Wordsworth's 'Intimations of Immortality' which presents an idealised view of childhood:

> But trailing clouds of glory do we come
>   From God, who is our home:
> Heaven lies about us in our infancy!

– a view which Greene, with his Catholic preoccupation with original sin, must have loathed.

In line with his socialism of that time he is seeing young lives blighted by squalid early years in overcrowded slums. As late as 1979 he felt able to say to Marie-Françoise Allain: 'I don't think that Pinkie was guilty of mortal sin because his actions were not committed in defiance of God, but arose out of the conditions to which he had been born.'[31]

Perhaps, but Pinkie is not merely a victim of the slums. Central to this novel is the Boy's passionate desire to commit evil. This is his private temperament and thus there is never a sense that Pinkie is Pinkie because of his social background. Part of the rich power of the novel derives from the fact that Pinkie is defiant and seeks with a religious passion his own damnation. The sociological fact of slum life is better revealed in the total apathy of Rose's parents in Nelson Place, and their willingness to sell their daughter to Pinkie for fifteen guineas. Moreover, there are elements of the human spirit that are made, not deformed, by such a background. Rose is an example of the slum having no corrupting influence on her natural purity of mind and spirit.

Greene had foreseen the development of the religious theme as early as 9 April 1937 when he wrote to Nancy Pearn enclosing the first 30,000 words of the novel plus a synopsis. The synopsis, unfortunately, has not survived, but in his letter he writes: 'Here is a rather confusing summary of what may or may not happen next. The real point – not to be breathed into *Nash's* ears – is the contrast between the ethical mind (Ida's) and the religious (the Boy's and Rose's) in thriller terms.' This, as Arthur Calder-Marshall said, was a long way from the Brighton race-course gangs, and it would seem to be a working out of the relationship between Good and Evil, God and Satan, and the precarious and continuous balance between the two: a world view presented in what to Greene was really neutral ground – beyond his personal experience, but tapping his own fundamental view of mankind and religious beliefs. What he is demonstrating in the novel is the limitations of religious beliefs which do not accept the existence of innate evil.

In August 1932, he records in his diary how he was given a lift by a driver of a Lyons' van on one of his long walks. The driver was also a member of Toc H (a society for the maintenance of comradeship after the First World War), but his views did not please Greene:

> 'Service', [the driver] said, was the motto, & told of the little innocuous services done to individuals, reading to sick men in bed, the bringing of flowers, comparable to the Scout's daily good deed . . . they are doing good, but it is good to the individual: they exaggerate the importance of the individual . . . they are as harmless and useless as their non-sectarian prayers; they have no enemies, in the same way as the devil has none.

Perhaps Greene's attitude comes out most strongly in Rose Macaulay's account which appears in her *Letters to a Friend*: 'Graham Greene is somewhat different! I was dining with him last Friday. An amusing little company . . . It was in a restaurant, and . . . I was upholding the Anglican point of view against Graham's assertions that only R.C.s were capable of real sin because the rest of us were invincibly ignorant.'[32] So Ida is invincibly ignorant. She has no religious sense – she is for life with a capital L: 'Life was sunlight on brass bedposts,

Ruby port, the leap of the heart when the outsider you have backed passes the post and the colours go bobbing up. Life was poor Fred's mouth pressed down on hers in the taxi, vibrating with the engine along the parade.'[33]

Neither has she any idea of the spiritual life, of heaven or hell. She believes 'only in ghosts, ouija boards, tables which rapped and inept little voices speaking plaintively of flowers'. Nothing is more comic than Ida and Old Crabbe playing the board and seeking guidance as to how to act. 'History has many cunning passages, contrived corridors', and Ida has gone down one of them, but she has retained a strong, pragmatic sense of Right and Wrong and so, because there is no one to see the murdered Hale off, she will go to the funeral and pay her last respects – ' "Someone ought to be *there*." "He won't care who's putting him in the ground," her companion objects, but "You never know", Ida said, remembering the ghost by the radio set. "It shows respect. Besides – I *like* a funeral." '[34]

There were 'no unhygienic buryings' in the suburb where Hale had lodged – only cremations, and for the scene at the crematorium Greene goes back to his experience of his mother-in-law's cremation. There are the 'Two brick towers . . . cloisters with little plaques along the walls like school war memorials, a bare cold secular chapel which could be adapted quietly and conveniently to any creed: no cemetery, wax flowers, impoverished jam-pots of wilting wild flowers.'[35] This, of course, is not part of Brighton except in the sense that it is part of the religious dimension, or rather the unreligious dimension, of the fictional town, and leads the author into a critical assessment of the pretence at religion which smooths out the difficult facts of life and death with which true religion deals. The clergyman tells the congregation that ' "our belief in heaven . . . is not qualified by our disbelief in the old medieval hell . . . We believe that this our brother is already at one with the One" . . . He stamped his words like little pats of butter', and claimed, ' "the certainty that our brother is at this moment reabsorbed in the universal spirit" . . . He touched a little buzzer, the New Art doors opened, the flames flapped and the coffin slid smoothly down into the fiery sea.'

Such strong religious condemnation would seem out of place in a thriller if it were not that the religious connotations of the world of *Brighton Rock* are primary and that they stem from the author's own strong convictions.

As Ida leaves the crematorium, 'from the twin towers . . . fumed the very last of Fred, a thin stream of grey smoke . . . Fred dropped in indistinguishable grey ash . . . he became part of the smoke nuisance over London, and Ida wept.'[36] So here we have another ironic reversal: out of the ouija boards and table-tapping and the thinly disguised scientific and hygienic disposal of the human remains, comes Ida's revenge, and her decision about what must be done to avenge Hale's murder.

It is only towards the end of the novel that Pinkie becomes aware of the potential threat of Ida: 'The Boy looked across the tea-room and the empty tables to where the woman sat. How she hung on. Like a ferret he'd seen on the Downs, among the chalky holes, fastened to a hare's throat.' Years earlier, when he was researching for his first novel *The Man Within*, Greene wrote to Vivien about a ferret he had seen on the Downs with its teeth fastened into a hare's throat.

*

Ida's view of life and death is protected not only by spiritualism but also by sentimentality: 'she cried in cinemas at *David Copperfield* . . . her homely heart was touched by the word "tragedy", easy pathos touched her friendly and popular heart.'[37] And she has a remorseless and dangerous optimism: 'To lose your lover – "broken hearts," she would say, "always mend", to be maimed or blinded – "lucky," she'd tell you, "to be alive at all." ' She considered that Papists treated death with flippancy, 'life wasn't so important perhaps to them as what came after: but to her [in spite of spiritualism] death was the end of everything', and so she took life with a deadly seriousness: 'she was prepared to cause any amount of unhappiness to anyone in order to defend the only thing she believed in.'[38]

Opposed to her secular view is Pinkie's Catholic heritage which includes a firm belief in Hell: 'These atheists, they don't know nothing. Of course there's Hell. Flames and damnation . . . torments', a concept which reflects Pinkie's sadism. Heaven he does not concede fully: ' "And Heaven too", Rose said with anxiety . . . "Oh, maybe", the Boy said, "maybe".'[39] And when his crooked lawyer says to him, quoting the dramatist Marlowe: 'You know what Mephistopheles said to Faustus when he asked where Hell was? He said, "Why, this [world] is Hell, nor are we out of it," ' he is obviously putting into words a further extension of Pinkie's experience – 'The Boy watched him with fascination and fear.'[40] Pinkie shows not so much the sadness of corruption, but the vicious childishness of it and its persistence, in deliberately seeking out the worst actions for sadistic pleasure: 'Life was good walking outside the white sun-drenched wall . . . towards the finest of all sensations, the infliction of pain.'[41]

Today Greene would say – and has – that he does not believe in Hell, but he did believe in it, not after death, but as a condition of human life, and he believed, long before Hitler appeared, in the existence of evil. In an interview with Marie-Françoise Allain he asked, after rejecting the idea of eternal damnation, 'How can one deny the existence of total evil?' Pinkie's vision of the human condition is one of evil, from birth to death, and beyond. There are and have to be, 'Flames . . . damnation . . . torments', or Pinkie could not enjoy his sadistic way of life or justify his existence. Rose, speaking as Ida would have spoken, says, 'Life's not so bad', but the Boy's answer is: 'Don't you believe it . . . I'll tell you what it is. It's gaol; it's not knowing where to get some money. Worms and cataract, cancer. You hear 'em shrieking from the upper windows – children being born.'[42] This probably derives from Greene's experience on returning from Africa and hearing the wail of a child in a tenement, 'too young to speak, too young to have learnt what the dark may conceal in the way of lust and murder, crying . . . because it still possessed the ancestral fear, the devil was dancing in its sleep.'[43] But if so, it has become linked with a sociological explanation of Pinkie's Satanism, the inversion of 'I believe in one God' to 'Credo in unum Satanum'.

When Pinkie returns to Nelson Place, near to where he was born, he sees children: 'A child with a leg in an iron brace limped blindly into him; he pushed it off; someone said in a high treble, "Stick 'em up". They took his mind back and he hated them for it; it was like the dreadful appeal of innocence, but *there* was not innocence; you had to go back a long way further before you got to innocence, innocence was a slobbering mouth, a toothless gum pulling at the teats; perhaps not even that; innocence was the ugly cry of birth.'[44]

Greene does explain Pinkie in sociological terms, eventually, returning to his own experience: 'The impressions of childhood are ineffaceable', and what is distinctive about Pinkie and Rose is that they appear to be so young, a fact commented upon by several characters. Indeed when the manageress of Snow's restaurant finds them together in the basement, where Rose had been tending the injuries Pinkie received in the fight at the race-course, she says, 'Child . . . what are you doing here? and who's the other child?' 'If you weren't so young', she tells Pinkie, 'I'd call the police . . . You're both too young for this sort of thing' – implying sex, ironic given Pinkie's hatred of it.

Pinkie is in one sense a puritan – he doesn't drink or bet (though he makes a living forcing bookies to pay for 'protection'), but he has a delight in the infliction of pain and also an aversion to sex, a desire to retain his virginity that goes beyond the normal and stems from the conditions of his childhood home and the 'frightening weekly exercise of his parents which he watched from his single bed': 'the stealthy movements of his parents in the other bed. It was Saturday night. His father panted like a man at the end of a race and his mother made a horrifying sound of pleasurable pain. He was filled with hatred, disgust, loneliness: he was completely abandoned: he had no share in their thoughts – for the space of a few minutes he was dead, he was like a soul in purgatory watching the shameless act of a beloved person.'[45]

Greene had on several occasions watched the sexual activities of others. Moreover, his glimpse of the governess, Gwen Howell, on the beach showing a length of naked thigh becomes part of Pinkie's experience – with a certain difference: 'he saw the skin of [Rose's] thigh for a moment above the artificial silk, and a prick of sexual desire disturbed him like a sickness.'[46] The idea of marriage fills Pinkie with nausea: 'He didn't want *that* relationship with anyone: the double bed, the intimacy, it sickened him like the idea of age. He crouched in the corner . . . vibrating up and down in bitter virginity. To marry – it was like ordure on the hands.'

Pinkie's horror at the thought that Rose might be pregnant might derive from a totally different angle, from Greene's own anxiety at his wife's second pregnancy and the difficulties he felt he had in providing for a family: 'He had never thought of that. He watched her with terror as if he were watching the ugly birth itself, the rivet of another life already pinning him down.' We know how distressed Greene was over Vivien's suffering at the birth of their first child.

It is perhaps impossible to know what made Greene turn *his* gangster into a young sadist but we can speculate. When Greene was planning the novel he reviewed in the *Spectator* of 1 May 1936 a film innocuously entitled *These Three*, which probably opened old wounds he had received at school from his enemy Carter: 'These three [adults] represent innocence in an evil world – the world of childhood, the world of moral chaos, lies, brutality, complete inhumanity. Never before has childhood been represented so convincingly on the screen, with an authenticity guaranteed by one's own memories. The more than human evil of the lying sadistic child is suggested with quite shocking mastery . . . it has enough truth and intensity to stand for the whole of the dark side of childhood.' Pinkie indeed stands for 'the more than human evil'.

There is much that is odd about this novel. It may start out as simple feuding between rival gangs but that is not how it ends. Instead of continuing the gang war Pinkie turns against his own, killing Spicer, excluding Cubitt, and cleverly devising a suicide pact with Rose, with the proviso that she shoots herself first. John Lehmann may be right to say that Greene knew very little about the mentality of gangsters, but he knew about Pinkie, because his source, in part, lies in Carter and in himself. The aspect of Pinkie which reflects Carter's character most nearly is his ability to toy with his enemies, pretend a friendship, hint a danger, humour his victim:

> 'We'll be going, Fred,' the Boy said.
> Hale rose. His hands were shaking. This was real now . . . The ground moved under his feet, and only the thought of where they might take him . . . saved him from fainting. But even then common pride, the instinct not to make a scene, remained overpoweringly strong; embarrassment had more force than terror, it prevented him crying his fear aloud, it even urged him to go quietly.

Perhaps the ground moved under Graham Greene when, as a boy, Carter approached him. Or witness Pinkie's playing with poor Spicer:

> 'You'll have to disappear, Spicer.'
> 'What do you mean?' . . . 'Disappear? . . . You wouldn't do anything' . . .
> 'Why,' the Boy said, 'what do you think I mean? I mean take a holiday' . . . 'And where will you go, Spicer?' . . . His mind was quite made up, and for the second time in a few weeks he looked at a dying man. He couldn't help feeling inquisitive.

These are reflections of Greene's own experiences thrown over the life of his characters, giving them credibility. It does seem that the interest in and motivation of sex in the novel stems from Greene's own strong sexuality, as Otto Preminger has observed in his autobiography: 'Though he gives a first impression of being controlled, correct, and British, he is actually mad about women. Sex is on his mind all the time.'[47]

*

The influence of the rites of the Roman Catholic Church and Greene's fascination with the chastity of priesthood are also sources of Pinkie's disgust with sex, and of his sadism and Satanism. 'Why, I was in a choir once', he confides to Rose, and 'suddenly he began to sing softly in his spoilt boy's voice: "Agnus dei qui tollis peccata mundi, dona nobis pacem." In his voice a whole lost world moved – the lighted corner below the organ, the smell of incense and laundered surplices, and the music.'[48] And he tells Dallow that when he was a kid he swore he would be a priest:

644

'A priest? You a priest? That's good,' Dallow said. He laughed without conviction, uneasily shifted his foot so that it trod in a dog's ordure.

'What's wrong with being a priest?' the Boy asked. 'They know what's what. They keep away' – his whole mouth and jaw loosened: he might have been going to weep: he beat out wildly with his hands towards the window . . . *Married Passion*, the horror – 'from this.'[49]

In plotting Pinkie's descent into corruption Greene was assisted by his study of a failed priest, for a source for the overall conception was the life of Frederick Rolfe, self-styled Baron Corvo, who fascinated Greene. He reviewed Rolfe's work twice in 1934 and once in 1935, and also A. J. A. Symons's biography of Rolfe, *The Quest for Corvo*. Rolfe was 'born for the Church'; he wanted to be a priest but was expelled from Scots College in Rome, from which tragedy he never recovered, for Rolfe's vice was 'spiritual more than it was carnal'. Like Pinkie, Rolfe loathed female flesh and took an oath to remain twenty years unmarried.

The uniqueness of Rolfe to Greene was that he was an example of someone living life on a different, even heroic level – a return to the days of Dante or Milton: 'Temptation, one feels, is seldom today so heroically resisted or so devastatingly succumbed to.' Both Pinkie and Rolfe actively seek their own damnation. Through Rolfe, Greene was able to perceive that during the period of the Edwardians, 'the age of bicycles and German bands and gold chamber ware, of Norfolk jackets and deerstalker caps', there could be a battle for the soul, 'of eternal issues, of the struggle between good and evil, between vice that really demands to be called satanic and virtue of a kind which can only be called heavenly.' Compared to Rolfe, those ordinary men he had to deal with – Monsignor Benson, Mr Pirie-Gordon, the partners of the publishers Chatto and Windus – 'beckon and speak like figures on the other side of a distorting glass pane. They have quite a different reality, a much thinner reality, they are not concerned with eternal damnation.'[50] Out of this struggle Pinkie and Rose were born: ' "You don't want to listen too much to priests," [Pinkie said]. "They don't know the world like I do. Ideas change, the world moves on . . ." His words stumbled before her carved devotion. That face said as clearly as words that ideas never changed, the world never moved: it lay there always, the ravaged and disputed territory between the two eternities. They faced each other as it were from opposing territories.'[51]

It is stressed often enough in the novel that the battle in which

Pinkie and Rose are involved is not between the Right and Wrong of human justice, but the spiritual one between Good and Evil. Greene concluded his third review of Rolfe with a quotation from T. S. Eliot: 'Most people are only a very little alive; and to awaken them to the spiritual is a very great responsibility: it is only when they are so awakened that they are capable of real Good, but that at the same time they become first capable of Evil.'[52]

Eliot's essay on Baudelaire, a Satanist, suggests a further significant source for Greene's vision in *Brighton Rock*: 'Baudelaire has perceived that what distinguishes the relations of man and woman from the copulation of beasts is the knowledge of Good and Evil . . . which are not natural . . . Right and Wrong.'[53] Baudelaire's view of sex is Pinkie's: 'la volupté unique et suprême de l'amour gît dans la certitude de faire le mal.' (The sole and supreme pleasure in love lies in the absolute knowledge of doing evil.)[54] For Pinkie, marrying Rose is simply another act of evil: 'He had a sense now that the murders of Hale and Spicer were trivial acts, a boy's game, and he had put away childish things. Murder had only led up to this – this corruption. He was filled with awe at his own powers.'[55] He knows that what he had started had not ended: 'It wasn't only Spicer. He had started something on Whit Monday which had no end. Death wasn't an end; the censer swung and the priest raised the Host.'[56]

When Rose begins to suspect she might be pregnant – '"You don't want a murderer's baby"', Ida says – she has a 'sense of glory. A child . . . and that child would have a child . . . it was like raising an army of friends for Pinkie'.[57] But Pinkie even then is plotting her death because she might, innocently, give him away to the police, though whether 'she were straight and loved him' didn't matter – he is determined to kill again. And he decides on the means – 'suppose she killed herself? And an insane pride throbbed in his breast; he felt inspired: it was like a love of life returning to the blank heart.'[58] He persuades her to agree to a suicide pact (which he will not in fact take part in) because Ida will one day get the evidence against him and that would separate them, forever.

There is a battle for Pinkie's soul between the powers of Good and Evil, as there was in the case of Marlowe's Dr Faustus, but in *Brighton Rock* it shows itself through his recollections of his childhood experiences of the Catholic Church ritual. A curious aspect is that as he moves towards acts of increasing evil he unconsciously recalls religious phrases: 'He began softly to intone – "Dona nobis pacem".' 'He won't', says Rose. 'What do you mean?' 'Give us peace.' A sentimental, romantic film inexplicably makes him weep, his mind giving him a vision of 'limitless freedom: no fear, no hatred, no envy.

It was as if he were dead and were remembering the effect of a good confession, the words of absolution: but . . . he couldn't experience contrition – the ribs of his body were like steel bands which held him down to eternal unrepentance.'[59] Which is what he is doomed to.

He reaches the Peacehaven Hotel (there was a Peacehaven Hotel along the coast from Brighton) and persuades her to write a suicide note. 'Say you couldn't live without me, something like that.' As he brings himself closer to the killing of Rose, the pressure on him grows and the supernatural battle for his soul proceeds: 'He found that he remembered it all without repulsion; he had a sense that somewhere, like a beggar outside a shuttered house, tenderness stirred, but he was bound in a habit of hate . . . Going down stairs to her and getting his story right for the authorities: "He hadn't known she was all that unhappy, he would say, because they'd got to part she must have found the gun in Dallow's room and brought it with her."' Pinkie's determination to do evil does not waver. Nevertheless there is this sense of more than human powers hovering – 'the huge darkness pressed a wet mouth against the panes and again he felt the prowling presence of pity.' They drive away from the hotel. God's angel, this time in the form of wings, comes to him:

An enormous emotion beat on him; it was like something trying to get in; the pressure of gigantic wings against the glass. Dona nobis pacem. He withstood it . . . If the glass broke, if the beast – whatever it was – got in, God knows what it would do. He had a sense of huge havoc – the confession, the penance and the sacrament – and awful distraction, and he drove blind into the rain.

The words of the Mass touch him for the last time: 'He was in the world and the world was made by Him, and the world knew Him not.' But he gives her precise instructions: '"All you need do is pull on this. It isn't hard. Put it in your ear – that'll hold it steady."' '"When it's over, I'll come back an' do it too"' . . . He says, '"It'll be too dark for me to see much."'

Such is the power of this scene that one feels that Greene is living out his own instructions to himself when, at twenty, he tried Russian roulette. Instructions to oneself are terrible enough, but turn those instructions around, apply them to another, act out the part of the devil's advocate and they become evil indeed: 'Put it in your ear – that'll hold it steady.' The inner journey of a novelist sometimes means mentally roaming in consort with the evil of a psychotic killer: 'Answer how well or ill he steered his soul', wrote the authors of *The Witch of Edmonton*, 'By Heaven's or by Hell's compass.'

As he tried to persuade Rose to shoot herself near the cliffs, Dallow (his one loyal friend) and Ida (his persistent enemy) appear together with the police. Pinkie takes out a bottle of vitriol he always carries:

'Where's that gun?' Pinkie said again. He screamed with hate and fear, 'My God, have I got to have a massacre?' . . .

She could see his face indistinctly as it leant in over the little dashboard light. It was like a child's, badgered, confused, betrayed: fake years slipped away – he was whisked back toward the unhappy playground. He said, 'You little . . .' he didn't finish . . . he left her, diving into his pocket for something. 'Come on, Dallow,' he said, 'you bloody squealer,' and put his hand up. Then she couldn't tell what happened: glass – somewhere – broke, he screamed and she saw his face – steam. He screamed and screamed, with his hands up to his eyes; he turned and ran; she saw a police baton at his feet and broken glass. He looked half his size, doubled up in appalling agony; it was as if the flames had literally got him and he shrank – shrank into a schoolboy flying in panic and pain, scrambling over a fence, running on.

'Stop him,' Dallow cried: it wasn't any good: he was at the edge, he was over: they couldn't even hear a splash. It was as if he'd been withdrawn suddenly by a hand out of any existence – past or present, whipped away into zero – nothing.[60]

The major question put in the novel is the nature of God's mercy, both on earth and in the after-life, working on the assumption that there is one. It is presented through the phrase, 'Between the stirrup and the ground', which occurs on at least six occasions, the first one being when Pinkie (an unlikely fellow to have known it) says to Rose, 'You know what they say – "Between the stirrup and the ground, he something sought and something found".' 'Mercy', she says. 'That's right: Mercy.' This is a quotation from a poem by William Camden (1551–1623): 'Betwixt the stirrup and the ground/ Mercy I asked, mercy I found.' But mercy, both human and divine, is a questionable factor in the world of *Brighton Rock*. After Pinkie's death, Rose goes to St John's (an actual Catholic church in Brighton) to confess, but she does not want absolution: 'I want to be like him – damned.' The priest gives her the example of Péguy: 'There was a man, a Frenchman . . . who had the same idea as you. He was a good man, a holy man, and he lived in sin all through his life, because he couldn't bear the idea that any soul could suffer damnation . . . This man decided that if any soul was going to be damned, he would be damned too . . . You can't conceive, my child, nor can I or anyone the . . . appalling . . . strangeness of the mercy of God.'[61]

Rose is convinced that Pinkie is damned. Not only did he die without absolution, but: 'He knew what he was about. He was a Catholic too.' The priest's response is, 'Corruptio optimi est pessima.' (The corruption of the best is the worst.) 'Hope and pray,' he tells her. 'If he loved you, surely, that shows there was some good . . .' And so she goes home looking forward to playing the record Pinkie made on their wedding day and hearing the message she had not yet heard. She goes with hope, but she is walking 'towards the worst horror of all'. What Pinkie had recorded was, 'God damn you, you little bitch, why can't you go back home forever and let me be?'[62] So much for hope.

*

Brighton Rock was written as a thriller and described by Greene as one of his 'entertainments', but its religious theme, its examination of the Roman Catholic religion, makes it his first Catholic novel, his first enquiry into the ways of man and God, and the novel obviously was inspired by his own conversion and his own questioning of those ways. It was to lead on to *The Power and the Glory* and *The End of the Affair*.

Rose Macaulay, after reading the novel, wrote to a friend: 'I wonder if you have yet finished *Brighton Rock*. The end is horrifying; the suicide pact, the horrible death, and then poor little Rose left alone with that awful gramophone record . . . Pinkie is allowed to die in mortal sin, without time to save himself by absolution as he had counted on. This is certainly poetic justice.'[63] Marghanita Laski, almost twenty years later, concluded that 'the ending is most memorable, the most painful any novelist has ever written.'[64] In whatever way Greene has reassessed his religious beliefs over the years, it is certain that the new dimension his conversion brought to his view of man and God brought also a new dimension to his fiction.

He finished writing the novel soon after the closing down of *Night and Day*. He and his friends had lost their jobs, and his income was worryingly reduced. He must have felt bitter. Mexico was ahead, but it was not then certain that a publisher would stake him for the trip. On 17 January 1938 he wrote to his publisher about *Brighton Rock*:

The novel in its last 5,000 words has turned round and bit me. (I've never had such a bother with a book: I suppose because I've never been able to concentrate on it for two months together), so I'm going off to a country pub, I hope, tomorrow evening to finish it.

As usual Greene decided on the title for the novel: 'I've made Frere quite happy about the title which I'm convinced is a good one.' In *Ways of Escape*, he records that the Brighton authorities 'proved a little sensitive to the picture I had drawn of their city, and it must have galled them to see my book unwittingly advertised at every sweetstall – "Buy Brighton Rock".'[65]

PART 8

Mexico

40

'I want to get out of
this bloody country'

Boredom – so often the mask of fear.
— MONICA FURLONG

Soon after his twenty-first birthday, Greene wrote to Vivien, 'as long as I can remember I've had a certain instinct that I should be killed before I was 32. I can't remember the time when I wasn't certain. Like the Apostolic Succession, it fades into the mists.' Perhaps that was why he went to Liberia when he was thirty-one – in order to test the validity of this instinct. It was not valid: in this case his mediumistic powers failed him. In the month of his thirty-third birthday a sketch of him done by Geoffrey Wylde appeared in the *London Mercury*. What is remarkable about this is that though *Night and Day* had then closed down and he was without a job, his reputation as a novelist, poet and literary editor was such that the sketch simply carried his name and the date when it was done – no other information seemed necessary.

The sketch shows a man with the touch of youth still about him – the youthfulness that had led him to rush the boy he was tutoring round the garden in an old pram and, after a rather alcoholic lunch with Patrick Ransome (who had shares in *Night and Day* and who was confined to a wheel-chair), led him to run him 'at top speed in his chair down Cecil Court while he shrieked at the astonished shoppers with laughter and fear'. But the Wylde drawing reveals other aspects of Greene.

There is the transparency of his eyes as he leans backwards and to his right side (waistcoated with the bottom button, according to custom, unbuttoned). Young in the face, he is not young in the eyes, which are wide-awake, expectant, with a strange fixed look as if he were anticipating future experiences and terrors. Elizabeth Montagu, who knew him in Vienna at the time of the making of *The Third*

Man, recalled going with him to the night-clubs which spawned in Vienna: 'Hideous they were . . . where did such hags come from? – this was February 1948, and four years into peace. Hour after hour in such dives. It was always late and I longed to prop my eyes open with a matchstick – such hags: I couldn't understand his interest. He looked old for his age and strained – he still had to grow into his face.'

The critic and novelist Walter Allen met Greene when he was editor of *Night and Day*. He had gone with an introduction to their offices in St Martin's Lane hoping to persuade Greene to let him be their soccer correspondent: 'He was not yet famous, was still merely "promising", but I read everything he had written . . . Of my near contemporaries he excited me more than anyone except Auden, and . . . they had more in common than I [then] realised. They shared an obsession with frontiers, spies, and betrayals . . . With both of them, whether in the flesh or on the page, I knew I was in the presence of powerful idiosyncrasy. Meeting Greene for the first time, with his account in *Journey Without Maps* of his march through Africa vivid in my mind, I remember thinking: how could this man have made such an expedition? He was very tall and thin; one felt a gust of wind would blow him over. His face was lined, as though he were under strain or perhaps in some pain, and his smile seemed somehow reluctant, as though he were using facial muscles not much exercised.

His voice, which was [a] lightish tenor, was not so much high-pitched as curiously strangled.'[1]

When Greene was twenty-one, he had written to Vivien:

I have three determinations:
1. And most important. To marry you.
2. To make a lot of money.
3. To edit the Spectator.

By the age of thirty-three he had achieved the first of these aims, and although he had not been editor of the *Spectator*, he had been literary editor of *Night and Day*, and enjoyed it: 'It was for all four of us who made up the staff a happy experience. I cannot believe that any paper has been so completely free from personal antagonisms.' He had not made a lot of money but he had worked on films with Korda, and apart from the three documentaries previously mentioned he wrote the commentary for *The Future's in the Air* (January 1937) which celebrated the Empire Air Mail.

But in December 1937 *Night and Day* collapsed, he was faced with a libel case and *Brighton Rock* was giving him trouble. He complained to Hugh on 16 January 1938: 'My damned novel is giving me worse hell than any other . . . my nerves as a consequence are in tatters.'[2] He was tired of England: 'I want to get out of this bloody country', but it seemed that his plans for Mexico were falling through – he had no way of escape.

He does himself less than justice in insisting that he always sought ways of escape. Usually he was seeking not so much a way out of a situation as a way into another, a new, more interesting, more dangerous situation, as with Liberia. There was also, as he wrote, 'a desire to be a spectator of history'. He had failed in that aim with Spain but Mexico, if he could get there, offered the same conflict as in Spain – religion versus atheism, but in a stranger, more stimulating environment. Though he did not get to Spain, the Spanish Civil War had nevertheless been an important influence, as he wrote in *Ways of Escape*:

My professional life and my religion were contained in quite separate compartments, and I had no ambition to bring them together. It was 'clumsy life again at her stupid work' which did that; on the one side the socialist persecution of religion in Mexico, and on the other General Franco's attack on Republican Spain, inextricably involved religion in contemporary life.

It was under those two influences, and the backward and forward sway of his sympathies, that he began to examine more closely the effect of faith on action:

> Catholicism was no longer primarily symbolic, a ceremony at an altar with the correct canonical number of candles, with the women in my Chelsea congregation wearing their best hats, nor was it a philosophical page in Father d'Arcy's *Nature of Belief*. It was closer now to death in the afternoon.[3]

It has been claimed that Greene went off to Mexico to escape the consequence of the Shirley Temple libel case, but this is not true. *Night and Day* stopped publication at the end of the year, but the libel case did not come up until March 1938 and Greene left for Mexico at the end of January 1938 to begin a journey he had been planning for over two and a half years. The closure of *Night and Day* had given him the freedom to do it; his persistence in attaining his object had borne fruit; his release from a busy but boring life had come about.

What seems to have been an obsession with going to Mexico was first mentioned in a letter to Hugh of 24 May 1936, before *Night and Day* and *Brighton Rock* had been thought of and when he was involved in making films and writing 'In the Night Coach' ('Fanatic Arabia') and reviewing for the *Spectator*. To Hugh he wrote, 'Later in the new year I may be getting off to Mexico; negotiations are on hand for a book on the Mexican Revolution and the Catholic church.' He had already been in touch with the Catholic publisher Sheed about this: 'Sheed promises an introduction to one of the heads of the Catholic party,' he told Hugh, and suggested that if they could manage a holiday together it should be in Spain, since he would have to learn Spanish for the Mexican trip and would need to practise it.[4] By July there were uncertainties and mysteries: 'Mexico remains uncertain. My agent's asked Sheed for £500 and Sheed can't make up his mind till he's been across to New York again and talked with the mysterious Fr Miranda.'[5]

The trip to Spain with Hugh did not take place because of Vivien's pregnancy, but his enthusiasm for Mexico continued. In July he was cock-a-hoop: 'I've just heard that Sheed has agreed to terms for the Mexican book, an advance of £500, so I shall be off after the new year [1937].' And he was reading about Mexico with that curious delight he seemed to take in facing adverse conditions: 'The reading is as morbid as Liberia's. There seem to be even more diseases, and an average of one shooting a week. This is a conservative estimate by a pro-Government writer! I hope you'll be able to give me a sofa in New York.' In the same letter, he put to Hugh what appears to be the kernel of *Brighton Rock* with the warning: 'Don't let out the idea if you can help it. There are plenty of literary sharks ready to get ideas for thrillers, who are quicker producers than I am.'[6]

A letter to his mother of 29 August 1936 gives an insight into his customary complexity of purposes: 'I shall go via New York to pick up introductions and information and try to arrange a lecture tour for later in the Catholic states. I can't help hoping too that something might turn up from Hollywood when I'm actually in America. If I get across to Sonora in Mexico, where they had the Indian war in 1928, I shall be only about 300 miles from Hollywood.'

Not only was Hollywood in his sights, but Hugh appears to have been netted as well. He was then in Berlin as a correspondent for the *Daily Telegraph*, and Greene seems to have hoped that the paper might finance his brother for a Mexican trip, or that, alternatively, Hugh might fund himself by writing a successful play: 'This is all very sad about The Telegraph's attitude to your coming to Mexico. However, a lot may happen before it becomes possible for me to go and . . . I shall hope for the best. Do write the play quickly and sell it for a lot of money.'[7] Hugh wrote the play, which was based on a novel by Roy Horniman, but it was not produced until 1977 in Lübeck with the German title *Gesellschaftspiel*. It did not make money, as the film *Kind Hearts and Coronets*, based on the same novel, had done.

It must have seemed to Greene that fate, perhaps even God, was against his Mexican trip. Because he felt it was the responsible thing to do, he took on the literary editorship of *Night and Day* ('A horrid decision. I'd much rather have Mexico,' he wrote to his mother) and Sheed was put on hold. And so *Night and Day* lived its short life. Thirteen days before the fatal Shirley Temple review appeared, Nancy Pearn wrote to Greene about a meeting with Sheed, doing her best to temper things: 'I was seeing Sheed yesterday and he enquired about your plans for Mexico, saying that if persecutions were to stop there, the book would lose its value. I said I couldn't tell him anything but I knew you had the whole thing in mind and believed you hoped to go in the New Year.'

It is apparent from the surviving correspondence that Sheed was losing interest but not taking a decision until he had consulted his American contacts. Greene was having his doubts about Sheed on two grounds: 'Personally, I would much rather be published in this country by Longman's [he wrote to David Higham], it would brand one less in the public eye as a Catholic writer. Also if the nature of the book when it was written offended Sheed's susceptibilities . . .'[8]

And he began a tentative approach to Longman's through his friend Tom Burns who was working there and was later to become the owner of the *Tablet*. Greene was proved right in his doubts about Sheed. On 10 December, David Higham received a letter from Sheed telling him that when he heard of the original postponement of Greene's book on Mexico, he had got in touch with what he calls 'the Mexican people who had been behind the original suggestion' but that they were no longer in favour of the scheme: 'The situation has changed in the last year and they would not be prepared to co-operate now. I am afraid therefore we shall have to drop it.'

Sheed was being rather astute here. Not only did he imply that the original idea for the book had come from Mexico via him and that he had chosen Greene as a suitable person to write it (though it had been Greene's idea), but he got out of the contract by laying the blame firmly on Greene and also rubbing salt into the wound by referring to the demise of *Night and Day*: 'It seems particularly unfortunate that the Editorship of *Night and Day* should have prevented his going [to Mexico] when we had arranged, and then proved impermanent.'

Greene's agent then asked, 'Shall I get straight in touch with Burns and see whether they won't take the contract over? I won't quite put it that Sheed has pulled out.' So Burns was approached, David Higham explaining that he wasn't doing Graham Greene a favour by taking over the book since he, the agent, was sure that he could sell it elsewhere, and that indeed Greene would insist that he approach his usual publisher Heinemann.

But there was an even more serious aspect to Sheed's withdrawal, for he had the Mexican contacts as we can see from an early letter (September 1936) Greene wrote to his mother: 'I had lunch with Sheed yday to talk over the Mexican book. My trip apparently has the blessing of the [Catholic] hierarchy, who are going to open their secret archives for me.' Greene must have felt that with Sheed dropping out, his valuable contacts would disappear.

Many people at this point, having lost a publisher, Mexican contacts and access to archives, would have given up – not Greene! There were other ways of getting to Mexico, including suggesting a different book. His friend, David Mathew, 'a wily and intelligent priest . . . a first class historian', thought that Greene could get all the help he needed from the Mexican mission college in Texas:[9] 'You needn't wash out Mexico altogether: this cold weather makes me feel more friendly towards it,' he told his agent. And he proposed extending the scope of the book which had initially the dull (and limiting) title approved by Sheed, *The Position of the Church in Mexico*:

'The other places I'm interested in are Paraguay – remains of old Jesuit missions, five revolutions or attempted revolutions since 1935, the totalitarian state transported to the centre of South America; and Ecuador, a half unexplored country, opera bouffe politics, a purely Indian state.'[10]

The elusive Sheed, as Higham called him, was again approached but had 'departed to America without [Higham] being able to get any word out of him about his American firm's attitude to a different Mexican book'. Other publishers were approached and David Higham was hoping that Frere at Greene's regular publishers, Heinemann, would give a satisfactory offer, but Greene was not happy about this: 'I feel very strongly', he responded to Higham, 'that it's not worth jockeying Heinemann's into a book which doesn't really interest them; I'd really rather give it up, or if it's financially practicable, take Longman's offer'; for he had told Higham on 17 January 1938 that he had talked to Frere and found under the surface that Heinemann did not really want it: 'With such a big amorphous overwritten scene as Mexico the only treatment . . . is a particular one – in this case religious. And Frere admitted that he hadn't the faintest idea how to sell a religious book. Why they even sell the Bible as literature!!'

Greene was in a mood: he was still smarting from having lost *Night and Day*; he was having a great struggle to finish *Brighton Rock* while these scattered negotiations were going on; and the bitterly cold winter was getting him down. His nerves were ragged and truly he wanted to get out of 'this bloody country'.[11] To his agent he gave vent to his feelings: 'I'm feeling rather bored with everything. I don't know how I shall get the vitality to think of another novel unless I can get out of bloody Europe.' His agents, trying desperately to assist him (as usual), suggested an approach to the publisher Collins. Greene replied: 'Collins is not a suitable publisher for the book I have in mind, but I daresay none is. Let's call it a day till after the world war.'[12] And war was certainly on the European horizon.

Although the general public in England, following its newspapers, developed a passionate interest in whether Princess Juliana of The Netherlands was pregnant, and if she was, whether the baby would be a boy or a girl (if it should be a girl then the Dutch would have a succession of Queens whose lives would span a century), there were more important political issues – namely the rise of Hitler in Germany and Mussolini in Italy. Winston Churchill, speaking of the new German air force as early as November 1934, when he was in the political wilderness soon after the Nazis had come to power, forecast that in a few years Germany could have 10,000 planes: 'Beware:

Germany is a country fertile in military surprises', he warned. In 1938 Prime Minister Neville Chamberlain would be pursuing a policy of appeasement towards both Hitler and Mussolini, but already by April 1937 an Air Raid Precautions service had been set up in Britain and in the same year police and local government employees were being given training in anti-gas measures.[13] The ranting speeches of Hitler could be heard on British radio and in May 1937, following Chamberlain's attempt to placate Mussolini, Foreign Secretary Anthony Eden resigned, declaring that 'we must not buy goodwill'. The next year saw the occupation by the Nazis of Austria, and the Austrian Chancellor's imprisonment in the concentration camp at Dachau.

However, by January 1938, Greene had found publishers for his Mexican book and finally sailed for America. 'Mexico', he wrote jubilantly to Hugh, 'has suddenly come off after all. Longman's here, Viking in America. I'm off with V[ivien] at a week's notice to New York; then I'm taking her to New Orleans, she's finding her way home, I'm going to San Antonio, Texas, where there's a mission college for Mexico, to get some dope [confidential information], and on down. Back middle of May. I wish you could meet me in Mexico City.'[14]

Greene's going to Mexico was evidence of a more serious and intense compulsion than this letter might suggest. Only weeks before his departure he wrote in his diary: 'And they say that religion is an escape. The man who believes in eternity must often experience an acute nostalgia for atheism to indulge himself with rest. There is the real escape.'[15] Perhaps already he was thinking of what he would find in Mexico – extremes of religious martyrdom and atheism. In the preface to *Ways of Escape* Greene writes: 'I can see now that my travels, as much as the act of writing, were ways of escape . . .'[16] He was, in his sense, escaping to Mexico. The tone and content of his letters tell us what he was escaping from – the incessant work, the loss of *Night and Day*, being cooped up in London and living the life of a 'gentleman' author in a 'gentleman's establishment'. Arthur Calder-Marshall regarded Greene as the epitome of the 'Established Writer', with his stylish home in Clapham Common. He added:

I was particularly impressed by Vivien's behaviour as the Protective Wife. One could not telephone Graham in the morning, because he was writing. Messages would be taken and passed on at more convenient times. (This, when I was writing short stories on marble topped tables in Lyon's Corner House, or over sixpenny pints of bitter in the Wells Hotel saloon bar).

Yet, at the same time, when we met (preferably in pubs) I was conscious that there was another part of Graham which felt imprisoned by the comfort of the house in Clapham and his protective wife, which yearned for the seedy, the dangerous, the uncomfortable.[17]

Maclaren-Ross, on visiting 14 North Side, gained a similar impression. An elderly housekeeper treated him on the doorstep as if he were a salesman: 'I said, "Could I see Mr Graham Greene please?" She said, "We don't want anything today, thank you." I said: "He's expecting me to lunch."' She said, '"Oh. Well why didn't you say so then. Come in."'

The housekeeper pointed to the drawing room at the top of the Adam staircase and left saying, 'He's out. You'll have to wait.' Maclaren-Ross waited upstairs for a while and glanced round, and as he did so Greene appeared quite silently in the open doorway: 'I was startled because not even a creak on the stairs had announced his approach. Seeing me there gave him also a start, and he took a step back. He was wearing a brown suit and large horn-rimmed spectacles, which he at once snatched off as if they had been his hat . . . this was the only time I saw him wearing spectacles. I had not expected him to be so tall. "I hope you haven't been waiting long," he said. He had a spontaneous pleasant smile. "Nobody told me you were here. Would you like a cigarette? Something to drink?" "Something cold if possible," I said accepting the cigarette avidly.'[18]

There was no beer in the house and so they set off to the pub on the other side of the Common, each carrying a large jug. In the course of conversation Maclaren-Ross disclosed that he supplemented his salary from writing plays for the B.B.C. by selling vacuum cleaners from door to door. Greene was interested – was he doing it to get material? He was doing it for money. Did he earn much at it? Eight to ten quid a week. 'I thought', said Greene, 'of signing up myself at one time. To write a book about it afterwards of course. I never knew one could actually sell the things.' He was intrigued by Maclaren-Ross's use of the term 'dem-kit' – the suitcase containing the demonstration machine – and Greene recalled that a salesman who came to their house carried his machine in a golfbag – 'I suppose less heavy. I used it in a novel of mine [*England Made Me*].' He also began to understand Greene's obsessive search for useful experience and copy – in the pub he attempted to smoke a Menzala to get used to Mexican tobacco as he was going out there, but he let it burn out in an ashtray on the bar.

There is some difficulty in dating this meeting, even though Greene is quoted as saying that he was off to Mexico soon, since Ross says that he had with him a review by James Agate of *Brighton Rock* which appeared in the *Daily Express* of Thursday 14 July 1938. Ross's account might well be, therefore, a compilation of two separate visits to 14 North Side. Certainly a number of irritations made Greene wish to get out of the country at that time (including the fact that Viking weren't 'exactly snatching at Mexico'); he came up with yet another idea for escape which he put to his brother: a collaboration with Malcolm Muggeridge – the two of them doing 'a fairly light book on the Palestine civil war', with Greene coming from Syria and Transjordan with Arab introductions and Muggeridge from Tel Aviv with Jewish. They would meet at the Holy Sepulchre and argue, Muggeridge being pro-Arab and Greene pro-Jew at that point. But they could not find a publisher to support the idea.[19]

Escape was obviously essential, but what was he escaping to? It would seem to be a long-held dream. In 1926, when he was twenty-one, having read D. H. Lawrence's novel about Mexico, *The Plumed Serpent*, he developed a yearning to see Mexico, and wrote to Vivien: 'When you feel it's about time for me to go off on an adventure, alone, I'll visit it.' They sailed on the *Normandie* on 29 January 1938.

*

It was not an entirely enjoyable trip. Even in good weather the *Normandie* was likely to produce a rocking sensation on the high seas, and they were disturbed by the noise and vibration of the ship. Moreover, they ran into an awful gale – 'For 56 hours we lay in bed', he wrote to his mother from the Bedford Hotel on East 40th Street, New York, though afterwards they enjoyed the food and life on board. They arrived in New York a day late, having been stuck in a fog on the river and missing the tide. Even after they landed, Vivien still felt the world wobbling under her feet.

They liked New York. The weather was lovely and Vivien was having an orgy of shopping. Unexpectedly they found Arthur Calder-Marshall staying at their hotel. Calder-Marshall and his wife were returning from Hollywood in January 1938 and by chance 'stayed in the same New York City hotel as Graham, who was en route for Tabasco'. He added, though Greene has denied it, that: 'He already had the germ of the whisky priest story and his research consisted in gaining the material to flesh it out.'[20]

The Greenes attended several parties in New York: 'We are having dinner with Felix [Greene] tonight, my agent [Mary Pritchett] is giving a party for us tomorrow, & on Friday my new publisher

[Viking]. We are also seeing a film friend Paul Rotha who is working here. So life is busy.'[21]

During their seven days in New York it is likely that Greene had some discussions with the 'mysterious Father Miranda' and he was very interested in learning anything he could about the conditions of the Church in Mexico. Some of the information he was given was obviously false. For example, he was told that a General Rodriguez had 40,000 armed men on the Texas border and he would be missing everything if he missed Rodriguez. He never found Rodriguez or his army of discontented farmers, but he discovered that he lived, in fact, by 'having fool newspapermen in New York write about him'.[22]

On Sunday night, 13 February, the Greenes left for Washington, where Graham was hoping to meet a Father Parsons at Georgetown University. Parsons had written *Mexican Martyrdom* (1936), a book which Greene must have read, in which is recorded the history of the political suppression of the Church in Mexico – families invaded, churches and haciendas confiscated, bishops exiled. In 1936 Parsons had returned to academic life as Professor of Political Science at Georgetown, and Greene had written to him: 'Could I trespass a very little on your time & hear from you some news of Mexico?' He enclosed a letter from his publisher, Tom Burns, which in effect indicates the terms on which Greene's projected book had been accepted. Greene was 'to study the present conditions in the country with a special eye to the religious situation for a book which Longman's will publish.' 'Greene', Burns states, 'is in the first rank of novelists here, a good journalist as well, and a Catholic', and he asked Parsons to put Greene 'on to people who would be useful to him in Mexico'. There is a warning: 'I want his book to be unofficial and quite personal in character, so I will trust you not to put him in touch with any quarters which might impose inconvenient restrictions on his movements or sources of information.' Burns stressed that: 'The book will be very good if he is given a free hand . . . and would be quite spoilt if his attitude were to be dictated to him by any officialdom.'[23] One can detect Greene's voice behind this.

Greene cannot recall meeting Parsons, yet he had been at pains to engage his interest before going to Washington, and he would have been a valuable contact since he was constantly receiving documented reports about the political and religious situation inside Mexico – no one in Washington would have more up-to-date information since his couriers in Mexico brought him private dispatches across the border at El Paso and the secret details were then sent to Parsons by telegraph wire.

They did meet, though it appears from Parsons's unpublished

autobiography that he was very circumspect and what he told Greene was limited, reflected in some vague remarks in *The Lawless Roads*: 'there seemed to be no priests at all in Tabasco . . . they believed not a church was left standing – not even the cathedral.'[24] Parsons may, however, have provided some useful contacts in Mexico.

From Washington, the Greenes went on to New Orleans. In a letter to his mother from New York, he says, cryptically: 'Our address will not be c/o Cooks – there is no Cooks. But Poste Restante, G.P.O., New Orleans. We'll cable you Vivien's return from there.'

*

Greene went on from New Orleans to San Antonio, having taken Vivien to the airport hotel, from which she wrote to him: 'After I saw you go away, dear heart, yesterday, I got 2 magazines & a Taxi to Canal Street (a long detour because of crowds) & got a most curious silver or nickel brooch for Aunt Nono.' It was their custom, when they were to be separated, for the one departing to leave a secret letter for the other, and in her letter, which gives us an impression of her feelings of loss and loneliness, she wrote: 'I waited as long as I could & finally I read [your letter] after dinner in our room, with the fire on, & again lots of times & finally before I put out the light, while the dance band was playing . . . A liner came in this morning & woke me up – almost sounded as if it was going to alight in my bath. So loud. After breakfast it was "All Aboard. All Aboard", calling in the hall: it is still exciting however often it happens.' She spent the following day reading Trollope and watching the planes come in: 'The little green plane has arrived & a pillar-box scarlet one is off. The airport is buzzing with people – I think mostly to see planes or have a Coca Cola . . . Now an all-scarlet one: Oh dear, you would like all this activity so much, dear, dear, love. The little green one is off again already & so is a yellow one.'

Very movingly at the beginning of his second long journey which was to separate them she wrote: 'I wanted to tell you at once how dear you are and how happy I've been with you for years & years & especially on this trip & the bits of New York . . . It's funny that to me the strangeness of it all, & loveliness of being with you are almost concentrated in that first evening in the Yama tea-room & seeing R[ockefeller] Center in the dark with the skaters . . . I wish I were back with you on Fifth Avenue in the evening, or with you anywhere at all.'[25] And when he was deep in the jungles of Chiapas, between Palenque and Salto de Agua, Greene's mind also went back to that occasion. He was in a hammock slung under a verandah with the sound of animal movements around him in the dark – pigs with pointed tapir snouts, turkeys with hideous Dali heads, a great storm starting them hissing and scurrying: 'Rockefeller Plaza rose in icicles of steel towards a cold sky; the ice-skaters moved in the small square under the stars.' This was not the same world, he thought, as he hit furiously at a pointed snout.

Forty years later, reflecting on that separation, Vivien said:

> I'm sure Graham has a lot of courage – takes risks. About Mexico, he took me as far as New Orleans, and I was left at the Shushan airport for about five days – it's about 10 miles out of New Orleans, and of course that was a bit queer. I was all by myself – I had enough money. I had to wait. I never questioned any of this. He presumably had to go – timetables and things – there was nothing to do – nothing to read. I was going back by Dutch cargo boat. It was terrible. There were three others, rather doggy sort of people on board, but it was awful – it took 19 days – unbelievable.

Greene had asked an agent to book the passage. Someone telephoned, collected Vivien and put her on the boat:

> It was tiny – it was a small cargo boat which took 4 passengers . . . the most terrible storm . . . the cabin was awash, the suitcases were all soaked and I was so ill . . . When I got back, I didn't know where Graham was because he was moving about. There was trouble with Shirley Temple and I came back into the blast of it. I can hear the judge saying why was he out of England, but that's all I remember.[26]

With hindsight she felt that Greene was a person who should never have married: 'It took me some time to understand that. I understood it but not consciously. I was unsophisticated and didn't think that he was somebody who was always wandering. When they were writing in the Sunday papers about the death of the last Marx brother, one of whose film characters was Otis P. Driftwood, I thought "That's the name for Graham" – never staying in the same place for more than weeks together.'[27]

*

Greene's search for experience brought an immediate return on the train journey to San Antonio. When he arrived there he sent a postcard to his wife: 'Had a pleasant journey with a sad gentle turkey breeder who lives alone with his [1,100] turkeys all the year round, unable to leave them even at night. He has a little house fastened to a motor car & follows them through the fields without any human company.'

This sad little story is faithfully recorded in *The Lawless Roads*, the voice of the nameless breeder forever preserved in Greene's travel book: 'You see', he said, 'you're at it night and day. You can't trust a hired man. The birds are so sensitive they get nervous and sick if a stranger's around.'[28]

But it is with his impressions of San Antonio that one begins to wonder whether experience is seeking him out or he is seeking it; whether he is also touching up his material for effect.

This raises the issue which has long disturbed Greene – the authenticity of what critics have named 'Greeneland', 'a strange violent "seedy" region of the mind'. His response is, '"This is Indo-China . . . this is Mexico, this is Sierra Leone carefully and accurately described. I have been a newspaper correspondent as well as a novelist. I assure you that the dead child lay in the ditch in just that attitude. In the canal of Phat Diem the bodies stuck out of the water . . ." But I know that argument is useless. They won't believe the world they haven't noticed is like that.'[29]

The world they had not noticed (in San Antonio) began when he went at night to where the West side begins – 'Wooden houses and raw shows and the brothels in Matamoras Street where the hold-ups happen nightly and the local paper prints a column of them at the week-ends' – and where he 'went into a freak show in a little booth . . . one got an awful amount for ten cents in the stuffy booth':

I was the only person there; I had a sense that nobody had been for a long while – it couldn't really compete with Matamoras Street – the dry exhibits were dusty with neglect. There were a Siamese sheep – eight legs sticking out like octopus tentacles – and calves with so-called human heads (like those of morons), and dogs created upside down rolling glass eyeballs towards legs that sprouted from somewhere near the backbone, and 'a frog baby born to a lady in Oklahoma'.

The high point of the freak show was two dead gangsters:

Dutch Kaplan and Oklahoma Jim, his henchman, lying in open coffins, mummified. Jim was dressed in rusty black, with a loose fly button and the jacket open to disclose the brown hollow arch of the breast, and his former leader was naked except for a black cloth across the loins. The showman lifted it to disclose the dry, dusty, furry private parts. He showed the two scars upon the groin through which the taxidermist had removed all that was corruptible and put his fingers there (a terrible parody of St Thomas) and urged me to do the same – it was lucky to touch the body of a criminal. He put his finger in the bullet-hole where the brains had been blasted out and touched the dingy hair.[30]

Greene asked him where they got the bodies from. The question irritated the showman, who replied 'The Crime Prevention League', and promptly changed the subject. In the corner of his postcard to Vivien, posted later in the Mexican border town of Laredo, he wrote: 'I spent the evening at a grim Barnum show – mummified gangsters – & a Mexican cinema & variety.'[31]

The freak show with the mummified gangsters did exist then in San Antonio. In an earlier edition of *The Lawless Roads* he evokes the 'hideous vision' of Dutch Kaplan and Oklahoma Jim: 'a hundred years hence, sanctified by age and ritual, with ten thousand invisible finger marks upon the groin.' The vision was untrue. The mummified figures have long since disappeared.

There is no record of a Dutch Kaplan and an Oklahoma Jim in any almanac of the underworld; but the showman could have invented the names. The freaks, according to Greene, were created by man to satisfy some horrifying human need for ugliness.

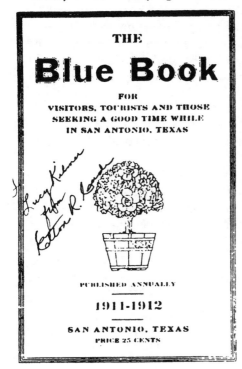

THE

Blue Book

FOR
VISITORS, TOURISTS AND THOSE
SEEKING A GOOD TIME WHILE
IN SAN ANTONIO, TEXAS

PUBLISHED ANNUALLY

1911-1912

SAN ANTONIO, TEXAS
PRICE 25 CENTS

DIRECTORY OF HOUSES AND WOMEN

Class—A

NAME	STREET	Old Phone New Phone
Arlington, The	507 Matamoras	1035
Benedict, Beatrice	421 Matamoras	2371
Benedict, Beatrice	309 South Pecos	2133
Benedict, Beatrice	501 Durango	499
Campbell, Maud	217 South Santa Rosa	563
Carson, Belle	526 Matamoras	4480
Clarke, Hazel	316 South Concho	48

Class—C

NAME	STREET	NEW PHONE
Brewer, Sallie	216 South Concho	1952
Dupree, Anita	220 " "	1952
Durant, Marian	220 " "	248
Duval, Aleese	307 " "	1605
Duval, Cecile	312 " "	
Duval, Georgette	226 " "	
Denman, Pebble	224 " "	
Davis, Ada	224 " "	
Edwards, Bessie	405 " "	2344
Garza, Margarita	410 " "	
Jennings, Grace	305 " "	248
Kato, Tama	220 " "	
Legal, Tender	216 " "	

667

The brothels in Matamoras Street, though remembered by some citizens of San Antonio, have long since disappeared, but the top end of the street was inhabited by the Class A prostitutes, followed by Class B, then the lowest, Class C. Before Greene arrived, a 'Directory of Houses and Women' had been published, listing the girls in alphabetical order from The Arlington (a Class A) living at 507 Matamoras Street to Bell Wilson (Class C) living at number 209. No doubt some of those girls were still there when Greene went to explore the street. The 'Mexican cinema & variety' he discovered must have been one of the 'Carpas', tent shows, once popular in the town, which were usually followed by a festival.

During his short stay in San Antonio there was also a strike of the workers at the pecan canning factory who had had their wages cut, even though they earned less than fifty cents a day. The strike had been originally led by a Father López and it was the first example Greene had come across of genuine Catholic Action on a social issue – 'a real attempt . . . to put into force the papal encyclicals which have condemned capitalism quite as strongly as Communism'. But he had to admit that 'there was something a little pathetic about Catholic Action in San Antonio'. Father Lopez had a naïve belief that the employers could be persuaded to open their books to the workers' representatives and restore wages if the books did not justify a cut.*

In his condemnation of employers' greed Greene quotes St James: 'Go now, ye rich men: weep and howl in your miseries which shall come upon you. Your riches are corrupted, and your garments are moth-eaten. Your gold and silver is cankered: and the rust of them shall be for testimony against you, and shall eat your flesh like fire . . .' Greene comments, 'Those are the words of revolution – not the dim promise that account books shall be inspected (how can a Mexican worker living on thirty-five cents a day trust an account book?).'[32]

But he liked San Antonio, describing it on a postcard to his wife as lovely: 'Very hot, palmy, old Spanish Cathedral, a river winding in & out of the town, very clean & skyscraping & ancient at the same time. Mass in Spanish, the old Archbishop very sweet & useless.'

*

On Sunday 27 February he 'got a seat in a car going to Laredo. Doc Williams drove it, with an unlit cigar stuck in the corner of his mouth

---

* Thirty thousand people were eventually involved in the strike which ended after eighteen months when a federal law set the minimum wage. Tragically, soon afterwards, automatic equipment for shelling nuts was introduced and the work force was reduced to about 600 girls.

... A shabby man with a hacking cough sat in the back seat; he had come down from Detroit without luggage and his sister was dying in Laredo.'[33] To Vivien he wrote jubilantly that he had heard of a cheap way of getting to Mexico City by buying a seat in a car for about fifteen dollars. He had been told in San Antonio that if he waited at the border he would catch a fine German car on its way to Mexico City.

In Laredo he waited all day: 'Every half-hour I walked down to the river bank and looked at Mexico.' He went to the cinema to kill time. He went to Pete's Bar and had a brandy. He went down to the river bank again and when the lights were coming out on the other side of the Rio Grande he caught a taxi and crossed into Nuevo Laredo, depositing 500 pesos at the customs. He was now in Mexico and he put up for the night. He had crossed the border into a different world: 'There was a large cockroach dead on the floor of my room and a sour smell from the water closet.' He was getting deeper into Greeneland.

Travelling and sight-seeing did not stop his writing. Before leaving Monterrey for Mexico City he sent a story to Nancy Pearn which he hoped might have 'enough action for the *Strand*' and sent a small descriptive article to the *Spectator*, 'A Postcard from San Antonio', and proposed sending another article, 'A Day at the General's' – both articles he thought would suit the *New Statesman* and *Time and Tide*, and, 'If anything should be printed – proofs to my wife.'

Vivien was not to receive them. Nancy Pearn wrote to her that although the *Strand* had an increasing interest in Greene as a short story writer, 'Across the Border' was not their type of thing – 'this editor regards him as so essentially one of the front rank fiction writers of the day, that he never ceases to hope that sooner or later he will turn his attention to writing for the *Strand*.' The *Spectator* turned down 'A Post-card from San Antonio' and the *Daily Telegraph* was 'not very interested in Mexico until something really happens. As you know, there are events of some importance nearer home. I suggest', Nancy Pearn went on, 'that you from your end cable if you know any decisive factor which at a given moment is going to result in revolution.'

Vivien could not contact Greene about these things, a letter from Nancy Pearn sent Post Restante, General Post Office, New Orleans, arrived after he had left; her report on the *Strand*'s rejection only reached him when many weeks later he arrived in Mexico City suffering from dysentery. And there was no revolution in Mexico. Although President Cardenas expropriated foreign oil companies and foreigners withdrew great sums of money from the banks and the British Ambassador, Owen St Clair O'Malley, behaved arrogantly, the Mexicans were persuaded that they must tighten their belts and accept that this was an indication of their independence from foreign influence.

At Monterrey Greene felt he 'had been whisked back . . . to Texas – one of those bad dreams where you never reach your destination . . . The hotel was American, the rooms were American, the food and the voices all American,'[34] but he was being drawn into Mexico.

In the first week of March in San Luís Potosí he interviewed the rebel General Cedillo, an Indian who had refused to enforce the anti-religious laws, though the Catholics he defended did not trust him – many people had an affection for him, 'an affection for an animal whose cage you enter with caution'.[35] Greene got on the wrong side of Cedillo for, having spent a week waiting to interview him, he went on to Mexico City the next day: 'The General blew himself out: his neck and cheeks extended like rubber. I could see . . . that I had committed an atrocity.'[36]

His account of Mexico City shows that he is still a tourist there, though trying to get into the true Mexico as a traveller (like George Borrow whose *Travels with the Bible in Spain* he makes reference to). He describes the city as being 'elongated and lopsided on its mountain plateau'; there is the great square with the Cathedral and the National Palace close to each other, the high, dark stony streets near the university quarter, tramways, red-light districts, street markets; 'a whole family of Indians eating their lunch on the sidewalk edge'; near the Cathedral the remains of an Aztec temple Cortés destroyed; hidden behind the new American hotels old baroque churches and convents; Cinco de Mayo and the fashionable streets and shops; the Avenida Hidalgo 'where hideous funeral wreaths are made, ten feet high and six across, of mauve and white flowers'.

Trotsky was there, living upstairs in Rivera's villa in a suburb, revising his *Life of Stalin*, 'a revolver on his desk, reporters searched for arms, the villa floodlit at night and guarded by Federal soldiers – the papers . . . full of a Stalinist plot against his life'.*[37] It seems a shame in retrospect that Greene did not interview Trotsky rather than the insignificant rebel Indian General Cedillo.

In Mexico City he changed his hotel for a dustier, noisier brand (probably the Hotel Canada, for a letter has survived on this hotel's notepaper), and obtained a room with a shower, plus three meals a day for 5.50 pesos (7s.). Lunch consisted of six courses with a cocktail and coffee. Music was supplied through the street door; a succession of marimba players took up a collection . . .[38] which does not sound like the Hotel Canada.

He explored the city, visiting a cinema, a cabaret (where 'a Mexican dancer with great bold thighs', pleased the men and troubled the women in the audience),[39] a picture gallery, and discovered a dark winding passage which 'at every curve disclosed a brightly lighted cell – with a monk in a cowl flogging a naked woman or interrogating one by torchlight, whip in hand. The women's bodies had been constructed with tender sensuality – pink haunches and round breasts.'[40]

He visited priests secretly at work; Father Q. who had suffered imprisonment for his beliefs: '"It was the happiest time," Father Q. said, chuckling, remembering the camaraderie of the cells, the hope and exultation, under the light of death.'[41] He visited the Bishop of Chiapas, now exiled from his state, old, thin, and dressed in 'seedy black': 'he looked like a village priest and showed a kind of humble confused embarrassment at my genuflexion.'

One has the impression that all was not well with Greene, and indeed it was not. It was not a matter, as it had been in Liberia, of encountering the primitive, danger, fear, discomfort and total uncertainty: it was that his long-cherished dream of Mexico was turning into disillusion and nightmare – even hatred for the country, a hatred which began in San Luís Potosí when he witnessed a cockfight.

* After many attempts on Trotsky's life, finally a man posing as an associate attacked Trotsky with an ice-pick on 20 August 1940 and he died two days later. During the attack, portions of his manuscript on Stalin were splattered with blood and other portions of the unrevised manuscript destroyed.

Men in big decorated cartwheel hats and tight charro trousers were watching. A procession of horsemen entered with a band of fiddlers. Then two of the charros (horsemen) 'took little bright spurs out of beautiful red leather cases and bound them on the cocks' feet with scarlet twine, very slowly, very carefully', preparation for 'the scurry on the sand, pain in miniature, and death on a very small scale.' Granted that Greene was aware of the significance of the ritual ('Men make rules and hope in that way to tame death'), the cocks crowing and a brass band blaring from stone seats, he suddenly felt an impatience with all 'this mummery, all this fake emphasis on what is only a natural function; we die as we evacuate; why wear big hats and tight trousers and have a band play? That, I think was the day I began to hate the Mexicans.'[42]

He was troubled by Mexico City beggars. The kind he saw at Huichapan station, north of Mexico City, horrified him. These were not the resigned patient kind waiting dumbly for alms, but the 'get-rich-quick' type 'scrambling, and whining and snarling with impatience, children and old men and women . . . pushing each other to one side, lifting the stump of a hand, a crutch, a rotting nose'. He gives an example of what he saw:

> A middle-aged paralytic worked himself down the platform on his hands – three feet high, with . . . feet twisted the wrong way. Someone threw him a coin and a child of six or seven leapt on his back and after an obscene and horrifying struggle got it from him. The man made no complaint, shovelling himself farther along; human beings here obeyed the jungle law, each for himself with tooth and nail.[43]

After five weeks away from Mexico City, Greene saw on his return a beggar woman bent double by some hideous disease: 'She could only beg your boots for alms. Sweeping round towards fresh pairs of feet she slipped and fell. She lay there with her mouth and nose pressed on the paving, unable to move and unable to breathe until she was lifted.'[44]

Nothing in Mexico seemed to please, even the food he found awful, tasteless and repellent: 'just a multitude of plates planked down on the table simultaneously, so that five are getting cold while you eat the sixth; pieces of anonymous meat, a plate of beans, fish from which the taste of the sea has long been squeezed away, rice mixed with what looks like grubs – perhaps they are grubs . . . a little heap of bones and skin they call a chicken . . . It is all a hideous red and yellow, green and brown . . .'[45] In Cuernavaca there were 'little obscene bone figures of men with movable phalli sold secretively by small boys near the bus stop';[46] in Mexico City 'dead fleas dressed up as little people inside walnuts';[47] in Taxco, there was an American colony 'for escapists with their twisted sexuality and their hopeless freedom. The place has rotted – the soldiers lie about in the streets at night with their women like dogs.'[48]

Even the Mexican greeting between friends, the *abrazo*, upset Greene: 'this immaturity, which gets most on the nerves in Mexico. Grown men cannot meet in the street without sparring like school-boys. One must be as a little child, we are told, to enter the kingdom of heaven, but they have passed childhood and remain for ever in a cruel anarchic adolescence.'[49]

Returning from Chiapas by train from Oaxaca to Puebla, he describes with venom a black-clothed old woman with grey straggly hair, his attitude no doubt due in part to his being sick with dysentery:

[an] old woman . . . removing a tick – blowing her nose – trying to put up a blind or open a lemonade bottle, mooing with her mouth wide, fixing her eyes on people meaninglessly for minutes at a time, slowly revolving her black bulk all of a piece like a mule . . . The hideous inexpressiveness of brown eyes. People never seem to help each other in small ways, removing a parcel from a seat, making room with their legs. They just sit about. If Spain is like this, I can understand the temptation to massacre.

[An] odious child takes all the paper cups from the water-tap by the lavatory and destroys them one by one. Nobody stops him. The white dust from the appalling plain blows against the glass. The heat, with the windows shut, is stifling.[50]

When he was in Palenque and down with fever Greene found his guide looking at him. He could see the man was troubled: 'He had a feeling of responsibility, and no Mexican cares for that. It's like a disused limb they have learned to do without.'[51]

There is no doubt about the genuineness of Greene's reactions during that journey through Mexico. For him to write 'if Spain is like this, I can understand the temptation to massacre' is a measure of the almost pathological hatred that developed during the journey.

Yet there were moments of pleasure. One came after he was able to seek out a priest and go to him for confession. It was in Orizaba, the main stopping place before reaching Veracruz, where he expected to take a ship across the Gulf of Mexico to the port of Frontera in Tabasco. Greene quotes what Mauriac wrote about a Catholic who frequently changed his confessor and how, suddenly, he received

673

from a strange priest an unexpected consolation. In Orizaba, the priest was thin, unshaved, impoverished, and yet he 'gained a sense of peace and patience and goodness', and even a sense of 'courage and endurance'. He was to need these qualities in travelling to Tabasco across the Gulf of Mexico and on into Chiapas.

It was one of those evenings 'that conspire for happiness' and he did experience peace. That night a crowd collected outside the Church. The air was warm and fresh and 'little braziers burned along the pavement, and the bell clanged in the tower . . . A Catherine wheel whirled in the road, and the rockets hissed up into the sky and burst in flippant and trivial stars . . . between the dark shoulders of the crowd you could see a dark Joseph surrounded by light; the noise of the bell and the rockets and the crowd faded out at the church door and inside was quiet and the smell of flowers. This, he felt, was how a saint's day should be celebrated – "joyfully, with fireworks and tortillas, domestically." '52

*

He had hoped to stay in Veracruz for a while but discovered that a boat was leaving for Tabasco that night – it was a boat with a bad, if unspecified, reputation. An American consul regarded him as a fool – he had never known a foreigner to use one of those boats before: 'You don't know what you are in for,' he said. Greene asked whether they were small. 'Small?' Words failed him, but he said he 'wouldn't go in one of those boats for a thousand dollars'. Greene asked whether they were unsafe – 'They don't often sink', the consul conceded, 'unless you hit a norther . . . Anyway . . . they insure you for five thousand pesos when you buy your ticket.'53

Since the 'norther' season was over, Greene decided to risk it and hired 'a bright dapper young man like a hair dresser's assistant' to take him round the town during the afternoon. They saw the small squat church built by Cortes, the oldest in America, and very generously, when the guide's allotted time was up and it was too late to find another customer, he stayed on with Greene as a friend, and he must have been able to give Greene some useful information since he came from Tabasco and had, moreover, travelled in the boat Greene was to travel in – the *Ruiz Cano*, though what he had to say must have been unnerving: 'Nothing – nothing will ever make me go on that boat again. You don't know – it's terrible.' Greene suggested changing to another boat, but the others were smaller: 'The *Ruiz Cano* has a flat bottom. That is good. It will not sink easily.' Moreover, if anything happened, they would pay 5,000 pesos to Greene's family, though that would involve a lot of lawyers' fees to prove who they were. His guide did offer to see the consul next day to tell him that if anything happened he must get the money for Greene's family.[54] In fact, after a meal with tequilas and beer mixed, his guide offered to accompany him to Tabasco, as a friend not a guide: 'I will prove that a Mexican is as good a sport [as an Englishman].' They pledged themselves in beer and shook hands drunkenly.

They went by taxi to the quay with the guide's ten-year-old nephew, full of hero-worship for his uncle, his dog running behind, 'gate-crashing past the sentry at the entrance to the docks'.

There was an English liner there from which the sound of music came, but there were no lights on the *Ruiz Cano* – 'a flat barge with a few feet of broken rail, an old funnel you could almost touch with your hand from the shore, a bell hanging on a worn piece of string, an oil-lamp and a bundle of turkeys. One little rotting boat dangled inadequately from the davits.' Groups of people stood on the quay, somebody wept on board and the turkeys rustled. Greene confessed he had never been more frightened than at the idea of spending 'Forty-two hours or so in the Atlantic, in the Gulf of Mexico', in a boat in which he would not have gone down the Thames.[55]

His guide, having gained much admiration from his nephew and the crowd on the quay in telling them of his journey, once the boat was moving, the engine shaking, everything knocking and rattling and the two of them sitting shivering on a bench, lost his courage – 'a sudden wild doubt came into his eyes like a face at a window' and he scrambled on to a lifeboat – 'The old davits cracked under the strain' – and leapt the three feet to the quay landing on his knees – ' "If I had any clothes," he called out . . . and we waved shamefacedly to each other.'[56]

Greene catches here the pathos of the situation and something of the adolescent nature of a certain type whose genuine urge to help and to offer friendship comes up against an inability to sustain it when reality has to be faced, but he never made use of this experience in his novels. The incident, though he does not mention it, suggests his own need for companionship now that he was embarking on the most dangerous part of his journey, though in writing to Nancy Pearn before he left Mexico City, he gave no indication of the dangers he might face: 'I'm off again to Veracruz in a day or two: thence to Tabasco, & then a fortnight's ride by horse across T[abasco], & Chiapas to the road & rail again. It should be interesting – almost untouched ground.'[57] He did not mention that once he reached Chiapas he would be among Mexicans who spoke only Spanish and Indians who did not speak it, and that he had no companion – Hugh being increasingly involved in the situation in Germany as a

correspondent for the *Daily Telegraph*. In Liberia it had been dangerous, but he had a companion – important in an alien world – and
servants who knew the country and the native dialects and could help
him. From his embarkation on the *Ruiz Cano* he would lead an
increasingly lonely existence, yet if he had been accompanied he
could not have written *The Power and the Glory*.

The *Ruiz Cano* sailed in almost complete darkness into the Mexican
Gulf.

*

Greene wrote to his mother on 13 April and on Hotel Español
notepaper, deliberately playing down the danger and discomfort: 'I
had a rather wearing trip, especially the journey from Veracruz to
Frontera, Tabasco, in a 30 ton Mexican barque about as big as a
canal barge. 42 hours on the sea & then 10 hours up the river to
Villahermosa.'

The boat had two cabins situated close to the engines – 'dark
padlocked cells with six wooden shelves in each'. In the bunk below
Greene, a woman lay, never stirring, never eating, for the whole
journey. The boat rolled horribly all night. Greene lay in his clothes
on his wooden shelf. On his right hand, a young girl lay on her face,
'her legs exposed up to the thighs'. That part of his luggage which
he could not get into his suitcase – riding boots, the ham bought
before boarding, a sun helmet and electric torch – rolled with the roll
of the ship on the Atlantic.

The next morning under a grey sky, they were provided with breakfast handed through a hatch in the deck from the engine-room. It was
a loaf of bread and a plate of fish scraps from which the eyeballs stood
mournfully out. Greene could not face it. He made his way down to
the only lavatory which was a horrible cupboard in the engine-room
with no ventilation, no flushing, and the ordure of many days and
voyages. That finished him for the rest of the day. He lay on his shelf,
like the woman below him, morning and afternoon.

The next day the sun was out but it sucked out all the smells in
the boat. Twice he dashed for the privy and the second time the
whole door came off in his hands and fell on to the engine-room
floor. He suffered from hunger but even more from thirst for, apart
from a frightful kind of coffee, there was no beer or mineral water
and the water available was from a tin filter above the wash-basin
which, in any case, only lasted for the first twelve hours. By late
morning of the second day, the coast came in sight reminding Greene
of the West African coastline – a long low line of trees and sand –
they had arrived at Tabasco's port of Frontera.

41

The Lawless Roads

Go where thou wilt . . . if thy soul is a stranger to thee,
this world is unhomely.
— FROM SEVENTEENTH–CENTURY INDIA

A T Frontera it was appallingly hot, but he was later to know
'how hot the world can be' when he arrived at the capital,
Villahermosa.

Frontera, on the Grijalva River, was the scene of the Conquistadores' first landing in Mexico in March 1519. The town itself was
out of sight round a river bend and when they turned the bend Greene
saw 'the Presidencia and a big warehouse and a white blanched street
running off between wooden shacks – hairdressers and the inevitable
dentists, but no cantinas anywhere, for there is prohibition in
Tabasco.'[1]

This was his first sight of Dictator Garrido Canabal's 'isolated
swampy puritanical state' where every church had been destroyed
and every priest had been chased out of the state. Greene noticed the
lily plants floating by, how the river divided round a green island
half a mile from the shore and, Greene's *bête noire*, 'the vultures came
flocking out, with little idiot heads and dusty serrated wings, to rustle
round the shrouds.'[2] He noticed that the soldiers stood in the shade
of the Presidencia and watched the boat edge in towards the river
bank.

They unloaded beer on the quay, 150 dozen bottles, the only liquor
available and sold by the government at a peso a bottle. This was a
ruinous price in Mexico, and Greene commented, 'puritanism pays'.

To the authorities, he had given as his reason for visiting that he
wished to see the ruins at Palenque. His real purpose was to visit the
only two states left where Catholics could not receive the Sacrament
except secretly. His intention was to discover the extent of the
persecution of the Church and the secularisation imposed on the

people. As a foreigner, considered undesirable under Clause 33 of the Constitution, he could have been expelled from the country.

Having reached Tabasco, his difficulties seemed to be only beginning. The owner of the warehouse to whom he had an introduction explained that while Palenque was only 100 miles away, getting there was not easy. There were no railways or roads and you had to travel by water to Villahermosa, the capital, and then by water again to Montecristo on the other side of the state. From there he had to get horses to the ruins of Palenque in Chiapas. Greene went back to the boat discouraged. There was a 10-hour passage the following day to the capital. He spent the night on the shelf in the boat and at sunset the mosquitoes began 'a terrifying steady hum like that of a sewing-machine'. He had only two choices, 'to be eaten on deck (and probably catch malaria) or to go below to the cabin and the appalling heat'. The only porthole was closed for fear of marauders, and mosquito nets seemed to shut out all the air. Greene lay naked under the net and sweated and every ten minutes he dried himself with a towel.[3]

Whatever the discomforts, it was on that boat, crowded next morning with passengers on their way to the capital, that he met the original for the seedy dentist Dr Tench in *The Power and the Glory*. He was an American, and was on his way to see a Dr Fitzpatrick, an Englishman, because of serious stomach trouble. He obviously made an impression on Greene as he kept on exclaiming, 'God, what a country!' and complaining at having to use dentists' drills made in Japan which were then cheap but never lasted, sometimes breaking down after a single use. He had been the dictator Garrido Canabal's dentist, though he longed now to leave the country, but whenever he thought he had saved enough money a revolution would break out. When Greene met him, because of the government's expropriation of the oil fields, the exchange was falling rapidly. Because of his stomach trouble and his hopeless memory Dr Winter (as Greene called him) remained firmly in the novelist's mind:

> Something – perhaps the heat – had destroyed memory. Every few minutes he would bring out the one fact he had caught hold of, 'You going off by aeroplane, eh?'
> 'That's right.'
> 'Where to? Frontera?'
> 'No. I told you. Salto – for Palenque.'
> 'You don't want to go to Salto. You want to go to Zapata.'
> 'But I told you. I can't get reliable guides there to Las Casas.'
> 'Las Casas? What you want to go there for?'

He would pause for what seemed hours at street corners, unable
to remember, I really believe, where he was going, standing like
a cow chewing. 'So you're off by plane, eh?'
'Yes.'
'To Frontera.'
And the whole explanation would begin again. It was inexpressibly tiring.[4]

Twice during that journey the barge went aground. Darkness fell
quickly. Sometimes a canoe passed, paddled by Indians – white and
silent and transparent like a marine insect – and the roar of the
mosquitoes nearly extinguished the sound of the engines. The heat
increased, and suddenly Villahermosa, capital of Tabasco, appeared.
After long hours of darkness, the passengers were startled by the
lights of the city burning down into the river, 'a great crown outlined
in electricity' and 'they called, triumphantly, "El puerto, el puerto."'[5]

*

He had reached what his confessor in Orizaba had described as a
very evil land, the Godless (and puritan) socialistic state. Then, at
nine-thirty, all the lights went out and the passengers walked 15 feet
along a plank bridging the mud river to the mud bank. By the light
of an electric torch he saw a policeman take his case and shake it,
listening for the clink of illicit bottles of alcohol – Tabasco was strictly
teetotal but he did not find Greene's secreted bottle of brandy.
Villahermosa did nothing to improve his view of Mexico. The only
possible hotel, its hallway filled by a dynamo, though it gave him
the luxury of a bedroom with a shower (which did not work), did
not provide meals. He ate, in the only restaurant in town, the worst
food he was ever to eat in the country – 'flies and dirty tablecloths
and meat on the point of turning in this wet oven of a place.'
He was in the town a week and describes what a camera panning
round the small plaza would have recorded: 'a dentist's with a floodlit
chair of torture; the public jail, an old white-pillared one-storey house
which must have dated back to the Conquistadores, where a soldier
sat with a rifle at the door and a few dark faces pressed against the bars;
a Commercial Academy, the size of a village store; the Secretariat; the
Treasury, a florid official building with long steps leading down
to the plaza; the Syndicate of Workers and Peasants; the Casa de
Agraristas.'[6]
He gained some information about the situation of Catholics in
the state when he visited a Catholic family and was told by the wife,
'we die like dogs here', no religious ceremony being allowed at the

grave.[7] He also met Dr Fitzpatrick and the chief of police, a big, blond, cheery creature with curly hair, dressed too tightly in white drill, with a holster on his fat hip, to whom he did not warm – 'He laughed aloud when he saw my passport, putting an arm round my shoulder with that false Mexican camaraderie' – but who told him: 'You've come home. Why, everybody in Villahermosa is called Greene – or Graham.' Greene thought there must be English people in the town, but no – the Greenes were Mexican and if he came back to the police station at 4 p.m. he would be introduced to them.[8]

Greene's hatred for the Villahermosa police festered. The police chief, his men, and the police station all find their way into *The Power and the Glory*: 'The appointment was for four; I sat on a bench in the courtyard of the police station for an hour. The dirty whitewashed walls, the greasy hammocks, and the animal faces of the men – it wasn't like law and order so much as banditry. The police were the lowest of the population: you had to look for honesty on the faces of the men and women waiting to be fined or blackguarded. You gained an overwhelming sense of brutality and irresponsibility as they took down their rifles from the rack and sloped away on patrol or ambled drearily across the yard in the great heat with their trousers open.'[9]

One policeman was assigned to hunt out the chief of police for Greene, and they walked from one end of the town to the other through the hot afternoon, looking in all the billiard rooms, but no chief was to be found.

He did meet one rather scared Greene. His name was De Witt Greene and he had Dutch, American, English and pure Indian blood in him. His grandfather had come from Pennsylvania after the Civil War. De Witt Greene, walking across the plaza, pointed to a seedy Mexican, with drooping hat and a gun on his hip: 'There's another Greene,' he said.

The heat must have been very distressing. A year before Greene's arrival, de Joaquin Bates, later to become secretary to the Governor, wrote this descriptive poem about Villahermosa:

Casas Viejas,	Old houses
Diez fordcitos,	Ten small Fords
Muchachitas sin color,	Little girls without colour*

* Without colour because of worms. In Yajalon, Chiapas, Greene met and was befriended by a Norwegian lady who had two young blonde children. One is the source for the wonderful child Coral Fellows in *The Power and the Glory*. Her mother once purged her of twenty worms, some of them a foot and a half long. They seldom evacuated more than half a dozen worms at a time: Greene writes: 'It was like the grave, the earth taking over before its day.'[10]

| Uno, Dos, Tres Parquesitos | One, Two, Three tiny parks |
| Millonadas de Mozquitos y Calor, Calor, Calor | Millions of Mosquitoes and Heat, Heat, Heat. |

And on Sundays, without cantinas or churches, which at the least had provided the poor with 'one spot of coolness out of the vertical sun, a place to sit, a place where the senses can rest a little while from ugliness', there was no escape. One could only sit in a rocking-chair waiting for the sunset and the mosquitoes and the vultures: 'The tiny moron head, long neck, masked face, and dusty plumage peering this way and that attentively for a death.'[11]

On his last night in Villahermosa, he sat on a rocking-chair at the head of the stairs with the old proprietor of the hotel and they swung back and forth, trying to stir a breeze. It was 'an awful night'. There was a storm but the air in Villahermosa never cleared. The pavement 'was black with beetles. They lay on every stair up from the electric dynamo to the hotel; they detonated against the lamp and walls and fell with little plops like hailstones.' Greene went to his bedroom and killed seven beetles and the corpses moved as rapidly as in life across the floor pushed by the swarms of ants. He lay in bed and read Trollope, with nostalgia.[12]

What was wrong with Tabasco, among other things, Greene felt, was a terrible lethargy: 'the Catholics died slowly out – without Confession, without the Sacraments, the child unbaptized, and the dying man unshriven.'[13] Greene put it down to the swamp and the extreme heat. In Chiapas there were mountains and less lethargy and there were Indians 'with their wild beliefs and their enormous if perverted veneration [who] shamed the Catholics into *some* action'.

Knowing that he faced a long, tough journey into Chiapas, Greene jettisoned everything he thought unnecessary, including dirty socks, and replaced these with a hammock, a serape (a brightly coloured blanket cloak), a kettle and a snake-bite remedy. He put on riding breeches and boots, in which he was to live for the next ten days, and went out to the airport on top of the hill beyond the cemetery with its blind wall, 'where Garrido shot his prisoners', and its white classical portico with its legend, 'Silencio', written in big black letters. He took off in a little, cramped, red, six-seater plane: below him was the Godless state.

*

The journey by air took a mere fifteen minutes. They came down first in a tiny clearing in a forest for a short stop: 'Three people left the plane, a peasant woman with a basket and two men carrying leather satchels and umbrellas; they walked off – like season ticket holders – into deep forest.'[14]

Then they were up again crossing the mountains. Salto de Agua lay right under the mountains on a bluff above a rapid green river. Travellers come down on a rough landing field and then cross the river in a dug-out canoe. After he watched the little red plane move back across the sky Greene felt marooned, very much alone and troubled by his poverty of Spanish in a land where few spoke English and a mistake could land him anywhere.

He had a letter of introduction to a store-keeper asking him to find a reliable guide – to Palenque. A man carried his suitcase into the dark store with its back to a tiny dry plaza. He wondered why he had started on this journey.

Now that he was in Chiapas he could drop the pretence that he wanted to see the ruins of Palenque, but it took a long time to explain in his poor Spanish that it was to the 'very Catholic' city of Las Casas that he wanted to go and not to Palenque – could he find a guide to take him as far as Yajalon, en route to Las Casas? The store-keeper said he would try.

Every few hours Greene turned up at the store to see whether a guide had been found. But by nightfall, after spending most of the day in the single cantina, drinking expensive warm beer (expensive because it had to be brought over the mountains on muleback), no guide was to be found for Yajalon, the route which would take him in the direction of Las Casas. In desperation he fell back on Palenque and the store-keeper encouraged him with the story that there was a German-American there with a beautiful daughter and a fine *finca*, but Greene doubted this having heard such a rumour ever since Mexico City. When he returned from Palenque he was promised there would be a guide for Yajalon.

Although he spent only one night in Salto, he felt he knew it as well as if he had been there years – a tiny barren place, the row of huts by the river, two parallel tracks running into the little plaza (not a soul there), the palms and the cantina, the eternal mineral water stand, the wooden bridge over a small ravine with a track running off into the hills; some mangy dogs, and flies of course, the tin-roofed shacks where men lay in hammocks swinging in the great heat. The little town was dead by midday.[15]

His lodging was a room partitioned off with plywood from the rest of the house, with a bed made out of packing-cases, a straw mat laid on the top of them. Surprisingly he slept well, his mackintosh cape folded up as a pillow, his mosquito net in place, but then he heard rattling on his door, 'something animal' muttering and stamping and blowing windily. It was his young guide who, just after four o'clock in the morning, took him to his father's home where he had coffee and biscuits.

Everyone was asleep as he left Salto to embark on a journey he would never forget, he suffering extreme discomfort and sickness; but which was to be the basis of *The Power and the Glory*. They crossed the river by canoe, the two mules swimming beside them, 'with just their muzzles and their eyes above the water like a pair of alligator heads, and then the long banana plantations on the other bank, the fruit plucked as we rode tasting tart and delicious in the open air at dawn.'[16]

Greene had never ridden a mule before. That day was to be one of the worst he spent in all his thirty-three years, for the route lay across a bare exposed plateau and there was rarely any shade and only a few patches of forest. By nine in the morning the sun was blindingly up. In the heat, his sun helmet, bought for a few pesos in Veracruz, turned into damp, hot cardboard. He found riding the mule was like riding a camel – the whole back heaving and straining: 'There is no rhythm you can catch by riding in the stirrups; you must surrender yourself to a merciless uneven bump.' Travelling over the mountain in that brutal sun with his neck stiffening and his head aching, Greene learnt of the stubbornness of mules, the impossibility of getting out of them anything more than a walk, the eternal call in the mountains: 'Mula. Mula. Mula. Echa, mula.'

After six hours they reached a couple of wattle huts, chickens and turkeys tumbling across the dusty floor, a pack of mongrels, a few cows listless in the heat. Greene longed to stay the night. With immense difficulty he dismounted; his whole body had stiffened and they swung a string hammock up for him. He rested for half an hour. The urge to stay in that bare Indian hut was overpowering, anything was better than that baked plateau, but the guide, who had never himself travelled to Palenque and only knew the general direction, wanted to reach it that day. There were another eight hours to travel.

Greene remembered little of the rest of the journey, raising his helmet for coolness and dropping it back for fear of sunstroke, his head aching, his mind becoming a blank. He did remember the guide 'getting smaller and smaller in the distance', and having to flog the mule into a backbone wrenching trot to catch up with him, and a man with the mails travelling at a smart canter on a pony in the opposite direction. Then:

somewhere on that immense rolling plain, in a spot where the grass grew long, the mule suddenly lay down under me. The guide was a long way off; I felt I could never get up on that mule again; I sat on the grass and tried to be sick and wanted to cry. The guide rode back and waited patiently for me to remount, but I didn't think it was possible – my body was too stiff.[17]

By 2 p.m. they had been riding for nine hours and according to his guide, Palenque was still about five hours away. Could they stay the night somewhere and go on the next day? There was nowhere to stay until they reached Palenque. String their hammocks on the tree and sleep there? But the guide had no hammocks 'and besides, there was no food, no drink, and lots of mosquitoes, perhaps a leopard'. Greene recalled, 'It was rather terrifying to believe you cannot go on, and yet have no choice.'[18] The mule lay down four times.

Eventually, after a patch of forest, they came to the dividing of the ways. The guide told him one way led to a German *finca*, the other to Palenque. This was the *finca* he had heard of so often but believed to be legendary, particularly because the pilot of the little red plane had made light of it, and so he chose the path to Palenque.

The sun sank; night fell; the flies came out thick and sank into the mule's neck, grappled and sucked until a stream of blood flowed down. Greene tried to dislodge the flies with his stick without success. He recalls that the smell of the blood and the mule was sickening. The journey went on and on and he felt that he had become a bundle of flesh and bone without a brain. The stars came out. Ahead, along a slope of grass, was a cemetery on a hill, abandoned, wall broken, crosses at angles also broken, the result of the useless persecution. They rode among mud huts where, on a little hill, there was a big, plain, ruined church. It was a scene he was to remember, and they arrived at Palenque, staggering off their mules, legs as stiff as stilts. They found a store near the church and had three warm beers and raw tequila which hardly quenched their thirst. That night they slept in a hut, once a stable, beside the ruined church, divided into three by thin partitions. Greene could hear small children crying behind one partition and the slow movements and regular coughing of cows behind the other.

At midnight came the sound of a horse outside, of a fist beating on the bolted door, of shouting, 'Con amistad – with friendship.' The stranger moved heavily round the room, tied up a hammock, and took off his revolver holster. It was all very Mexican and somewhat romantic, but Greene had a touch of fever, needed to vomit, and was too tired to move.

He went the next morning, absurdly after such a body-breaking journey and a fever, to see the ruins. They passed a bleached skeleton on the path. Periodically, the guide had to stop to cut a way through with his machete. After two and a half hours the ruins appeared, but Greene merely hung on to the pommel of his saddle for he was almost beyond caring. With an effort of will he climbed up two slopes and peered into cold snaky chambers. He sat on a stone and later slid to the ground while the guide set off with an Indian to explore another palace. He struggled to an Indian hut, a twig shelter without walls, with chickens scratching in the dust, a hammock and a packing case.

Greene is not certain what happened next but thinks he must have dozed for he remembered the Indian and the guide looking down at him, troubled. They got him to another hut and gave him corn coffee. Again he wanted to sleep but the guide complained of mosquitoes and suggested the German *finca* and the beautiful daughter. Greene lay on his back still disbelieving. The *finca* they said was only a little way from Palenque, and they would take him in the cool of that evening. They pushed him back on the mule and on to Palenque where he fell off the mule, made for the village schoolmaster's hammock and lay down. He could hear the plump complacent schoolmaster talking to a passing peasant about the sun as the origin of life; that without the sun we should cease to exist. Greene drank cup after cup of coffee, but was unable to eat. Liquid poured out of him and he lay in sweat for hours. Outside the street was silent.

*

The *finca* was not a myth, it did exist and it was paradise. Greene recalled, 'It was like heaven' finding that *finca* only fifteen minutes out of Palenque – the rolling down, the stream, a broken bridge, cows grazing, orange trees at the gate, a tulipan in blossom and a woman knitting on the verandah, a man beside her reading his paper. There was no beautiful daughter, that part of the story was untrue but the rest was no fantasy. They were a German farmer and his sister, good Lutherans. There was a big earthenware jar of fresh water with a dipper beside it, there was a soft bed with sheets and 'most astonishing luxury of all' a little clear sandy stream to wash in, six-week-old copies of New York papers, the tulipan which dropped its blossoms at night and prepared to bloom again with the day: 'Only the bullet-hole in the porch showed the flaw in Paradise – that this was Mexico.'[19]

At the *finca* Greene recovered from his fever, had his first feeling of happiness in Chiapas, and experienced a sense of remarkable peace. And it was there that he must have decided to take two days over the return journey to Salto de Agua, spending the night at the Indian hut where he had rested for half an hour, a bare Indian hut surrounded by chickens, pigs and turkeys with the 'mauve surrealist flaps of skin they . . . toss aside to uncover the beak or eyes'. The old Indian lady with 'a burnt pinched face and dry hair, like the shrivelled human head in the booth at San Antonio', gave him corn coffee and stringy chicken. Greene lay all afternoon and evening in his hammock under the palm vine verandah. It might not have been unpleasant but he had an unreasonable and deeply superstitious dread of the movement of animals in the dark and feared that when darkness fell the turkeys might decide to perch on his hammock.

At 2 a.m. came the sound of horses beating up across the plain and again there were armed strangers at the door: 'A horse whistled, stirrup irons jangled; when the lightning flared I could see four horses, and a man dismounting. He felt his way across the verandah and knocked at the door – "*Con amistad*". His belt drooped with the weight of his gun. He seemed to be the leader; the three others dismounted and unsaddled . . .'[20]

Men were disturbed; the turkeys lumbered down from the tree hissing and squawking, candles were lit and coffee served. There was political and incomprehensible talk around the table – hammocks were slung. One stranger was asked by the owner of the hut to take off his gun belt: 'The stranger laughed, took off his belt, and tossed it into his hammock; the bearded arrogant faces shone in the candlelight.'[21]

Then a storm broke, the lightning striking the ground within a hundred yards. It was bitterly cold and the rain poured in under the verandah, wetting the hammock. Greene had left his mackintosh cape at Salto. Soaking and frightened by the storm, he said 'Hail Mary's' to himself like a good Catholic, dozed till four, wakened his guide at four-thirty and was off, tired and stiff, for the last part of the journey. They reached Salto just before nine and crossed the river by canoe, the mules swimming as before, just their muzzles and eyes above the water, again like a pair of alligator heads.

Lifeless and drab as Salto was, it felt like home. Greene found ticks wedged firmly into his arms and thighs and buttocks and swore he would never ride a mule again! 'There is a kind of cattle tick you catch in Chiapas, which fastens its head in the flesh,' he writes. 'You have to burn it out, otherwise the head remains embedded and festers.' Forty years later, Greene told Marie-Françoise Allain how they had burrowed into, and remained in, his backside.

Writing to his mother from Las Casas, he gave a much played-down account of his experiences: 'I . . . took a mule & guide to Palenque – unwisely I did it in one day – 13 hours of riding & by the time I'd done another 4 hours to the ruins & back, I was very knocked up. However, I stayed a couple of days on a *finca* owned by a German & that put me right & I made the return journey in two days.'[22]

Again, his luck changed. Having vowed never to ride a mule again he was saved from having to. His friend José Ortega, pilot of the little red plane, had landed at Salto and was to have taken off again for Yajalon the day before, but was grounded by low clouds. Greene had a quick lunch, walked down to the river bank and saw across the river the red plane and the pilot giving its propeller a twist. He ran for a canoe, sent for his suitcase and hurried across.

Greene recalled that from the plane the river dropped away like a knife; a magnificent landscape opened up of rock and forest and sharp precipitous ridges. They climbed in that tiny red plane over 3,000 feet but still the mountains on both sides were above the propeller and the pilot flew, not over the mountains but between them, the world slanting up all round as if they were diving. Ortega, over the wind and clouds, shouted in Greene's ear that they were through the mountains and close to Yajalon: 'We bumped downwards towards a white church on a little plateau completely surrounded by mountains; we were like a billiard ball dropping into a pocket.'[23]

*

Yajalon held pleasant surprises. Through an open door, Greene came suddenly on a tall woman with hollow handsome features and a strange twisted mouth. The odd shape of her mouth was due to food poisoning which had paralysed her for eight months. He stayed in a lodging (it is there to this day) with Sr Lopez and was taken there by the daughters of the handsome lady. Her husband was dead and his grave was in the cemetery above the town. Greene calls her Fru R. She and her husband were Norwegian and her real name was Rasmussen. Greene makes especial reference to her two little blonde daughters, fourteen and eleven, 'startlingly beautiful in a land where you grow weary of black and oily hair and brown sentimental eyes'. Greene believed that the elder girl disliked him on sight: 'I was the stranger breaking their narrow familiar life with demands – for lodging, conversation, company.'

Fru Rasmussen was a tragic figure, left alone in the mountains with her two young daughters after her husband's death, trying to carry on her husband's coffee farm, all their savings stolen by her god-parent (a spiritual relationship regarded in Mexico as a close one) while her husband was dying. She was to be a saviour to Greene, the second kind Lutheran family he had met on his journey.

Greene hoped to stay in Yajalon for only three days, when a plane was expected to arrive to take him to Las Casas, that town which had been praised by the German living at the *finca* as 'a very moral town', in Yajalon as that 'moral' city, that 'very Catholic' town; and Greene was longing to reach it during Holy Week to see how Catholics might practise their religion under severe restrictions, where, though the churches might well be open, no priest would be allowed to enter or offer the sacraments. In Yajalon, in the great square, the church was shuttered, weeds growing out of the bell towers.

Meanwhile Greene visited Fru Rasmussen at tea-time. She always had coffee and cake ready for him, and he looked forward to his daily visit as the days went by and still no plane had arrived; he felt it impossible to repay her kindness adequately. But he did repay her in his next novel with his portrait, not of the tragic Norwegian woman herself, but of the elder daughter. She is the model for Coral Fellows in *The Power and the Glory*.

On the first night he walked back to the hotel in the dark – there was no street lighting – and met his fellow lodgers. They were eating at a table under the verandah by the light of an oil-lamp: 'a stout, white-toothed mestizo school teacher with an air of monotonous cheeriness (and one obscene English word which he repeated, with huge amusement, day after day), his pregnant wife, and his small son of a year and a half . . . And there were others who dropped in for meals only – a few grizzled, friendly men, a young married couple with their baby, and a clerk I grew to loathe, a mestizo with curly sideburns and two yellow fangs at either end of his mouth.'[24]

The town was so small that Greene saw these faces whenever he walked out – 'the mestizo looking up from his typewriter in the Presidencia and showing his fangs as I went by, a grizzled man waving a hand from a doorway, the schoolmaster's rich, powerful voice sounding all across the little plaza from his schoolroom, and the young married man pulling up his horse outside the cantina. It gave one the sensation of being under observation all the time.'[25] He did not like the Mexicans he met there. But he did not feel a forceful current of enmity towards himself until he reached Las Casas. The schoolmaster the night before had made an impassioned speech at a fiesta on the oil expropriations and urged people to 'Get rid of the gringoes'. There were, in any case, only three gringoes in Yajalon – Fru Rasmussen, a German photographer, and Greene.

Most of the schoolmasters had taken over the functions once filled by priests, but unlike the priests they could not speak the Indian dialects, and Greene recalls that the schoolmaster told him how the Spaniards had oppressed the Indians, making them into 'mere beasts of burden', but as he spoke, Greene could not help but notice the sad, patient procession of Indians bowed double under enormous crates supported by a leather belt across the forehead, plodding by.

The lodging house was infested with rats – at night he could hear them chasing one another in the *sala*. Rats terrified him. One evening he borrowed an Elizabeth Bowen novel from Fru Rasmussen. Sitting in the *sala* he saw a rat, small, black and elongated, run up the wall and in through the open door of his bedroom. He went to his plank bed and shut his door – better one rat than a family of them – and spent 'an awful and absurd night', candle stuck in wax on his chair, with the brandy he'd bought in Veracruz, reading Elizabeth Bowen. The plane did not appear; the weather worsened; the rains were coming and soon the roads would be impassable.

After lunch, the schoolteacher played the guitar, singing, among other songs, 'Have I a Rose in My Field?' Greene felt a growing claustrophobia in this small place wedged in among the mountains round its locked decaying church. To his mother he wrote: 'I got stuck at Yajalon a week – I'd sworn never to go on a mule again, and they said there'd be an aeroplane tomorrow & tomorrow, but it never came & I got desperate with boredom & rats in my room.'[26]

Greene sought out his previous guide to Palenque. He implored young Gomez to find him mules and offered him an exorbitant sum if he could start next morning early. A promise was made to have mules ready at six. He hardly slept, not only because of the rats but because of hope. Next morning the rain was pouring down and no mules came. Everyone, including Gomez, said that it was impossible to travel in the mountains in this rain. At López's the schoolmaster argued that Greene did not realise how bad the road was; it was precipitous, dreadful. He stressed that he would never go that way himself, the paths were so narrow (and he showed Greene with his hands just how narrow and precipitous they could be). Greene almost became resigned but then:

> rather terrifyingly everything altered. Fru R.'s little blonde daughter stood in the dripping rain with a stranger, a small scrubby-bearded man. He would go with me in spite of the rain and for ten pesos less than Gomez's muleteer.[27]

The muleteer went off into the rain to find his mules to return at midday. Greene played a last game of chess and the schoolmaster checkmated him in six moves. Greene was distracted by the German photographer's* comments about how crazy it was even to dream of travelling in this weather. The mountains would be impassable and the guide did not know the way to Las Casas (which turned out to be true).

Then the strange muleteer returned. Fru Rasmussen packed him a rucksack, with a kind of home-made advocaat, two sausage sandwiches, some candles, cheese, a serape and 'a great lump, the size of a doll's head', of brown sugar. This huge sugar lump was not forgotten and later appeared in *The Power and the Glory*.

*

There were three mules, one for each rider and one for Greene's suitcase. For two hours they proceeded slowly, step by step, through drenching rain while the scrubby-bearded little muleteer lashed and dragged and lashed, calling out in a high hysterical voice, 'Mula. O Mula.'

That journey to Las Casas equalled in difficulty the journey to Palenque. Moreover, it took three days, each day on the mule increasing in length, until they reached the 'Holy City'. There were no roads. 'People said the paths would be impossible after two days of rain', he afterwards wrote to his mother, 'but we got out of the storm area & after three days riding reached here [Las Casas] the first day 1.p.m. to 7; the 2nd day 6 a.m. to 7.30 p.m. & 3rd, 6.45 to 9 p.m. Palenque had toughened me, & I was no more than very tired.'

It was a remarkable journey and it says something for Greene's strength and health that he could, even after a recent fever, do such a journey and be only 'very tired'. Parts of the journey were stored in his memory, and later used in his novel.

They climbed in long spirals, up into the mountains. A thousand feet above Yajalon, the mule with the suitcase ran off. The guide, having dismounted to adjust his load, lost his head and set off on foot (instead of on his mule) chasing after the disappearing mule 'crying and praying hysterically to the Mother of God down the mountainside'. It was comic but also disturbing. Greene last caught sight of the mule climbing up the opposite slope with the muleteer ·

---

* The German photographer was still in his store forty years after Greene's visit, and still, 'The wooden wall of his . . . shack was covered with innocent pictures of naked girls and Plaisirs de Paris torn off the covers of magazines; among them, rigidly, the face of Hitler' – though the face of Hitler had gone. But Greene also looked at films, badly washed, of weddings, funerals and fiestas which the German store-keeper expected him to buy at an exorbitant price. When I was there, I bought some of those badly washed photographs. The price *was* exorbitant.

50 yards behind – the mule in the distance a toy animal, the muleteer a toy man.

Darkness fell; the opposite slope 'dropped into obscurity, untenanted'. Greene was left trying to push the spare mule; it dug its heels in, while his own mule went forward. Greene felt himself being dragged backwards out of the saddle, which was dangerous because of the narrow path and the second mule which he could not handle. But then his guide returned. He had obviously taken his revenge on the mule for there was a big bleeding gash in the mule's neck – prompt punishment, indeed.

They lost their way to a *finca* where they had hoped to stay and went on and on, climbing and descending, the mules slipping on tree-roots. About 7 p.m. they came upon four mud-and-wattle huts 'black and silent in the moonless dark'. An old man tended them. He was on the edge of starvation, living in a hut with rats, welcoming the strangers without a word about payment, gossiping gently in the dark: 'I felt myself', writes Greene movingly, 'back with the population of heaven.'[28] The old man was also to be remembered.

They started again for 13½ hours on muleback to Cancuc – an incredible feat for an unseasoned gringo. At 11 a.m. they reached a village and ate dry strips of bacon and tortillas. They were climbing, but for every 1,000 feet they rose, they also had to drop down 600. The landscape was spell-binding – huge gorges covered with forest, sheer walls of rock, trees grasping a foothold in the cracks. To reach Las Casas they had to climb at least 7,000 feet. There were no more villages before Cancuc and only occasional Indian settlements perched on the rocky plateau above the path. One of these was to be used later as an important meeting place and crisis in *The Power and the Glory*: 'One with a little wattle watch-tower from which an Indian stared down at us as we climbed wearily upwards.'

After eleven hours Cancuc could be seen in the distance and especially what looked from afar 'a great white cathedral' flashing in the late sun. Greene was touched by faint feelings of romance. Years ago, he could not doubt that this would have seemed romance to him, to be riding slowly at evening through the mountains, going south towards he did not know what in an unfamiliar land, the crack and pad of the mules' feet on stone and turf, and the immense serrated waste of almost uninhabited country, only an Indian watch-tower leagues away.[29]

That day they must have climbed 3,000 feet and the night was bitterly cold and windy. Keeping on, they suddenly came round the rock to the 'great cathedral' which turned out to be a small square white-washed church. He was desperately tired. It was an uncomfortable night, also remembered and later used. They rode on. Almost the only light came from fireflies, and then outside the cantina a huge bonfire. The cantina was an unwalled shelter filled with men, beds raised on stakes from the ground and covered with serapes, not an inch of space for more bodies.

Finally, they were put in the mayor's office, though the beds there were already occupied. Greene chose a bench to sleep on, putting on more clothing – a vest, two shirts, two pairs of pants, his leather jacket. He drank admirable coffee, had bacon and fried eggs eaten with the fingers. Again he fell asleep and again came the romantic surprising fist beating on the barred door – the password '*Con amistad*' softening men's fears. It was the mayor himself, not the least disturbed that four strangers were sleeping in his office. Greene heard his horse whinnying in the dark.

The guide woke at 3 a.m. They had a mere thirty odd miles to travel to Las Casas, yet in those hills and in those conditions, it was to be a long day, the more so because they discovered that the mules had disappeared – they did not start until after 6 a.m.: 'The muleteer went wailing through the darkness with my torch; I could see it flash across the bone-white church; he was praying and close to tears, as he had been that first day when the mule ran away. Poor man, he was highly wrought; he wasn't cut out for a muleteer. There was nothing to do but wait for daylight on the mayor's bench. The next time I got up, the stars were still out, but a great fire was blowing beside the eating hut, playing on the white-washed ghost of a church.'[30]

Then they were off winding round huge hairpin bends along the edge of the barranca, a path cut in rock. After two terrible hours, Cancuc was still just opposite them. Greene grew desperately weary:

> Just weariness shot through occasionally with flashes – not exactly of beauty, but of consciousness, consciousness of something simple and strange and uncomplicated, a way of life we have hopelessly lost but can never quite forget. There was a moment at a little · brown pebbly river when the guide took a bowl from his saddle-bag and filled it with water from the stream and made himself a kind of gruel with a ball of corn – the mules drank and I stood on a stone and washed my face and hands and the shadow played on the stream, and it was like peace and natural happiness.[31]

Towards evening they came out of the forest on to a plateau, meeting up with a curious Indian cemetery which keenly impressed Greene (also remembered). He was struck by the magic of it, the magic element of Christianity.

After almost twelve hours on the road, Las Casas came into view:

> Suddenly we came out of the forest on to the mountain edge, and there below us were the lights of the town – the long lines of streets laid out electrically. It was extraordinarily dramatic to come on a city like this, eight thousand feet up, at the end of a mule track, a city of fourteen thousand inhabitants with a score of churches, after the hairpin bends round the mountainside, after the precipices and the foot-wide tracks, the climbs and the descents. It was like an adventure of Rider Haggard – coming so unexpectedly out of the forest above this city, once the capital of Chiapas and the home of Las Casas.[32]

'Extraordinarily dramatic', the very words used in *The Lawless Roads* but which he had used in a letter to his mother on the day he arrived at Las Casas and the Hotel Español: 'It was extraordinarily dramatic arriving at a place of this size at the end of a mule track in a cup of the mountains – and only a road out the other side to Tuxla [and the coast and home]. One came down to it, as it stands over 8,000 feet up.'

They had ridden for almost fourteen hours; they went down a seemingly endless cobbled street and finally they rode into the little flowery patio of the hotel:

> A room with a bed and sheets, a beautifully cooked meal, steak and greens and sweet bread, a bottle of beer, and the radio playing: I was drunk and dazed with happiness. The neighbours sat round the radio listening to news of Spain, picking out the ravaged villages on a map hung on the wall, marking with enthusiasm Franco's advance. Somebody said, 'Turn on the news from London,' and 'This is London,' they said to me. It was still a Spanish voice speaking in Spanish, but it came from London. It welled out of that solid and complacent building in Portland Place, over the Queen's Hall and Oxford Circus, over the curve of the world, the Atlantic and the Gulf and the Tropic of Capricorn, over the cemetery with 'SILENCIO' in black letters and the wall where Garrido shot his prisoners, over the swamps and rivers, the mountains and the forests, where the old man slept with the rats beside his corn and the flames beat against the front of the locked-up church. 'This is London,' they assured me again because I doubted it.[33]

He fulfilled his ambition to spend Holy Week in Las Casas. Mass was held in an anonymous house in a side street – 'a closed door, nothing to mark the presence of God . . . the priest . . . his face hideously disfigured with mauve patches' and Mass without the sanctus bell. On Holy Thursday, after early morning Mass, it was like an invasion, 'The Indians were pouring in from the mountains, down the long cobbled streets from Guadalupe . . . they came in thousands to see the crucified Christ.'[34]

*

He went on, completing his arduous and dangerous journey of five weeks, ill with dysentery. He travelled by bus, and at the village of San Lorenzo, when they stopped, he had to go into a stony field to relieve himself and be sick. The journey was an interminable winding descent to the tropics and Tuxtla, then an old plane to Oaxaca and a final train journey to Puebla, where he visited a hidden convent which had been discovered by the government and was now run as an anti-God museum, and the final run by bus to Mexico City.

He had looked forward to that goal throughout his journey – there his troubles would be at an end – it would be 'so fine, easy, and luxurious, all brandy cocktails and bourbon and Coca Cola'. But it wasn't. The cares, irritations and responsibilities he had left were waiting for him. The American proofs of *Brighton Rock* had not arrived but there were newspaper clippings about the Shirley Temple libel case. He was worried that he might be arrested on his return to England. He lay in bed that night in the Hotel Canada, reading again what counsel and Judge had said, and on the floor below 'a hysterical woman screamed and sobbed and a man spoke every way in vain . . . God knows what relationship was breaking up so publicly in the hotel room.'[35] He had come full circle and returned to what he had temporarily escaped from.

He left by liner from Veracruz, still full of loathing for Mexico, but in London he wondered what he had come back to: the A.R.P. (Air Raid Precautions) posters were new and ominous.

42

The Power and the Glory

I must lie down where all the ladders start,
In the foul rag-and-bone shop of the heart.
— W. B. YEATS

W HEN, in 1978, I went to Tabasco, retracing Graham Greene's journey through Mexico forty years after the publication of *The Lawless Roads*, the then Governor of Tabasco said to me: 'Mr Greene had nasty things to say about us; we hope his biographer will say nice things.' The critics had nasty things to say about *The Lawless Roads* when it was published in 1939. 'One tires', wrote one reviewer, 'of Mr Greene's dyspeptic descriptions of the hotels, the meals, and the sanitary facilities of Mexico.' The *New York Times* pointed out the strange fact that 'wherever he went, ugliness stalked him and leered at him from things and beasts and humans', and that he appeared to be 'one who infallibly attracts to himself bad food and bad smells and bad people. One suspects that, even at the North Pole, Mr Greene would be harassed by mental mosquitoes.' An anonymous reviewer, commenting on the oddity of the fact that this loveliest of all American countries should have filled Greene's soul with rage and that he experienced little joy in travel and adventure, nevertheless concludes: 'Yet *The Lawless Roads* is more worth reading than a hundred other books of travel.'

Greene had allowed Mexico to make its own impression on him. He had undoubtedly prepared for the journey by reading and making contacts and he had not one but two purposes in going there – not only to look into the state of religion but by travelling alone, by taking the lawless roads, to enter as far as he was able into the experience of the country and its people. Joy in travel and adventure was not his object.

What is extraordinary about *The Power and the Glory* is that it should have been written by a man who spent only five weeks in Mexico, one week in Villahermosa and one night in Frontera, and

695

yet re-created the country and situation so convincingly in his novel
that he won the praise of a Mexican priest. Father Munos, who knew
Frontera where the novel begins, said in Mexico City in 1978, 'I
think his masterpiece is *The Power and the Glory* – for myself it is
extraordinary. As a Mexican I travel in those regions. The first three
paragraphs of [the novel], when he gives you camera shots of the
place, why it is astounding. You are *in* the place.' Father Munos also
felt that he owed Greene 'a great debt in [his] own religious make-up',
since he had influenced him as a Catholic priest. In 1960, a Catholic
teacher from San Lorenzo, California, wrote to Greene:

> One day I gave *The Power and the Glory* to an even more specialized
> reader – a native of Mexico who had lived through the worst
> persecutions. She was so moved by your story that she volunteered
> to come into my classes with souvenirs of the period – photographs,
> communist propaganda, etc., to fill in the background of the story.
> She confessed that your descriptions were so vivid, your priest so
> real, that she found herself praying for him at Mass. I understand
> how she felt. Last year, on a trip through Mexico, I found myself
> peering into mud huts, through village streets, and across impass-
> able mountain ranges, half-believing that I would glimpse a dim
> figure stumbling in the rain on his way to the border. There is no
> greater tribute possible to your creation of this character – he lives.

Absorption of a place and its atmosphere is one thing; the creation
of convincing characters within that place is another. Out of his
Mexican experience came a priest, a policeman and a Judas figure,
central to the theme he found in Mexico. Where did he discover them
in such a short time? Their origins must go back a long way in
Greene's psyche, as far back as Berkhamsted, the villain Carter
and the traitor Wheeler with himself as victim – the basic pattern
established. In Mexico he found surrogate figures, to whom in some
sense he could transfer his childhood emotions. He also experienced
a strengthening of his own religious beliefs.

The effect of his experiences makes *The Lawless Roads* his personal ·
credo. It is significant that at the beginning of the book he quotes a
poem by Edwin Muir describing a landscape in which everything is
lawless, and also quotes Cardinal Newman in his assessment of the
human condition – 'a reason-bewildering fact': 'either there is no
Creator, or this living society of men is in a true sense discarded from
his presence . . . *if* there be a God, *since* there is a God, the human
race is implicated in some terrible aboriginal calamity.' Not a hopeful
diagnosis but probably a valid reflection of Greene's religious views

at that time. It is interesting that the title of the novel that came from his Mexican experience gives this world and the fictional world he had created back to the Creator: 'For Thine is the Kingdom, the Power and the Glory'. For Greene's is an unstable universe – not only 'if' but also 'since' there is a God; not only is human political power a fragile matter, but glory is an even more fragile and ambiguous state – a whisky priest who dies reluctantly for his faith, a lieutenant of police who lives as a puritan with total devotion to his beliefs. On the boat Greene returned home in there were Catholic volunteers from Havana going to support the Fascism of Franco in Spain who were disconcerted by the Fascist German farmer from Chiapas who hated Christianity.[1] In an unstable universe, giving back to God (*if* there is or *since* there is one) a picture of his kingdom, one can only present things as they appear to a single human observer.

For this reason Greene has to experience the human condition at all possible levels, he has to experience hate and anger and degradation. Though, of course, it is a quest: he is not locked into a specific situation, he can and will retreat with his spoils. But his anger is always directed against what he sees as injustice – and such anger often demolishes the mask of the quiet Englishman (as opposed to the quiet American), the English upper-class civility and control. For example, he attacked Reginald Maudling, the then British Home Secretary, over methods of interrogation of I.R.A. suspects:

> If I, as a Catholic, were living in Ulster today I confess I would have one savage and irrational ambition – to see Mr Maudling pressed against a wall for hours on end, with a hood over his head, hearing nothing but the noise of a wind machine, deprived of sleep when the noise temporarily ceased by the bland voice of a politician telling him that his brain will suffer no irreparable damage . . . How can any Englishman now protest against torture in Vietnam, in Greece, in Brazil, in the psychiatric wards of the USSR, without being told, 'You have a double standard: one for theirs and another for your own country'?[2]

In Mexico the Roman Catholic Church was the underdog, but he was antipathetic to Mexico – its food, beggars, rats, fleas, mosquitoes and the Mexican man's greeting – the *abrazo*:

> I have never been in a country where you are more aware all the time of hate. Friendship there is skin deep – a protective gesture. The motion of greeting you see everywhere upon the street, the

hands outstretched to press the other's arms, the semi-embrace –
what is it but the motion of pinioning to keep the other man from
his gun? There has always been hate, I suppose, in Mexico, but
now it is the official teaching: it has superseded love in the school
curriculum.[3]

Hate and suspicion were what (among much else) he brought out
of Mexico, but if you are writing a novel about religious fundamen-
tals, and enquiring into the human soul and its manipulation by a
secular power, perhaps a basis of hate and suspicion is not a bad
thing, neutralising partisanship and sentimentality. *The Power and the
Glory*, after all, deals with a cosmic war in human terms.

Greene insisted, however, that he had no idea, even after he
returned home, that a novel would emerge from his Mexican experiences or that he was seeking one: 'do you imagine I knew I was going
to write *The Power and the Glory*? No, I'd never consent to appropriate
other people's political sufferings for literary ends.'[4] He does not
mention religious sufferings, and perhaps destiny conspired to give
him the inspiration for the novel, but Calder-Marshall probably had
some justification in saying that Greene took the germ of a story he
wanted to write about Mexico with him. Moreover, he was able to
flesh it out, not simply by his own experiences, but by an interest in
martyrdom that went back a long way. Mexico drew him because it
had been, and to some extent still was, a battlefield where war was
waged between a form of paganism and Christianity – the fiercest and
most successful persecution of the Roman Catholic religion anywhere
since the reign of Queen Elizabeth I of England. By the time Greene
arrived in Mexico the religious persecution was to all intents and
purposes over, but the tradition of martyrdom was still there. One
might say that in Mexico he was seeking martyrs and persecutors, but
however much he brought out of Mexico, he took a lot into it.

*

When in 1927 the priest Padre Pro was executed in Mexico City,
Graham wrote to his wife-to-be: 'Yes I saw the article on the Mexican
martyrs. I read all that number because I pulled it in pieces page by
page.' Nine years later there is an extract in his diary, probably copied
from the *Tablet*: 'Two priests were recently murdered in Durango.
In the same town an officer knocked the Vicar of Toniola down with
the butt of his pistol and ordered his battalion to shoot him . . . In
Tacamachaleco soldiers entered the church whilst the congregation
was reciting the Rosary. As the officer pulled the priest out of the
pulpit, the congregation rushed to his defence; the soldiers fired into

the crowd, wounding some fifty people . . . In general, the women show greater pluck in resisting the tyranny of the troops.'

Greene, because he had no inclination to be a martyr himself (except perhaps when in search of material), developed a strict view of the nature of martyrdom. In his 1936 diary, under the heading 'Notes for Mexico', he wrote of the only martyr he could remember meeting – a Jew imprisoned by Hitler and called Lorant – at a 'party at a female novelist's & he was very proud of his book, very conceited about himself; a stout middle-aged man he had a great opinion of his sexual ability & martyrdom had given him no end of a kick.' Which leads him to a consideration of the nature of true martyrdom: 'The church's martyrs are saved from this publicising; unless they are killed. They usually remain anonymous, & if they escape they are reabsorbed into the organisation for future use.' There remains the question of the validity of violent response to violence, and this involves a consideration of Communism, Fascism and Catholicism. Following Malraux's opinion in *Days of Contempt*, Greene sees Communism, unlike Fascism, as being based to some extent on love: 'Comrade, the type word cf. with the leader'. Communist atrocities seem at first inevitable – 'how can the tortured man help killing if he has the chance?', but 'Hate . . . of the oppressor & torturer: violence the result of violence: these things are not inevitable. The seventeenth-century Jesuit martyr Edmund Campion told his persecutors "to win you heaven or die upon your pikes", and this spirit at that period *did* communicate itself to some laymen . . . The priests in Mexico & Spain who take to arms only demonstrate that the Church is out of practice in martyrdom.' Greene's reaction to a poster in the Catholic newspaper, the *Universe* – 'Five Bishops killed in Spain' is: 'One feels wrong about the Catholic press trumpeting its martyrdoms. You don't *complain* about a death of that kind. It should be taken for granted.'

When he wrote *The Lawless Roads* he recorded the comments of a Catholic priest who was in prison at the time Padre Pro was shot, and who was later released: 'Pro was not a solitary victim – he counted over others he had known as we went for a drive together out to Chapultepec, sitting square, talking with immense satisfaction of death. "The Church needed blood," he said. "It always needs blood." It was the duty of priests and bishops to die; he had no sympathy for complaint and pious horror.'[5]

Greene found the nature of the true martyr in part in what his friend Herbert Read wrote:* 'Glory is now a discredited word, and

---

* Essay on Vauvenargues, a French moralist (1715–47), known for his *Introduction à la connaissance de l'esprit humain* with *Réflexions et maximes* appended.

it will be difficult to re-establish it. It has been spoilt by too close association with military grandeur; it has been confused with fame and ambition. But true glory is a private and discreet virtue, and is only fully realised in solitariness.'[6]

The glory of true martyrdom is its influence on others – 'when an eyewitness observed the leap of Southwell's torn-out heart'; 'when the spot of blood from Campion's entrails splashed Henry Walpole's coat, so that the course of the young man's life changed towards Tyburn'.* And, to illustrate the personally felt unworthiness of the martyr, Greene quotes a poem by Southwell, emphasising his sense of sin, unworthiness and betrayal, yet foreshadowing the whisky priest, dogged by Grace, with his 'greatness in decay . . . possessed by compassion':[7]

> At Sorrowe's door I knockt: they crav'd my name:
> I answered, one unworthy to be knowne:
> What one? say they. One worthiest of blame.
> But who? a wretch, not God's, nor yet his owne.
> A man? Oh no! a beast: much worse: what creature?
> A rocke: how call'd? The rock of scandale, Peter.

In the same review, Greene compares the Jesuit martyrs crossing the Channel with the young soldiers from Britain who went to the battlefields in France in the First World War – lightness of spirit in both, but 'For these recruits [the seventeenth-century Jesuits] there were no leave trains. They simply had to stay in line till death.' The same comparison occurs in *The Lawless Roads*, when in the heat and darkness of a night in Villahermosa, he turned out the light and 'as the cockchafers buzzed and beat one felt the excitement of this state where the hunted priest had worked for so many years, hidden in the swamps and forest, with no leave train or billet behind the lines.'[8] His whisky priest was coming to life.

Given his relentless pursuit of experience in Mexico, his long enquiry into the nature of glory and martyrdom, and his imaginative identification with the hunted, Greene might well have said, following Flaubert's Madame Bovary – 'c'est moi', 'the whisky priest c'est moi'.

*

In March 1939, a month after the publication of *The Lawless Roads*, Greene sat down to write his Mexican novel and he conceded, in

---

* Greene's review of Evelyn Waugh's *Life of Campion* and Pierre Janelle's *Life of Robert Southwell*, the *Spectator*, 1 November 1935.

1980, 'Now, of course, when I reread *The Lawless Roads*, I can easily detect many of the characters in *The Power and the Glory*.'⁹ Many, but not all: one wonders whether he detected himself among them. Was he, in part, 'the small man in a shabby dark city suit, carrying a small attaché case', a stranger without a name but with protuberant eyes like Greene, who meets, as Greene did, the dentist at the port? Greene, of course, is anything but small, but the priest's experiences and Greene's are very similar. When Greene wrote his novel, he probably worked with carefully documented accounts of his journey to hand – possibly a diary (now lost), from which the travel book was written up. Without these records of his experience, such a powerful and convincing novel could not have been written, for the godless land the priest travels through is the godless land Greene travelled through, and the bed-rock of the novel was to be those unplanned, perilous and exhausting journeys on muleback with inexperienced guides. Without them he could not have created his priest's flight from the police and his discovery of his parish, his lawless kingdom. Greene was almost as lonely and lost as his hero and could pass on his physical sufferings and minor enjoyments to the priest from his own experience of the situation in Tabasco and Chiapas. There are numerous instances of Greene's almost word-for-word transference of what he recorded in *The Lawless Roads* to *The Power and the Glory*.

*

The novel begins with a dentist, Mr Tench, walking into the blazing Mexican sunlight in search of an ether cylinder which should be in the cargo of the vessel *General Obregón*, now in port. Seeing vultures on the roof, he throws a piece of the road at them and one rises and flaps across the town, over the bust of an ex-president towards the river and the sea, but we are told that the vulture would not find anything there, 'the sharks looked after the carrion on that side.'¹⁰ We are certainly in Frontera – Greene wrote more briefly in *The Lawless Roads*: 'The vultures squatted on the roofs. It was like a place besieged by scavengers – sharks in the river and vultures in the streets.'¹¹ The bust of the ex-president is in fact that of ex-President, ex-General Obregón, a one-armed soldier and politician, which Greene observed when walking through the town – 'a bust of Obregón on a pillar'. He had been assassinated in 1928 and in 1931 Garrido Canabal had the bells of the Cathedral, when it was destroyed, melted down to make the bust.

Frontera was to be re-named Obregón: Greene re-named the *Ruiz Cano*, in which he sailed to Frontera, the *General Obregón*, but they are the same vessel – a few feet of broken rail, a bell hanging on a rotten cord, hobbled turkeys on both. Greene was told the *Ruiz Cano* would be safe if she did not meet a Norther, and he wrote of her fictional counterpart: 'She looked as if she might weather two or three more Atlantic years.' The *Ruiz Cano* did not in fact. She sank in the gulf a year after Greene sailed in her.

The English dentist Tench is, of course, the American dentist 'Dr Winter' who practised in Frontera, was concerned about Japanese drills, not ether cylinders, who boarded the *Ruiz Cano* on his way to consult his doctor, and who skulked 'abstractedly round the corner of the hotel spitting at the street corners, suddenly lost to all the world humming in the plaza, "I don't like the food. I don't like the food," without a memory and without a hope in the immense heat; he loomed during those days as big as a symbol – I am not sure of what, unless the aboriginal calamity, "having no hope, and without God in the world".' (Note the repetition of Newman.)[12]

We have yet another example of Greene's economical re-use of his personal experience. The stained glass windows of the dentist Greene hated when he was a boy, representing the laughing Cavalier, which were passed on to Pinkie in *Brighton Rock*: 'a stained-glass door (the laughing Cavalier between Tudor roses)', becomes one of Tench's memories of dentists' houses in England with their stained glass – 'it was generally the laughing Cavalier . . . or else a Tudor rose.' But Tench also has a piece of stained glass obtained when the church was sacked.

The Rasmussen family in Yajalon is reconstructed with the name of Fellows, the father still alive, returning home from the city and taking over Dr Winters's song, 'I don't like the food. I don't like the food.'[13] The family's plantation is not of coffee but bananas, Fru Rasmussen is reduced to a weakly, frightened shadow, but her elder daughter, now Coral Fellows, becomes a young heroine, unafraid. Like her source she is being taught by her mother through postal lessons (from England not America now), and is learning the poems of Victor Hugo (the younger Rasmussen child was learning 'The Charge of the Light Brigade'). She is also, like the Rasmussens' child, coming, even at so young an age, to maturity, which worries her father as it had worried Fru Rasmussen:

> As she walked in front of him, her two meagre tails of hair bleaching in the sunlight, it occurred to him for the first time that she was of an age when Mexican girls were ready for their first man. What was to happen? He flinched away from problems which he had never dared to confront.[14]

702

Just as Fru Rasmussen's elder daughter led Greene to shelter for the night, so Coral Fellows finds shelter for the hunted priest – her independence and courage heightened for the purposes of the novel, the police lieutenant does not frighten her and she can feel sympathy for the priest's desire for alcohol, bringing him a bottle of Cerveza Moctezuma. In the novel she dies mysteriously and her death, though alluded to, is never explained.*

What Fru Rasmussen's daughter would not have been is an atheist, but by making Coral Fellows into one Greene gives resonance to the theme of atheism in the book, strengthened by the fact that it is a young girl who says, 'You see, I don't believe in God. I lost my faith when I was ten', and urges the priest to renounce his faith to save his life. She is a pragmatist: being a priest, she concludes, must be like having a birthmark, you can't get rid of it, and when he says he will pray for her, she promises to teach him the Morse code – 'It would be useful to you.' But also, if his hunters kill him, she will never forgive them: 'She was ready to accept any responsibility, even that of vengeance, without a second thought.' Another revelation of the uncertain universe.

The *finca* belonging to the Lutheran brother and sister, only a quarter of an hour out of Palenque, provides also a resting place for the priest when he is at the end of his tether, and a brief escape from persecution before he has to face martyrdom. The *finca* in fact and fiction is a place of peace, beauty and civilisation. Herr R. and his sister in *The Lawless Roads* are first seen 'sitting side by side in rocking chairs on the veranda – as it might be the States, the woman knitting and the man reading his paper'.[15] In the novel a 'middle-aged woman sat on the veranda darning socks . . . Mr Lehr, her brother, read a New York magazine – it was three weeks old, but that didn't really matter.' In *The Lawless Roads*: 'It was like heaven'; in the novel, 'the whole scene was like peace.' There was 'a big earthenware jar of fresh water with a dipper beside it' (*L.R.*): 'A huge earthenware jar stood in a cool corner with a ladle and a tumbler' (*P.G.*). In both, a tulipan tree dropped its blossoms at night and bloomed again next day, and there was a little stream in which to bathe: 'and, most astonishing luxury of all, a little clear sandy stream to wash in with tiny fish like sardines pulling at the nipples . . . Next day I lay up at Herr R.'s – a bathe at six in the stream and another in the afternoon at five . . . you went to bathe in the little stream barefooted across the grass in spite of snakes.' (*L.R.*): ' "Well, I guess it's time for a bath now. Will

---

* I visited Yajalon in 1978 and learnt that Fru Rasmussen had died in California, and her elder daughter, Astrid, had died before her.

you be coming father?" and the priest obediently followed . . . Mr Lehr barefoot across . . . the field beyond. The day before he had asked apprehensively, "Are there no snakes?" and Mr Lehr had grunted contemptuously that if there were any snakes they'd pretty soon get out of the way . . . At the bottom of the field there was a little shallow stream running over brown pebbles. Mr Lehr . . . lay down flat on his back . . . Tiny fishes played over his chest and made little tugs at his nipples undisturbed.' (*P.G.*)

Herr R./Lehr had also his experiences of the revolution, losing crops and cattle – there were bullet holes in the posts of his verandah,★ but he used craft to avoid losing valuable land and having to pay taxes by giving over to 'the agraristos' 50 acres of barren land he had not the means to develop.[16]

On the first leg of his mule journey to Las Casas (a place the priest desperately hopes to reach but never does), Greene and his guide, having lost their way, were forced to spend the night at a place where there were four huts of mud-and-wattle, standing black and silent in the darkness, and where an old man on the verge of starvation gave up his bed in his rat-infested hut to Greene, without payment. His hands 'were like last year's leaves' and he had no food but 'set a small boy to boiling some thick black coffee'. This becomes the priest's experience with the addition that the priest has to hear confessions while a boy keeps watch through the night for soldiers. Both Greene and the priest ask if they can have a hammock and are told they must go to a town for that – 'here you must take only the luck of the road'. The priest asks for spirits: Greene gave brandy to the old man.

There were people and experiences important to the novel that Greene could not have known at first hand. Apart from his reading of newspaper accounts of the situation in Mexico, he had probably prepared for his journey by reading such works as Wilfred Parsons's *Mexican Martyrdom*, Francis McCullagh's *Red Mexico* and F. C. Kelley's *Blood-Drenched Altars*, which recorded the persecution of the Catholic Church begun by the Mexican President Calles in 1926. This involved the desecration and destruction of churches and cathedrals and the hunting down and killing of priests – the creation of a Godless country. By the time he went to Mexico in 1938, as Greene himself admits, the Godless country had been established: 'Calles had been flown over into exile by his rival, Cardenas', and the period of persecution had ended. 'The anti-religious laws were still enforced,

---

★ Forty years after Greene's visit, in 1978 nothing had changed. The marks in the verandah posts were made by bullets, though not from the guns of Villa's men, as Greene suggested, since Villa's army never got south of Mexico City.

Herr R./Lehr's real name was Ernst Raiteke.

except in . . . San Luís Potosí. Churches – now Government property – were allowed to open in most of the states except for the hundreds that had been turned into cinemas, newspaper offices, garages. Priests were allowed to serve (though only one priest to ten thousand people).' Thus it could be said that since the anti-religious laws had been softened, the carpet had been taken from under Greene's feet so far as his search for persecution and martyrs was concerned and this probably accounted for the lack of interest by publishers in articles about Mexico. It also accounted for his determination to make the dangerous journey into the two southern states, Tabasco and Chiapas, where the laws of Godlessness were still strictly maintained. Granted, 'The world is all of a piece . . . engaged everywhere in the same subterranean struggle . . . There is no peace anywhere where there is human life.'[17] But 'where the eagles are gathered together' we can expect to find 'the Son of Man as well'.[18]

In Tabasco and Chiapas he would reach 'an active sector of the line', though even then he arrived too late for the main action since the creator of the Godless state of Tabasco, Garrido Canabal, had already been exiled. So *The Power and the Glory* is in one sense an historical novel, re-creating vividly and convincingly, and with an atmosphere of immediacy, a period of past persecution.

*

In *Ways of Escape* Greene tells us that he had to invent 'the idealistic police officer who stifled life from the best possible motives: the drunken priest who continued to pass life on',[19] and this is true, but he found live models in Mexico on which to build. In Tabasco there was Garrido Canabal who, it was said, 'had destroyed every church; he had organized a militia of Red Shirts, even leading them across the border into Chiapas in his hunt for a church or a priest. Private houses were searched for religious emblems, and prison was the penalty for possessing them.'[20]

Who was Tomas Garrido Canabal who challenged God and made a Godless state out of Tabasco? He was born in 1890, the son of a wealthy farmer. In 1922 he was elected Governor of Tabasco and having served four years put in his place his supporter, Ausencio Cruz, and became Governor again in January 1931 and then Minister of Agriculture in President Cardena's government in December 1934. His power did not end there. A relative followed as Governor in January 1932, and indeed Garrido's family exercised much power throughout Tabasco – brothers, cousins, uncles and all.

He was in some ways a remarkable leader and brought about important reforms in agriculture, but he had two hatreds: one was alcohol; the other organised religion. His hatred outdid that of all other leaders in his campaign against the Church and its priests. Before he left Villahermosa for Mexico City to become Minister of Agriculture he organised a great burning of the statues of saints from the churches by 1,000 women and there was mass singing of atheistical songs. The Red Shirts, his private army of 6,000 young men, shouted in unison against *Los Fanáticos* (those who still believed in God) and searched private homes for statues of saints. Churches left standing were used for fiestas, socialist meetings, meetings for re-educating the population from their long-standing faith. A Christian burial became impossible. The *New York Times* of 3 June 1934 reported: 'MEXICAN GOVERNOR BANS GRAVESTONES' and went on to say: 'Tomas Garrido Canabal, Governor of the State of Tabasco, has issued a decree . . . that all monuments on graves within his jurisdiction shall be removed and that in the future graves shall be plain earth mounds without even crosses to mark them. No names shall appear in any manner over the graves which are to be marked by numbers.'

In the churches where once, in Communion, bread and wine were transformed into the body and blood of Christ, livestock would be exhibited (usually the fine beasts would be from the farms of Garrido Canabal). A bull would be named God, a donkey Christ, a pig the Pope, and the Virgin of Guadalupe represented by a cow. All religious observances were outlawed and a cross or religious ornament would be torn off the wearer's throat and the wearer would at the very least be imprisoned. Greene himself recalls a story (one of many about the curious incorruptibility of Garrido Canabal) of a family friend of Garrido, imprisoned for three days for wearing a cross under his shirt.[21] No favouritism was shown. One could no longer say, 'Adios', because it means 'To God'.

The 'genuine man of the Revolution', as he was called in songs sung by choirs of little girls, the antichrist, 'God's enemy number one', as he was referred to by his critics, was conducting an experiment in Godlessness, creating a new humanity, as was also being attempted then in Spain, Russia and Hitler's Germany. He replaced the worship of God with the worship of the yucca plant or pineapple. He named one of his sons Lenin, a daughter Zoila Libertad (I am Liberty – a humorist said she was the only free person in the state), and his nephew was Luzbel (Lucifer). In February 1925, the legislature passed a law defining the necessary qualifications for priests practising in Tabasco: they must be of Tabascan or Mexican birth with five years' residence in the state; they must be older than forty; they must have studied in official (i.e. anti-religious) schools; and they had to marry – 'an effort', as Garrido described it, 'to legitimize the existing children'. As a result, priests were hunted down and executed – Tabasco was freed from 'clerical opium, ignorance and vice'.

It was also freed from alcohol, and Garrido's rule was equally without favouritism in this respect. The leader of an orchestra about to play in a concert was caught with the smell of brandy on his breath and was ducked in water and imprisoned.

The source of such a combination of atheism and puritanism was said to be Garrido's father. Fitzpatrick, the doctor, told Greene: 'the priests in Tabasco were good men. There was no excuse for the persecution in this state – except some obscure personal neuroses, for Garrido had been brought up as a Catholic: his parents were pious people.'[22] But a Mexican in Las Casas said that Garrido's change to atheism began when his brother fell off his horse and broke his neck and 'his father burned all the saints in the town because he thought the Church had failed him. They had been a religious family and look what happened to them . . . His father was the first to burn plaster and wooden saints.' Also: 'His father drank too much. Yes, there is very likely a good reason why Tomas Garrido launched prohibition. Garrido himself abstained. He couldn't drink – it upset his stomach.' When Garrido was interviewed by George Creel (who thought he looked like a Wyoming cattleman in town for Saturday night, though he could also be taken for a Mexican dandy), he said: 'How can any sane person read history without coming to the fixed conclusion that religion and alcohol have ever been humanity's greatest curses?'[23] In line with his atheistical puritanism, he told his father to stop drinking or leave the country – his father left. Garrido was intense, direct, had a sense of integrity, and, uniquely, persuaded his officers to remain in office without taking bribes – something rare in Mexican public life. Garrido Canabal was exiled to Costa Rica in August 1935. He returned to Mexico in 1940, but took little part in politics and died in Los Angeles, California, in 1943. The Godless state he established and his rigorous persecution of priests and church gave Greene the material to create his martyr, the whisky priest, and he was himself the source for Greene's Lieutenant of Police.

Greene fleshed his man out, stressing the police lieutenant's honesty and obsession, his disinterested ambition to catch the last hunted priest in the state, and his unbending puritanism, but he elevated his model by giving him a different religious fervour – he had 'something of the priest in his intent observant walk'. He lived simply as a saint might: inside his room 'there was a bed made of old packing cases' (the kind of bed Greene slept on during his journeys). He took pleasure in 'the cement playground where the iron swings stood like gallows in the moony darkness', where once there had been a cathedral. Unlike the policemen Greene saw in Villahermosa with their trousers unbuttoned, he is clean, his gaiters polished. But when he looks at the photograph of the priest he is hunting with his well-shaved and well-powdered jowls (Greene may well have had a photograph of the martyr Padre Pro in mind here) 'a natural hatred as between dog and dog stirred in [his] bowels'. The newspaper photograph is of a first communion party and 'something you could almost have called horror moved him when he looked at the white muslin dresses', remembering his boyhood – 'the incense in churches, old, tired peasants kneeling before holy images, their arms held out in the attitude of the cross . . . a further mortification' squeezed out by a priest from the altar steps, coming round with the 'collecting-bag, abusing them for their small comforting sins, and sacrificing nothing in return – except a little sexual indulgence.' The lieutenant 'felt no need of women'.

Coming from a convert to Roman Catholicism, this is strong stuff, though we have to remember that as a student Greene put forward atheistic views. But the lieutenant's atheism is a kind of mysticism: 'what he had experienced was a vacancy – a complete certainty in the existence of a dying, cooling world, of human beings who had evolved from animals for no purpose at all. He knew.'[24] This philosophy seems to have been derived from a Wisconsin police commissioner with whom Greene fell into conversation on the train journey to Monterrey:

And suddenly – I can't remember how it happened – the old, good, pink face disclosed the endless vacancy behind. You expected somebody of his age – from Wisconsin – an honorary police commissioner with a badge – to believe in God – in a kind of way, a vague, deistic way. I had imagined him saying you could worship God as well in your own home as in a church; I had taken him already and made a character of him, and I had got him entirely wrong. He didn't believe in any God at all – it was like suddenly finding a cruel intelligence in a child. For one can respect an atheist as one cannot respect a deist: once accept a God and reason should carry you further, but to accept nothing at all – that requires some stubbornness, some courage.[25]

Another piece in the unstable universe of the novel.

*

It seems natural that Greene's basic model for his priest should be Mexico's most famous martyr, Padre Pro, who died eleven years before Greene went to Mexico and so appears in the second part of the Prologue to *The Lawless Roads*, 'The Faith', which is set against the first part, 'The Anarchists' which gives examples of Newman's 'corruptions, the dreary hopeless irreligion'. Greene's account of Padre Pro is succinct, and probably derives from several sources though the main one was McCullagh's *Red Mexico*. Padre Pro is not the whisky priest, though he was a martyred priest who had great courage, devotion and self-sacrifice.

Padre Miguel Pro, a twenty-five-year-old Jesuit, returned to his own country, Mexico, from a foreign seminary in 1926, much as Edmund Campion had returned from Douai to England. President Calles began his persecution of the Church two months later. 'The prisons were filling up, priests were being shot, yet on three successive first Fridays Pro gave the Sacrament to nine hundred, thirteen hundred, and fifteen hundred people.'[26] McCullagh puts it only slightly differently: 'He gave Holy Communion to about three hundred persons daily, and on the first Friday of three months, the numbers ran successively to 900, 1,300 and 1,500.'[27] It hardly needs saying that Greene's account is briefer, more forceful, as sharp as chipped granite. Pro, never dressing as a priest, which would have led to immediate arrest, continued to hear confessions in half-built houses, in darkness, in retreats held in garages. He was an amateur actor and had a remarkable capacity for escape; finding a police officer at a house where he was supposed to say Mass, he posed as another police officer, remarking, 'There's a cat bagged in here.' Greene's account shows his skill as a journalist. It is a little too deft on occasion, terse, dramatic, like a well-made film: 'In July 1926 Father Miguel Pro landed at Veracruz . . . We know how he was dressed . . .' the dramatically placed contrasts: 'They got him, of course, at last', and he was shot wearing, as Greene writes, 'a dark lounge suit, soft collar and tie, a bright cardigan'. Except for his fatal encounter with Calles's regime, an ability as an actor to deceive the police and his constant need to evade them, he has only one other resemblance to the whisky priest – being revered as a martyr. One religious account of the execution states that Pro's body was not crumpled by the bullets but retained 'the rigid form of the Cross quite unaffected by the fall'. Photographs of Pro 'praying for his enemies beside the pitted wall, receiving the *coup de grâce*', were published by the Government, 'but within a few weeks it became a penal offence to possess them for they had an effect which Calles had not foreseen'.[28]

Similarly, at the end of *The Power and the Glory*, the whisky priest is accepted as a martyr by the woman, pieces of a handkerchief soaked in his blood being sold, her young son carrying on the Catholic tradition by spitting on the police lieutenant and admitting another priest in hiding to their home.

If, however, Greene is accurate in his account of his experience of Tabasco in *The Lawless Roads*, it would seem that he came there with some foreknowledge of a fugitive priest, the one he refers to when he spends his first night in Villahermosa: 'one felt the excitement of this state where the hunted priest had worked for so many years, hidden in the swamps and forest'; and it is likely that he picked up this information in Mexico City where he met the young man who was imprisoned for three days for wearing a cross. What follows would seem to be an extension of the young man's account of Tabasco: 'Every priest was hunted down or shot, except one who existed for ten years in the forests and the swamps, venturing out only at night; his few letters, I was told, recorded an awful sense of impotence – to live in constant danger and yet be able to do so little, it hardly seemed worth the horror.'[29]

Then, in Villahermosa, he asked Dr Fitzpatrick about the priest in Chiapas who had fled: '"Oh," he said, "he was just what we call a whisky priest." He had taken one of his sons to be baptised, but the priest was drunk and would insist on naming him Brigitta. He was little loss, poor man . . . but who can judge what terror and hardship and isolation may have excused him in the eyes of God?'[30]

There would seem to be enough here, given Greene's imaginative flair, for the creation of his whisky priest, a man forced into fear and hardship developing the 'private and discreet virtue' of true glory in solitariness. He must also have heard other rumours of such a priest. One possible source is Father Parsons in Washington to whom Greene had a letter of introduction. In the unpublished account of his life, Parsons denies giving Greene information, but after the publication of the novel, because there were in Parsons's view two unworthy priests in the novel, he was troubled that it might be thought that he had told Greene about the hunted priest. He asserted that he did not 'tell Mr Greene that there actually was a priest at that very time in Tabasco. He was a Belgian and had heroically volunteered his services to work for the people and guaranteed that he would not marry any woman.' He goes on: 'What became of him I never knew, but he did, as I know from Archbishop Diaz, perform a number, a large number, of heroic acts during his ministry in that State. I do not know if he was ever caught or if he is still alive.' Perhaps all we can conclude from this is that there was indeed one priest working in secret and that his reputation was vouched for.

In Mexico forty years after Greene's trek I asked many Tabascans and Chiapans about that single hunted priest and heard a number of stories. There was one such priest, but he was Mexican not Belgian. He was an alcoholic and his name was Father Macario; for safety's sake he would often work near the border of Tabasco so that he could slip over into Chiapas and therefore, in a sense, he belonged more to the state of Chiapas. He certainly fits Dr Fitzpatrick's priest in that he drank. My source told me: 'He was a real drunk. He drank the best and the cheapest. He was a bad priest because he was a drunk.' At the same time there was another priest called Isidro González. He was not a drunk but he had women. It might be that Graham Greene, when developing the priest in his novel, given his character's attachment to alcohol and his illegitimate child, had simply combined Isidro and Macario.

Instinct told me that the hunted priest was Macario and that in the short unnamed descriptions Greene gives in *The Lawless Roads*, he has Macario in mind. Parsons was probably mistaken when, in old age, he thought the hunted priest was Belgian (for in his taped autobiography there are numerous lapses of memory). Parsons may never have learnt what happened to the hunted priest – 'I do not know if he was ever caught or if he is still alive' – but recently, in reading the diary of an uneducated but devout Indian, Gabriel, (who was finally killed by Garrido's men because he refused to give up his religion),★ I came across a short reference to our hunted man – 'only one of them, Father Macario Fernandez Aguado, remained one jump ahead for fear of punishment, always in the swamps or in the jungle helping within its desolate loneliness those Catholics who still had the courage to confess their faith.'[31] It cannot be that two priests with the same name, Father Macario, could have been operating in the jungles of Tabasco.

What happened to Macario Aguado? Did he live on or was he brought to account by Garrido Canabal's government? The diary is vague. One entry is critical of Archbishop Díaz, saying that 'he [Father Macario] laid before him all his complaints and he did not have the dignity to pay attention to him.' It then goes on to relate how, at one time, he was on the point of falling into the hands of the Governor in the town of Atasta, but that by Divine Providence, the guard, instead of coming to the house where he was, stopped at

---

★ According to Gabriel's brother: 'Gabriel found himself cornered [by Garrido's Red Shirts] and on 30 September he was butchered with machetes in front of the ranch "La Argentina" in the State of Chiapas in a place called "El Tigre" and his remains thrown into the river.' Father Macario Fernandez Aguado, watching from the ranch, saw a canoe with the remains of the prisoner and from there he gave him absolution. The next day, Gabriel's brother, not knowing what had happened to the body, picked up the bloodied soil, and gave it a Christian burial.

a house near by, thereby saving him, and that this took place on 4 March 1930. This is followed by the all too brief account of his death in the same year: 'He and the people from La Argentina in the State of Chiapas witnessed his apprehension and death and that was on the 1st of October 1930 and they can give exact information.'

From this account, the source for the protagonist in *The Power and the Glory* was not brought to the capital to be executed, but was despatched, probably with machetes, by Garrido's killers, the Red Shirts. It has been said by Garrido Canabal's Catholic enemies outside his state that he had Catholics killed and then fed the corpses to pigs so that no trace of them was left behind. Mexicans in Las Casas have told of bodies of dead Catholics floating in the rivers. Either method of disposal could account for the lack of any known grave for Father Macario Fernandez Aguado.

*

Greene's priest suffers his greatest degradation in jail and this episode owes a good deal to Greene's experiences in Villahermosa, though in the geography of the novel it could not have been Villahermosa. The priest goes to the town in search of wine for the Mass and is also, illegally, sold a bottle of Veracruz brandy (the same brand of brandy Greene carried with him) by a cousin of the Governor (in the same hotel, with its electric dynamo and wide stairs leading to the first floor, in which Greene stayed). Just as Greene did in *The Lawless Roads*, so the priest saw the young men and women promenading in two concentric circles. The priest and the Governor's cousin get drunk on the brandy and wine, joined by the chief of police, who suffers from toothache throughout the novel and who is based on the corrupt chief of police Greene met (and his assessment of him was sound). He was corrupt, jovial, drank and played billiards in life as in the novel. His name was Carlos Jordán and his nickname was Mito, Spanish for myth, because his famed generosity was a myth.

The priest is picked up by the Red Shirts and the police lieutenant who – even though his picture is on the prison wall – does not recognise him and jails him for a night for being drunk. This provides a key scene in the novel. He is pushed into an open cell, treading on a hand, an arm: 'An appalling smell lay on the air and somebody in the absolute darkness wept'; and he hears a woman's 'muffled painless cries'. He realises with horror that pleasure was going on even in this crowded darkness: 'This place was very like the world: overcrowded with lust and crime and unhappy love, it stank to heaven.'[32] The priest is moved by an enormous and irrational affection for the inhabitants of the prison: 'He was just one criminal among a herd of criminals . . . he had a sense of companionship which he had never experienced in the old days when pious people came kissing his black cotton glove.'[33] His compassion grows during his evening in the dark jail, but another prisoner, a pious woman, in contrast hates the sounds of 'hooded and cramped pleasure'. When she learns he is a priest, she demands: 'Why won't they stop it? The brutes, the animals? . . . Stop them. It's a scandal', and as the priest finds further compassion, she threatens she will write to his bishop: 'You sympathize with these animals,' she ends. 'The sooner you are dead the better', and the priest thinks:

> He had always been worried by the fate of pious women: as much as politicians, they fed on illusion: he was frightened for them. They came to death so often in a state of invincible complacency, full of uncharity.[34]

> He couldn't see her in the darkness, but there were plenty of faces he could remember from the old days which fitted the voice. When you visualized a man or woman carefully, you could always begin to feel pity . . . that was a quality God's image carried with it . . . when you saw the lines at the corners of the eyes, the shape of the mouth, how the hair grew, it was impossible to hate. Hate was just a failure of imagination.[35]

Next morning, his suit fouled by the cell floor, he is forced to take out and empty the pails of excrement and clean up the vomit.

The realism of this scene did not derive from Greene's personal experience, though he had spent some time in the courtyard of Villahermosa prison while waiting for the chief of police, and the priest's view through the grille of the hammocks outside is part of that experience: 'The dirty whitewashed walls, the greasy hammocks, and the animal faces of the men [police] – it wasn't like law and order so much as banditry.'[36] The source of his information about the inside of the prison is surely to be found in the Epilogue to *The Lawless Roads*.

Greene travelled back to England from Veracruz on the German liner, *Orinoco*. He met on that ship a German whom he calls Kruger, and perhaps this is his name since he calls him 'K' in the *Spectator* in which this section of the travel book was first printed.[37]

Kruger had had an unusually painful experience in Mexico. He could hardly have failed to interest Greene, who is a collector – not of pictures, or stamps, or fine porcelain – but of acquaintances. Kruger had spent three months in a Mexican prison in an open cell. His story was that he had strolled into Tapechula in Chiapas to listen

713

to the marimbas, had sat down in the plaza, and two plain-clothes men came and put revolvers to his head. His papers had been stolen, so he was put in jail and was in an open cell for three months, for the first eight days of which he was given no food or water; the floor crawled with worms, and what Greene described as 'other things', presumably urine and excrement. A man jailed for being drunk, on his release, took out a letter from Kruger to the German consul, who brought him money for food, but could not arrange his release since he had no papers. Kruger lived in semi-starvation among thieves and murderers until he managed to smuggle a letter out to the Mexican Government who sent an agent down, and Kruger was taken to Veracruz where he served another two months of imprisonment before being put on board the German liner.

Greene was struck by Kruger's gentleness, 'his quiet gentle way, playing with the children' on board the ship; his amazing gratitude for life; and the extraordinary sense of goodness surrounding him. Kruger longed to settle on the Amazon and tried to persuade Greene to return with him: 'You will never want to go home, never. You can get another wife there.'

Greene probably made no substantial use of Kruger as a character, yet something of the growing gentleness of the hunted priest might derive from him, but it must have been from Kruger that Greene learned details of the sordid conditions of an open cell in a Mexican jail.

*

The impression made on Greene by the Chamula Indians' version of Christianity became part of his priest's experience. Greene's contact with it began on the way to Las Casas when he and his guide came at evening out of a forest, 'on what seemed to be at last the top of the world nine thousand feet up', upon 'a great plateau of yellow grass', lit by the 'last pale golden light' of a sun dropping over the ridge, 'as if over the world's edge, so that you thought of the light going on and on through quiet, peaceful, uninhabited space'. It was 'like a scene from the past before the human race had bred its millions'. And 'a grove of tall black crosses stood at all angles like wind-blown trees against the blackened sky.' 'This was the Indian religion – a dark, tormented, magic cult'[38] – as it certainly was. It led Greene to consider that Christians were too apt to minimise the magic element in Christianity: 'the man raised from the dead, the devils cast out, the water turned into wine. The great crosses leaned there in their black and windy solitude, safe from the pistoleros and the politicians, and one thought of the spittle mixed with the clay to heal the blind man, the resurrection of the body, the religion of the earth.'[39] Magic might be 'a short cut to the dark and magical heart of the faith'.

This is, perhaps, a romanticised view of the primitive, inspired by the atmosphere and unexpected vision of a place. In fact, after the Spanish conquest of Mexico, the Chamula Indians had accepted only part of the Christian faith – the saints, the rosary, medals, incense, banners and processions, but the rituals were adapted to their own beliefs. Each saint became an individual god: the Virgin Mary was to them the Goddess of the Sun, and their wooden, plaster or clay images have their hands cut off (so that they would be safe from theft) and wear mirrors on their chests to ward off evil spirits. The graves of their dead in their cemetery, at the foot of the 20-ft-high crosses, have boards placed on top of them through which the spirits have exit and entrance – they are not evil spirits but everyone is afraid of them. The Chamulas have no understanding of the Stations of the Cross, but on 2 November they come to the cemetery to celebrate the Catholic day of the dead, bringing food for the dead, renewing the graves and cutting down huge pine trees (always pine as pine needles are a sacred offering) and tying them to the crosses. But alcohol has become an unfortunate part of such observances – on Saints' Days it is poured on the candles and there is drinking, smoking and chanting to the point of collapse: and on the day of the dead there is a fiesta, drinking and eating all day.

The atmosphere of that cemetery was the same when I visited it in 1978*. In Yajalon, a Catholic priest who knew the Indians told me that three policemen had been killed only days before by Chamula Indians in the mountains and that we should stay away from that sacred place with its 20-ft-high crosses. But we did visit it to photograph those giant crosses leaning at different angles, as night fell. It was a deeply moving and religious experience, but not a Christian one. The silence at that height was eerie and there was a strong sense of being watched.

Greene made good use of his brief experiences of the Indian cemetery in *The Power and the Glory* in a scene which combined Christian and pagan and a leavening of realism. The priest is followed by an Indian woman carrying her dying baby – it had been shot during an exchange of fire between the police and the American gunman. The woman, recognising the word 'priest', follows him in the direction of the mountains and the border, the dead child strapped to her back. They walk on and on and for the last thirty hours they have only had sugar to eat, 'large brown lumps of it the size of a baby's skull'. They travel by the sun until the black wooded bar of

---

* In the company of scholar and traveller Dr Richard Sinkin.

mountain tells them where to go: 'They might have been the only survivors of a world which was dying out – they carried the visible marks of the dying with them.'

There were no visible boundaries and: 'There seemed to be so little progress: the path would rise steeply, perhaps five hundred feet, and fall again, clogged with mud. Once it took an enormous hairpin bend, so that after three hours they had returned to a point opposite their starting-place, less than a hundred yards away.'[40]

This was Greene's experience in setting out from Cancuc on the last track to Las Casas, and it leads to an Indian cemetery.

At sunset on the second day they came out on to a wide plateau covered with short grass: an odd grove of crosses stood up blackly against the sky, leaning at different angles – some as high as twenty feet, some not much more than eight. They were like trees that had been left to seed. The priest stopped and stared at them: they were the first Christian symbols he had seen for more than five years publicly exposed . . . No priest could have been concerned in the strange rough group; it was the work of Indians and had nothing in common with the tidy vestments of the Mass and the elaborately worked out symbols of the liturgy. It was like a short cut to the dark and magical heart of the faith – to the night when the graves opened and the dead walked.[41]

Now the priest observes the Indian woman and dead child:

The woman had gone down on her knees and was shuffling slowly across the cruel ground towards the group of crosses: the dead baby rocked on her back. When she reached the tallest cross she unhooked the child and held the face against the wood and afterwards the loins: then she crossed herself, not as ordinary Catholics do, but in a curious and complicated pattern which included the nose and ears. Did she expect a miracle? and if she did, why should it not be granted her, the priest wondered? Faith, one was told, could move mountains, and here was faith – faith in the spittle that healed the blind man and the voice that raised the dead. The evening star was out: it hung low down over the edge of the plateau: it looked as if it was within reach: and a small hot wind stirred. The priest found himself watching the child for some movement. When none came, it was as if God had missed an opportunity. The woman sat down, and taking a lump of sugar from her bundle began to eat, and the child lay quietly at the foot of the cross. Why, after all, should we expect God to punish the innocent with more life?[42]

There is no miracle; the priest and the Indian woman part; the child is left alone beside the cross. It is raining; the priest feels fever – conscience-stricken that he has left the Indian woman alone – and climbs in his soaked condition back up to the top of the plateau. Only the dead child is there and a huge lump of sugar. Guilty, but desperately hungry, the priest eats the sugar (like that given to Greene by Fru Ramussen). It sticks in his throat. He feels an appalling thirst and sucks at his soaked trousers. The child lies under the streaming rain like a dark heap of cattle dung. He walks away. He has the sense that he is moving across a blank white sheet, going deeper every moment into the abandoned land. The journey becomes more terrible for him. He feels himself to be in a mine shaft, going down into the earth to bury himself. He meets a man with a gun who asks him who he is, and the priest gives his name to a stranger for the first time in ten years. He expects doom. He tries to run away and comes to the edge of the forest and a whitewashed building (which Greene in his original travels thought from a distance was a cathedral and which the priest in his fever thinks is a barracks). 'Father, it is our church,' says the man with the gun. The priest runs his hands over the wall like a blind man and suddenly sits down on the rain-drenched grass and falls asleep in absolute exhaustion with 'home behind his shoulder-blades'.

*

The priest is being hunted not only by the police lieutenant but also by God. On two occasions he deliberately seeks martyrdom. He is to find it, not by his own will but through betrayal by a Judas for the reward. He first encounters his Judas in the town of La Candelaria: 'a man lay in [a hammock] bunched diagonally, with one leg trailing to keep the hammock moving up and down . . . He had only two teeth left – canines which stuck yellowly out at either end of his mouth like the teeth you find enclosed in clay which have belonged to long-extinct animals.'[43] This reflects Greene's arrival in Salto de Agua where he passed 'tin-roofed shacks where men lay in hammocks, drearily swinging in the great heat'. The Judas figure has his source in the mestizo clerk he encountered in Yajalon and whom he hated on sight, a clerk he 'grew to loathe, a mestizo with curly sideburns and two yellow fangs at either end of his mouth. He had an awful hilarity and a neighing laugh which showed the empty gums.'[44] He wore a white tennis shirt open at the front and he scratched himself underneath it. 'After a week of his company I would find it impossible to abandon him forever, and so he became the Judas of my story.'[45] The 'inane laugh' (*Ways of Escape*) or 'neighing laugh' (*The Lawless Roads*) becomes our recognition sign of the Judas and he is to take on some of the characteristics of Greene's guides through Mexico. Greene's experience of not being able to go about Yajalon without seeing 'the mestizo looking up from his typewriter and showing his fangs as I went by',[46] becomes the priest's inability to shake off his Judas, who immediately recognises him as a priest and follows him. When they stop to spend the night in a hut, the mestizo goes out to look after the mule and to hide the saddle in case the priest escapes him in the night and he loses much more than thirty pieces of silver.

He tries his best to trap the priest into a confession of his calling, but the priest resists: 'He was determined not to sleep – the man had some plan . . . his conscience ceased to accuse him of uncharity. He knew. He was in the presence of Judas.'[47] He recalls how in Holy Week 'a stuffed Judas was hanged from the belfry and boys made a clatter with tins and rattles as he swung out over the door'[48] – a reflection of Greene's experience at Las Casas during Holy Week when 'the Guadalupe Christ was led in chains by two tiny soldiers . . . and up on the roof between the bell towers under the white dome they were hanging Judas on the cross – a hideous figure in a straw sombrero . . . while youths on the roof beat a tin tray and rattled wooden clappers, to tell the town that Judas . . . was properly hanged.'[49]

The Power and the Glory is a remarkable and convincing amalgam of Greene's researches, his experiences and his convictions, interpreted by his skill and imagination as a creative writer. One might add that without his success in writing a thriller with a strongly religious theme, *Brighton Rock*, this novel might not have been so successful, for on the level of plot he again uses the chase of the hunted by the hunter, but he extends it by another dimension – the hunted who wants to be caught, but cannot give himself up. The priest is hunted not only physically but also by his own conscience and by God – he has to suffer, he has to be betrayed. There is a reward on his head and he tries to persuade the villagers where his 'wife' lives to take it: 'Why don't they catch me?' he asks, 'I did my best . . . It's *your* job – to give me up. What do you expect me to do? It's my job not to be caught.'[50] But the villagers advise him to go over the mountains to Las Casas where Mass can be celebrated again, not on an altar made of packing cases, but 'a proper altar and the priest all dressed up like in the old days. You'd be happy there, father.'[51] And the mother of his child saves him from the police by making sure he looks and smells like a peasant. He attempts again to bring martyrdom upon himself through the agency of others when he is in jail and confesses to the other prisoners that he is a priest: 'The ten years' hunt was over at last . . . "They are offering a reward for me. Five hundred, six hundred pesos, I'm not sure," ' he tempts them, but ' "nobody here," a voice said, "wants their blood money." ' Perhaps this is an illustration of Greene's comment: 'I had also observed for myself how courage and the sense of responsibility had revived with persecution.'[52]

*

The priest's final meeting with the mestizo comes when he is preparing to leave the *finca* for Las Casas: 'Two men waited beside the mules; the guide was adjusting a stirrup, and beside him, scratching under the arm-pit, awaiting his coming with a doubtful and defensive smile, stood the half-caste. He was like the small pain that reminds a man of his sickness.'[53] He rejects the mestizo's plea to go with him to give absolution to a dying American bandit (the one who had shot the Indian baby) for the priest knows it is a trick to betray him – only the mestizo can identify him as the hunted priest. But then the mestizo shows him a piece of paper with, 'For Christ's sake, father', written on it and, knowing the man has much on his conscience, he goes willingly into the trap, and is quite cheerful: 'he had never really believed in this peace . . . never really believed he would ever get back to parish work and the daily Mass and the careful appearance's of piety.' Seeing the schoolmaster who had railed at him, he gives him all the money he has made out of the baptisms. He begins to whistle a tune he had heard somewhere: 'I found a rose in my field' – a song which Greene had heard the schoolteacher in Yajalon singing as he played his guitar: 'Have I a Rose in My Field?'[54]

For the scene of the priest's capture, Greene transferred a setting well within Chiapas and near the Indian graveyard where a priest would have been safe, to a point in Tabasco near the border with Chiapas – a setting he knew personally. 'There are no more villages before Cancuc,' he wrote in *The Lawless Roads*, 'only occasional Indian settlements, perched on rocky plateaux . . . one with a little wattle watch-tower from which an Indian stared down at us as we climbed wearily upwards.'[55] In the novel, the mestizo and the priest make their way to just such an Indian settlement. Its apparent emptiness makes the priest suspicious: 'Even the look-out, the little platform of twigs built on a mound above the huts, was empty.'[56] The mestizo responds typically to his questions: 'There you go again . . . Suspicion. Always suspicion. How should I know where the Indians are? I told you [the American gangster] was quite alone, didn't I?'

The dying man *is* there and the priest tries to hear his confession, but the gangster only wants the priest to take his gun and escape. As he dies, the priest gives him conditional absolution and prays for him: 'O merciful God, after all he was thinking of me, it was for my sake . . .' The police are waiting and, his work done, his reward obtained, the Judas disappears from the novel.

*

Of the mestizo I heard from many people. His name was Don Porfirio Masariegos, but he was known everywhere as Don Pelito, born on 5 February 1902. He was educated at the Catholic school in Yajalon, was organist at the church and sang the Mass, which was how he earned his living. Don Pelito's handwriting was beautiful, he was popular, always singing songs in a particularly attractive voice, was very political, articulate and knew what was going on; but then he began to show signs of mental instability, which, it was rumoured, was due to a love affair that went wrong. The first sign was when he began a massive letter-writing campaign to artists when he was twenty-five, but he was trusted in the town and was found to be absolutely reliable in delivering a message even if it involved him in a plane ride. He ran errands for the two Rasmussen daughters and some said he fell in love with Astrid; others said it was possible that he came away with the wrong idea about some relationship with the family.

When Greene was in Yajalon in 1938, Don Pelito was working in the Presidencia as a clerk-typist (as Greene has it in *The Lawless Roads*) but that lasted only six months as he did not know how to type. After that he began to deteriorate and took to getting up at five in the morning, knocking on doors to collect garbage. He began to eat filth and stopped washing.

*

In 1978 Father Loren, priest at Yajalon, and I met Don Pelito. We were walking towards the Plaza and the church. Dogs slept in the shade of lime trees; in the bell tower small boys leapt up on to the bell ropes; in the church peasants sat on marble seats, white shirts hanging over white trousers, sombreros in hand.

Don Pelito was sitting on a wooden bench. He was only 4 ft 6 in. tall. His hair was dirty; everything about him was dirty; there was soft grit on his hand. (I realised afterwards that it was excrement.) His trouser legs were rolled up. His pockets were capacious and his black coat stretched down to his knees. He had a thin black moustache. As I approached he stood up, took off his hat and bowed – no doubt recognising me as a gringo with pesos to spare. I knew he was seventy-six and although his face was deeply lined he looked surprisingly young – perhaps his layer of grime protected him. Only his turkey neck gave his age away. His ears stood out and he was toothless – no yellow fangs at each end of his mouth.

He answered questions in a slow, mumbling, yet rather delicate voice, but nothing made sense, though about simple matters he could be lucid. When asked if he was well he replied that he was, but troubled because his feet were being bitten by rats.

The last view of the mestizo in the novel is when the priest, now captured, with police in front of and behind him, looks back as his horse is poised for the steep descent between the rocks:

> The half-caste stood alone among the huts, his mouth a little open, showing the two long fangs. He might have been snapped in the act of shouting some complaint or some claim – that he was a good Catholic perhaps; one hand scratched under the arm-pit. The priest waved his hand; he bore no grudge because he expected nothing else of anything human and he had one cause at least for satisfaction – that yellow and unreliable face would be absent "at the death."[57]

Everyone at the mission in Yajalon had read *The Power and the Glory* in translation without recognising the original of the Judas figure walking in their streets, but then how could they have connected this little, innocuous, put-down and isolated man with the mestizo Graham Greene had disliked yet elevated into a prime mover in his novel?

*

The lieutenant and the priest, in spite of their total authority, come strangely together when they reach the prison. Atheist though he is, the lieutenant himself seeks out the married, cowardly priest, Padre Jose, to ask him to hear the whisky priest's confession, but Jose cannot withstand his wife's authority: ' "Perhaps, my dear," Jose said, "it's my duty . . ." "You aren't a priest anymore," the woman said, "you're my husband." She used a coarse word. "That's your duty now." ' The lieutenant breaks a second of his country's laws when he leaves the priest a bottle of brandy, and the priest says: ' "You've seen people shot. People like me." "Yes." "Does the pain go on – a long time?" "No, no. A second," he said roughly and closed the [cell] door.'

The priest spends a night of misery and drunkenness alone in the cell, condemning himself because the love he had for his sullen, knowledgeable, illegitimate child should have been felt for 'every soul in the world' – the lieutenant, the half-caste, the dentist he once met, the child at the banana station – they were in as much danger as his child, but always his prayers come back to her: 'Another failure'. He complains about his coming execution: ' "It's all very well . . . for saints . . . How does he know it only lasts a second? How long's a second?"; then he began to cry, beating his head gently against the wall.'[58] The thought that he might yet escape death calms him and he falls asleep. He dreams of the child at the banana station. The child and the congregation are tapping along the aisles the morse code – three long and one short. He asks what it is and the child responds with her responsible gaze, 'News', and he awakens at dawn with a huge feeling of hope – suddenly lost as he wakes to the sight of the prison yard. It is the morning of his death and he is crouching on the floor with an empty brandy-flask. He struggles with the Act of Contrition and he realises that it will not be the good death for which he had always prayed. He catches sight of his own shadow on the cell wall: 'it had a look of surprise and grotesque unimportance.' He realises his uselessness: 'I have done nothing for anybody. I might just as well have never lived.' His parents were dead – soon he would not even be a memory – perhaps after all he was not really Hell-worthy. Tears poured down his face; he was not at the moment afraid of damnation but felt only 'an immense disappointment because he had to go to God empty-handed with nothing done at all . . . It would only have needed a little self-restraint and a little courage [to have been a saint] . . . [he had] missed happiness by seconds . . . there was only one thing that counted – to be a saint.'[59]

That is the reader's last glimpse into the priest's mind. Skilfully, Greene backs away from his torment, and his execution is witnessed by Mr Tench, the dentist, looking down into the prison yard, the chief of police in his chair crying with the pain of having a tooth out: 'A small man came out of a side door . . . held up by two policemen . . . his legs were not fully under his control . . . They paddled him across to the opposite wall; an officer tied a handkerchief round his eyes . . . the rifles went up, and the little man suddenly made jerky movements with his arms. He was trying to say something . . . nothing came out except a word that sounded like "Excuse". The crash of the rifles shook Mr Tench . . . Then there was a single shot . . . and the little man was a routine heap beside the wall.'[60]

*

Greene's most personal experiences are an important ingredient in *The Power and the Glory*. They led to an empathy with his three major characters, the lieutenant, the mestizo and the whisky priest. They are hinted at in the Prologue to *The Lawless Roads*, when he returns to his school days and to Carter who 'practised torments with dividers'. Into the lieutenant, the priest and the Judas went some of the insight into human nature gained from his experience with Carter and Wheeler, which had involved him in persecution, self-doubt, feelings of cowardice and the fear of betraying.

The dialogue between the priest and the Judas with his constant lies and denials perhaps originates in Wheeler's own lies and denials and his attempts to trap Greene into admissions that could be passed on to Carter. There is a certain coming to terms with each other, a certain understanding between the priest and the lieutenant which was part of the Greene/Carter antagonism: 'there was an element of reluctant admiration, I believe, on both sides. I admired his ruthlessness, and in an odd way he admired what he wounded in me.'[61]

The basic theme of the novel, the examination of the nature of goodness and evil and the conclusion that there can be no clear definition of either, is one of Greene's strongest convictions. 'The greatest saints have been men with more than a normal capacity for evil, and the most vicious men have sometimes narrowly evaded sanctity.'[62] An extension of this is the stress in the novel on the fact that there can be a difference between a man and his vocation – they can be two entities. 'The whole argument in *The Power and the Glory*', he told an interviewer, 'was deeply rooted in me from childhood . . . I remember members of my family coming back from their holidays in Spain, sometimes terribly shocked because in some little village they had come across a priest living with his housekeeper, or keeping a mistress . . . I found their indignation exaggerated because . . . I saw no reason why a man should not be different from his function, that he could be an excellent priest while remaining a sinner.'[63]

Edith Sitwell's comment to Greene was, 'what a great priest you would have made',[64] and in Nottingham, at the time of his conversion, Greene had fears that he might discover in himself a vocation for the priesthood. Certainly there are times when he smiles, with his transparent blue eyes giving an impression of blindness, when he unquestioningly looks beatific, as if he had never experienced the corrupt reality he portrays so convincingly. But he was aware by 1938 that he would never have made a good priest for, as he once said, 'chastity would have been beyond my powers'. Again, at the time of his conversion, there are indications in his letters to his future wife and in autobiographical pieces which suggest that, like the priest, he was filled with actual physical dread the first time he had 'consumed the body and blood of God in a state of mortal sin: but then life bred its excuses'.[65] Writing of the humiliating ordeal of his First Confession as a convert, he recalls that promises were then made which he 'carried . . . down with [him] like heavy stones into the empty corner of the Cathedral'. Later he was to abandon Confession and Communion because of his continual failure to keep his promises.[66] The guilt of the whisky priest on his last night on earth reflects Greene's own sense of guilt: 'I've betrayed a great number of things and people in the course of my life . . . It still torments me often enough before I go to sleep.'[67]

*

From Mexico City Greene had written to Hubsch of Viking Press:

I got back here last night from Chiapas with a lot of material and a little dysentery . . . I feel rather tired, I never want to ride a mule again (I feel for my relative who travelled with a donkey in Cevennes) [Robert Louis Stevenson, *Travels with a Donkey*, 1879] – I hate this country and this people. Hatred at any rate will be a new angle for you.

His publisher had suggested that he had better stay away from England for a while because of the Lord Chief Justice's comments during the Shirley Temple libel case – 'it looks as if I shall be arrested when I land if the L.C.J.'s bite is as bad as his bark.'[68] Nevertheless, he sailed on the *Orinoco*, longing to see his wife and children again, arriving in England on 25 May 1938, only to suffer another culture shock: 'one jolted through the hideous iron tunnel at Vauxhall Bridge, under the Nine Elms depot and the sky-sign for Meux's beer. There is always a smell of gas at the traffic junction where the road is up and the trams wait; a Watney's poster, a crime of violence, Captain Coe's Finals . . . In the grit of the London afternoon, among the trams, in the long waste of the Clapham Road, a Baptist chapel, Victorian houses falling into decay in their little burial grounds of stone and weed, a coal merchant's window with some fuel arranged in an iron basket, a gas showroom.'[69]

'How could a world like this end in anything but war?' He began to wonder why he had disliked Mexico so much, as he compared the religious observances in England with those in Mexico: 'Mass in Chelsea seemed curiously fictitious; no peon knelt with his arms out in the attitude of the cross, no woman dragged herself up the aisle on her knees. It would have seemed shocking, like the Agony itself. We do not mortify ourselves. Perhaps we are in need of violence.'[70]

In London, the telephones were cut off, the anti-aircraft guns set up on the Common, and trenches were being dug. Air Raid Wardens had been appointed and Air Raid Posts set up in anticipation of the onslaught of German bombers. In spite of Neville Chamberlain's attempts to avert it, war was inevitable – and Greene would welcome it, in spite of the disruption it was to cause. It would be a new experience, another way of escape.

Notes

Wherever possible in the following notes I have referred to the Penguin editions of the works of Graham Greene because these are the most accessible and widely distributed. Although the pagination of some Penguin editions has remained unchanged for decades, others have been reset in recent years. Neither of these, however, contain the introductions in the Heinemann and Bodley Head uniform and collected editions. A full Bibliography of Greene's works and the sources used in this book will appear in Volume Two.

Our Man in Antibes

1 Malcolm Muggeridge, *Like it Was, Selected Diaries*, ed. John Bright-Holmes, Collins, 1981, p. 374.

1 Beginnings – Comfort and Fear

1 Graham Greene, 'Behind the tight pupils', *The Month*, July 1949, pp. 7–8.
2 Raymond Greene, untitled typescript.
3 *A Sort of Life*, Penguin edition, 1974, p. 43.
4 *Ibid.*
5 *Ibid.*, p. 57.
6 *Ibid.*, p. 12.
7 Letter, 14 January 1926.
8 Steedman booklet, 'All About Baby'.
9 *A Sort of Life*, p. 14.
10 *Ibid.*, p. 13.
11 *Journey Without Maps*, Penguin edition, 1978, p. 36.
12 *The Confidential Agent*, Penguin edition, 1971, p. 73.
13 *Journey Without Maps*, p. 36.
14 MS 'Fanatic Arabia', housed at the Humanities Research Center, Austin, Texas.
15 *The Lawless Roads*, Heinemann uniform edition, 1955, p. 6.
16 Interview with Sir Hugh Greene, 19 May 1981.
17 *A Sort of Life*, p. 15.
18 *Ibid.*, p. 22.
19 'Sad Cure', 'The Life and Death of John Perry-Perkins', *The Cherwell*, 20 February 1926.
20 *A Sort of Life*, p. 37.
21 *Ibid.*
22 *Ibid.*, p. 24.

23 *Ibid.*, p. 13.
24 *The Quiet American*, Penguin edition, 1975, pp. 110–11.
25 *Brighton Rock*, Penguin edition, 1975, p. 186.
26 *A Sort of Life*, p. 18.
27 *Ibid.*, pp. 23–4.
28 *The Ministry of Fear*, Penguin edition, 1972, pp. 137–8.
29 *Ibid.*, p. 88.
30 *A Sort of Life*, p. 28.
31 Marion Greene to her husband Charles, Easter 1909.
32 *The Ministry of Fear*, p. 68.
33 *The Quiet American*, p. 108.
34 *A Sort of Life*, p. 19.
35 Letter, 2 October 1912.
36 *The Berkhamstedian*, 1913.
37 *A Sort of Life*, p. 47.
38 *Ibid.*, p. 40.
39 'The Lost Childhood', *Collected Essays*, Penguin edition, 1970, p. 13.
40 *A Sort of Life*, p. 46.
41 *Ibid.*, p. 39.
42 'The Lost Childhood', p. 13.
43 *A Sort of Life*, p. 40.
44 'The Lost Childhood', p. 15.
45 *The Ministry of Fear*, pp. 88–9.
46 *Ibid.*, p. 11.
47 'The Lost Childhood', p. 16.
48 *The Power and the Glory*, Penguin edition, 1977, p. 12.
49 Letter, 1926.
50 *A Sort of Life*, p. 14.
51 Marion Greene to her husband Charles, Easter 1909.
52 Interview with Eva Greene, 23 January 1977.
53 *A Sort of Life*, pp. 18–19.
54 *Ibid.*, p. 28.
55 *Ibid.*, pp. 52–3.
56 *Ibid.*, p. 34.
57 *Ibid.*, p. 29.
58 *Ibid.*, p. 37.
59 Letter, 1926, to Vivien Dayrell-Browning.

2 Personal Map

1 *A Sort of Life*, Penguin edition, 1974, p. 12.
2 'The Innocent', *Twenty-One Stories*, Penguin edition, 1973, pp. 47–8.
3 'Across the Border', *Penguin New Writing*, Vol. 30, 1947, p. 72.
4 *A Sort of Life*, p. 23.
5 *Ibid.*, p. 35.
6 *Ibid.*, pp. 12–13.
7 *Ibid.*, p. 35.
8 *Ibid.*, p. 11.
9 *Ibid.*, p. 12.
10 *Ibid.*, p. 26.
11 *Ibid.*, p. 33.
12 'Across the Border', p. 70.

13 *A Sort of Life*, pp. 34–5.
14 *Ibid.*, p. 25.
15 *Ibid.*, p. 42.
16 Interview with Mrs Mervyn Peake, January 1976.
17 *A Sort of Life*, p. 45.
18 *Ibid.*, p. 42.
19 Letter from Olga Franklin, 26 November 1980.
20 *A Sort of Life*, p. 11.

3 Charles and Marion Greene – and Dr Fry

 1 *A Sort of Life*, Penguin edition, 1974, p. 15.
 2 *Ibid.*, p. 22.
 3 *The Ministry of Fear*, Penguin edition, 1972, pp. 63–4.
 4 *A Sort of Life*, p. 15.
 5 Interview with Trevor Wilson in 1976.
 6 *A Sort of Life*, p. 19.
 7 *Ibid.*, pp. 33–4.
 8 *Ibid.*, p. 21.
 9 *Ibid.*
10 *Ibid.*, p. 20.
11 James Hilton, *Goodbye Mr Chips* (Macmillan, 1934), a best-selling novel of the 1930s, later a box-office success as a film.
12 B. N. Garnons Williams, *History of Berkhamsted School – 1541–1972* (The School, 1980), p. 217.
13 *Ibid.*, p. 210.
14 The following ten gave me valuable accounts: Raymond Greene (elder brother of Graham), Ben Greene (Graham's cousin), James Wilson, in early life asst. manager of a huge cotton estate in Peru, R. S. Stanier (who became a distinguished headmaster himself), Sir Cecil Parrott (one-time British Ambassador to Prague), Eric Guest (retired London Magistrate), Anthony Nichols (a well known TV actor), Felix Greene (Graham's cousin, an authority on China), S. R. Denny, (one-time senior minister of the Northern Rhodesian administration) and Claud Cockburn (one of the most brilliant journalists of his age).
15 Christine Keeler had an affair in 1963 with John Profumo, War Minister in the Macmillan government. She was also involved with Yegeny Ivanov, assistant naval attaché to the Russian Embassy. It became headline news. When Profumo initially denied his involvement this was publicly accepted by Macmillan on the grounds that his War Minister, as a man of honour, would not lie to him.
16 Derek Winterbottom, *Doctor Fry, Berkhamsted*, Clanbury Cotterell Press, 1977, p. 28.
17 *A Sort of Life*, pp. 57–8.
18 *Ibid.*, p. 57.
19 Alec Waugh was nineteen and wrote *The Loom of Youth* while waiting to go into the Army in 1917.
20 Letter to Marion Greene, 2 January 1905.
21 Interview, 19 May 1981.
22 Interview, 23 January 1977.
23 Telephone conversation, 6 July 1984.
24 *A Sort of Life*, p. 15.
25 Letter to author, January 1976.
26 *A Sort of Life*, p. 50.

27 *Ibid.*, pp. 50–1.
28 Derek Winterbottom, *op. cit.*, p. 8.

4 The First World War and the School

1   *A Sort of Life*, Penguin edition, 1974, p. 18.
2   Raymond Greene, untitled typescript.
3   Letter from Cecil Hodges, 12 June 1981.
4   *A Sort of Life*, p. 52.
5   *Ibid.*, p. 48.
6   Letter, 30 August 1925.
7   *A Sort of Life*, p. 51.
8   *Ibid.*, p. 25.
9   *The Berkhamstedian*, November 1914, p. 132.
10 Edmund Blunden, *Undertones of War*, Cobden-Sanderson, 1928, pp. 15–16.
11 Paul Fussell, *The Great War and Modern Memory*, OUP, paperback edition, 1977,
    p. 49.
12 *A Sort of Life*, p. 63.
13 Letter, 12 June 1981.
14 Letter, 4 May 1927.
15 *A Sort of Life*, p. 49.
16 Interview with Claud Cockburn, 18 June 1977.
17 *A Sort of Life*, pp. 83–4.

5 The Greening of Greene

1   *A Sort of Life*, Penguin edition, 1974, pp. 58–9.
2   Interview with Countess Strachwitz, 1976.
3   *A Sort of Life*, p. 54.
4   *Ibid.*
5   *The Lawless Roads*, Penguin edition, 1979, p. 14.
6   James Joyce, *A Portrait of the Artist as a Young Man*, Penguin edition, 1965,
    p. 120.
7   *A Sort of Life*, p. 54.
8   *England Made Me*, Penguin edition, 1970, pp. 17–18.
9   *The Lawless Roads*, p. 13.
10 'The Last Word', *The Old School*, Jonathan Cape, 1934, p. 252.
11 Interview with Sir Cecil Parrott, 1977.
12 Interview with R. S. Stanier, 1976.
13 Interview with J. B. Wilson, 1977.
14 *The Berkhamstedian*, April 1919.
15 *Ibid.*, December 1919.
16 *A Sort of Life*, p. 59.
17 *Ibid.*, p. 55.
18 *The Lawless Roads*, p. 14.
19 'Prologue to Pilgrimage' (typescript), p. 74.
20 *England Made Me*, p. 86.
21 *Ibid.*, p. 85.
22 *A Sort of Life*, p. 47.
23 Interview with Sir Cecil Parrott.

24 'The Lost Childhood', *Collected Essays*, Penguin edition, 1970, pp. 16–17.
25 *Ibid.*, p. 17.
26 *A Sort of Life*, p. 60.
27 Extract from an address given by Graham Greene on receiving the Shakespeare prize from the University of Hamburg on 6 June 1969.
28 *The Ministry of Fear*, Penguin edition, 1972, p. 43.
29 *A Sort of Life*, p. 60.
30 *Ibid.*
31 'Prologue to Pilgrimage', pp. 80–1.
32 *England Made Me*, p. 83.
33 *Brighton Rock*, Penguin edition, 1975, p. 106.
34 'Prologue to Pilgrimage', p. 94.
35 *Ibid.*
36 *Ibid.*, p. 75.
37 *The Confidential Agent*, Penguin edition, 1971, p. 24.
38 *A Sort of Life*, p. 55.
39 'Prologue to Pilgrimage', p. 133.
40 *The Ministry of Fear*, pp. 203–4.
41 *The Berkhamstedian*, March 1921.
42 Ronald Matthews, *Mon Ami Graham Greene*, Desclée De Brouwer, 1957, pp. 49–50. 'On ne savait pas où on en était, et cela pourrait faire une bonne définition du cauchemar. Le monde du cauchemar est un monde sans défenses, parce que chaque défense peut y être tournée. A quoi sert de se préparer, de prévoir une attaque, quand notre meilleur ami peut, tout soudain, sans aucune raison, se muer en notre pire ennemi?'
43 *A Sort of Life*, p. 56.
44 *Ibid.*, p. 55.
45 *The Man Within*, Penguin edition, 1977, p. 67.
46 'Prologue to Pilgrimage', p. 78.
47 *A Sort of Life*, p. 60.
48 'Prologue to Pilgrimage', p. 170.
49 *England Made Me*, p. 86.
50 'Prologue to Pilgrimage', pp. 72–3.
51 *The Lawless Roads*, p. 14.
52 *A Sort of Life*, p. 62.
53 *Ibid.*, p. 64.
54 Letter to Vivien Dayrell-Browning, 1925.
55 *A Sort of Life*, p. 64.
56 *The Old School*, pp. 250, 252.
57 *Ibid.*, p. 286.
58 See Derek Winterbottom, *Doctor Fry, Berkhamsted*, Chanbury Cotterall Press, 1977.
59 *A Sort of Life*, p. 60.
60 Interview with Eric Guest, 1976.
61 *The Man Within*, p. 74.
62 *Ibid.*, p. 71.
63 Interview with Elisabeth Dennys, August 1983.
64 *A Sort of Life*, p. 61.
65 'The Young Dickens', *Collected Essays*, p. 83.

6 Psychoanalysed

1   *A Sort of Life*, Penguin edition, 1974, pp. 67–8.
2   *Ibid.*, p. 64.
3   Interview with Zoe Richmond, January 1985.
4   *A Sort of Life*, p. 73.
5   Interview with Zoe Richmond.
6   *A Sort of Life*, p. 74.
7   Interview with Zoe Richmond.
8   *A Sort of Life*, p. 73.
9   Interview with Ave Greene, 1976.
10 Interview with Zoe Richmond.
11 Interview with Ave Greene.
12 *A Sort of Life*, pp. 74–5.
13 Interview with Ave Greene.
14 *Spectator*, 20 June 1941, p. 657.
15 *A Sort of Life*, p. 75.
16 Interview with Zoe Richmond.
17 *A Sort of Life*, p. 73.
18 *Journey Without Maps*, Penguin edition, 1978, p. 181.
19 *Ibid.*
20 *A Sort of Life*, pp. 73–4.
21 *Journey Without Maps*, p. 181.
22 J. D. Beresford, *W. E. Ford: A Biography*, Doran, 1917, with Kenneth Richmond; a semi-autobiographical fiction.
23 *The Confidential Agent*, Penguin edition, 1971, p. 147.
24 *A Sort of Life*, p. 74.
25 *Ibid.*, p. 43.
26 *Ibid.*, p. 74.
27 *Ibid.*, pp. 75–6.
28 Interview with Zoe Richmond.
29 *Ibid.*
30 *A Sort of Life*, p. 80.
31 *Ibid.*, p. 72.
32 Letter written in 1921 but dated only 'Wednesday'.
33 *A Sort of Life*, p. 24.
34 Letter to Vivien Dayrell-Browning, 11 December 1925.
35 This letter was shown to me on my last visit to Zoe Richmond in 1986.
36 *The Old School*, Jonathan Cape, 1934, p. 256.

7 Realism and Fantasie – a Reconciliation

1   Letter, 29 June 1948.
2   Interview, June 1977.
3   *A Sort of Life*, Penguin edition, 1974, p. 75.
4   *Ibid.*, p. 77.
5   *Ibid.*, p. 78.
6   Letter from Colonel A. L. Wilson, 3 October 1976.
7   *A Sort of Life*, p. 33.
8   Peter Quennell, *The Marble Foot*, Collins, 1976, p. 98.
9   Interview with R. S. Stanier, 24 August 1977.
10 Letter to Vivien Dayrell-Browning, 16 November 1925.

11   *A Sort of Life*, pp. 80–1.
12   *Ibid.*, p. 81.
13   *The Lost Childhood and Other Essays*, Eyre and Spottiswood, 1951.
14   'The Tyranny of Realism', *The Berkhamstedian*, March 1922.
15   Interview with R. S. Stanier, 24 August 1977.
16   *The Berkhamstedian*, March 1922.
17   *Ibid.*, July 1921.
18   *The Ministry of Fear*, Penguin edition, 1972, p. 36. In the Authorised Version, Psalm 141, Verse 3, we have the phrase closest to Greene's quotation:

> 'Set a watch, O Lord, before my mouth,
> Keep the door of my lips.'

19   Interview with J. B. Wilson, 7 June 1981.

8   Freshman at Balliol

1   *A Sort of Life*, Penguin edition, 1974, p. 87.
2   *Ibid.*, p. 108.
3   The name given to a club of reckless young men early in the eighteenth century. Peter Quennell, 'A Kingdom of Cokayne', *Evelyn Waugh and his World*, ed. David Pryce Jones, Weidenfeld and Nicolson, 1973, p. 35.
4   *Ibid.*, p. 36.
5   Peter Quennell, *The Marble Foot*, Collins, 1976, p. 115.
6   Tom Driberg, Ruling Passions, Stein and Day, 1979, p. 55. The Hypocrites' Club (fairly innocuous by today's standards) was suppressed and the suppression was suitably celebrated: 'The Club had given a funeral dinner at an hotel in Thame, and leading members had driven back to Oxford riotously in a glass hearse', Claud Cockburn, *I, Claud*, p. 43.
7   Anthony Powell, *Infants of the Spring*, Heinemann, 1976, p. 182. (Penguin edition, 1967).
8   *Ibid.*, pp. 167–8 and Peter Quennell, *The Marble Foot*, p. 117.
9   *Oxford Now and Then*, Duckworth, 1970, p. 56.
10   *A Sort of Life*, pp. 87–8.
11   Interview with Sir Harold Acton, 11 May 1977.
12   Letter, 24 October 1922.
13   'I had failed to win a scholarship, so why to Balliol? I think my father wisely plumped for a college which at that period was anti-athletic. Also the number of students there, as in a great city, offered the shelter of anonymity', *A Sort of Life*, p. 87. Greene had lodgings in Beechcroft Road, north Oxford, during his first two terms. *A Sort of Life*, p. 89.
14   Interview with Claud Cockburn, 18 June 1977.
15   Interview with Sir Harold Acton, 11 May 1977.
16   Robert Scott became a distinguished Consular official and was High Commissioner for Kenya when Greene visited that country in 1963 and their friendship was renewed.
17   Interview with Lord Tranmire, April 1977.
18   Evelyn Waugh wrote: 'There is a jolly problem Club run by some men at Balliol. Their last competition was to receive the offer of the queerest job', *The Letters of Evelyn Waugh*, ed. Mark Amory, Weidenfeld and Nicolson, 1980, p. 10. The editor's dating of these letters (1922) is speculative and this could be a reference to the Mantichorean Society.
19   Interview with Lord Tranmire, April 1977.

20 *Daily Telegraph*, 15 November 1971.
21 Letter to his mother, November 1922.
22 *Ibid.*
23 Letter to his mother, 19 May 1923.
24 Interview with Lord Tranmire, April 1977.
25 Interview with Claud Cockburn, June 1977.
26 This fact remained in the mind of Graham Greene's brother Raymond when I interviewed him. At the age of eighty he was still the most handsome man in London. He died in December 1982.
27 Unsigned article by Greene in *The Times*, 27 December 1928.
28 Interview with Lord Tranmire, April 1977.
29 Interview with Sir Harold Acton, 11 May 1977.
30 Interview with Lord Tranmire, April 1977.
31 'The Trial of Pan', *The Oxford Outlook*, V., February 1923, pp. 47–50.
32 15 November 1924.
33 Interview, April 1977.
34 *Ways of Escape*, Penguin edition, 1981, p. 25.
35 22 October 1922.
36 Letter to his mother, 3 May 1923, quoting from one of the judges, of whom Harley Granville-Barker was one.
37 24 January 1923.
38 Letter to his mother, 11 February 1923.
39 Interview with Sir Harold Acton, 11 May 1977.
40 Letter to Vivien Dayrell-Browning, January 1926.
41 Interview with Joseph Macleod, 13 May 1977.
42 Letter to Evelyn Waugh, 10 September 1964.
43 *A Sort of Life*, p. 99.
44 Claud Cockburn gave me an account of his own drinking habits at Oxford: 'I got up fairly early, 8 a.m., I would then drink a large sherry glass of neat whisky before breakfast and go on for an hour and drank heavily throughout the day. I drank approximately a bottle and a half of whisky every day, exclusive of wines and beers. God the amount of liquor one took on board. How the hell could I notice how much Greene had. I suppose I was two-thirds stewed the whole time. It seems to me I remembered everything – perfectly alert and so on. In those days it was all right.' (Interview, June 1977.)
45 Letter to Vivien Dayrell-Browning, 13 February 1926.

9 The Art of Spying

1 *A Sort of Life*, Penguin edition, 1974, p. 104.
2 *Ibid.*
3 *Ibid.*, pp. 35–6.
4 Interview with Ave Greene, January 1977.
5 Interview with Claud Cockburn, 18 June 1977.
6 *A Sort of Life*, p. 100.
7 Letter to Vivien Dayrell-Browning, 24 September 1925.
8 *Harper's Magazine*, April 1985, p. 44.
9 'The Revolver in the Corner Cupboard', *The Lost Childhood and Other Essays*, Eyre and Spottiswood, 1951, and *A Sort of Life*, p. 95.
10 Letter to his mother, 9 June 1923.
11 *Ibid.*
12 *Ibid.*

13   Letter to Vivien Dayrell-Browning, 24 September 1925.
14   *A Sort of Life*, p. 100.
15   Interview, 18 June 1977.
16   Letter, 12 March 1924.
17   *A Sort of Life*, pp. 100–1.
18   Letter, 12 March 1924.
19   *A Sort of Life*, p. 101.
20   Interview, 18 June 1977.
21   *A Sort of Life*, p. 101.
22   Letter to his mother, 17 April 1924.
23   *A Sort of Life*, p. 102.
24   *Ibid.*
25   Letter, 17 April 1924.
26   *A Sort of Life*, p. 102.
27   Interview, 18 June 1977.
28   Letter to his mother, 17 April 1924.
29   *A Sort of Life*, p. 102.
30   *Ibid.*, p. 103.
31   Letter to his mother, 13 June 1924.
32   *A Sort of Life*, p. 104.
33   Letter to his mother, 17 April 1924.
34   Interview with Edward 'Tooter' Greene, 19 December 1976.

10   Apprenticeship

1   In a letter to Nancy Mitford, Evelyn Waugh writes: 'Did you know that the Sitwells only trace their descent through the female line. The real name is Hurt. They took Sitwell quite lately – about 1800.' (*Letters of Evelyn Waugh*, ed. Mark Amory, p. 274.)
2   *Oxford Outlook*, February 1924. He also insisted on the catholicity of his taste: 'There is no greater admirer of the Sitwells than myself, but I do not understand why this should prevent my being also an admirer of Mr. Drinkwater. Poetry would indeed be dull if all were revolutionaries, none conservatives.'
3   Letter to Vivien Dayrell-Browning, 21 November 1925.
4   *Twenty Five: Being a Young Man's Candid Recollections of his Elders and Betters*, Penguin, 1973, p. 38.
5   G. M. Trevelyan (1876–1962) was Regius Professor of Modern History at Cambridge (1927–40).
6   In spite of Greene's comment, Quennell's piece was by no means his best. It was entitled 'Toad': 'The cuckoo, whose bed God has made of brass,/Rouses to wake his doubtful agony.'
7   Louis Golding (1895–1958) a popular novelist best known for *Magnolia Street* (Gollancz 1932), a provincial street with Jews living on one side and Gentiles on the other.
8   Letter to his mother, 4 November 1923.
9   Letter to his mother, 27 April 1924.
10   Here is a longer quotation from Cavafy's 'Come Back':

> Come back often and take me,
> Beloved sensation come back and take me –
> When awakens the body's memory,
> And an old desire again courses through my blood,

When the lips and the skin remember
And the hands feel as though they were touching again.

Come back often, at night, and take me
When the lips and the skin remember . . .

11 Letter to Hugh Greene, January 1925.
12 'Poetry by Wireless', *Oxford Chronicle*, 30 January 1925, p. 15.
13 *A Sort of Life*, Penguin edition, 1974, p. 91.
14 A. L. Rowse, *A Cornishman at Oxford*, Jonathan Cape, 1965, p. 206–7.
15 *A Sort of Life*, p. 91.
16 *Ibid.*

11   Love and Death – a Flirtation

1 *A Sort of Life*, Penguin edition, 1974, pp. 89–90.
2 *Ibid.*
3 *Ibid.*, p. 92.
4 *Ibid.*, p. 90.
5 Letter, 1983.
6 *The Ministry of Fear*, Penguin edition, 1972, p. 130.
7 *A Sort of Life*, p. 90.
8 *The Ministry of Fear*, pp. 132–3.
9 *Ibid.*, p. 67.
10 Letters from Conway Spencer.
11 In spite of his quiet manner, his unfailing modesty (to which many people attest), Greene, once having entered the lists, was and is a fighter. When he was sixty-seven he wrote to Hugh Delargy, M.P.: 'It's good to be fighting again if even in a smaller cause.'
12 Letter, 24 April 1982.
13 *Babbling April*, Blackwell, 1925, p. 14.
14 *A Sort of Life*, p. 91.
15 Interview with Graham Greene, 25 April 1981.
16 *A Sort of Life*, pp. 93–4.
17 *Ibid.*, p. 92.
18 *Ibid.*, p. 95.
19 Letter, 12 January 1925.
20 *A Sort of Life*, p. 94.
21 Interview with Claud Cockburn, 18 June 1977.
22 *Babbling April*, p. 32.
23 *A Sort of Life*, p. 93.
24 *Ibid.*, p. 94.
25 'The Electric Hare', *The Month*, September 1951, p. 147.
26 Interview at the Savile Club, London, 20 January 1977.
27 Marie-Françoise Allain, *The Other Man: Conversations with Graham Greene*, trans. Guido Waldman, Bodley Head, 1983, p. 49.
28 B.B.C. Television *Omnibus* programme, 'The Hunted Man', November 1968.
29 Interview with Claud Cockburn, 18 June 1977.
30 Interview with Sir Harold Acton, 11 May 1977.
31 *A Sort of Life*, pp. 94–5.
32 Interview with Lord Tranmire, 2 June 1977.
33 *A Sort of Life*, p. 93.

12 A Seminal Year

1 Interview with Joseph Macleod, 13 May 1977.
2 Letter to Vivien Dayrell-Browning, 26 November 1926.
3 *Ibid.*, 29 December 1925.
4 *Journey Without Maps*, Penguin edition, 1978, p. 36. *Enchanted Castle* by E. Nesbit (1858–1924).
5 *Journey Without Maps*, p. 36.
6 *A Sort of Life*, Penguin edition, 1974, p. 98.
7 *Rumour at Nightfall*, Heinemann, 1931, p. 235.
8 *Brighton Rock*, Penguin edition, 1975, p. 109.
9 *A Sort of Life*, p. 97.
10 *Ibid.*, p. 98.
11 Letter, 6 March 1925.
12 Letter, November 1923.
13 Letter from Joseph Macleod, 24 November 1980.
14 Letter, 24 February 1924.
15 Letter to his mother, 14 November 1924.
16 Letter, 22 November 1924.
17 Letter to his mother, 29 November 1924.
18 *Ibid.*, February 1925.
19 *Ibid.*, August 1925.
20 Letter to his mother, 16 February 1925.
21 *Ibid.*, 14 April 1925.
22 *Ibid.*, 6 March 1925.
23 *Ibid.*, 18 May 1925.
24 *Ibid.*, 24 January 1926.
25 *Ibid.*, 26 January 1926.
26 Letter to Vivien Dayrell-Browning, 16 November 1925.
27 Letter to Evelyn Waugh, 26 October 1950.
28 Letter to Vivien Dayrell-Browning, 11 November 1925.
29 Letter to his mother, 6 November 1925.
30 *Ibid.*, 18 May 1925.
31 *Ibid.*
32 *Ibid.*, 22 May 1925.
33 *Ibid.*, 3 June 1925.
34 *Ibid.*, 22 May 1925.
35 *Ibid.*, 25 May 1925.
36 *Ibid.*, 19 July 1925.
37 *A Sort of Life*, p. 106.

13 'Some Ardent Catholic'

1 *A Sort of Life*, Penguin edition, 1974, p. 86.
2 *Ibid.*, p. 87.
3 The typescript is housed in the Humanities Research Center, Austin, Texas. Greene originally called the novel 'Anthony Sant'.
4 'Prologue to Pilgrimage', TS, p. 148.
5 *Ibid.*, p. 149.
6 *The Ministry of Fear*, Penguin edition, 1972, pp. 66–7.
7 *A Sort of Life*, p. 88.
8 *Ibid.*

9 'The Innocent', *Twenty-One Stories*, Penguin edition, 1973, p. 47.
10 *Ibid.*, p. 50.
11 *A Sort of Life*, p. 25.
12 'The Innocent', p. 51.
13 *Ibid.*
14 Letter to Vivien Dayrell-Browning, 26 June 1925.
15 *Oxford Outlook*, March 1925.
16 Letter to author, 12 August 1980.
17 *Ibid.*
18 Letter to Vivien Dayrell-Browning, 13 January 1926. This was the time when Graham Greene was becoming infatuated with the cinema – his innocence belongs to the days before high tech: 'Dear Miss Dayrell . . . have you been to the Capitol cinema? It's simply glorious. You are taken up to the circle in a lift!' (Undated letter, probably early May 1925.)
19 *Ibid.*, 18 November 1925.
20 *Ibid.*, 19 May 1925.
21 *Ibid.*, 21 August 1926.
22 Letter to author, 12 August 1980.
23 Undated letter but probably immediately after his return from his unsuccessful interview with Asiatic Petroleum, 21 May 1925.
24 A later letter to Vivien gives more details of this event and does suggest that it might have inspired Greene to propose: 'I'd just got into my digs. I was feeling miserable because I hadn't said anything, which I'd wanted to say (to you) and I was beginning to scrawl a note to you (it was a Thursday night) begging you to let me see you next day . . . I was just writing this, when I heard Macleod tapping (he has a tap of his own) on the outer door . . . He was in a perfectly ghastly condition . . . he was patchy in colour and in a dinner jacket he looked ludicrous and yet one couldn't laugh because his state of mind was too evidently genuine. He'd been to a theatre with someone of whom he was very fond and was miserable because he'd simply funked saying anything he'd wanted to say. He felt sure, almost, that she was fond of him, and had been waiting, and was now probably furious with him. I tried to laugh him out of his mood, by offering him a revolver to shoot himself, but he looked so fearfully inclined to accept the offer that I hastily shut it away again, & gave him whisky. Then came my advice. He mentioned he'd left proofs of some long poem of his for her to look at, so I commanded him to rush round to her digs now, say that he'd found a note from Monkhouse [Monkhouse had become editor of *Oxford Outlook* in succession to Greene] saying he must have them back first thing in the morning, and could he take them away now. I pointed out that she'd probably see through it, and that he could leave the rest to the inspiration of the moment. So off he went, and I sat down and finished the note to you, saying I must see you once more, before I went home. And then as I finished came a tap on the door again, and Macleod beaming gratitude and happiness. It's a dead secret. You are the only person who knows.'
25 Letter to Vivien Dayrell-Browning, 8 June 1925.
26 *Ibid.*, 6 June 1925.
27 *Ibid.*, 8 June 1925.
28 *Ibid.*
29 *Ibid.*, 25 June 1925.
30 *Ibid.*, 26 June 1925.
31 *Ibid.*
32 Interview with Claud Cockburn, 18 June 1977.

14   The World Well Lost

1   Letter to Vivien Dayrell-Browning, 29 June 1925.
2   *Ibid.*
3   *A Sort of Life*, Penguin edition, 1974, p. 108.
4   Reference from his Balliol tutor Kenneth Bell, 18 January 1926.
5   Letter to Vivien Dayrell-Browning, 13 July 1925.
6   *Ibid.*, 22 July 1925.
7   *Ibid.*, 17 July 1925.
8   *Ibid.*, 11.30 a.m., 26 July 1925.
9   *Ibid.*, 26 July 1925.
10   *Ibid.*, 24 July 1925.
11   *Ibid.*, 27 July 1925.
12   *Ibid.*, 30 July 1925.
13   *Ibid.*
14   This was printed later in the *Weekly Westminster Gazette*, 24 October 1925.
15   Letter to Vivien Dayrell-Browning, 6 August 1925.
16   'Ford Madox Ford', *Collected Essays*, Penguin edition, 1970, p. 127.
17   Letter to Vivien Dayrell-Browning, 7 August 1925.
18   *Ibid.*, 9 August 1925.
19   *Ibid.*
20   This letter also dated 9 August 1925: the second letter he wrote to Vivien that day.
21   Letter to Vivien Dayrell-Browning, 11 August 1925.
22   *Ibid.*, 10 August 1925.
23   Greene's name did not appear on the title page of the first edition, only that of Dorothy Craigie, the illustrator. His name has appeared in all subsequent editions.
24   Shuttleworth and Raven interview with Graham Greene, *The Paris Review*, No. 3., Autumn 1953, pp. 24–41.
25   Letter to Vivien Dayrell-Browning, 16 August 1925.
26   *Ibid.*

15   Late Summer at Ambervale

1   Letter to Vivien Dayrell-Browning, 17 August 1925, Monday, 2 p.m.
2   Letter to author, 12 August 1980.
3   *A Sort of Life*, Penguin edition, 1974, p. 112.
4   *Ibid.*, pp. 111–14.
5   Letter to Vivien Dayrell-Browning, 20 August 1925.
6   Letter to his mother, 15 May 1925.
7   Letter to Vivien Dayrell-Browning, 20 August 1925.
8   *Ibid.*, 25 August 1925.
9   *Ibid.*, 12 September 1925.
10   *A Sort of Life*, p. 114.
11   *Ibid.*, p. 113.
12   Letter to Vivien Dayrell-Browning, 31 August 1925.
13   *Ibid.*, 12 September 1925.
14   *Ibid.*, 11 September 1925.
15   *Ibid.*, 10 September 1925.

16   In Search of a Career

1   Letter to Vivien Dayrell-Browning, 30 September 1925.
2   Letter from Vivien Greene to author.
3   Letter to Vivien Dayrell-Browning, 22 October 1925.
4   *Ibid.*, 31 August 1925.
5   *Ibid.*, 24 September 1925.
6   *Ibid.*, 12 October 1925.
7   *Ibid.*, 21 October 1925.
8   *Ibid.*
9   *Ibid.*, 22 October 1925.
10   *Ibid.*, 10 November 1925.
11   *Ibid.*, 24 September 1925.
12   *Ibid.*, 8 October 1925.
13   *Ibid.*, 15 October 1925.
14   *Ibid.*, 7 October 1925.
15   *Ibid.*, 12 October 1925.
16   *Ibid.*, 21 October 1925.
17   *Ibid.*, 28 October 1925.

17   Sub-editing in Nottingham

1   Letter to Vivien Dayrell-Browning, 3 November 1925.
2   *A Sort of Life*, Penguin edition, 1974, p. 116.
3   Letter to Vivien Dayrell-Browning, 20 January 1926.
4   *A Sort of Life*, p. 115.
5   *A Gun for Sale*, Penguin edition, 1974, p. 40. The 'smell of bad fish' is taken out of the Heinemann and Bodley Head collected edition of the novel.
6   *Journey Without Maps*, Penguin edition, 1978, p. 101.
7   *A Gun for Sale*, p. 122.
8   *Ibid.*, p. 131.
9   Letter to Vivien Dayrell-Browning, 3 November 1925.
10   *A Sort of Life*, p. 117.
11   Letter to Vivien Dayrell-Browning, 19 November 1925.
12   Interview with V. S. Pritchett, *The Times*, July 1978, p. 29.
13   *A Gun for Sale*, pp. 72–3.
14   *A Sort of Life*, p. 124.
15   *Brighton Rock*, Penguin edition, 1975, p. 207.
16   *A Gun for Sale*, pp. 92–3.
17   *Brighton Rock*, p. 56.
18   *Ibid.*, p. 208.
19   Interview with V. S. Pritchett, *The Times*, July 1978, p. 29.
20   *Ways of Escape*, Penguin edition, 1981, p. 57.
21   *Brighton Rock*, p. 209.
22   *It's a Battlefield*, Penguin edition, 1981, p. 98–9.
23   *Brighton Rock*, p. 211.
24   *A Sort of Life*, p. 117.
25   Quoted in *A Sort of Life*, p. 124.
26   *Brighton Rock*, p. 212.
27   Letter to Vivien Dayrell-Browning, 14 January 1926.
28   *Ibid.*, 24 January 1926.
29   *Ibid.*, 15 January 1926.

30 *Ibid.*, 18 November 1925.
31 *Ibid.*, 4 November 1925.
32 *Ibid.*, 24 February 1926.
33 *Ibid.*, 12 February 1926.
34 *Ibid.*
35 *Ibid.*, 23 November 1925.
36 *Ibid.*, 18 January 1926.
37 *Ibid.*
38 *Ibid.*
39 *Ibid.*
40 'Turton had been doing law & had just dropped it for journalism, and though he had intros to every editor in London he had had even less success than I. So he was going off to Hungary for a year, in order to come back and apply as a Hungarian specialist. Hearing from Gorham I had reached a dead end, he suggested that I should go too.' (Letter to Vivien, 18 January 1926.)
41 *Ibid.*, 27 January 1926.
42 *Ibid.*, 9 February 1926.
43 *Ibid.*, 10 February 1926.
44 *Ibid.*
45 *Ibid.*, 11 February 1926.
46 *Ibid.*, 17 February 1926.
47 *Ibid.*, 21 November 1925.
48 Cecil Roberts, *The Bright Twenties*, Hodder and Stoughton, 1970, pp. 257–8.
49 *Ibid.*
50 Letter to Charles Greene, 28 February 1925.
51 Letter to Vivien Dayrell-Browning, 21 November 1925.
52 *Ibid.*, 21 October 1925.
53 *Ibid.*, 23 November 1925.
54 *A Sort of Life*, p. 117.

18 Thomas the Doubter

1 *A Sort of Life*, Penguin edition, 1974, p. 121. In a letter to Vivien Dayrell-Browning, 1 March 1926, he writes, 'I haven't taken any other names yet . . . I think Sebastian is a good idea.'
2 *Ibid.*, p. 118.
3 TS p. 189. The typescript is housed in the University Library of Boston College, Boston.
4 *The Lawless Roads*, Heinemann uniform edition, 1955, p. 5.
5 *A Sort of Life*, p. 118.
6 Letter, 2 November 1925.
7 Second letter of 2 November 1925.
8 *A Sort of Life*, p. 118.
9 Letter to Vivien Dayrell-Browning, 8 November 1925.
10 *Ibid.*, 13 November 1925.
11 *Ibid.*
12 *Ibid.*, 14 November 1925.
13 *Ibid.*, 16 November 1925.
14 *A Sort of Life*, p. 119.
15 *Ibid.*, pp. 118–19.
16 *Journey Without Maps*, Penguin edition, 1978, p. 101.
17 *A Sort of Life*, p. 119.

18 *Ibid.*
19 *Ibid.*, p. 120.
20 Undated letter to Vivien Dayrell-Browning, probably written during the first week of December 1925.
21 *Ibid.*, 7 December 1925.
22 *Ibid.*, 13 December 1925.
23 *Ibid.*, 24 December 1925.
24 *Ibid.*, 21 November 1925.
25 *Ibid.*, 13 January 1926.
26 *Ibid.*, 27 February 1926.
27 *Ibid.*, 23 February 1926.
28 *A Sort of Life*, p. 121.
29 Letter to Vivien Dayrell-Browning, 27 February 1926.
30 *Ibid.*
31 *Ibid.*
32 *Journey Without Maps*, pp. 101–2.
33 *A Sort of Life*, p. 122.
34 *Ibid.*, p. 121.
35 *The Potting Shed*, Act II, Scene 1, Penguin, 1971, p.46.
36 Letter to Vivien Dayrell-Browning, 1 March 1926, from 141 Albert Palace Mansions, Battersea Park, S.W.11.

19   Between the Tides

1   Letter to Vivien Dayrell-Browning, 8 November 1925.
2   Letter to his mother, 29 January 1926.
3   Letter to Vivien Dayrell-Browning, 7 January 1926.
4   *Ibid.*, 9 January 1926.
5   *Ibid.*, 10 January 1926.
6   *Ibid.*, 11 February 1926.
7   *Ibid.*, 5 November 1925.
8   *A Sort of Life*, Penguin edition, 1974, p. 91.
9   And other quotations, even when expressed in gaiety as in the passage below, do show his continuing attachment to children's books – Baroness Orczy? Alexandre Dumas? Stanley Weyman?
    'Do you call your love a small thing, foolish one? I should like to call you out to fight with rapiers at dawn in a forest glade, with no witnesses. And I should run you through the heart, & flee to Dover, with horses waiting at every inn.' (30 September 1925.)
10 Letter to Vivien Dayrell-Browning, 12 October 1925.
11 *Ibid.*, 29 December 1925.
12 *Ibid.*, 11 November 1925.
13 *Ibid.*, 26 October 1925.
14 *Ibid.*, 18 January 1926.
15 *Ibid.*, 11 December 1925.
16 *Ibid.*, 5 November 1925.
17 *Ibid.*, 22 February 1926.
18 *Ibid.*, 24 February 1926.
19 *Ibid.*, 9 February 1926.
20 *Ibid.*, 14 November 1925.
21 *Ibid.*, 2 February 1926.

22 *Ibid.*, 27 February 1926. 'After all you are helping the lame soul to walk . . . It's you who are the guardian.'
23 *Ibid.*, 11 November 1925.
24 *Ibid.*, 7 December 1925.
25 *Ibid.*, 21 August 1925.
26 *Ibid.*, 23 January 1926.
27 *Ibid.*, 12 October 1925.
28 *Hamlet*, Act I, Scene 4.
29 Letter to Vivien Dayrell-Browning, 17 November 1925.
30 *Ibid.*, 18 August 1925.
31 Interview with Michael Meyer, February 1977.
32 Letter to Vivien Dayrell-Browning, 12 February 1926.

20   *The Times*

1   Letter to Vivien Dayrell-Browning, 1 March 1926.
2   *Ibid.*, 10 March 1926.
3   *Ibid.*, 8 February 1927.
4   *A Sort of Life*, Penguin edition, 1974, p. 125.
5   Letter to Charles Greene, 28 February 1926.
6   Letter to Vivien Dayrell-Browning, 24 June 1926.
7   *Ibid.*, 2 March 1926.
8   *Ibid.*, 3 March 1926.
9   Letter from the Appointments Manager, 9 March 1926.
10 Letter to his mother, 9 March 1929.
11 Letter, 4 May 1926.
12 *A Sort of Life*, typescript p. 200.
13 Letter, 8 March 1926.
14 Letter, 10 March 1926.
15 *Ibid.*
16 Letter, 9 March 1926.
17 Letter, 24 June 1926.
18 'The News in English', *Strand Magazine*, June 1940.
19 *A Sort of Life*, Penguin edition, 1974, p. 124.
20 Letter, 11 March 1926.
21 Letter, 10 March 1926.
22 Undated March 1926 letter.
23 Letter, 11 March 1926.
24 *A Sort of Life*, p. 125.
25 *Ibid.*, p. 131.
26 Douglas Woodruff, 'Times Remembered', *The Times*, 2 May 1977.
27 Letter from Leslie Smith, 23 February 1977.
28 Letter from G. L. Pearson, 11 February 1977.
29 *Ibid.*
30 *A Sort of Life*, p. 130.
31 Obituary, *Times House Journal*, June 1951.
32 Letter from Leslie Smith, 23 February 1977.
33 Letter to Vivien Dayrell-Browning, 14 April 1926.
34 *Ibid.*, 10 March 1926.
35 *Ibid.*, 11 April 1926.
36 *Ibid.*, 13 April 1926.
37 *Ibid.*, 9 April 1926.

38 *Ibid.*, 16 March 1926.
39 *Ibid.*, 5 April 1926.
40 *Ibid.*, 15 March 1926.
41 *Ibid.*, 12 May 1926.
42 *Ibid.*, 17 May 1926.
43 *Ibid.*, 10 July 1926.
44 *Ibid.*
45 *Ibid.*, 1 April 1926.
46 *Ibid.*, 10 July 1926.
47 *Ibid.*, 6 April 1926.
48 *Ibid.*, 10 April 1926.
49 *Ibid.*, 25 May 1926.
50 *Ibid.*, 26 July 1926.
51 *Ibid.*, 12 August 1926.
52 *Ibid.*, 21 March 1926.
53 *Ibid.*, 23 March 1926.

21   The General Strike

1   John Paton, *Left Turn*, Secker & Warburg, 1936, p. 254.
2   Arnold Bennett, *Journals, 1921–1926*, Cassell, 1933, entry of 5 May 1926.
3   Sir Philip Gibbs, *Philadelphia Evening Bulletin*, 5 May 1926.
4   G. D. H. Cole and Raymond Postgate, *The Common People, 1746–1938*, Hutchinson, 1946, p. 567.
5   *A Sort of Life*, Penguin edition, 1974, p. 127.
6   *Ibid.*
7   Letters, 4 May 1926.
8   Christopher Farman, *The General Strike, May 1926*, Hart-Davis, 1974, p. 200.
9   *Strike Nights in Printing House Square*, privately printed, 1932, p. 16.
10 Letter, 5 May 1926.
11 Letter, 6 May 1926.
12 *A Sort of Life*, pp. 126–127.
13 Interview with Colonel Maude, January 1977.
14 *Strike Nights in Printing House Square*, p. 15.
15 Farman, *op. cit.*, p. 179.
16 Letter to Vivien Dayrell-Browning, June 1926.
17 *Ibid.*, 6 May 1926.
18 *A Sort of Life*, p. 127.
19 *Ibid.*
20 Letter to Vivien Dayrell-Browning, 11 May 1926.
21 *Ibid.*
22 *Ibid.*, 5 July 1926.
23 Undated letter from London.
24 Letter, 16 July 1926.

22   'The beastly Episode'

1   Interview with Walter Allen, 1976.
2   Letter to Vivien Dayrell-Browning, 5 July 1926.
3   *Ibid.*, 15 February 1926.

4 *Ibid.*
5 *Ibid.*
6 *Ibid.*, 29 December 1925.
7 *Ibid.*, 5 July 1926.
8 *Ibid.*
9 *Ibid.*, 11 December 1926.
10 *Ibid.*, 12 April 1926.
11 *Ibid.*, 11 December 1925.
12 'George Darley', *Collected Essays*, Penguin edition, 1970, p. 224.
13 Letter to Vivien Dayrell-Browning, 25 December 1926.
14 *Ibid.*, 9 December 1925.
15 *Ibid.*, 16 December 1925.
16 *Ibid.*, 21 December 1925.
17 *Ibid.*, 16 March 1926.
18 *Ibid.*, 23 February 1926.
19 *Ibid.*, 3 March 1926.
20 *Ibid.*, 8 November 1925.
21 *Ibid.*, 8 July 1926.
22 *Ibid.*, 26 February 1926.
23 *Ibid.*
24 *Ibid.*, 16 March 1926.
25 *Ibid.*, 18 March 1926.
26 *Ibid.*, 19 April 1926.
27 *Ibid.*, 31 March 1926.
28 *Ibid.*, 22 April 1926.
29 *Ibid.*, 23 March 1926.
30 *Ibid.*, 29 March 1926.
31 *Ibid.*, 21 April 1926.
32 *Ibid.*, 22 April 1926.
33 *Ibid.*, 20 April 1926.
34 *Ibid.*, 24 January 1926.
35 *Ibid.*, 19 May 1926.
36 Letter to his mother, 30 March 1926.
37 Letter to Vivien Dayrell-Browning, 22 April 1926.
38 *Ibid.*, 29 April 1926.
39 *Ibid.*, 28 June 1926 from the Embankment at 3 p.m.
40 *Ibid.*, 27 May 1926.
41 *Ibid.*, 31 May 1926.
42 *Ibid.*, 2 June 1926.
43 *Ibid.*, 5 July 1926.
44 Letter to his mother, 4 June 1926.
45 *A Sort of Life*, Penguin edition, 1974, p. 131.
46 Letter to Vivien Dayrell-Browning, 15 July 1926. Later it transpired that he did not send it first to Heinemann.
47 TS., Boston College, Boston.
48 *Ways of Escape*, Penguin edition, 1981, p. 13.
49 *A Sort of Life*, p. 132.
50 Letter to his mother, 21 April 1927.
51 *A Sort of Life*, p. 133.
52 Letter to Vivien, 29 September 1926.

23 In Hospital and Suspected Epilepsy

1 *A Sort of Life*, Penguin edition, 1974, p. 133.
2 *Ibid.*, p. 134.
3 *A Gun for Sale*, Penguin edition, 1974, p. 28.
4 Letter to his mother, 30 September 1926.
5 Letter to Vivien Dayrell-Browning, 2 October 1926.
6 *Ibid.*, 5 October 1926.
7 *Ibid.*, 7 October 1926.
8 *Ibid.*, 3 October 1926.
9 *Ibid.*, 8 October 1926.
10 *Ibid.*, 4 October 1926.
11 *Ibid.*, 18 October 1926.
12 *A Sort of Life*, p. 134.
13 *Ibid.*
14 Letter to Vivien Dayrell-Browning, 3 October 1926.
15 TS, p. 231.
16 Letter to Vivien Dayrell-Browning, 15 October 1926.
17 *It's a Battlefield*, Penguin edition, 1981, pp. 194–6.
18 *Ibid.*, p. 197.
19 Letter to Vivien Dayrell-Browning, 13 October 1926.
20 *Ibid.*, 15 October 1926.
21 *Ibid.*, 6 November 1926.
22 *Ibid.*, 7 November 1926.
23 *Brighton Rock*, Penguin edition, 1975, p. 154.
24 Letter to Vivien Dayrell-Browning, 17 November 1926.
25 *Ibid.*, 18 November 1926.
26 *Ibid.*, 19 November 1926.
27 *Ibid.*
28 *Ibid.*, 24 November 1926.
29 *Ibid.*, 25 November 1926.
30 *A Sort of Life*, p. 136.
31 Letter to Vivien Dayrell-Browning, 25 November 1926.
32 *Ibid.*, 26 November 1926.
33 *Ibid.*
34 *Ibid.*
35 *A Sort of Life*, p. 136.
36 *Ibid.*
37 Letter to Vivien Dayrell-Browning, 18 January 1927.
38 *Ibid.*, 19 January 1927.
39 *Ibid.*
40 *Ibid.*, 25 January 1927.
41 *Ibid.*
42 *A Sort of Life*, pp. 137–8.
43 *The Living Room*, Act I, Scene 2, Viking edition (U.S.A.), 1954, p. 55.
44 Letter to Vivien Dayrell-Browning, 24 January 1927.
45 *A Sort of Life*, p. 121.
46 The dummy collection has survived and is housed at the Humanities Research Center, Austin, Texas.
47 Letter to Vivien Dayrell-Browning, 15 December 1926.

24 Marriage at Last

1 Letter to Vivien, 10 January 1927.
2 *Ibid.*, 17 February 1927.
3 *Ibid.*
4 *Ibid.*, 21 March 1927.
5 *Ibid.*, 12 April 1927.
6 *Ibid.*, 1 June 1927.
7 *Ibid.*, 13 May 1927.
8 *Ibid.*, 13 March 1927.
9 *Ibid.*, 26 April 1927.
10 *Ibid.*, 1 March 1927.
11 *Ibid.*, 4 March 1927.
12 *Ibid.*
13 *Ibid.*, 19 March 1927.
14 *Ibid.*, 30 March 1927.
15 *Ibid.*, 26 June 1927.
16 *Ibid.*, 18 June 1927.
17 *Ibid.*, 20 June 1927.
18 *Ibid.*, 9 September 1927.
19 *Ibid.*, 17 June 1927.
20 *Ibid.*, 30 May 1927.
21 *Ibid.*
22 *Ibid.*, 9 June 1927.
23 *Ibid.*, 5 January 1927.
24 *Ibid.*, 18 June 1927.
25 *Ibid.*, 11 June 1927.
26 *Ibid.*
27 *Ibid.*, 18 June 1927.
28 *Ibid.*, 11 September 1927.
29 *Ibid.*, 22 September 1927.
30 *A Sort of Life*, Penguin edition, 1974, p. 21.
31 Letter to Vivien, 18 June 1927.
32 *Ibid.*, 31 August 1927.
33 *Ibid.*, 27 September 1927.
34 *Ibid.*, 30 August 1927.
35 *Ibid.*, 11 September 1927.
36 *Ibid.*, 23 June 1927.
37 *Ibid.*, 24 April 1927.
38 *Ibid.*
39 *Ibid.*, 21 February 1927.
40 *Ibid.*
41 *Ibid.*, 1 September 1927.
42 *Ibid.*, 26 September 1927.
43 *Ibid.*, 14 June 1927.
44 *Ibid.*, 27 September 1927.
45 *Ibid.*, 20 September 1927.
46 *Ibid.*, 25 September 1927.
47 *Ibid.*, 27 September 1927.
48 *Ibid.*, 1 June 1927.
49 *Ibid.*, 19 March 1927.
50 *Ibid.*, 10 June 1927.
51 *Ibid.*, 28 May 1927.

52 *Ibid.*, 2 February 1927.
53 *Ibid.*, 22 April 1927.
54 *Ibid.*, 14 June 1927.
55 *Morning Post*, 17 October 1927.
56 Letter from Elisabeth Dennys, 18 March 1983.
57 Interview with Vivien Greene, 10 August 1983.
58 Letter to his mother, 21 December 1927.
59 *Ibid.*
60 *Ibid.*

25 'Pussy' and 'Tiger' and *The Man Within*

1 *A Sort of Life*, Penguin edition, 1974, p. 138.
2 Interview with Helga Guinness, 19 January 1977.
3 Interview, January 1977.
4 Interview with David Higham, July 1977.
5 Interview with Helga Guinness.
6 *Ibid.*
7 Letter to his mother, February 1928.
8 *Ibid.*, 18 March 1929.
9 *Ibid.*, 27 September 1928.
10 *Ibid.*, 12 April 1928.
11 *Ibid.*, 14 January 1929.
12 *Ibid.*, 31 May 1928.
13 *Ibid.*
14 *Ibid.*, 23 July 1928.
15 *Ibid.*, 9 May 1928.
16 This appeared in *Nineteen Stories*, Heinemann, 1947.
17 Letter to Vivien, September 1926.
18 *Ibid.*, October 1926.
19 *Ibid.*, 8 November 1926.
20 *Ibid.*, 13 May 1927.
21 Letter to his mother, 20 February 1927.
22 *Ibid.*, 27 September 1928.
23 *Ibid.*, middle of November 1928.
24 *A Sort of Life*, p. 139.
25 Letter from Grace Cranston, Archivist for Heinemann, 27 May 1982.
26 Letter to his mother, 7 January 1929.
27 *Ibid.*, 5 June 1929.
28 *Ibid.*, 24 May 1929.
29 *Ibid.*, 28 June 1929.
30 *Ibid.*, 3 October 1929.
31 Introduction to Margaret Lane's *Edgar Wallace: Biography of a Phenomenon*, Hamish Hamilton, 1964.
32 Letter to his mother, 21 October 1929.
33 *Ibid.*, 29 October 1929.
34 Interview with Helga Guinness, 19 January 1977.
35 *Outlook and Independence*, 25 December 1929.
36 *Letters of Aldous Huxley*, ed. Grover Smith, Chatto & Windus, 1969, p. 330.
37 David Higham, *Literary Gent*, Jonathan Cape, 1978, p. 170.
38 *A Sort of Life*, p. 139.

39 *Ibid.*, p. 140.
40 *The Man Within*, Penguin edition, 1977, p. 86.
41 *Ibid.*, p. 200.
42 Letter to Vivien, 11 June 1927.
43 *Ibid.*, 9 January 1927.
44 *Ibid.*, 31 January 1927.
45 *Ibid.*, 21 February 1927.
46 *The Man Within*, p. 84.
47 *Ibid.*, p. 85.
48 *Ibid.*, pp. 200–1.
49 Letter to Vivien, 20 June 1927.
50 *The Man Within*, p. 167.
51 Interview with Edward Greene, 19 December 1976.
52 *The Man Within*, p. 121.

26 A False Start

1 Letter to his mother, 14 January 1929.
2 *Ibid.*
3 *Ibid.*, 13 August 1929.
4 *Ibid.*, 3 October 1929.
5 *A Sort of Life*, Penguin edition, 1974, p. 141.
6 Letter to his mother, 29 October 1929.
7 Letter to *The Times*, October 1929.
8 *Ibid.*
9 *A Sort of Life*, pp. 141–2.
10 *Ibid.*, pp. 128–9.
11 Interview with Vivien Greene, 23 June 1977.
12 Letter from Leslie Smith, 1977.
13 Interview with the Rt Hon. Douglas Jay, 1977.
14 *A Sort of Life*, p. 142.
15 Letter to his mother, 29 March 1929.
16 'Save Me Only from Dullness', *Evening News*, 23 January 1930.
17 Letter to his mother, 11 February 1929.
18 *Ibid.*, 13 August 1929.
19 The postcard's date is indecipherable.
20 Letter to his mother, 2 February 1930.
21 *Ibid.*, 23 March 1930. On the last page of the manuscript of *The Name of Action* are the following dates: 'March 1929–July 1930'.
22 'Oberammergau', *The Graphic*, 17 May 1930, p. 345.
23 *A Sort of Life*, p. 144.
24 *Ways of Escape*, Penguin edition, 1981, p. 16.
25 Letter to his mother, 18 August 1930.
26 *Ibid.*
27 *Ibid.*, 5 August 1930.
28 On the last page of the manuscript are the following dates: '1930 September–1931 April 27'.
29 Letter to his mother, 20 October 1930.
30 *Ways of Escape*, pp. 15–16.
31 *A Sort of Life*, p. 144.
32 Undated letter to his mother, probably March 1931.
33 *Spectator*, 1 June 1934, p. 864. Graham was discussing Dennis Kincaid's dis-

appointing second novel after his brilliant first but he had his own case very much in mind.

34 *Spectator*, 5 May 1933, p. 654.
35 Letter to his mother, 2 October 1930.
36 Letter to Hugh Greene, undated.
37 Letter to his mother, 22 January 1931.

27 Down and Out at Chipping Campden

1 Letter to his mother, 2 March 1931.
2 *Ibid.*
3 *Ibid.*, 12 June 1931.
4 Diary, May 1932.
5 Undated letter to Hugh Greene – the date on the envelope is not easy to read but is probably 17 April 1931.
6 Letter to his mother, 28 April 1931.
7 Interview with Vivien Greene, July 1979.
8 Letter to his mother, 2 March 1931.
9 *Ibid.*, 31 May 1931.
10 Letter to Hugh Greene, 15 November 1930.
11 *Lord Rochester's Monkey: Being the Life of John Wilmot, 2nd Earl of Rochester*, Bodley Head, 1974, p. 13.
12 Letter to his mother, 12 June 1931.
13 *A Sort of Life*, Penguin edition, 1974, p. 151.
14 *Lord Rochester's Monkey*, p. 9.
15 'John Hayward, 1904–1965: Some Memories', ed. John Carter, *Book Collector*, XIV (Winter), 1965, pp. 443–86.
16 *Ibid.*
17 *Ibid.*
18 *New Statesman and Nation*, 14 November 1931, p. 614.
19 *The Nation*, 3 May 1932, p. 578.
20 *Spectator*, 26 December 1931, p. 892.
21 *Ways of Escape*, Penguin edition, 1981, pp. 17–18.
22 *A Sort of Life*, p. 151.
23 Letter from Frank Swinnerton, 2 January 1977.
24 Diary, 19 July 1932.
25 Letter to Vivien, 11 December 1925.
26 Letter to his mother, 11 October 1930.
27 Interview with Vivien Greene, 10 August 1983.
28 A term used by Groucho Marx.
29 Letter to his mother, 11 September 1931.
30 Letter dated only Monday 1931, but obviously a response to his mother's dismay at his seeming to agree with the porter.
31 Interview with Vivien Greene, July 1979.
32 *Ibid.*
33 *Ibid.*, August 1977.
34 *Ibid.*
35 Diary, 20 September 1932.
36 *Ibid.*, 4 July 1932.
37 *Ways of Escape*, p. 17.
38 *A Sort of Life*, p. 145.

28 *Stamboul Train/Orient Express*

1   Letter to Vivien, 1 January 1926.
2   Letter to his mother, 2 February 1930.
3   Letter to Vivien, 18 March 1927.
4   *Ways of Escape*, Penguin edition, 1981, p. 23.
5   Undated letter to Vivien.
6   *Ways of Escape*, p. 22.
7   *Stamboul Train*, Penguin edition, 1981, p. 169.
8   *Ibid.*, p. 165.
9   *A Sort of Life*, Penguin edition, 1974, p. 147.
10 *Spectator*, 20 October 1933, p. 538.
11 Diary, 1 July 1932.
12 *Spectator*, 17 November 1933.
13 *A Sort of Life*, pp. 146–50.
14 *Stamboul Train*, p. 35.
15 *A Sort of Life*, p. 134.
16 *Stamboul Train*, p. 168.
17 *Ibid.*, p. 71. See also *The Lawless Roads*, Heinemann uniform edition, 1955, p. 5.
18 *Stamboul Train*, p. 48.
19 *Ibid.*, p. 14.
20 Letter to his mother, 31 May 1928.
21 *Stamboul Train*, pp. 16–17.
22 'The Sense of Apprehension', *The Month*, July 1951, p. 51.
23 Diary, 6 June 1932.
24 *Ways of Escape*, p. 25.
25 Letter to his mother, 15 March 1932.
26 Undated letter to Hugh Greene.
27 Diary, 7 June 1932.
28 *Ibid.*, 1 August 1932.
29 *Spectator*, 26 July 1935.
30 Diary, 3 June 1932.
31 *Ibid.*, 28 February 1933.
32 *Ibid.*, 25 February 1932.
33 *Ibid.*, 8 August 1932.
34 *Ibid.*, 28 June 1932.
35 *Ibid.*, 7 July 1932.
36 Letter to author, 13 March 1986.
37 Diary, 9 July 1932.
38 John Dos Passos, *Orient Express*, Harper & Row, (U.S.A.), 1927, p. 3.
39 Interview with author, 23 June 1977.
40 Dos Passos, *op. cit.* pp. 10–12.
41 H. E. Bates, *The Blossoming World*, Michael Joseph, 1971, p. 123.
42 Diary, 21 July 1932.
43 *Ibid.*, 4 August 1932.
44 *Ibid.*, 13 August 1932.
45 Interview, 23 June 1977.
46 Diary, 14 August 1932.
47 *Ibid.*, 17 August 1932.

29 The Book Society and the J. B. Priestley Affair

1 Letter to his mother, 22 August 1932.
2 *Stamboul Train*, Penguin edition, 1981, p. 22.
3 Diary, 18 August 1932.
4 *Ibid.*, 19 August 1932.
5 *A Sort of Life*, Penguin edition, 1974, p. 153.
6 Diary, 1 September 1932.
7 *A Sort of Life*, p. 153.
8 Diary, 1 September 1932.
9 *Ibid.*, 2 September 1932.
10 *A Sort of Life*, p. 154.
11 *Ibid.*
12 *Sunday Telegraph Magazine*, 20 December 1974.
13 Diary, 12 September 1932.
14 *Ways of Escape*, Penguin edition, 1981, p. 18.
15 Diary, 10 September 1932.
16 Rupert Hart-Davis, *Hugh Walpole: A Biography*, Macmillan, 1952, p. 299.
17 'Casanova and Others', *Spectator*, 9 July 1932.
18 Diary, 19 June 1932.
19 *Ibid.*, 24 September 1932.
20 Letter to Hugh Greene, 22 October 1932.
21 Interview with Vivien Greene, 1987.
22 Diary, 10 October 1932.
23 *Ibid.*, 3 November 1932.
24 *Ibid.*, 28 November 1932.
25 *A Sort of Life*, p. 155.
26 Undated letter.
27 *A Sort of Life*, p. 155.
28 *Ways of Escape*, p. 24.
29 Rupert Hart-Davis, op. cit., p. 316.
30 Diary, 2 December 1932.
31 Undated letter to his mother.
32 *The Times*, 3 December 1932.
33 Diary, 4 January 1933.
34 *Spectator*, 29 December 1933.
35 'A Typewriter in the Desert', *London Mercury*, April 1937, p. 635.
36 Graham Greene, *Footnotes to the Film*, ed. Charles Davey, Lovat Dickson (U.S.A.), 1938, p. 58.
37 *Brighton Rock*, Penguin edition, 1975, p. 140.
38 *Spectator*, 10 November 1939, p. 662.
39 'A Lost Leader', *Spectator*, 13 December 1940, p. 646.
40 *Ways of Escape*, p. 24.
41 Diary, 12 December 1932.
42 *Ibid.*, 17 December 1932.
43 *Stamboul Train*, p. 24.
44 *Ibid.*, p. 31.
45 *Ibid.*, p. 32.
46 *Ibid.*, p. 47.
47 *Ibid.*, pp. 215–16.
48 Diary, 13 December 1932.
49 Diary, 19 July 1932.
50 *Ways of Escape*, p. 27.

30   1933

1   Diary, 30 January 1933.
2   *Sunday Telegraph*, 30 September 1979.
3   Diary, 14 February 1933.
4   Letter, 3 March 1933. The contract was not in fact forthcoming.
5   Diary, 1 March 1933.
6   *Ibid.*, 19 January 1933.
7   H. E. Bates, *The Blossoming World*, Michael Joseph, 1971, pp. 174–5.
8   'I'm an angry old man, you see', *Spectator*, 14 June 1986, p. 9.
9   Letter to his mother, 25 October 1932.
10   Diary, 24 October 1932.
11   *Ibid.*, 20 January 1933.
12   *Ibid.*, 21 January 1933.
13   *Ibid.*, 21 March 1933.
14   *Ibid.*, 22 March 1933.
15   *Ibid.*, 29 April 1933.
16   Diary, 5 January 1933.
17   *Ibid.*, 25 July 1932.
18   *Ibid.*
19   *Ibid.*, 6 July 1932.
20   'Fiction', *Spectator*, 7 April 1933, p. 508.
21   *Ibid.*
22   *Ibid.*, 22 September 1933.
23   *Ibid.*, 21 April 1933.
24   *Ibid.*, 3 November 1933.
25   *Ibid.*, 22 September 1933.
26   *Ibid.*
27   *Ibid.*
28   *Ibid.*
29   *Ibid.*, 19 May 1933.
30   *Ibid.*, 28 July 1933.
31   *Ibid.*, 21 April 1933.
32   *Ibid.*, 5 May 1933.
33   *Ibid.*, 10 February 1933.

31   *It's a Battlefield*

1   Letter to Mary Pritchett, 25 February 1933.
2   Introduction to the Heinemann and Bodley Head collected edition, *It's a Battlefield*, 1970, p. viii, also *Ways of Escape*, Penguin edition, 1981, pp. 27–8.
3   Introduction to collected edition, p. viii, also *Ways of Escape*, p. 27.
4   Diary, 23 June 1932.
5   *Ways of Escape*, p. 28.
6   *It's a Battlefield*, Penguin edition, 1981, p. 59.
7   *Ibid.*, p. 180.
8   Letter, 7 July 1926.
9   *Ibid.*, 13 May 1926.
10   *It's a Battlefield*, pp. 62–3.
11   *The Times*, October 1932.
12   Marie-Françoise Allain, *The Other Man: Conversations with Graham Greene*, trans. Guido Waldman, Bodley Head, 1983, p. 55.

13 Diary, 10 November 1932.
14 *Ibid.*, pp. 27–8.
15 *Ibid.*, p. 29.
16 Interview, 2 March 1977.
17 Interview, 19 December 1976.
18 Sandra Jobson Darroch, *Ottoline*, Coward, McCann & Geoghegan, 1975, p. 251n.
19 *Ibid.*
20 *Ibid.*, p. 274.
21 Michael Holroyd, *Lytton Strachey*, Holt, Rinehart and Winston (U.S.A.), 1980, p. 448.
22 Interview, 23 June 1983.
23 *It's a Battlefield*, p. 188.
24 *Ibid.*, p. 192.
25 *Ibid.*, p. 87.
26 Jeffrey Meyers, *Katherine Mansfield*, A New Directions Book, 1980, pp. 145–6.
27 *It's a Battlefield*, p. 34.
28 Katherine Mansfield's diary entry, 8 February 1922.
29 Meyers, *op. cit.*, p. 75.
30 Aldous Huxley, *Point Counter Point*, Penguin edition, 1974, p. 170.
31 *It's a Battlefield*, p. 58.
32 *Ibid.*, pp. 106–8.
33 Diary, 10 April 1933.
34 *Spectator*, 21 April 1933, p. 579.
35 *It's a Battlefield*, p. 39.
36 *Ibid.*, p. 189.

32 'The skeletons of other people's people'

1 Diary, 4 August 1932. Samuel Pepys, in his diary, expressed his curiosity as to how the Italian sport of buggery was performed: 'Blessed be God, I do not to this day know what is the meaning of this sin, nor which is the agent nor which is the patient.'
2 *Ibid.*, 6 April 1933.
3 *Ibid.*, 12 July 1933.
4 *Ibid.*, 2 August 1933.
5 *It's a Battlefield*, Penguin edition, 1981, p. 125.
6 *Ibid.*, p. 126.
7 Diary, 12 July 1932.
8 *Ibid.*, 5 October 1932.
9 *Ibid.*, 12 February 1933.
10 *Ibid.*, 2–10 September 1932.
11 Letter to his mother, 21 April 1933.
12 Letter, 4 October 1925.
13 Interview, 26 July 1979.
14 Interview, 10 August 1983.
15 Diary, 21 May 1933.
16 *Ibid.*, 24 May 1933.
17 *The End of the Affair*, Heinemann, 1951, pp. 192–3.
18 Letter to his mother, 5 May 1933.
19 Diary, 27 February 1933.

20 *Ibid.*, 16 June 1933.
21 *Ibid.*, 10 July 1932.
22 *Spectator*, 15 December 1933.

33 *England Made Me* – and the Black Sheep of the Family

1 'Gold Bricks', *Spectator*, 3 March 1933, p. 308.
2 Diary, 1–6 July 1933.
3 *Ibid.*, 13 July 1933.
4 *Ibid.*, 21 July 1933.
5 *Ibid.*, 28 July 1933.
6 Michael Tracey, *A Variety of Lives: A Biography of Sir Hugh Greene*, Bodley Head, 1983, p. 27.
7 Interview with Sir Hugh Greene, 19 May 1981.
8 Letter, 18 August 1932.
9 *Ways of Escape*, Penguin edition, 1981, p. 30.
10 *Ibid.*
11 'Two Capitals', *Spectator*, 20 October 1933, pp. 520–1.
12 *Ways of Escape*, p. 31.
13 *England Made Me*, Penguin edition, 1970, p. 15.
14 *Ibid.*, p. 83.
15 'Fiction', *Spectator*, 30 June 1933, p. 956.
16 Diary, 22 July 1933.
17 *The Old School*, Jonathan Cape, 1934, p. 253.
18 *Ways of Escape*, p. 31.
19 *England Made Me*, pp. 9 & 14.
20 *Ibid.*, p. 16.
21 *Ibid.*, p. 21.
22 *Ibid.*, p. 10.
23 'Across the Border (an unfinished novel)', *Penguin New Writing*, Volume 30, 1947, p. 73.
24 *Ibid.*, pp. 69–70.
25 *England Made Me*, p. 184.
26 'Across the Border', p. 70.
27 Letter from Olga Franklin, 26 November 1980.
28 Interview with Edward Greene, 19 December 1976.
29 Interview with Felix Greene, 2 March 1977.
30 Letter to Vivien, 10 March 1926.
31 *Ibid.*, 22 March 1926.
32 *Ibid.*, 31 May 1926.
33 *The Old School*, p. 248.
34 Postcard to his mother, August 1933.
35 *A Sort of Life*, Penguin edition, 1974, p. 21.
36 *England Made Me*, p. 63.
37 'Across the Border', p. 70.
38 Letter to Vivien, 22 February 1927.
39 *England Made Me*, pp. 13–14.
40 *Ways of Escape*, p. 31.
41 *England Made Me*, p. 17.
42 *Ibid.*, pp. 16–19.
43 *Ibid.*, p. 141.
44 *Ibid.*, p. 201.
45 Letter to his mother, 2 January 1934.

34   Champagne and Fate

1   *Ways of Escape*, Penguin edition, 1981, p. 37.
2   Barbara Greene, *Land Benighted*, Geoffrey Bles, 1938, p. 1.
3   *Ways of Escape*, pp. 37–8.
4   *News Chronicle*, 4 January 1935.
5   Letter to Hugh Greene, 18 August 1934.
6   *Ibid.*
7   *Ways of Escape*, p. 37.
8   Papers Concerning Affairs in Liberia, December 1930–May 1934, HMSO, May 1934, p. 61.
9   Postscript to letter to Hugh Greene in Berlin, 26 November 1934.
10   *Journey Without Maps*, Penguin edition, 1978, p. 23.
11   *Ways of Escape*, p. 38.
12   *Land Benighted*, p. 6.
13   *Journey Without Maps*, p. 30.
14   Diary, p. 1.
15   *Land Benighted*, p. 5.
16   *Journey Without Maps*, p. 37.
17   *Ibid.*, p. 38.
18   *Ibid.*
19   *Ibid.*, p. 53.
20   *The Pleasure Dome*, Oxford University Press, 1980, p. 157.
21   *Journey Without Maps*, p. 43.
22   'The Soupsweet Land', *Collected Essays*, Penguin edition, 1970, p. 343.
23   *Journey Without Maps*, p. 43.
24   *Collected Essays*, p. 343.
25   *Time and Tide*, 19 October 1940.
26   Interview, 1976.
27   *Land Benighted*, p. 6.
28   *Ibid.*
29   *Journey Without Maps*, pp. 49–50.
30   *Ibid.*, p. 51.
31   *Ibid.*, p. 53.
32   *Ibid.*
33   *Ibid.*, p. 54.
34   *Ibid.*, p. 53.
35   *Ibid.*, p. 55.
36   *Ibid.*, p. 54.
37   *Ibid.*, p. 59.
38   *Land Benighted*, p. 14.
39   Diary, p. 19.
40   *Journey Without Maps*, p. 64.
41   *Ibid.*, p. 68.
42   Diary, p. 10.
43   *Journey Without Maps*, p. 68.
44   Diary, p. 10.
45   *Journey Without Maps*, p. 78.
46   Diary, p. 16.
47   Diary, p. 11.
48   *Land Benighted*, p. 18.
49   Diary, p. 6.
50   *Journey Without Maps*, p. 79.

51 *Ibid.*, pp. 79–80.
52 *Ibid.*, p. 80.
53 *Ibid.*, p. 81.
54 *Ibid.*, p. 82.
55 *Ibid.*
56 *Ibid.*
57 *Land Benighted*, p. 9.
58 *Ibid.*
59 *Journey Without Maps*, p. 83.
60 *Ibid.*
61 Diary, p. 12.
62 *Land Benighted*, p. 21.
63 *Journey Without Maps*, p. 86.
64 *Ibid.*
65 *Ibid.*, p. 87.
66 Jeremy Gavron, 'Dark Journey into Greeneland', *Daily Telegraph*, 16 January 1988.
67 *Journey Without Maps*, pp. 98–9.
68 *Ibid.*, p. 95.
69 *Ibid.*, p. 97.
70 *Ibid.*
71 Diary, p. 27.

35   Whisky and Epsom Salts

1 Barbara Greene, *Land Benighted*, Geoffrey Bles, 1938, p. 32.
2 *Journey Without Maps*, Penguin Books, 1978, p. 85.
3 *Ibid.*, pp. 103–4.
4 *Ibid.*, p. 85.
5 *Ibid.*, p. 105.
6 *Ibid.*
7 *Ibid.*, p. 108.
8 *Ibid.*, p. 105.
9 *Ibid.*, p. 110.
10 *Ibid.*
11 *Ibid.*, p. 111.
12 *Ibid.*, p. 112.
13 *Ibid.*, p. 115.
14 *Ibid.*, p. 118.
15 *Ibid.*, pp. 119–20.
16 *Ibid.*, pp. 120–1.
17 *Ibid.*, p. 122.
18 *Ibid.*, p. 124.
19 *Ibid.*, p. 125.
20 Diary, p. 31.
21 *Journey Without Maps*, pp. 126–7.
22 Undated letter to her mother from Monrovia.
23 *Journey Without Maps*, p. 129.
24 *Land Benighted*, p. 55.
25 *Journey Without Maps*, p. 132.
26 *Ibid.*, p. 133.
27 *Land Benighted*, p. 69.

28 *Ibid.*, pp. 63–4.
29 *Journey Without Maps*, p. 134.
30 *Ibid.*
31 *Land Benighted*, p. 61.
32 *Ibid.*, p. 68.
33 *Journey Without Maps*, p. 137.
34 *Land Benighted*, p. 72.
35 *Ibid.*, p. 65.
36 *Ibid.*
37 *Journey Without Maps*, p. 137.
38 *Ibid.*, p. 141.
39 *Land Benighted*, pp. 79–80.
40 *Ibid.*, p. 81.
41 *Ibid.*, p. 86.
42 *Ibid.*, p. 88.
43 *Ibid.*
44 *Journey Without Maps*, p. 150.
45 'A Chance for Mr Lever', *Twenty-One Stories*, Penguin Books, 1973, p. 101.
46 *Land Benighted*, p. 96.
47 'A Chance for Mr Lever', p. 99.
48 *Journey Without Maps*, p. 154.
49 *Ibid.*
50 *Ibid.*
51 *Ibid.*, p. 155.
52 *Ibid.*, p. 162.
53 *Land Benighted*, p. 109.
54 *Ibid.*, p. 112.
55 Diary, pp. 44–5.
56 *Land Benighted*, pp. 118–19.
57 *Journey Without Maps*, p. 171.
58 *Ibid.*, p. 183.
59 Diary, pp. 51–2.
60 *Land Benighted*, p. 136.
61 *Ibid.*, p. 137.
62 *Ibid.*, p. 135.
63 *Journey Without Maps*, p. 157.
64 *Ibid.*, p. 192.
65 *Ibid.*, p. 193.
66 *Ibid.*, p. 200.
67 'At Home', *Collected Essays*, Penguin Books, 1970, p. 335.
68 *Journey Without Maps*, pp. 205–6.
69 *Ibid.*, pp. 200–1.
70 *Ibid.*, p. 211.
71 *Land Benighted*, p. 159.
72 Diary, p. 67.
73 *Journey Without Maps*, p. 211.
74 *Land Benighted*, pp. 173–4.
75 *Ibid.*, pp. 176–7.
76 *Journey Without Maps*, p. 213.
77 'A Chance for Mr Lever', p. 107.
78 *Journey Without Maps*, p. 215.
79 *Land Benighted*, p. 179.
80 Diary, p. 68.

81 *Journey Without Maps*, p. 220.
82 *Land Benighted*, pp. 189–90.
83 *Ibid.*, p. 192.
84 *Journey Without Maps*, p. 224.
85 *Land Benighted*, p. 193.
86 *Journey Without Maps*, p. 226.
87 *Land Benighted*, p. 194.
88 *Journey Without Maps*, p. 228.
89 *Ibid.*, p. 235.
90 *Ibid.*, p. 234.
91 Diary, entry on last page.
92 *Land Benighted*, p. 202.
93 *Journey Without Maps*, p. 248.
94 *Land Benighted*, p. 204.
95 *Journey Without Maps*, pp. 248–9.
96 *Ibid.*, p. 250.
97 'Books in General', *New Statesman and Nation*, 21 June 1952, p. 745.
98 *Journey Without Maps*, p. 19.
99 *Ibid.*, p. 244.
100 *Ibid.*, p. 21.
101 *Ibid.*, p. 249.
102 *Ibid.*, p. 248.
103 *Ibid.*, p. 21.
104 *Ibid.*, p. 250.
105 *Spectator*, 5 July 1935.
106 Letter to Hugh Greene, 19 December 1937.
107 Letter to Louise Callendar, 11 October 1946.
108 *Spectator*, 15 May 1936.
109 Letter to Countess Strachwitz, 11 January 1975.

36 14 North Side

1 Letter to his mother, 18 April 1935.
2 *Ibid.*
3 Interview with Vivien Greene, 10 August 1983.
4 Letter to his mother, 18 April 1935.
5 'West Coast', *Spectator*, 12 April 1935.
6 Letter to his mother, 8 September 1936.
7 'Two Tall Travellers', *Spectator*, 11 September 1936.
8 Letter to his mother, 9 May 1935.
9 *Ibid.*
10 'The Basement Room', *Twenty-One Stories*, Penguin edition, 1973, p. 19.
11 *Ibid.*, p. 17.
12 Undated letter of 1935.
13 *Ibid.*
14 The review entitled 'The Domestic Background' appeared in the *Spectator*, 26 July 1935.
15 Undated letter of 1935.
16 *The Times Literary Supplement*, 23 November 1935.
17 William Plomer, *Spectator*, 22 November 1935.
18 *The Times Literary Supplement*, 4 June 1935.
19 *Spectator*, 28 June 1935.

20 Letter to David Higham, 26 March 1939.
21 Letter to Nancy Pearn, 20 October 1935.
22 *Ibid.*, 21 October 1935.
23 *Ibid.*, 11 November 1935.
24 Letter to his mother, 3 April 1936.
25 Letter to Nancy Pearn, 13 January 1936.
26 *Ibid.*, 7 January 1936.
27 *Ibid.*, 11 January 1936.
28 *The Times*, 23 January 1936.
29 Letter from Nancy Pearn, 10 February 1936.
30 Letter to Nancy Pearn, 13 March 1936.
31 Letter from Nancy Pearn, 8 May 1936.
32 Letter to his mother, 3 April 1936.

37   The Pleasure Dome

1   Letter, 9 May 1936.
2   Letter, January 1936.
3   *Ways of Escape*, Penguin edition, 1981, p. 45.
4   'Screen Greene', *London Magazine*, April 1968, p. 54.
5   *Spectator*, 11 October 1935.
6   Letter to his mother, 3 November 1935.
7   *Spectator*, 25 December 1936.
8   *Night and Day*, 30 September 1937.
9   *Spectator*, 22 May 1936.
10 *Ibid.*, 18 December 1936.
11 *Night and Day*, 29 July 1937.
12 *Ibid.*, 26 August 1937.
13 *Spectator*, 20 November 1936.
14 *Ibid.*, 11 December 1936 and 18 December 1936.
15 *Ibid.*, 4 October 1935.
16 *Journey Without Maps*, Penguin edition, 1978, p. 27.
17 *Ibid.*, pp. 28–9.
18 *Night and Day*, 22 July 1937.
19 *Ibid.*
20 *Ibid.*, 4 November 1937.
21 *Ibid.*, 7 October 1937.
22 *Ibid.*
23 *Spectator*, 6 September 1935.
24 *Ibid.*, 2 April 1937.
25 *Ibid.*, 5 July 1935.
26 'Subjects and Stories', *Footnotes to the Film*, ed. Charles Davey, Lovat Dickson (U.S.A.), 1938.
27 *Spectator*, 17 April 1936.
28 *Ways of Escape*, p. 47.
29 *Spectator*, 27 December 1935.
30 *Ibid.*, 5 March 1937.
31 'Ideas in the Cinema', *Spectator*, 19 November 1937.
32 *Footnotes to the Film*.
33 *Ibid.*
34 Letter to Hugh Greene, 29 February 1936.
35 *Ibid.*

36 *Spectator*, 4 September 1936.
37 *Ways of Escape*, p. 50.
38 *Ibid.*
39 'The Novelist and the Cinema – A Personal Experience', *International Film Annual*, No. 2, ed. William Whitebait, Calder, 1958.
40 Basil Dean, *Mind's Eye*, Hutchinson, 1973, p. 251.
41 *Ibid.*, p. 252.
42 *Spectator*, 12 January 1940.
43 'The Novelist and the Cinema'.
44 *Ways of Escape*, pp. 50–1.

38   *Night and Day*

1   Letter from Arthur Calder-Marshall, 8 October 1977.
2   Basil Dean, *Mind's Eye*, Hutchinson, 1973, p. 250.
3   Letter to Hugh Greene, 11 June 1936.
4   Letter in Graham Greene's possession. Also quoted in *The Letters of Evelyn Waugh*, ed. Mark Amory, Weidenfeld and Nicolson, 1980, pp. 108–9. Amory dates the letter 30 July 1936.
5   Letter to his mother, 29 August 1936.
6   Letter to Hugh Greene, 31 August 1936.
7   Letter to his mother, 8 September 1936.
8   *Ibid.*
9   Letter from Ian Parsons, 30 December 1976.
10 Letter undated, but Mark Amory dates it March or April 1937.
11 Waugh's letters to Graham Greene are still in Greene's possession. Not all of them have been published. They are all undated.
12 Dated by Amory, August 1937.
13 Quoted by Hugh Thomas in his *Spanish Civil War*, Billing & Sons, 1961, pp. 171–5, from Antonio Montero's study *La Persecucion religiosa en España*.
14 Alan Jenkins, *The Thirties*, Heinemann, 1976, p. 85.
15 Hugh Thomas, op. cit., p. 410.
16 *Ways of Escape*, Penguin edition, 1981, pp. 59–60.
17 Interview with Sir Hugh Greene, 19 May 1981.
18 A selection from the entire run of the magazine was published in 1985. Well edited by Christopher Hawtree, preface by Graham Greene.
19 Quoted by Hawtree in his wide-ranging introduction to the selection of *Night and Day*.
20 Preface to *Night and Day*, Chatto & Windus, 1985, p. vii.
21 Walter Allen, *As I Walked Down New Grub Street: Memories of A Writing Life*, University of Chicago Press, 1982, pp. 64–5.
22 Interview with Lady Read, June 1977.
23 *Night and Day*, 19 August 1937.
24 *Ibid.*, 21 October 1937.
25 *Spectator*, 24 May 1936.
26 Anne Edwards, *Shirley Temple: American Princess*, William Morrow & Co., (U.S.A.), 1988, p. 105.
27 Diary, 24 September 1938.
28 *Night and Day*, 18 November 1937.
29 Letter to Hugh Greene, 16 January 1938.
30 *Diaries of Evelyn Waugh*, ed. Michael Davie, Penguin Books, 1976, p. 426.
31 Quoted by Hawtree in his introduction to the selected *Night and Day*.

32 Letter from Ian Parsons, 30 December 1976.
33 *Ibid.*
34 John Atkins, *Graham Greene*, Calder and Boyars, 1969, p. 86.
35 Letter to Mrs Stine, 21 April 1969.
36 Letter to Hugh Greene, 16 January 1938.
37 *Spectator*, 5 August 1938.

39 Brighton Rock

1   Martin Shuttleworth and Simon Raven, 'Graham Greene Interviewed', *Graham Greene: A Collection of Critical Essays*, ed. Samuel L. Hynes, Prentice-Hall, 1973, pp. 161–3.
2   Letter to Vivien, 15 December 1925.
3   J. Maclaren-Ross, 'Excursion in Greeneland', *Memories of the Forties*, Alan Ross, 1965, p. 25.
4   Letter from Nancy Pearn, 25 July 1936.
5   *Ways of Escape*, Penguin edition, 1981, p. 62.
6   Letter to Hugh Greene, 30 July 1936.
7   *Brighton Rock*, Penguin edition, 1975, p. 129.
8   *Ways of Escape*, p. 61.
9   *Brighton Rock*, pp. 99–100.
10 J. Maclaren-Ross, op. cit., p. 21.
11 *Brighton Rock*, p. 102.
12 *Ibid.*, p. 5.
13 *Ibid.*, p. 6.
14 *Ibid.*, p. 86.
15 *Ibid.*, p. 140.
16 *Ibid.*, p. 64.
17 *Ways of Escape*, p. 61.
18 *A Gun for Sale*, Penguin edition, 1974, p. 127.
19 *Ways of Escape*, p. 61.
20 *Spectator*, 22 May 1936.
21 *Brighton Rock*, pp. 6–7.
22 *Ibid.*, p. 80.
23 *Ibid.*, p. 10.
24 *Ibid.*, p. 146.
25 *Ibid.*
26 Letter from Arthur Calder-Marshall, 8 October 1977.
27 *Brighton Rock*, p. 106.
28 *Ibid.*, p. 102.
29 *Ibid.*, p. 101.
30 *Ibid.*, p. 68.
31 Marie-Françoise Allain, *The Other Man: Conversations with Graham Greene*, trans. Guido Waldman, Bodley Head, 1983, pp. 158–9.
32 Rose Macaulay, *Letters to a Friend 1950–2*, ed. C. B. Smith, Collins, 1961, p. 124.
33 *Brighton Rock*, p. 36.
34 *Ibid.*, pp. 34–35.
35 *Ibid.*
36 *Ibid.*, p. 36.
37 *Ibid.*, pp. 32, 34.
38 *Ibid.*, p. 36.

39 *Ibid.*, p. 52.
40 *Ibid.*, p. 210.
41 *Ibid.*, pp. 101–2.
42 *Ibid.*, p. 226.
43 *Journey Without Maps*, Penguin edition, 1978, p. 250.
44 *Brighton Rock*, p. 141.
45 *Ibid.*, p. 186.
46 *Ibid.*, p. 92.
47 Otto Preminger, *An Autobiography*, Doubleday (U.S.A.), 1977, p. 153.
48 *Brighton Rock*, p. 52.
49 *Ibid.*, p. 164.
50 'Frederick Rolfe: Edwardian Inferno', *Collected Essays*, Penguin edition, 1970, pp. 130–2.
51 *Brighton Rock*, p. 139.
52 'Frederick Rolfe: A Spoiled Priest', *Collected Essays*, pp. 137–8.
53 T. S. Eliot, *Selected Essays*, Harcourt Brace (U.S.A.), 1950, p. 380.
54 Charles Baudelaire, *Intimate Journals*, trans. Christopher Isherwood, City Lights Books, 1983, p. 24.
55 *Brighton Rock*, p. 167.
56 *Ibid.*, p. 104.
57 *Ibid.*, p. 200.
58 *Ibid.*, p. 203.
59 *Ibid.*, p. 179.
60 *Ibid.*, p. 243.
61 *Ibid.*, p. 246.
62 *Ibid.*, p. 177.
63 Rose Macaulay, *Letters to a Friend*, p. 135.
64 *The Times*, 17 February 1966.
65 *Ways of Escape*, p. 61.

40 'I want to get out of this bloody country'

1 Walter Allen, *As I Walked Down New Grub Street: Memories of A Writing Life*, University of Chicago Press, 1981, p. 100.
2 Letter to Hugh Greene, 16 January 1938.
3 *Ways of Escape*, Penguin edition, 1981, p. 59.
4 Letter to Hugh Greene, 11 June 1936.
5 *Ibid.*, 30 July 1936.
6 *Ibid.*, 31 August 1936.
7 *Ibid.*, 19 August 1937.
8 Letter to David Higham, 8 December 1937.
9 *Ibid.*, 3 January 1938.
10 *Ibid.*, undated but probably 8 January 1938.
11 Letter to Hugh Greene, 16 January 1938.
12 Letter to David Higham, 11 January 1938.
13 T. H. O'Brien, *Civil Defence* (HMSO), 1955, p. 101.
14 Letter to Hugh Greene, 22 January 1938.
15 Diary entry, 12 January 1938.
16 *Ways of Escape*, p. 9.
17 Letter from Arthur Calder-Marshall to author, 8 October 1977.
18 J. Maclaren-Ross, 'Excursion in Greenland', *Memories of the Forties*, Alan Ross, 1965, p. 15.

19 Letter to Hugh Greene, 16 January 1938.
20 Letter from Arthur Calder-Marshall, 8 October 1977.
21 Letter to his mother, 7 February 1938.
22 *The Lawless Roads*, Heinemann uniform edition, 1955, pp. 17, 27.
23 Letter to Father Parsons from Tom Burns, 5 January 1938.
24 *The Lawless Roads*, p. 76. Parsons's unpublished autobiography is housed in the archives of Georgetown University Library.
25 Letter to Graham from Vivien, 27 February 1938.
26 Interview with Vivien Greene, 23 June 1977.
27 Interview with Vivien Greene, August 1977.
28 *The Lawless Roads*, p. 19.
29 *Ways of Escape*, p. 60.
30 *The Lawless Roads*, pp. 24–5.
31 Letter to Vivien, 28 February 1938.
32 *The Lawless Roads*, p. 23.
33 *Ibid.*, p. 26.
34 *Ibid.*, p. 35.
35 *Ibid.*, p. 59.
36 *Ibid.*, p. 62.
37 *Ibid.*, p. 100.
38 *Ibid.*, pp. 76–7.
39 *Ibid.*, p. 87.
40 *Ibid.*, p. 100.
41 *Ibid.*, p. 86.
42 *Ibid.*, pp. 49–50.
43 *Ibid.*, p. 70.
44 *Ibid.*, p. 262.
45 *Ibid.*, pp. 32–3.
46 *Ibid.*, p. 268.
47 *Ibid.*, p. 107.
48 *Ibid.*, p. 268.
49 *Ibid.*, p. 78.
50 *Ibid.*, pp. 255–7.
51 *Ibid.*, p. 176.
52 *Ibid.*, pp. 114–15.
53 *Ibid.*, p. 119.
54 *Ibid.*, pp. 120–1.
55 *Ibid.*, pp. 121–2.
56 *Ibid.*, p. 125.
57 Letter to Nancy Pearn, 7 March 1938.

41   *The Lawless Roads*

1 *The Lawless Roads*, Heinemann uniform edition, 1955, p. 128.
2 *Ibid.*
3 *Ibid.*, pp. 130–1.
4 *Ibid.*, p. 154. When I went to Frontera and Villahermosa in 1978 I could find no record of a Dr Winter, not surprisingly since, with the Shirley Temple libel case looming up, Greene would have been circumspect and changed the dentist's name. Perhaps Dr Winter's real name was related to the weather – Snow? – though I am still searching for evidence. There was, however, a dentist in the area called Carter!
5 *Ibid.*, p. 135.

6 *Ibid.*, pp. 137–8.
7 *Ibid.*, p. 139.
8 *Ibid.*, p. 140.
9 *Ibid.*, p. 143.
10 *Ibid.*, p. 196.
11 *Ibid.*, p. 152.
12 *Ibid.*, p. 158.
13 *Ibid.*, p. 151.
14 *Ibid.*, p. 162.
15 *Ibid.*, pp. 164–6.
16 *Ibid.*, p. 167.
17 *Ibid.*, pp. 168–9.
18 *Ibid.*, pp. 169–70.
19 *Ibid.*, p. 178.
20 *Ibid.*, pp. 182–4.
21 *Ibid.*, pp. 184–5.
22 Letter to his mother, 13 April 1938.
23 *The Lawless Roads*, p. 188.
24 *Ibid.*, p. 192.
25 *Ibid.*, p. 193.
26 Letter to his mother, 13 April 1938.
27 *The Lawless Roads*, p. 204.
28 *Ibid.*, p. 209.
29 *Ibid.*, p. 211.
30 *Ibid.*, p. 214.
31 *Ibid.*, p. 215.
32 *Ibid.*, p. 217.
33 *Ibid.*, p. 218.
34 *Ibid.*, p. 228.
35 *Ibid.*, p. 265.

42 *The Power and the Glory*

1 *The Lawless Roads*, Heinemann uniform edition, 1955, p. 279.
2 *The Times*, 1971.
3 *The Lawless Roads*, p. 157.
4 Marie-Françoise Allain, *The Other Man: Conversations with Graham Greene*, trans. Guido Waldman, Bodley Head, 1983, p. 118.
5 *The Lawless Roads*, p. 270.
6 Quoted in *Ways of Escape*, Penguin edition, 1981, p. 35.
7 Marie-Françoise Allain, op. cit., p. 159.
8 *The Lawless Roads*, pp. 138–9.
9 *Ways of Escape*, p. 64.
10 *The Power and the Glory*, Heinemann uniform edition, 1960, p. 1.
11 *The Lawless Roads*, p. 130.
12 *Ibid.*, p. 156.
13 *Ibid.*, and *The Power and the Glory*, p. 34.
14 *The Power and the Glory*, p. 42.
15 *The Lawless Roads*, p. 178.
16 *The Lawless Roads*, p. 180 and *The Power and the Glory*, p. 208.
17 *The Lawless Roads*, pp. 29–30.
18 *Ibid.*, p. 30.
19 *Ways of Escape*, p. 66.

20 *The Lawless Roads*, p. 129.
21 *Ibid.*
22 *Ibid.*, p. 150.
23 George Creel, *Collier's Weekly*, 23 February 1935.
24 *The Power and the Glory*, p. 25.
25 *The Lawless Roads*, pp. 34–5.
26 *Ibid.*, p. 12.
27 Francis McCullagh, *Red Mexico*, Louis Carrier & Co., 1928, p. 235.
28 *The Lawless Roads*, p. 13.
29 *Ibid.*, p. 129.
30 *Ibid.*, p. 150.
31 'solo uno de ellos, el Padre Macario Fernandez Aguado, permanecio a salto de mata, siempre en el monte o en la selva, auxiliando dentro de su desoladora soledad a aquellos catolicos que todavia tenian el valor de confesar su fe.'
32 *The Power and the Glory*, p. 161.
33 *Ibid.*, p. 166.
34 *Ibid.*, p. 164.
35 *Ibid.*, pp. 169–70.
36 *The Lawless Roads*, p. 143.
37 'The Escapist', *Spectator*, 13 January 1939, pp. 48–9.
38 *The Lawless Roads*, pp. 215–16.
39 *Ibid.*, p. 216.
40 *The Power and the Glory*, p. 200.
41 *Ibid.*, p. 200–1.
42 *Ibid.*, p. 201.
43 *Ibid.*, pp. 105–6.
44 *The Lawless Roads*, p. 192.
45 *Ways of Escape*, p. 65.
46 *The Lawless Roads*, p. 193.
47 *The Power and the Glory*, p. 115.
48 *Ibid.*
49 *The Lawless Roads*, pp. 229–30.
50 *The Power and the Glory*, p. 97.
51 *Ibid.*, p. 98.
52 *Ways of Escape*, p. 66.
53 *The Power and the Glory*, p. 228.
54 *The Lawless Roads*, p. 195.
55 *Ibid.*, p. 210.
56 *The Power and the Glory*, p. 236.
57 *Ibid.*, p. 256.
58 *Ibid.*, p. 271.
59 *Ibid.*, p. 273.
60 *Ibid.*, p. 281.
61 *A Sort of Life*, Penguin edition, 1974, p. 60.
62 'Frederick Rolfe: Edwardian Inferno', *Collected Essays*, 1970, p. 131.
63 Marie-Françoise Allain, op. cit., p. 160.
64 Letter from Edith Sitwell to Graham Greene, 11 April 1945.
65 *The Power and the Glory*, p. 87.
66 *A Sort of Life*, p. 121.
67 Marie-Françoise Allain, op. cit., p. 20.
68 Letter to Ben Hubsch, 25 April 1938.
69 *The Lawless Roads*, pp. 287–8.
70 *Ibid.*, p. 289.

Acknowledgments

First, I must thank my subject Graham Greene, not only for his enthusiasm and his patience but for allowing me access to all his private papers and complete freedom to do as I would with all his copyright works. He promised not to interfere with what I made of all this material so generously given, and he has been as good as his word, correcting only a few small errors of fact that crept into the proofs of my book. Thanks also to Vivien Greene, who over many years withstood the fossicking of a literary detective and remained throughout generous and warm.

I am also grateful to Auberon Waugh for allowing me to quote from his father's letters, and to Sir Harold Acton for permission to quote from his letters to Greene. Peter Quennell kindly let me use some lines from his works and the Countess Strachwitz (Barbara Greene) gave her consent to my quoting from her book *Land Benighted*. Above all, I must thank Sally Leach, Katherine Henderson and Carey Thornton for steering me through the Greene archives at the Harry Ransom Humanities Research Center at the University of Texas, Austin, and supplying me with countless photocopies and photographic prints.

For generously allowing me to use so many photographs from the Greene family collection, I must warmly thank both Vivien Greene and Elisabeth Dennys. Anne Forbes kindly sent me the picture of her father Kenneth Richmond, and James Wilson, the most selfless of men, allowed me to plunder his family collection. The Countess Strachwitz also generously allowed me to use a few of her African photographs alongside those Graham Greene took himself. Nicholas Dennys sent me the rare photograph of Graham Greene being sketched by Geoffrey Wylde.

My thanks are also due to the Bell family, Nigel Finch (BBC 'Arena' programme), John W. F. Dulles, Richard Sinkin and Jan Rus for photographs so freely given, and to the United Methodist Mission (New Jersey) for the picture of Dr Harley with his children. Permission has also been sought and given for pictures from the archives of the following: Bassano Studios/National Portrait Gallery, London – no. 1; Nottingham Diocesan Archives – no. 22; Brompton Oratory – no. 38; the Hulton Picture Company – nos 28, 29, 37, 39; courtesy the British Library – no. 30 and the illustration on page 508; 20th Century Fox Films – no. 57, Shirley Temple in a scene from *Rebecca of Sunnybrook Farm*; and Weintraub Screen Entertainment – nos 55, 56, filming *Brighton Rock*. Feliks Topolski gave me permission to use his cover drawing for the first issue of *Night and Day*, and a few of my own pictures are included in the book.

Many others over a period of thirteen years have made a contribution to this book: not least the former Vice-Chancellor of the University of Lancaster, Professor Philip Reynolds, who took an active interest in my early efforts, read the first eighty pages and gave me invaluable advice. Dr Ronald Calgaard, President of Trinity University, San Antonio, Texas (an administrator characterised by the qualities of vision and drive) followed closely the book's development and strenuously supported it to the end. Dr Ram Singh made himself, as only a friend can, ever available, ever useful. My twin brother Alan was always ready to meet me returning from abroad, at sea ports and airports, and continues to face the awkward destiny of being identical. Bernard Lifshutz never wavered, never failed in his support, whilst Richard Sinkin brought me through some tight scrapes as I followed Greene's footsteps and he mine, in sometimes difficult jungle or mountainous conditions. His parents, Fay and William Sinkin, have been surrogate parents to me. And finally, Dr Robert Still has kept me alive during a succession of illnesses brought about by the difficulties of travel.

Over the years I have had the invaluable support of a number of secretaries – Elaine Layer, herself a poet; Dee Escobedo; Anne Dalton; Elisa Albert Bass; Grace Alaquinez. I would especially like to thank Lucy Kilmer for her unstinting involvement and passionate interest in the book. My new secretary Linda Clark helped in the final stages of Volume One and has already accepted the responsibilities of Volume Two.

I have to thank my publishers for the help they gave me, especially during 1988. Anthony Colwell has gone on working well past midnight, ever watchful of textual and printing difficulties; one was aware of his knowledge and skill in all branches of publishing. Anne Chisholm made some very necessary changes to the final text, and Jill Sutcliffe showed an uncanny ability for spotting errors. But it has been Graham Carleton Greene's support throughout the writing of the book that has been an absolute necessity, particularly during those periods when I seemed unable to bring the work to a successful conclusion. His patience has bordered on the miraculous and I am happy to call him friend.

For a short period in 1977 I had the assistance of Susan August Brown who read Greene's difficult handwriting (sometimes, in its worst moments, it takes on the character of the scratchings of a chicken); and at the period when I was partially blinded Liz Smith also deciphered and typed Greene's manuscript writings. I owe much to Carmen Flores's assistance during my research. Russ Newell's early morning reveilles in North Carolina spurred me to begin writing the book.

Some people took on willingly the onerous task of reading the typescript in its first draft – its original length being one thousand and five hundred pages – and these I salute, in particular David Holloway, formerly literary editor of the *Daily Telegraph*; Jonathan Clowes, my literary agent; Nicholas Scheetz, the archivist of Georgetown University Library; and the following brilliant scholars, Professors Peter Balbert, Robert ter Horst, John Halperin, Kenneth Muir, Ian Watt and Cedric Watts. Watts also read the proofs and checked the index and his intimate knowledge of Brighton is apparent in important aspects of Chapter 39. My distinguished colleagues, Professors William Breit and John Stoessinger both read the first nineteen chapters and made highly constructive comments. Edwin Thumboo, Dean at the National University of Singapore, read the typescript long into the night. Graham Greene's bibliographers, the late Alan Redway and Dr Neil Brennan, were selflessly helpful. Sylvia Sherry was in on the book's conception and saw it through to the end and where there is special evidence of good sense, tact and intelligence, it must be said that she is the original owner of these qualities.

I am conscious that I may have failed to recall all those who, in these long years of research, have assisted me. I ask their forgiveness. However, I can record my indebtedness to the following: Victoria Aarons, Walter Allen, James Andrew, Farid Anthony, Father Joseph Appleyard, Clemonceau Ari, Mr and Mrs Armstrong, Francis Arnold, Merton Atkins, Monsignor Atkinson, Harold Atkins who helped me in my study of Nottingham, Arthur Abrams and Moses Dumbuya (who shared my Liberian adventures), G. E. Brice, A. R. C. Bolton, Mrs Blom, Tom Burns, Mrs Ave Barham, the late Sir Basil Blackwell, Rene Berval, Professor Tony Bottomley, Dr Jacques Barzun, Professor Muriel Bradbrook, Sir Thomas Bazeley, Charles Blitzer, Jane Bywaters, Hon. Thomas Brima, Miss Phyllis Calvert, Claud Cockburn, Canon Cummins, Dr Mario Curreli, John Caincross, Roger Coster, Elton R. Cude, Ian Carr, Nigel Cottam, Dr Frank Cancian, the late James Carr, Arthur Calder-Marshall, Josine Couch, Carla v Delft, Bernard and Mercedes Darbyshire, S. R. Denny, Guy Denison, Bernard Diederich, the late Basil Dean, Nigel Dennis, Ian Dalrymple, Hon. Fulton Dumbar, Peter Duffell, Father Leopoldo Duran, Canon Brian Dazely, Dr John Donahue, Father Dike, D. J. Enright, Alicia and Raul Ezquerro, the late A. S. Frere, Philip French, Brito Fonchez, Sr Figuerrero, Olga Franklin, Gabriel Fielding, Hon. Joseph M. N. Gbadyu, H. R. Gaines (better known as Ill-gotten), Eva Greene, Edward Greene, E. R. Guest, the late Dr Raymond Greene, the late Sir Hugh Greene, the late Ben Greene, Kate Greene, the late Felix Greene, Francis Greene, Edward Paul Greene, Audrey Greene, De Witt Greene, Peter Glenville, Tom Guinzburg, Harry Gottlieb, James Greene, Dr Gary Gossen, R. J. B. Granville, Simon Grove, Tom Greene, Mr G. E. B. Harrison, Father Hamilburg, the late Miss Caroline Hill, the late Trevor Howard, Douglass Hunt, Professor David Leon Higdon, Jim Hopkinson, Cecil Hodges, Professor Samuel Hynes, William Igoe, the Rt Hon. Douglas Jay MP, Adam Jones, Henry and Charlotte Jordan, Harry Johnson, Michael Korda, Justin Kell, Marie Karim, Frank Kersnowski, Mrs Kelly, John Keen, Margarete Kleiber, the late Leland Lyons, the late John Lehmann, Leslie Horace Leslie-Smith, Nigel Lloyd, David Low, Dr Michael Lechat, the late Harold Lee, Irwin C. Lieb, John Leefe, David and Jo Lopez, Tom Laughton, the late Manuel Landa, Rey Leal, the late Col Alan Maude, Col Murray, Michael Meyer, Malcolm Muggeridge, the late Patrick Monkhouse, Sr Pedro Sanchez Mejorada, Michael Mewshaw, Ambassador Joseph G. Morris, Gordon Morris, Dr Paul Murray, Dr Mark Magenheim, Richard Muirie, Kent Mullikin, Eric Morris, The Rt Rev. James T. McGuinness, the late Joseph G. MacLeod, the late Monica McCall, Juan Torres Morales, the late Tom McGann, Mario Maurino, Major J. McGregor-Cheers, Dr Davidson Nicol, the late Beverley Nichols, Anthony Nichols, Rigel and Edwin Newman, Erik Nielsen, the late Miss C. O'Grady, the late Sean O'Faolain, Ian Ogilvie, Dr Marion Oettinger, Thomas F. O'Connell, Charles Orsinger, the late Ian Parsons, the late Mrs Mary Leonard Pitchett, G. L. Pearson, Don Pelito, the late Otto Preminger, M. B. Pescod, Charles Pick, Gerald Pollinger, Mrs Mervyn Peake, the late Sir Cecil Parrott, Professor Clive Probyn, Señora Pro, Sir V. S. Pritchett, Gordon Phillips, Rev. Gene D. Phillips, SJ, Keith Reeson, A. L. Rowse, the late Cecil Roberts, W. Rees Mogg, Piers Paul Read, Lady Read, the late Sir Ralph Richardson, the late Mrs Zoe Richmond, Jeffrey Richards, Ruben Munguia, Dianne Ramirez, Hannah Strauss, Mrs Joy Ross, R. S. Stanier, the late Frank Swinnerton, John Spencer, the late John Sutro and Gillian Sutro, the Hon. Mrs Stoner-Saunders, Ragnar Svanstrom, Mario Soldati, Irene Selznick, Betty Saunders, Shamay Scimeca, Bill Scanlan, Philip Stratford, Scott Steves, Willis Salomon, R. R. Timberlake, the Rt Hon. Lord Tranmire, the late A. J. P. Taylor, Alun Thomas, Keith Cross Thompson, Clemenceau Uri, Peter Ustinov, the Hon. Mrs Elizabeth Varley, Dr James Vinson, the late Rex Warner, Mrs Caroline Weston, H. I. Willis, the late Col A. L. Wilson, the late Alec Waugh, the late Antonia White, Dr Carl Wood, Dr Harry Wilmer, Derek Winterbottom, Trevor Wilson, Harvey Curtis Webster.

Finally, I owe a debt of gratitude to the National Humanities Center, Research Triangle Park, North Carolina, which granted me a fellowship in 1982-3 allowing me to begin the book's first draft. Two institutions in particular are holders of Greene research and Manuscript material essential to a biographer; Boston College Library in Boston and Georgetown University Library in Washington. This last institution, through the prodigious efforts of the librarian, Joseph Jeffs, now has an unrivalled collection of Greene material. All deserve my deepest thanks.

Norman Sherry

Trinity University
San Antonio, Texas
1989

Index

Index

Index

Index

Index

Index

Index

Index